THE DRAMA OF POSSIBILITY

THE DRAMA OF POSSIBILITY

Experience as Philosophy of Culture

JOHN J. McDERMOTT
Edited by Douglas R. Anderson

FORDHAM UNIVERSITY PRESS   NEW YORK   2007

Library of Congress Cataloging-in-Publication Data

[[To come]]

Printed in the United States of America
09 08 07   5 4 3 2 1
First edition

Contents

Part 5: Teaching

Acknowledgments

The preparation of this volume is due to the initiation, encouragement, editing, and indefatigable patience of Douglas Anderson. Equivalently essential was the extreme care given this manuscript by my loyal research assistant, David Henderson. It was he who scanned this material for transmission and who presided over the quality of the submission from my side of this endeavor. Gratitude is given, as well, to James Campbell and Robert A. McDermott. *The Drama of Possibility*—I write here that this title was suggested by Patricia A. McDermott, who, in my life, has made possibility possible.

THE DRAMA OF POSSIBILITY

READING McDERMOTT
Douglas Anderson

Editing a book requires an economy of judgment and patience. This is especially true when, as in the present instance, the pool of essays from which one is selecting runs rich and deep. As editing goes, this has certainly been the most rewarding endeavor in my career. John J. McDermott's presence is not captured by the numerous titles, professional awards, and teaching citations he has earned over the years; nevertheless, these titles, awards, and citations serve as signs of that presence. They tell us to investigate further what this McDermott thing is about. Teacher, philosopher, historian, editor, *teacher*, social critic, mentor, poet, teacher—and here, essayist. Professor McDermott writes philosophy aboriginally, as Emerson might have said. He writes through his experiences, with his reading and learning, and about his culture and history. His essays are philosophically down-to-earth but never without the presence of a deep learning and an attentive familiarity with the history of thought. The essays take us into the presence of John McDermott and reveal to us that whatever else he might be up to, he is always in the act of teaching.

In the classroom and at the podium, Professor McDermott is electric—not paying attention is *not* an option. His essays are likewise pedagogical and bear some of this electricity, but they also exemplify what William James called the "strenuous." They have an energy, a solidity, and a sense of resistance to that which would take the life out of things. McDermott believes it when he says that "experience is pedagogical." In short, for those of us who work both on the back roads of American philosophy and on the main streets of American culture, it is difficult not to work under the influence of John McDermott. But here is where Professor McDermott's presence inserts itself—even as we come under its influence, it resists cult-building. In thinking of how John McDermott has influenced my own thinking, I am always reminded of Emerson's description of Nature in "Experience": "Nature, as we know her, is no saint. . . . She comes eating and drinking and sinning. Her darlings, the great, the strong, the beautiful, are not children of our law, do not come out of the Sunday School, nor weigh their food, nor punctually keep the commandments." It is precisely his experiences with finitude and his deep sensitivity to these experiences that make Professor McDermott's work so powerful. To be under his influence is to be sent on a quest for one's own possibilities. McDermott will assess where and how we live, but what we will do with our futures is always up to us. In the classroom and in his essays, John McDermott is an exceptional teacher—one who teaches of experience and through experience.

John E. Smith has rightly noted that among the American philosophers whom John McDermott studies, he has perhaps the strongest affinity for William James. Yet McDermott is also Deweyan to the extent that he is a social critic, a commentator on the way things go in American culture. But it is important to note that he is never a cultural technician; Professor McDermott is more of a social aesthetician. He searches out the beauties and blemishes in our everyday practices, and he discloses an exceptional knack for seeing and describing how a culture feels—its moods, temperaments, and relations. He exhibits what Dewey often called a "wide sympathy" for things going on around him. When he tells a doorman at a Houston skyscraper that he has "an appointment with the building," he in one stroke tells us of urban life, of corporate life, of urban fears, of class structure, and of twentieth-century American aesthetic sensibilities. A Deweyan critic with the eye of a Jamesian radical empiricist, Professor McDermott converts his experience into philosophical essays.

As essayist, John McDermott is not merely a social aesthetician but an artist of possibility. He is a champion of the dynamic, the open, and the ongoing. He is a welcome companion to the transitory, the vagrant, and the adrift. "The crucial factor in our understanding of the world in which we live," he says, "is the affective experiencing of relations." A kind of Johnny Cash of American thought and culture, McDermott finds relations where others find barriers, he crosses disciplinary and stylistic boundaries that are the arbitrary results of a particular academic history, and he engages human difference as the ordinary fact that it is—something to be amazed by and lived with, but not to be feared or idolized. In the essays at hand, as in personal conversation, John McDermott not only experiences relations but builds them. Without religion, with assurance, without prophecy, his is a philosophy of hope and possibility:

> The most perilous threat to human life is secondhandedness, living out the bequest of our parents, siblings, relatives, teachers, and other dispensers of already programmed possibilities. We should be wary of the inherited, however noble its intention, for it is the quality of our own experience which is decisive. Failure, deeply undergone, often enriches, whereas success achieved mechanically through the paths set out by others often blunts sensibility. We are not dropped into the world as a thing among things. We are live creatures who eat experience. (140, *Culture*)

And so to the essays at hand. With the help of Professor McDermott and in consultation with some of his former students, I have put together a set of essays that I hope will capture the central themes of his thought as well as the power of his style. Some of the essays are occasional, marking some feature of Professor McDermott's own career. Some are more traditionally philosophical, aiming at a diagnosis of a wider culture. To address the temporal spread and thematic variety of the essays, Professor McDermott has, in the prescript that follows, provided the reader with an overview of the circumstances in which the essays were written. This seemed a more prudent route to maintaining the authenticity of the pieces than rewriting for a different time and cultural setting.

The essays reveal the breadth of Professor McDermott's interests. Acknowledging with James and Dewey that philosophy begins with primary experience, he provides ongoing commentary on the meanings of American culture and its history, social and intellectual, to show the context in which his own thinking develops. As one who lives without belief in the supernatural, Professor McDermott also writes about our actual, finite victories and losses, and about the possibilities that these victories and losses suggest for our contingent futures. The moral, the aesthetic, the religious, the political all take place for McDermott as a drama of possibility, and he repeatedly calls our attention to the dynamic interplay of loss and hope this drama presents. Finally, Professor McDermott's awareness of our precarious setting leads him to a Deweylike commitment to pedagogy. Only through meaningful transactions across generations and cultures will we remain alive as a people and not resort to social stagnation or fall into cultural chaos. In the end, for McDermott, it all comes down to our willingness to learn and to teach—these are our most elemental existential projects.

My hope in collecting these essays is that yet another generation of students can catch a glimpse of another way of doing philosophy, one that leads not to cultural invisibility but rather brings us into daily engagement with questions of importance for the making of our own futures. Reading the work of John McDermott has the curious effect not only of bringing us into his presence but, in the manner of Thoreau, of awakening us to our own senses.

REMARKS UPON RECEIVING THE 2004
PRESIDENTIAL TEACHING AWARD

I try to live and teach on behalf of the democratic maxim that every-one is educable. More, I believe that each person who comes to me in a pedagogical setting has the ability to turn their experimental history into an abiding nutritional resource such that they can live on behalf of a reflective intelligence, an aesthetic sensibility, and a commitment to the well-being of the commonweal. In this setting, my task, my responsi-bility as a teacher is crystal clear—to help. Since my first day of teaching in January 1953, I have not wavered in my conviction that pedagogy is the centerpiece of the human community. Pedagogy is the way in and through which I and my students become connected with our human, planetary past and it is how we build our personal presence into the vast complexity of contemporary culture.

My teaching proceeds from the legacy of the humanities, with my choice of fulcrum philosophy, both historically and speculatively. Con-sequently, dependent on the issues of the moment, we discuss Plato's *Euthyphro*, or Arthur Miller's *Death of a Salesman*. Herein, the issue is loyalty. In short, I bring to bear the most searingly incisive texts and traditions to illuminate the tangles, the traps, and the sadness which dog us at every turn. The upshot here of the more than 20,000 students which I have taught face to face is vocal and consistent: "McDermott, you helped me do this on my own."

The teaching that I espouse, that I do and encourage others to do as well, requires patience, compassion, and an alert sense of what is happening in the lives of students. I consider it to be a serious mistake to underestimate the prevalence of spiritual and intellectual restiveness in our students. When I teach the philosophy of literature, with a focus on family—for example, the work of Aeschylus, James Baldwin, Eugene O'Neill, Carson McCullers, and Sylvia Plath—the resonance of these "stories" with my students is startling. They write themes for me every two weeks and after a month of denial, self-aggrandizement, and sloganeering, a deeper, more troubled, more questioning, more generous self begins to emerge. So, too, with my teaching of medical students here at Texas A&M; a more difficult undertaking, to be sure, but over time, say ten years after our course in Interpersonal Medical Diagnosis, there drifts back to me that yes, the practice of medicine does indeed involve the insights of literature, history, and philosophy. One major issue in medical education is that of the distinction between healing and curing. This discussion involves not only coming to grips with the mortality of the patient but, signally and disturbingly, the mortality of the physician. Philosophically, the effort here is to develop the worthiness of amelioration and remission, both virtues of time rather than of eternity.

In my hundreds of presentations in an array of educational, professional, and cultural settings, I have come to believe that the audience responds to existential authenticity and has little patience with frills, techniques, or short-cuts. I have found this to be true in Budapest, where students carried chairs from one unkempt room to another. And in the Kingdom of Tonga, where the venue was an ad-hoc "college" in the "bush," featuring students from thirty nations. So, too, in Manila, Shanghai, the medical school in Nanjing, and in work with the Montessori movement and The National Faculty of Humanities, Arts, and Sciences. In these endeavors, I found myself in schools, prisons, half-way houses, and programs for the disabled. Being able to connect was a requisite for these pedagogical situations. So long as I was able to marry the rich historical and philosophical versions of the wisdom literature with an affective reconnoitering of my own experiences and those of my family, my children, my students, and my friends, the pedagogy took place and the possibilities for growth became extant. Consequently, for me, teaching is not a "job" or merely a profession. Teaching is a calling, a *vocare*, one which is intellectually sophisticated in practice, sacred in intent, and affectionate in transaction. . . .

Not a year goes by that I do not have a letter or a phone call from students taught by me twenty, thirty, forty years ago. The message from them is revealingly similar. Something happened in their life forcing them to reach far, go deep, hold on, whatever. They thought of something that we read together, some walk we took, some event we shared. They were grateful for that help, then and now, and they were quick to say that they try to do that for others in their own way, their own lives. That is the kind of teaching I do and that is the kind of teaching I shall continue to do until I die.

Prescript

I am privileged to have these essays published once again, this time in a volume which brings some coherence to my work over the last fifty years. Surely, I and my editors are aware of the difficulties extant in the presentation of material from the past, especially as our cultural situation moves with increasing speed sufficient to convince some among us that only recent reflections have purchase or merit.

As a help to the reading of these essays, I offer here four areas of adumbration. The first has to do with the noxious virus of obsolescence as a destructive touchstone for evaluation. Second, I present some comments on the essay as a genre. Third, I acknowledge the presence of some repetitions, especially stories. And, fourth, I make a plea for this approach to philosophical inquiry as one very important way to write philosophically in response to the calling of the public.

I take this obsolescence to mean that if a piece does not acknowledge developments in attitude, changes in focus, or the latest mode of expression, it is written off (pun intended). Of note here is the focus of my essay on "An American Angle of Vision," conceived in the late 1950s and published in 1963–64. By the lights of today's cultural critics, this essay limps to one side, forgoing border literature, the narrative of African American slaves, and the stories of Native Americans. Had I written this essay today, I would certainly point to these now-central events in our understanding of American culture; that is, I would have widened the focus, but I would not change the contention—namely, the irreducible significance of "covenant" in the American social and political psyche. Ironically, when first published, "An American Angle of Vision" was received as a radical defense of a secular interpretation of our Puritan heritage. To this day, I hold that attempts to understand America without a grasp of the insights and perils of this Calvinist bequest court vincible historical ignorance. I add here, that my enclosed poem "Roots/ Edges" is a clear indication of the subsequent widening of my historical tapestry.

So, too, can the scythe of obsolescence block us from the importance of events, places, and themes no longer in vogue. Instance here my reference to the destruction of the Republic of Biafra in West Africa, 1967–70. If written in 1994, the location would have been Rwanda and, as of this day, Darfur. By analogy, such placeholders are not to be read as anachronistic but rather as revelatory events in the systemically pockmarked history of our planet.

It may be of note to indicate that the present publication is composed of essays, loosely gathered thematically, and does not have the intention often present in an historical monograph. Holding, as I do, to the maxim of William James that we should abide by an "ever not quite" to our formulas, judgments, and, perforce, opinions, I choose the essay to be my genre. An essay is a trying, a probing, an attempting to cast light on the forgotten, the opaque, and to generate worry about the hidden dangers of the assumed, the status quo. Over against the monograph, the massive tome, the definitive magnum opus, the essay can appear as slight, casual, and of seemingly lesser import. I believe this attitude to be mistaken. Of course, I do not gainsay the merit of longer, more thorough studies. Yet the essay thrives on the directness of intention and the intensity of scrutiny. In an essay, the tapestry under consideration is asked to yield its central upshot, directly. One thinks of Ralph Waldo Emerson and William James, for whom it is the occasional piece, the reflection on a single issue, which characterizes much of their work. Of moment here is Emerson's "Nature," "The American Scholar," and "Experience." From James, we have "The Sentiment of Rationality," "The Dilemma of Determinism," and "The Will to Believe." Nothing is "wrapped up" in these essays. Still, the perspective taken, the way of inquiry, and the elucidation turn out to be rich, far beyond their girth. I make no comparison of my work to these masters of the philosophical essay but simply point to the tradition out of which I write.

Another consideration for the reader of these essays is the presence of some repetition. The editors and I have made every effort to excise from inclusion those pieces which are obviously repetitive of material found elsewhere in this volume. Nonetheless, some repetition remains, namely, an occasional paragraph and a few stories, notably that of the Cigar Man. It was decided that the stories were axial to the essay in question and could not be removed without severe interpretive damage. Further, for me, stories are not incidental or decorative. Rather, they are constitutive of the spiritual marrow of my person. Many of them I shall take to my grave as linchpins in my personal history.

My last prescriptive remarks have to do with the necessity of rendering accessible to the public the fruits of philosophical inquiry. When it comes to the study of philosophy, I am comparatively orthodox, holding that one should know the text, know the problem, and know the cultural context from which philosophical claims, contentions, and criticisms are bequeathed. Having done that, I believe that some of us are able to make public, in an accessible way, the wisdom of the philosophical tradition. Unfortunately, this involvement in the public sphere is not characteristic of contemporary philosophical activity, which, to the contrary, seems to be increasingly arcane and rhetorically "in house." I lament this situation. This is not to say that I have in mind philosophy as a magic bullet or a curative, a nostrum for what ails us. However, following William James, I believe that philosophers can "thicken the discussion," widen horizons and bring the long and storied history of philosophical reflections to bear in contemporary discussions which are often jejune and ahistorical.

I have in mind a revisiting of Plato's *Euthyphro* and his cave, the warnings of the Stoics, and the high political intelligence of the Roman and medieval jurists. Think here as well of Spinoza's "healing" of understanding and Kierkegaard's devastating critique of *our* time, *The Present Age*, written in 1846. So, too, of moment is existentialism's stress on personal freedom within the emerging presence of self-deception, as also Emerson's cautionary remarks about the danger of half-gods and the entire tradition of classical American philosophy, with its emphasis on the messagings of experience and the implacable necessity of integrating the antennae for consequences into all human decisions.

Whence has come the common assumption that the practice of philosophy is confined to an academic setting. For those of us who have been deeply fortunate to understand and teach matters philosophical, we should remind ourselves that this rich quality of knowing is most alive when shared with those for whom philosophy is a closed door. My personal assumption is that the marching order given at birth is to *help*. Ultimate resolutions, canopies of ultimate explanation, and eschatological redoubts are but gossamer wings, ephemerally dangerous and dangerously ephemeral. It has long been my experience that speaking to and writing for audiences of high culture and academic sophistication differs only in choice of rhetoric from doing so before audiences of the ad hoc public; I refer to those gatherings of intentional communities found in medical settings, schools, prisons, political activities, or the arts. All of this speaking and writing counts. How much it counts is not for me to say, for I long ago adopted as my personal mantra the refrain from "East Coker" by T. S. Eliot: "For us there is only the trying. The rest is not our business."

When this volume is published, I shall have celebrated my diamond-year birthday. For me, therefore, my time is more spent than prospective. I shall continue trying, perhaps, to finish my "America Poem" and a few essays, one on loneliness and one on addiction. Far more important, however, than my future efforts is the clarion call to my readers, pace Kierkegaard: speak, write, and show up. The global human community of the early twenty-first century is in a fractious state, striated by large pockets of barbarism and constant, terrifying threats to our planetary well-being. The task before us is to generate patterns of amelioration. Solutions tend to generate violence, and so a studied modesty of intent is in order. In the language of recovery, there is work to be done.

As a sign of continuity in these essays and in my thoughts, I return here to a suggestion that I set forth in 1976, one that I still embrace: do not await salvation while the parade passes by. Surprise and mystery lurk in our experiencing the obvious, the ordinary. Salvation may be illusory, but salving experiences can occur day by day.

Benedicite,

John J. McDermott
Texas A&M University

PART ONE

AN AMERICAN ANGLE OF VISION

Roots/Edges

The past as Prologue to creative oblivion
And so—America
One of a kind, but special
Nonetheless—
Pockmarked, heroic, bewildered,
Arrogant, sensitive, never
Plodding
Aboard the Arbella—Bible in hand
Rickets, scurvy and rats
Everywhere
We shall be a City on a Hill
The Lord's Plantation
And the eyes of all the
World
Shall be upon us.
No easy burden, that.
Redeemed
Only somewhat, they, we, say—
John Winthrop to his
Beloved Margaret
How fortunate—fortunate indeed
Are we.
Half of my siblings, half of our
children,
One of my three wives, you
still alive.
God is good
From Sudbury to Marlborough
A stone taken from
Meeting House hill
A new start, the Alleghenies,
The Appalachians

On to the alleged
Northwest Territory
O'MacKinac
O'Saginaw
The great plains await
As white man and white woman
Bible in hand, once again
Forage and deforest
Oblivious
To the red that floods the land
Amerindian—Amerindian
Shoshone, Osage, Apache
Iroquois, Blackfeet
The Christian Chief Joseph
Betrayed by us
As the Nez Perce bite the dust
Victims of cultural genocide
Listen—Listen to the Jesuit
Father Hennepin
Why, Why, he plaintively asks?
How is it that our Indian
Brothers and Sisters, pagans all,
Be more Christian than we,
How. Yes How!
At that point, nothing, nothing
Said about the browning of
America
Yet, try the Camino Real
Try the Santa Fe Trail
Try the Rio Grande
To this day
By fatal boxcar
By car trunk
By wading among the snakes
Slicing through the anchor fence
America—and ye shall be free

Maybe—
Roots, Ah roots—
The deep irony of Haley's Roots
No! Not Haley's comet
Haley's Roots
The Dahomean—kidnapped
Look to it—Boy!
Come here—Girl!
Leroy! a slash for that clandestine
Reading
Trapped between the scissoring
From a magnificent
Non-literate gesture culture as
Embodied, and so liturgically,
Ritually thick
As in the world of Africa
Yet prevented, a euphemism for
Slavery
From getting it on with the book.
Rachel! Do not let me catch you
Ever, Ever
Reading
Across the Great Plains
Bush by brackish water
Trapped in the Humboldt Sink
The pregnant Sara Royce
The Donner party (now the
Recipients of ORV)
Ate each other.
From St. Jo to Sacramento
Arrows in the neck, Pony
Express—detritus
Horses presaging the telegraph
Pole
From Peck Slip to the Barbary Coast
O Columbia—Gem of the Ocean.

Stained with heroism and
Madness
The American Frontier
Frontier of Valor
Frontier of Sadness
Frontier of Violence
Frontier of Courage
Frontier of Trashing
Of beginning again and again
Of novelty
Of loneliness
America, America, America
Named for a pickle dealer
In need of a Latin feminine case ending.
Cosmographicae Introductio of 1507
Europa, Asia, Africa and
America.
Oy Vey—and who are they?
Not a new place, not a new thing
Nay—A mundus novus
A new world
America.
A truck-stop outside of Des Moines
The blitzed copper veins of
Anaconda and Butte,
Montana
Whitesand, corn rows, endless
Wheat, breezing in the Iowa still.
Gunnison, San Joaquin
Even Hoosiers
Franconia Notch, Pennsylvania Station
Hatteras and Everglades
A brace of panhandles
Chattanooga, parden me boy
Kimosabe
Hi Ho Silver—Away

The silver bullet of
The midnight special
Dens of crack
Crinolines and bouffant
For the day will live in
infamy
As will My Lai
From the LBJ lie, low to Haiphong
Who would have thought
He was such a nice boy
The McDonalds of San Ysidro
as Beirut
When black boys and black girls
Hold hands with white boys
and white girls
From the granite hills of
New Hampshire
To Stone Mountain of Georgia
To the curvaceous shores
of California
A King among pygmies
Gun him down
Ask not what your country
can do for you
But ask what you can do
for your country
Gun him down
We can do better
Gun him down
The 'Natural' as Ruthian
Greta and Marilyn
Clark and Gary
Here's looking at you
As time goes by with
A grapefruit in your face
You can of course, go uptown

Or downtown—by the
A train
Unless you come from Wharton
Or the B. school
Complete with Wall Street
Attache
Cocaine-lined, white collared
Subtle violence
Hey there, can you spare a dime
Over there, over there
Let us make the world
Safe for democracy
As we wallow in our
Augean stable.
Many mice make a Meese
Tammany and Teapot Dome
Karl Marx said it was a sell-out
The lefties call it co-optation
But my Mama lives on your
Social Security
Only in America—says
Harry Golden
As Niagara Falls into
The wedding gown
Flivvers and flappers
Bathtub gin
Shitkickers and yuppies, the latter
alas
Edison and Lincoln
The Jeffersonian City as a canker
Land, always land,
But only for the few
Burn baby burn
The arch—the sluices in the
High Missouri
Burn baby burn

After all, business is business
The business of America
is Business.
Bible in hand, preaching the
Carnegie Gospel of wealth
On the road and by the
Way
Can you spare a dime.
The word is German
Heimlosigkeit
The phenomenon is American
I ain't got no place to go
Homeless!
The world at large, the planet
Global culture
Chastises America
Get your act together
Confusion reigns, they say.
Not confusion, say I
Ambiguity
Say I
Despite the philosophers of the new
stripe
The big questions are irresolute
Should we emulate Famulus in
Goethe's *Faust*
Who, upon peering into the world of
Intellect
Announced and pronounced
How impressed he was with how
Wondrously far he has come
Or, should we emulate that
Stunning vignette of
Camus in *L'Etranger*
Until now I have not thought about it;
But now that I have thought about it, No!

I want to live only with that which I know.
Derby day, Dr. J.
Why is the American National pastime
A game that can be tied to infinity
Schenley, Shaker and Scarsdale
Hough and Watts
White and Black
Can you spare a dime
The braggart Swaggart
Does not know a red light from
Bible in hand.
Why not listen to Matisse
L'exactitude ne pas verité
America—ambiguity
Quo vadis. I have not the slightest
idea.
Why go—then?
Precisely.
As the parade goes by
Hey Camerado—
I love you.
They do not answer—
Hey there—no matter.
When you come, as you will,
to look for me—
Find me under your boot soles.
I am—will be
the leaves of grass—

Benedicite

ONE

THREADBARE CRAPE

Reflections on the American Strand

For my head-text, I take a passage from Hobbes's *Leviathan*. At the end of the last chapter of part 2, "Of Commonwealth," Hobbes writes as follows:

> I recover some hope, that at one time or other, this writing of mine may fall into the hands of a sovereign, who will consider it himself (for it is short, and I think clear) without the help of any interested, or envious interpreter, and by the exercise of entire sovereignty, in protecting the public teaching of it, convert this truth of speculation, into the utility of practice.[1]

The admonishing word is practice. No less than the austere, American theologian Jonathan Edwards holds that "holy practice" is the "greatest sign of grace" and that "Christian practice" is the principal sign of those twelve which distinguish "Truly Gracious and Holy Affections." Of a profoundly different cast of mind and presentation, Immanuel Kant tells us likewise. For those intrepid souls who make it to the closing pages of Kant's epochal work, *The Critique of Pure Reason*, they read his telling us that the upshot of both the speculative and the practical reason come to these three questions: "What can I know?"; "What ought I to do?"; and "What may I hope?" For Kant, the doing is "practical" and he adds, warningly I take it, that we can only "hope" if we do what we "ought to do." Enough—although more, much more in this ameliorative vein could be cited, for it has struck me over and again that most of the major figures in the history of thought, despite their often dazzling speculative forays, maintain the abiding presence of the need for practice, the need to *do* something, to forage, to nurture, to sustain, to maintain, and to build. Sooner or later, sheer talk runs out and the great conversation becomes solipsistic.

I turn now to the title of this presentation. Following the wisdom of Kierkegaard, who tells us that we should "live forward" but "think backwards," I start with the second line, "Reflections on the American Strand." This is a play on the opening of the *Magnalia* by Cotton Mather, a work as fascinating as it is arcane. Quite directly, Mather writes of us as "flying from the Depravations of Europe, to the American Strand." Equally direct, almost three hundred years later, my reflections tell me that it is increasingly apparent that we have turned in on ourselves such that the "Depravations" allegedly left behind have become reincarnated in this contemporary version of our American Strand, once so promising. In turn, these reflections then generate the first line, the head-line of my discussion, namely, "Threadbare Crape." As you would expect, it comes from our American poet, Walt Whitman. I exhumed this phrase from a line suppressed by Whitman in subsequent editions of *Leaves of Grass*, a line which holds of life that "nothing remains but threadbare crape and tears."

Now, let us bring the title to storied life. On behalf of the memoried tradition of Whitman, this story is deeply personal and yet is revelatory of all of us together in our contemporary American time. I was a young child in the bleak decade of the American 1930s. Three of my grandparents were dead. My paternal grandfather was buried on the nasty January day that I was born in 1932. My remaining grandparent was my maternal grandmother, known in our family as Nana. Widowed at an early age with three young children, she made a living for them by scrubbing fire-house floors and sewing men's ties. She was a follower of

the New York Giants, of John McGraw, and a whiz at pinochle. My entire extended family was shanty Irish. We had nothing, except the American dream, Irish style.

I correct myself, for I should not say "nothing." For the shanty Irish
did manage to obtain, grab, or perhaps even purloin one precious possession, lace curtains, to be had no doubt in defiance of our often offensive and patronizing peers, the lace-curtain Irish. My Nana had such a
set of curtains. Each spring they would be ceremoniously washed,
starched, and tacked to a long, nail-pronged stretcher. For decades, I
helped to do that. And then, as she failed in strength, I did them for her.
Some thirty years ago, when she was in her eighties, I said to her, "Time
for the curtains." Nana replied, "Not this year." What! Why not? They
were threadbare. A stretch was beyond their reach. They would fray and
the threads would unravel, spinning dizzily out of control, dangling,
footless, homeless, anomic, and pathetically lonely, each and all of them,
lonely together. Nana Kelly was dead within the year.

I think here of America, our "strand" of hope, and I ask: do we still
have that long-standing, self-announcing confidence in our ability to
meet and match our foes, of any and every stripe—political, economic,
natural, and, above all, spiritual—arising from without and within our
commonwealth? I do not ask this as a rhetorical question but rather one
of direct, existential contemporaneity, the intention of which is to elicit
an equally direct response. For most of my life, even through the turbulent and bewildering decade of the 1960s, I would answer yes. Subsequently, my reply became halting and had the corresponding cloak of
"maybe" about it. Of late, I carry with me, resonant of many others
among us, a lamentable dubiety about whether, in fact, we are still able
to tap that eros of community which has served us so well for the past
three centuries.

This dubiety does not trace to events so much as to mood. To be sure,
events such as the Oklahoma City bombing and the escalating, precipitous rise in acts of violence traceable to the increasing presence of estrangement, and ontological, rather than functional, frustration, are of
central moment. The issue in question, however, cuts deeper and may
presage our having lost the capacity to rework and reconstitute the viability of a pluralistic and mosaic communal fabric which, in truth, is
simply quintessential if we are to survive as a nation.

Taking heed of botanical and physiological metaphors, far more help-ful in telling us what is happening than is the language of logic and con-ceptual schemas, I hear the following conversations. After an ice storm, a flood, a fire, or just the constant, searing sun of the Texas summer, one asks of the tree, the plant, the bush, or perhaps a tendril or two, can it come back, will it come back? I do not know. There exists a line of viability, for the most part invisible, and even, despite modern science, mysterious. Cross that line and the leaves wither, announcing the death of the botanical life-form. So, too, with physiological metaphors. We speak of atrophy, as when a muscle loses its febrility. The common watch in our mediated society is for the rampant, destructive cell, as in cancer. Far more present, however, is the malodorous activity of inani-tion, wasting away, loss of tone; in short, he/she seems to be failing. In what, of what, we ask? I do not know, just failing, in general. You can tell. The many diseases of the central nervous system carry on by *via negativa*. Neurons do not fire. Cellular messages are not sent, or, if sent, are not received, or, if received, are not heeded, as in the biblical admo-nition, they who have eyes, but do not see, they who have ears, but do not hear. The terror of Alzheimer's disease is that we do not know how far to go with it until it is too late, and we cannot turn back for a fresh start. You say to me, what does this have to do with fascism? What does this have to do with America? I say to you, it has to do with both!

Fascism, akin to substance addiction, is a "subtle-foe." It comes bear-ing gifts, especially the treacherous ones, seen as an escape from seem-ingly intractable difficulties and the promise of a quick fix—the trains to run on time, courtesy of Benito Mussolini. Subtle, indeed. As late as 1993, the vaunted *Columbia Encyclopedia* devotes but two columns to a discussion of fascism. This is equivalent to the two columns addressing the Etruscans. I do have interest in the Etruscans but fascism, after all, is the major social and political virus of our century, garbed alternately as statism, nationalism, ethnocentrism, racism, and the religiously hege-monic. It is a fuse which lurks everywhere, inclusive of our souls, were we honest to so admit. I tend to see the fascist temperament as au na-turel, alas.

Etymologically, the word fascism traces to the Latin *fasces*, a cylindri-cal bundle, not of a Monet haystack, but of wooden rods, from "which an axe projected." Originally in its Roman form the "fasces" denoted "regal and magisterial authority." In our time, it means authority seized, usually, and this is very significant, with widespread compliance. How and why does this happen? What is it about human history that finds us so prone to being "taken over," marshalled, managed, coerced, and rent one from the other, on behalf of one or the other transient, episodic excuse? How does it come to be that generation after generation, having undergone profoundly sorrowing, disabling and hurtful experiences with oppression, finds a way to engender it once more? Is there no escape from our propensity to "escape from freedom," to use the baleful and trenchant phrase of Erich Fromm?

At this point, a voice from the audience is heard to say, that of which you speak is not America. We know of freedom, it is our birthmark. We know of this subtle foe, the fascists, and we are guarded against them. We have a name for them: tinhorn, a bleater, pompous and empty. Trust us, this is America. I know my rights! I have my rights! And we can see through this fascist threat, as echoed in that self-preening refrain, "it can't happen here." In therapeutic parlance, all this chatter adds up to the devastating presence of denial. Instance, for example, that the declarative phrase "it can't happen here" rarely follows the question, rarely asked, "can it happen here?" What is the status of an answer to a question not seriously posed, let alone explored? Bogus! So, for me, at least as a participant-observer, it *can* happen here. Let us take a look at why. Certainly, several replies could be positive, some even hopeful. Some could be cheering or possibly cheerful. Yet, when visiting, a young Russian philosopher told me that he has never been in the presence of people who had so much and yet were so interiorly tense. He lives in Moscow!

Visitors come from far-away places. The most recent to my home came from China and Russia. They ask of me, so what do you think of America? What's going on? Now there are many, many replies possible. The three perceptions that I offer here should come as no surprise. Yet stringing them together may be of help to us, analogous to the effort of Karl Jaspers, who in 1930 wrote of *Die Geistige Situation der Zeit*. That did not work! For the present context, however, let us isolate the most nefarious responses. First, in America we seem not to like each other.

Contentiously divided by skin-color racism, narrowing religious ideology, gender conflicts, and an increasing class-consciousness, we have come to view the "other" as alien, not only to ourselves, to our own groupings, but alien, as well, to the very mission and meaning of America. In this setting, one which is profoundly ahistorical as to our originating intentions, America is conceived in a way that is simply self-serving, merely a locale for our personal ambition. Rather than seeing the "other" in terms of enlightening and enriching difference, we find ourselves responding with indifference, stereotypical ignorance, or adversarially. It seems to occur less and less to us that for the "other," we are their "other."

In this vein, obviously I am supportive of multicultural education, though I find the fracas over its implementation appalling. How did we get ourselves into a situation whereby we must legislate, by curriculum no less, that we should have an interest in the historical and cultural lineage of those whose lives and roots differ from ours? For all of my life, I have taken such affectionate curiosity as a given, as in, what do they do and why? The expectation was that they would do likewise!

The attempt to legislate moral sensibility has been and can only be but a prod, a DEW line that signals the presence of trouble ahead. Only by a turning of the heart, a *teshuvah*, as bequeathed to us by ancient Jewish wisdom, will we be able to effect a healing of this body politic. Only by a realization that pluralism means living harmoniously with those with whom we disagree, permanently and intractably, will it be possible to protect ourselves from that internecine strife that previews a "takeover." Pluralism is not a fall from the grace of unity, not a step on the way to final resolution of disagreement, difference, or conflict. Pluralism is an ontology, a "form of communal life," without which neither this American nation nor the planet can survive, humanly.

A second perception in this jeremiad addressed to contemporary America has to do with the erosion of compassion. In its stead, we find ourselves, virtually all of us, including me, using the language of punition. The basic human approach of rehabilitation, the sense of the redemptive, is now regarded as the acme of liberal naiveté. In its place, we turn to the lockup, solution by capital punishment, and, most frightening, scapegoating by race, religion, economic class, or virtually any category of a gathered "other," cited euphemistically as "those people." It is of dolorous note that most fascist movements of the modern time began with scapegoating as a self-denying cover for internal, spiritual emptiness.

The steady disappearance of compassion has gone beyond a response to those who commit asocial acts and who are obviously at fault. It now extends to the impoverished, the homeless, those in need of economic assistance and to the underclass, *uberhaupt*. We continue to be flooded with social science research about "these people," now numbering in the millions, offering us profiles, statistics, and gloomy prospects about their future and the cost to us, the good others. The gap between the announcements of peril from the research cadre and actual, hard-core institutional acts to effect remediation and help looms larger with each passing decade.

A story. When I was a teenage youth, I worked in a supermarket, the A&P. After the store closed on Saturday evenings, I had the task of running an errand. I took the day-old bread, cakes, and the perishable vegetables to the Odd Fellows home, a considerable distance away. I thought to myself, who are these Odd Fellows, living in this giant Edward Hopper–like red brick building? I never met one. I never saw one. Were they Odd because they were left over? Were they Odd because they acted strange but not so strange as to join the 100,000 persons locked up in three mental hospitals on Long Island? Or were they simply homeless and therefore cared about in a domestically gentler time—the 1940s?

If one were to spend participatory time, as I have, in a mission, shelter, halfway house, prison, or support group, nothing becomes more apparent than the utterly complex, gnarled, and bewildered faces of "these persons," so faceless in the media and in research case studies. One meets here the emotionally, physically abused; the ambulatory schizophrenic numbed by thorazine; abandoned infants and children; the chronically, clinically addicted; the deracinated; and those whose lives have unraveled, plunging them into a farrago of rules, regulations, and closing doors everywhere around them. Despite the heroic, although given the scale of diremption, spasmodic efforts of those who come to help and who still have compassion as their raison d'être, the unspoken word, more often than not, is hopeless. We have constructed a social service bureaucracy that has taken on a life of its own, one which tramples the lives of those it was created to serve.

It is of note that this macabre version of an allegedly compassionate society has begun to infiltrate the middle class. Pensions are cut and even disappear. Necessary routes of transportation are obviated and legitimate expectations for geriatric health care are threatened. The canopying words emerge as a broken promise, a reneging, a distancing of understanding. In the face of this development, we scapegoat those worse off rather than challenge those who profit from our demise. These are the circumstances which historically seed and feed incivility and oppression.

Our third perception is dramatically factual. As a society, we are awash in weapons of violence (read "guns") of all kinds, sizes, and power, everywhere and available to everyone. The fist, even the clenched fist, has been reduced to mush. Vigilantes on behalf of well-being urge the forbiddance of boxing matches and we worry about helmet laws. In the midst of this, one state after another, now more than twenty, passes a law allowing concealed weapons—guns, that is. We had a conference here at Texas A&M where we were told that the carrying of concealed weapons will make Texas a more polite society. The authenticity of that *politesse* eludes me. Also, just recently we received a "public service" announcement from the cafeteria chain known as Luby's, well-known for apple pie. Their spokesperson told us of a decision made by them on our behalf; namely, it is acceptable to dine at Luby's while in possession of a concealed weapon.

(Scenario: Hey dad, it's Saturday. What are we going to do tonight? We are going to Luby's for a Saturday night special—apple pie. Dad, supposing they run out of apple pie? Then we shall have our own Saturday night special.) Was not this the message of an angry man a generation ago, Rap Brown, who told us violence was as American as apple pie! Luby's, of course, holds that it is simply responding to its own history, the massacre of innocent patrons in its cafeteria located in Killeen, Texas. And that outburst takes its place in a series of equally violent and inexplicable assaults, beginning with the one at McDonald's in San Ysidro, California, and now coming at the rate of one every few weeks. Take the latest. A "guy" is a waiter for nine years—continuously employed, as they say. He hears bad news from the IRS, a draconian and Orwellian institution if ever there were one. He loses it. What is the "it" that he loses? Balance, context, a belief that time is on his side. He has had deep feelings of being hunted. Have you been hunted? He seizes a school bus with disabled children. Everyone thinks he has a gun, a bomb, a nuclear bomb. Such is our climate. He goes down in a hail of bullets—over, it is over. Is it? Who are these persons that erupt in episodes of maiming and killing? Their profile is not that of the thug, the criminal. Rather, they are of us, one of us, known to us. Who would have thought. We just experienced a savage murder here in this town, perpetrated by a "nice guy," one very active in a student religious center. Who could figure. Again, he lost it, whatever that mythic "it" may be.

I have had the experience of a daughter so assaulted, complete with guns and firebombs, smack in the middle of an upscale neighborhood in Houston. There are now more private security guards than public police in this nation. Gated and protected communities are springing up everywhere. Do not walk after dark, park next to the building. What is remarkable about this situation is that we seem to think that this is the way it was and that this is the way it has to be. Recall that when we first put metal detectors in airports, there came to be a great deal of grumbling, staccatoed by that self-deceiving line, "this is a free country." Now we are mute when metal detectors are placed in schools, hospitals, and courthouses. These devices of surveillance are not in response to international terrorism, but clearly are directed at local violence, inclusive of that perpetrated by children.

Obviously, something very, very serious has gone awry in the American frame of mind, in the American set of expectations, in, dare we say it, the American way. "Back to basics," we hear, meaning language and numbers. I think that it would be more salutary if we returned to that subject, jettisoned for more contemporary needs, known simply as Civics. Democracy is fragile. Fascism is a bully. We must avoid sentimentalism. Overturning the bully is rare. We treasure the David story but in truth, in fact, Goliath pervades the schoolyard, the work force, and the establishment. Some twenty years ago, I traveled alone through the communist states of Eastern Europe. In the main, that was a hoary and terrifying experience but for now I tell only one story. As I stepped off the little plane, late at night, at the Bucharesti airport, much to my surprise and considerable consternation, I was "met" at the bottom of the stairs by several *polizei*, complete with M16s and shepherd dogs. "Good evening," they said. I assure you, I also said good evening. On to the once-mysterious, now-browned-out city of Bucharest; decades later, after the curtain fell or was lifted, I saw a CNN clip of that very same central square in Bucharest. Citizens were gathered and they sang the Romanian national anthem—children sang that anthem. How did they know the words; it had not been sung for some forty years. I was deeply moved by this scene. Not as moved backward, however, as I was a month later. Another clip—same place, the square in Bucharest, featuring a riot, notably, Romanian boots on the prone bodies and faces of ethnic Hungarians. Democracy is fragile. The bully always finds an allegedly acceptable excuse to justify oppression. And so, my colleagues in this human odyssey, I see us, America, at a self-conscious, self-diagnosing crossroad. For us, there have been many crossroads before this one. Yet they had an obviousness about them, a sort of historical awareness of the way we were, even given their complexity, as in the period leading to our Civil War. This time, however, I see a difference in that I do not see the obviousness of this subtle foe, fascism.

The philosopher G. W. F. Hegel is of assistance here. In his *Phenomenology* Hegel writes of the "unhappy consciousness," one which has been self-satisfied such that it is unaware of its capacity to self-destruct from within. He details the presence of an insidious "invisible and unperceived spirit" which "insinuates its way through and through the noble parts," the "vitals," of our unconscious idolatry. And then Hegel draws on the wisdom of Diderot in *Rameau's Nephew*: "some fine morning it gives its comrade a shove with the elbow, when bash! crash! and the idol is lying on the floor."[2]

Given the present discussion, my reading of the above is simply that fascism will not come to America as an antidemocratic movement. Quite the reverse! If it comes, it will be as an eruption from within our self-preening, self-deceiving confidence in our own "practice" of democracy. So, in the concrete, although I find the militia movement in America unsettling, I do not see it or them as the harbinger of fascism. I do see, however, the contemporary crusading religious fundamentalist coalition as deeply foreboding, for they parade under the anthem of God and Country, thereby replicating the most dangerous of the historically numbing and oppressive movements. Hegel speaks of the cunning of history and here we face just that! Under the fake guise of pure American values and traditions, we are being coaxed into patterns of separation in our schools, opposition to gun-control laws, and a morally self-righteous smear on all alternate lifestyles. The insidious and seditious hook in this movement is its ability to convince many that their positions are not only authentically American but exclusively so. If ever there were the warning signs of an unhappy consciousness about to detonate itself, these are now before us.

Heeding the cultural self-diagnosis sketched above, the persuasions of this coalition sit in the belly of our democratic society as all right. Akin to the AIDS virus, their penetration into the center of our body politic is cloaked until they have clasped themselves to our immune system. As any clinical viral diagnostician will tell you, that is how it happens and that is why it is then too late![3] Is it too late? Who is to know the whereabouts of a thief in the dark of night? On the hopeful but tenuous assumption that it is not too late, I offer these suggestions on behalf of what John Dewey calls "funded experiences"—that is, the bequest of accrued, national wisdom.

There is a caveat and I have written it before, in fact, fifteen years ago: "The stark and startling residual wisdom of our collective past tells us that, for the most part, by far, all great movements of the past have been on behalf of a definite goal—in short, an eschatology. Further, conversely rare has it been for the multitude to devote themselves to a cause whose message was the celebrating of the finite, the generational, and especially, sheer transiency."[4] I believe this judgment still to hold, only more so, alas. And it is of serious note to realize that American thought, historically, does not feature a major ideological strand; nay, we do not have an embracing philosophy of history. In our pantheon of thinkers, gifted though they be, we do not have a Hegel, a Marx, nor even a Spengler or a Toynbee. The only powerful thinker in our history who set out to provide a *strengwissenschaftliche Geistesgeschichte* was Josiah Royce. After heroic intellectual efforts, he abandoned that European calling and mission under the experiential press of things and events American. As a reflective tradition, by far, we are chary of ideology, eschatology, and final words on anything important. I see this cultural and intellectual attitude as profoundly salutary. Yet it leaves us with a spiritual tapestry as exquisitely open as it is dangerously loose. And as William James once cautioned, into these openings flow threatening fictions of every kind. To which we add, especially those with false promises and short-term resolutions, both the hallmark of fascist strategy.

We cannot abandon our loyalty to these openings to novel experience. Nonetheless, we must be wary of our penchant to indulge the phrase of Kurt Vonnegut, "and so it goes," for, in time, it is we who will go—nowhere. I believe that on this treacherous issue of the rhythm existent between opening and closure in the affairs of the body politic, it is John Dewey who has it right. I offer you a passage of vintage Dewey:

> Life itself consists of phases in which the organism falls out of step with the march of surrounding things and then recovers unison with it—either through effort or by some happy chance. And, in a growing life, the recovery is never mere return to a prior state, for it is enriched by the state of disparity and resistance through which it has successfully passed. If the gap between organism and environment is too wide, the creature dies. If its activity is not enhanced by the temporary alienation, it merely subsists. Life grows when a temporary falling out is a transition to a more extensive balance of the energies of the organism with those of the conditions under which it lives.[5]

And that precipice is exactly where we are. So, what to do? In 1922, Dewey published his *Human Nature and Conduct*. The last three lines of that work I take as my understanding of an American secular liturgy: "Within the flickering inconsequential acts of separate selves dwells a sense of the whole which claims and dignifies them. In its presence we put off morality and live in the universal. The life of the community in which we live and have our being is the fit symbol of this relationship. The acts in which we express our perception of the ties which bind us to others are its only rites and ceremonies."[6]

Can we live with this commitment to the affairs of time? Can we live with this secular liturgy, stunningly apart from a meaning transcendent of our everyday affairs? As Americans, can we start over? Why not? Why not start over? Why not build an America which speaks the voice of the forgotten, the voice of the repressed, the voice of the new beginning? We, after all, are the supreme new beginners of the modern world. Why not tell the truth? Human life is fraught with conflict and oppression. Why not say that we will share our struggles as well as our accomplishments? We are the home of the proletarian individual. Any nation can be the home of the bourgeois individual, the few. We, historically, have celebrated the many—individuals en masse—and it would be in keeping with our best wisdom if we were to export that globally. We are the people who believe in the educability of all, no matter what the origin, situation, or previous failure. We are the champions of surprise.

A community, be it local, natural, or global, is worth its salt only insofar as it can provide for an integral voice of its members, no matter what their persuasion. The individual is paramount. Yet without a communal sanction the individual festers, often in self-deception about his or her worth. America has the potential capacity to structure a communal forum for individual life second to none. We cannot deny that the American dream has lost much of its glitter. Nor can we deny that our role in the global scene is infinitely more complex and controversial than we had expected. Yet no nation in the history of the earth has ever undertaken a more arduous and worthwhile task. We seek nothing less than to enable a wide variety of peoples, rooted in virtually every racial, ethnic, religious, and political tradition, to form a community in which each person lives out the uniqueness of his or her heritage and persuasion in a spirit of harmony and justice. This American nation cannot expect such communities to occur at the end of a gun or a rocket, nor can this nation use economic and legislative manipulation to carry such a profound message. To the contrary, only complete equity of opportunity for the individual will assure that America is building a bona fide community, one that will cast spiritual light on a deeply troubled world. We should seek to be emulated not for our power, but for our compassion. We should not seek to create a Leviathan, which features the war of all against all and mindless violence. Let us pursue the path of Royce's beloved community and let us reinvigorate the advice of Dewey, building slowly, from the ground up, face to face, and with empathy for one another. Without the other person, there is no community. The quest for America, resembling the human quest, is often lonely and ultimately sad, for, being finite, the quest ends in death. The nectar, therefore, is in the journey, and only the community can sustain that nectar by the presence of sharing, thereby assuaging our loneliness.[7] Warily the specter of fascism also offers an end to loneliness, although history has told us that such a promise is both ephemeral and devastating to all that we hold sacred.[8]

TWO

AN AMERICAN ANGLE OF VISION, PART 1

Introduction

In that land the great experiment of the attempt to construct society upon a new basis was to be made by civilized man; and it was there, for the first time, that theories hitherto unknown, or deemed impracticable, were to exhibit a spectacle for which the world had not been prepared by the history of the past.

—Alexis de Tocqueville, *Democracy in America*

I t is of singular importance that within the past half decade, two massive institutional structures, the Roman Catholic Church and the United States of America, have raised, under the aegis of charismatic leadership, the question of renewal. In both instances, there has arisen strong opposition, although the reasoning behind this has differed. In the case of the church, opposition has proceeded from a reading of the historical past to the conclusion of institutional immutability. The opposition on the American scene, however, while claiming historical antecedents, derives its strength far more from an analysis of the dangers in our contemporary situation. It can be said of the Roman Church that, for the most part, her past is on the side of doctrinal unity, reaction as a sociological cast of mind, and a correlative refusal to be led by the press of the wider cultural experience in which she finds herself. The American tradition, by contrast, is characterized by an historical series of compromises and adjustments, called by some a declension in doctrine, be it religious or constitutional, and a general responsiveness to environmental pressures.

Now the fascinating dimension in this issue, and the reason for introducing a comparison of these otherwise disparate institutional traditions, is that the crisis of the church in the modern period and the
parallel evolution of American culture are rooted in the same historical
matrix, the sixteenth-century reformulations of Western experience.
The same events that signalized the *fons et origo* of America sounded the
death knell for the medieval church. The structuring of a "New World,"
the Protestant Reformation and Copernicanism, are sixteenth-century
phenomena that sooner or later force a reconstitution of every major
discipline and perspective in the Western mind. The position here is that
the Roman Church, beginning with this period and until the present,
symbolizes the stance of tradition over against experience, while graphically revealing the infertility of "truth" defended apart from the historical context in which it is set.[1] By contrast, the American tradition,
awkward in doctrinal unity and vague in goal, not only symbolizes the
supremacy of experience over tradition but offers the management of
experience for human ends—that is, experiment—as the most genuinely
human endeavor.[2] A further contention would be that the American
style, particularly as characterized by its quality of irresolution on the
ultimate issues, is the style of the future, wherein experience, process,
and plurality are the leading and formulating metaphors, while structure, order, and unity are the derivative metaphors.[3] Put another way,
America tends to understand itself in behavioristic rather than in con-
ceptualistic terms. This is not to say that in the most general sense, the
American approach to the human situation is superior to other cultural
attitudes. Like all cultural formulations, it is an interweaving of advantages and disadvantages relative to the needs of human life. We seek here
only to explore the qualities at work in the American angle of vision, so
as to encourage their articulation for purposes of their assimilation into
world culture.

In order to sustain these judgments, two areas of inquiry come to the
fore: first, what are the generalized implications of the sixteenth-century
"breakthrough"; second, where do we turn for an adequate, though admittedly not exclusive, articulation of the dimensions peculiar to this
American approach?[4] The second concern is especially thorny since
America is a snarl of seeming contradictions. This can be seen not only

in terms of the evaluation of historical events, but even with regard to the interpretations of what we claim to be our most basic traditions. Seldom has a culture so expansive as ours been so hard-pressed to establish clear lines of origin and development. Speaking of the "ambiguity of the American experience," one recent commentator goes on to state that "its complexity lies below the surface and therefore makes a special demand on the historical imagination."[5]

Parenthetically, for those seeking some understanding of American culture, two major difficulties soon become manifest. In the first place, an analysis of the simply conceptual or intellectual tradition in America is more deceptive than in perhaps any other modern culture. The tools of analysis are themselves honed out of the European intellectual framework; while making contact with American experience on a terminological level, they rarely, if ever, pierce through to those processes that yield the qualitative characteristics at work in the development of American civilization. Continuity of language is no guarantee of a continuity of experience.[6] A revealing instance in point is the frequency with which American cultural and intellectual historians speak of an "American Enlightenment," thereby attempting to indicate the similarity of philosophical problems and resolutions in both European and American political and social writing of the eighteenth century.[7] Except for showing semantic continuity, this approach would seem to be very misleading. The problems that are at the heart of the genesis of the European Enlightenment are decidedly native to that culture. By contrast with the European context, nowhere in eighteenth-century America do you encounter the difficulty of calling for reform in the face of a geographically claustrophobic situation, with its ensuing burden of upending the conceptual and political dominance of two historically entrenched institutions. Reform in such a context demands not simply transformation but rather extirpation, to which the checkered history of the French Revolution bears eloquent witness. And, relative to those problems pertinent to the new notions of reason and nature, how could eighteenth-century America be said to grasp the gravity of the European philosophical revolution engendered by Hume, Rousseau, and Diderot, a revolution against an attitude that not only pervaded all fundamental endeavors of European life but was also allied with the political and religious powers

of the European tradition?[8] Although, historically, the American situation has to be seen in a quite different light, the absence of any as yet
indigenously American conceptual tradition (and this is a story in itself)
forced American eighteenth-century thought to express itself, whatever
the problem, in a language quite foreign to the kinds of experiences it
was undergoing. Isn't this what Emerson meant when he predicted that,
in time, "the writers of the English tongue shall write to the American
and not to the island public, and then shall the great Yankee be born."[9]
A neglect of such critical differentiations in cultural history, in what is
an all-too-frequent effort to offer a superficial cultural continuity, only
prevents our seeing the more fruitful continuity characterized by the activities of disparate cultures which, in a wider relational setting, opens
new possibilities directed toward the resolution of those tasks facing
man at large in any given century.

Continuing our parenthesis relative to the methodological questions
involved in any approach to the analysis of American culture, we see
that a second stumbling-block is the claim made for uniqueness.[10] The
interpretation of American civilization that long featured the simple
continuity of European and American values and institutions has again
seen the pendulum swing in the other direction. This shift can be seen
in the reading of the prefaces to the first and second editions of Herbert
Schneider's classic work, *History of American Philosophy*. In 1946 he
stated that "in America, at least, it is useless to seek a 'native' tradition,
for even our most genteel traditions are saturated with foreign inspira-
tions." And again, "We still live intellectually on the fringe of European
culture."[11] In 1963, however, he has this to say:

> I have inserted at the beginning of the bibliographical section, con-
> trary to my taste, a miscellaneous list of generalizing works on Amer-
> ican thought and culture. Having been called to task by a respectable
> number of earnest Americans, for emphasizing in the Preface the Eu-
> ropean context and matrix of philosophy in the colonies and in the
> subsequent United States, I am referring to recent works which,
> yielding to the temptation created by de Tocqueville and perhaps by
> the Garden of Eden, profess to understand the basic meaning and
> values of American existence and offer a certain amount of circum-
> stantial evidence for their insight.[12]

In our time this dialectic of continuity and discontinuity with regard to European culture is central to the history of American historiography.[13] Actually, we have never been able to agree upon an adequate and articulated response to Emerson's call for our structuring of "an original relation to the universe."[14] But such either/or efforts as we have been discussing here only emphasize the artificiality of such an approach. Certainly American cultural uniqueness cannot be isolated out by analysis of those historical events and attitudes which do not seem to occur elsewhere. There is strong doubt as to whether any important event could have such absolute uniqueness. It would seem that the approach should be quite different. Given a wider philosophical setting for an analysis of cultural life than the category of uniqueness or the aforementioned examination of the conceptual tradition at face value, the real task would emerge. It would be one which directs itself to an analysis of those qualitative happenings, in their most expansive historical setting, both cultural and extracultural, that show themselves to be new to the human situation as a whole. In this way, those energies heretofore devoted to setting up polar similarities or dissimilarities of one culture to the other fade into the background in favor of historical analysis that yields insight to the specific characteristics of any culture, in this case American, that are seminal for understanding the total contemporary situation. We are not, in other words, attempting to view America as a disjunct historical entity but rather as a world phenomenon. While heeding these methodological warnings, we should seek out those original qualities in American culture that maintain themselves as originating qualities for world culture. What, then, seems to be the most fruitful way to enable us to better understand the American angle of vision?

Certainly the analyses of the evolution of American religion and American political institutions have yielded the genesis and character of an American way of responding to the increased complexities of contemporary society. And American literature, although often a dissenting voice to the direction taken by American institutions, offers, nonetheless, a searing insight into the nature of American culture. This is to say nothing of those revealing local traditions, such as the development of American jazz,[15] or the peculiarly American experience of community.[16] Fundamentally, however, it is a shift in the mode of inquiry that is at stake here, and thus, in the most profound sense, it is a philosophical revolution that is structured by the development of American culture. Daniel Boorstin, for one, contends that "the most fertile novelty of the New World was not its climate, its plants, its animals, or its minerals, but its new concept of knowledge."[17] He offers a maze of fascinating data to support this position and yet is insistent that this is an antiphilosophical tradition.[18] No doubt this traces in part to his abandoning at this point his otherwise persistent fidelity to the American context in assessing the major metaphors of explication. Thus, nature, self-evidence, and culture itself are handled, by Boorstin, and correctly I believe, in a peculiarly American way. Philosophy, by contrast, is utilized in a purely European sense, with pejorative overtones.[19] The irony here is that the one discipline specifically structured for an analysis of the problem of knowledge is banished from the discussion. We would hold, to the contrary, that the most immediate and revealing way to analyze the quality of this American mode of inquiry would be to examine and utilize that tradition in America for which this question is central—namely, American philosophy from James through Peirce, Royce, and on to Dewey.[20] The themes engaging these thinkers, despite their philosophical complexity, can be seen as American writ large: the pluralistic and unfinished universe; the world and the individual; loyalty and sectionalism; and especially the concerns of Dewey, who ties us back to the sixteenth century by affirming that we must cease the quest for certainty as though we lived in a pre-Copernican world and turn instead to the dramatic interactions of experience and nature.

Although by no means an exclusive point of departure, it can be said that the sixteenth-century revolution in thought and the American classical tradition, coupled together for purposes of analysis, yield a unique perspective from which to reconstruct the major characteristics of the American angle of vision. And it should be emphasized that genuine historical continuity exists between these two foci, for if the sixteenth century is a revolution in the kind of experiences to be had, American classical philosophy devotes its energies, in the main, to a delineation of the ramifications for human inquiry when experience is taken to be the seminal metaphor. Indeed, the history of American life can be viewed as a struggle to maintain order and a sense for tradition while holding to an ever more self-conscious affirmation of the supremacy of experience.[21] Let us examine the first of these two areas of concern in some detail.[22]

The Historical Dimension

Historical generalizations are always easy to formulate, but increasingly more difficult to sustain.[23] No longer do we hold to radical breaks in historical continuity or hold to the absolute novelty of positions taken by individual thinkers. The roots of given events are found imbedded deep in the historical past. But, dependent on the type of problem with which we are concerned, some events are more important than others. Dewey tells us that "there is no event which ever happened that was merely dynastic, merely scientific, or merely technological. As soon as the event takes its place as an incident in a particular history, an act of judgment has loosened it from the total complex of which it was a part, and has given it a place in a new context, the context and the place both being determinations made in inquiry, not native properties of original existence."[24] As an illustration of this, we can say that the history of Western civilization is not without its irrational conflicts and severe shifts in value structure. But the vicissitudes of such a context are often not apparent to narrative history, despite the considerable quantity of historical data that we accrue. And while the historical origins of such happenings are complex and often reach beyond the immediate context, such historical causation, even if verifiable, is not equivalent to the quality of the experience in question. Such an identification of the experience undergone with its historical roots is a subtle version of the genetic fallacy and to commit it is to substitute explanation for experience.[25]

Although we should proceed within the framework of a fundamental narrative history, let us invoke the principle of contextualism as a legitimate method to elucidate those specific problems pertaining to the origin and development of American culture. The primary problem has to do with the American awareness of the pre-American past. It is important to realize that America has no experience of Greek or Medieval roots, geographically considered. Her entire experience of Western civilization is distilled through post-sixteenth-century men; indeed, for the most part, her own tradition originates with the seventeenth century. The Western culture that is assumed by early America is a tradition that had been critically reformulated in the sixteenth century. And even though these reformulations do not show up in America in a one-to-one correspondence, they preclude the possibility of the classical-medieval position functioning as the total point of departure in the formation of a new culture. In that sense, America differs profoundly from the modern European West.

A specific question now comes to the fore: what were the major qualities to emerge from this reconstitution of experience that characterized Western civilization when America came into being and began her own tradition of self-consciousness? It is, after all, only this version of the West that is immediately pertinent to an understanding of the genesis of American culture. And it is within these terms that we can focus on those decisive changes in the Western world which occur just prior to the origin of America. They can be summarized as (1) the cartographical revolution brought on by the awareness of a new continent, (2) Protestantism, and (3) Copernicanism.[26] In each instance they signalize a new start, a new order, and, most important, a new locus for human activity and inquiry.[27] Together they undo the religious, philosophical, cosmological—and in the long run, sociological—fabric that characterized the West until that time. While not separable from the cultural transformations that reach back into the medieval world, particularly in the areas of science and political order, these three major events play the fundamental role in structuring all subsequent Western experience, and to this day, mark the dividing line between the classical world and modernity.

1. The New World

First, chronologically, and, so far as America is concerned, in order of importance, is the acknowledgment of a *mundus novus*. This awareness is graphically demonstrated by the publication in 1507 of the *Cosmographiae Introductio*, with the accompanying Waldseemuller-engraved world map, in which a "fourth" part has been added to Europe, Asia, and Africa as constitutive of the "Island of the Earth."[28] Much of the literature about this event has focused on the Columbus-Vespucci controversy as to the priority of discovery, or even as to the intent of discovery. This need not occupy us here, for that on which all commentators agree, no matter their persuasion, is of much more significance. "Columbus's 'other world' and Vespucci's 'New World' meant one and the same thing: a world unknown to Ptolemy or the ancients."[29] Relative to the very framework of the world, in geographical terms, man had to abandon his belief as to its insularity and was forced to see his previously privileged *insularum Domini* extended on through the sea, and after Magellan, even turning round on itself. O'Gorman gives eloquent testimony to this transformation:

> It is clear, then, that in the thesis of the *Cosmographiae Introductio* the crisis which ever since Columbus' third voyage had threatened the ancient concept of the world reached its final climax. The moment that the *Orbis Terrarum* was conceived as transcending its ancient insular bounds, the archaic notion of the world as a limited space in the universe assigned to man by God wherein he might gratefully dwell lost its *raison d'être*. Since then man has been in a position to comprehend that his world has really no bounds because it is in any and every part of the universe of which he can possess himself; that the world is not something that was providentially given to him as a dwelling-place but something of his own making, and therefore something for which he is responsible as owner and master. From the moment that the *Orbis Terrarum* was conceived as embracing the whole globe, both land and sea, and no longer circumscribed only to the Island of the Earth, man opened for himself the road to the conquest of the universe. The universe no longer appears to him as a strange, alien and forbidden reality belonging to God and made for His sake, but as a vast inexhaustible quarry of cosmic matter out of which man may carve out his world, depending not on divine permission, but solely on his own initiative, daring, and technical ability.[30]

Given such an upheaval in man's fundamental way of relating to his "world," it was but a short time until the exploratory thrust passed from the intrepid soldiers of fortune to become more of a collective experience, in which the possibility of an alternative geographical setting became mythologized into the paradise theme so inextricable from

European responses to the New World. And so, through a tangled skein of motives—religious, economic, political, and social—there begins what may have been the last great migration of peoples upon the earth.[31] Significantly, it is directed toward a New World and a fresh start. De Tocqueville, retrospectively, describes this experience.

> Everything is extraordinary in America, the social condition of the inhabitants as well as the laws: but the soil upon which these institutions are founded is more extraordinary than all the rest. When the earth was given to men by the Creator, the earth was inexhaustible; but men were weak and ignorant and when they had learned to take advantage of the treasures which it contained, they already covered its surface and were soon obliged to earn by the sword an asylum for repose and freedom. Just then North America was discovered as if it had been kept in reserve by the Deity and had just risen from beneath the waters of the Deluge.
>
> That continent still presents, as it did in the primeval time, rivers that rise from never-failing sources, green and moist solitudes, and limitless fields which the plowshare of the husbandman has never turned. In this state it is offered to man, not barbarous, ignorant, and isolated, as he was in the early ages, but already in possession of the most important secrets of nature, united to his fellow men, and instructed by the experience of fifty centuries.
>
> Thus the European leaves his cottage for the transatlantic shores, and the American who is born on that very coast plunges in his turn into the wilds of central America. This double emigration is incessant; it begins in the middle of Europe, it crosses the Atlantic Ocean, and it advances over the solitudes of the New World. Millions of men are marching at once towards the same horizon; their language, their religion, their manners differ; their object is the same. Fortune has been promised to them somewhere in the West, and to the West they go to find it.[32]

If for some, this wending to the West culminated in their arrival in America,[33] for many more it was the beginning of a continuous process that remains at work throughout American history.[34] And in our time when we can speak of "a new frontier," it symbolizes the inseparability of growth from horizon.[35] In a broad historical sense, the affirmation of a deeply felt tie between American life and the cartographical revolution of the sixteenth century is inescapable. But such a tie was no static thing;

rather should it be seen in terms of the continual reconstitution of experience.[36] The wending to the West is an attitude, a reflection of what Karl Jaspers calls an "epochal consciousness," and, in this particular instance, its decisive quality is found in the emphasis given to the response to novelty.[37] The affirmation of a new continent offers a new option for bypassing the series of interiorized revolutions that characterized the history of European culture. The locus of experience now shifts and Western man confronts what William James is later to call the "push and press of the cosmos."[38] The previous historical continuity, particularly as characterized by an increasing self-consciousness within the European tradition, is now broken into on behalf of a geographical revolution. It is of the utmost importance to realize that this relocation of the primary resource for experience and the very coming into being of America are conjoined on the one matrical stem, historically considered. This double dimension—of European consciousness of its future and American consciousness of its past—yields a dialectic that forms the substance of the Euro-American world. Depending on the position, European or American, from which perspective is taken, the nature of this dialectic shifts its meaning.

Proceeding here, from the American side,[39] the major questions emerge as to how that Euro-American continuity was originally understood by the first settlers, or during the revolution, or subsequently, with nineteenth-century immigration and a further trek West; or how it is understood when such movements are no longer directed to "free land" but to new ways of structuring the human community as a geopolitical society; or finally, its ultimate implication for the relationship to be forged between earthly man and the astral settlements on which we now plan. Whatever be the qualitative changes in the concerns of American life, it can be safely said that thus far the American way is a continuing reflection of its continuity with this sixteenth-century geographical upheaval, for it still looks to the immediate future as a more seminal resource than its structured past. In her conclusion to *Meetinghouse Hill*, Ola Winslow offers us this text: "March 5, 1770 (The day of the Boston Massacre): Voted that the committee appointed to underpin the new meeting house shall take as many of the stones under the old meetinghouse as they think proper."[40]

2. The New Religion

We come now to the second major breakthrough in the sixteenth century: namely, the Reformation. Granted the myriad of diverse phenomena that can be gathered under this event, one can still hold to the historical reality of a Protestant response to, and reconstruction of, experience. Furthermore, while it should be acknowledged that the development of European Protantism is but a large strand in a very complex total culture—featuring, among other elements, residual Roman Catholicism, the tremendous thrust of modern philosophy, and the evolution of scientific method—it can be stated that no such extrinsic complexity engulfs the Protestantism that begot America. Indeed, if there is one historical event that yields an all-too-infrequent clarity, it is the way in which the Protestant approach to experience holds sway over the early development of American culture.[41] This is not to contend that the Protestant temper was a univocal affair, for even a casual reading of American Puritan history would disabuse one of that simplistic notion. But it is to say that there existed a Protestant angle of vision, particularly to be differentiated from pre-Reformation Christianity, and more particularly as the former works itself out in the American context.[42] Here again, we have the double dimension of a sixteenth-century breakthrough: first, the ending of a classical European tradition; and second, its most obvious meaning found in a new approach to experience, as primarily located on the American scene.

The first aspect of the Reformation was to rend the allegedly seamless garment of the Church of Christ. That such a claimed Catholicity was not in keeping with total historical fact—witness the Orthodox schism, as well as the basic irrelevance of the church to the vast population of the non-European world—is really not to the point. Given the European culture under analysis here, the Roman Catholic Church exercised a hold on religious consciousness and persuasion. The Reformation, especially as it worked itself out, put an end to that tradition and more significantly, although often not by intent, raised the ominous question as to whether any single version could ever again, in any legitimate sense, hope to be solely responsible for the working out of the biblical deposit. Originally seen as in large measure a return to the spirit of the early church, the Reformation in its European setting was faced with the awesome problem of reconstituting a society, which even in its secular manifestation, yielded at every turn an imaging of the Catholic tradition. After the Counter-Reformation and after the Thirty Years' War with its Treaty of Westphalia, and especially when contrasted with previous power, there is something pathetically ineffectual about the entire effort of European Christianity. Relative to the critical questions, an entirely new frame of reference for European culture, rooted in philosophy, science, and secular political thought, had passed it by.

Such was not the case, however, with the other thrust of Protestantism—namely, its errand into the American wilderness. Of significance here is the problem of growth or decline relative to the development of American Protestantism. An analysis of this question yields much insight into the peculiarities of American life and to the basic question of the best methodological approach to the problematic of American culture.

In his interpretive essay on a 1670 election sermon, significantly entitled by Samuel Danforth "A Brief Recognition of New England's Errand Into the Wilderness," Perry Miller raises the problems centering on the double meaning of "errand." Was the burden of the errand to be found in what was brought to America, or rather to be found in what was accomplished in America? In this essay, and elsewhere in his writings, Miller seems to waver between holding, on the one hand, that the tradition which founded America suffered subsequently from severe doctrinal erosion, declension, or, more bluntly, a loss of faith, and, on the other, that "under the guise of this mounting wail of sinfulness, this incessant and never successful cry for repentance, the Puritans launched themselves upon the process of Americanization."[43] In short, they became more intrigued with what they found than with what they brought. It is true that Miller, emphasizing the wilderness as he does, offers the most sophisticated version of this alleged declension of Protestant life. We must emphasize "alleged," however, because the charge of declension has to rest upon the evaluation of an ongoing historical experience in the light of one extrapolated stage of its development. This approach is, I believe, generally unjustifiable, but notably so relative to Protestantism in the New World. After all, the stage chosen is one barely

out of the infancy of the Reformation itself, relocated in a totally different physical environment, and forced to start from scratch on almost
every major question, particularly the fundamental and pressing problem of generating a polis. "Declension" is obviously a relative term, and
it can be held that the decisive contribution to the formation of the
American approach to experience is a richer, and ultimately more consistent, doctrinal continuity for Protestant thought than the effort to
duplicate the patriarchal tradition. One thing is sure: to effect a comparison between the several generations, ostensibly committed to the same
doctrine but operative in considerably different sociological contexts, is
to subscribe to a "vicious abstractionism." A context is no separate thing
or container in which doctrinal persuasions play themselves out; rather,
it is of the very structure of the doctrine itself and in changing such
context, there is generated a like change in doctrinal meaning, although
the mode of expression often hangs on. In any event, what we hope to
break open here is the underlying problem of tradition and change, or,
more specifically, of novelty and continuity.

In order to come adequately to grips with the historical dimensions
in such a complex experience as the coming to America of Reformation
thought, one must not only acknowledge the diversity of Protestant
strains represented in such an event, but also must be willing to abandon
what could be called the "Euclidean" mode of inquiry.[44] In the latter
approach, the development of a tradition follows the character of a line,
with before and after, given and imposed, inside and outside as legitimate metaphors for purpose of evaluation. In taking such an approach—unhappily the prevalent one in most narrative history—we act
as if neither Hegel, who viewed history as dialectic, nor William James,
who held to a streaming relational field as the mode of inquiry, had ever
appeared upon the scene. It is of note that both these approaches,
among others equally non-Euclidean, are widely accepted by disciplines,
other than history, which deal with human behavior.

Let us be more specific here and analyze the problem of novelty, with
the Protestant experience in early America as the focal point. The major
difference that emerges from the Protestant experience in America, as
over against its European origins, has to do with the distinct, and ultimately more expansive, field of experience in which it works itself out.

The very phenomenon of the Reformation, in its European setting, was inseparable from the historical traditions, both religious and civil, from which it claimed to be a departure. Although in formulation and mode of expression this dialectic seemed also to characterize early American religious concerns, we would argue—and here is the critical point—that in the American situation the historical tradition had a minimal *experiential* significance that decreased rapidly.[45] Thus the field of experience in which the Protestant vision found itself in America had so shifted in all the decisive areas as to render the ostensible doctrinal continuity actually novel in implication. Thereby what is seen as declension from the perspective of straight historical narrative takes on more complex, and perhaps more fecund, dimensions when one admits to an elementary principle of the sociology of knowledge—namely, to the fundamental inseparability of "meaning offered" from the setting in which it is to be evaluated.

Novelty, then, from this perspective, is not necessarily separate from continuity, but may very well be the most genuine formulation of it. Novelty as distinct from the "old" in some separate way is a phenomenon different from the novelty that shows itself to be a realization of those things implicit in the tradition that emerge under the pressure of new events. The second type of novelty is best understood by a doctrine of relations rather than by a doctrine of separateness.[46]

Once again, we would maintain that the full continuation of the Reformation is to be found not in the attempt to keep alive a literal version of the particular positions taken by the pioneer reformers, but rather in continuing the basic attitude which holds that we must turn from an already-structured version of experience (this latter is historically the Roman Catholic position, although it may be untrue to the deeper insight of the church) to opening ourselves to wholly new resources for salvific sustenance. A statement of Paul Tillich has meaning here: "The inner dilemma of Protestantism lies in this, that it must protest against every religious or cultural realization which seeks to be intrinsically valid, but that it needs such realization if it is to be able to make its protest in any meaningful way."[47] Such a position seems to persist throughout the many variants of the Protestant persuasion. One sees it at work in the stress on conversion that signalizes early Puritan life, the emphasis on the "inner light" of the Quaker tradition, and the thirst for a new "awakening," or awareness, which features in revivalistic activities. Indeed, it is of paramount concern in that continuing and intensive struggle over the inter-relationship between a "covenant of grace" and a "covenant of works" that begins with the Hutchisonian controversy of Massachusetts Bay and lasts on into the very fabric of American life, recast as the tension between thought and action.[48] Actually each in its own version starts anew on the question of whence salvation, thereby choosing to bypass the long-standing contention of historical Christianity that it had settled such a question long ago.[49] More revealing still is the development of denominationalism and the persistent shift from one denomination to the other, pointing as a consequence to the conviction that the institutional framework is but a point of departure for placing us in touch with saving experience rather than that by which we are necessarily circumscribed.[50]

It could be said that, in speaking this way, we are describing the American temperament as much as historical American Protestantism. As hinted before, this is very much so, for American Protestantism and the formulation of America, in its most instinctual sense, are inseparable one from the other. The New England Puritans did not, as Miller contended, begin the "process of Americanization," for there was no such resource to put into operation. Rather, maintaining the revolutionary break with the classical West, they opened themselves to new experience and, in so doing, saw the full continuity of their doctrine, in time, beget the historical event that is America. If this fundamental approach to experience is of critical religious import, as Protestantism holds—or as John Dewey thought, as witness his plea for an "intellectual piety toward experience"—then in the most profound sense, the marrow of the American tradition is religious in implication.

On the other hand, the entire American tradition, as herein described, can be read as a fall from grace. The contemporary jeremiad takes the form of lamenting the successful assimilation of the Protestant tradition into the American cultural fabric. This is a particular concern of those for whom the "success" of American Protestantism is a sign of the erosion of its spiritual qualities.[51] We would argue the reverse and hold that the most positive qualities of American life are inseparable from the experimental and evolutionary attitudes of the Protestant persuasion. It may very well be, however, that the contemporary scene, no longer simply Protestant in religious conviction, demands a quite different type of religious response to the problems at work in American culture. Whatever this may come to upon further analysis, one thing emerges as clear: America, in its most original leanings, is inconceivable without the Protestant Reformation.

3. A New Cosmic Order

And now to the third of the great revolutions in the sixteenth century, Copernicanism. This sixteenth-century breakthrough differs from the two just discussed in that it is not, as such, one with the formulation of America. Yet, from a more expansive point of view, the novelty that is America could only be fully realized in a post-Copernican setting. If Christianity, in its original import, signalized the breaking into nature on the part of a radically reconstituted doctrine of the human person as an *imago Dei*, the historical development of Christianity chose, more often than not, especially in its Thomistic expression, to tie itself to the Greek doctrine of nature. However organic the interplay within *physis*,[52] the world of Ptolemy and Aristotle was cosmologically self-contained and had as its correlate a cyclic theory of history.[53] But if any one doctrine can be said to identify America, a first choice would be the affirmation of an "open nature," both writ large, as on the frontier, and microcosmically, as in the stress on individual resources, religious in origin, political in development. The correlate in this case differs, for, rather than being cyclic, the American tradition features an ongoing lineal doctrine of history, with its antagonism to hierarchies, as concretized in the elimination of economic and political feudal patterns. The American temper, relative to an active participation in nature, with its rhythm of stability and precariousness, and with the assumption of an enriched future, once engaged—in short, its emphasis on growth and change—without a framework of full intelligibility would have been sheer illusion in a Ptolemaic world. It is granted that such a confidence is not guaranteed by a post-Copernican world, but significantly, neither is it rendered utopian in the pejorative sense. Once the Greek view of nature had been broken,[54] America then symbolized not an aberration or an overly optimistic vision, but rather a genuine alternative to the classical Christian position on the complex entwining of history and eschatology. In commenting on this interaction of the geographical revolution and the Copernican revolution, O'Gorman has this to say:

> This formidable ideological revolution, so quietly brought about in the *Cosmographiae Introductio*, soon found its better-known expression in the new astronomical ideas that unchained the hitherto immobile terrestrial globe and made it a winged observatory of the heavens. But this revolution went even deeper; the world has ceased to be considered as a sort of cosmic jail, man was able to picture himself as a free agent in the deep and radical sense of possessing unlimited possibilities in his own being, and as living in a world made by him in his own image and to his own measure. Such is the profound meaning of this historical process which we have called the "invention of America," a process which implies modern man's contempt for, and his rebellion against, the fetters which he himself has forged under pressure of archaic religious fears. It was not by a chance coincidence that America appeared on the historical scene of Western culture as the land of opportunities, of the future, and of freedom.[55]

Perhaps a further comparison could be made. Just as Greek culture was the medium through which emerged the philosophical metaphor that played such a decisive role in the formation of European culture, so, too, it may be that American culture is the medium through which will emerge the philosophical metaphor utilized in the formation of the new geopolitical man. The difference between these two situations, at this writing, has to do with the absence, thus far, of an adequate articulation of the American tradition in its full philosophical implications.

What, then, is this Copernican revolution that we make such extensive claims for it? Copernicanism is the watershed of the modern world.[56] Severing the tie of man to the world that had existed since the Greeks, the Copernican revolution thrust to the fore the conviction that man, whatever his reluctance or his protest,[57] is the center of the universe and the source of its meaning.[58] Quite aside from the technical astronomical difficulties that resulted from the ending of the geocentric

universe, there existed also the stubborn refusal on the part of the European West to face the human import of the new cosmology. The often
repeated lament of John Donne from his "Anatomy of the World" is
pertinent here:

> . . . new Philosophy calls all in doubt,
> The Element of fire is quite put out;
> The Sun is lost, and the earth, and no man's wit
> Can well direct him where to look for it.
> And freely men confess that this world's spent,
> When in the Planets, and the Firmament
> They seek so many new; then see that this
> Is crumbled out again to his Atomies.
> 'Til all in pieces, all coherence gone;
> All just supply, and all Relation:
> Prince, Subject, Father, Son, are things forgot,
> For every man alone thinks he hath got
> To be a Phoenix, and that then can be
> None of that kind, of which he is, but he.[59]

With the shattering of the former intimacy between man and what he
thought to be the physical presence of paradise, cosmically considered,
he had now to account for his centrality by turning to wholly new resources. Randall will go so far as to say that "The whole impact, in fact,
of the Copernican revolution was humanistic, and pointed to a new
glory of man in this world."[60] And although Protestant thinkers bitterly
opposed Copernicanism,[61] they had already, no doubt inadvertently,
opened the way to one of the most powerful alternatives—namely, a
radical doctrine of self-sustenance. Further, the concern for science as a
New Organon and especially the Cartesian revolution, with its emphasis
on the tremendous power of mind, point to this tireless effort to replace
the former source of meaning with one equally potent, and, ironically,
equally certain. The history of modern philosophy in the West can be
incisively analyzed with the problem of Copernicanism as a backdrop,
yielding in turn various ways to circumvent the ever-persistent possibility that man could not count on a meaning found but only on a meaning made. The familiar contemporary claim that human life is alienated
from the world of meaning is in large measure due to the overextended

and illegitimate expectations that characterized the traditional thought of the West. Refusing to go it alone, Western thought had, in general, alternated a series of salvific structures, hoping to bypass the inevitable tension that exists between the persistent search for complete certitude and the experiential presence of the equally persistent, limited meaning. After the seventeenth century, the full inadequacy of the Greek under-pinnings, particularly with regard to the doctrine of nature, made itself felt. It is Hume, over against the Newtonians and the Deists, who forces philosophy, and in the long run, science, to abandon the quest for abso-lute certitude.[62] From that point forward, European thought, within its own categories, has waged a tremendous struggle on the side of a hu-manly constructed and genuinely post-Copernican version of the world, over against the rationalist residue of a fully intelligible reality, explica-ble through the analysis of the "laws" of nature.

As one might expect, Hegel puts both positions into the same para-graph. "Still, however, knowledge of essential reality stands secure above vain and empty knowledge; and pure insight only appears in genuinely active form in so far as it enters into conflict with belief."[63] Bothered not a whit by the classical problems of philosophy, the American tradition until the mid-nineteenth century assumed, as a matter of course, that meanings were made rather than found.[64] And more significantly, when Americans became concerned with philosophy at the end of the nine-teenth century, they developed a metaphysics of "meanings made" and a cosmology that was explicitly and radically post-Copernican.

The perhaps fatal difficulty, of course, is that in withdrawing from "the quest for certainty," to use Dewey's phrase, and introducing the notion of compromise into metaphysics itself, the American tradition has moved toward an abandoning of what is still a major question for religion and philosophy: the ultimate formulation of the question of human destiny. In effect, how long can a culture structure its inner life and its responses to the major questions on what seems to be an ad hoc metaphysics? If European thought has had difficulty in concretizing in-sights through an ordered transformation of institutions, the American philosophical tradition has had the corresponding burden of having to accept the "price to be paid for making our thoughts speak to a limited experience and circumstance, the price of being so tied to the moment that we lose sight of the perennial or universal elements that bear on all moments."[65] Yet, it has to be said, that human values, in America, are most often and most seriously threatened by those who offer some ultimate principle of judgment.

Furthermore, although reluctant to resolve any question for all time, and chary of speculative systems,[66] this American temper may very well be more sustaining than at first appears. It should not be forgotten that since Copernicanism, there can be no turning back from this admission of an open universe. In a very real sense, European *thought* since Copernicus has simulated American *experience*, and attempted a "pioneer metaphysics" to respond to the staggering horizon of a universe whose experiential origins, reach, and ultimate end are shrouded in what looks to be permanent mystery.[67] Isn't this why Kant asked us to proceed *snit den ersten Gedanken des Kopernikus?*[68] And isn't this largely the approach of modern science, reluctant to discuss causality and opposing the position that the universe will again be seen as explicable from a single vantage point or reducible to a single theory or known once and for all?[69] Is William James so different, then, when he dovetails a cosmology and an American cultural attitude, concluding, from what he calls our "multiverse," that life is "or at least [involves] a muddle and a struggle, with an 'ever not quite' to all our formulas, and novelty and possibility forever leaking in."[70] This belief in a "multiverse" or "pluralistic universe," and the corresponding American penchant for an opened-out view of nature, is neither a romanticized nor mythologized position when contrasted with the actual contemporary scientific view of the world. The American view of nature, so poetized as an indigenous phenomenon, should be seen also as having, in our time, profound correlation with the directions taken by world culture relative to cosmic nature. Depending on our religious or philosophical persuasion we may balk, but like it or not, since Copernicus and with increasing force and rapidity, the American tradition of a broadly experimental participation in an unsettled and vague future is more deeply rooted in experience than what can only be called the antiquated belief in a "universe" and in the corresponding abstraction of ultimate intelligibility.[71]

A New World, a new religion, and, indeed, a new cosmos. Could we ask for a more auspicious setting for a new culture? Is it any wonder that as late as the nineteenth century, Lyman Beecher could say that we wanted to "show the world by one great successful experiment of what man is capable"?[72] And if America is such an experiment, why shouldn't it be vague as to the ultimate goal, especially born as it was of the upending of the major mythological and conceptual moorings of the West? There was nothing necessary about the direction of American culture, for it could have as easily justified a bemoaning of its outcast fate, cut off from the great riches of European culture. Although America never fulfilled the "exotic dream" intended for it by European culture,[73] it brought off something quite different. The American experience showed that tentativeness, rather than a fall from grace, could become the framework for the optimum realization of growth.[74]

Conclusion

If such an historical setting as the sixteenth century provides the backdrop to the origin of America, there remains, for subsequent analysis, the qualities that characterize the concrete activity of early American experience and their explication in the nineteenth century, particularly by philosophy. We are given the fact that an articulate and enlightened seventeenth-century generation submitted itself to the rigors of a totally primitive environment. In his address to the Philosophical Union of California in 1911, Santayana tells us that

> As much as in clearing the land and fighting the Indians they were occupied, as they expressed it, in wrestling with the Lord. The country was new, but the race was tired, chastened, and full of solemn memories. It was an old wine in new bottles; and America did not have to wait for its present universities, with their departments of academic philosophy, in order to possess a living philosophy—to have a distinct vision of the universe and definite convictions about human destiny.[75]

The ramifications of this reflective primitivism, so characteristic of the seventeenth century, and a factor in the continuing frontier experience, are considerable, for they intensify the effort to force nature to do the bidding of human concern, pose a radically different view of ideation, and point to the introduction of the experimental temper as central to human inquiry, rather than as simply an aid to the codification of a real world.[76] One could say, further, that the affection for context as the determinant for doctrine yields in the long run an explicit acknowledgment of the primacy of time as the source of intelligibility. Over against the doctrine of obsolescence in which the history of man waits patiently for a paradisiacal Deus ex machina, the American temper points to a temporalized eschatology in which the Spirit manifests itself generation by generation and all counts to the end.

Now whatever may be the richer implications of these dimensions in American thought,[77] further analysis should be carried on within the context of that triple revolution in the European sixteenth century, so inseparable from the origin of America and from the genesis of its peculiar angle of vision.

THREE

AN AMERICAN ANGLE OF VISION, PART 2

When a way of thinking is deeply rooted in the soil and embodies the instincts or even the characteristic errors of a people, it has a value quite independent of its truth; it constitutes a phase of human life and can powerfully affect the intellectual drama in which it figures.

—George Santayana, *Character and Opinion in the United States*

I n the case of America, to which Santayana's text primarily refers, the stakes are somewhat higher than that of an intellectual drama. For better or worse, the American perspective is engaged with other major cultures in formulating the dominant metaphors for world culture.[1] As with all massive cultural formulations, we find in America the perils and fruits of original attitudes not institutionalized elsewhere. Having already sketched some of the historical and methodological factors pertinent to the analysis of American culture,[2] we turn now to the major philosophical assumptions and implications of this tradition. Naturally, there can be no exhaustive treatment here of any of these issues; we wish rather to emphasize the confusion that frequently exists between the analysis of American philosophy and the philosophical analysis of American culture. Categories and persuasions often taken to be characteristic of the former are actually found to be broadly based attitudes of the culture at large.

During the classical phase of American philosophy, as well as in the subsequent work of Dewey, the culture and its philosophical tradition shared basic concerns and methods of articulation. The studied neglect of the American philosophical tradition by all but a handful of contemporary American thinkers cuts us off, then, not simply from a philosophical option, but from the articulation of basic culture categories. Philosophy in America has made tremendous strides in a professional and technical way; but with rare exceptions, it has failed to address itself to the exigencies of the culture in a language commensurate with the way in which the culture understands itself. A major reason for this is the increased sophistication of philosophical discourse, which renders the work of Edwards, Emerson, James, and even Dewey inadequate and infelicitous in expression.

What is not adequately realized, however, is the fact that these thinkers, among others, have their hands on a large set of basic, even primitive, reconstitutions of the way in which men structure inquiry, of the values they seek, and a fortiori of the role of philosophy. These concerns and their imaginative, though admittedly often vague, versions are indigenous to a culture which was attempting, within the ever-present framework of Western European civilization, to work out what Emerson plaintively called "an original relation to the universe."[3] While not always explicit, this theme is basic to American thinkers, at least until World War I. In the long run, when one considers that it involves such questions as the meaning of nature, time, experience, and the experimental attitude, this cultural development should prove to be more important than the various responses given by individual philosophers. Granted that we cannot nostalgically return to the alleged "Golden Age" of American philosophy, it remains that the questions which bound those thinkers to their culture are still with us, and, as with all important questions, are badly in need of ever-renewed philosophical analysis. The remarks which follow are an attempt to reopen some of these questions from the perspective of philosophy, always recalling their broader cultural significance.

The Ambiguity of the Spiritual Pilgrimage

In speaking of the American people during their formative years, Sidney Mead opens up the question that should increasingly occupy us now that we have obviously and irrevocably come to the end of any cultural and political separation from the pressing burdens of world culture.[4] We are, in a word, faced anew with the problem of national identity.

> Their great and obvious achievement was the mastery of a vast, stubborn, and ofttimes brutal continent. This is the "epic of America," written with cosmic quill dipped in the blood, sweat, and tears of innumerable nameless little men and women and a few half-real, half-legendary heroes. . . . This is the mighty saga of the outward acts, told and retold until it has *over-shadowed and suppressed the equally vital, but more somber, story of the inner experience. Americans have so presented to view and celebrated the external and material side of their pilgrims' progress that they have tended to conceal even from themselves the inner, spiritual pilgrimage, with its more subtle dimensions and profound depths.*[5]

The question at issue has to do with the qualities of this "inner experience." Are they distinctive enough to add dimension and insight to the human endeavor, as understood from a wider cultural perspective? Many would answer in the negative, seeing America as primarily a derivative culture with its strengths in the area of applied wisdom, both political and technological. There is a long tradition of such criticism, which the following remark of Walter Rathenau accurately sums up: "America has no soul and will not deserve to have one until it consents to plunge into the abyss of human sin and suffering."[6]

On the other hand, a case can be made for the original and seminal aspects of what Mead calls the "spiritual pilgrimage," although the commentator must scrupulously avoid any chauvinism in his analysis. Speaking of our tendency to harbor a "cultural hypochondria," particularly among intellectuals, Daniel Boorstin states:

> The cure for our hypochondria is surely not chauvinism. That simply adds one real ill to the many unreal ills of which we already accuse ourselves. Waving a flag cannot cure inner uncertainty. One possibility, at least a little more fruitful, is to try to discover the peculiar virtues of our situation, the special character of our history: to try to judge ourselves by the potentialities of our own peculiar and magnificent continent. We may then discover that our virtues, like our

ills, are actually peculiar to ourselves; that what seem to be inadequacies of our culture, if measured by European standards, are nothing but our differences and may even be virtues.[7]

This is also the intent of John Kouwenhoven's work in *Made in America: The Arts in Modern Civilization*. He writes in his preface that it is a book about America that

> assumes that the elements of creative vitality in American civilization matter a great deal, not only to Americans but to other people as well. It was written in the conviction that we cannot understand either the limitations or the achievements of that civilization if we continue to think of it solely as the product of Western European culture, modified by the geography and the climate of the New World.[8]

In the final analysis, a continual reassessing of the significance of any cultural lineage is actually a function of a more broadly based human endeavor. And it is not so much a question as to whether the American tradition is radically different from other cultures but whether, in its emphases, concerns, and blindspots, as generated by its historical situation, such a tradition doesn't offer options of a profound kind for the immediate human future. But the great obstacle to the articulation of such "inner qualities," at least in the American context, is that they do not lend themselves to any consistent ideological formulation. At times, this is a sign of great cultural insight: a living dialectic between a series of equally humanizing alternatives. Witness, for example, this perceptive commentary on the twofold reaction of the American people to Lindbergh's flight:

> One view had it that America represented a brief escape from the course of history, an emergence into a new and open world, with the self-sufficient individual at its center. The other said that America represented a stage in historical evolution and that its fulfillment lay in the development of society. For one, the meaning of America lay in the past; for the other, in the future. For one, the American ideal was an escape from institutions, from the forms of society, and from limitations put upon the free individual; for the other, the American ideal was the elaboration of the complex institutions which made

modern society possible, an acceptance of the discipline of the machine and the achievement of the individual within a context of
which he was only a part. The two views were contradictory but both
were possible and both were present in the public's reaction to Lindbergh's flight.[9]

At other times, however, the articulation of our experiences remains
trapped in a layer of self-deception that has often shrouded the way in
which we understand and value ourselves. And this becomes a particularly crucial problem as our society relies increasingly on the activities
of mass media for the development of self-understanding. In an incisive
and exacerbating treatment of contemporary American culture, Daniel
Boorstin shows how the externalized "image" of our experience has replaced the driving "ideal" that once motivated us:

> Of all nations in the world, the United States was built in nobody's
> image. It was the land of the unexpected, of unbounded hope, of
> ideals, of quest for an unknown perfection. It is all the more unfitting
> that we should offer ourselves in images. And all the more fitting that
> the images which we make wittingly or unwittingly to sell America
> to the world should come back to haunt and curse us. Perhaps, in-
> stead of announcing ourselves by our shadows and our idols, we
> would do better to share with others the quest which has been
> America.[10]

Can we offer another and more sanguine interpretation of the American
penchant for mirroring itself in what often becomes a series of fake versions of deeply felt needs and ambitions? Perhaps this imaging of which
Boorstin speaks is actually a degenerate form of a persistent symbolizing
activity, an activity so necessary for a culture whose bounds are set out
of events, often arbitrary, rather than as a response to deeply ingrained
traditional mores.[11] Recalling the historical dimensions of the origin of
America, particularly the influence on it of the origin of modernity and
the end of the fully intelligible universe, we must realize that the correlative upheaval in Western values could manifest itself in a series of ways.
In effect, given the American context, an underlying doctrine of an open
nature and an anthropomorphic view of historical destiny can generate

either a bold, ongoing symbolization of man's humanizing his environment, or a self-deceiving, pollyanna version of the world in which the
major dimensions of human life are lived vicariously.

American culture is, of course, shot through with these alternative
formulations and it is not adequately realized that they both proceed
from the same originating qualities and concerns, intrinsic to its historical development. Those who oppose the tawdry and seductive dimensions of contemporary American culture by appealing to a nostalgic
view of morally integral old America should be aware—as was Melville
in his *Confidence Man*—that the very trust in experience, so indelibly
and fruitfully American, was also the gateway to sham, corruption, and
the ultimate dissolution of the very fabric of truth in human affairs.[12]
Boorstin's *Image, or What Happened to the American Dream* can be read
as a modern version of Melville's critique, and although not as philosophically incisive, it is ultimately more terrifying, for it draws on the
wiles of the revolution in mass media, engendered by modern technology.

In order to come to grips with this basic ambiguity that surrounds
the fundamental categories of self-understanding in American life, we
have to analyze assumptions about "knowing," which are actually the
decisive factors in the framing of our fundamental value systems. In
contemporary terms, we must begin to utilize the perspective of a "culture-
epistemology." It is true that, taken in its widest ramifications, this
problem yields only to a thorough cultural history, but from the single
perspective of philosophy, several critical dimensions are opened up.
First, the emergence of an attitude toward knowledge, which results
from the concrete historical situation and its entwining of a primitive
environment with reflective and religiously wise settlers. This "reflective
primitivism" ultimately forges a new doctrine of the relationship between nature and experience. Secondly, in the cultural and historical development of this novel setting, there is manifested a basic rephrasing of
the fundamental relationship between thought and experience. To focus
on these concerns is to come to grips with one major strand of those
"inner qualities" central to American life; a strand which, when improp-
erly assessed, leads to much that is shallow and dehumanizing on the
American scene.

Reflective Primitivism: The Experience of Experience

In the American seventeenth century, philosophy was all but nonexistent; yet reflection was intense and self-conscious, primarily as a response to a pressing and omnipresent collective experience of a situation that was novel at every turn. And although that period in American history offered no articulation of the notion of experience as such, there was a correspondingly rich awareness of the significance of this situation over against the tradition of reflection. It was a period that dealt with profound philosophical themes without an articulated philosophical language. In effect, the American seventeenth century realized a broadly based cultural experience of experience. Santayana saw this clearly when he stated that "the country was new, but the race was tired, chastened and full of solemn memories."[13] And in a different context, Dewey offers this revealing comparison:

> In a certain sense the motif of American colonial history and of Defoe's *Robinson Crusoe* are the same. Both represent man who has achieved civilization, who has attained a certain maturity of thought, who has developed ideals and means of action, but is suddenly thrown back upon his own resources, having to cope with a raw and often hostile nature, and to regain success by sheer intelligence, energy and persistence of character.[14]

The most obvious and persistent import of this dialectic between the reflective tradition, as carried by the settlers, and the "new world" was the dominance of "experience" over any conceptual anticipation of "how things should be." The original situation had a clarity to it: "For summer being done, all things stand upon them with a wetherbeaten face; and the whole countrie, full of woods & thickets, represented a wild & savage hiew. If they looked behind them, ther was the mighty ocean which they had passed, and was now as a maine barr & goulfe to separate them from all the civill parts of the world."[15] Theory broke down here and "what one could build on this continent tended to become the criterion of what one ought to build here."[16] A factor in this development may very well have been the inability of colonial Americans to initially duplicate the English version of cultural proprieties. Thus "the American, 'this new man,' was early conceived in relation to civilized Europe, if not to the savage frontier, as a primitive."[17] This change in the spectrum of possibilities is engagingly caught in this excerpt from the *Autobiography of Sam Houston*: "And yet, this running wild among the Indians, sleeping on the ground, chasing wild game, living in the forests, and reading Homer's *Iliad* . . . seemed a pretty strange business, and people used to say that I would either be a great Indian chief, or die in a mad-house, or be governor of the State—for it was very certain that some dreadful thing would overtake me!"[18]

The cultural rejection by Europe fostered a sense of inferiority, but at the same time encouraged the colonial man to justify the richness of his own situation, making him open to new resources and ultimately to a different way of evaluating his needs and hopes. In this vein, Sanford states:

> The chosen people of the American colonies increasingly looked upon their mission into the wilderness not merely as the continuation of something old but as the beginning of something new: they were to usher in the final stage of history. They had inherited a new world in a physical sense, and in order "to vindicate the most rigorous ideal of the Reformation" they felt it necessary, in Jonathan Edwards' words, "to begin a new world in a spiritual respect."[19]

The literature of early America—John Smith, the Puritans, and subsequent commentaries on the continuing waves of settlement of "free land"—attests to this re-formation, and ultimately re-formulation, of basic value structures under the press of a new setting. The realization of this new setting was the dominant theme of the second-generation Puritans, of whom Perry Miller said: "Having failed to rivet the eyes of the world upon their city on a hill, they were left alone with America."[20] The stage was set for a long series of interactions between theoretical structures and a primitive but malleable environment.

Nowhere is the epistemological implication of this persistently renewed interaction between reflection and environment more cogently phrased than in this passage from the Virginia Convention of 1830. A spokesman from West Virginia states:

> But, sir, it is not the increase of population in the West which this gentleman ought to fear. It is the energy which the mountain breeze

and western habits import to those emigrants. They are regenerated, politically I mean, sir. They soon become *working politicians*; and the difference sir, between a *talking* and a *working* politician is immense. The Old Dominion has long been celebrated for producing great orators; the ablest metaphysicians in policy; men that can split hairs in all abstruse questions of political economy. But at home, or when they return from congress, they have negroes to fan them asleep. But a Pennsylvania, a New York, an Ohio, or a western Virginia statesman, though far inferior in logic, metaphysics, and rhetoric to an old Virginia statesman, has this advantage, that when he returns home he takes off his coat and takes hold of the plow. This gives him bone and muscle, sir, and preserves his republican principles pure and uncontaminated.[21]

It is not necessary to adopt Frederick Jackson Turner's often too optimistic view of the results of this exposure to the primitive situation. Rather, the persistent tension between ideas and experience should be the focal point, a tension that led Henry Nash Smith to write "Daniel Boone: Empire Builder or Philosopher of Primitivism?"[22] This is the tension which is so clearly caught by Arthur K. Moore in his book on Kentucky:

Thus, the real frontiersman, obsessed with the garden myth, and behaving accordingly, became entangled in several versions of the same myth projected into the wilderness by the romantic imagination. Existing both as abstractions derived from European ideas about nature and man and as objective realities embodying the practical consequences of those ideas, Kentucky and the Kentuckian may be said to have mediated between Western civilization and the civilization which evolved in the American West.[23]

What is crucial here, from the philosophical side, is that the press of environment as a decisive formulator of thought about the basic structures of the world became the outstanding characteristic of the American temperament. Pragmatism, so often regarded as the typically American philosophical product, is but a pale reflection of an ingrained attitude affirming the supremacy of experience over thought. It should be emphasized that this sense of the ineptness of anticipatory and defining concepts for managing experience was not only paramount in the early colonial period but was characteristic of the growth of American culture until the end of the nineteenth century. This is true not only for those who lived at the level of popular culture but also for those whose responsibility involved an articulation of general responses to the life-situation. The tension between beliefs held and experiences generated by incessantly novel circumstances, often of a physical kind, is a central theme in the thought of John Winthrop, Jonathan Edwards, Horace Bushnell, Emerson, Whitman, and, of course, James and Dewey, to say nothing of the major lines of political literature. For the most part, that tradition of American *thought* which we now regard as seminal, and even patriarchal, clearly sides with experience over reflection as the primary resource in formulating beliefs.

Contemporary America, however, has grave doubts about the present viability of this tradition, seeing it as no longer adequate to the complex ideational demands that confront us on every level. There is certainly a legitimate aspect to this contention, particularly if the meaning of experience remains fixed in the romantic metaphors of an earlier American version, or in the unimaginative formulations of British empiricism. But a careful analysis of the history of the notion of experience in American thought would show previous instances where outworn and sterile terminology was successfully reconstituted.

In a very real sense each generation is faced with using the method of experience to develop a language that is consonant with the events and potentialities of its own situation.[24] Such a transformation of the meaning of experience was accomplished by American philosophy at the end of the nineteenth century.[25] Not only did this tradition, beginning with Chauncey Wright, effect a total reworking of the properly philosophical meaning of experience, but it also provided a large set of metaphors capable of being utilized at the level of popular culture. Some of these, as for example Dewey's suggestions about education, have been worked into the fabric of American life. But others, like James's views in the "Moral Equivalent of War" and Dewey's "Common Faith," have only now been put to the test of relevance. Still others, such as Royce's doctrine of community and James's insight into individual energies within a fully cosmic scheme, can still serve in the future reconstitution of experience along lines consistent with the still-active assumptions of the culture.

The point at issue is that the reflective primitivism so deeply imbedded within the culture is primarily an attitude, which more than in any
other version of Western culture forces theoretical statements to respond more to the language of events than to its own mode of discourse.
What must not be forgotten is the primal fact that the American tradition of which we speak, due to its aversion to any separate mode of discourse, cannot be adequately confronted simply by an epistemological
critique of its shortcomings. Historically considered, this tradition was
faced with an ever-shifting scene, characterized by widespread geographical, political, and spiritual upheavals. These crises were built into
the very continuity of the culture, and it was thereby fitting that basic
and even primitive categories of understanding were transformed. The
meaning of the reflective experience is to point precisely to the fact that
such a transformation had its basis in the willingness of the culture, over
a sustained period of time, to listen to the informing character of
experience.

This was a culture which knew what learning meant and, significantly, was heir to a great tradition of learning. But it was also able to
accept the press of experience without submitting such an interaction to
a conceptual framework. Such an openness to experience has been well
documented in terms of the development of our political institutions,
but it has not been adequately understood as a broader doctrine of inquiry. Efforts in this latter direction have too often separated the concern for experience from the reflective attitude, thereby failing to realize
that in the American context reflection is not necessarily the bearer of
traditional intellectual values. What is needed is an understanding of the
tremendous effort within American culture to relocate the role of learning, and even to provide for a different method of generating basic principles—both seen as a function of the method of experience. In our
immediate cultural situation, we would have to admit that speculation
which is not linked to this persistent dialectic of reflection and experience
does not obtain an adequate hearing, but the charge of anti-intellectualism
against the culture is simply not to the point.

It might be said that the originality and power of the early formulation of American culture was inseparable from the mobility resulting
from its almost continental status and from the ever-present contiguous

"free land." Since such a situation no longer holds true, perhaps it would be wise to abandon the attitudes developed in that situation and make a fresh start. But any attempt to redirect American culture has to confront several deeply rooted metaphysical beliefs that are not easily gainsaid by traditional philosophical or theological terms. Furthermore, with events of staggering human importance manifesting themselves with unprecedented speed on the contemporary scene, in a world shrunken to geopolitical intimacy, there is neither time nor space to bring off a total, yet continuous, reconstitution of our entire lineage. Seemingly aware that we cannot effect such a momentous realignment of our tradition, and yet obviously dissatisfied with what seems to be an increasingly shallow way of responding to the larger questions of our time, we may very well be wise to prescind from traditional canons of interpretation and take a fresh look at what we articulate only vaguely but actually hold to be our basic beliefs. A primary example might be our understanding of nature, seen pre-eminently as space and as subject to man's fabrication. A second could be our understanding of time, seen as option, rather than as the measure of man's entropic situation. Both perspectives, although rooted in the early American experience, can claim powerful and direct relevance to the situation in which we now find ourselves.

Reflective Primitivism: Nature and Time

> The influence of the land is sometimes looked upon as significant only in primitive conditions of life. With the coming of "civilization"; that is to say, trade and manufacture and organized cities, the land is supposed to diminish in importance. As a matter of fact, the importance of the land increases with civilization: "Nature" as a system of interests and activities is one of the chief creations of the civilized man.[26]

The literature pertaining to the meaning of nature as an American motif is extensive.[27] It often involves an analysis of the relationship between the experience in America and the corresponding myth of the Garden or the quest for Eden. Following Sanford, this relationship includes the activities of both the "philosophers of primitivism" and the "trailblazers of progress":

The Edenic image, as I have defined it, is neither a static agrarian image of cultivated nature nor an opposing image of the wilderness, but an imaginative complex which, while including both images, places them in a dynamic relationship with other values. Like true myth or story, it functions on many levels simultaneously, dramatizing a people's collective experience within a framework of polar opposites. The Edenic myth, it seems to me, has been the most powerful and organizing force in American culture.[28]

A much less adequately analyzed notion is that of time. Of particular concern is the separation of the analysis of time from that of nature, as though honoring a dualism between the inner and outer man.[29] Sidney Mead, for example, in a penetrating essay on the role of space in the development of the American people, asserts that "Americans have never had time to spare. What they did have during all their formative years was space—organic, pragmatic space—the space of action. And perhaps this made the real difference in the formation of 'this new man.'"[30] The "space of action," however, should be seen as fundamentally a "time" category, for it structures possibility and gives to the immediate situation a quality of human participation that renders meaningful the temporal process.

Space is not a sufficiently humanizing context for man's situation. When events are framed against novel occurrences, the experience of ordinary living takes on the hue of an imaginative reconstruction of life. James has told us that "according to my view, experience as a whole is a process in time."[31] But if the setting for this process, relative to each life lived, is characterized by repetition and by the plodding dullness of a context that rarely, if ever, is broken into by basic shifts in direction, then the "process" may be aeonically viable but of little import in immediate terms. Tillich sees this clearly. He holds that "while time and space are bound to each other in such an inescapable way, they stand in a tension with each other which may be considered as the most fundamental tension of existence."[32] But this tension is not one of a simple standoff, for it can be recast from the side of the human endeavor: "In man the final victory of time is possible. Man is able to act towards something beyond his death. He is able to have history, and he is able to transcend even the tragic death of families and nations, thus breaking through the circle of repetition towards something new. Because he is able to do so, he represents the potential victory of time; but not always the actual victory."[33]

We would argue that this statement of Tillich is a precise description, writ small, of the historical American interaction between institutional possibilities and the setting of nature. Tillich, himself, after his American experience, seemed to arrive at the same viewpoint:

> But in spite of these permanent contacts with the Old World, the New World grasped me with its irresistible power of assimilation and creative courage. . . . I saw the American courage to go ahead, to try, to risk failures, to begin again after defeat, to lead an experimental life both in knowledge and in action, to be opened toward the future, to participate in the creative process of nature and history.[34]

Nature, as understood within the American tradition, was open and seminal for human life. This is not to say that nature, so understood, was simply and necessarily beneficent. It is to say, however, that the simple fact of prodigal space yielded a sense of fecundity, possibility, and, above all, the challenge that was to be associated with man as "engaged" with nature. This fundamental attitude is phrased by the American explorer John Wesley Powell in an address in 1883 on the "Methods of Evolution":

> When a man loses faith in himself, and worships nature, and subjects himself to the government of the laws of physical nature, he lapses into stagnation, where mental and moral miasma is bred. All that makes man superior to the beast is the result of his own endeavor to secure happiness. . . . Man lives in the desert by guiding a river and fertilizing the sands with its waters, and the desert is covered with fields and gardens and homes.[35]

Not only did this tradition deny that conforming to nature was the highest wisdom, it even awarded ultimate authority to the needs, admittedly often ostensible, of human activity. John Anderson speaks of eighteenth-century American thought as offering us "an original insight" into the relationship between man's nature and the order of nature.

> Thus American thinkers including John Adams and Thomas Jefferson made explicit the focus of men's attention upon the New World

by describing the individual in the setting of the order of nature; and, in Jefferson's case at least, contributing an original interpretation of the moral problem of man's free natural action by describing the New World as the matrix required for the emergence of man's moral nature.[36]

This anthropocentric approach to nature yields in turn a deep-seated paradox, still active in the American temperament. On the one side, the Edenic myth of the "garden," while, on the other, a systematic destruction of natural resources under the press of an aggressive and collective adolescence in which liberation from feudal and antique political patterns generated a hostility to any structure, even the rhythm of the forests. Negative also was the cultural worship of youth, the absence of a *De Senectute*, and the refusal to recognize the price to be paid for squandering resources and doing often irreparable damage to the fabric of nature on which subsequent generations depended. In commenting on this situation, Anderson says, "Consider as one typical example the development of the Great Plains in the late 19th century. Here the effort to conquer the land was successful when reinforced by the Industrial Revolution; and the ultimate social effects were realized in the Dust Bowl of the 20th century."[37] Charles Sanford states the cultural significance of this relationship between unlimited possibility and the accent on youth:

> The newness of the country, the expectation of some kind of rebirth or beatitude in the near future, and the eternal promise of future blessings associated with the land produced a distinct emphasis on youth in America. . . . A psychic primitivism of youth replaced or accompanied geographical and cultural primitivism. . . . The cult of newness followed the pioneers westward; it fortified bumptious individualism in its never-ending contests with authority; it contributed to a characteristically American disrespect for tradition and history; it minimized fatally the large contribution which European civilization has made to our culture; it served as an important basis for criticism of the "new" industrial order and supplied the moral and intellectual framework within which it was to operate. Finally, it continued to haunt the American mind long after, conceivably, it should have reached maturity.[38]

There is considerable truth in these remarks. We should not forget, however, that the cult of youth is a reflection of a more important and far-reaching dimension of the American doctrine of nature. The emphasis on the immediate, on the good of *this* generation, and the absence of concern for the larger future is a symptom of a specific doctrine of "local time." The significance of man, in this view, proceeds from his immediate situation rather than from his place in any metahistorical scheme. We could describe this as an American stoicism, wherein human life is inextricable from its relationship with nature, but yet free to formulate the character of this relationship, with increasing control, from the human side. This dialectic is expressed in an incisive text by John Anderson:

> Thus both Emerson and Thoreau accepted the insight of their time, that man's nature was that of a shaper, a constructor and maintainer. But they focused attention upon man's autonomous nature, his intrinsic self; they insisted that each man saw himself not only as a part of the creative flow of experience but as a universal reference point in this flow. Viewed in this way, man was seen not as identical with the evolution of a novel strand in experience, but as a jewel which might reflect an inclusive and eternal meaning. Asked who he was, man could then reply, I am this universal spark. And with this statement he could maintain in principle his integrity in the course of his creative action wherever in particular this might lead him.[39]

In such a view, man has a future, but its prognosis should never be uprooted from the actual situation in which he finds himself. The future is to be realized generation by generation and its goals constantly reworked in the light of man's needs and capacities. "Experience had taught Americans," Bryce reported, "that though the ascent of man may be slow it is also sure."[40] How "sure" it is remains open to serious question. But it may be generalized that the American tradition can be understood as the first posthistorical and communal rejection of an eschatological framework, which yet retains an aggressive doctrine of the meaning of history.[41] Granted that there often is a shallow side to thinking simply in terms of generation to generation; nonetheless, such an attitude avoids the type of absolutist ideology, whether in the name of religious, metaphysical, or utopian political beliefs, that so often yields an oppressive immediate social order so as to guarantee some future way of life.

The American view is that nature is pliant and at the service of the community of men who, although mindful of the past, are committed to build a city out of response to contemporary needs. There is irony here, since this view, often described as short-sighted and even "materialistic," is actually an embodiment of what is now the "sophisticated" interpretation of Christianity—namely, the emphasis on the sacramentality of time redeemed. It is difficult to see how one could structure a doctrine of the primacy of individual life, operative within a community of men devoted to human amelioration, if the overall setting were not characterized by an openness of nature and an admission that the created world served the needs and vision of the human quest. Some have answered that such a view is too anthropomorphic and lacks patience with a beneficent God; but history has told us a different story, for such beneficence is all too obscure. This is especially so when one realizes that the notion of God is often inseparable from doctrines such as that of the cyclic nature of ancient man, with its inexorable reduction of human life to an aeonic fragment,[42] or with the later Scholastic view of natural law, supposedly more reflective of man's actual nature, while really manifesting the sociological boundaries in which he was placed by ingrained institutional power. It recurs finally in the modern world, where it is found in the inverted forms of varying ideologies, all offering a total resolution of man's plight if he would but conform to the latest sociological or political myth.

Analysis of such previous interpretations of man's fate shows them to be just as anthropomorphic as the doctrine of an open nature, with man as the giver of "forms."[43] But there is this salutary difference: the admission of man's pre-eminence over nature, when joined to an acknowledged irresolution relative to the ultimate questions, makes possible the building of the principle of self-correction into our basic framework as a metaphysical category. At its most fruitful, this attitude is unfettered by prejudices or by a worship of the past. It finds its concrete expression in experiment as directed to an ever-richer expression of human life and human institutions. This is the kind of America envisioned by Dewey. At its worst, it is characterized by an arrogant usurpation of natural processes, simply for the purpose of pandering to the narrowest range of human needs. This is the America so legitimately held up to ridicule by Boorstin and so often scorned by the American intellectual. In Tillich's view, America "can be both a world power politically and a provincial people spiritually. Will the emphasis on the 'American way of life' produce such a situation?"[44]

Repeating our opening analysis, the nub of the problem is that both cultural attitudes proceed basically from the same set of assumptions, generally understood. The doctrine of an open nature, romanticized as unfettered freedom and self-reliance, when assimilated without cognizance of the major problems inseparable from such a view, supports only a superficial version of cultural life. On the other hand, when understood in its full significance and admitting to the burdens of holding to such a perspective, the American tradition can sustain an approach to cultural life as rich as the great versions of the past.

If experience, nature, and time as historically undergone constitute the basic framework through which the qualities of the American tradition developed, the articulation of these categories constitutes still another aspect of this problem. The full implications of the historical events in American life, worked out within the broad perspective of a reflective primitivism, are not realized until one binds such developments to their subsequent articulation, particularly by philosophy. This is especially true of our leading metaphor, experience.[45] The development in American consciousness—from the "experience of experience" to the "notion of experience" and finally, with Dewey, to the "method of experience"—is of crucial importance from both the cultural and philosophical viewpoint. The question, of course, is whether the articulation of these deeply felt cultural traditions maintains the richness and immediacy of the original responses. Secondly, if such an articulation does keep fidelity with the tradition, can it also show relevance to the more specifically intellectual dimensions of its own mode of discourse? In a word, can American philosophy *do* philosophy and yet remain within the traditional cultural dispositions of the American cultural past? It would seem that while doing other things, American philosophy must do at least this much, if we are to avoid what Tillich fears—a future characterized by spiritual provincialism.

The Articulation of Experience

American philosophers, young and old, seen scratching where the wool is short . . .

—William James

In a recent essay on "The Return to Experience," Robert Johann tries anew to open up the importance of a shift away from "reflective thought" to that of the method of experience as the distinctively, personal activity of human life.[46] He tells us that "any effort to locate the real in a realm distinct from everyday experience and somehow accessible only to thought will bypass the real altogether."[47] Although the notion of experience has roots in Greek philosophy, and was a central concern for Kant as well as for Locke and Hume, it is clear that Johann places himself in the tradition of James and Dewey as another in a long line of commentators who attempt to break open this most obvious and yet most obscure of philosophical notions.[48] James was right when he spoke of experience as a double-barrelled word, figuring as both thought and thing,[49] as also Dewey, when he added:

> Like its congeners, life and history, it includes what men do and suffer, what they strive for, love, believe and endure, and also how men act and are acted upon, the ways in which they do and suffer, desire and enjoy, see, believe, imagine—in short, processes of experiencing. . . . It is "double-barrelled" in that it recognizes in its primary integrity no division between act and material, subject and object, but contains them both in an unanalyzed totality. "Thing" and "thought," as James says in the same connection, are single-barrelled; they refer to products discriminated by reflection out of primary experience.[50]

Now, whatever the difficulties in the tangled philosophical literature about experience, a constant theme emerges, warning us against the intellectualizing of our situation to the extent that we cut ourselves off from the richer and unfettered immediacies of living. But these warnings themselves often take on a highly speculative character and soon become shadows of the very intellectualism they oppose. A fascinating parallel to this problem of "thinking about experience" is found in the brief history of postwar existentialism. In the effort to elucidate the full burden of living in tension between *l'etranger* and *l'homme revolte*, philosophy, omnivorous to the end, blanketed the problem with a host of distinctions and clarifications, worthy of analytic philosophy, but hardly of the thrust of the existentialist concern. So, too, with the method of experience: easy to claim as a touchstone but exceedingly difficult to abide by within the very fabric of inquiry. Johann warns of this difficulty when he states that "the proper role of reflection is not to construct an escape from experience, but by seeking to formulate the links and connections that experience presents to us, gradually to enrich our awareness of what it is we are about and what is at stake, so that life itself, in the light of this awareness, can be lived with greater meaning and purposefulness."[51]

Within the American context, the effort to remain faithful to the demands of experience has constantly been entangled with the assertion that the culture is fundamentally "anti-intellectual." Much has been written about this theme in American culture, and no doubt there are complex reasons for much of the antagonism shown the intellectual, particularly when one analyzes the political ramifications of class structure emanating from distinctions derived from education.[52] In his comprehensive study of this problem, Hofstadter sees the roots of such an attitude in the primitive and evangelical dimensions of early America and its realization in the subsequent growth of the business mentality:

> If evangelicalism and primitivism helped to plant anti-intellectualism at the roots of American consciousness, a business society assured that it would remain in the foreground of American thinking. Since the time of Tocqueville it has become a commonplace among students of America that business activism has provided an overwhelming counterpoise to reflection in this country. Tocqueville saw that the life of constant action and decision which was entailed by the democratic and businesslike character of American life put a premium upon rough and ready habits of mind, quick decision, and the prompt seizure of opportunities and that all this activity was not propitious for deliberation, elaboration, or precision in thought.[53]

There is much to be said for this interpretation from the perspective of straight historical narrative, but its underlying philosophical assumption is open to question. Too often, the perspective from which evaluation is made accepts the classical distinction between the speculative and practical as permanent deposits in the activity of inquiry. In a general way,

Hofstadter recognizes this and attempts to redress such abstract dualisms as "intellect and emotion" and "intellect and practicality" by reworking the category of intellect. This approach is, however, an uphill struggle given the implicit philosophical framework of American culture. We should offer here a reworking from another perspective, namely, the refusal to accept any dualism at all, while yet trying to locate the life of reflection in terms of the wider context of experience. In this way, the history of those movements often thought to be anti-intellectual, if given a different setting for analysis, can perhaps be shown to have made decisive contributions to the way in which men seek and ground knowing.

It is not unimportant that in a general way, the American tradition involves a crucial shift in the method for ascertaining the major focus of inquiry. Because of the pre-eminence of the experience of nature as open and as subject to reconstruction, the prime analogates for inquiry have centered on life metaphors. From the very outset, the notions of growth, experiment, and liberty, along with a host of derived metaphors, have characterized inquiry in American life. This holds not only for those endeavors traditionally directed to so-called practical concerns but equally constitutes the very fiber of religious thought. Indeed, more revealing, such metaphors comprise the major language of the American philosophical tradition, when it finally emerges in the nineteenth century. With Emerson and again with Dewey, we have a philosophical concern that uses the language of cultural cliché. In a word, the *problematic* assumes the primary role, reserved elsewhere for the ineffable, the Good, or the language of being. In such a worldview, the most profound recesses of reflection are themselves burdened by the obligation to reconstruct experience so as to aid in the resolution of those difficulties seen to hinder growth. In an address at Union College in 1836, Gulian Verplanck carefully analyzes this attitude:

> But it has often been objected that this all-absorbing gravitation towards the useful, the active, and the practical, in our country, propels every student from his most favorite studies into the struggles, the competition, and tumult of life, and is thus fatal at once to all recondite and curious learning, to deep attainment in pure science or polished excellence in elegant art and literature. There is certainly

some portion of truth in this objection, and yet but a portion only. . . .

The experience of scientific investigation has shown that such application of the test of reality and experiment to theoretic truth, has not only often thrown a clearer light on that theory, at once limiting its generalities and confirming its evidence, but has also evolved new combinations, suggested new inferences, and manifested higher laws. . . . Thus contemplations, apparently the most shadowy, have often operated with the greatest efficiency upon the most engrossing concerns of daily life.[54]

The passion for amelioration of the human plight, so carefully nurtured by the French *philosophes*, becomes almost a total cast of mind within the American tradition. Such a view is clearly put by Dewey, when he states that "Philosophy recovers itself when it ceases to be a device for dealing with the problems of philosophers and becomes a method, cultivated by philosophers, for dealing with the problems of men."[55] Or again, with James, who tells us that "knowledge about life is one thing; effective occupation of a place in life, with its dynamic currents passing through your being, is another."[56]

Thus American classical philosophy comprises a highly original effort to maintain a genuinely metaphysical concern within the limits of time and nature. Such an approach is most obviously characterized by the refusal to separate the efforts of intellectual life, including those of philosophy, from the burden of resolving concrete problems. Following James: "Ideals ought to aim at the *transformation of reality*—no less."[57] This attempt at amelioration, which burdens the processes of thought, even those of so-called basic research, should not be seen as simply a pragmatic reductionism, directed to what James called the American "moral flabbiness born of the exclusive worship of the bitch-goddess Success."[58] Rather than honoring a simple dualism between thought and action, the American bent toward the practical should be viewed from a wider perspective. Both the method of reflection and the method of action are to be seen as conjoined and rotating functionaries of an experimental approach. Neither method is self-contained or totally reliable but assumes priority relative to the nature of the problem to which it is directed. It is the problem and its resolution, or at least reconstruction on more enhancing terms, that occupies the place of importance in this approach to inquiry. The rotating priority of thought and action covers an important and infrequently analyzed assumption in American life; the contention that experience, as such, has informing, directive, and self-regulating qualities which are ordered and managed as subject to intelligence and as responsible to the burdens of the various contexts in which inquiry finds itself. Thought and action are functionaries of the method of experience in a culture which gives to experience qualities and powers usually denied in the larger tradition of Western thought. It is this underlying assumption as to the seminal character of the method of experience for both theory and practice that has to be isolated and reworked in the light of contemporary problems and language. Failure to do this results not only in our falling back into a crippling dualism between practical and speculative activity, on cultural lines, but also, as Dewey warns, denies us the riches of immediate experience in favor of an ever more vacuous conceptual tradition:

> The serious matter is that philosophies have denied that common experience is capable of developing from within itself methods which will secure direction for itself and will create inherent standards of judgment and value. No one knows how many of the evils and deficiencies that are pointed to as reasons for flight from experience are themselves due to the disregard of experience shown by those peculiarly reflective. To waste of time and energy, to disillusionment with life that attends every deviation from concrete experience must be added the tragic failure to realize the value that intelligent search could reveal and mature among the things of ordinary experience.[59]

A brief commentary on this modern jeremiad by Dewey should put the question of the articulation of experience into some perspective. It is clear that Dewey, for one, accepts the assumption about the power of experience which is basic to American life. But he demands also an articulation of this assumption relative to the major problems faced by each generation and subject to the logical structures of the various methodological approaches as embodied in the disciplines of intellectual life.[60] And his major concerns were with the notions of nature, growth, and human interaction with institutional life, often phrased out in the vein sketched here as characteristic language of the American temperament.

What Dewey laments is the separation of reflection from the method of experience. In a brilliant statement of the meaning of experience, "congenial to present conditions," Dewey contrasts his position with the "orthodox" view. The latter, in general terms, sees experience as blunt and always in need of conceptual formulation before performing any significant cognitive function. Dewey, on the contrary, sees experience as richly informing on its own terms, shot through, as it were, with implicitness and meaning.[61] He offers that in his view "experience in its vital form is experimental" and has as its "salient trait" "connection with a future." For Dewey, experience is not antithetical to thought; he holds that there exists "no conscious experience without inference; reflection is native and constant."[62]

Upon more careful analysis Dewey's view would be seen as incomparably richer than other statements of experience. Dewey, however, has presented a view of experience deeply rooted in a cultural attitude, as against a philosophical statement of what has always been a derivative rather than primary notion in Western thought. Dewey fails to realize that his lamentation about the separation of reflection from the method of experience is far more of a sociological problem than one to be explicated in philosophical terms.[63] From the point of view of contemporary philosophical thought, experience is simply too vague and bumptious a term to be used as the central category for structuring a logic of inquiry. For one recent commentator, "The most basic principle of this 'minimal' empiricism is that all ideas are derived from experience and the vagueness and ambiguity of the expression 'ideas', 'derived from', and 'experience', pretty well account for the history of modern empiricism."[64]

We do not, however, discover the reason for the extraordinary priority given to the method of experience in American philosophy by restricting our analysis simply to philosophical language. The setting, after all, was quite different with philosophy elsewhere.[65] Randall sees it this way: "American philosophy, come of age by the end of the nineteenth century, could draw on all the different European traditions. That has something to do with the fact that the giants of the last generation could bend them all to the illumination of American experience, in creating a distinctively new and American philosophical attitude and approach."[66]

Perhaps the major thrust of this illumination is the place given experience itself. In a somewhat different vein, Tillich, in discussing the "pragmatic-experimental approach of American theology," can speak of the "emphasis on religious experience in the movements of evangelical radicalism that have largely formed the American mind and have *made of experience a central concept in all spheres* of *man's intellectual life.*"[67]

Although the history of the meaning of the notion of experience in American life has yet to be written, the American mood, even at the outset, more often than not anticipated the later contention of Emerson that "every ingenious and aspiring soul leaves the doctrine behind him in his own experience."[68] The question, of course, is whether this is simply a philosophical correlate to the attitude of ingrained condescension to speculative learning—an attitude so cogently expressed in the commentary on a failure in a colonial Massachusetts iron works, wherein "experience hath outstripped learning here, and the most quick-sighted in the theory of things have been forced to pay pretty roundly to Lady Experience for filling their heads with a little of her active afterwit."[69]

Or is Emerson's text to be read rather as an affirmation of the informing richness of experience as such; indeed, of the cognitive thrust in all events, particularly those through which we locate ourselves as persons? Originally biblical in meaning,[70] the experience of the new world viewed the "land" as but the site on which the New Jerusalem was to be founded. Given the press of events, however, the focus of expectation soon shifted, and located around the land itself.[71] In one of his poems, Thoreau calls for a new future by pointing to possibilities hardly credible anywhere else in nineteenth-century Western civilization:

> All things invite this earth's inhabitants
> To rear their lives to an unheard of height
> And meet the expectation of the land.[72]

And in our time, Robert Frost, celebrating what he hoped was a new beginning, significantly repeats the refrain of Thoreau:

> To the land vaguely realizing westward,
> But still unstoried, artless, unenhanced,
> Such as she was, such as she would become.[73]

The energizing to meet and engage the "expectations of the land" is but one version of the overreaching dominance of situation over theory. Experience as sociological environment trumps philosophical thought at every turn. This is stated with clarity by Boorstin:

> Through the eighteenth and nineteenth centuries—from Creve-coeur's notion that America had produced a new man, through Jefferson's belief in the wealth, promise, and magnificence of the continent, and Turner's faith in a frontier-born culture and frontier-nourished institutions—runs the refrain that American values spring from the circumstances of the New World, that these are the secret of the "American Way of Life." This refrain has been both an example of our special way of dealing with ideas and an encouragement to it. For lack of a better word, we may call this a leaning toward implicitness, a tendency to leave ideas embodied in experience, and a belief that the truth somehow arises out of the experience.
>
> This carries with it a preference for the relevance of ideas as against their form and a surprising unconcern for the separability of ideas. We have seldom believed that the validity of an idea was tested by its capacity for being expressed in words. The beliefs that values come out of the context and that truth is part of the matrix of experience (and hardly separable from it) become themselves part of the way of American thinking—hence, the formlessness of American thought, its lack of treatises, schools, and systems.[74]

It would seem that we should more openly admit that vision is most creative when it acknowledges an interaction within the actual limitations of our situation. In writing of James, Robert Pollock clarifies this problem:

> James was endeavoring to take seriously the fact that reality does not address itself to abstract minds but to living persons inhabiting a real world, to whom it makes known something of its essential quality only as they go out to meet it through action. It is this concrete relation of man and his world, realized in action, which accounts for the fact that our power of affirmation outruns our knowledge, as when we feel or sense the truth before we know it.[75]

The work of analysis in American life has to take into account the powerful assumption about experience as self-revealing as well as the living inseparability of world and action. Thought, traditionally, has no privileged place in the American scheme. The burden of this essay is that such an arrangement has been fortunate in relation to our culture, and should be abandoned only with great caution.

Conclusion

At times contemporary reflective thought in America seems to identify itself only by locating around a response to what is considered the traditional hostility to the intellectual. Such a response only confronts a by-product of what is actually a long-standing and general cultural effort to rework the nature of thought in terms of its functional role within the total human endeavor. From the Puritans to Dewey, one is offered a series of efforts, alternating in stresses and varying in success, to account for man's most profound difficulties and concerns within the context of ordinary experience. In that tradition, all-embracing systematic truth, whether it be theological, philosophical or political, was consistently submitted to the broadly based canons of a constantly shifting collective experience. Inevitably these doctrinal stances were broken under the pressure of having to support a more than simply theoretical posture. But there developed a highly sensitive feeling for the riches of experience as a way of reconstructing doctrine rather than as a malleable resource awaiting clarification. The doctrine of an open nature and the perpetual return to the invigoration of frontier language provide a sense of renewal and local horizon which serve to constantly galvanize energies. As a consequence, what appear to be more basic questions are often left to fend for themselves in the rush of events. Is it not significant that the major thinkers in the American tradition are recalled more for their attitude and openness to possibility rather than for the specific resolution of the problems they faced? This would seem particularly true of Emerson, James, and Dewey, who, despite their concern with matters philosophical, have a mythic type of existence in the American tradition. Vaguely understood as thinkers, but personally imbedded in the popular consciousness as classic representations of the American mind, they seem to serve in a nostalgic way as the redoubt against the increased complexity of the modern world. Precisely because of this new role as played out in popular culture, technical thought, especially philosophy, tends to by-pass such versions of man's situation.

In failing to recognize that the American tradition in its emphasis on the method of experience, for purposes of human inquiry, constitutes a contention of the highest philosophical priority, contemporary American thought has driven a new wedge between the role of philosophy and the affairs of men. The going assumption often seems to hold that the affection for experience, so notable in earlier American philosophical thought, has a naive and propaedeutic ring to it. As such, it cannot continue as the basis for a response to the increasingly complex dimensions which manifest themselves as characteristic of inquiry in our time. If this assumption is basically sound, then we must conclude that no matter what its verve and boldness in avoiding systematic thought, the emphasis on experience in previous American thought, while remaining a cultural deposit in the wide sense, has only peripheral philosophical significance. Such a bifurcation, however, falls prey to Dewey's warning that "philosophy in America will be lost between chewing a historic cud long since reduced to woody fiber, or an apologetics for lost causes (lost to natural science), or a scholastic, schematic formalism, unless it can somehow bring to consciousness America's own needs and its own implicit principle of successful action."[76]

By way of summary, our position here contends that the separation of the method of analysis, be it historical or philosophical in concern, from the basic leaning of the culture, has two pejorative results. First, widening Dewey's concern, analysis (particularly so in the academic formulation increasingly characteristic of it) finds itself caught in a circle of self-sustenance, using the same language for both criticism and description with only rare and ineffectual points of contact with the wider culture. Secondly, as the culture develops an increased dependence on intellectual expertise, there is a tendency to neglect the obligation to conjoin analysis and the reconstruction of experience. It is, after all, far easier to confront the interiorized difficulties relative to each discipline, particularly those of the humanities and social sciences, than it is to take full cognizance of actual events, which by their very nature occur as interdisciplinary phenomena. It can be granted that the penchant for experience as the major source for the language of inquiry often leads to a lack of rigor and precision in speculative formulations. Yet such an approach has the important advantage of avoiding the deception that accrues to those who assume that events happen readymade for analysis within the striated limitations of single disciplines.[77] Openness to experience, with its historical roots in an anthropomorphic view of nature and a sense of frontier as human horizon, is to be understood as more than an outdated cliché. It should be seen rather as a fundamental attitude through which are strained the tasks of intellect, ever pressed to take account of the novelty that is manifested in the onrush of events. Above all, we should accept the stricture of James that "experience, as we know, has ways of *boiling over*, and making us correct our present formulas."[78] Such corrections are at the behest of experience but their articulation is the task of reflective reconsideration and reformulation.[79] We must strive to institutionalize this dialectic between the press of experience and the wisdom of reflection.

Let Peirce have the last word. An American philosopher of the first rank and no sentimentalist on these matters, he tells us that "without beating longer round the bush let us come to close quarters. Experience is our only teacher." And "how does this action of experience take place? It takes place by a series of surprises."[80]

FOUR

SPIRES OF INFLUENCE

The Importance of Emerson for Classical American Philosophy

And, striving to be man, the worm
Mounts through all the spires of form.
　　　—Ralph Waldo Emerson, "Nature"

I

Perhaps the title of this chapter should be "Why Emerson?" as that would better reflect how I came to write this piece. It is not so much that I have had to become convinced of the singular importance of the thought of Emerson, for the writing and teaching of Joseph Blau,[1] as well as that of Robert C. Pollock,[2] long ago made that clear to me. Rather the query about "Why Emerson?" proceeds from my study of the classic American philosophers, especially William James, Josiah Royce, and John Dewey. Despite their differences and disagreements, often extreme in both personal style and doctrine, these powerful and prescient philosophers did have at least one influence in common—the thought of Ralph Waldo Emerson.

　　Another major figure of the American classical period, George Santayana, seems to be a case apart. Santayana had an abiding interest in Emerson's thought and refers frequently to Emerson in his own writings. His judgments on Emerson vary from admiration and affection to pointed, and even harsh, criticism. I do not think that Emerson was a significant influence on Santayana. Nonetheless, his published assessments of Emerson at the beginning of the twentieth century are contextually interesting, especially as they contrast with those of James, Royce, and Dewey. The remaining two major figures of the classical period, C. S. Peirce and G. H. Mead, appear to be much less directly influenced by Emerson.[3]

Parenthetically, however, we do find a text in Peirce about Emerson which is intriguing and perhaps merits further inquiry in another context. In "The Law of Mind," published in 1892, Peirce wrote:

> I may mention, for the benefit of those who are curious in studying mental biographies, that I was born and reared in the neighborhood of Concord—I mean in Cambridge—at the time when Emerson, Hedge, and their friends were disseminating the ideas that they had caught from Schelling, and Schelling from Plotinus, from Boehm, or from God knows what minds stricken with the monstrous mysticism of the East. But the atmosphere of Cambridge held many an antiseptic against Concord transcendentalism; and I am not conscious of having contracted any of that virus. Nevertheless, it is probable that some cultured bacilli, some benignant form of the disease was implanted in my soul, unawares, and that now, after long incubation, it comes to the surface, modified by mathematical conceptions and by training in physical investigation.[4]

The wary and tough-minded response of Peirce is not atypical of a philosophical assessment of Emerson. Indeed, even those philosophers who acknowledge their debt to Emerson lace their remarks with dubiety about his fundamental assumptions and unease about much of the rhetoric of his formulation. Nonetheless, James, Royce, Dewey, and Santayana, each in his own way, find it necessary to evaluate the importance of Emerson in the light of their own developing positions. Before turning to these judgments, it should be helpful if I sketch the Emersonian project in cultural and philosophical terms.

The central theme of Emerson's life and work is that of possibility. In an anticipation of the attitude of Martin Buber, Emerson believes that "we are really able," that is, we and the world are continuous in an affective and nutritional way. It is human insight which is able to "animate the last fibre of organization, the outskirts of nature."[5] Emerson's persistent stress on human possibility is fed from two sources: his extraordinary confidence in the latent powers of the individual soul when related to the symbolic riches of nature, and his belief that the comparatively unarticulated history of American experience could act as a vast resource for the energizing of novel and creative spiritual energy. The often oracular style of Emerson should not cloak the seriousness of his intention when he speaks of these possibilities. In this regard, the key text is found in his introduction to the essay "Nature."

> Our age is retrospective. It builds the sepulchres of the fathers. It writes biographies, histories, and criticism. The foregoing generations beheld God and nature face to face; we, through their eyes. Why should not we also enjoy an original relation to the universe? Why should not we have a poetry and philosophy of insight and not of tradition, and a religion by revelation to us, and not the history of theirs? Embosomed for a season in nature, whose floods of life stream around and through us, and invite us, by the powers they supply, to action proportioned to nature, why should we grope among the dry bones of the past, or put the living generation into masquerade out of its faded wardrobe? The sun shines to-day also. There is more wool and flax in the fields. There are new lands, new men, new thoughts. Let us demand our own works and laws and worship.[6]

We of the twentieth century may not grasp the radical character of Emerson's invocation, standing as we do on the rubble of broken promises brought to us by the great faiths of the past, be they scientific, social, or religious. But Emerson made no such promise and cannot be accused, retroactively, of bad faith. His message was clear. We are to transform the obviousness of our situation by a resolute penetration to the liberating symbolism present in our own experience. We are not to be dependent on faith hatched elsewhere out of others' experiences, nor, above all, are we to rest on an inherited ethic whose significance is due more to longevity and authority than to the press of our own experience. Surely, Emerson's nineteenth century, which was barely able to absorb the recondite theology responsible for the transition from Presbyterianism to Unitarianism, had to blanch at his bypassing the issue entirely, while calling for a homegrown "revelation." The radical character of

Emerson's position at that time was given historical credence by the reception given to his "Divinity School Address," delivered two years after "Nature" and one year after "The American Scholar." Using a tone more modest than either of those, Emerson in effect told the graduating class of Harvard Divinity School that the tradition they had inherited was hollow and the church to which they belonged "seems to totter to its fall, all life extinct."[7] As in "Nature," he again called for a "new hope and new revelation."[8] The upshot of this address was that for nearly thirty years Emerson was unwelcome as a public figure in Cambridge.

Now, more to the point of the present discussion is Emerson's doctrine of experience and his emphasis on relations, both central concerns of the subsequent philosophical thought of James and Dewey. In his essay "The American Scholar," Emerson points to three major influences on the development of the reflective person: nature, history, and action or experience. In his discussion of the third influence, Emerson provides a microcosmic view of his fundamental philosophy. He makes it apparent that he does not accept the traditional superiority of the contemplative over the active life. Emerson tells us further that "action is with the scholar subordinate, but it is essential. Without it he is not yet man. Without it thought can never ripen into truth."[9] It is noteworthy that accompanying Emerson's superb intellectual mastery of the great literature of the past and his commitment to the reflective life is his affirmation that "character is higher than intellect."[10] Living is a total act, the functionary, whereas thinking is a partial act, the function. More than twenty years after the publication of "The American Scholar," Emerson reiterated his commitment to the "practical" and to the "experiential" as the touchstone of the thinking person. In his essay "Fate" he considers those thinkers for whom the central question is the "theory of the Age." In response, Emerson writes: "To me, however, the question of the times resolved itself into a practical question of the conduct of life. How shall I live? We are incompetent to solve the times."[11] The human task for Emerson is not so much to solve the times as to live them, in an ameliorative and perceptive way.

Emerson's generalized approach to inquiry is clearly a foreshadowing of that found subsequently in James, Dewey, and Royce. Too often, Emerson's anticipation of these thinkers is left at precisely that general bequest, whereby the undergoing of experience is its own mean and carries its own peculiar form of cognition.[12] What is less well known is that Emerson also anticipated the doctrine of "radical empiricism," which is central to the philosophy of James and Dewey. I do not contend that Emerson's version of relations had the same psychological or epistemological genesis as that of either James or Dewey.[13] Yet, mutatis mutandis, Emerson did affirm the primary importance of relations over things and he did hold to an aggressive doctrine of implication. Further, his metaphors were more allied to the language of continuity than to that of totality or finality. Finally, Emerson shared that modern assumption which began with Kant and is found repeated in James and Dewey—namely, that the known is, in some way, a function of the knower.

Emerson's attitude toward implicitness, relations, and the partially constitutive character of human inquiry helps us to understand him in other ways as well. Why, one might ask, would Emerson, a New England Brahmin, have a proletarian epistemology? That is, how could Emerson write as he did in "The American Scholar," a paean of praise to the obvious, to the ordinary? The text, as read to the audience at the Phi Beta Kappa celebration of 1837, was startling. "I embrace the common, I explore and sit at the feet of the familiar, the low. Give me insight into to-day, and you may have the antique and future worlds. What would we really know the meaning of? The meal in the firkin; the milk in the pan; the ballad in the street; the news of the boat; the glance of the eye; the form and gait of the body."[14] Emerson immediately provides the response to the rhetorical question posed above. For the "ultimate reason" why the affairs of the ordinary yield insight traces to Emerson's belief that "the sublime presence of the highest spiritual cause lurks, as always it does lurk, in these suburbs and extremities of nature."[15] His version of the world is not characterized by hierarchies, nor by fixed essences, each to be known as an object in itself. Rather he stresses the flow of our experience and the multiple implications of every event and every thing for every other experience had or about to be had. Nature brings with it this rich symbolic resource, enabling all experiences, sanctioned and occasional, to retract potentially novel implications of our other experiences. The novelty is due both to the unpredictability of nature and to the creative role of human imagination.[16] Of the first Emerson writes:

Nature hates calculators; her methods are saltatory and impulsive. Man lives by pulses; our organic movements are such; and the chemical and ethereal agents are undulatory and alternate; and the mind goes antagonizing on, and never prospers but by fits. We thrive by casualties. Our chief experiences have been casual. The most attractive class of people are those who are powerful obliquely and not by the direct stroke; men of genius, but not yet accredited; one gets the cheer of their light without paying too great a tax. Theirs is the beauty of the bird or the morning light, and not of art. In the thought of genius there is always a surprise; and the moral sentiment is well called "the newness," for it is never other; as new to the oldest intelligence as to the young child.[17]

The malleability and novelty-prone capacity of nature feeds the formulating and constructive powers native to the human imagination. Emerson, like James and Dewey, sees this transaction between the open nature of nature and the "active soul" as the necessary context for meaning. In his Journals, Emerson writes: "This power of imagination, the making of some familiar object, as fire or rain, or a bucket, or shovel do new duty as an exponent of some truth or general law, bewitches and delights men. It is a taking of dead sticks, and clothing about with immortality; it is music out of creaking and scouring. All opaque things are transparent, and the light of heaven struggles through."[18] We should not mistake Emerson's position for a flight of fancy or for the poetic stroke, in the pejorative sense of that word. Emerson is a hardheaded empiricist, reminiscent of the Augustinian-Franciscan tradition, for whom the world was a temporal epiphany of the eternal implications and ramifications of the eternal ideas. For Emerson, "A fact is the end or last issue of spirit."[19] Such facticity, paradoxically, comes to us only on behalf of our grasping and formulating the inherent symbolic features of our life. We learn nothing rightly until we learn the symbolical character of life. Day creeps after day, each full of facts, dull, strange, despised things, that we cannot enough despise—call heavy, prosaic, and desert. The time we seek to kill: the attention it is elegant to divert from things around us. And presently the aroused intellect finds gold and gems in one of these scorned facts—then finds that the day of facts is a rock of diamonds; that a fact is an epiphany of God.[20]

The epiphanic, for Emerson, is not a result of human quietism. It is we who constitute these "facts" by our forging of relations. "Every new relation is a new word."[21] The making of words for Emerson, as for James, is the making of the world of meaning. Words are not simply grammatical connectors. As the embodiment of relations they do more than define. They make and remake the very fabric of our world as experienced. "The world is emblematic. Parts of speech are metaphors, because the whole of nature is a metaphor of the human mind."[22] This text mirrors the binary strands found in subsequent American philosophy: the idealist-pragmatic epistemology of James, Royce, Dewey, and Peirce, each with an original emphasis of one strand over another.

If we read the Emersonian project as one which focuses on the dialectic between the raw givenness of nature and the symbolic formulations of the human imagination, then we have a direct line of common interpretation from Emerson to the classic American philosophers. I grant that each of the American philosophers in question contexts this dialectic differently, yet even a cameo version reveals the similarity. The thought of Peirce, for example, exhibits a life-long tension between his acceptance of the irreducibly "tychistic" (that is, chance-ridden) character of the world and of the inevitably fallibilistic character of human knowledge, and his extreme confidence in the method of science. And it is the tough-minded Peirce who writes that "without beating longer round the bush let us come to close quarters. Experience is our only teacher." And "how does this action of experience take place? It takes place by a series of surprises."[23]

The philosophy of John Dewey reflects a similar tension between a confidence in empirical method and the acknowledgment of novelty and unpredictability as indigenous to the history of nature. Dewey states that "man finds himself living in an aleatory world; his existence involves, to put it baldly, a gamble. The world is a scene of risk; it is uncertain, unstable, uncannily unstable. Its dangers are irregular, inconstant, not to be counted upon as to their times and seasons. Although persistent, they are sporadic, episodic."[24]

Still, when faced with this extremely open and even perilous version of nature, Dewey calls upon philosophy to act as an intelligent mapping, so as to reconstruct, ameliorate, and enhance the human condition.

Dewey's project is Emersonian, for the affairs of time and the activities of nature are the ground of inquiry, rather than the hidden and transcendent meaning of Being. Just as Emerson broke with the theological language of his immediate predecessors and many of his peers, so, too, did Dewey break with the ecstatic religious language of Emerson. This break in language should not hide from us that Dewey's understanding of the relationship which exists between nature and human life echoes that of Emerson: always possibility, often celebration, frequently mishap, and never absolute certitude.

As for an Emersonian analogue in Royce, readers of that indefatigable polymath know that cameo versions of any of his positions do not come easy. Nonetheless, Royce's long speculative trek away from the absolute and toward a theory of interpretation, ever reconstructed by the community, echoes Emerson's emphasis on the conduct of life. Royce was forced to abandon the doctrine of the absolute mind because he finally accepted the judgment of his critics that he could not account for the experience of the individual on either epistemological or metaphysical grounds. In his last great work, *The Problem of Christianity*, Royce has come full circle and awarded to the individual the task of formulating the "real world" by virtue of the relationship between "self-interpretation" and the "community of interpretation." Emerson wrote that "we know more from nature than we can at will communicate."[25] Similarly, Royce writes that "the popular mind is deep, and means a thousand times more than it explicitly knows."[26] In my judgment, Royce's mature thought, under the influence of Peirce, structures philosophically the earlier informal approach of Emerson. Although the content is Emersonian, the following passage from Royce brings a heightened philosophical sophistication.

> Metaphysically considered, the world of interpretation is the world in which, if indeed we are able to interpret at all, we learn to acknowledge the being and the inner life of our fellow-men; and to understand the constitution of temporal experience with its endlessly accumulating sequence of significant deeds. In this world of interpretation, of whose most general structure we have now obtained a glimpse, selves and communities may exist, past and future can be defined, and the realms of the spirit may find a place which neither

barren conception nor the chaotic flow of interpenetrating perceptions could ever render significant.[27]

It is with William James, however, that the Emersonian dialectic between the creative and constructive character of the human mind and
the apparently intransigent character of the physical world most explicitly comes to the fore. James, like Emerson, holds to a relationship of
congeniality between nature and human power. They both avoid the alternate interpretations, which, in turn, would stress either the complete
objectivity of the meaning of nature or a completely subjective version,
in which nature has an existence only at the behest of the human, or,
failing that, the absolute mind. In some ways, James outdoes Emerson
in his stress on the "powers" and "energies" of the individual, although
we should remember that he also emphasizes "seeing and feeling the
total push and pressure of the cosmos."[28]

William James is profoundly aware of these alternate versions of our
situation and often evokes them in an extreme way. Two texts from
Pragmatism stand out in this regard, and if we put them back to back,
the poles of the Emersonian dialectic are thrown into bold relief.

> Woe to him whose beliefs play fast and loose with the order which
> realities follow in his experience: They will lead him nowhere or else
> make false connexions.[29]

> In our cognitive as well as in our active life we are creative. We add,
> both to the subject and to the predicate part of reality. The world
> stands really malleable, waiting to receive its final touches at our
> hands. Like the kingdom of heaven, it suffers human violence will-
> ingly. Man engenders truths upon it.[30]

Obviously, both of these texts cannot stand at one and the same time.
James was very much aware of this conflict and continued to pose it,
even though he was simultaneously working his way out of the dilemma.
In an earlier entry in an unpublished notebook, he gives a reason for
maintaining this conflict. "Surely nature itself and subjective construction are radically opposed, one's higher indignations are nourished by
the opposition."[31] Emerson, of course, would approve of both the "in-
dignation" and the "nourishment." It should be noted, however, that

James goes beyond Emerson at this point and develops his formal doctrine of radical empiricism to mediate this "opposition." The genesis
and content of James's radical empiricism is a long and complicated
story, but in his conclusion to the essay "A World of Pure Experience,"
James sets out the dramatic presence of the knowing self in a world both
obdurate and malleable.

> There is in general no separateness needing to be overcome by an
> external cement; and whatever separateness is actually experienced is
> not overcome, it stays and counts as separateness to the end. But the
> metaphor serves to symbolize the fact that experience itself, taken at
> large, can grow by its edges. That one moment of it proliferates into
> the next by transitions which, whether conjunctive or disjunctive,
> continue the experiential tissue, cannot, I contend, be denied. Life is
> in the transitions as much as in the terms connected; often, indeed,
> it seems to be there more emphatically, as if our spurts and sallies
> forward were the real firing-line of the battle, were like the thin line
> of flame advancing across the dry autumnal field which the farmer
> proceeds to burn. In this line we live prospectively as well as retro-
> spectively. It is "of" the past, inasmuch as it comes expressly as the
> past's continuation; it is "of" the future in so far as the future, when
> it comes, will have continued it.[32]

So much for the refractions of the Emersonian dialectic in some of
the classical American philosophers. At this point, the reader may well
ask why I have not cited these philosophers on this central theme in
Emerson. The response, alas, is quite simple. Our philosophers did not
write very much on Emerson, and when they did, the focus was often
on other, if related, themes. I turn now to James, Santayana, Royce, and
Dewey on Emerson, directly.

II

At the age of three months, William James was visited by Ralph Waldo
Emerson at the James family's home on Washington Square in New
York City. This prepossessing and perhaps burdensome presence of Emerson lasted throughout most of the life of William James. In the decade
following 1870, James read virtually everything Emerson wrote, and at
one point, in 1873, made the following entry in his diary: "I am sure that

an age will come when our present devotion to history, and scrupulous care for what men have done before us merely as fact, will seem incomprehensible; when acquaintance with books will be no duty, but a pleasure for odd individuals; when Emerson's philosophy will be in our bones, not our dramatic imagination."[33] Apparently, Emerson's thought had already reached the "bones" of James, for the above sentiment about the past is shared by Emerson. In "The American Scholar" he wrote that "I had better never see a book than to be warped by its attraction clean out of my own orbit and made a satellite instead of a system. The one thing in the world of value is the active soul."[34]

Some thirty years after his diary entry, in 1903, James was called upon to deliver the address at the centenary celebration for Emerson in Concord.[35] This occasion caused James to reread virtually all of Emerson's writings. Frankly, with regard to the question of the influence of Emerson on James, the address is disappointing. As one would expect, James is laudatory of Emerson's person and work.[36] And, as he often did in such pieces of encomium, the text is largely made up of long passages from Emerson. Despite these limitations, an important theme runs beneath the baroque prose of James and that of Emerson as selected by James. As we might expect, it is the theme of "possibility," of the hallowing of the everyday. James is struck by the radical temporality of Emerson's vision. He offers a brief collage of that attitude: " 'The Deep today which all men scorn' receives thus from Emerson superb revindication. 'Other world! There is no other world.' All God's life opens into the individual particular, and here and now, or nowhere, is reality. 'The present hour is the decisive hour, and every day is doomsday.' "[37]

James cautions us that Emerson was no sentimentalist. The transformation of stubborn fact to an enhanced symbolic statement of richer possibility was an activity that James found very compatible with his own stress on novelty and surprise. Emerson had written, "So is there no fact, no event, in our private history, which shall not sooner or later, lose its adhesive, inert form and astonish us by soaring from our body into the empyrean."[38] On behalf of this and similar passages, James comments that Emerson "could perceive the full squalor of the individual fact, but he could also see the transfiguration."[39]

Aside from this important focus on Emerson's concern for "individuals and particulars," James's address is taken up with praise of Emerson's style as a literary artist. I note the irony here, for such praise of style is precisely what has taken up much of the commentaries on the thought of James, often to the detriment of an analysis of his serious philosophical intent. It is unfortunate that James never undertook a systematic study of Emerson, especially as directed to his notions of experience, relations, and symbol. James would have found Emerson far more "congenial" and helpful than many of the other thinkers he chose to examine.[40] A detailed study of Emerson as an incipient radical empiricist is a noteworthy task for the future.

The response of Santayana to Emerson's thought was more censorious than that of James and Dewey. On several occasions, James compared the thought of Emerson and Santayana, to the detriment of the latter. In a letter to Dickinson S. Miller, James comments on Santayana's book, *The Life of Reason*:

> He is a paragon of Emersonianism—declare your intuitions, though no other man share them. . . . The book is Emerson's first rival and successor, but how different the reader's feeling! The same things in Emerson's mouth would sound entirely different. E. receptive, expansive, as if handling life through a wide funnel with a great indraught; S. as if through a pin-point orifice that emits his cooling spray outward over the universe like a nose-disinfectant from an "atomizer."[41]

We learn from a letter written by Santayana that James apparently had expressed similar sentiments to him as he had in the letter to Miller. Santayana was not pleased and in his response issues a devastating criticism of Emerson.

> And you say I am less hospitable than Emerson. Of course. Emerson might pipe his wood-notes and chirp at the universe most blandly; his genius might be tender and profound and Hamlet-like, and that is all beyond my range and contrary to my purpose. . . . What did Emerson know or care about the passionate insanities and political disasters which religion, for instance, has so often been another name for? He could give that name to his last personal intuition, and ignore what it stands for and what it expresses in the world. It is the

latter that absorbs me; and I care too much about mortal happiness
to be interested in the charming vegetation of cancer-microbes in the
system—except with the idea of suppressing it.[42]

Although not quite so caustic as his rebuke to James, Santayana's writings on Emerson always had a critical edge to them. In an early essay,
written in 1886, Santayana comments judiciously on Emerson's optimism, which he traces more to his person than to his doctrine. Yet, Santayana's sympathetic treatment of Emerson concludes with a damaging
last line: "But of those who are not yet free from the troublesome feelings of pity and shame, Emerson brings no comfort, he is a prophet of
a fair-weather religion."[43]

In 1900, as a chapter in his *Interpretations of Poetry and Religion*, Santayana published his best-known essay on Emerson. This piece has been
frequently cited on behalf of those who are condescending to Emerson
or severely critical of him. I believe this use of Santayana's essay to be a
misreading. Certainly, Santayana was more indulgent of Emerson in
1900 than he was in 1911, when he published his famous essay "The Genteel Tradition in American Philosophy." In 1911 Santayana lumps Emerson with Poe and Hawthorne as having "a certain starved and abstract
quality." Further, their collective "genius" was a "digestion of vacancy."

> It was a refined labour, but it was in danger of being morbid, or tin-
> kling, or self-indulgent. It was a play of intramental rhymes. Their
> mind was like an old music-box, full of tender echoes and quaint
> fancies. These fancies expressed their personal genius sincerely, as
> dreams may; but they were arbitrary fancies in comparison with
> what a real observer would have said in the premises. Their manner,
> in a word, was subjective. In their own persons they escape the medi-
> ocrity of the genteel tradition, but they supplied nothing to supplant
> it in other minds.[44]

In 1900, however, when Santayana addresses Emerson's thought directly, his evaluations are more favorable. Admitting of Emerson that
"at bottom he had no doctrine at all," Santayana writes that "his finer
instinct kept him from doing that violence to his inspiration."[45] Santayana repeats his earlier contention that Emerson's power was not in his
"doctrine" but rather in his "temperament." And that Emersonian temperament was, above all, antitradition and antiauthoritarian. Even

though he was a classic instance of the "Genteel Tradition" and held many positions which were anathema to Santayana, Emerson nevertheless pleased Santayana by his refusal to professionalize and systematize his thought. Further, Santayana, with poetic sensibilities of his own, was taken with Emerson's style. He writes of Emerson: "If not a star of the first magnitude, he is certainly a fixed star in the firmament of philosophy. Alone as yet among Americans, he may be said to have won a place there, if not by the originality of this thought, at least by the originality and beauty of the expression he gave to thoughts that are old and imperishable."[46]

Still more to the point, and less known, is that Santayana shared Emerson's celebration and embracing of the "common." In 1927, as part of a chastising letter sent to Van Wyck Brooks, Santayana writes: "I therefore think that art, etc., has better soil in the ferocious 100 percent America than in the intelligentsia of New York. It is veneer, rouge, aestheticism, art museums, new theatres, etc., that make America impotent. The good things are football, kindness, and jazz bands."[47] It turns out that Santayana, like Whitman, learned something from Emerson.

Before examining John Dewey's essay on Emerson, I offer a brief interlude with a comment on Josiah Royce's assessment of Emerson. Although Royce was a voluminous writer and ventured interpretations of an extremely wide range of problems and thinkers, he rarely spoke of Emerson.[48] And yet Royce thought far more of Emerson than we could have divined from his publications. In 1911, Royce delivered a Phi Beta Kappa oration in honor of William James, who had died the previous year. The theme of Royce's essay was that James was the third "representative American Philosopher." It was in Royce's opening discussion of the first two candidates that his version of Emerson emerged:

> Fifty years since, if competent judges were asked to name the American thinkers from whom there had come novel and notable and typical contributions to general philosophy, they could in reply mention only two men—Jonathan Edwards and Ralph Waldo Emerson. For the conditions that determine a fair answer to the question, "Who are your representative American philosophers?" are obvious. The philosopher who can fitly represent the contribution of his nation to the world's treasury of philosophical ideas must first be one who

thinks for himself, fruitfully, with true independence, and with successful inventiveness, about problems of philosophy. And, secondly,
he must be a man who gives utterance to philosophical ideas which
are characteristic of some stage and of some aspect of the spiritual
life of his own people. In Edwards and in Emerson, and only in these
men, had these two conditions found their fulfillment, so far as our
American civilization had yet expressed itself in the years that had
preceded our civil war. . . . Another stage of our civilization—a later
phase of our national ideals—found its representative in Emerson.
He too was in close touch with many of the world's deepest thoughts
concerning ultimate problems. Some of the ideas that most influenced him have their far-off historical origins in oriental as well as
in Greek thought, and also their nearer foreign sources in modern
European philosophy, but he transformed what ever he assimilated.
He invented upon the basis of his personal experience, and so he was
himself no disciple of the orient, or of Greece, still less of England
and Germany. He thought, felt, and spoke as an American.[49]

Again, we are left with a judgment as to Emerson's importance, notably in this case as a philosopher, but without subsequent or sufficient
analysis. A search through the papers and publications of Royce does
not cast much more direct light on this influence of Emerson. Royce's
remarks do convince me, however, that Emerson wrought more in the
lives of the classical American philosophers than written evidence can
sustain. Among the centenary addresses of 1903, we find another by an
American philosopher, John Dewey. This essay sets out to rescue Emerson from the condescension implied when he is described as not a philosopher. Dewey complains that "literary critics admit his philosophy
and deny his literature. And if philosophers extol his keen, calm art and
speak with some depreciation of his metaphysic, it is also perhaps because Emerson knew something deeper than our conventional definitions."[50] The first of Dewey's complaints is now out of date, for Emerson
is taken very seriously as a literary artist. The second complaint still
holds, although with important exceptions, as noted above in the work
of Blau and Pollock.

In Dewey's judgment, Emerson has been misread and misunderstood. He takes as Emerson's project the submitting of ideas "to the test
of trial by service rendered the present and immediate experience."[51]

Further, Dewey contends that Emerson's method is consistent with this experimental endeavor. "To Emerson, perception was more potent than reasoning; the deliverances of intercourse more to be desired than the chains of discourse; the surprise of reception more demonstrative than the conclusions of intentional proof."[52]

It is intriguing that Dewey, whose own style is anything but oracular, would praise this approach of Emerson. One might rather expect this indulgence from those reared in the language of the existentialists or of twentieth-century religious thinkers, such as Buber, Berdyaev, and Marcel. A closer look at Dewey's text, however, provides some source of explanation. Similar to James's emphasis, Dewey states that the locus of Emerson's inquiry is the "possibility" inherent in the experience of the "common man." Against the opinions of other commentators, Dewey holds that Emerson's "ideas are not fixed upon any Reality that is beyond or behind or in any way apart, and hence they do not have to be bent. They are versions of the Here and the Now, and flow freely."[53]

Dewey is especially sympathetic with Emerson's attempt to avoid the "apart."[54] And he is convinced that Emerson knew, as few others, of the enervating and diluting effect often had by theory on the richness of common and concrete experience. Dewey's text on this issue is crystal-clear and can be read as well as a critique for much of what passes for philosophical discourse in our own time.

> Against creed and system, convention and institution, Emerson stands for restoring to the common man that which in the name of religion, of philosophy, of art, and of morality has been embezzled from the common store and appropriated to sectarian and class use. Beyond anyone we know of, Emerson has comprehended and declared how such malversation makes truth decline from its simplicity, and in becoming partial and owned, become a puzzle of, and trick for, theologian, metaphysician, and litterateur—a puzzle of an imposed law, of an unwished for and refused goodness, of a romantic ideal gleaming only from afar, and a trick of manipular skill, of specialized performance.[55]

Dewey took Emerson's task as his own. Although his prose lacked the rhetorical flights so natural to Emerson, he, too, wrote out of compassion for the common man and confidence in the "possibility" inherent in every situation. By the time of Dewey's maturity, the world of New England high culture had passed. Dewey, despite being born in New England, was a child of industrial democracy. He alone of the classic American philosophers was able to convert the genius and language of Emerson to the new setting. John Dewey, proletarian by birth and style, grasped that Emerson's message was ever relevant. In the conclusion to his essay on Emerson, Dewey captures that message and carries it forward to his own time. I offer that we should do likewise. "To them who refuse to be called 'master, master,' all magistracies in the end defer, for theirs is the common cause for which dominion, power and principality is put under foot. Before such successes, even the worshippers of that which to-day goes by the name of success, those who bend to millions and incline to imperialisms, may lower their standard and give at least a passing assent to the final word of Emerson's philosophy, the identity of Being, unqualified and immutable, with Character."[56]

FIVE

JOSIAH ROYCE'S PHILOSOPHY
OF THE COMMUNITY

Danger of the Detached Individual

The popular mind is deep and means a thousand times more than it knows.

—Josiah Royce

I

It is fitting that the Royal Institute of Philosophy series on American philosophy include a session on the thought of Josiah Royce, for his most formidable philosophical work, *The World and the Individual*,[1] was a result of his Gifford lectures in the not-too-distant city of Aberdeen in 1899 and 1900. The invitation to offer the Gifford lectures was somewhat happenstance, for it was extended originally to William James, who pleaded, as he often did in his convenient neurasthenic way, to postpone for a year on behalf of his unsettled nerves. James repaired himself to the Swiss home of Theodore Flournoy, with its treasure of books in religion and psychology, so as to write his Gifford lectures, now famous as *The Varieties of Religious Experience*. In so doing, however, James was able to solicit an invitation for Royce to occupy the year of his postponement. Royce accepted with alacrity, although this generosity of James displeased his wife, Alice, who ranted, "Royce!! *He* will not refuse, but over he will go with his Infinite under his arm, and he will not even do honor to William's recommendation."[2] Alice was partially correct in that Royce, indeed, did carry the Infinite across the ocean to the home of his intellectual forebears, although on that occasion, as on many others, he acknowledged the support of his personal and philosophical mentor, colleague, and friend, William James.

We note a philosophical irony in Royce's lectures in Scotland, for if ever there were a book to arouse the wrath of the great Scottish philosopher David Hume it was *The World and the Individual*, representing as it did the acme of the metaphysics destined for the Humean bonfire. Fortunately for Royce, Hume was dead and as yet unrecovered, else his Gifford lectures would have been severely challenged. Instead, they have fallen into comparative neglect, although they represent one of the most ambitious philosophical attempts to ground the existence of the individual self within the context of an all-knowing Absolute Mind. I shall return to an analysis of that effort by Royce, but first let us place Royce in the setting of classical American philosophy and detail his personal and philosophical journey.

II

Most commentators agree that classical American philosophy is comprised of six figures: Charles Sanders Peirce (1839–1914), William James (1842–1910), Josiah Royce (1855–1916), John Dewey (1859–1952), George Herbert Mead (1863–1931), and George Santayana (1863–1952). All but Santayana were native-born; Santayana was born in Spain and did not come to America until he was eight years of age. Santayana lived in America until 1912, when he retired to Europe, permanently. Some commentators include Alfred North Whitehead (1861–1947), who was born in England and did not come to America until 1924, at the age of sixty-three. It is true that Whitehead, when in America, wrote in the tradition of James and was fond of the thought of Mead, but he more properly belongs to the later period known as the Silver Age of American philosophy, rather than the Golden Age as herein described.

As in all great philosophical clusters of the past, and this one was truly distinguished, one can trace strands of continuity among the group and one can elicit profound philosophical differences in their thought, one against the others. As an instance of commonality, I point to the fact

that with the exception of John Dewey, the classical American philosophers either studied or taught at Harvard University. The abiding presence of Harvard in this tradition is extraordinary, as has been detailed
by Bruce Kuklick in his brilliant and contentious *The Rise of American
Philosophy*.[3] In keeping with the Cambridge ambience, the thought of
Ralph Waldo Emerson was very influential on these philosophers.[4]

Differences abound, as, for example, with regard to the influence of
Hegel. Royce and Dewey began as neo-Hegelians, with Royce maintaining that position until midcareer. James and Peirce, to the contrary, had
nothing but contempt for Hegel. All but Royce adopted a pragmatic
epistemology and fought against idealism, although idealist tendencies
remain in the work of James and Dewey.

The upshot of this set of relationships is that classical American philosophy resembles a many-colored mosaic, something like a wall painting by Marc Chagall. The strident differences in their philosophical
views are held together by their constant refraction of the American
scene, often enthusiastic, often critical, but distinctively American in
their pluralism, meliorism, and temporalism. Even Royce, long an Absolute Idealist, adopts these American strategies for a creative philosophical future.

III

Focusing now on Royce, it is notable that he alone among the six philosophers was neither born nor raised in the Northeast. In fact, he was a
child of the frontier, a Californian by birth and by deepest inclination.
One cannot understand America without understanding the frontier experience, and one cannot understand the life and thought of Josiah
Royce without a grasp of his version of that experience. Despite the influential hegemony of the Northeast, and especially New England, on
the intellectual life of America, the long-standing experience of wester-
ing and trekking is a far deeper factor in the evolution of American self-
consciousness.

In detailing this experience we must be aware that despite the presence of the Spanish and the French, America was founded by English
Calvinist Puritans. The fathers and founders of America are not Jefferson and Adams, but John Winthrop, Roger Williams, and Thomas

Hooker. It was they who bequeathed the congregational insight of a cov-enanted community to the forbidding rigours of the wilderness, that is, of western Massachusetts and in turn, West Virginia, western New York, the original northwest territory of the Great Lakes, the Plains, Texas, the northwest of Lewis and Clark, California, and finally, the interior west of Oklahoma in 1907. This dramatic odyssey lasted for two centuries and it left a permanent deposit on the American soul.

The English Puritans were masters of the interior life. They recorded the struggle of their anxiety for a conversion experience as taking place within their own self-consciousness. Their diaries and letters are exqui-site testaments to their introspective sophistication and contain ample description of the false conviction, self-deception, and hypocrisy which richly limn the thicket of the inner personal wilderness. In the early seventeenth century, some of those English Puritans became children of the new world, of America. It soon became clear, as in clearing, that the wilderness existed, but it was spatially external and it lay to the immedi-ate west, rather than festering within the breasts of Puritan men and women.

The conquering and cultivation of the land became the major sign of conversion as the itinerant and trekking Baptist and Methodist ministers replaced the staid, fixed congregations of the Presbyterians. A dialectic soon set up between the systemic loneliness of the frontier and a devel-oping sense of possibility, to be realized over the next hill, across the next river, atop the next mountain. The experience of the inner wilder-ness of the depraved Calvinist soul gave way to the potential fertility of the American settler, always on the move, perennially restless, while searching for the signs of salvation, on, in, of, and about the land.

Just as the founding and/or invention of the New World rendered the European world old, so, too, did the American West find itself in relationship to the East Coast. The Europeans interpreted Americans, and America, variously: as barbarians over against their long-standing civilization; as children over against the parentage of the mother coun-try; as noble savages over against their jaded ways; as a source of hope over against their cynicism; and, finally, as physical paradise over against their intractable inner wilderness. It is striking that these polarities are duplicated in the relationship between the western settlers and the Brahmins of American East Coast sensibility. The transition from spiritual transformation to agrarian realization is put well by Charles Sanford. "The most popular doctrine in the colonies was that America had been singled out, from all the nations of the earth, as the site of the Second Coming; and that the millennium of the saints, while essentially spiritual in nature, would be accompanied by a paradisiac transformation of the earth as the outward symbol of their inward state."[5]

Josiah Royce was born amidst the high point of the trek west—namely, the Gold Rush of 1849 and the immediately subsequent years. His mother, Sarah Royce, was a remarkable woman: literate, educated, and deeply religious in the best tradition of American puritanism. She detailed the perilous family journey in a memoir,[6] written at Royce's request when he was preparing his history of California in the 1880s. Leaving Iowa in April of 1849, the Royce family made their way across the Plains, the Nevada desert, and the high Sierra mountain range until, in October of 1849, they arrived in a California mining camp, named Hangtown, for therein thieves were regularly hung on recognizance. It was in a similar mining camp at Grass Valley, California, in the Sierra mountains, that Josiah Royce was born in 1855. Some sixty years later, on December 29, 1915, less than a year before his death, Royce recalled the message of his childhood.

> My earliest recollections include a very frequent wonder as to what my elders meant when they said that this was a new community. I frequently looked at the vestiges left by the former diggings of miners, saw that many pine logs were rotten, and that a miner's grave was to be found in a lonely place not far from my own house. Plainly men had lived and died thereabouts. I dimly reflected that this sort of life had apparently been going on ever since men dwelt in that land. The logs and the grave looked old. The sunsets were beautiful. The wide prospects when one looked across the Sacramento Valley were impressive, and had long interested the people of whose love for my country I heard much. What was there then in this place that ought to be called new, or for that matter, crude? I wondered, and gradually came to feel that part of my life's business was to find out what all this wonder meant.[7]

Assisted by the *Recollections* of his mother, Royce movingly details the terror and the spiritual quality of the trek west, from wilderness to the alleged paradise of California.

On the plains journeyed, meanwhile, in the summer of 1849, and in a number of subsequent summers, vast crowds of weary emigrants, who faced disease, hunger, and Indians for the sake of the golden land. . . . As my own parents were of this great company, I have taken a natural interest in following their fortunes, and have before me a manuscript, prepared by my mother for my use, wherein, as an introduction to her own reminiscences of early days in San Francisco and elsewhere in California, she has narrated, from her diary of that time, the story of the long land journey. . . .

The route taken and the general sequence of events in the early part of the journey do not vary much in her account from the ordinary things narrated by all the emigrants of that year. There was the long ascent of the Rocky Mountains, with the cholera following the trains for a time, until the mountain air grew too pure and cool for it. A man died of cholera in my father's wagon. There were also the usual troubles in the trains on the way, among such emigrants as had started out in partnership, using a wagon in common, or providing one a wagon, and another the oxen or mules. Such partnerships were unstable, and to dissolve them in the wilderness would usually mean danger or serious loss to one of the partners. In settling these and other disputes, much opportunity was given to the men of emigrant trains for showing their power to preserve the peace and to govern themselves. There was also the delight at length, for my mother as for everybody, of reaching the first waters that flowed towards the Pacific Ocean. And then there was the arrival at Salt Lake, the meeting with the still well-disposed Mormons, and the busy preparation for the final stage of the great undertaking.

From Salt Lake westward my parents, with their one child, my eldest sister, then but two years old, traveled apart from any train, and with but three men as companions. Their only guide-book was now a MS. list of daily journeys and camping-places, prepared by a Mormon who had gone to California and back in 1848. This guide-book was helpful as far as the Sink of the Humboldt, but confused and worthless beyond. The result was that, after escaping, in a fashion that seemed to them almost miraculous, an openly threatened attack of hostile Indians on the Humboldt River,—an attack that, in their weakness, they could not for a moment have resisted,—they came to the Sink, only to miss the last good camping-place there, by reason of their vaguely-written guidebook, to find themselves lost on the Carson desert. They erelong became convinced that they had missed their way, and that they must wander back on their own trail towards the Sink. It was a terrible moment, of course, when they thus knew that their faces must be turned to the east. One was confused, almost stupefied, for a while by the situation. The same fatal horror of desolation and death that had assailed the Donner party in the Truckee Pass seemed for a while about to destroy these emigrants also. They knew themselves to be among the last of the great procession. Many things had concurred to delay and to vex them. It was now already October, and there was not a moment to waste. To turn back at such a crisis seemed simply desperate. But the little water carried with them was now nearly exhausted, and their cattle were in hourly danger of falling down to die. Dazed and half senseless, the company clustered for a while about their wagon; but then a gleam of natural cheerfulness returned. "This will never do," they said, and set about the work of return. On the way they met by chance another lonesome little party of emigrants, who, with very scant supplies, were hurrying westward, in fear of the mountain snows. These could not help my father, save by giving him a few new directions for finding water and grass at the Sink, and for taking the right way across the desert. As the slow wagon neared the long-sought camping-place, my mother could not wait for the tired oxen, but remembers hurrying on alone in advance over the plain, carrying her child, who had now begun to beg for water. In her weariness, her brain was filled with nothing but one familiar Bible story, which she seemed to be dreaming to the very life in clear and cruel detail. But the end of all this came, and the party rested at the little pasture-ground near the Sink.

These details I mention here, not for their personal interest, but because they are so characteristic of the life of thousands in the great summer of 1849. My mother's story goes on, however, to yet another characteristic experience of that autumn. Once supplied at the Sink, my parents, still as nearly alone as before, set out once again across the fortymile desert, and, after more hardships and anxiety, reached the welcome banks of the Carson. But the mountains were now ahead, the snows imminent, and the sand of the Carson Valley, under the wagonwheels, was deep and heavy. On October 12, however, they were opportunely met by two mounted men detailed from

Captain Chandler's detachment of the military relief party which General Smith had sent out to meet and bring in the last of the emigration. The newcomers, riding at full speed, seemed to my mother, in her despair, like angels sent from heaven down by the steep, dark mountains that loomed up to the westward. They were, at all events, men of good mountaineering experience and of excellent spirit, and they brought two extra mules, which were at once put at my mother's own service. By the peremptory orders of these relief men, the wagon was forthwith abandoned. What could be packed on the still serviceable animals was taken, and the rest of the journey was made by the whole party mounted. They arrived safely in the mines a little before the heavy snows began.

Socially considered, the effect of the long journey across the plains was, of course, rather to discipline than to educate; yet the independent life of the small trains, with their frequent need of asserting their skill in self-government, tended to develop both the best and the worst elements of the frontier political character; namely, its facility in self-government, and its over-hastiness in using the more summary devices for preserving order. As for the effect on the individual character, the journey over the plains was, at least as a discipline, very good for those who were of strong and cheerful enough disposition to recover from the inevitable despondency that must at first enter into the life of even the most saintly novice in camping. Where families were together, this happy recovery happened, of course, more quickly. One learned, meanwhile, how to face deadly dangers day by day with patience and coolness, and to strongly religious minds the psychological effect of this solitary struggle with the deserts was almost magical. One seemed alone with God in the waste, and felt but the thinnest veil separating a divine presence from the souls that often seemed to have no conceivable human resource left. This experience often expresses itself in language at once very homely and very mystical. God's presence, it declares, was no longer a matter of faith, but of direct sight. Who else was there but God in the desert to be seen? One was going on a pilgrimage whose every suggestion was of the familiar sacred stories. One sought a romantic and far-off golden land of promise, and one was in the wilderness of this world, often guided only by signs from heaven,—by the stars and by the sunset. The clear blue was almost perpetually overhead; the pure mountain winds were about one; and again, even in the hot and parched deserts, a mysterious power provided the few precious springs and

streams of water. Amid the jagged, broken, and barren hills, amid
the desolation of the lonely plains, amid the half-unknown but always horrible dangers of the way, one met experiences of precisely
the sort that elsewhere we always find producing the most enthusiastic forms of religious mysticism. And so the truly pious among these
struggling wanderers gained from the whole life one element more
of religious steadfastness for the struggle that was yet to come, in
early California, between every conservative tendency and the forces
of disorder.[8]

Royce's search for the meaning of his childhood in the mining camp
became an obsession for him—personally, morally, and philosophically.
His adolescence was difficult, especially as his physiognomy and body
image lent themselves to mockery. He was short of stature, rotund, with
orange hair, an enormous forehead and a high-pitched voice. Shall we
say simply that he was the butt of much abuse, some of it physical, on
the part of his more macho peers. Money was hard to come by for Royce
and he began his life much as he finished it, under financial pressure for
one reason or another. He did manage to attend the brand-new University of California at Berkeley, where he became competent in Greek
literature, although overall his grades were not outstanding. Yet he impressed sufficiently to be given assistance to study philosophy in Germany in 1875–76. Imbued with the thought of German idealism, he
returns to the first graduate program in America at Johns Hopkins University, where he completes his PhD degree in 1878. His only opportunity is to return to Berkeley as a lecturer in the Department of English.
Cut off from his European experience as well as the intellectual excitement of Hopkins, where, among others, he met William James, Royce
became very depressed in California. Actually, Royce was of two minds,
for he had an abiding "loyalty" to California and he treasured its topography and physical beauty.[9] Yet, distant from philosophical conversation, he became increasingly lonely, insecure, even alienated from
himself. Two texts reveal this Picassoesque "boy in the mirror" image of
the reflective Royce. The first is on behalf of California, written in 1879
as a hymn to the Golden Gate, that is, to the magnificent promontory
which from on high affronts the entrance to San Francisco Bay by the
vaunted majesty of the Pacific Ocean. The text is as follows:

"Meditation before the Gate"

I am a Californian, and day after day, by the order of the World Spirit (whose commands we all do ever obey, whether we will it or no), I am accustomed to be found at my tasks in a certain place that looks down upon the Bay of San Francisco and over the same out into the water of the Western Ocean. The place is not without beauty, and the prospect is far-reaching. Here as I do my work I often find time for contemplation. . . .

That one realizes the greatness of the world better when he rises a little above the level of the lowlands, and looks upon the large landscape beneath, this we all know; and all of us, too, must have wondered that a few feet of elevation should tend so greatly to change our feeling toward the universe. Moreover the place of which I speak is such as to make one regret when he considers its loveliness that there are not far better eyes beholding it than his own. For could a truly noble soul be nourished by the continual sight of the nature that is here, such a soul would be not a little enviable. Yet for most of us Nature is but a poor teacher.

Still even to me, she teaches something. The high dark hills on the western shore of the Bay, the water at their feet, the Golden Gate that breaks through them and opens up to one the view of the sea beyond, the smoke-obscured city at the south of the Gate, and the barren ranges yet farther to the left, these are the permanent background whereon many passing shapes of light and shadow, of cloud and storm, of mist and of sunset glow are projected as I watch from my station on the hillside. The seasons go by quietly, and without many great changes. The darkest days of what we here call winter seem always to leave not wholly without brightness one part of the sky, that just above the Gate. When the rain storms are broken by the fresh breezes from the far-off northern Sierras, one sees the departing clouds gather in threatening masses about the hilltops, while the Bay spreads out at one's feet, calm and restful after its little hour of tempest. When the time of great rains gives place to the showers of early spring one scarcely knows which to delight in the more, whether in the fair green fields, that slope down gently to the water, or in the sky of the west, continually filled with fantastic shapes of light and cloud—nor does even our long dry summer, with its parched meadows and its daily sea winds, leave this spot without beauty. The ocean and the bay are yet there; the high hills beyond change not all for any season; but are ever rugged and cold and stern; and the long lines of fog, borne in through the Gate or through the depressions of the range, stretch out over many miles of country like columns of an invading host, now shining in innocent whiteness as if their mission were but one of love, now becoming dark and dreadful, as when they smother the sun at evening. So, while the year goes by, one is never without the companionship of nature. And there are heroic deeds done in cloud-land, if one will but look forth and see them.

But I have here . . . to speak not so much of Nature as of Life. And I shall undertake to deal with a few problems such as are often thought to be metaphysical (whereby one means that they are worthless), and are also often quite rightly called philosophical (whereby one means that it were the part of wisdom to solve them if we could). With these problems I shall seek to busy myself earnestly, because that is each one's duty; independently, because I am a Californian, as little bound to follow mere tradition as I am liable to find an audience by preaching in this wilderness; reverently, because I am thinking and writing face to face with a mighty and lovely Nature, by the side of whose greatness I am but as a worm.[10]

On another occasion, however, in the very same year as the "Meditation," 1879, Royce writes in the following letter to William James.

There is no philosophy in California—from Siskiyou to Ft. Yuma, and from the Golden Gate to the summit of the Sierras. . . . Hence the atmosphere for the study of metaphysics is bad, and I wish I were out of it. On the other hand, I am at home and so among good friends; and further, as to my work, I am entirely free to arrange my course as I please, and to put into it a little philosophy. . . . I trumped up a theory of logical concepts last term and preached it to the seniors. It was a kind of hybrid of Hume and Schopenhauer, with an odor of Kant about it. It was somewhat monstrous, and, in this wilderness with nobody to talk with about it, I have not the least idea whether it is true or not.[11]

William James, ever responsive to a plaintive cry, soon arranged for a temporary appointment for Royce in the Harvard University Philosophy Department. Royce arrived in 1882 and did not leave until his premature death in 1916, some thirty-four years later. Royce, the indigenous Californian, found himself among the New England Brahmins. Try as he might, he never quite fitted that august, precious, and self-serving intellectual world. A rocky marriage to Katharine Head and a severe mental collapse by his oldest son increased the tensions in Royce's life. His other two children did not fare very well and he had the burden of a severely retarded grandchild. Money problems often plagued Royce and he seemed caught in a tangle between paying his creditors and struggling to obtain a public reputation judged worthy of a Harvard professor. George Herbert Palmer, a mainstay of the Harvard Philosophy Department, stated that Royce was visited by "afflictions sorted, anguish of all sizes."[12] Royce had fled the loneliness and alienation of the sparse intellectual life on the Pacific rim of California, only to have these deep self-doubts reappear in the cozy, but yet forbidding, interpersonal terrain of New England high culture. In 1888, when under severe mental strain, Royce took a year away from Harvard and sailed around the world, with a prolonged intermediate stay in Australia and New Zealand. From 1882 until 1888, Royce had taught full-time at Harvard and at an earlier version of Radcliffe, as well as having published three books: *The Religious Aspect of Philosophy* (1885);[13] *California* (1886);[14] and *The Feud of Oakfield Creek: A Novel of California Life* (1887).[15] With financial assistance from Harvard and from his friend, Charles Rockwell Lanham, Royce attended to his breakdown by leaving home, a routine he was to adopt periodically in the future. Some commentators, such as Frank Oppenheim, see Royce's trip to the South Seas as extraordinarily important for the development of his mature philosophical position.[16] We do know that he returned to Harvard refreshed and anxious to once again take on his many duties and begin to fashion a metaphysical response to the always underlying theme of his life—why suffering?

IV

In a famous statement of the moral quandary which results from the existence of evil, Dostoevsky sharpens the issue by involving us in the death of an innocent child. Surely such a tragic occurrence makes necessary the existence of an all-good God who will, in the canopy of eternity, make right this flagrant injustice. Yet Dostoevsky holds simultaneously that given such an event, an all-good God could not exist, for if He did and did not prevent this outrage, then that God would be evil. In my reading of Royce, I have come to believe that this moral dilemma is at the center of his life and thought. Further, I believe that he takes a double route to resolve the problem. The first is metaphysical and, in turn, the utilization of modern mathematics and logic. The second way is through social philosophy, laced with homilies and pleas for tolerance and the willingness to develop a community. The most notorious single obstacle to the building of a great and beloved community, according to Royce, is the existence of the detached individual. That person who lacks loyalty and concern is fair game for seduction by those nefarious movements which seek to wreck the community on behalf of some political, social, or religious ideology, all of them self-aggrandizing. Royce seeks to overcome this loneliness of the detached individual, a characteristic of his own life, experientially learned and observed in the course of his mining-camp childhood. The parallel strategies of Royce to deal with this matter find him concentrating on metaphysics and logic, on the one hand, and a philosophy of community, on the other. They are not brought together until the publication of *The Problem of Christianity* in 1913. A break-out of this parallel, citing the major writings of Royce (with abbreviations of titles in parentheses), looks as follows:[17]

SOCIAL PHILOSOPHY	METAPHYSICS AND LOGIC
Fugitive Essays (on Pessimism and Romanticism)—1879–80 (FE)	*The Religious Aspect of Philosophy*—1885 (RAP)
California—1886 (CAL)	*The Spirit of Modern Philosophy*—1892 (SMP)
The Feud of Oakfield Creek—1887 (FOC)	*The Conception of God*—1897 (CG)
Studies of Good and Evil—1898 (SGE)	*The World and the Individual*—1899–1901 (WI)
The Philosophy of Loyalty—1908 (PL)	*The Conception of Immortality*—1900 (CI)
Race Questions, Provincialism, and other American Problems—1908 (RQP)	*Lectures on Modern Idealism*—1906 (1919) (LMI)
William James and other Essays on the Philosophy of Life—1911 (WJO)	*The Principles of Logic*—1913 (PrL)
The Sources of Religious Insight—1912 (SRI)	
The Problem of Christianity—1913 (PC)	
The Hope of the Great Community—1916 (HGC)	

If we weave together a commentary on each of the two approaches taken by Royce, the development of his thought takes on the following cast. The young Royce is very taken by the seamy side of human life. In 1879, after having returned to California, he writes an essay, "The Practical Significance of Pessimism." In a remarkably pessimistic text, Royce delineates the human condition from his perspective.

> Contemplate a battlefield the first night after the struggle, contemplate here a vast company the equal of the population of a great town, writhing in agony, their groans sounding at a great distance like the roar of the ocean, their pain uneased for many hours, even death, so lavish of his favors all day, now refusing to comfort; contemplate this and then remember that as this pain to the agony of the world, so is an electric spark drawn from the back of the kitten to the devastating lightning of many great storms; and now estimate if you can the worth of all but a few exceptional human lives, such as that of Caius.
>
> Briefly and imperfectly I state the case for pessimism, not even touching the economical and social argument, drawn from a more special consideration of the conditions of human life. Such then, is our individual human life. What shall we call it and whereunto shall it be likened? A vapor vanishing in the sun? No, that is not insignificant enough. A wave, broken on the beach? No, that is not unhappy enough. A soap bubble bursting into thin air? No, even that has rainbow hues. What then? Nothing but itself. Call it human life. You could not find a comparison more thoroughly condemning it.[18]

For the next five years, Royce attempts to overcome this perspective by appealing to his philosophical conviction that the doctrines of Absolute Idealism can successfully account for evil and error, sufficient to render it meaningful. The fruition of these reflections is published in 1885 under the title *The Religious Aspect of Philosophy*. Royce was never pollyanna about the existence of evil, stating in his essay "The Problem of Job" that "I regard evil as a distinctly real fact, a fact just as real as the most helpless and hopeless sufferer finds it to be when he is in pain."[19]

The epistemological version of evil is the existence of error. Royce sees this perennial human activity as potentially undermining any philosophical effort to ground religious truth, such that one could account

for evil. Consequently, before addressing the problem of evil in *The Religious Aspect of Philosophy*, Royce attends to the problem of error. Holding that we cannot ascribe error to any judgment, unless it be compared
to an Absolute Truth, Royce sees error as a torso, a fragment of the
seamless garment of Truth. He writes:

> That there is error is indubitable. What is, however, an error? The
> substance of our whole reasoning about the nature of error
> amounted to the result that in and of itself alone, no single judgment
> is, or can be, an error. Only as actually included in a higher thought,
> that gives to the first its completed object, and compares it therewith,
> is the first thought an error. It remains otherwise a mere mental frag-
> ment, a torso, a piece of drift-wood, neither true nor false, objectless,
> no complete act of thought at all. But the higher thought must in-
> clude the opposed truth, to which the error is compared in that
> higher thought. The higher thought is the whole truth, of which the
> error is by itself an incomplete fragment.[20]

What is intriguing here is that Royce is pursuing an inductive argument,
to wit, the existence of error as a particular, empirical artifact is able to
be so judged if, and only if, a total fabric exists in which all of the possibilities extant are known, by someone, somewhere, somehow, somewhen. This latter capacity must exist because we do come to know about
counterfactuals. Thus, from a single miscreant event, claim, or judgment
we can conclude to a wider, all-embracing whole which gives credibility
to our decision on the veritability of the particular in question.

Turning from epistemological error to moral and metaphysical evil,
Royce attempts the same strategy—namely, to turn the very existence of
particular evil into a proof for the existence of Absolute Good. For
Royce, the acknowledgment that an act is morally evil is a sign that it is
being overcome on behalf of a good will. Such a designation Royce calls
a "moral insight."

> The moral insight condemns the evil that it experiences; *and in con-
> demning and conquering this evil it forms and is, together with the evil,
> the organic total that constitutes the good will. . . . I here directly experi-
> ence how the partial moral evil is universal good*; for so it is a relatively
> universal good in me when, overcoming myself, I choose the univer-
> sal will. The bad impulse is still in me, but is defeated. In the choice

against evil is the very life of goodness, which would be a pale, stupid abstraction otherwise.[21]

Frankly, even for sympathetic students of Royce, these arguments are not convincing. In the first place, the prose of *The Religious Aspect of Philosophy* is bloated, much like an English-language redaction of what William James used to call, condescendingly, "teutonic metaphysics." Secondly, the claim of Royce that particulars, be they judgments, acts, or events, are meaningful only if they are understood as parts of a whole, is plausible but not apodictic. It is possible, after all, that William James is right in holding that totality and finality are constructs of an insecure human temperament. Third, and in his deeper, more reflective, less cerebral self, Royce knows it to be true that systemic evil is not whitewashed or even made acceptable by philosophical principles of accountability. Yet, during this period from 1878 until 1885, Royce walks the double path of acknowledging the existential presence of pessimism, the violence perpetrated in the struggle for a human community, as, for example, on the California frontier, and the philosophical attempt to render the entire scene, all for the good, *sub specie aeternitatis.*

In that decade of the late nineteenth century, few, if any, commentators knew that Royce was treading a double path: of experiential, empirical reportage of evil, and of a complex intellectual attempt to render the filled bulb of everyday human interaction as, somehow, meaningful.

The next steps in this parallel journey occur in the years 1897–1901. In a command performance, Royce was invited back to the University of California at Berkeley in 1895 in order to defend his Absolute Idealism against critics, especially the gifted American philosopher, George Holmes Howison. The invitation was accepted by Royce with enthusiasm, for he enjoyed the prospect of returning home to California as a representative of his Brahmin nest at Harvard University. He met more opposition than he anticipated, however, as Howison, still smarting over being bypassed by Royce for the Harvard appointment, went on the attack. In a perceptive critique of Royce's position, Howison asks rhetorically:

> *Whose* omniscience is it that judges the ignorance to be real?—*whose* absolute experience pronounces the less organised experience to be

really fallacious? Well,—whosesoever it may be, it is certainly acting in and through my judgment, if I am the thinker of that argument; and in every case it is *I* who pronounce sentence on myself as really ignorant, or on my limited experience as fallacious. Yes,—and it is I who am the authority, and the only direct authority, for the connexion put between the reality of the ignorance or of the fallacious experience, on the one hand, and the reality of the implicated omniscience, on the other.[22]

Royce begins to see cracks in his Absolute Idealism as the antidote for an understanding of systemic evil. In response to Howison, he pleads that his critic does not realize that the individual and the particular are not obliterated by the Absolute, which, although transcendent, does not destroy its components.[23] In *The Conception of God*, Royce makes a valiant effort to defend his position, even though he is aware that Howison and others have struck a deadly blow against him, for he cannot account for the irreducible character of particulars, especially persons and personal acts. It is not irrelevant that in 1898 Royce publishes his moral and social, existentially sensitive essays on Good and Evil, inclusive of commentaries on Job, Bunyan, and the relation between self and social consciousness.[24] Yet, Royce, stung by the criticism at Berkeley, devotes his Gifford lectures on "The World and the Individual" to a resolution of his difficulty in maintaining a fidelity to the personal, acting, willing self, while yet holding to a principle of final accountability as found in the existence of an Absolute Mind. In the preface to the published version of his Gifford lectures in *The World and the Individual*, Royce plots his course as a response to the earlier objections of Howison and, increasingly, William James:

> While this central matter regarding the definition of Truth, and of our relation to truth, has not essentially changed its place in my mind, I have been doing what I could, since my first book was written, to come to clearness as to the relations of Idealism to the special problems of human life and destiny. In my first book the conception of the Absolute was defined in such wise as led me then to prefer, quite deliberately, the use of the term Thought as the best name for the final unity of the Absolute. While this term was there so defined as to make Thought inclusive of Will and of Experience, these latter terms were not emphasized prominently enough, and the aspects of

the Absolute Life which they denote have since become more central in my own interests. The present is a deliberate effort to bring into synthesis, more fully than I have ever done before, the relations of Knowledge and of Will in our conception of God. The centre of the present discussion is, for this very reason, the true meaning and place of the concept of Individuality, in regard to which the present discussion carries out a little more fully considerations which appear, in a very different form of statement, in the "Supplementary Essay," published at the close of *The Conception of God*.[25]

In this massive and complex work of metaphysics and epistemology, Royce attempts to work out a strategy for dealing with one of the most stubborn of all philosophical questions, known to the ancients as that of "the one and the many." Do we begin with an experience of many singles, particulars, and put a conceptual blanket over them, so that they be one? If so, does this principle of unity exclude significant individual characteristics, such that the unity be a sham, a mere gathering of the obvious? Or do we begin with an intuition of unity and come serially to distinguish particularity, by accrued sense experience? If so, is this grasp of unity to be trusted? Is it the same for all persons? Are the resulting singulars truly distinctive or are they only figments of a roving imagination which is bored with the principle of unification? These rhetorical questions mask the philosophical dramatis personae from Heraclitus and Parmenides to Quine. Intermediate pauses with the thought of Plato, Aristotle, Scotus Erigena, Aquinas, Duns Scotus, Descartes, Spinoza, Leibniz, Kant, and Hegel only prepare us for the recent debate as carried on by Bergson, Whitehead, Russell, James, Heidegger, and, of course, by Royce.

Speaking now only of Royce, he takes the position of an epistemological voluntarist, which is to say that for him particulars exist precisely because they are the constituency of the Absolute. A particular—that is a person, an individual self—is as it is precisely because in its purpose as being, it fulfills the portion of reality necessary to a realization of the Absolute as all that has been, is, or can be. In a clever turn of phrase and idea, Royce holds that the particular is particular for the reason that the Absolute is a realization of all particulars. In his analysis of the conception of being as found in the meaning of ideas, Royce writes:

First, *the complete fulfilment of your internal meaning*, the final satis-
faction of the will embodied in the idea, but secondly, also, *that absolute determination of the embodiment of your idea as this embodiment
would then be present,—that absolute determination of your purpose,
which would constitute an individual realization of the idea*. For an
individual fact is one for which no other can be substituted without
some loss of determination, or some vagueness.[26]

As he hinted in his preface, Royce now makes the will a knowing probe
of the self. Ideas become neither copies nor representations nor even
intuitive flashes, but rather probes which carry the self into uncharted
and rich areas of potential meaning. This voluntarism has a pragmatic
tone and the influence of William James is beginning to be felt on the
formerly impervious Absolute Idealist conceptual hide of Royce. Yet the
time for capitulation to the pragmatic and totally empirical-experiential
approach is not yet present for Royce. He thinks that he has one last
card to play, and among recent philosophers he is one of the few who
could play it; that is, a formal logical and mathematical resolution of
the problem. Stated simply, Royce's difficulty is, how can you have an
Absolute, an infinite series, and still have a bona fide individual, self, or
particular? His metaphysical effort to resolve this has been herculean,
yet he is not satisfied with the result, nor should he be. Perhaps logic
and mathematics holds the key. Under the influence of Charles Sanders
Peirce and the early-twentieth-century mathematical explorations of the
infinite, Royce makes one last-ditch effort to ground his Absolute without simultaneously destroying the individual person in all of his/her distinctive and unrepeatable experiences.

Paradoxically, Royce looked to logic as the way to provide a still more
voluntaristic, constructive character to human inquiry. In this effort,
Royce was prescient, for he grasped the little-known character of modern logic as a method for "building" versions of the human quest rather
than as a form of denotation of that already in place. Even Morton
White, no champion of Royce or of his approach to philosophy, cites
him as a forerunner of the twentieth-century revolution in logic:

For Royce was more than a metaphysical soothsayer, more than a
philosopher of religion and of loyalty to loyalty: he was also a logician and a philosopher of science. He was one of the first American

teachers of philosophy to recognize the importance of research in symbolic logic and to encourage its study both for its own intrinsic intellectual importance and as a tool. Some of his pupils, like C. I. Lewis and H. M. Sheffer, became distinguished Harvard contributors to this subject and founders of one of the most influential centers of logic in the twentieth century.[27]

Despite the many logical and mathematical byways taken by Royce in his attempt to forge a new logic, known to him as "system sigma," Royce had his eye on the problem which had vexed him from the beginning—namely, the possibility of an individual, or particular, if, in logical fact, there is an infinite system. It is intriguing that Royce hoped to show that modern logic and the modern logician proceeds from a world which is "empirical."[28]

Royce filled hundreds of pages with logical notations, most of them on behalf of an original system, in an effort to fuse his developing philosophical empiricism and his recent pragmatic sensibility with that of his long-standing commitment to Absolute Idealism. By 1913, in *The Principles of Logic*, Royce capitulates to a pragmatic grounding of the Absolute. Clearly anticipatory of the work of W. V. O. Quine, Royce clings to the Absolute only in a functional way, and as a result of successful reporting or activity. In the last section of *The Principles of Logic*, "The Logical Genesis of the Types of Order," Royce makes his last, valiant effort to preserve both an empirical and constructive epistemology and a doctrine of Absolute Truth:

> In brief, whatever actions are such, whatever types of action are such, whatever results of activity, whatever conceptual constructions are such, that the very act of getting rid of them, or of thinking them away, logically implies their presence, are known to us indeed both empirically and pragmatically (since we note their presence and learn of them through action); but they are also absolute. And any account which succeeds in telling what they are has absolute truth. Such truth is a "construction" or "creation," for activity determines its nature. It is "found," for we observe it when we act.[29]

In the meantime, with the other hand/person, as it were, Royce was continuing his social philosophical writings. In 1908, he published *Race Questions, Provincialism and other American Problems*, which was a volume of sermonic essays. "Provincialism" is still viable, for Royce put his finger on a serious dilemma in the pedagogy of culture. Surely we cannot be closed off from other cultures, persuasions and ideas, if we are to achieve a human community in the fullest sense, as, for example, in Royce's vision of the "beloved" or "great" community. Yet, Royce warns us, as paraphrased, that to love the world and detest one's brother or sister is to be a hypocrite. For Royce, community is a flowering of deeply and integrally held commitments to one's local environment. The underpinning of the attempt to structure a community is what Royce details as "loyalty." In 1908, the same year as the publication of *Race Questions, Provincialism and other American Problems*, and in the midst of his intense personal work on logic and mathematics, Royce publishes *The Philosophy of Loyalty*.

Actually, the misunderstandings of Royce's doctrine of loyalty are easily traceable to the fact that his critics read only that work or, at best, knew little of Royce's philosophical work and vision. In fact, *The Philosophy of Loyalty* is vintage Royce, being an attempt to justify personal experience as an anticipation of eternal meaning. I must grant that Royce's phrasing is not always sufficiently cognizant of the short-sighted opponent and, therefore, his doctrine of loyalty is often subject to critical abuse. He writes, for example, that loyalty is "the willing and practical thoroughgoing devotion of a person to a cause."[30] The uninitiated will immediately challenge on behalf of the obvious fact that some causes are worthy and others are not worthy. It is not until some three hundred pages later that Royce also writes: "Loyalty is the will to manifest, so far as is possible, the Eternal, that is, the conscious and superhuman unity of life, in the form of the acts of an individual Self."[31]

The second text merely opens the first text, in a way that Royce, in 1908, takes for granted; that is, all personal acts take their meaning from a more expansive context, one which casts approving or disapproving light on their intentionality. In obvious terms, if one is "loyal" to an evil cause, there is no self-transcendence and no commitment to the other person or persons. Consequently such activity is not loyalty for Royce but rather self-aggrandizement and, indeed, disloyalty to the potential for personal growth. To the contrary, loyalty to a cause, de facto, is a commitment to an idea, event, or person, which forces upon the human self a willingness to transcend the narrow boundaries of self, be they preservation, reputation, or success. In a paraphrase of an earlier text in *The Religious Aspect of Philosophy*,[32] Royce sees loyalty as an activity whose eternal end-in-view renders the temporal act meaningful, even though confusion may reign as to what one is to do or believe at any given time. So much does Royce believe in this possibility of the capacity of human life to transcend the pitfalls of seductive allegiance that he insists that, with the passing of time, the eternal fragrance will make itself felt among the thorns and vicissitudes of daily demands. Royce sees a unity of persons who so believe in this hidden but palpable capacity of the loyal to experience the eternal. On behalf of this spiritual loyalty, he writes:

> Moreover, that which I have called the cause of all the loyal, the real unity of the whole spiritual world, is not merely a moral ideal. It is a religious reality. Its servants and ministers are present wherever religious brotherhood finds sincere and hearty manifestation. In the sight of a perfectly real but superhuman knowledge of the real purposes and effective deeds of mankind, *all the loyal, whether they individually know the fact or not, are, and in all times have been, one genuine and religious brotherhood.* Human narrowness and the vicissitudes of the world of time have hidden, and still hide, the knowledge of this community of the loyal from human eyes. But indirectly it comes to light whenever the loyalty of one visible spiritual community comes, through any sort of tradition, or custom, or song or story, or wise word or noble deed, to awaken new manifestations of the loyal life in faithful souls anywhere amongst men.[33]

Up to this point, Royce kept the two aspects of his thought and person in a tolerable and creative relationship. Yet, surely he knew that despite his conceptual brilliance, the gnawing intractability of human suffering could not forever be "transcended" by a philosophical protocol, however logical it might seem to its polymathic author. Consequently, in 1913, Royce publishes his attempt at bridging his two parallel approaches to the problem of suffering, namely, *The Problem of Christianity*. This book is somewhat mistitled, for it is not so much about Christianity as it is about the Pauline doctrine of the beloved community, a notion inspired by Jesus, but hardly representative of the history of Christianity except for an occasional Benedictine or Franciscan monk.

The most important aspect of Royce's book is his utilization of Peirce's doctrine of signs, converted by Royce into a method of interpretation. Royce finally gives way in his fealty to the language of Absolute Idealism and begins to speak more of the "community," in process, than of the Absolute. Royce, despite his prodigious knowledge, or maybe because of it, was a learner. Peirce had stung him by giving faint praise to the publication of *The World and the Individual*, saying that it was a good effort given that the author knew no logic.[34] Royce responded by making an effort to understand the logic of Peirce, despite its complexity and comparative unavailability in published form. One cardinal tenet of Peirce's logic did become accessible to Royce: that of the doctrine of third-term mediation. For every A in relationship to B, there is needed a third, interpretive term, C. Royce converts this triadic logic into a doctrine of interpretation, wherein protagonists in an otherwise communal setting take it upon themselves to listen to a third party, one who has the sense of both missions, both allegedly viable and praiseworthy, so as to render a *vade mecum*, for purpose of amelioration. Royce details the "world of interpretation" as follows:

> We all of us believe that there is any real world at all, simply because we find ourselves in a situation in which, because of the fragmentary and dissatisfying conflicts, antitheses, and problems of our present ideas, an interpretation of this situation is needed, but is not now known to us. *By the "real world" we mean simply the "true interpretation" of this our problematic situation.* No other reason can be given than this for believing that there is any real world at all. . . .
>
> In brief, then, the real world is the Community of Interpretation which is constituted by the two antithetic ideas, and their mediator or interpreter, whatever or whoever that interpreter may be. If the interpretation is a reality, and if it truly interprets the whole of reality, then the community reaches its goal, and the real world includes its own interpreter. *Unless both the interpreter and the community are real, there is no real world.*[35]

What, then, can be rendered significant by interpretation? Surely Royce has the intention of bequeathing a way to build a truly human community. To this end he offers these conditions for the existence and well-being of a community.

The *first* condition upon which the existence of a community, in our sense of the word, depends, is the power of an individual self to extend his life, in ideal fashion, so as to regard it as including past and future events which lie far away in time, and which he does not now personally remember. That this power exists, and that man has a self which is thus ideally extensible in time without any definable limit, we all know. . . .

The *second* condition upon which the existence of a community depends is the fact that there are in the social world a number of distinct selves capable of social communication, and, in general, engaged in communication.

The *third* of the conditions for the existence of the community which my definition emphasizes consists in the fact that the ideally extended past and future selves of the members include at least some events which are, for all these selves, identical. This third condition is the one which furnishes both the most exact, the most widely variable, and the most important of the motives which warrant us in calling a community a real unit.[36]

If we look carefully at these three Roycean conditions for the existence of a community, rather than being simply a human conglomerate, a thread appears throughout. One could call it "transcendence," or "reaching" or "getting," "going beyond oneself," but whatever the description it is clear that Royce expects us to enter into a form of interpretation so that our jealously guarded turf—beliefs, commitments, and assertions—is, at the very least, subject to the viewpoint of another, distant, although concerned participant. This process does not end in any form of closure, for Royce holds that we always have the possibility of "an endless wealth of new interpretations."[37] The building of the human community becomes for Royce nothing less than the meaning of the world, in the most profound sense of "meaning," as in metaphysics. Royce writes:

Metaphysically considered, the world of interpretation is the world in which, if indeed we are able to interpret at all, we learn to acknowledge the being and the inner life of our fellow-men; and to understand the constitution of temporal experience, with its endlessly accumulating sequence of significant deeds. In this world of interpretation, of whose most general structure we have now obtained a glimpse, selves and communities may exist, past and future can be defined, and the realms of the spirit may find a place which neither barren conception nor the chaotic flow of interpenetrating perceptions could ever render significant.[38]

Royce wrote the above text at the dawning of a great calamity, the First World War, a conflict which was to begin the erosion of confidence in the classical values of Western civilization.[39] In failing health and enormously depressed by the sinking of the *Lusitania* in May of 1915, Royce nonetheless clung to the possibility of rebuilding a sense of community. To that end, in 1916, the year of his death, Royce published a paper, "The Hope of the Great Community," in the prestigious *Yale Review*. At the very end of his successful but deeply troubled life, Royce wrote:

> The citizens of the world of the future will not lose their distinct countries. What will pass away will be that insistent mutual hostility which gives to the nations of to-day, even in times of peace, so many of the hateful and distracting characters of a detached individual man. In the case of human individuals, the sort of individualism which is opposed to the spirit of loyalty, is what I have already called the individualism of the detached individual, the individualism of the man who belongs to no community which he loves and to which he can devote himself with all his heart, and his soul, and his mind, and his strength. In so far as liberty and democracy, and independence of soul, mean that sort of individualism, they never have saved men and never can save men. For mere detachment, mere self-will, can never be satisfied with itself, can never win its goal. What saves us on any level of human social life is union.[40]

It is fitting that we have a discussion of the philosophy of Josiah Royce in this international setting, characterized as it is by an effort to reach out and transcend our parochial sentiments by sharing the wisdom of American philosophy with a culture whence it originated, England. On this matter of classical American philosophy, it has been too long detached from other cultures, for it has much to learn and much to teach. I appreciate the opportunity for both experiences, here in the great city of London.

SIX

POSSIBILITY OR ELSE!

The Philosophy of William James

Philosophy is the habit of always seeing an alternative.
> —William James, "The Teaching of Philosophy in Our Colleges" (1876)

I am pleased and privileged to be a guest at Blinn College, which is doing fine work in the educating of many persons here in the Brazos Valley and central Texas. Now, speaking for myself, I have trouble getting through the day, while maintaining some semblance of personal *equilibrium*. If this is also your wont, your need, I have a suggestion: read and reflect on the philosophy of William James. You could try Camus and be happy as the rock of your life rolls down the hill once again, infinitely. Or Freud, where you could spend your day wary of secrets. You could follow Marx and thereby duke it out with whatever establishment comes your way. Try Aristotle and you would be busy, very busy, memorizing millions of descriptions and definitions. How about Descartes, enabling you to doubt everything, including the necessary presence of your own body? Each of these philosophers and many others, as well, offer diagnostically accurate versions of one or more ways to be in the world. Their very brilliance, however, seems to cause us to "list" in one direction or another and their power is too strong to get us through the day. Although I am enchanted with the canonical thinkers of our culture, and of other cultures, for example, Lao Tzu, author of the *Tao Te Ching*, I choose a more modest helpmate for my journey. The thought and writings of William James offer us a philosophical take equivalently canonical, but along the way, his work is laced with aperçus, gleanings, quick shots of wisdom that strike at the heart of the everyday: that is, the fabric in and through which we live our lives. Here is one—"Nothing so fatiguing as the eternal hanging on of an unfinished task."[1] If that does not speak directly to you, it will.

Let us return to the substance of our discussion, the philosophy of William James, by glossing the epigraph to this essay, to wit: "Philosophy is the habit of always seeing an alternative."[2] Quite directly, aside from being good advice, James has deep philosophical reasons for this judgment—namely, his abiding dubiety about finality, totality, closure: in a word, certitude. Also, he had a commitment to the doctrine of possibility, to the persistent presence of novelty and to the wisdom of taking a chance on there being more than is in our present sight. James tells us that "experience has a way of *boiling* over and flooding all our categories."[3] This flooding washes over our habits, our addictions, and yes, our beliefs. Get by yourself with a notepad. Write down all of your beliefs—theological, religious, moral, political, economic, social, sexual, personal lifestyle—and then separate them into those inherited and those chosen in response to your actual experience and the experience of others.

While doing this, keep in mind a notebook entry by William James:

> All neat schematisms with permanent and absolute distinctions, classifications with absolute pretensions, systems with pigeon-holes, etc., have this character. All classic, clean, cut and dried, "noble," "fixed," "eternal" *weltanschaungen* seem to me to violate the character with which life concretely comes and the expression which it bears of being, or at least involving, a muddle and a struggle, with an "ever not quite" to all our formulas and novelty and possibility leaking in.[4]

Consequently, and I use this word advisedly, we should live on the edge, with the attitude of *un tentativo*, open to novelty, surprise, and the dismaying message that my beliefs may have been self-foreclosing.

The reigning assumption here is that experience speaks, such that by and of itself experience is pedagogical. In response to the question What is nature?, Shakespeare tells us that it is its own mean that is speaking to us as indigenous to its very being. So, too, with the ancient Greek philosophical notion of the "logos," found dramatically in Heraclitus and throughout the philosophy of the Stoics.

Yet, not so easy, not so quick, for even if you believe, as I do, that both nature and experience speak, major obstacles remain. First, as hinted earlier and as Heraclitus warned, the logos speaks but no one listens. And even if we listened, the need before us is how to read our experiences. There is much data that we load on our children but precious little time and effort is given on behalf of teaching our children to read their own experiences. On this issue, William James is the master. To have James help us to help ourselves with regard to the pedagogy of experience, I offer you three cardinal texts from his work. The first is from his essay "The Sentiment of Rationality" in 1879, and the remaining two excerpts are from his famous and infamously conflicted book, *Pragmatism*, of 1907. The first text, indebted to Goethe, is as follows: "The inmost nature of reality is congenial to powers which you possess."[5] If we were to ask of this sentence to yield the most significant words, the following reading could take place. "Inmost nature"— interesting but woolly. "Powers," a word gratuitously overused in our time. For William James and for McDermott, hear "possibilities," "energies." Although those just cited are helpful words, they are not central to our reading. Although modest in intonation, the explosive word is "congenial," by which James means that we are "in on something." Physiologically, psychologically, and spiritually we carry, and are carried by, the flow, by James's "stream of experience." In short, we belong, and in our journeying need not be rendered either flotsam or jetsam (willy-nilly or hanging on a twig). Retrospective and reminiscent of the aforementioned antique doctrine of the logos, we are not ontologically—that is, utterly—disconnected. This is an assumption, one which not all philosophers share. Should you invite me next week to speak about Camus, I would tell you that he believes radical disconnection to be our lot and that the lodestone of our life rolls back down the journeying hill always and forever. Not so, William James and, I add, not so John Dewey.

Please keep this text in mind on behalf of the mission before us—namely, how to read our experiences. We need a philosophical bedding, an assumption submitted to intense self-reflection and concomitant with the wisdom of others. Also we need not a modus operandi so much as a modus vivendi, a way of life, a TAO. To further this end, again assisted by James, we look at two more texts, both, paradoxically, occurring in his *Pragmatism* (1907). The first is bold, promethean, and continuous with his stress on powers, energies, possibilities, and our capacity to forge what Emerson called "an original relation to the universe." "In our cognitive as well as our active life we are creative. We add both to the subjective and to the predicate part of reality. The world stands really malleable, waiting to receive its final touches at our hand. Like the kingdom of heaven, it suffers violence willingly. Man [woman] engenders truths upon it."[6] In technical philosophical terms, we find here a "constructivist epistemology," which means, following Immanuel Kant, in my, in your, seeing, hearing, touching, knowing, doing is the constituting, the making, "in some way" of *what* we see, hear, touch, know, and do. This text is extraordinarily liberating, for it gives license to my imagination, to my creative presence in the world. The text awards dignity to my reflective life. In short, James tells me and now he tells you that we count and we are "able." I hear you say, so far, so good. Lay it on me. I say, hold the phone. Stop the wagons—here. I have another text from William James: "Woe to (those) whose beliefs play fast and loose with the order which realities follow in (their) experience; they will lead (them) nowhere, or else make false connexions."[7]

Our stream of experience is malleable and open to creative infusion. Yet the stream is not without dangers, laced with false leads, dead-ends, and traps of every imaginable and, yes, unimaginable locus. For William James, the "stream of experience" is best described as a series of alternating perches and flightings. Should we remain perched, caught in our own self-aggrandizement, our own shrunken version of the world in which we find ourselves, then we shall fester and die spiritually of inanition. Contrariwise, if we flit from one experience to another, more as a surfer than as a knower, this approach by saturation renders us a honey bee without any blossoms. For those of you who pride yourselves on the skill of multitasking, beware. I know aggressive multitaskers who have disappeared as persons. They have scads of antennae but no digestive tract. What is a carotid or an aorta without a heart? With each oncoming generation, access to experience multiplies, exponentially, while the capacity to read experience, to diagnose experience, and to eat experience as embodied, declines, precipitously. The baleful result is that we become as ciphers, or, in medieval parlance, as ghouls, someone who is human but vacant within. We find here much ado in the face of personal emptiness.

This "woe"-text warns us that the most dangerous development in our journey is to make false connections or to be led nowhere. For "false," read "seduction," whether it be ambition or addiction. And to be led nowhere is to have lost all hooks, all signs, hints, hunches, and, in effect, hope, the most devastating of all spiritual maladies. (I trust that you recall the name of the protagonist in the Beatles's "Yellow Submarine"—he was Mr. Nowhere Man and he was the philosopher!)

If a person perches on behalf of a closed mind, a stinginess with regard to the having of experience, especially those had as novel and against the grain, then heed the advice of William James—stick out your neck and take a chance by an experimental exploration of experiences beyond your present sight. Make no mistake here, he tells us that all which we believe—whether it be the alleged truths of our social, political, moral, and religious history, or traits of habituation and addiction— they should be submitted to the crucible of alternatives. He does not tell us to abandon our perch and subsequently lose our way pursuing instant gratifications and quick fixes. James suggests that we move through the world avoiding a canopy of ultimate explanation by which we shut out novelty and possibility. Nonetheless, to do this we must maintain a personal presence such that we are not seduced by glitter, by false promises, and, above all else, by a failure to heed the *consequences* of every experience, every belief, and every decision. This is the major pragmatic maxim.

I return now to the major theme of this discussion: how can William James help us learn to read our experiences and to perform a self-diagnosis that is free of both the arrogance of certitude and the seduction of the ephemeral? The tapestry that he has sketched for us replaces the classical philosophical metaphor of substance with that of process. And he replaces our long-standing version of consciousness as a thing or a container with the metaphor of a stream, an ongoing, multiconstitutive, self-making of the self. In short, we have no fixed self. We are selving, richly or by impoverishment. If we live, think, and act deeply, then we have access to experiences that do not show their hand to a shallow living. I use the word "deep" advisedly, thinking here of ourselves as earth persons, with the hands and feet more to the point than the eyes, the ethereal. Recall here the poetry of Gerard Manley Hopkins, who urges us to tread the earth with heavy feet, to feel the ground, the bottom, "for there lives the dearest freshness deep down things."⁸ Or look at the exquisite painting by Jackson Pollock, entitled simply *The Deep*. I offer that William James is well aware of these covert messages. In his magisterial *Principles of Psychology*, James urges us to pay attention to the vague (and the inarticulate) in our mental life.

Elsewhere he points to the "more," the penumbra, the shading, the "inchoate" that resides and resonates in our "getting through the day" lives. Following Emerson here, James stresses that openness to experience is the way in which we come upon possibility. Possibility is potentially fructifying. It is also personally necessary. Without possibility, the soul desiccates, for we live our lives cornered, trapped, and in time we become that person dangerous to ourselves and to others; that is, we become one of Josiah Royce's "detached individuals." Possibility gives James's "will-to-believe" its viability. The possibility of possibility requires that novelty can occur. Novelty here is not a trinket in Wal-Mart, nor is it a gizmo, nor an iPod. Rather, novelty is an eruption in the allegedly ascertained flow, one which forces us to reconnoiter, regather, regroup, and reconstruct, dependent, always dependent, on heeding the consequences. If a person lacks a sense of horizon, the gate is closed. If all of our experiencing turns back on itself, the gate is locked and our possible access to possibility starts to shrivel. In time, we begin to hear ourselves utter that dreaded and dreadful phrase "been there, done that," as if there were old, finished experiences. All experience, even that had by recollection, is potentially new, fresh, revivifying. The reconnoitering of our past, the telling of our *tale* in the search for our *tail*, finds every experience once had to change the undergone landscape of experiences we are now having.

A story should help here. When my five children were young, they were frolicking on the floor with our iguana. In so doing, the iguana became caught in the baseboard heating panel. I came to the rescue and extricated the iguana, only to realize, alas, that I had severed his tail. Efforts at reattachment failed, but the veterinarian cauterized the wound, applied healing cream, and prescribed antibiotics. It was assumed that all would go well. Although lavished with attention and fancy, special food, the iguana began to show a foreboding lassitude and an unhealthy skin color. In a few days, the iguana was dead. Hey, Dad, we gave our iguana the best of care. Why did it die? I said that the iguana died of a broken heart. How come? It turns out an iguana cannot live without a tail and the message is that neither can you. We do not have a tail. Indeed, you do and it is your tale which will reveal your tail, the personal sign of your vulnerability, or your "needs," not your "wants." The latter are short-run and erode. Your needs are long-run and your personal, ontological signature. Now get busy and search for your tail.

Percepts lead, concepts chase. Charles Sanders Peirce: "Experience is our only teacher . . . and how does experience teach? It takes place by a series of surprises."[9] For William James, experiences are cognitive of one another, for experience is pedagogical. Literal-mindedness and the quest for objectivity in matters human constitutes the death of the soul. The distinctively personal ingredient should color all of our activities; otherwise, we live in the gray of correctness, external and dead to the world and to ourselves. We should widen the frame of relations and avoid being hung out to dry, like jetsam, or carried by the mob or by the occult or by the socially acceptable, like flotsam. Reach and touch. When you are touched, touch back. The key is not in objects, names, and definitions. The key is in the relations and symbols. Not by the obvious, alone, doth man live.

Feelings speak and no deeper question exists than to ask yourself, "how do I feel?" So, too, is it with asking of another, how do you feel? Almost sixty years ago, I failed to ask a damaged person, how did he feel. He was my cigar man and after many decades, in retrospect, he taught me that feelings speak.

In that regard, I close with the story of the cigar man. Long dead, long ago on a dreary Sunday morning, he taught me about the difference between the literal and the symbolical. In 1948, I was a volunteer at the *Catholic Worker* in New York City, headed by the indefatigable and famous Dorothy Day. One of my tasks was to visit hospitals and to attend to the indigent sick. On early Sunday mornings, I would go to Bellevue Hospital and do what I could to assuage the suffering in the cancer ward, known as the death ward, because this was before contemporary therapies were available. Among my assignments was the pathetic effort to fit the patients with appropriate reading glasses, collected randomly at the *Catholic Worker*. I also made phone calls, ran errands, and assisted the crippled patients to chapel services.

One rainy Sunday morning, I came on a quadruple amputee sitting totem-like on the bed, as if he were a runaway torso. He was Puerto Rican, and his black eyes had the defiance known only to a beaten person, for he was terminal. I passed by his bed, at a quickened pace, afraid to look or stare. He called to me in Spanish. Not knowing the language, I asked a nurse for help. Our patient wanted two cigars. It was a rainy Sunday morning and not propitious for finding a store open. I groused but said I would try to get them for him.

As I was about to leave, he barked again to the nurse. He wanted a special cigar, a Puerto Rican cigar. At that point, I became stressed, for the task was becoming onerous. I told the nurse to tell him I would try for his cigars, but failing, I would bring him some American cigars. On being told that, he became furious and all of his anger, as befits a quadruple amputee, rushed to his face. He blurted: no Puerto Rican cigars, no cigars at all. As embarrassing as it now seems to me, I became irritated at his obduracy. After all, I was doing a "good thing," being helpful and solicitous. But enough is enough. Yet, as an Irish Catholic, I had been steeped in guilt and the moral obligation of service. So I set out to get two Puerto Rican cigars—no easy task. After much hassle, I did obtain the cigars and brought them back. I placed one in his mouth and lit it. His face shone like an evening star.

It was not until fifteen years later that I realized what had happened, what I had missed, and what I had to learn. I was teaching the philosophy of Albert Camus, and the theme was personal authenticity. In a flashback, my Puerto Rican patient taught me of authenticity, of the aesthetic moment, and of the quality of life in a pretechnological medical setting. His message came to me as a revelation, an epiphany. Surely, only those special cigars would do, for only they, their smell and taste, would bring back the rich memories of Puerto Rico: the cocoa-brown skin of the women, the mist hanging over the coast between the Condado of San Juan and the city of Mayaguez. Only those cigars were authentic, existential, freighted with experienced relations. Only they sang his song, his personal song.

I missed the meaning in 1948. Now I have it. No pedagogy is worth its salt if it does not know the difference between one cigar and another, between the literal and the symbolical. As help to being sensitive to this difference, I carry with me always the admonition of William James, who asks us to be alert to "an 'ever not quite' to all our formulas, and novelty and possibility forever leaking in."

PART TWO

ENVIRONING

The Professional Tin Cup

Poor John
How
Very busy
You
Are
Are
You
So just say
No
Tho
Not to me!!!
For
Just this favor
Quite now
So
That Later
You
Can Say
No
To all other
Than I
Tho
They too
Say
Not me
Just
This time
For me
Do
A favor
before
You

Do yourself
in
And thereby
Be
Out of favor
With
Us
No?

SEVEN

A RELATIONAL WORLD

The Significance of the Thought of William James and John Dewey for Global Culture

Real culture lives by sympathies and admirations, not by dislikes and disdains: under all misleading wrappings it pounces unerringly upon the human core.

—William James, *Memories and Studies*

One can say with confidence, alas, that systemic intractability, ethnic and religious self-righteousness, and wholesale hubris are now endemic to global society. We have only to witness contemporary Lebanon in order to realize how a people can become victimized by the hanging on of ancient rivalries, hates, and jealousies, especially when these are combined with more recent ideological conflicts as sponsored within, as well as by scavenging neighbors from without. Like instances abound, east and west, north and south. Lamentably, no end to this strife seems to be in sight, and conflicts like it distract us from the truly awesome problems of population, world hunger, depletion of natural resources, and, of course, the specter of nuclear conflagration.

The thought of a single tradition, much less of single thinkers, seems powerless when placed in the context of these sprawling human brush fires, which are both geographically widespread and chronologically repetitive. The extraordinary influence of Buddha, Jesus Christ, Mohammed, and Karl Marx, among others, however, attests to the capacity of one person to offer a message, a viewpoint, a claim that becomes the staple of common wisdom for subsequent generations. Yet the difficulty with many of the charismatic figures of the past, sometimes through no fault of their own, is that they have generated intense allegiance but precious little tolerance for competing views and persuasions. The contemporary scene requires a very different type of insight, one characterized less by exclusivity and more by relationship and pluralism. This approach to human conflict, as desirable as it may be, is not easily obtainable. Yet there are thinkers whose work can make a contribution to this dilemma, namely, William James (1842–1910) and John Dewey (1859–1952).

In my judgment, James's thought is the vestibule to the thought and values of the twentieth century. He does not have the philosophical intensity or genius of Heidegger, nor does he have the scope and social-political sophistication of Dewey; but he anticipates much of the contemporary temper—its weaknesses as well as its strengths. In his 1891 essay "The Moral Philosopher and the Moral Life," James reveals his habit of thinking into the future: "All the higher, more penetrating ideals are revolutionary. They present themselves far less in the guise of effects of past experience than in that of probable causes of future experience, factors to which the environment and the lessons it has so far taught us must learn to bend."[1] James's potential contribution to twentieth-century culture is at least fivefold: his doctrines of relations, pluralism, pragmatic contextualism, temporalism, and his suggestion of a moral equivalent to war. Taking them in turn, I shall draw out the ramifications of James's ideas for a viable philosophy of culture.

The metaphysical basis for James's entire philosophical program is to be found in his doctrine of relations, which he called "radical empiricism." In 1909, a year before his death, in a preface to *The Meaning of Truth*, James clarified his meaning of radical empiricism. The tenets of this position constitute a partial philosophical mapping of the twentieth-century intellectual terrain.

> Radical empiricism consists first of a postulate, next of a statement of fact, and finally of a generalized conclusion.
>
> The postulate is that the only things that shall be debatable among philosophers shall be things definable in terms drawn from experience. [Things of an unexperienceable nature may exist ad libitum, but they form no part of the material for philosophic debate.]

The statement of fact is that the relations between things, conjunctive as well as disjunctive, are just as much matters of direct particular experience, neither more so nor less so, than the things themselves.

The generalized conclusion is that therefore the parts of experience hold together from next to next by relations that are themselves parts of experience. The directly apprehended universe needs, in short, no extraneous trans-empirical connective support, but possesses in its own right a concatenated or continuous structure.[2]

For James, the direct and affective experiencing of relations obviates the position which holds that the world comes ready-made in a series of objects, essences, or as if we lived in a "block-universe." To the contrary, objects are mock-ups, structured by the mind as a means of managing the perceptual flow. James writes that "the only meaning of essence is teleological, and that classification and conception are purely teleological weapons of the mind."[3] The "meaning" of reality is a function of the constitutive activity of the human mind. Existence is finite and unformed, but meaning is constructed and subjected to personal, social, and historical predilection. Above all, we are not trapped in any form of determinism, be it theological, scientific, or historical. The widest and most profound obligation of human pedagogy is to teach ourselves and others how to make relations—that is, how to diagnose both the continuity and discontinuity in our experiences, which he contends are "cognitive of one another." Experience, as such, is potentially pedagogical, if we but pay attention. Everything we perceive teems with relational leads, many of them novel, and therefore often blocked from our experience by the narrowness and self-defining, circular character of our inherited conceptual schema. The human task is to let our experiences speak to us in all of their manifold vagueness. Naming, defining, cataloging, quantifying are activities of a last resort and have justification only for purposes of organization—necessary for enabling us to move on to still richer fields of experience—or of survival.

James's doctrine of relations unseats the dominance of the Aristotelian conceptual framework that has suffused common Western consciousness for more than 2,000 years.[4] Further, James's stress on relations rather than objects, and on percepts rather than concepts, is congenial to cultures other than that of Western civilization; he espouses a congeniality far more in keeping with the contemporary reality of a truly global culture.

Actually, the most singularly informative breakthrough in our recent understanding of the world is to be found in the works of cultural and social anthropologists. It is now obvious that the peoples of the world have been engaged in creating a dazzling array of formulations of what it is to be human. On a close, reflective, and patient look, it is apparent that novelty rather than similarity is the hallmark of human civilization. Following James, if we cast off our conceptual and habitual cultural predispositions, we find that ritual, dance, food, costume, language, myth, architecture, artifacts, and an original sense of space and time revel in as many rich subtleties as there are gatherings of people who trace themselves to a wide variety of ethnic, religious, and climatic origins. These subtleties are primarily relational, tied as they are to expectations, responses, and to a vast range of aesthetic manifestations. The traditional penchant for reducing differences to similarity and novelties to familiarity destroys the panoply of meanings that lurk in all of our observations, all of our listening, all of our touching—in short, in all of our experiencing. In 1907, James tells us in *Pragmatism*: "There can be no difference anywhere that doesn't make a difference elsewhere—no difference in abstract truth that doesn't express itself in a difference in concrete fact and in conduct consequent upon that fact, imposed on somebody, somehow, somewhere, and somewhen."[5] Fascination with these differences and respect for their messaging enables us to live and let live. Moreover, such an attitude enables us, by contrast, to enrich the fabric of our own lives and to become more aware of the relationships at work in our own experience, especially those which disappear from our purview because they do not conform to the a priori range of accepted names for things and events undergone.

The interpersonal arena and the descriptions of social and cultural anthropology are not the only areas of human activity which sustain James's prescient judgment about the primary character of relations. Both modern art and modern science have abandoned classical descriptive terms in favor of relational and process metaphors.[6] This is especially true of modern painting, jazz music, modern dance, and modern physics, all of which stress happenings, events, and processes rather than objects or things. The influence of the thought of James on the physicist Niels Bohr and quantum mechanics is one powerful example of a twentieth-century realization of the significance of radical empiricism. A still more pervasive salutary fallout from James's doctrine of relations is his evocative description of our mental life as a "stream of consciousness," whereby we alternate between things and relatings, between perches and flights. Movement, change, and occasional moorings are the richer stuff of life than the time-honored boxes in which so many of us, lamentably, spend so much of our lives. James celebrates "streaming" and process, as does much of the creative, imaginative, and frontier thinking of the twentieth century. The bequest of the philosophy of William James in this regard is the call to close the gap between the processive, dynamic way in which our life flows and the way in which we came to experience it, burdened by the closed concepts that often render our experiences as repetitive, even trite.

A second important contribution of William James to the life and thought of the twentieth century is his notion of pluralism. The generalized conclusion of James's statement on radical empiricism emphasized that he saw no need for any "extraneous trans-empirical connective support." James conceived this sense of openness as an antidote to both cosmological and theological closure. He also viewed this commitment to processive continuity rather than ontological unity as a counter to philosophical monism and closed systems of any kind. James had both a temperamental and philosophical aversion to finality, ultimate solutions, and any interpretation of our human situation which forbade loose ends, discontinuity, or embarrassing, unclassifiable remainders. As he put it in *A Pluralistic Universe* (1909):

> Pragmatically interpreted, pluralism, or the doctrine that it is many, means only that the sundry parts of reality may be externally related. Everything you can think of, however vast or inclusive, has on the pluralistic view a genuinely "external" environment of some sort or amount. Things are "with" one another in many ways, but nothing includes everything, or dominates over everything. The word "and" trails along after every sentence. Something always escapes. "Ever not quite" has to be said of the best attempts made anywhere in the universe at attaining all-inclusiveness. The pluralistic world is thus more

like a federal republic than like an empire or a kingdom. However much may be collected, however much may report itself as present at any effective centre of consciousness or action, something else is self-governed and absent and unreduced to unity.[7]

Pluralism is the pragmatic result of James's doctrine of relations. Things, events hang together by relations, in a network which in the long run is empirically vague, no matter what proximate clarity we may attain. Nothing can be fully understood by itself, for every experience we have reaches, potentially, every other perceivable aspect of reality. Closure, names, and definitions are merely pragmatic strategies to construct a viable finite world in an infinite abyss. The perspective of other persons is partially constitutive of their reality and, therefore, by shared custom, partially constitutive of ours as well. If there is no single vantage point from which the world can be seen or interpreted or experientially had as whole, then every person makes his or her contribution to the ongoing statement as to how it is with the world, and how the world comes to be for me is in some way due to how the world has come to be for the other, for you.

In order to understand James's pluralism, it is crucial to realize that this multiplicity of interpretations, perspectives, and realizations is not a temporary fall from grace. James does not hold that pluralism is a waiting game, a temporary aberration until the archons of clarity—theological, scientific, or ideological—can rescue us from confusion. No, it is quite the opposite, for pluralism is the irreducible characteristic of not only the human presence but also of the evolutionary and developmental character of reality. In James's philosophy, closure and finality "violate the character with which life concretely comes . . . with an 'ever not quite' to all our formulas, and novelty and possibility forever leaking in."[8]

One could hardly overestimate the importance of James's pluralism as a basic strand of personal, social, political, and national policy on the contemporary world scene. Given the strident and long-standing homage to self-righteousness, along with the appropriate defensive propaganda, it would take a major change of heart for the present human community to take seriously even the possible plausibility of positions,

claims, and attitudes to be inevitably pluralistic and therefore not subject to agreement in any form or for any reason. This situation leaves us
in a serious quandary, for the absence of compromise seems to foretell
a permanent and irresolute struggle, on the one hand, or the demolish-
ing of difference, on the other hand. In this vein, recent events in both
Vietnam and Afghanistan come all too readily to mind.

Relative to this thorny and inflammatory issue, the thought of William James can make a contribution. He offers us not the pragmatism
identified with Realpolitik, but a pragmatism forged from his pluralism,
his commitment to irreducible ambiguity and his conviction that the
truth of the matter is not to be found in either a definition or in agreement between concepts and the alleged object. Rather, the truth emerges
from working out a hypothesis as subjected, tested, and revised in the
light of ongoing experience. Pragmatic epistemology is a contextualism
that not only brings to the fore the events before us but takes into consideration the possible future ramifications of the position taken.

If James is correct, as I think he is, that reality is evolutionary, developmental, and processive rather than static or complete in any way, then
it is imperative to realize that positions taken by human diagnosis and
human intervention are significantly, although partially, constitutive of
the future course of events. Nowhere is this more apparent than in the
activities of contemporary science and its application, contemporary
technology. Classical realist epistemology held that the world exists as
an object for us to "learn about." Once we knew the laws and principles
governing reality, we could then follow them in a series of applied strategies, so as to effect salutary results. Recent science, however, is not simply realist or descriptive. To the contrary, it is intrusive and constructive,
as is dramatically shown by modern medicine and modern physics. The
principles behind the use of antibiotics, gene-splicing, pharmacology,
and organ transplants take into account both the given stubbornness
of nature and our capacity to effect the very laws which govern nature.
Contemporary physics and chemistry provide similar examples of our
capacity to transform reality, as witness the creation of artificial, "unnatural" entities, such as plastics.

Unless we accept a retrograde, and politically unfeasible, Luddite position and abandon the march of modern technology, it is clear that we

need a different epistemology than that of traditional realism. If science and technology continue to be intrusive, it is necessary that we include potential future ramifications as relevant to decision making. It is not sufficient to make a decision based on the simple face of the matter. Future implications must be taken into consideration. A baleful example of this warning is to be found in the use of therapeutic drugs and pesticides. Both strategies are for the purpose of alleviation or amelioration of an undesirable situation found either in human life or in nature. Both strategies, however, have spawned results often far more deleterious than the original object of concern; witness the responsibility of the drug thalidomide for massive birth defects, or the concentration of DDT in so many of the organisms of the world.

Although James had no such extensive crises in mind, his pragmatic and contextualist epistemology is of direct relevance. With James, we hold that all events, all decisions are pregnant with connections, many of which show themselves only subsequent to the human plan enacted. Granted that it is impossible to predict safely or accurately all of the implications of any decision, far greater attention must now be paid to future fallout from our attempt to "manage" nature. Truth as the mere correspondence between a concept and its object is far too narrow and inept when used as the method for evaluating the proper approach to the scale of problems now confronting world civilization. It would be far better if we were to develop an epistemology which accepted surprise, novelty, and potential mishap as permanent ingredients of human inquiry. In so doing, our decisions would be more tentative, less absolute, and consequently truer to the actual situation in which we find ourselves.

In addition to his doctrines of relations, pluralism, and pragmatic contextualism, James offers one further philosophical contribution to our effort at understanding and meliorating life in the twentieth century. James is a temporalist, by which I mean that he holds the affairs of time to be sacred. Further, according to James, the flow of historical experience is not tied to some fixed, determined master plan. The world is real and human intervention is real. The ultimate reach of reality may be infinite, but the human condition is clearly played out on a finite stage and all of its characteristics—theological, scientific, philosophical, and ideological—are finite in origin, intent, and significance. In his preface to a series of essays collected as *The Will to Believe*, James puts forth his unwavering commitment to his belief that the "crudity of experience remains an external element" of our experience of the world. He continues: "There is no possible point of view from which the world can appear an absolutely single fact. Real possibilities, real indeterminations, real beginnings, real ends, real evil, real crises, catastrophes, and escapes, a real God, and a real moral life, just as common-sense conceives these things, may remain in empiricism as conceptions which that philosophy gives up the attempt either to 'overcome' or to reinterpret in monistic form."[9]

The full meaning of this text is extremely instructive. If we are finite, if our experiences are finite, and if there is no higher meaning which transforms these experiences into something other than the way in which we undergo them, then the affairs of time, our things and events, are to be taken at face value. The flow of time is the only setting for judging the worth of human life and human activity. James reverses the assumptions of much of the history of religion and philosophy. The transcendent and infinite are abstractions, ways of compensating for the opacity and ambiguity in our human experience. Time is all we have and, as we know all too well, human time is finite, irreversible. Above all, time is terminal so far as individual life is concerned.

From this metaphysical temporalism of James there proceed two radically different interpretations. The first holds that the necessarily terminal character of finitude—graphically spelled out by the words, *organic death*—renders human life trivial and human activity absurd. The second interpretation holds that the absence of a transcendent resolution of finitude, the absence of a transcendent principle of explanation, paradoxically forces us to value the history of human life as the only source of the sacred. Consistent with James's basic metaphysical position, this latter view regards the human affairs of time as worthy of total devotion on behalf of melioration and, where and when appropriate, celebration. Therefore, starvation, interpersonal violence, and repression are not only morally evil, but metaphysically evil as well, for they offend human life within the fabric of time, knowing full well that there we have no future recourse to any salvific resolution that transcends our human lives. In my judgment, this second interpretation is an accurate diagnosis of our actual situation. If we were to truly believe this, we would take vigorous steps to eradicate the systemic evil which continues to plague global culture. Not only is this evil harmful to human life and aspiration, it further mocks the only way we have to account for why, in an infinite cosmological setting, the activities of finite creatures have purpose.

For the most part, James was a nineteenth-century person and, as such, he did not have access to the cataclysmic events of our own century, for example, two world wars, the Holocaust, and Hiroshima. Had he experienced those events, he may have provided us with a more detailed and rigorous application of his philosophical wisdom to concrete and massive human disasters. Shortly before his death in 1910, he did write a suggestive piece, which, despite its pre–World War I innocence, does provide us with perhaps a viable approach to human violence. Entitled "The Moral Equivalent of War,"[10] it offers a pragmatic approach, in which James contends that the martial habituation of human nature has to be reoriented rather than simply lamented, for the lamentation about the evil of war seems to be followed, inevitably, by more war. The key word, of course, is "equivalent," and faced as we are with the specter of potential nuclear conflagration, we might well intensify our efforts to develop a globally applicable equivalent. Surely, the energy, intelligence, vast economic resources, and sophisticated systems of surveillance that have been marshalled to produce a tenuous stalemate could be an extraordinary "weapon" for technological and economic assistance to the millions of human beings for whom life is a bitter struggle against disease, poverty, and malnutrition.

No more than any other single source of philosophical wisdom is the thought of William James to be taken as a panacea. His approach, however, to the relationship between thought and action and his profound distrust of absolutes and final solutions are extremely significant for us in the twentieth century, since we have been seduced over and again by nostrums and dangerously false promises. James's pragmatic temper is the proper mood for contemporary society. His stress on the experience of relations and connections provides us with the metaphysical subtlety necessary as an antidote to the single vision which dominates so many of our endeavors. James's spiritual vision is also of note, for he insists that we celebrate the affairs of ordinary experience and that we realize it is we, and we alone, who are responsible for the course of human history. Due to the power of modern technology, we are now, for better or worse, the lords of history. If we have the "will to believe" in both our capacity to effect human healing of unnecessary suffering and in our responsibility to do so, then we shall, in time, create a human community worthy of the rich human tradition of hope, aspiration, and wisdom.

I turn now to the work of John Dewey and its significance for world culture. Dewey absorbed the basic assumptions and claims of William James, and, indeed, saw earlier and more perceptively than most that James's thought was the direction the future should take. In a 1931 essay, "The Development of American Pragmatism," Dewey affirms the stress on the future as found in James's thought:

> Pragmatism thus has a metaphysical implication. The doctrine of the value of consequences leads us to take the future into consideration. And this taking into consideration of the future takes us to the conception of a universe whose evolution is not finished, of a universe which is still, in James' term, "in the making," "in the process of becoming," of a universe up to a certain point still plastic. Consequently reason, or thought, in its more general sense, has a real, though limited, function, a creative, constructive function. If we form general ideas and if we put them in action, consequences are produced which could not be produced otherwise. Under these conditions the world will be different from what it would have been if thought had not intervened. This consideration confirms the human and moral importance of thought and of its reflective operation in experience. . . . One will understand the philosophy of James better if one considers it in its totality as a revision of English empiricism, a revision which replaces the value of past experience, of what is already given, by the future, by that which is as yet mere possibility.[11]

Dewey, however, differed from James in that he was neither a New England Brahmin nor a Europhile like James. To the contrary, long before it became either fashionable or necessary, Dewey was involved globally. His travels on educational matters took him to South Africa, Turkey, the

Soviet Union, Japan, and China. In a venture that can be described as a one-person educational peace corps, Dewey realized the necessity of serious transactions with a world theretofore ignored or victimized by cultural imperialism. Dewey had nothing of the preacher or the vigilante in his makeup. He was careful to indulge the cultural priorities of his host country and merely suggested that democratic strategies could be developed as consonant with local prerogatives.[12] In retrospect, it is true that Dewey had none of the anthropological sophistication now available to us, yet he made an effort to reach out and test his educational and political theories and practices in some of the most volatile areas of the world between the two great wars.[13]

I have detailed above the significance of James's contributions in the form of pluralism, pragmatic contextualism, and temporalism. Dewey continues these insights of James and attempts to build them into a social and political fabric in a far more extensive and sophisticated way than did James. Influenced in his early work by the sense of the social and the historical in the thought of Hegel, Dewey always demanded of himself that his judgments about personal possibility be realistic in the light of institutional limitations. Although he shared with James a lifelong commitment to the need for individual and personal growth and for the necessity of liberation from false gods, Dewey also knew that the enemies of such growth were not simply errant or bad persons, but more often the very way in which we constructed our social, political and, above all, economic and educational institutions. His pragmatic temper was instinctual, as when he writes: "To fill our heads like a scrapbook, with this and that item as a finished and done-for thing, is not to think. It is to turn ourselves into a piece of registering apparatus. To consider the bearing of the occurrence upon what may be, but is not yet, is to think."[14] Dewey has in mind here an intellectual ingredient essential to a pragmatic epistemology—namely, the sharp sense of implicitness, which yields insight only to the alert. One has to keep a wary eye on the implication of decisions, warnings, and even suggestions. Both James and Dewey are chary of final solutions or a priori prognostications, both of which deny the inevitable role of chance in the human and natural equation of events. In this regard, Dewey is uncanny in his awareness that human plans for the future are necessarily fraught with obstacle, for any intrusion into the status quo generates responses and mishap precisely in proportion to the imaginative cast of the intention. For Dewey, as for James, neither optimism nor pessimism are the proper empirical response to the actual situation of the human condition. To be optimistic is to be potentially naive about the vagaries of natural forces which often presage disaster. It is also to be blithely unaware of the human capacity to act in a self-aggrandizing manner, even at the expense of the community or of those values which most of us cherish. On the other hand, to be systematically pessimistic is to draw the curtain on possibility, on growth, on novelty, and on the most indomitable characteristic of the human spirit: the ability to begin again, afresh, with hope for a better day.

Better than most major thinkers, Dewey understands the pitfalls of these two traditional options to the future of human activity. In response, he adopts the approach of James, which is also indicative of the American temperament when it is at its best, namely, meliorism. Put simply and etymologically, the attitude of meliorism is to make things better. At a deeper and more profound index of analysis, the attitude of meliorism acknowledges both sin and possibility. Dewey is adamant in his conviction that nothing will go totally right in either the short or the long run. He is equally convinced that all problems are malleable and functionally, although not ultimately, resolute, even if they are sure to appear in another guise at another time. I refer to this as a metaphysics of transiency, in which human life is seen as a wandering, a traveling, a bemusement which rocks from side to side, comedy and tragedy, breakthrough and setback—yet, in all, a purposive, even progressive, trip, in which the human endeavor makes its mark, sets its goals, and occasionally scores, an event which Dewey calls a "consummatory" experience, as in "that was an experience."

Truly, then, meliorism is a salutary human approach, despite its lacking the drama of either pessimism or optimism. It takes no captives, makes no excessive claims, nor bows out in frustration at the opposition. Dewey evokes the deepest sentiments of human life, too often unsung and too often derided: that the nectar is in the journey, that ultimate goals may be illusory, nay, most likely are but a gossamer wing. Day by day, however, human life triumphs in its ineluctable capacity to hang in and make things better: not perfect, simply better. Dewey has no illusions about the danger of this attempt to change institutions, habits, and attitudes. He is aware of the guarded response to any effort at change. In an affectionate and prescient text, Dewey confronts the opponent to change: "Let us admit the case of the conservative; if we once start thinking no one can guarantee where we shall come out, except that many objects, ends, and institutions are surely doomed. Every thinker puts some portion of an apparently stable world in peril and no one can wholly predict what will emerge in its place."[15]

Dewey's awareness of the unpredictability of the future, especially when subject to human attempts at intervention, planning, or reconstruction, is refreshing in a period of time when we seem to replace one forecast with another without taking any responsibility for our role in the different and frequently contradictory results. We live in a time when futurology is in vogue and when the mighty forces of the computer and modern statistics combine to predict our future, day by day, detail by detail. That such predictions often go awry does not seem either to deter our confidence or to chastise our arrogance. Dewey has a clue to these mishaps, for in true pragmatic style he is aware that to effect change in one area is to court disaster in another. Also, pragmatic sensibility has as a cardinal tenet that only consequences can effectively validate the truth or even the propitiousness of a claim. Part of the disparateness in the relation between intention and realization has to do with the early abandonment of the quest in favor of some poor simulation. Dewey writes, "Men hoist the banner of the ideal, and then march in the direction that concrete conditions suggest and reward."[16]

Why is Dewey so tough on the viability of prediction and yet so sanguine on the possibility of human growth? My response is that Dewey has a doctrine of creative transiency, wherein the journey is its own mean and does not take its significance from a hoped-for, wished-for paradisaical future. In the language of medieval Christian theology, Dewey is clearly an incarnationalist and not an eschatologist. For him, the affairs of time are sacred, precisely because of human involvement, human care, and human intrusion. Now, how does John Dewey set the stage for this creative transiency? At first blush, the context is quite straightforward. The human organism, embodied, transacts with the affairs of nature. This transaction is double-barrelled, for it is both a doing and an undergoing. As dramatically distinct as may be our personal experiencing, it is precisely the having of experience, each in our own way, which binds all of us together, no matter what our place on the planet earth.

These commonplaces prove that experience is *of* as well as *in* nature. It is not experience which is experienced, but nature—stones, plants, animals, diseases, health, temperature, electricity, and so on. Things interacting in certain ways are experience; they are what is experienced. Linked in certain other ways with another natural object—the human organism—they are how things are experienced as well. Experience thus reaches down into nature; it has depth. It also has breadth and to an indefinitely elastic extent. It stretches. That stretch constitutes inference.[17]

The fascinating aspect of global culture is the dialectic in the life of each culture between what is experienced and how it is experienced. Dewey realizes that the differences in what we experience are clearly palpable, as in the contrast between the mountains of mountain people and the desert of desert people. Similar palpability is available in the contrasts of rural/urban, coastal/plains, frigid/torrid, and other macroscopic matrices for undergoing experience. That palpability, however, only masks the deeper novelty, which emerges when we attempt to understand how others have their experiences: that is, how they do the world in which they find themselves and how that world, literally, does to them—or better, does them.

The master anthropologist of our time, Clifford Geertz, maps the perils and pitfalls of one of us seeking to know how another of us has his or her experience:

> The tension between the pull of this need to penetrate an unfamiliar universe of symbolic action and the requirements of technical advance in the theory of culture, between the need to grasp and the need to analyze, is, as a result, both necessarily great and essentially irremovable. Indeed, the further theoretical development goes, the deeper the tension gets. This is the first condition for cultural theory: it is not its own master. As it is unseverable from the immediacies thick description presents, its freedom to shape itself in terms of its

internal logic is rather limited. What generality it contrives to achieve
grows out of the delicacy of its distinctions, not the sweep of its
abstractions.[18]

As Geertz notes, this obfuscation, which blocks our effort to understand
another's experience, is heightened incomparably when we are involved
in a different linguistic, environmental, and ritualistic setting—in short,
in a distinctively different culture.

Dewey's message is more general and more applicable to our present
need to forge a genuinely global culture. "Respect for experience is
respect for its possibilities in thought and knowledge as well as an en-
forced attention to its joys and sorrows. Intellectual piety toward experience is a precondition of the direction of life and of tolerant and
generous cooperation among men. Respect for the things of experience
alone brings with it such a respect for others, the centres of experience,
as is free from patronage, domination and the will to impose."[19] There
is clearly a deep sense of trust here in the quality of the experience of
other persons and cultures. Dewey always invokes a sense of potential
rejuvenation, despite the fact that he regards the transaction of the
human organism and nature as necessarily and irreducibly problematic.
The rejuvenation proceeds from the gains made in the fabric of time
and is sullied by an indulgence of overbeliefs, pinings for immortality,
and other assorted escapes from the grinding obviousness of our situation. Still, the will to adjudicate, heal, and advance the human cause in
its temporal bind is not without celebratory occasions. Happiness, in the
Aristotelian sense, is not hereby envisioned by Dewey, whose approach
is more empirical, more realistic, and more attuned to the crushing sadness which visits most of our lives, most of the time. No, Dewey focuses
rather on the occasional but crucial moments of celebration, joy, and
the ability to break through the ersatz and the habitual. Dewey is cognizant of the surprises which lurk in everyday experience, but he also
knows that we must be ever on the alert for these possibilities. Depressing though it be, most of us, the world over, spend days upon days simply fulfilling obligations of one kind or another, in a vast global fidelity
to rote. Even the lives of the storied have such long patches of boredom,
as witness historically the efforts of empresses and kings to entertain

themselves, with spectacles, usually of an inhumane and oppressive nature. Surely, their unhappiness, widely documented, does not trace to the absence of opportunity or of creature comforts, but rather to their inability to convert their experience to sufficient experiential nutrition for a human life.

In Dewey's metaphysics, the cognitive linchpin and the source of the major metaphors used to describe our place and activity in the world is the human body. Like James, Dewey paid close attention to the physiological process as a way of learning how we came to be in, of, and about nature. The alteration of nutrition and inanition is as true of our person as it is of our body. The respect for, and piety toward, experience, cited earlier, reveal that Dewey sees values and judgments as profoundly contexted by the variety of cultural experiences operative in the world. It is the liturgy, the celebration of these experiences, which holds his attention, for it is that which reveals the trust, the treasure, and the momentous in the lives of the participants.

Dewey was not taken by either Plato or Aristotle, but he was enamored of the alleged lesser figures in the Greek philosophical pantheon, namely, the Sophists and the Stoics. In fact, Dewey's thought is that of a latter-day Stoic, for he believes that we are tied inextricably to the fabric, and subject to the wiles, of nature. Yet Dewey's Stoicism is an American version rather than one of Greece or Rome. Consequently, it includes apertures of opportunity in a natural setting, which yield possibilities for the recreation of nature in the name of human needs. The politics of managing these possibilities are fraught with danger, for historically the definition of human needs does not elicit wide agreement. The give and take in the scramble to both survive and celebrate constitutes a secular liturgy the world over. Dewey implores us to enter this fray alert and with our most formidable weapon, creative intelligence, which enables us to plot, to plan, to express opinions, and to reconstruct, always mindful of the twin obduracy of institutions and natural forces. The problems of food, population, sporadic regional violence, and the dark specter of nuclear obliteration demand of us that we invoke our creative intelligence on behalf of humane response. The first task is to learn from our past, for human history sets out the glories, the mishaps, the violence, and the achievements in our endeavor with a chilling accuracy. Better than most, Dewey knows of the wisdom of the past, for he converts it into currency for the future.

> Most mortals are conscious that a split often occurs between their present living and their past and future. Then the past hangs upon them as a burden; it invades the present with a sense of regret, or opportunities not used, and of consequences we wish undone. It rests upon the present as an oppression, instead of being a storehouse of resources by which to move confidently forward. But the live creature adopts its past; it can make friends with even its stupidities, using them as warnings that increase present wariness. Instead of trying to live upon whatever may have been achieved in the past, it uses past successes to inform the present. Every living experience owes its richness to what Santayana well calls "hushed reverberations."[20]

The second task is to knit together those traditional opponents: education, politics, and aesthetic consciousness. Dewey has little patience with the compartmentalization of human activity into areas divined by a conceptual scheme rather than by the integral continuity of our experience as undergone. The baleful characteristic of our century is that, for the most part, the educational and political institutions of the planet do not meet the expectations or possibilities of the cultures which they control. Aesthetic sensibility and the engendered art forms are infinitely richer than the educational and political institutions through which they are filtered. Dewey's message is to return the educational and political processes and their institutions to a supportive relationship with the affective feelings, gestures, and aesthetic sensibilities of the culture in question. The separation of education and politics from the celebration of the everyday, an occurrence endemic to most of the cultures of the world, constitutes a blight on human feeling and on the conditions necessary for making human life tolerable. For Dewey, philosophy must insist on the renovation and celebration of those experiences which constitute the rhythm of our daily experience of the world. He insists that the alleged "commonplace" is a strategy devised by high culture to maintain an experiential caste and class system, one that perpetuates a hierarchy of values independent and ignorant of the richness found in our toil, our conversation, our gestures, and the happenstance of doing a day's work.

I am loath to conclude without reference to the larger liberal humane value of philosophy when pursued with empirical method. The most serious indictment to be brought against non-empirical philosophies is that they have cast a cloud over the things of ordinary experience. They have not been content to rectify them. They have discredited them at large. In casting aspersion upon the things of everyday experience, the things of action and affection and social intercourse, they have done something worse than fail to give these affairs the intelligent direction they so much need. It would not matter much if philosophy had been reserved as a luxury of only a few thinkers. We endure many luxuries. The serious matter is that philosophies have denied that common experience is capable of developing from within itself methods which will secure direction for itself and will create inherent standards of judgment and value. No one knows how many of the evils and deficiencies that are pointed to as reasons for flight from experience are themselves due to the disregard of experience shown by those peculiarly reflective. To waste of time and energy, to disillusionment with life that attends every deviation from concrete experience must be added the tragic failure to realize the value that intelligent search could reveal and mature among the things of ordinary experience. I cannot calculate how much of current cynicism, indifference and pessimism is due to these causes in the deflection of intelligence they have brought about.[21]

Global pedagogy must attend to affording us the ability to read the revelations of ordinary experience to be had in a ken, a clime, and a cultural setting diverse from our own. To be open to the experience of another is of double salutary significance. Not only do we apprise, learn, and participate in diversity but, perhaps paradoxically, we come to appreciate the novelty, singularity, and preciousness of our own experience. To participate in the plurality of experiences is personally explosive, for it trims our sails and curtails our arrogant provincialism while it widens our horizons and indirectly sanctions those experiences which are mundane to us, but exotic to others. Perhaps a global pedagogy should focus on precisely that relationship—namely, the shared experience of diverse experiences, such that the everyday would be experienced by others as exotic, and therefore cast refreshing light on what we take to be routine.

There is nothing sentimental in these views of Dewey, for he regards them as essential to a democratic polity. On many occasions in his writing, Dewey stresses the relationship between a respect for ordinary experience, work, and the affairs of the everyday and the formulation of a society in which personal growth, dignity, and a creative advance become staples in the social fabric. For example, in *Democracy and Education* (1916) he writes, "Democracy cannot flourish where the chief influences in selecting subject matter of instruction are utilitarian ends narrowly conceived for the masses, and, for the higher education of the few, the traditions of a specialized cultivated class."[22] Dewey has in mind here the subtle but pervasive political management of curriculum, present in an obviously nefarious way in fascist states but operative as well in allegedly more enlightened nations. It is rare for a culture to sanction the quality of its ordinary experiences in a reenforcing curriculum structure. To the contrary, most cultures tend to ignore their own personal strengths and predilections in favor of a more embracing, yet inevitably more abstract, scholastic presentation. Nonetheless, unless we celebrate what each of us does, day by day, we run the risk of extensive cultural condescension. Furthermore, the efflorescence of artistic, literary, and scientific genius seems to always have its roots in the most apparently routine and mundane of cultural contexts. In his eightieth year, John Dewey points to the salutary effect of an environment in which each person can articulate his or her deepest feelings about experience. He writes that "a society of free individuals in which all, through their own work, contribute to the liberation and enrichment of the lives of others, is the only environment in which any individual can really grow normally to his own stature."[23]

Dewey was enamored of growth and perceptive about both the obstacles to and the goals of its development. Although he had an irreducible commitment to the educability of all human beings, each to his or her potential ability, Dewey was aware also of the patterns of condescension and the class-oriented assumptions about human potential which so often scar an educational and social structure. He was convinced, as few before or since, that education, if structured in genuinely democratic ways, could overcome even the most oppressive and debilitating of regimes. In effect, with Dewey, we find a heightened version of the conflict between the imposition of rote, provincial, and self-serving values and interpretations, on the one hand, and, on the other, free inquiry and the roaming of the unfettered mind, alert to its experiences, sensitive to its past, affectionate toward its future but distrustful of draconian and magisterial pronouncements about the necessity of preserving the present.

Some think that our time on earth is but a vale of tears, and that we shall be healed only *sub specie aeternitatis*. In this regard, I report a moving allegory of the early third century AD—the tale of Perpetua, awaiting death as a Christian martyr:

> I had this vision: I saw Dinocratus coming out of a place of darkness, where he found himself in the midst of many others, all burning and parched with thirst, filthy and clad in rags, bearing on his face the sore that he had when he died. Dinocratus was my own brother. He died of illness at age seven, his face eaten away by a malignant canker, and his death repulsed everyone. I prayed for him: and between me and him the distance was so great that we could not touch. In the place where Dinocratus was there was a basin full of water, whose lip was too high for a small child. And Dinocratus stood on the tips of his toes, as though he wanted to drink. It caused me pain to see that there was water in the basin but that he could not drink because the lip was so high. I woke up with the knowledge that my brother was being tried.

A few days later Perpetua has another vision:

> The day we were put in irons, this is what I saw: I saw the place that I had seen before, and Dinocratus, his body clean, well dressed, refreshed [*refrigerantem*], and where the sore had been I saw a scar; and the lip of the basin that I had seen had been lowered to the height of the child's navel, and water flowed out of it continuously. And above the lip there was a golden cup filled with water. Dinocratus drew near and began to drink from it, and the cup never emptied. Then, his thirst quenched, he began playing happily with the water, as children do. I awoke and I understood that his penalty had been lifted.[24]

Of such allegories was born the belief in purgatory, later so brilliantly detailed by Dante. Now neither John Dewey nor I believe in purgatory.

Yet we both believe that the planet earth could become a *locus refrigerium*, a place of refreshment and healing, one in which the water of life might always run clear and sweet. Dinocratus is everywhere in our world, most often a victim of mindless internecine strife. A social philosophy, if it is to be truly helpful, must focus on the ways in which we can heal Dinocratus, face to face, during and in time.

EIGHT

NATURE NOSTALGIA AND THE CITY

An American Dilemma

That men shall say of succeeding plantacions: the lord make it like that of New England: for we must Consider that wee shall be as a Citty upon a Hill, the eies of all people are uppon us.

—John Winthrop

The only room in Boston which I visit with alacrity is the Gentlemen's Room at the Fitchburg Depot, where I wait for cars sometimes for two hours, in order to get out of town.

—Henry David Thoreau

G eneralizations about national cultures are notoriously inexact, for exceptions abound. The judgments of a single perceiver, however imaginative, are often narrowing. This is especially true of interpretations of a culture as vast and complex as America. Nonetheless, cultures often subsequently live out these generalizations, for they are frequently articulations of deeply held images, projected onto the stream of history. In many instances, whatever the paucity of facts at the origin of the generalization, its power soon engenders the sustaining empirical support.[1] So true is this of analyses of American culture that one recent commentator, Daniel Boorstin, can hold that we live in terms of "pseudo-events,"[2] mock-ups which take their place in our consciousness as reality.

Despite the methodological problems and the warning of Boorstin, and while not oblivious to the risk of self-deception, I offer that the following generalization has uncommonly profound and expansive empirical roots: American urban man has been seduced by nature.[3] By this I mean that at the deepest level of his consciousness urban man functions on behalf of nature metaphors, nature expectancies, and a nostalgia for an experience of nature which neither he nor his forebears actually underwent. For contemporary America, the implications of this situation are significant. In the first place, we are blocked off from understanding the dramatic and necessary conflict with nature, which characterized American life until recently. Indeed, we have become naive and ahistorically sentimental about that conflict. Second, we have often failed to diagnose the limitations and strengths of our present urban context on its own terms, rather than as a function of the absence of nature.

I am not, of course, claiming that this contention about the role of nature is the only, or even the major, key to the solution of the American urban crisis. On the other hand, I do hold that much contemporary diagnosis, whether of ecology, youth culture, or alienation, is woefully out of context without some grasp of the significance of this theme in the development of American consciousness. The basic problem is not one of general inattention, for we have a rich and long-standing literature on the meaning of nature and, of more recent vintage, an escalating literature on the city. We do not, however, have a broad tradition of analysis which focuses on their interrelationship, especially as written from the side of the urban experience. So as not to be waylaid by the vastness of our theme, let us consider the fundamental meaning of nature in American culture and its import for our understanding of time and the related possibilities for institutional transformation. If we then contrast this analysis with similar themes at work in urban consciousness, we should have some insight into the subtle but powerful role of nature in our present urban difficulties.

Nature as Context

For it is the wilderness that is the mother of that nation, it was in the wilderness that the strange and lonely people who have not yet spoken but who inhabit that immense and terrible land from East to West, first knew themselves, it was in the living wilderness that they faced one another at ten paces and shot one another down, and it is in the wilderness that they still live.

—Thomas Wolfe, *Men of Old Catawba*

Even the slightest familiarity with the history of American culture, especially its literary stand, will yield an awareness of the extraordinary importance of the nature motif. The philosophical dimensions of the meaning of nature are deeply rooted in European thought, beginning with the notion of *phusis* in Greek culture and reconstituted subsequently as *natura* in medieval and early-modern philosophy. The complexities of the development of this notion are endless, as an analysis of that aspect called "natural law" will readily reveal. This tradition does not account, however, for the meaning of nature in American culture.

In America there was an originating clarity to the experience and understanding of nature; it meant land, ferocious but untrammeled and free. The experience of nature in the early history of American culture was set in a dialectical tension between wilderness and paradise, or perhaps more accurately, a dialectic *inside* wilderness between desert and garden, between terror and salvation.[4] The odyssey of the Puritan is instructive in this regard. The Puritan had a profound sense of unregeneracy built into the very fabric of his being, as if the struggle between wilderness and paradise were being played out within his own autobiography.[5] On the American scene, the Puritan confronted wilderness as an external phenomenon, and its presence within his own soul slowly became eroded. In time, American man saw himself, his very presence, as the salvific factor in an unregenerate wilderness: paradise as the planting of a garden in the wild. Change these terms to the language of the expanding frontier and you have an intriguing insight into the American drive to conquer nature.[6]

From the time of the Puritans to the beginning of our century, despite vast geographical differentiae, nature experienced as land was held to be the fundamental locus for symbolic formulations of our cultural and religious life. The struggle for survival in a physical sense was undoubtedly an irreducible matrix in this confrontation with the land. Morton and Lucia White write that "land ruled supreme, and seemingly limitless untamed nature, rather than the city, was the gigantic obstacle that confronted the five million people who populated the United States of America in 1800."[7]

Beginning with the Puritans, however, there was another and deeper sense of that obstacle: one which saw the land as nothing less than the New Jerusalem. For the Puritans, if the kingdom is to come, it will come upon the land and show itself as continuous with the rhythms of nature. At the close of a moving paragraph on the correspondence of nature to salvation, Samuel Sewall writes in "Phaenomena" (1697): "As long as nature shall not grow old and dote but shall constantly remember to give the rows of Indian Corn their education, by Pairs: So long shall Christians be born there; and being first made meet, shall from thence be Translated, to be made partakers of the Inheritance of the Saints in Light."[8] The role of nature in personal regeneration becomes tremendously intensified on the American scene. It is a dominant theme in the life and conversion experiences of Jonathan Edwards, for whom the "doctrines of the gospel" were to his soul as "green pastures."[9] And in the nineteenth-century revisiting of the paradise theme, we witness the harrowing journey of the Mormons from Nauvoo, Illinois, to the Great Salt Lake as quest for salvation, "a stake in Zion," played out against the backdrop of an alternating violence and beneficence of the land. In 1835, James Brooks sees Nature as the guarantor of our salvation:

> God has promised us a renowned existence, if we will but deserve it. He speaks this promise in the sublimity of Nature. It resounds all along the crags of the Alleghenies. It is uttered in the thunder of Niagara. It is heard in the war of two oceans, from the great Pacific to the rocky ramparts of the Bay of Fundy. . . . The august TEMPLE in which we dwell was built for lofty purposes. Oh! that we may consecrate it to LIBERTY and CONCORD, and be found fit worshippers within its holy wall.[10]

In commenting on this and similar assertions, Perry Miller writes, "so then—because America, beyond all nations, is in perpetual touch with Nature, it need not fear the debauchery of the artificial, the urban, the civilized." And, he adds, that nature "had effectually taken the place of the Bible."[11] Closer to our time, at the beginning of this century, John Muir, under the rubric of conservationist language, sees salvation as tied to the preservation of wilderness and the American struggle as one "between landscape righteousness and the Devil."[12] Muir had also written

about how "thousands of nerve-shaken, over-civilized people are beginning to find out that going to the mountains is going home; that wildness is a necessity; and that mountain parks and reservations are useful
not only as fountains of timber and irrigating rivers, but as fountains of
life."[13]

The messianic interpretation of the land was not always cast in biblical, or even religious, language. In a parallel development, the history of
American thought also brought forth a tradition which understood the
land as an ethical and political resource able to transform human nature
for the better. Nowhere is this more obvious than in the early writings
of Thomas Jefferson. In his *Notes on the State of Virginia*, Jefferson offers
that "those who labor in the earth are the chosen people of God. . . .
While we have land to labor, then, let us never wish to see our citizens
occupied at a work bench, or twirling a distaff."[14] Jefferson sees the
workshop as associated with cities, and it is thereby better to have them
remain in Europe, for "the mobs of great cities add just so much to the
support of pure government as sores do to the strength of the human
body. It is the manners and spirit of a people which preserve a republic
in vigor. A degeneracy in these is a canker which soon eats to the heart
of its laws and constitution."[15]

In a strain anticipatory of much of later American thought,[16] Jefferson
sees the commitment to the land as passionate and moral. John Anderson, in *The Individual and the New World*, writes that

> Jefferson found in his American experience a faith that man's egoism
> might disappear under some conditions of human commitment to
> the new land. In his conception that man's commitment to the New
> World might contain the principle for the control of man's natural
> egoism, Jefferson not only re-directed attention to the environment
> of the American continent, he suggested that man's true nature
> emerged for this reference. Jefferson sought thus to formulate those
> conditions of human acceptance of the New World under which
> man's moral nature might emerge and effectively control his egoism.[17]

The experience of the land as a basis for a democratic ethos, as articulated by Jefferson, remained a deep characteristic of American political
literature throughout the nineteenth century, but it did not negate completely the earlier biblical dimension which saw the land as the readiness

for the coming of the kingdom of time. The convergence of these attitudes toward the land are found not only in the evangelical interpretation of frontier experience but in the symbolic versions of man's place in nature as found in Emerson and Thoreau. Writing in 1927, Lucy Lockwood Hazard in *The American Frontier and American Literature*, stated that "it is time to strip from the Emersonian hero the decorous toga and conventional mask with which rhetoric and philosophy have disguised him, and show that 'the American Scholar' and Davy Crockett are brothers."[18] It was, after all, in the address on "The American Scholar" that Emerson told us "so much only of life as I know by experience, so much of the wilderness have I vanquished and planted, or so far have I extended my being, my dominion."[19]

Emerson has a deep feeling for what Leo Marx refers to as the "metaphysical powers of landscape."[20] And this sensibility lends to him an abiding hostility against the city. In "Culture," Emerson writes:

> Whilst we want cities as the centres where the best things are found, cities degrade us by magnifying trifles, the country man finds the town a chop-house, a barber's shop. He has lost the lines of grandeur of the horizon hills and plains, and with them sobriety and elevation. He has come among a supple, glib-tongued tribe, who live for show, servile to public opinion. Life is dragged down to a fracas of pitiful cares and disasters. You say that God ought to respect a life whose objects are their own; but in cities they have betrayed you to a cloud of insignificant annoyances.[21]

In a note to that text, Emerson is cited as having commented that on his passing the woods on Walden Ledge, "on the way to the city, how they reproach me!"[22] The land, then, was more than open space and sylvan woods; it was a spiritual resource and a moral challenge. Thoreau offers us the most perceptive phrasing of this power of the land: "All things invite this earth's inhabitants / To rear their lives to an unheard of height / And meet the expectation of the land."[23]

It is the "expectation of the land" which has driven us, notwithstanding repeated disappointments in the realization of these expectations. In Perry Miller's phrase, we are "nature's nation."[24] And for John Anderson, our visions about the possibility of the land "express an intuition of the reflexive direction of human energy necessary to freedom. In such intuitions, Americans have seen themselves as marching across the wilderness and with more or less clarity have conceived of themselves as representative of mankind's ultimate place in the unknown universe."[25] The empirical basis for these mythic interpolations of our experiencing the land was the sheer prodigality of space and the related reconstituting of our experience of time. The importance of this interrelationship of space and time within the context of our experience of nature cannot be overestimated, for the experience of time is a crucially distinctive characteristic of any culture, and as we replaced nature experience with urban experience, we failed to reorient our sense of space and time in a way consistent with this shift in context.

In specific terms, the experience of nature as open and free space generated for Americans a sense of time as option, as possibility. In "The American People: Their Space, Time and Religion," Sidney Mead comments that Americans never had time to spare. What they did have during all their formative years was space—organic, pragmatic space—the space of action. And perhaps this made the real difference in the formation of "this new man."[26]

Space, however, is time undergone. The absence of "time to spare" really means the absence of time as introverted experience—that is, the absence of the struggle to achieve identity while subject to the contours of fixed options. Spatial claustrophobia turns us in on ourselves, interiorizing the landscape so that it is continuous with our imagination rather than with our vision. Over against this, in a context of open space, there is the possibility of projecting oneself outward and achieving identity as subject to the emerging novelties of the space of action. The presence of options gave dignity to events, for they were chosen rather than inherited. Put otherwise, a man could come to himself by relocating. The "space of action" was the locus of novelty and, paradoxically, the locus of self-awareness. Growth was inseparable from shifts in spatial contours, thereby indirectly transforming our experience of time from that of waiting, backing, and filling to that of anticipating and the structuring of possibility. The shift in the word "trip" is instructive here, for its present meaning of a hallucinogenic visit to our inner landscape contrasts starkly with its open-ended spatial exploration in the vernacular of nature language.[27] Nature experienced as open space was not a nature

in which man sat, derivative and self-preening. On the contrary, the undergoing of nature of which I speak found man grappling and reaching,
fed always by shifts in location, even when such shifts came to him vicariously, as in the influence of the legendary evocations of the "mountain
men" on the consciousness of the eastern seaboard.[28]

It is important to realize that the space of which I speak was riddled
with drama, not only of natural origins (mountain. forests, and great
rivers) but of sociopolitical origin (the presence of Indians and the
struggles over territory and gold). Space, flat and boxed, is not a sufficiently humanizing context for man's situation. The drama of space is
proportionate to its capacity for novelty. In the experience of nature,
movement is necessary whether it be real or vicarious, the assumption
being that something new, different, better is out there, just over the
next ridge. In that tradition we are riven with the need of beginning
again and again. Commenting on Emerson's oracular text, "why
should not we also enjoy an original relation to the universe?"[29] Frederick Jackson Turner answers, "Let us believe in the eternal genesis, the
freshness and value of things present, act as though, just created, we
stood looking a new world in the face and investigate for ourselves and
act regardless of past ideas."[30] It is this quest for novelty, expressed
while he was still a young man, that we should read into Turner's later
designation of the meaning of American space as a frontier—namely,
as a series of options.

When events are framed against novel occurrences, the experience of
ordinary living takes on the hue of an imaginative reconstruction of life.
William James, for example, has written that "according to my view,
experience as a whole is a process in time,"[31] but if the setting for this
process, relative to each life lived, is characterized by repetition and by
the plodding dullness of a context that rarely, if ever, is broken into by
basic shifts in direction and possibility, then, however eschatologically
viable, our lives experience little of import in immediate terms.[32] The
sense of option, as created by the novelties of open space, enabled American man to ground a deeply felt, but rarely sustained, religious belief—
namely, that the passing of time was a healing and liberating experience.

By way of specifying this contention, let us take as example one of
America's most profound, although unappreciated philosophers, Josiah

Royce. A Californian and a child of the frontier, Royce was born in the mining camp of Grass Valley, high in the Sierras. His early experience bequeathed to him a fascination with the evolution of American communities, especially their combination of moral imagination and novel physical settings. Royce believed that landscape and climate were constitutive of consciousness, and given man's efforts, time was a healing force. In his *History of California*, Royce describes the evolution of a mining community in a section he entitles "The Struggle for Order: Self-Government, Good Humor and Violence in the Mines." Royce's conclusion to this chapter illustrates the earlier commitment to a salvific future as witnessed and sustained by the possibilities inherent in an open and fecund nature (though the last line of this text is depressing, for, as we too well know, rivers no longer purify themselves):

> The lesson of the whole matter is as simple and plain as it is persistently denied by a romantic pioneer vanity; and our true pride, as we look back to those days of sturdy and sinful life, must be, not that the pioneers could so successfully show by their popular justice their undoubted instinctive skill in self-government—although indeed, despite all their sins, they showed such a skill also; but that the moral elasticity of our people is so great, their social vitality so marvelous, that a community of Americans could sin as fearfully as, in the early years, the mining community did sin, and could yet live to purify itself within so short a time, not by a revolution, but by a simple progress from social foolishness to social steadfastness. Even thus a great river, for an hour defiled by some corrupting disturbance, purifies itself, merely through its own flow, over its sandy bed, beneath the wide and sunny heavens.[33]

Now the history of Royce's California is the history of relocated Americans, pulled by the land and the chance of a fresh start. Whatever the persuasion (and the spectrum embraced a wide number of social, political, and religious convictions), the operative assumption was an acceptance of the dramatic enhancement of one's possibilities by the presence of uncommitted land and a variety of nature experiences. Such an assumption was operative earlier in the century on the eastern frontier, as witnessed by a text on the comparatively simple move from old Virginia to western Virginia. What greater testament to the moral and political liberation which results from the experience of nature than at the Virginia Convention in 1830, when a western Virginia delegate was heard to say:

> But sir, it is not the increase of population in the West which this gentleman ought to fear. It is the energy which the mountain breeze and western habits import to these emigrants. They are regenerated, politically I mean, sir. They soon become *working politicians*; and the difference, sir, between a *talking* and a *working* politician is immense. The Old Dominion has long been celebrated for producing great orators; the ablest metaphysicians in policy; men that can split hairs in all abstruse questions of political economy. But at home, or when they return from Congress, they have negroes to fan them asleep. But a Pennsylvania, a New York, an Ohio or a western Virginia statesman, though far inferior in logic, metaphysics, and rhetoric to an old Virginia statesman, has this advantage, that when he returns home he takes off his coat and takes hold of the plow. This gives him bone and muscle, sir, and preserves his republican principles pure and uncontaminated.[34]

The theme of "regeneration," spurred on by land, uttered here in a traditional political setting, reached its zenith of intensity in the hundreds of nineteenth-century American experimental communities. What had been European visions, festering with frustration, found their way into American life as communities capable of covenanting on available land, often free. These communities, most often extremely critical of American society, had the possibility of working out a range of beliefs relative to free love, socialism, or the mysteries of diet. The availability of land enabled a fair test to be made of the claims for viability of these lifestyles.[35] Furthermore, the ensuing relevance of certain aspects of their vision was made possible by the stretch of time, in some cases several generations, during which they could maintain the original character of their communities.

Given the opportunities of land and the extensive time in which to operate, the failure of a new community, experimental or otherwise, was not a crushing blow. Failure was not due to repression or the absence of opportunity but rather to the inadequacy of the idea and its implementation before the test of time. Even as late as the depression of the 1930s in our century, Americans were not prone to the experience of alienation and cynicism, now so deeply rooted in American life.[36] But the erosion of belief in endless options, generated by nature, and in the passing of time as liberating has now become a major touchstone of contemporary American society. This development is not unrelated to the fantastic growth of the American city and the begrudged emergence of urban man.

In a word, we have lost our access to experimental space. This is true not only of the great cities, where the vast majority of us now live, but of Butte, Montana, or Burlington, Iowa, or Zuni Pueblo, New Mexico, where the disenfranchised huddle together under the ironically cruel aegis of an extraordinary yet private natural setting managed by absentee ownership. The revisionist historians notwithstanding, Frederick Jackson Turner was correct; the closing of the frontier, however symbolic rather than statistical it may have been at the turn of the century, was to spell the inevitable end of a deeply ingrained style. The deeper problem is whether the loss of experimental space will spell also the loss of the experimental temper in America. To put it idiomatically, can rehabilitation replace relocation as the locus for prophetic vision and even more broadly based experimental communities? Or must we accede to those culture prophets, powerful and incisive in their own way, like N. O. Brown, for whom the city is already an Armageddon from which we must take nomadic flight, or Charles Reich, who offers us a quasi-revolutionary re-Greening of America?

The new rhetoric is often fed from two sources: nature nostalgia and a long-standing corollary, the conviction that the city is a trap. So long as our image of the city is a function of our image of nature, we shall intensify our hostility to urban life and our negative judgment will be self-fulfilling. As the actuality of nature recedes in our life, our nostalgia for it becomes increasingly riddled with unreality and innocence about its complexity and dangers. Only a radically reconstituted image of the city will provide us with a new resource for structuring once again a sense of option and experiment as continuous with everyday life. Let us sketch some of the obstacles to such a reconstitution.

The City as Context

And the critical rhythm of a city is the sequence of closing hours,
the city's play with the order of the eternal sun.

—Robert Kelly

I isolate several characteristics of our image of the city, which, though by no means exhaustive, are nonetheless revealing. Even a brief analysis of these characteristics will provide us with a different perspective from which to view both the plight of urban man and some of the direction necessary for the melioration of his future. The first characteristic is double-pronged, with the interacting resonance of a tuning fork. On the one hand, we lament the city as being without nature. On the other hand, the nature we have in mind in such a lamentation and about which we are nostalgic is stripped of its most forbidding qualities: loneliness, unpredictability, and the terrors of the uninhabitable. Witness the innocence of this comment from Dallas Lore Sharp, a turn-of-the-century commuter from a suburb just outside of Boston. "And this our life, exempt from public haunts and those swift currents that carry the city-dweller resistlessly into the movie show, leaves us caught in the quiet eddy of little unimportant things—digging among the rutabagas, playing the hose at night."[37] For the most part, the nature envisioned by urban and suburban man is one that has been domesticated by the very qualities of the city which we take to be unnatural. Commenting on an earlier form of nature nostalgia, Lewis Mumford points to the too-often-overlooked grubbiness of the open road. He writes in *The Golden Day*:

> The vast gap between the hope of the Romantic movement and the reality of the pioneer period is one of the sardonic jests of history. On one side the bucolic innocence of the eighteenth century, its belief in a fresh start, and its attempt to achieve a new culture. And over against it, the epic march of the covered wagon, leaving behind it deserted villages, bleak cities, depleted soils, and the sick and exhausted souls that engraved their epitaphs in Mr. Masters' Spoon River Anthology.[38]

And recall Van Wyck Brooks's description of the America of Emerson's time: "Alas for America! An air loaded with poppy and all running to leaves, to suckers, to tendrils, to miscellany, dispersion and sloth. A wilderness of capabilities, of a manyturning Ulyssean culture; an irresistibility like Nature's, and, like Nature, without conscience."[39]

I make no attempt here to deprecate the majesty of nature or, as I tried to make clear above, to deny its real capacity as a setting for distinctive social and political growth. Under the press of nostalgia, however, we strip both nature and city of ambivalence, in a bizarre reversal of the wilderness-paradise theme. We now name the city a jungle and ascribe habitability in proportion to our distance away from it. Indeed, we often seem to give the city credence only to the extent that we are able to import nature, to "green" it. Vest-pocket parks and isolated city trees receive our affection while we allow public conveyances, building facades, and other urban artifacts to deteriorate. We seem oblivious to the fact that efforts at "greening," such as Golden Gate Park in San Francisco, are often masterpieces of artifact and directly attributable to urban man's management of nature.

As a matter of fact, in our time artifacts shape the entire context of nature. Our American culture has long succumbed to the principle of accessibility on demand, and as heightened by modern technology, particularly the automobile and the airplane, has successfully driven out nature in the sense of "wilderness," which, a fortiori, denies accessibility. We resist facing up to the loss of wilderness in America. In the more than two hundred photographs accompanying Freeman Tilden's *The National Parks*, hardly an automobile is to be seen, but for those of us who have visited those parks and natural monuments, automobiles are omnipresent, along with the roads, souvenir stands, and the apparently self-propagating beer can.[40] Turning a wilderness into a park is, after all, a gentle form of urbanization.

Our innocence about the artifactuality of our experience of nature interacts with our failure to form any better image of the city. On one side, we harbor a deep conviction (perhaps "prejudice" is a better word) of the superiority of the organic over the inorganic, of the natural over the artifactual. Nonorganic material becomes at best functional and at worst dehumanizing, saved only by the arbiters of the aesthetics of high culture as it is present in acceptable architecture, museums, and outdoor sculpture. The latter become for many critics of the city the only re-deeming features of urban life. Peter L. Marks, for example, in "A Vision of Environment," tells us that New York is "far too large" but that one should have a city the size of Minneapolis so as to preserve the "urban amenities," which he lists as "museums, galleries, theaters, opera, etc."[41] Such amenities are sought by a very small percentage of city people, and they in no way represent the marvels of urban design, the intensity of urban interaction, or the complexity of urban possibility. Many critics of the city have no sense of the pulse of city life except that prescribed by those cultural canons continuous with the lives of the critics.[42] Given such an interpretive context, as we move through the alleged travail of everyday experience, we seem reduced to the impropriety of generating, and social inability to generate, nonorganic aesthetic metaphors able to provide the security and affection nostalgically traceable to nature metaphors.[43]

The contrasts between "naturals" and urban materials are inevitably invidious. Grass is soft whereas wood and metal are hard. The sense of touch has either eroded, as with regard to cloth and wood, or never de-veloped, as with regard to aluminum, plastics, and the vast range of syn-thetics. Woodland light is diaphanous and playful, but city light, as refracted from giant slabs of glass, is arching and brittle. Dung is earthy and a sign of life, whereas axle grease is dirty and a necessary burden. Many of us were taught as children to distinguish between the clean dirt of nature and the dirty dirt of the playground and the street. Why is it that "swinging on birches" is affectionate and wistful but sitting on curbs is pouty and "hanging out"? Such contrasts are endless and they are maddening because they distort and repress one entire side of our experience—or, more accurately, if we are honest with ourselves, for most of us our *only* direct experience.

The source of this prejudice is only partially nature nostalgia and the historical seduction of its metaphors. From another vantage point, a more decisive characteristic emerges—namely, that we have failed to ar-ticulate our distinctively urban experience in aesthetic terms. Just as for decades we have taught multiracial, multiethnic children in the context of a bland WASPish world, so, too, have we taught children in a vague combination of a gentle nature setting and appeals to the value of high

culture. Such a pedagogy continues to be oblivious to the teeming relational fabric of urban experience and to the rich nutrients of technological style which children would soak up, as if to the "manor born," if so
encouraged. Unfortunately, we have held fast to the style and language
of traditional pedagogy and, as such, have missed the startling idiomatic
evolution from nature language to industrial language, to say nothing of
the recent emergence of electronic language.

Urban alienation proceeds from the bifurcation of lived experience
and institutional formulation, particularly on the part of the schools,
churches, and social-political agencies. The truth is that for hordes of
urban children, the argot of street language provides their fundamental
education, their coming to consciousness. Unsanctioned as experiences,
these sensibilities and insights ride beneath the surface of personal life,
unable to bring the person into an acceptable creative life. Our task is to
sanction and celebrate these processes of urban living, within the confines of urban institutions. Speaking only of the schools, we must learn,
for example, how to integrate the powerful message of jazz, with its emphasis on improvisation, processive unity, and indirect communication
(each an urban style). We must learn of the vast array of city materials
and generate novel non-nature metaphors to describe our ways of experiencing them. We must learn how to personalize our evaluations of ordinary experiences to render them aesthetic, commensurate with new
materials, new techniques, and new anticipations. Could not our watchword be the penetrating remark of John Dewey—"even a crude experience, if authentically an experience, is more fit to give a clue to the
intrinsic nature of esthetic experience than is an object already set apart
from any other mode of experience"?[44] These strategies will aid in overcoming one of the deepest and most pervasive sources of our alienation:
the separation of the affective life from the processes of urban experience. As strategies, they assume, however, a turning back of still another
characteristic of our image of the city, that is, our sense of space.

City space is enclosed space, and therein we find a crisis for urban
man. As we have attempted to show above, the primary meaning of nature for America has been the presence of open space, with its corollary,
a sense of time as prospective and fruitful. In the last twenty years, as
the diagnosis of the city has become increasingly negative and we have

made attempts to restructure it subtly but powerfully under the rubric of urban reclamation and renewal, we have re-embodied this hankering for open space. We have failed to realize that people brought to consciousness in enclosed space have interiorized their sense of time and endowed the immediate environment with the drama of landmarks, whether they be funeral parlors, candy stores, playgrounds, or street processes. Largely unarticulated, this sense of time has been a way of protecting the city dweller from the rapid but pyramidal pace. Experience in the city was hectic, intensive, and escalatory, but not spatially expansive. Entire lives, even generations, were lived out on a single street, known affectionately as the "block."[45] In such an environment it was necessary to structure "stabiles," moments of security and repetition, as a base from which to participate in activities which far outstripped the natural sense of pace and which multiplied novelties at a rate quite beyond personal absorption, let alone comprehension.

Many years ago, the building of the then-great apartments on Riverside Drive in New York City occasioned Henry James's comment that they were merely holding the spot for whatever was to replace it.[46] As the pace quickened, each city dweller structured his or her own version of the environment, developing in either personal terms or in closely knit communal terms what Kevin Lynch has called "nodal points," ways of comfortably and knowingly experiencing the environment. Nodes are points, "the strategic spots in a city into which an observer can enter and which are the intensive foci to and from which he is traveling."[47] These nodal points, not to be confused with landmarks, are too often assumed to be large and obvious, as squares, powerful buildings, or boulevards; more often they are intensive refinements of one's movement through city-space—the feel of a small street, a lobby, a stoop, a bar, a subway stop, refined even to the north or south entrance. In effect, they are embodiments of intimacy, urban style. They are ways of domesticating the rush of city life. They are sources of affection. Listen to a young black student at Queens College conclude his poem of praise to Harlem.

> 'Cause we own the night
> And the streets and the sounds and the air itself
> And the life is there

And the movement is there
And all of our energy
And the spirit is there
On through the night
And right through the dawn
Through those wide/funky/
Bad/
   Black/
     Streets[48]

Any attempt at massive urban transformation which fails to take into account the deep feeling that people have for their environment, however objectively inadequate, is doomed to failure. The difficulty with extensive relocation is not simply the wait to enter a new home, although that wait is often cruel and abortive. Nor is it simply the loss of an apartment or dwelling. It is the destruction of those nodal points which not only took generations to web into the seam of personal experience but also acted as a subtle resource for coping with the massive energy of the city at large.[49] Home, then, is not simply the apartment or even the building. Rather, it is correlative with a wider range of experience, including neighborhood and city region or just accessibility to the familiar. In his profound essay "Grieving for a Lost Home," Marc Fried evokes the sadness of those residents who were bullied out of their homes in the West End of Boston.[50] Although many interpersonal relations could be kept in the new location, it was the loss of spatial identity for which they grieved. What is striking about Fried's findings is the extensive presence of bodily responses to the loss. Many persons reported serious depression, nausea, and weeping. Deep in our psyche we are profoundly attached to the allegedly lifeless forms of the urban scene—our streets, lights, and sounds.

The need would seem to be to learn the techniques of rehabilitation rather than fall prey to the precipitous use of the scissoring of spatial relocation. We have some small signs of an increased sensitivity to this need. In New York City, fifty-nine residents of a neighborhood called Corona, in Queens, led by the urban rhetoric of Jimmy Breslin, staved off relocation and are now struggling to maintain their community against the power of official policy. Even minor relocation was thought to be painful and excessive, for as Francis X. Clines wrote in the *New York Times*, the relationships were, after all, "structural as well as human."

The job of relocating houses could prove as delicate as heart surgery, for there is an attractive crazy-quilt of structural and human relationships present. For example, Mrs. Thomas Manfre has a house, marked by a lawn madonna, that looks to the rear onto her husband's boyhood home, where a niece now lives. Her seventy-year-old mother lives off to the side in a separate home, small and brown with a pigeon coop on the roof. All three are as one in her family's diary, Mrs. Manfre explained: "There have been deaths here and my brother Joey was born here," she said.[51]

We are under obligation to develop an enriched understanding of the relationship between urban structure and urban person. We must develop insight into the time of city-space and the space of city-time. And we must search for a way to render our bodies as continuous with technological artifact as they were with the environs of nature. We have to celebrate this continuity and build accordingly. If we fail in these tasks, contemporary urban man will simply be in place, and as such detached from the processes of living. But, as Royce warns us, the detached individual without deep feeling for his environment dilutes the energies necessary to build communities.[52] He cautions also that when under duress, the detached individual abandons restraint and, out of disrespect for the variety of lifestyles, moves to suppress them. We should be warned that nature nostalgia detaches us from the urban present and promulgates condescension, disinterest, and, eventually, hostility. For better or worse, American man is now urban man, or at the least, megapolitan man. Nature nostalgia, no matter how subtle, does not serve him well. It is time for a turning and a celebrating of the dazzling experiences we have but do not witness for all to share. The city is now our home; in the most traditional and profound sense of the word, it is our land.

NINE

SPACE, TIME, AND TOUCH

Philosophical Dimensions of Urban Consciousness

As man is a responsible constructor of the environment he is unavoidably in-
fluencing his own genetic structure.

—Paolo Soleri

U rban experience is a vast and complex process of interwoven institutions, events, and perceptions. It can be subjected to analysis
only from a wide range of perspectives and disciplines, each of them
limping in turn from an unavoidable narrowness, although each providing necessary data and, hopefully, vision. Urban studies, itself a comparatively new endeavor, seems to have no methodological uniqueness or
consistency, borrowing from one or another of the social and applied
natural sciences. In this present essay, we do not attempt to resolve that
difficulty in any detail, although our approach hints at the direction
such a methodology would take—namely, to treat the city as an interdisciplinary phenomenon, yielding to no single discipline or to a gathered
potpourri of several disciplines, but rather as the source of an entirely
new language and set of assumptions and criteria. Such a need calls for
philosophical contributions, to this point starkly absent.[1] By way of a
context for our present discussion, I offer the following generalized attitudes as operative in our approach to urban experience.

Consciousness-Raising and Disaffection

The major difference between consciousness-raising and coming-to-consciousness, or awareness, is that the former pertains to experiences long since undergone but unappreciated or repressed, whereas the latter connotes novelty of perception. In the past decade the poor (unsuccessfully), and black Americans and women (each with some success), have participated in the experience of consciousness-raising. One of the dramatic and salutary characteristics of such efforts at consciousness-raising is the upending of stereotypes and the concomitant revolution in self-image and sense of worth. Central to this endeavor is the significance of the aesthetic dimension, understood as both environmental and as embodied in personal style. Indeed, it can be argued that the strategy which engenders a transformation of aesthetic sensibility is more praiseworthy and long-lasting than one which effects a change in political sensibility, as witness the debate between Norman O. Brown and Herbert Marcuse on precisely this issue.[2]

More specifically, I offer here that a necessary and even crucial addition to the recent occasions of consciousness-raising has to do with our response to urban experience. Stated simply, urban consciousness in America is usually secondhand consciousness, derivative from a defensive attitude and lacking in deeply rooted patterns of pride, responsibility, and distinctive sensibility. Of particular concern in this regard is the absence of an articulated urban aesthetic and the bizarre domination of a high-culture aesthetic, through which cities become known and evaluated by their museums, monuments, and other replications of an aesthetic past.

It is true, of course, that to avoid the perils of self-deception, consciousness-raising of any sort has to be accompanied by an ongoing internal critique, especially of pretense and false claims. We are not about to hide from view, therefore, the painful awareness of what few or any would deny: the extensive afflictions found in the contemporary American city. In fact, one of the most severe and pressing social problems of contemporary America is the deep discontent pervasive of urban life, especially as it is expressed in the apparent opposites of boredom and violence. Regarded by many as a pathological situation of epidemic proportions, urban discontent is fostered by schools and by social agencies, remains unameliorated in hospitals let alone prisons, and has been largely ignored as a problem by traditional religious and political institutions.[3] In keeping with the sociology of the vicious circle, this urban discontent festers and generates hostility and violence, which in turn escalates fear and promotes still wider patterns of alienation and anomie.[4] In New York City at the present time, one of the most distinctive urban artifacts is the fox-lock, a metal rod from door to floor signaling that others are locked out but symbolizing as well that we are locked in. Recent events in the city of Boston, mindless stonings and burnings of persons, remind us again of the message delivered in the 1960s, showing us how close to the surface rides the explosive and destructive response of the often bitter and repressed urban mass. That message rings loud: if we loathe our environment, in time we shall destroy it.[5] The underlying questions, then, are why we have allowed our cities to be objects of hate and sources of alienation, and what are the means by which we can turn that situation around so that celebration and affection become the governing attitudes.[6]

It is obvious that such a major undertaking as the reconstituting of urban life cannot yield to a single nostrum, no matter what its potential or the commitment of its supporters. An integration of basic political, social, educational, economic, and ecological strategies is necessary if the city is to be healed. What strikes us as odd, however, is that little attention has been given to how urban people actually "feel" about the city.[7] When they leave, what do they miss? Do they stay on account of necessity, or do they stay on account of affection? For the most part, do urban people share those variable approaches of urbanologists who see the city as being viable if it were cleaner, or less noisy, or less polluted, or less crowded? Do flamboyant buildings, trade and culture centers, bypass expressways penetrate to the core of perceptions held by urban people about their city? Are the tangles over neighborhood schools and community control explicable in racial, or even educational, terms, or do they reveal other, distinctively urban needs? Does urban transportation perform basically as a "people mover" or does it operate in other fundamental human dimensions, such as the social and the aesthetic? More such questions abound, which, if posed in the right vein to urban people themselves, would in my judgment elicit some surprising responses.[8]

The fundamental problem has to do with those who see themselves as responsible for curing the ills of the city, for, even when genuinely concerned, they tend to proceed from perceptions other than those of the people affected. We point, then, to an unfortunate gap between the urban experience and its articulation, and again between the articulation and how it is heard by those with the power of decision. That gap spawns distrust, an erosion of confidence, and an abandonment of commitment by all concerned. More care must be addressed to the area where that gap most often occurs, namely, in the affective dimension of experience which more often is referred to philosophically as the "aesthetic."

The Urban Aesthetic and Nature Nostalgia

The meaning of the "aesthetic" in its widest and most general sense has to do with human feeling as enhanced by transaction with nature, an event, or an artifact. In its more restricted sense, the "aesthetic" has reference to matters of taste, works of art, and art-events, such as theater and dance. One of the more creative implications of the development of "modern art" over the last seventy-five years was the shattering of a constricted and proprietary approach to art and to the aesthetic. Endowed with the riches of new materials and techniques, largely due to advances in technology, the forms that art may take now are virtually as extensive as the number of participants. Of even more importance in this development is the stress given to the aesthetic significance of ordinary experience and to the artifacts of everyday life, thereby giving rise to an appreciation of the enormous increase in our own experience of shapes, sounds, colors, textures, and patterns of mediation. Nowhere is this development more apparent than in the experience of our cities, which can be described, in contemporary terms, as a vast assemblage, undergone kinetically, laced throughout with the tensions, mishaps, celebrations, and fulfillments worthy of any rich assemblage.

In my judgment, then, the scope of an "urban aesthetic" is nothing less than all the affective transactions experienced in urban life, and the task of an "urban aesthetic" is to articulate those transactions in a language as close to the quality of urban experience as spoken and written discourse will allow. Grady Clay states this task as follows:

Most Americans are captives of an object-ridden language which they must awkwardly manipulate to deal with a changeable, process-ful thing called "city." They speak of "downtown" as a place, but it is many places, scenes of overlapping actions, games, competitions, movements. There are many towns: downtown, uptown, cross-town, in town, out-of-town, old and new town, smoketown, honkytown, shantytown. A city is not as we perceive it to be by vision alone, but by insight, memory, movement, emotion, and language. A city is also what we call it and becomes as we describe it.[9]

While this approach does not preclude the possible importance of the arts and of the urban centers for the arts, an "urban aesthetic" is both a more extensive and a more fundamental response to urban life. It can be argued that concentration on the role of the arts as equivalent to the aesthetic character and quality of a city has worked to the disdvantage of urban sensibilities: in funding, for example, or in the frequent gener-ating of attitudes of condescension to more "proletarian" aesthetic needs. Concretely, in aesthetic terms, I find the refurbishing of Yankee Stadium as equal to the construction of Lincoln Center.

Before proceeding to the main theme of this essay, on the experience of urban time and space, one further methodological caution should be flagged. While it is simple to urge, as being essential to the development of an "urban aesthetic," that we utilize a distinctively urban language, the undertaking is more difficult than appears at first reading. A basic obstacle emerges when we realize that the American mind is overrun with nature metaphors and with a deep bias for the superiority of nature experience over urban, artifactual experience. There resides behind this fundamental American attitude a complex cultural, social, and intellec-tual history,[10] and we repeat here a previously stated generalization about the significance of American nature nostalgia for the development of a new urban consciousness.

American urban man as been seduced by nature. By this I mean that at the deepest level of his consciousness urban man functions on behalf of nature metaphors, nature expectancies, and a nostalgia for an experi-ence of nature which neither he nor his forebears actually underwent. For contemporary America, the implications of this situation are sig-nificant. In the first place, we are blocked off from understanding the dramatic and necessary conflict with nature, which characterized American life until recently. Indeed, we have become naive and ahistorically sentimental about that conflict. Second, we have often failed to diagnose the limitations and strengths of our present urban context on its own terms, rather than as a function of the absence of nature.[11]

Given this historical attitude in America, it is not, therefore, coincidental that two of the more discussed writers of the last five years, Theodore Roszak and Charles Reich,[12] have incorporated antiurban, aintitechnological attitudes into their blueprints for an ameliorated future.[13] If, by the most cautious of statistics, more than 80 percent of Americans live on 10 percent of the land, what are urban dwellers to think of the relevance of a strategy for the future which calls for the "Greening of America," let alone the belief that cities should be abandoned? Even in incomparably more profound thought than that found in the commentators on the counterculture, we find a deep disquiet and even hostility to the city as over against nature. There is a direct and acknowledged reflective line from Emerson, who "shuddered when he approached New York,"[14] to Norman O. Brown, who writes, "hence a city is itself, like money, crystallized guilt."[15]

Returning to the contention that nature nostalgia presents an obstacle to the development of an urban aesthetic, we may complain here not only of the obvious innocence of the belief that cities can become humanized and aesthetized in direct relation to their ability to "green" the environment, as in vest-pocket parks or sporadic splurges of tree planting, but also of the much deeper difficulties which attend any attempt to articulate urban experiences from such an alien social-psychological context. Let us be quite specific at this point. If an effective and genuine urban aesthetic depends on the utilization of distinctive urban metaphors,[16] we have to cut deeper than the unreflective use of urban argot like "street rat," "corner boy," "kiosk," or "pushcart."

I contend, rather, that virtually all of our language is contexted by our urban setting and has a different implicitness when so grasped, as, for example, in the language of urban time and urban space. Indeed, I would point even to the language of urban nature, for we experience rain differently in a street than in a field, while "slush" is urban snow. Kansas sunlight differs obviously from the sunlight which arches off

great slabs of glass or darts furtively through alleys and plays on para-
pets. Mutatis mutandis, the affairs of nature vary with the cities in which
they are experienced. More helpful, however, to our effort to develop
the language of an urban aesthetic are the fundamental contexts of experienced time and space, in terms of which we communicate our needs,
anticipations, and generalized sensibilities. Timed bodies, we touch and
are touched by the things of space, human artifacts. What are the originating qualities of this process when it dwells within the matrix of urban
experience? We turn first to urban space and urban artifact.

Urban Space and Urban Artifact

Perhaps it would be helpful to begin with a brief summary of the meaning of "nature space," a theme developed elsewhere.[17] In American experience, nature space is endowed with the character of the sacred, for
salvation, historically and religiously, was thought to take place on the
land. This judgment is true not only of the American Puritans of the
seventeenth century but of, for example, James Brooks, who in 1835 tells
us that "God has promised us a renowned existence, if we will but deserve it. He speaks the promise in the sublimity of nature."[18] In our own
time, the ecologist Eliot Porter is fond of citing Thoreau, "In Wildness
is the preservation of the world."[19]

Dwellers in nature space have a deep and abiding sense of the continuity of the body with the environment. Such continuity creates, in
turn, a confidence in the fertility of nature, elsewhere if not here, which
was so often expressed in the decision to relocate rather than to rehabili-
tate. In personal terms, the experience of vision is pre-eminently physical, spatial, expansive; it is characterized by horizontality and evaluated
by reach. While the environment of nature space is extraordinarily rich
in stimuli, much of it is hidden from the ordinary patterns of response.[20]
The more dramatic stimuli of nature space function at a distance, cutting the intimacy of tactile response, which more often reflects the ambience of wonder and awe, rather than of control. Although man dwells
more or less comfortably in nature space, the overarching awareness is
that the environment preceded us and will outlast us. We can say of our
experience of nature space that it involves body continuity, cultivation

skills, and a paradoxical alternation between the disparate responses of awe and boredom.

Our experience of urban space has a dramatically different point of origin. Urban space is not found space but chosen space, managed space, especially in the creation of a multiplicity of spaces within space. The most frequent way to manage space so as to create urban space is to move from horizontal experiencing to vertical experiencing. While it is not an absolute requisite for an environment to qualify as a city, verticality, however modest, is the seminal spatial characteristic of most cities. This is particularly true of American cities and, interestingly, it is rapidly becoming true of the American suburb.[21]

By virtue of tall buildings, we have created layers of livable or singly usable space which can simultaneously realize the needs of multiple numbers of people while yet insuring spatial proximity, and even providing for intimacy or solitude. We focus here not only on the prepossessing verticality of the skyscraper but also on the more subtle versions seen in subways, elevated trains, underground arcades, overhead walkways, elevated expressways, and multilayered bridges. Urban space as vertical space is radically pluralized on a single site. Urban place often cannot be identified with a single piece of land or with a single function. Although many people journey each day to the same urban building, they would not think of themselves as going to the same place. An urban place is a placeholder for a multiplicity of functions. so that the source of identification is less likely to be "where" than it is to be "what goes on." The event replaces the place as having priority in our consciousness; in the words of Kevin Lynch, "what time is this place?"[22] Despite the apparent heaviness of concrete and stone, large urban buildings are gatherers and dispatchers of urban personal processes, as much creatures of time as of space.[23]

Further intriguing implications emerge from the experiential dominance of verticality in city life. It becomes obvious, for example, that cities should be walked to be experienced fully, for automobiles are horizontally oriented, making rear vision hazardous and almost entirely blocking upward vision. In this regard we should lament the passing of the double-decker, open-top bus, for it so aptly symbolized the focus of urban visual action. A more important implication of verticality is that it develops in us a shorter vision-reach, yet one that is more intense and one that tends to interiorize itself. Stone, brick, concrete, metal, and building glass are not vision-penetrable. Buildings are clustered together, and the most we can see, boulevards excepted, is a block or so ahead. Our eyes confront and bounce off these massive, impermeable buildings, turning our vision back in upon ourselves, feeding imaginative relations. In effect, our eyes rarely "run on," wandering over great distances, as they do in nature space. Significantly, in order to do that in urban space, we must climb to the top of the tallest building and look out and over. The shrinkage of horizon and the impenetrability of urban objects combine to intensify the significance of what we *do* see in urban sight.

Urban life, therefore, leans more to the working of the imagination and to the development of often inarticulated but complex patterns of symbolization. Frequently dwarfed by immense artifacts, urban man has a constant sense of something hovering over him. The response to this huge presence is not quite that of awe, for it is, after all, man-made. Nonetheless, in an effort to assure human responsibility for this environment and to enhance participation in even its most prepossessing of architectural creations, urban man "blocks" out small pockets of lived space and endows them with deep symbolic meaning.[24] They, rather than the famous or honorific, are the true urban landmarks. We speak here of newsstands, tiny restaurants, bars, fruit stands, vendor spots, funeral parlors, playgrounds, lobbies, public bathrooms, and certain street corners. Such "landmarks" are anonymous and are described only by their location, which is only proximate to giant buildings or under bridges or eccentrically present in the midst of an urban complex devoted to more formal endeavors.[25] Symbolically, to meet someone at the pretzel vendor outside of the World Trade Center serves as a hopeful reminder that, no matter how awesome, the urban environment shall serve man and not the reverse.[26]

A further contributing factor to the urban introverting of spatial sensibility is the role of artifactual light. While it is true that we are the first century for whom night and darkness are not synonymous, we tend to forget the intervening array of shadows which exists between night and light. From the neon brightness of the center city, through the speckled light of the great apartments, those dozing day buildings, and along the bejeweled bridges, night light finally plays itself out on side streets, doorways, alcoves, stairwells, and alleys, only to break out again in the stark glare of the all-night cafeterias. The light we choose is the mood we seek, as we alternate between the disparate needs of intimacy and anonymity, heightened by the range of options which bear down upon us in urban life.

The response to artifactual light is only one of the multiple ways in which our bodies resonate to the urban environment. We may point to a widely held prejudice—that, in contrast to our experience in nature space, our bodies are fundamentally alien to the textures of urban space, that is, to technological artifact, media, and material. The sources of this prejudice are complex and varied, but in the main they can be traced to the deeply felt commitment we have to the superiority of the natural over the artifactual. This distinction, in keeping with our propensity for philosophical dualism, sets one category over against another; from such a method flows a series of invidious comparisons: the organic versus the inorganic, life versus death, natural versus artificial, and real versus ersatz. In turn, these distinctions spill over into aesthetic judgments having curious but revealing emphases. For the most part, the natural is associated with salutary endowments, such as "soft," "fertile," "rich," and "blooming." Even the apparently negative in nature, such as the "bleakness" of the moor or the "mystery" of the desert, is transformed in our affectionate version. With technological artifacts, on the other hand, the descriptive language is either prosaic, as in characterizations like "interesting," "clean," "necessary," "functional," or it is negative, as in "drab," "shabby," "dehumanizing," "noxious"; or again, if it is in praise, then it is not technology of which we speak but "art," as in a "beautiful" building, bridge, or monument. The operative assumption here is that we honor a hierarchy of favored materials, arranged according to their proximity to the organic—that is, the natural—as witness, in descending order, cloth, wood, stone, brick, aluminum, and plastic. In effect, we *render* our bodies alien to nonorganic materials.

Now this situation cuts deeper than it appears; it can only be attributed partially to nature nostalgia, or, for that matter, to a twentieth-century version of the ever-present temptations of a Neoplatonic hierarchy of forms.[27] The underlying question is whether man can be as continuous with urban artifact as he is with the affairs and creatures of nature. I believe that such continuity is both possible and desirable. In that vein I would hold, for example, that the Mississippi River and the Bitterroot Mountains are no more or less "alive" than Wrigley Field or Scollay Square, for they all "live" off the endowments of human history, although the latter pair owe their existence to us as well. It has to be admitted that this sort of statement runs against the grain of long-nurtured assumptions in common parlance. This is not to say that we do not feel affectionately about artifacts, but it is to say that we do not, in general, speak such affection. What is it, then, that prevents us from acknowledging, developing, and celebrating our intimate tactile relations with artifacts? Is it that we have defined our bodies too narrowly, too unimaginatively? Is it that we have underestimated the multiple ways in which we penetrate and are penetrated by the physical environment, taken in all of its artifactual manifestations, in contrast to the activites of nature? Is it that we have made too much of the eyes and not enough of the hands?[28]

No doubt each of these operative attitudes figures significantly in diluting our potential for developing richer relations with the world of artifacts. More extensive examination would most likely turn up other obstacles of similar character and importance. A continuation of such a list of obstacles does not, however, go to the heart of the matter; in a way somewhat reminiscent of the chiding given to Meno by Socrates, we should try to locate the fundamental source from which these obstacles proceed. In my judgment, this search leads to a set of metaphysical assumptions which, despite more than two thousand years of turbulent philosophical history, still undergird much of our consciousness. Put obviously and polemically, when discussing and analyzing the human condition, we have not integrated adequately into the language of description and response the shift from a metaphysics of substance, thing, and place to one of process, relations, and field. Nor have we absorbed significantly the evolution of the meaning of inquiry from primarily that of "looking at" to primarily that of "constituting." Whether the source be existential, phenomenological, depth-psychological, or "future shock" jargon, abundant testimonies acknowledge, and even take for granted, this shift in consciousness. Yet, despite this flamboyant rhetoric of the twentieth century, celebrating, as it does, "Protean man" and the endless possibilities of human creativity, it remains painfully true that contemporary institutions still sustain themselves on a jejune anthropology, characterizing and "dealing" with man in terms of obviousness and sameness. Our options seem pared to a virtual Scylla and Charybdis: either to celebrate our own ordinary experience and be rendered idiosyncratic, or to "get with it," and thereby abandon the originating qualities of our own perceptions. We have many incisive diagnosticians of this contemporary affront, and we do not have to accept their remedies in order to share their warning that, no matter how developed and confident in his self-consciousness, Protean man, self-making man, is not liberated if the world in which he lives is alien.[29]

Expanding the phrase "works of art" to mean the making of artifacts, the making of the city, the making of the world, we may accept John Dewey's judgment that the "task is to restore continuity between the refined and intensified forms of experience that are works of art and the everyday events, doings and sufferings that are universally recognized to constitute experience."[30] While undertaking this task, we should take heart from the fact that the recent revolution in modern art and modern design has pressed upon us a new realization of the aesthetic dimensions of ordinary experience, especially the impact of new materials and techniques inseparable from technological artifacts, and consequently holds out new options for the enhancement of the human condition. But as we have indicated earlier, because of philosophical presuppositions of long standing, the transformation of aesthetic sensibility with regard to artifacts has not received the wide endorsement necessary if it is to function within the fabric of common consciousness. On the contrary, such an awareness seems, ironically, to be the preserve of the devotees of high culture, for whom in general the urban artifact appears in museums, honored under the rubric of the latest art movement rather than as a living presence in their lives. This development is not what I had in mind when I echoed Dewey's call for celebration of the things of ordinary experience.[31] Perhaps even a brief excursion into the thought of William James and John Dewey will provide some direction for a richer philosophical inquiry into the meaning of "artifact."

Artifact as Relational

In 1951, at the age of ninety-two, John Dewey, in one of his last written comments, stated presciently the task of a contemporary philosophy of inquiry.[32] "If I ever get the needed strength, I want to write on *knowing* as the way of behaving in which linguistic artifacts transact business with physical artifacts, tools, implements, apparatus, both kinds being planned for the purpose and rendering *inquiry* of necessity an *experimental transaction*."[33] Such a relation-oriented, or "transactional," epistemology depends on a very different metaphysical underpinning than that dominated by the notion of substance in the history of Western philosophy.

Thinkers as diverse as James, Bergson, Whitehead, and Dewey have emphasized the move from substance to process as the basic metaphor in a metaphysics. Of these, James's thought was the most decisive, for he offered both the first and the most explicit statement that the most fundamental characteristic of reality is not substance, essence, or thing, but rather a relational manifold. James held that things were nothing "but special groups of sensible qualities, which happen practically or aesthetically to interest us, to which we therefore give substantive names, and which we exalt to this exclusive status of independence and dignity."[34] And later on he tells us that "there is no property *absolutely* essential to any one thing."[35]

Implicitly with James and explicitly with Dewey, inquiry becomes a transaction between the knowing self and the transactions carried on within the affairs of nature and culture. "Knowledge," then, is a knowing of processes rather than of objects, the latter being definitional loci, pragmatically constructed to effect optimum management of the transactional relationship between awareness and decision. Put differently, James contends that "perception and thinking are only there for behavior's sake."[36] Rather than being set over against the world, we find ourselves within its concatenated fabric, having to hook onto its flow so as not to be bypassed, while yet structuring a self-presence for purpose of evaluation and identity. Known as "radical empiricism," this philosophical approach proceeds from what he refers to as "a statement of fact,"[37] namely, that we affectively experience relations equivalent to our experience of things. He writes, "If there be such things as feelings at all, *then so surely as relations between objects exist* in rerum natura, *so surely and more surely, do feelings exist to which these relations are known.*"[38]

Following his affirmation that consciousness is a relational stream, affectively continuous, and that objects are human constructs, or perches, insulated within the stream by conceptual schema, James proceeds in a series of essays to an even more controversial assertion that matter and mind are not ontologically, but only functionally or behaviorally, different. Without our stopping here to comment on the difficulties involved in his underlying notion of "pure experience,"[39] James, in denying an ontological division between matter and mind, points to the extraordinary quality of the human being who has experience in both ways, simultaneously. Just as there is no ontological dualism within the self, classically known as "body" and "soul," so, too, there is no ontological dualism between the self and the world. Now the startling consequence of this view for the present context is that if man and the world are made of the same reality and only function differently, then the things of reality as made by man are ontologically similar. Artifacts, then, are human versions of the world acting as transactional mediations, representing human endeavor in relational accordance with the resistance and possibility endemic to both nature and culture.

So long as artifacts remained as obvious "utiles," enhancing human activity by virtue of increased leverage, strength, durability, or accessibility, the man-world polarity held firm as an exhaustive description. We can refer to this centuries-long tradition in terms of the human use of tools. Regarded for the most part as necessities, unless occasionally bestowed with something more by the aesthetic criteria of specific cultures, as, for example, culinary utensils, the presence of such artifacts rarely gave rise to philosophical discussions. Perhaps this is due in part to the fact that Western philosophy has been concerned far more with the eyes than with the hands and speaks of vision rather than of touch. It is noteworthy that the two most remarkable inventions of the early modern period, the telescope (1590) and the microscope (1608), both have to do with vision. And despite the enthusiastic response to the marvels revealed by these super-eyes, the epistemology remained the same: that is, man the viewer "unhiding" layers and outer reaches of the external world. Until the twentieth century, it did not occur to us to realize that not only did we see "more" but that the viewer became profoundly transformed at the level of consciousness. If, as I believe, Kant is correct in his assertion that consciousness informs the world "sensuously," prior to its being known specifically, then transformations of consciousness, are, in effect, transformations of the world. Taking artifacts as "relatings" in the Jamesian sense gives us the history of artifact as a major strand in the history of the formulation of the meaning of the world.

The significance of James's rational metaphysics for an understanding of artifact becomes much clearer when we cite the move from industrial, machine-oriented technology to electronic technology which has occurred within the past century, and which is essential to contemporary urban life. Electronic technological artifacts such as the telephone, radio, television, and computer terminals are "things" in the Jamesian sense—that is, perches or gathering places for ongoing relational processes. As perches, they exist in time and space, classically understood relative to motion and dimension, but as activities they defy those limitations and create for us entirely novel sense-relations to the world. What James regarded as the fringe of consciousness, or the wider range of consciousness, becomes concretized by the presence of electronic media, with Telstar performing as a global cerebral cortex.

At this point in our discussion, we should remind ourselves of the problem which led to this brief exploration of a different philosophical approach: that is, the alleged inferiority of man's relationship to artifacts when contrasted with his relationship to nature. Put differently, the point at issue is whether human artifacts, as they come to resemble less and less the natural environment as experienced originally, are an alienating factor in human life. I have referred here to the evolution from the age of tools to the age of the machine, the combustion engine, and on to highly novel contemporary forms, such as electronic media and the computer. My position is that this development of technology, far from being alienating, is in fact the most distinctively human activity, offering an originating aesthetic quality to our lives.[40] The significance of the natural environment as "natural" has been affirmed by contrast with the artifactual environment. It is, then, not at all surprising that, in our age of technological domination of the environment, a tremendous increase in the concern for the quality of the natural environment should come to the fore, although such concern ought not lead to the now-frequent disparaging of the artifactual environment. While it is a truism that man's history is inseparable from nature, it does not follow that man's history is explicable solely, or even mainly, in terms of nature. Furthermore, the uniqueness of the human organism, and of the human endeavor, could never be experienced if an absolute continuity of man with the affairs of nature were honored. In my judgment, technological artifacts served not only to manage nature as problem-solving devices but also to distance man from nature, thereby allowing the development of human history within a context which was sui generis. The most dramatic version of that uniquely human context was the creation of the supreme artifact thus far, the city, with which, we contend, our bodies are potentially as intimate as they are with the affairs of nature.

Urban Time

Having considered in some detail the experiencing of urban space and artifact as a context for human life, we turn now to a beginning analysis of some characteristics of urban time. Once again we must forgo a full discussion of the contrasting experience of nature time, offering only some contentions gleaned from previous consideration. Nature time can be described as fat time, running in seasons, even in years and decades. To a young city boy the prognostications of the *Farmer's Almanac* were as strange and alien as if they were made for a millennium hence. Nature time gives room to regroup, to reassess, featuring a pace and a rhythm tuned to the long-standing, even ancient, responsive habits of our bodies. Feeding off the confidence in the regenerative powers of nature, time is regarded as realizing, liberating, a source of growth.[41] The rhythm of nature time shares with nature space a sense of expansiveness, such that in nature we believe that we "have time" and that "in time" we, too, shall be regenerated. As exemplified by the extraordinary journey of the nineteenth-century Mormons, their "trek," a distinctive nature phenomenon, points to salvation "in time." Space is the context for "in time," both taken as a long period of time, walking from Nauvoo, Illinois, to the Great Salt Lake, Utah, and being saved "in the nick of time."

In nature time, undergoing, doing, and reflection function simultaneously, thereby providing little need for "high culture," chunks of reflection taken out of the flow of experience. Perhaps the most obvious way to describe nature time is to call it baseball time, referring to a game in which the clock technically plays no role and which conceivably could last to infinity, tied to the end.

By contrast, urban time is thin time, tense, transparent, yielding no place to hide. Urban time is clock time, jagged, self-announcing time, bearing in on us from a variety of mediated sources, so often omnipresent and obtrusive that many people refuse to wear watches in an effort to ward off its domination. Why are clocks when worn on our bodies called watches? The first meaning of "watch" was to go without sleep, that is, to beat nature. Is the urban "watch" to "watch" time passing or is it to make sure that no one steals our time, as when we hoard time by saying that we have no time?

Clock time, like clock games, carries with it the threat of sudden death, an increasing urban phenomenon. But sudden death can be averted with but "seconds" to go. Urban time is "second" time, which may very well mean "second chance" or "surprise" time. We now have clocks which tell time in hundredths and even thousandths of seconds, reminding us how much faster we must go if we are not to be made obsolete, left behind, for cities have little patience with the past. Some people in the urban environment like to think that they live by nature time, but this assumption is self-deceptive, for such claims are relative only to the frantic urban pace. Clock time, after all, overrides nature time, as, for example, when at one second after midnight, in the pitch dark, your radio announcer says good morning and describes the events of your life that day as having happened yesterday.[42]

Beneath this somewhat anecdotal discussion of urban time there reside some significant implications. The rapid pace of urban time radically transforms the experience of our bodies, which often seem to lag behind. The network of communication media, which blankets a city like a giant octopus, constantly tunes us in to sensorially multiple experience, even if vicariously undergone. In a broad sense, when the setting is urban we experience less identity in spatial terms than proximity to events; rather than having a place, we identify ourselves relative to events taking place. In a city, when giving directions, the question as to "how long it will take" is not answered by the spatial distance traversed; rather the allotted time is a function of potential interventions, for the time of city space is activity measured. Our imagination, fed at all times by the messaging of electronic intrusions,[43] races far ahead of our body, which we often claim to drag around. Yet, despite the pace, the apparent garrulousness and noise, urban life is extraordinarily introspective, enabling us to carve out inner redoubts of personal space. The urban person must protect himself against the rampaging activity of time, which dismantles our environment with alarming speed. It is a cliché that you can't go home again, for the spiritual and psychological experiences of childhood are unrepeatable; but further, for one seeking his urban childhood, there is added the almost-inevitable burden of having his physical environment obliterated. The urban past is notoriously unstable, so that in urban experience we often outlive our environment.

Just as the prepossessing verticality of urban space encourages us to endow body-scale places as experiential landmarks, so, too, in the rush of urban time is it necessary to further endow such loci with the ability to act as functional clots in the flow of time, in short, to stop time for a time. In urban argot we call this "hanging out," and we might reflect on how it differs from a new version, oriented toward nature and called "dropping out." The verticality of urban space turns vision inward, and the speed of urban time revs up our capacity for multiple experiences, thereby intensifying the need for inner personal space to play out the experiences subsequently in our own "good" time. More often than is supposed, urban man does attain management of his inner personal space, and, contrary to the offensive cliché of antiurban critics, anonymity is *not* a major urban problem. As a matter of fact, urban life is crisscrossed with rich interpersonal relations, brought about by the extraordinary shortcuts to interpersonal intimacy that flourish in the type of situation we have been describing—namely, a welter of experiences, rapidly undergone, yet transacted by the ability of the person to impact some of them in both space and time and convert them to sources of emotional nutrition. Having cut to a bare minimum the timespan required to forge urban interpersonal relationships, in general one does not expect that longevity be a significant quality of these relationships. The pace of urban time, coupled with the people-density of urban space, churns up tremendous possibilities for interpersonal life, for the multiplicity of relations widens considerably the range and quality of the intersections and transactions operative in our daily lives. As we see it, then, the major problem in urban life centers not in the relations between persons, but rather in the relations of persons to the urban environment and in the studied institutional insensitivity to the aesthetic qualities germane to the processes of urban space and urban time.[44]

If we come full circle and remind ourselves of the need for urban consciousness-raising, a warning is in order. The healing and amelioration of the contemporary American city will be stymied if our efforts betray an ignorance or insensitivity to the experiential demands of the original qualities of being human in urban space and in urban time. As in most human situations, the caution of William James is relevant here: "Woe to him whose beliefs play fast and loose with the order which realities follow in his experience. They will lead him nowhere or else make false connexions."[45]

TEN

GLASS WITHOUT FEET

Dimensions of Urban Aesthetics

S ome time last year, I made my way to the area adjoining the Galleria in the imposing new outer city of Houston. Entering one of the more formidable glass towers so as to experience its inside, I was stopped by a security guard, who asked me if I had an appointment with anyone in the building. I replied that my appointment was with the building—to see if it had a soul and was open to the presence of personal space. He tossed me out. I went looking for a newspaper, a sandwich, a personal opening to these jutting edifices of technological supremacy. No luck! No kiosk! No paper! No sandwich! No body! No place! Just a marvel of impersonal use of space. Consequently, no personscape.

I. Coming to Consciousness

Far from offering solid, impermeable barriers to the natural environment, [the building's] outer surfaces come more and more closely to resemble permeable membranes which can accept or reject any environmental force. Again, the uterine analogy; and not accidentally, for with such convertibility in the container's walls, man can modulate the play of environmental forces upon himself and his processes, to guarantee their uninterrupted development, in very much the same way as the mother's body protects the embryo.

—James Marston Fitch, "Experiential Basis for Aesthetic Decision"

The human body is neither a container nor a box in a world of boxes. To the contrary, our bodies are present in the world as diaphanous and permeable. The world, in its activity as the affairs of nature and the affairs of things, penetrates us by flooding our consciousness, our skin, and our liver with the press of the environment. We respond with our marvelous capacity to arrange, relate, reject, and, above all, symbolize these transactions. In effect, we as humans, and only we, give the world its meaning. Even as embryos in the comparatively closed environment of our mother's womb, we are open to the experience of the other. The quality of the other and how we transact with the other constitutes our very being as human. Let us diagnose some of these transactions in general terms, and then specify our relationship to the world as natural and to the world as artifact, as human-made—that is, as urban.

For the human organism, coming to full consciousness is an exquisitely subtle phenomenon. We are always enveloped by the climate, known in America as "the weather." We weather the world and the world weathers us. Except for the occasional outrageous performances of nature such as typhoons, hurricanes, earthquakes, and tornadoes, our experience of the weather is largely inchoate, that is, subliminally conscious. Unfortunately, inchoate also is our experience of most things, doings, happenings, events, and even creatures. I say that this is unfortunate because our tendency to categorize, name, and box the affairs of the world signifies a drastic decline from the alert consciousness of environment which characterized our young childhood.

The most telling way to realize how little we actually experience that which takes place within the range of our bodies is to focus on the very young child. For children, the world comes, as William James suggests, as a buzzing and blooming continuity. The nefarious dualisms between color and shape, past and present, even between organic and inorganic, are foreign to the child, who has an extraordinary capacity to experience relations, that webbing which holds the multiple messages of the environment in an organic whole.[1] Despite the ongoing richness of the child's experience of the world, adults quickly strike back. They have long been conditioned to see the world as disparate, each thing and event complete unto itself, each with an appropriate name tag courtesy of the fixed categories of Aristotle, Euclid, and linguistic syntax. The children soon yield and, like the rest of us, sink into the oblivion of the obvious. The occasional poets rise above this sameness of description, but their special place only reinforces the jejune character of how we feel and describe the world in which we find ourselves.

Allow me to offer a way out of this Platonic cave, in which we so often languish, cut off from the teeming richness so potentially present in our experience. Returning to the uterine analogy, I prefer us to experience the world as if we were in a permeable sheath rather than trapped in a linguistic condom. If we listen to the wisdom of the Greek and Roman Stoic philosophers, then we know that the world speaks to us from the very depths of being. The logos, the word, the utterance is meant for us if we but listen, feel, touch, see, and allow ourselves to be open to the novelty, originality, and freshness that is endemic to experience. Openness to experience is crucial, by which I mean that we must allow our perceptions a full run before we slap on the defining, naming, locating tags of place, thing, and object. Coming to consciousness in this way allows us to be bathed by a myriad of impressions, each of them too rich for the task of organization, a task which should follow far behind, gathering only the husks, the leftovers from what we have undergone in a personal and symbolic way.

All experience counts and counts to the end of our days. This includes the salamander who lives on my porch and dazzles me with its change of skin color; the forgotten rake which leaps up in the melting of an April snow; those lovely Georgian doors that front the row houses in Dublin city; Brahmin bulls with human visage; the Irish setter on its haunches, nose poised to spring in response to the advance of an impinging world; the great Gretzky streaking the ice and the soaring of the marvelous Dr. J.; or, more profoundly and demandingly, the crippled seventy-year-old mother who, upon learning of the impending death of her incontinent, cystic fibrosis–afflicted, totally retarded forty-eight-year-old daughter, cries out in anguish, "Not my baby, not my baby!"

Boredom and ennui are signs of a living death. In that the only time we have is the time we have, they are inexcusable faults. Sadness, and even alienation, given our personal and collective miseries, are proper responses, especially attenuated as they can be by occasional joy and celebration. Coming to consciousness has nothing to do with the traditional pursuit of happiness, an attempt illusory and self-deceiving for a human organism whose denouement is the inevitability of death without redemption. Rather, the signal importance of how we come to consciousness is precisely that such a process is all we are, all we have, and all we shall ever be.

The world appears to us as given, yet we knead it to our own image, for better and for worse. As we slowly awake to our environment, to our cosmic and planetary womb, we soon find that the more local arrangements are the ones which formulate how we come to know and feel ourselves. In American culture, one of the most prepossessing of these local contexts for consciousness is the dialectic between nature, on the one hand, and artifacts, especially those supreme artifacts, cities, on the other hand. Two hands, but one consciousness. Two hands, but one nation. For Americans, the experience of nature and city has been both actual and mythic, depending on the site in which a person came to consciousness. The difference between the experience of nature as primary and the experience of city as primary is not one between good and bad or positive and negative. It is, however, a difference which has important ramifications for our evaluation of the kind of environment we should seek to build and for a host of allied personal concerns, values, preferences, and attitudes. If nature is the environment we inherit and city is the environment we build, what, then, is the ideal relationship between them? What does nature teach us that we need to maintain if we are to remain human as we make an abode, a human place in which many of us live together? Further, what does the history of cities teach us about what we have discovered to be distinctively human and propitious in that which we have made for ourselves, undreamt by nature or by the animals or by the insects?

II. Nature and City

As in all such general terms of description, nature and city are herein used with a specific cultural context in mind: that of North America.[2] We have before our consciousness Boston and the Berkshire Mountains; Chicago and Lake Michigan; Denver and the Rocky Mountains; San Francisco and its bay; Miami and the Everglades; Missoula and the Lolo Pass; Houston and west Texas; the ocean cities, the river cities, the cities of the plains; and, of course, those dots of nostalgia from the event-saturated past as we traversed the land—North Zulch, Snook, and Old Dime Box, those representative Texas fables.

In American terms, nature was always writ large. The history of the meaning of nature for America is as old as our first settlements and as central to the meaning of America as is our vaunted political history. The stark generalization is that nature took the place of the Bible as the script by which Americans searched for the signs of conversion. How shall we know when we have been saved? This was the plaintive and genuine question most prominent on the lips and in the heart of the early American Puritans. Faced as they were, however, with an environment deeply forbidding and foreboding, as well as lushly promising, they soon began to equate their justification with their ability to bring nature to its knees and celebrate Zion in the Wilderness. Witness this revealing 1697 text from the "Phaenomena" of Samuel Sewall: "As long as nature shall not grow old and dote but shall constantly remember to give the rows of Indian Corn their education, by Pairs: so long shall Christians be born there; and being first made meet, shall from thence be Translated, to be made partakers of the Inheritance of the Saints in Light."[3]

As the American eighteenth century opened, the fixed meeting houses of the Congregationalists and Presbyterians were slowly but inevitably being replaced by the itinerant preaching of the Baptists and the Methodists. America was on the move! Nature was calling; the West was calling. First, the Berkshires, then the Alleghenies, the Appalachians, western Connecticut, western Virginia, Kentucky, the Northwest Territory, the Mississippi, the pony express to California, the Mormon trek, Texas, and—as late as 1907—the emergence of Oklahoma. This 200-year

history of frontier conflict, frontier conquest, and frontier failure became the central theme of American consciousness, lived in the "West"
in nature, and vicariously lived in the "East" in the cities which always
"trailed" behind, as redoubts, points of departure. It is essential to realize that the public story of the American odyssey was played out in the
clutches of nature, at war with nature's children, the American Indians,
and at war, internally, on the land, about the land, for the control of the
land.

To the West they wend. To the West is to be free. To the West meant
simply to leave the city, wherever it might be, and chase the setting of
the sun. This is why California, despite its protracted adolescence, symbolizes the end of continental America.[4] And this also is why Texas still
retains its mythic value, for Texas is endless, large, vast, and still provides
the scape for disappearance into the land and the chance to start over.
Further, this is why Americans are wary of cities, often seeing them as
vulgar necessities and as interruptions in the natural flow of persons in
nature. The public voice of America tells us that cities are places to go,
to sin, to buy, to sell—in short, to visit. The utter unreality of this judgment, given that 90 percent of all Americans live on but 10 percent of
the land, points to the inordinate power of our long-standing romance
with nature, especially as it is biblically sanctioned and artistically recre-
ated in story and film. This tradition confirms our indigenous belief that
mobility, exodus, change of place are necessary for salvation. Is it any
wonder, then, that despite the presence of historical monuments and
grandiloquent architectural sorties, we build our cities not as habitats
for persons but rather as pens for those waiting to leave, to leave for the
land where, allegedly, human beings truly belong?

III. The Space and Time of Nature and City

The most dramatic and long-lasting influences on persons coming to
consciousness are their senses of space and of time. What could be more
different for me as a person than if I came to believe that I was in space
as one creature among others, all of us with space to spare, rather than
if I came to believe that no space was present for me unless I seized it

and made it my own space, that is, my place? What could be more different for me as a person than if I believed that time was seasonal, repetitive, and allowed for reconnoitering over the same experienced ground again and again, rather than if I believed that time was by the clock, measured in hours, minutes, and even in rapidly disappearing seconds? The difference between the space and time of nature and the space and time of cities has its most important impact on our perceptions of the environment, sufficient to generate a very different experience of ourselves, our bodies, our memory, and our creative life.

The affairs of nature are inexorable. Even the intrusions, such as drought and tornadoes, follow the larger natural forces. Although spawned elsewhere, they occur periodically, loyal to conditions routinely present in nature. Cities, however, have no correlate to the seventeen-year cycle of the appearance of the cicada. Nature space is spacious, with room for recovery, for redemption, for second and third chances. Vision in the space of nature is predominantly horizontal, as though a person were on permanent lookout. The plains and the desert afford us an extraordinary visual reach, a field for our eyes to play upon, as in an endless cavorting through space with nothing definite, no things to obtrude. Still more powerful is the heightened sense of distance given to us from our mountain perch. This horizontality passes over the billions upon billions of individual items present in nature space, those of the flora, the fauna, and the living creatures of the soil and sky. But the very vastness of nature space requires a special attention, a special ability to grasp and relate the presence of the particulars. Thus, persons of nature space are homemade botanists, entomologists, ichthyologists, and animal scientists, constantly aware of variations which await the patient observer of what only seems to be stretches of sameness. For city dwellers, this potential richness of nature space is missed, for they have been schooled to confront the obvious in their experience—multiple sounds, objects, things, and events—all up front and requiring no search. Actually, persons of city consciousness often find the virtually endless sky of nature space, as in Montana and Texas, to be claustrophobic. This situation is obviously paradoxical but it is instructive. When a person experiences so vast a distance, a sky so wide that the eye reaches out endlessly with no end in sight and no grasp of the subtle particulars of shadow, cloud, and terrain, then that person shrinks back in an introverted, hovering manner, alone and fearful. The claustrophobia of open space for the person of urban consciousness is precisely the opposite of the experience of persons of nature consciousness, whose claustrophobia erupts when they first find themselves adrift in a teeming city street, cut off from sky and horizon by glass canyons.

The time of nature space is likewise special. I call it "fat" time, for it is measurable by seasons, even by decades. The shortest time in nature time is that of sun time and moon time, both of which are larger by far than the hurried ticks of clock time, so omnipresent in cities. Nature time is also consonant with body time, a rhythm akin to the natural processes of the physiology of the human organism. This rhythm is present in the daily transformation of night into day and then into night once more, just as our bodies sleep, wake, and sleep once more. These events mirror exactly the nutrition cycle in our bodies and more poignantly, more naturally, they are microcosmic instances of the life and death of crops, insects, the leaves of the trees and, on a larger scale, our own life, whose rhythm, like that of nature, turns over in a century.

If we are properly attuned, nature time, like nature space, affords an abode for a distinctively human marriage between the body and the affairs of the environment. Being in and of nature, then, seems to make sense. Yet not by matched rhythm alone doth we live. The human organism, on an even deeper personal terrain, historically and culturally has expressed a need to develop an interior life, singular and independent of the external world. For the most part, this possibility is absent in the time and space frameworks of nature. I see the result of this absence as twofold; first, a quiet yet present sense of personal loneliness and even alienation pervades much of the lives of nature persons; second, in response to that situation, from the beginning of humankind, we have abandoned the rightness of nature for us and huddled together by building cities. The great American philosopher Ralph Waldo Emerson, no lover of cities and a master delineator of the majesty of nature, writes: "We learn nothing rightly until we learn the symbolical character of life. Day creeps after day, each full of facts, dull, strange, despised things, that we cannot enough despise—call heavy, prosaic and desert. The time we seek to kill: the attention it is elegant to divert from things around us. And presently the aroused intellect finds gold and gems in one of these scorned facts—then finds that the day of facts is a rock of diamonds; that a fact is an Epiphany of God."[5]

It is this "aroused intellect" that is at work in the building and maintaining of cities, a homemade environment which demands human symbolization for purposes of survival. The space of city space is vertical rather than horizontal. The sky fades into anonymity, replaced by the artifactual materials of wood, concrete, mortar, steel, and glass, each married to the other in an upward spiral of massive presence and extensive height. Yet the massiveness and the height, even in the great towers of the John Hancock building in Boston, the Sears Tower in Chicago, and the twins of the World Trade Center in New York City, are human scale, for by our hands, and by the technological extension of our hands, we built them. They belong to us, they are our creation. The mountains, the great lakes, the rivers, the desert, belong to someone, somewhere, somehow, someway, somewhen else. They have mystery and distance from our hands. City space is not found space or space in which we wander. Nor is it space that fulfills the needs of our body, understood physiologically. Those, rather, are the conditions of the space of nature. Quite to the contrary, city space is space seized, made space, wrestled to a place, our place, a human place. A building is a clot, a clamp, a signature in the otherwise awesome, endless reach of nature space. City space as human place is rife with alcoves, alleys, streets, corners, backs and fronts, basements, tunnels, bridges, and millions of windows which look out on other windows. This introverting character of city space is the source of human interiority. The reach of vision is short-circuited by the obtrusion of objects: impermeable, stolid, and in need of symbolic regathering. Bus stations, train stations, cafeterias, urban department stores, pawnbrokers, betting parlors, ticketrons, stadia, bars, courthouses, jails, hospitals, and innumerable other "places" gather us in a ·riot of interpersonal intensity. These spaces, once they become places, colonize space with an intensity and a personal messaging which defy their comparatively small size, for they multiply meaning independent of both physics and geometry. These city places are spiritual places, transcending the body as a thing in space. City space is person-centered and symbolically rich. The accusation of anonymity as lodged against urban life is a myth of nature dwellers. Cities are fabrics, woven neighbor-hoods, woven covenants, each integral and thick in personal exchange, yet each siding up to the other, so as to knit a concatenated, webbed, seamed, and organic whole. If the truth be told, the capacity of genuine urban dwellers—as distinct from visitors, transients, or those on the make so they can return to the land—constitutes a most remarkable phenomenon in human history. The history of the city is a history of human organisms, ostensibly fit for nature, rendering the artifactual af-fectionate, sentimental, warm, and symbolically pregnant.

The mountains, rivers, streams, lakes, oceans, insects, animals, plants, stars all belong to nature. But the buildings, trolleys, depots, museums, and Hyatt Regencies belong to us. They are human versions of nature, found, so far as we know, on no other planet, in no other place, for there is no other place which is human place, our place. Emerson praises this human capacity to render the activities and things of the world as more than they be, as simply taken or simply had. With Emerson the task is to use our "power of imagination" so as to clothe the world of the every-day with immortality, else we become dead to ourselves.[6]

The activities that make a city out of nature—converting it to artifacts with distinctive human significance, function, and symbol—are charac-teristic of a millennia-long effort at transubstantiation, the effort to ren-der nature an abode for human life in its liturgy, its interpersonal transactions, and its artistic creations. The space of nature is aestheti-cally rich but it is never art unless rendered so by human ways. City space is artifact supreme, the most extensive, detailed, multimedia human creation in the history of what we do to nature, rather than our simply being in nature.

The time of city time also reverses that of nature. City time is "thin" time, transparent time, the experience of virtual instantaneity. Ruled by the clock rather than by the sun, city time measures out our experience in short bursts, such that we place ourselves under enormous pressure to make every minute count. City time seems to have no attendant space, no room to move around and idly look ahead. To exist sanely in city time requires that we build an inner life, an introspective fortress in which we can reflectively lounge, impervious to the din accompanying rapid time passing. Despite the rush of events and the multiplicity of persons transacting in an infinite number of ways, city persons soon develop a sense of privacy which they carry deep within them, even in the midst of public urban clamor. It is not ironic but rather fitting that America's most distinctive game, baseball, is usually played on a sylvan field smack in the middle of the city. It is a nature game, defying time, which has no permanent role to play, for a baseball game can be tied to infinity. Sitting in the afternoon sun in Wrigley Field in Chicago, where night baseball is forbidden, provides the urban dweller a natural cranny, nestled among the tenements and elevated trains, a space in which time is defeated, halted and sent scurrying.[7] This contrasts with the clock games—hockey, basketball, and football—which are so driven by time that they attempt to cheat its passing by asking for overtime.

The great Hawaiian sailors who, without instruments, charted the Pacific Ocean, seemingly had sun dials for souls. City persons hide their souls and chart their way with urban clocks, that is, watches, which they wear everywhere, even to bed. Analog, digital, bells, songs, faces of every kind; each way a way to tell the time and in so telling, tell ourselves where we are, how we are, and how much time we have left. Although for most of the past decade, I have been a resident of that recent category of the amorphous, a Small Metropolitan Statistical Area (SMSA), having a teeny population of only 100,000 people, I am by consciousness still an urban person. Consequently, when someone asks if they can see me, I respond, seriously and with conscious intent, that "I have a minute." What an extraordinary statement, and still more extraordinary that increasingly, even in an SMSA, people are not offended. Orthodox psychoanalysis, an urban phenomenon to be sure, features a couch with a large clock visible to the patient so that the hour of soul-searching wears down publicly. The urban factory introduced the tradition of punching the clock. If one were late, the clock would punch this out and you would be docked. Urban time has a fixed and narrow memory. It exacts its price twenty-four hours a day, seven days a week, year in and year out. This is wearing, and therefore urban persons hurry by you without a howdy, for they are carrying on a conversation with themselves, a dialogue that protects them spiritually from the ravages of urban time.

In this contrast between nature and city, one further contrast should prove helpful, that of the presence of nature in the city. I do not refer to the greening of the city, too often a euphemism for planting shrubs around ugly buildings. Rather, I mean those times when nature shouts at the top of its voice and does so in the confines of a city. Some years ago, with family, while traveling across the horizontal state of Kansas we came upon, in the distance, a magnificent tornado. It soaked up the sky and drew all of the horizon to its center. I subsequently learned that aside from some ranch fences and an errant cow, it played itself out without causing damage. The people of the city of Wichita Falls, Texas, have no such romantic memories. When a tornado visited their city, it cut a violent swath, scattering bodies, homes, and automobiles, and left a calling card of disaster. These comparisons are apt, for they provide insight to the relative imperviousness of nature as contrasted with the awkward vulnerability of the city when nature strikes. Two further examples will assist us here. A massive snowstorm on the plains is troublesome and causes some disarray, even death here and there. Yet, by contrast, the endless snow dumped on the city of Buffalo some years back created such havoc that the competition for scarce resources brought the viability of social cohesion into serious question. And a hurricane which dances its wild dance off the Gulf Coast is far different from the hurricane which visits Galveston Island or, as recently happened, has the temerity to blow out those archetypes of high technology, the windows of the Houston skyscrapers.

This contrast, however, need not always be frightening or deleterious to urban life. Fog in a woodland is eerie and moving. It takes a back seat, however, to the late summer fog which cascades in glorious tufts across the boulevards of the city of San Francisco, washing and whitening, along the way, those lovely row houses which face the Pacific Ocean. And few events can match the fall of a gentle and wet snow on a late-night city street, providing a white comforter for the sleepers and a glistening cover for the nocturnal walkers. One could replicate these appearances of nature in cities around the world: the overcast, ice-bound streets of Moscow in December; the gentle Irish rain on a pedestrian overlooking the River Liffey in Dublin; the London fog; and the rising sun over the River Ulna in the Prague of Franz Kafka, heightening the twin spires of the castle and the cathedral, church and state, yin and yang, the glory of medieval Christendom.

When cities intrude upon nature, it is an assault. When nature intrudes upon cities, it is a challenge, a transformation of urban life into still more imaginative forms.

IV. Personscape: "Building" the Future

It is now clear that the older cities of America are in serious trouble. The reasons for the decay of the inner city and the rise of anomie are now well documented. Despite the many discussions as to how to heal this situation, the problem remains critical, although glimmers of hope poke through, as, for example, in the exciting revitalization of the city of Baltimore. The financial recovery of the incomparable city of New York is also a cause for cheer, and efforts to transform Detroit, Philadelphia, and St. Louis are welcome. In this essay, however, the issue is quite different. What of the "new" southwestern cities like Houston, Dallas, and Tucson? Have they learned anything from the relative demise of their older peers? I think not.

The older American cities long ago learned from their European forebears that the most crucial characteristic of a viable city was human scale. I call this the presence of "personscape," by which I mean the urban ambience which affords the city dweller the same bodily continuity with the environment as that found in nature. Even New York City, despite its overwhelming population and the dominating presence of its huge buildings, has preserved the sense of neighborhood, intimacy, and personal accessibility. Until recently, the city of Los Angeles, a comparatively new city, failed in precisely the way that Boston, New York, and Chicago succeeded—namely, to be a resource for ordinary and local experience as well as for the glitter of being on the town. Los Angeles, in its reworking of downtown, has attempted to address that lack and become a city in reality as well as in claim.

Traditionally, our great cities have been water cities, adjacent either to oceans, to lakes, or to rivers. Water has the capacity to bathe the soul and to provide a stimulus for the symbolization of the environment. Water yields depth, fog, mist, the reflection of sun and moon, and especially the possibility of escape—by boat, by reverie, and by suicide. Many of our new cities, however, are land cities; these include Denver,

Tucson, Phoenix, Dallas, and even Houston, despite its ship channel and occasional bayou. Land cities as prepossessing and powerful constitute a new event for America. The city of Dallas is the locus classicus for this development. Deeply symbolic of the state of Texas, Dallas, like an oil well, erupts from the land rather than slowly oozing from the water. At the top of the hotel in the Dallas–Fort Worth Airport, there is a lounge surrounded by enormous picture windows. One can look out, as one does in many other similar settings in this nation. In this case, one sees nothing, nothing. Yet catching the cityscape of Dallas by air is an unusual experience. No matter how one approaches Dallas, its appearance is shocking, arising as if out of nowhere. Dallas is a land city, an urban bequest to the interior of America. It defies the loneliness of the plains and seeks to celebrate the land in a way different than ever before. Although water dominates the origin of American cities, it is intriguing to contemplate the metaphors which will feed the land cities, for the earth, the dirt, the plains hold their share of mysteries as well. And the sky, the sky of the land cities, is visible. Despite the reach of the new buildings, the Dallas, Houston, and Tucson sky holds its own. The old cities have no sky. Their citizens are introverted cellar dwellers, looking down and in, or when up, no further than the tops of closely packed buildings. It is novel and exhilarating to be in a major city and still be able to reach for the sky. Still more inviting are the cities of Austin and San Antonio, river cities yet surrounded by land, by vast stretches of openness. In those cities, the river, the sky, and the new buildings make for a scape original in America, powerful and rich in potential poetry.

So much for the possibilities. The actuality is troublesome. Only a few years ago, I was staying at a motel adjacent to the University of Arizona. I asked the bellman directions for visiting the city of Tucson. He warned me, gravely and sternly, of the dangers in such a trip. Rejecting those warnings as endemic to the long-standing myth about cities, I walked a gentle, suburban three miles into the city of Tucson, arriving at 9 P.M. This city of some half-million people was closed; not a light, not a joint, not a person. Stopping a police patrol car, I asked where was it happening? Answer: no happening, no shopping, no action, no nothing. I returned to the dreaded anonymity of my tacky suburban motel.

I close as I open, on the theme of glass without feet. A city, to be a city, must have a downtown. A city, to be a city, must have a residential downtown, a walking place. Pretentious buildings without arcades, without accessibility to the wanderer, the stroller, stifle the very meaning of a city. The contrast between the foreboding office buildings open only from eight to five, and the fancy hotels with their lineup of limousines and airport taxis, on the one hand, and the urine-stained bus stations, on the other, has become an unpleasant reality in the new cities. It is not that we are without historical wisdom. One of the truly great cities of the world, Rome, can teach us how to build a human city. In Rome, the old and the new, the elegant and the proletariat, the monumental and the occasional are married day by day as people of every persuasion, of every ability and every desire, mingle in a quest for the good life. The warning is clear, for those American cities which have abandoned their downtown areas for the ubiquitous external mall have become faceless, soulless blots on the landscape. Neither city nor nature, they are witnesses to the emptiness of contemporary American life. Heed the message; cities are for people, ordinary people who move through both the day and night in the search for nutrition, spiritual and aesthetic nutrition.

It would be ironic folly if the new land cities were to repeat the disasters of the older urban areas. Annexation of suburban land does not resolve the fundamental question of how to build a city. The inner city, downtown, is still the irreplaceable soul of urban life. The city of Houston, a masterpiece of transportation madness, seduced by glass towers dotting the sides of its ugly freeways, sprawling, struggling for identity, has recently looked within. Downtown Houston, as pathetic an area as can be found in a major American city, has become a cause for concern. Houston, alert to its major symbolic role in the new America, now has thoughts about invigorating its inner city. This is encouraging news, and it is to be hoped that the potential success of the city of Houston will be a model for new cities throughout the land. We come to consciousness in the grip of space, time, and touch. Nowhere is this more crucial than in the quality of urban life, where, it turns out, even in the Southwest, even in Texas, most of us live. Let us give the glass towers some feet, so that we may walk about in a genuinely human home, our city.[8]

PART THREE

TURNING

WAITING

Knowing that it
he, she, they
will
come
in time, as before
does not mean
that one, in fact, knows
that it, he, she, they
will
come
this time
for this time
is not before
but not yet
and
the yet
is a vast
hole
from which
by which
because of which
nothing
is promised
as
the promise of
nothing
hangs over
the wait
until
ended by
something.

ELEVEN

WHY BOTHER

Is Life Worth Living? Experience as Pedagogical

We must beware of our penchant to dismiss the cliché phrase, especially posed as a seemingly trite rhetorical question. At first glance, the query as to whether life is worth living strikes us as somewhat routinely jocular, a sort of throwaway question to which one would not expect a reply, let alone an answer. Nonetheless, if we take the question at dead reckoning (pun intended, for the inquiry, after all, is about death—that is, my death) then its seriousness leaps to the fore.

The Question

So, let us ask ourselves, each in turn, is my life worth living? Surely, we must avoid a present-minded response, for at some time, the yin and yang in most of our lives, the only appropriate refrain would have been, to wit: I wish I could die. Yet, even if we extricate ourselves from an immediate personal crisis, an identical plea, justifiably, could be entered. The arrangement of my own death, despite its chilling finality, does bring with it two salient advantages. First, it is a free act and, for that matter, perhaps my only free act, ever. Second, its very finality is also liberating, as in the sadly bravado comment, "Well, I shall not have to put up with that (or anything) anymore." If the reader-listener finds this too lachrymose or riddled with the allegedly nasty vice of systemic despair, I counter by offering a brief diagnosis of what it is to "do" living.

The Setting

The first, foremost, and permanent ontological fact of our human situation is that we were born to live but sure to die. The awareness of this central, irreducible, incontrovertible fact comes to each of us at different times in our lives. For me, being full-blooded Irish-American, the awareness came very early, at age four or five. The setting was traditional, no less than participation in that glorious linguistic piece of self-deception, the "wake." And just why, I would boldly ask, is Aunt Peggy asleep, here in the parlor? I was told that this sleep was necessary if she were to "wake" again, as in the powerful and oft-healing biblical motif, paraphrased as "if the seed does not die, ye shall not have eternal life."

I came to accept that explanation, albeit with the canny dubiety often found in the not-so-virginal mind of a child. And the click of tall glasses filled with rye and ginger created a domestic celebratory atmosphere that could only bode well for the future of Aunt Peggy. It was much later in my life that I became sadly aware that the alcohol was far less a celebratory liquid amulet than an attempt to deaden intractable pain. The searing truth of this reached a crescendo when I drank my way through my father's wake, a pain still throbbing. Some among us believe that in time we shall be redeemed; I do not so believe. Some among us believe that death is au naturel, or, as Marcus Aurelius contends, a sort of spiritual nitrogen cycle, knit by an inexorable and holy bond; I do not so believe. Still others refer to us in our future state of finality as "the grateful dead"; I do not so believe.

Neither you nor I were asked if we were willing to start on this journey. Our conception resulted from the acts of others. Is it not plausible, then, that we may come to resent being told that we must finish a journey begun tychastically by us, willy-nilly as it were. Our opponents charge us with *hubris*, an important Greek word which means "pride," nay "stubborn, self-destructive pride," as testated by Achilles sulking in his tent. My version of *hubris* is that it means the acting out of a perpetual adolescent protest. Yet is *hubris* an accurate description of those of us who have serious doubt about whether life is worth living and who refuse to accept a supine gentility as the appropriate response to mortality? I think not. To the contrary, and paradoxically, I offer that only a response of refusal to accept the righteous character of the inevitability of death can make it possible for life to be worth living.

The Problematic

So much for a general philosophical landscaping. Let us now come closer to hand by means of a phenomenological diagnosis of our "text"—namely, indeed, is life worth living? The term "life" can be only used retrospectively as in "my life," or "if you knew of my life," or "what a life I have had," or "I have no life," or, plaintively, "this is a life?" The term "living," on the other hand, is a process word, a present participle, a happening and a witness to the "specious present." Following John Dewey, we live only at this time and at no other time and so life is an abstraction, perched above our living as a desperate effort to identify ourselves, to become existentially instantiated. Yet the only part of our past which exists is the past that is present to us. And the future is but a "gossamer wing": vapid, elusive, and most always, by far, doomed to be different from the futured intentions of our present.

Our living is not out of something or in something. Nor is it about something, or on behalf of something. Rather, our living is constitutive of our person. Who we are at any moment is precisely our living. Obviously, spatial metaphors fail us here. Analogous to our physiological activity, which goes on always until it stops, forever, so, too, does our personal living proceed inexorably, without respite, without any extrapolation for purpose of an objective view; for that, too, is our living. Our language, especially in its fidelity to a subtle yet pervasive Aristotelean bequest, leads us to believe that stasis, substance, place, thing are where we are, what we hold as if we moved from box to box, external to the flow which courses through us. My version emulates the female body; that is, I see us as uterine, a permeable membrane, eating, breathing, "livening" all the while. For me living is a journey, the origin of which is not of our making. The goals are *en passant* and the end is ontologically tragic, although for many of us, alas, it may be salutary, even, unfortunately, welcome.

The Journey

If it is so that the meaning of the last, ultimate end is unknowable, then at best our human journey involves risk. More, the ultimate end, should there be such, seemingly has no significance for me, personally, at all. The philosophical question as to the "beginning" and the "end," if there be either, and the still deeper question, "Why is there something rather than nothing?" are precisely that, questions: fascinating, intriguing, nagging, perplexing in the sense of Maimonides, yet irresolute. Their obduracy is not due to our failure, thus far, to unlock the argument, but rather to being cast in such a way that however we turn, we face an experiential surd. Whatever else one wishes to say about Parmenides, he is right when he cautions us about the attempt to discuss *nothing*. In rough-house terms, with regard to the ultimate meaning of existence, we do not and cannot have a clue. Does it not follow that a homely question emerges, namely, why bother?

Yes, why bother? Why *should* we live it through to our end? This is a revealingly different question than why *do* we live it through. The answers to the latter question are as old as human consciousness. They appear as brilliant constructs, anthropologically, liturgically articulated and often accompanied by repressive totems, warnings, advice, and claims, none of which have any ultimate certitude. If I do not know the ultimate *meaning* of when, of how, of why, and I am deeply skeptical of the integrity of those efforts to explicate those questions so that I shall behave as cajoled, demanded, or in response to a promise, the most fake of all the attempted resolutions, then, again, our question comes to the fore, why bother?

It may justly be asked that if one does not bother, what else does one do? The answer is very singular and clear. One should commit suicide. Granted that this decision has to be a careful one, for it is the final insulating cut, the permanent withdrawal from the process, from the fray, and the end of hope for a way back in and out. We have no way of knowing whether those among us who have committed suicide have actually made a liberating decision, for the famous and infamous suicide note is always anticipatory. There can be no reportage on the aftermath from the doer of the deed. The assumption here is that the person committing suicide is fully aware of what he or she is doing. It is not true that suicides are "crazy" people, for the latter rarely kill themselves. It is also not true that suicide is necessarily a selfish act in that it leaves behind gaping wounds in the lives of others. Obviously, that can be, and often is, the scenario. Just as often, however, suicide is an act of moral courage and altruism, putting an end to the mayhem and hurt caused by the person who no longer believes that life is worth living. *Straight out, then, living should be a personal choice made over against the existential, viable, often plausible, and certainly liberating option of suicide.* Certainly, to choose to go on living should be more than a response to those quietest of phrases: "life goes on" and "so it goes," "round and round we have it," "as the world turns."

As of this moment, I am living. At one point in the recent past, I chose not to go on living. Before my decision was consummated, I was personally seized and forced to reconsider. Alike with Dax Cowart, a Galveston burn victim, I have mixed feelings about that reprieve. Still, having it granted, I now undertake to ground the decision to go on living, hoping to answer the question, "Is life worth living?" affirmatively. The sentence for which I reach to assist me does not come from the Bible or from the *Te-Tao Ching* or any other spiritual literature. It is from *The Myth of Sisyphus* by Albert Camus and reads, "I want to know if I can live with what I know and only with that." An understanding of the life and thought of Camus, especially as found in his early North African essays, makes it obvious that, for him, "to know" is not to be construed in a narrow, traditionally epistemological way. Knowing for Camus is ringed with ambience and is inclusive of the tacit, the inchoate. In my version, personal knowing is best found in our affective experiences, which, no matter how dangerous, how trivial, never lie. As we feel so do we know. Concepts, set in the brilliant schemata of the philosophers, trail our percepts, wooing them into coherence, correspondence, or, with Ockham, *flatus voci*. As with William James, when faced with the problem of living, I lean to "knowledge by acquaintance" rather than "knowledge about," unless by that latter word one means *to be up and about* or *hanging about.*

The Journey: Suffering as Texture

Now as I decide to bother, both by acquaintance and by "about," I ask myself the question, "Just what is it that is coming at me as I am living in the world?" Is there a message, an utterance, a voice from the logoi of persons, nature, things, and artifacts? As I listen, I hear, for the most part, the voice of unrequited suffering. If one does not believe, as I do not, that in the long run, sub specie aeternitatis, all will be well, be one, be redeemed, or, in the die-cast metaphysics of Las Vegas, even out, then the voice of the unrequited takes on a shrill, chilling, razor-sharp quality. The voice threatens to unseat any and all efforts at equanimity, let alone serenity. Those among us who are reflectively knowledgeable are all too aware of the grisly fact that since the beginning of human history, most persons did the living in a grinding, precarious, and repressed setting. In this century alone, yet to close, despite (or because of) its exquisite technical and scientific accomplishments, more than fifty million people have met death prematurely, violently, vulgarly, even obscenely at the hands and minds of other human beings, chasing one absolute or another due to religion, region, ethnicity, language, skin color, or race. Has life been worth living for those who for decades have suffered under periodic eruptions of attempted genocide, local internecine strife, or—as featured in the twentieth century—worldwide, narcissistic bathing in rampant destruction?

These disasters have not befallen me, thus far. And so, is this jeremiad on behalf of collective, long-standing, seemingly intractable suffering any skin off my nose? Question! To what extent should I allow the suffering of others to affect my version of life's being worth living? The responses to this question are very revelatory as to how we understand ourselves, have ourselves, as it were, as a human living creature, a person. (The ongoing destruction of our ecosystem and our treatment of all living creatures is surely germane to our question but is not of reach in the present context.) One response, callous but widespread, is that the suffering of others is neither our problem nor our concern. A second response—delusive, self-deceptive for me—is that there but for the grace of whatever, whomever, go I. This is a sort of talismanic approach in which the Greek notion of *moira* is transformed into the American notion of luck. Of this, I offer that Descartes was closer to the truth when he flirted with the possible existence of a *mal genie*. The Manicheans were closer still when they posited good and evil in an eternal, irresolute embrace. But did not the Calvinists, terrifying though they be, have it right when they held that some are saved and some are not and the reason is arbitrary?

A more affectionate position, despite its character of self-preservation, holds that we cannot afford (the pun is foreboding) to allow others' suffering to enter into our personal ken because its enormity will paralyze us or render us hopeless. There is again a strand of self-deception here, but this version at least acknowledges that not all is well. The upshot, however, of each of these responses is that we should do nothing or we can do nothing to resolve either the existence or the meaning of collective unrequited suffering.

One further and treacherous rationalization abides in the mind of our own self-styled mandarin class, planet-wide. I refer here to a legitimation of human history by virtue of our collective monuments, historical moments of dazzling heroism, reflective accomplishment, and human creations greater than the sun, the moon, and the earth, as John Keats once wrote. Just how does one reconcile the magnificence of the Pyramids, Angkor Wat, and the Great Wall with how they were built, by whom, and at what human price. Can we afford, spiritually, psychologically, to reflect on the plight of our Irish and Chinese forebears as we Amtrak our way from Chicago to Los Angeles? Do we not then invoke the Spartacus syndrome, forgetting the history of Thrace while thrilling to the courageous, if abortive, rage of one who carries for us just a glimmer of liberating possibility? I have no way out of this masking of the terror of our past. It would seem that Hegel was accurate when he described human history as a slaughter-bench, riven with victims, rescued only in meaning by those "heroes" who epochally embody the *Phenomenologie des Geistes*. And just what do we think, only recently, of the contrast between our being appalled at the potential destruction of the archaeological treasures of ancient Mesopotamia and the also present destruction of the lives of thousands of children, as innocent in that debacle as they have been in all of the pockmarked millenia preceding? Is it not true that deep within us, the cultural remains take precedence, for, after all, they are immortal, whereas the children, like we, are mortal? And so it goes.

The Journey: Amelioration as Nectar

Some decades ago, an unusual refrain was heard over and over as part of a political campaign. After a litany of problems and afflictions, Robert Kennedy would say that "we can do better." This is hardly the stuff of rhetorical flourish, and, yet, the use of the word "better" is a very important choice, for it replaces all of those halcyon words; "cure," "resolution," and those metaphors of comfort, as in to "straighten out" things, make everything "whole"—all on the way to a great society and a new world order. Unfortunately, these are the seeds of cynicism, for as I look over the wreckage of the human historical past, I see no hope for any resolution of anything humanly important. This baleful perspective does not, however, obviate other responses, such as healing, fixing *en passant*, rescuing, and yes, making, doing, having things better. These approaches are actions on behalf of metaphysical amelioration, which holds that finite creatures will *always* be up against it and the best that we can do is to do better.

Yes, I acknowledge that the strategy of amelioration is vacant of the ferocious energizing that comes with commitment to an absolute cause, ever justifiable for some, somewhere, in spite of the nefarious results that most often accompany such political, religious, and social self-righteousness. A moral version of the maxim of Camus, cited above, would read, "can I believe in helping when, sub specie aeternitatis, I hold that there is no ultimate resolution?" Put differently, the original meaning of the ancient medical maxim *primum non nocere* was to "do no harm." How and why did the maxim come to mean "keep the patient alive," at all cost, including the cost of dignity? What is it about us that cannot abide the sacrament of the moment as we reach for a solution, an end game, an explanation, a cure, nay, immortality?

I try as hard as I can to believe that the nectar is in the journey and not in its final destination. I stand with T. S. Eliot, who warns that "for us, there is only the trying. The rest is not our business." Perhaps I can describe my philosophical position as a Stoicism without foundation. Walt Whitman says it for me better than I can say it for myself: "The press of my foot to the earth springs a hundred affections, they scorn the best I do to relate them." For what it is worth—and that, too, is a perilous question—I now believe, shakily, insecurely, and barely, that life is worth living!

A Deweyan Pedagogical Appendix

Now if I choose to "bother," it becomes incumbent upon me to build out from the aforegoing diagnosis. In so doing, I try to leave no stone or thinker unturned in my search for a way to continue the journey, while not becoming unfaithful to my rejection of those traditional moorings which have now lost both their viability and their integrity for me. One version of the human condition that I find wise and energizing is the aesthetic pedagogy of John Dewey. In *Art as Experience*, Dewey issues a profound and yet stern warning with regard to the way in which we have our experiences. The time of consummation is also one of beginning anew. "Any attempt to perpetuate beyond its term the enjoyment attending the time of fulfillment and harmony constitutes withdrawal from the world."[1]

Before we break open this text of Dewey, which comes to us as an alternation between a source of liberation and a dirge, a dies irae, it will be necessary to understand Dewey's quadruple phases of "having an experience": the inchoate, the anaesthetic, the aesthetic, and the consummatory. These appellations of our experience as undergone are not to be taken as hierarchical, nor are they mutually exclusive, one of the other. Actually, the inchoate is always with us and its significance depends on our ability to flush out the hidden ambience that lurks in the everyday, the ordinary, the scene, the sounds, the smell, the feel, the dreams, the rich symbolic hinting as present in our time passing. To the contrary, an experience as consummatory is rare, whereas the aesthetic and anaesthetic versions of our experience are pervasive, a sort of systolic-diastolic rhythm in our personal living.

Taking these phases now in turn, what can we say of the inchoate as characteristic of our aesthetic sensibility? We each carry with us, subcutaneously, as Dewey would say, *all* of our experiences ever undergone. To retrieve them we have obvious activities, such as memory, and more determined attempts, such as retrospection. We are also subject to flashbacks, startling intrusions from our past into our present consciousness. At times, we can trace the relational netting that gave rise to these eruptions but at other times their origins are vague, unknown, as if they were self-propelled from our past into our present. What is startling and pedagogically crucial about our experience of the inchoate is that when it makes an appearance in our consciousness, we realize the originating power and the surprising novelty of experiences we once "had" and yet of which we were unaware in our daily consciousness. I offer as an instance that if we were to recollect a place in which we had spent long and intensive personal time—a home, a neighborhood, a city, a work-site—and then asked ourselves just what do we miss, the response is often jolting. Deep beneath and ambient to the layers of our everyday consciousness there resides and abides the inchoate fabric that subtly penetrated all that we did, thought, and underwent in that previous time and place.

Some years after moving from the sensorially rich environs of New York City to the, comparatively, profoundly sparse location of south-central Texas, I asked myself, what do I miss? Immediately, a flood of obvious, no-longer-present events and stimuli came to mind. Yet, in truth, I did not seem to miss them in a deeply sad and lachrymose way. Pressing further, the real loss came to the fore of my awareness—namely, the omnipresence of water. For forty-five years, I had lived and worked on the island of Manhattan and on Long Island, surrounded by rivers, a sound, and, most of all, the great Atlantic Ocean. When in New York City, this water presence, remarkably, was taken for granted and its deepest significance was inchoate. When in Texas, the absence of the water forced its earlier presence to "surface" and, paradoxically yet helpfully, I nostalgically brought its healing character to bear on my new life and situation.

Each of us, in our own way, can have access to the inchoateness of our past. I now find that by retrieving these heretofore vague experiences, I am able to thicken the frame of my person such that the possibility of spiritual nutrition is enhanced.[2] Striating everything we do, think, and in all of our experiencing are the crossover rhythms of the aesthetic and the anaesthetic. The former, for Dewey, is quite straightforward, a living-on-the-edge. He compares it to the ever-alert nostrils of a fine animal, whose quivers anticipate and attend the slightest perturbation. To be aesthetically alive is to be touched when we touch, and to allow each of our experiences to bathe us, penetrating our affective response and transforming all that we have experienced, no matter how distant from our present consciousness.

Yet, as Martin Buber wisely warned us, we have a melancholy fate in our inability to sustain a relationship that is sacred, with the world of "Thou." Often, very often, we find ourselves insensate and drifting in the world of "it." For Dewey, the abiding and notorious enemy is the humdrum, the routine, which lulls us into patterns of autonomic response such that experiencing becomes numb. The anaesthetic will cause the self-fulfilling nadir of inanition. Long before the spate of medical literature on the pathology of clinical depression, Dewey accurately diagnosed the perils which await us when we sever ourselves from the messagings of the everyday, the ordinary, from the indigenous aesthetic rhythm allowing our experiences to speak directly to us. A person knows that a negative answer awaits the question, why bother?, when even one's things—precious, personal things—no longer speak, no longer resonate, no longer matter. To the contrary, when a person is open to the multiple voices of experiences, inclusive of the apparently inert presence of things, the inchoate and the riot of sounds and colors, nutrition is at work such that one, indeed, might decide to bother.

Now as we pay increasing attention to the aesthetic rhythm of how we have our experiences, the possibility of profound enrichment emerges, called by Dewey "consummatory" experiences. They are not of the run of experience, even aesthetically undergone. Rather they are constituted as special, as *an* experience set off in verve, in implication, in sheer delight, in ambience, and in exquisite intensity. For some consummatory experiences we may prepare, while knowing full well the risk of failure and the collapse of our anticipation, our expectation, our thick, promissory dream. A second, ludic origin of consummatory experiences may be simply one of surprise. The only preparation here, although it is indispensable, is that we live our lives as always aware of the symbolic nuance that accompanies all of our experiences and we remain ever on watch for even the slightest novelty in the message. Further, to the extent that we allow ourselves to hope for that moment which sings uniquely—and to us, immediately, then significantly—such moments will occur with frequency.

Consummatory experiences may be large, even gigantic, in input, as, for instance, our presence at the winning, overtime goal in the Stanley Cup, or singularly personal, as in the surprise announcement that our underachieving child has been admitted to medical school. Or these consummations may be of a cameo nature, a chance meeting with a never-forgotten but long-lost friend. Or, again, serendipitously coming upon a once-treasured love letter or the return of our favorite bird from its winter habitat. Still, as Dewey has warned us in the text above, these consummations have their appropriate duration and then they, as we, in time cease to be. We cannot and should not attempt to string out a consummatory experience beyond its own distinctive presence and rhythm in our life. To do so will be an act of spiritual necrophilia as we try to suck life from the frayed, desiccated husks of once-glorious experiences. To know when to stop is as demanding a need as to know when to start. Consequently, it is the journey which yields the nectar. To ask of our journey that it yield surety as to its meaning other than its meaning *en passant* is to court spiritual arrogance. In time, the arrogance is sure to self-destruct, and then sets in for us the ultimate spiritual disease: cynicism. When cynicism arrives, the question, why bother?, is not only unaddressed, it is not asked. We close down and become helpless, hapless, and mean-spirited.

The thought of John Dewey does not answer the question, why bother?, in any peremptory or stentorian way. The question, however, pervades his life and his work. Of one thing we can be sure; for Dewey, cynicism is not a creative option but a deadening one. Pedagogically, it is salutary to teach ourselves, others, and especially the children that it is not necessary to have certitude in order for a person to live a meaningful life. It is a hallmark of the thought of C. S. Peirce, William James, and John Dewey that the risk of failure is attendant upon forays into the future. Our lives are riddled with the presence of the tychastic and no probability theory, however sophisticated, will obviate the persistence of that strand in all we do. And Dewey is especially helpful in his denotation of the ever-pervasive rhythm existent between the stable and precarious generic traits of existence.

Possibility cuts both ways, for it can be foreboding or enriching. Yet we have no guarantee of which direction our possibilities shall take. In short, we move slowly hand over hand, reading the consequences of our actions and our thoughts as they emerge in the crucible of existential experience. I tell myself to savor the nectar and bury the dross. And even when I founder in so doing, I do not fail to tell that to my children, to my grandchildren, and to my students. If the nectar is not in the journey, where else could it possibly be?

TWELVE

ILL-AT-EASE

The Natural Travail of Ontological Disconnectedness

Preamble

I am grateful for the honor and privilege of delivering the Annual Patrick Romanell Address. One accepts the invitation with alacrity and then, faced with the task of beginning to compose a text for such an auspicious occasion, insecurity sets in. One soon becomes, as it were, "ill-at-ease." Perhaps, taking a leaf from Kierkegaard, I should address my listener, herewith my reader, *der Einzelner*, directly. Given that I have to say something, do I tell you a story, as in "Grandpa, tell us a story." Which story, little ones? There are so many stories to tell. Tell us the one that has you falling through Grandma's ceiling, plummeting to the floor below, startling all of us, most of all, you. Good story, yet too blunt, too crass, and it lacks rhetorical flourish, verbal polish and, so, is inappropriate for this occasion. On reflection, most of my stories turn out to be inappropriate for any audience other than a few trusted companioning souls.

Well then, how about starting with a text, an epigraph. Such a beginning would provide me and the listener a sort of locus from which we can *eject*, or further; such a text would enable each of us to *conject*. The dreamers among us can *traject*, playing with their respective fantasies as I speak. The personally intense listeners can render our text a *subject* or turn it to an *object*, as in, I *object*. And, given that this performance is to be in a philosophical vein, tradition allows that the response individually and even collectively, alas, could be simply to *reject*.

Even though my intended literary lily-pond now seems to be faced with this series of respondent piranha fish, I push on. Ah! The text. Would it not be appropriate to begin with an excision from the codex of the philosophical tradition on nature, the *De rerum natura* of Lucretius?

> [A]ugescunt aliae gentes, aliae minuuntur,
> inque breui spatio mutantur saecla animantum
> et quasi cursores uitai lampada tradunt. (Book 11, 77–79)[1]

> The nations wax, the nations wane away; in a brief
> space the generations pass. And like to runners hand
> the lamp of life one unto another.

How could any start be more salutary than to begin with a text warning of cyclic inevitability, and yet affirming generational continuity, and in an affectionate way no less? Still, as soon as I begin to address the meaning of this text by Lucretius, there arises from within me still another ancient text, this from *The Meditations* of Marcus Aurelius: "life is a warfare and a stranger's sojourn, and after fame is oblivion" (Book 2, 17).[2] Surely, these two texts will take us in very different directions, and although moral and spiritual syncretists will find compatibility, I think not. Being torn between them brings to mind still another text, that of St. Augustine, who diagnoses our situation, or is it better called our "plight," as one which features an *irrequitur cor*, a restless heart.[3] For Augustine, the ultimate future can be salvific, for we can rest in a "Thee." Yet, for others, such a restlessness reveals what Martin Buber calls "the exalted melancholy of our fate,"[4] an oscillation between the poles of the sacred and the profane, between the enhanced and the obvious, a rhythm seemingly natural, intractable. Is this restlessness a harbinger of liberation or is it a malady, endemic to nature, when humanly had, as in you and me?

I could, of course, render this "melancholy" in a more terrifying way if I invoked a text of Nietzsche, who warns us that "since Copernicus man has been rolling from the center toward X."[5] He subsequently adumbrates that prophecy by claiming that we are "slipping farther and farther away from the center into—what? Into nothingness? Into a *penetrating* sense of his [our] nothingness?"[6] Nietzsche's subsequent remark that this sense "has been the straightest route to the *old* ideal" is not sufficiently cheering.[7] Consequently, I hark back to the death-bed lament of St. Francis of Assisi, who tells us that if he had it to do over, he would have loved brother ass more.[8] Now that is a text with which I can do something. But I shall not!

Lest I find myself ending at the beginning or beginning at the end, trapped in the circle set for us by the morbidly playful James Joyce of *Finnegans Wake*, I now make my move. Taking as my spiritual canopy the jeremiad of John Dewey in *Experience and Nature* that, in fact, I find myself "living in an aleatory world" and, forthwith, my "existence involves, to put it baldly, a gamble,"[9] I hereby invoke as my epigraphs three penetrating lines from William James, all found, startlingly, in one paragraph: "whatever separateness is actually experienced is not overcome, it stays and counts as separateness to the end. . . . Experience itself, taken at large, can grow by its edges. . . . Life is in the transitions."[10] Epigraph behind me, although it shall surface *en passant*, I turn now to the text itself.

I. Starting: In and Out

In the periwinkle of my life, now into its seventh decade, I am more bemused than mused by its never-ending foibles, dead-ends, and broken promises, some of which, alas, are mine.[11] Further, deeper, my response to the phrase and book of the same name (1913) of Miguel de Unamuno, "The Tragic Sense of Life" (*Del sentimiento trágico de la vida* . . .), cloaking as it does irreducibly tragic events, has moved from outrage, to inner rage, to a Jansenist softening brought on by incomprehensibility rather than by any appeal to the dodge of sub specie aeternitatis.

This is not to say that inanition is omnipresent, only frequently so. My determined, life-long attempt to find and absorb nutrition, spiritual and metaphysical nutrition, too often resembles the sidewinder drilling of the stubborn and lonely oil rigs that dot my local Texas landscape, erupting as they do from the acres of blossoming cotton and sorghum plants. In this quest, the experience of joy is epiphenomenal as in a phenomenal epic had fleetingly, occasionally, by me and, I suspect, by most of us.

Obviously, from the beginning of this journey, seemingly without a *terminus ad quem*, traveling companions, on occasion, would bite the dust, as did my friend young Lenihan, who was seized by polio at the age of eighteen in 1950, then took to an iron-lung in a brief respiratory respite before expiring—dying, that is. Of late, however, and the sad pun is intended, my journeying accomplices are vanishing with a frequency that is foretelling. Only this last July of 1993, did we lose the powerful and abiding presence of R. W. Sleeper. He was a philosophical naturalist of integral marrow and stripe, an authentic Yankee icon, steeped in Emerson and Dewey, who was slain by *adeno carcinoma*, naturing run wild. I spoke to Ralph on his deathbed as he clutched pieces of an overdue correspondence relative to an obligation for an essay on the thought of John Dewey. Groping through the morphine, palliating and yet a clear sign of his very near demise, he begged me to bail him out. I did, I am, and I shall. His last moments with me had him insisting that my wife, Patricia, now view his field of lilies, seen from the window to have been lovingly planted and nurtured so that all of us could have naturing exquisite.

Just what, then, is the significance of the relationship of naturing as carcinogenic and naturing as exquisite? Do they need each other, as the Manicheans contend? Is this what Spinoza meant by *natura naturans* and *natura naturata*, such that the done, the dying, the dead must follow the doing, the living? I do not know! Still, I must carry on, even if only to dally on or to tarry on. So I do.

II. Ill-at-Ease

It could be that a brief interlude here will be of assistance; namely, just what, in plain style, do I mean by my title, "Ill-at-Ease: The Natural Travail of Ontological Disconnectedness"? Quite simply put, it comes to this. I take as assumptive the direct experiential identity of the quality of our personal sensitivity and the correspondent thickness of our being ill-at-ease. Following the metaphor of Wilhelm Reich, if we did not "armor" ourselves, somewhat, we would find ourselves awash in stimuli far beyond our capacity to absorb. In fact, William James claims that we sensorially filter up to 90 percent of the stimuli which come at us, so that we rarely hear what we hear, see what we see, or touch what we touch. Yet we tell ourselves, of a person or an event, that "there is more there than meets the eye," and we urge ourselves to listen hard so that we "get" all of it. By the way, did you get it? Nonetheless, there is always something left over or left out and rather than our playing a Stradivarius violin to render the experiential acoustics of our living, we seem more to fiddle around, fiddle with, and, in the long run, just fiddle.

This mismatch between what we *can* get, physiologically, and what, in sum, we *do* get, consciously, causes us to be ill-at-ease, for we are living in a transaction that promises more than it delivers. The "educators" among us say that knowledge will obviate this gap, but knowledge is not *Verstehen*, and, as William James cautioned, "knowledge about" often denies immediacy. Rather than acquiring knowledge, the task is to learn how to eat experience, reflectively.

When the endemic state of ill-at-ease is given a jolt so that we now *have something*, for example, cancer, AIDS, or, again recently, tuberculosis, we say that we have a "dis-ease." The diagnosis is often frightening, yet the nomination is also often relieving. One thinks here of Alice James, who for many years took to her bed, neurasthenic and hypochondriacal, yet without a proper designation for her being systemically and functionally ill-at-ease. In May of 1891, she was diagnosed as having terminal cancer of the breast and of the liver. In her *Diary* on May 31, she writes: "Ever since I have been ill, I have longed and longed for some palpable disease, no matter how conventionally dreadful a label it might have." When informed of her "label," cancer, she tells us on June 1 of the "enormous relief" of this "uncompromising verdict, lifting us out of the formless vague and setting us within the very heart of the sustaining concrete."[12]

Alice James knew the difference between "ill-at-ease" and "dis-ease." For her, to be ill-at-ease was far more painful to her person than to be racked with a dis-ease afflicting her body. Try as we might, under the banner of the implacable and determined march of high medical technology, we can only postpone, stem the tide, temporarily detour the inevitable outcome of our disease, whatever it be named along the way. Its real, unchanging name is "mortality," and, medicine notwithstanding, it is natural. Dying is known to us, and we struggle to face it, manage it, deny it, or shrug it away as but a bad dream. Death, however, is beyond our ken. That, we do not understand. Consequently, the ongoing natural travail of being in the world demands our reflective attention. In my judgment—fed, fueled, and sustained by my personal experience—the core of natural travail traces to our being ontologically disconnected. Despite being orthographically and sonorously homely, I use "ontological" rather than the lovely word "metaphysical" because ontology is hard-boiled, of the bottom, and when the stakes are high, I look below. In short, the ontological is what we face—have, when, as we say, all is said and done. Or, when queried, we look up or look down and say, "I have nothing to say." Is not the fundamental question of ontology that which asks, does it work?

When I was a little boy, I would ask my father or my uncles, they of rich and favored memory, if they could fix something. Sometimes it was for them, sometimes for us, and sometimes for me—as in "just me." Whatever, however, a tire, a wheel bearing on the old Nash, a balky toilet bowl, or, most important, a crooked bicycle rim in need of "trueing."

My question to them was quite simple and direct. Can you fix it? Will it work? If the answer was yes, then, *rara avis*, anticipatory joy and familial pride seeped through my body. More often, the answer was "I do not know" or "we shall see," usually accompanied by the remonstrance, "You have to be patient." Occasionally, and dramatically for a little boy—of which, in more than one way, I still am—the answer would be no! To which I would say, can we buy a new one, a replacement? No! They do not make them any more and, further, the time being the dark days of the depressioned 1930s, we have no money. Well then, I implored, can you jerry-rig it, just for now, just for today, just for tonight, just for me? Can't you please do something, anything? No! We are licked. It doesn't work, and it won't work.

Now, I do not want to rain, excessively and hurtfully, on anyone's rationalizing and self-explanatory parade, yet I must offer that experiential evidence points to the baleful assumption that, insofar as our being human naturals, we find ourselves in a situation which, in its most profound sense, *does not work.* In short, I believe that the being of being is to be disconnected, ontologically adrift, casting a net here, a hook there, and all the while confusing a strategy with a solution. I realize that this position runs counter to most of the history of philosophy and virtually all of the history of theology. Also, I am aware that this can be read as a telling departure from the radically empirical, pragmatic metaphysics of James and Dewey. Certainly it would appall those who hold to the conservative metaphysics of Peirce. And, yes, it is Camus who is speaking here, the Camus who wants to know if he "can live with what I know and with that alone" and the Camus who tells us that for him, suicide is the "one truly serious philosophical problem."[13] More, it is the Camus of the early essays, for whom the naturals of sun, sand, and sweat speak for themselves, needing no further raison d'être.

Surely, given the living assumption just sketched, it is encumbent upon me to acknowledge that it is but a position, an angle of vision, or, better, a philosophical trampoline from which I can reach, bounce, gyrate, and, perhaps, to which I can return and on which I can intermittently land. It is, of course, given, that like an errant projectile, I miss and splat, just as the eschatologically confident paraders pass me by, moving on to one Valhalla or another. So be it! I never warmed to the Pascalian wager, for to eliminate risk is to die unworthy of the journey.

Contrary to the view of most respondents to the above position—namely, the contention that philosophically shies away, is chary of, or simply denies even the potential existence of ultimate intelligibility—one does not have to be a lone ranger, a solitary thinker, in order to bring to bear philosophical reflection on the meaning of life. Being a cultural and philosophical historicist, I hold that although it is unquestionably necessary to understand the intentions and conclusions of the historical thinker in the irreducible fabric of his or her cultural setting, it does not follow that one cannot appropriate that wisdom as a way, a Tao, for a cultural setting far different, far removed, as is mine and yours, from that of theirs. Thereby, I read the history of philosophy as a long prose poem, evoking the extraordinary, brilliant, provocative and contentious efforts to work out speculatively what does not work experientially—namely, totality, finality, or answers, once and for all.

The oft-spoken idiom reads, "what you see is what you get." Following Kant, for whom everything that is known is known *in aliquo modo*, I change that idiom to read, "what you get is how you see it." The shift from "what" to "how" is both pedagogically and philosophically crucial to the present discussion. If one were to read the history of philosophy as a "how to make sense" rather than "to make sense of a what," we could avoid absolutes of every kind and eliminate the offensive effort of each generation seeking to obsolete its past.[14]

Is not this precisely what William James means when he writes "the only meaning of essence is teleological"? In short, essences are "weapons of the mind."[15] Is not this a way to read the *Eidai* of Plato, the *ousia* of Aristotle, and the *essentia* of Aquinas? When Darwin entitles his work *Origin of Species*—that is, the medieval philosophical word *species*, or *essentia*—are we not being asked to cast an ancient insight into a profoundly different but yet continuous mode of discourse? When I make an effort to teach my grandson, James, how to pick up a contemporary instantiation of Mark Twain's jumping frog, molecular biology, however accurate, is of no help. The problem is clearly resolvable only by a knowledge of some primitive taxonomy. You pick up the frog with a deft placing of your fingers around his legs. That is a "natural" for as long as there have been frogs, which, we are told, has been forever. Although I do believe there to be "separateness to the end," and I do not believe in the possibility of ultimate intelligibility, or that, in the long run, so far as human naturals are concerned, it to work, I still take as a personal and philosophical obligation to seek ways of coping, ameliorating, and understanding in the short run.

Beginning here once again, I ask myself, what is it for me to be in the world as a natural, that is, as a creature? I take everything that we do—our activities, attitudes, and actions—as natural. They may be deleterious, baleful, self-destructive, and, for a variety of reasons, countermanding of one or more assumptions, mores, laws, or styles of whatever social and cultural matrix we inhabit. We cannot say with impunity that "anything goes," but we do know that in the eonic history of the kingdom of naturing, at one time or another, for one creature or another, everything and anything has "gone." It might help if we were to invoke the basic assumption of both Aristotle and Freud by repeating as a daily mantra that, ineluctably, we exist as *bodies*, as naturals.

As I have written elsewhere, "being in the world is not a cakewalk,"[16] although gratefully, it can have its celebratory perturbations and interpolations. If not a cakewalk, neither is it, for most of us, a walk on the wild side. Rather, the walk in the world turns out to be mostly a trudge, with occasional interstitial eruptions and an all-too-habitual tendency to live vicariously through the mediated ersatz reportage of persons and events "in the news," as we are fond of saying.

Our lives do not have to be that way and certainly that way is not a Tao. I think here of the opening stanzas of Walt Whitman's *Leaves of Grass*, wherein he asks of us that we "get at the meaning of poems."[17] In response to a question asked by a child—"what is the grass?"— Whitman offers that he does not know, and then ruminates on this or that possibility, moving from the affectionate "guess" that "the grass is itself a child" to the metaphysical version of the ancient nitrogen cycle of the Stoics: namely, that the grass "seems to me the beautiful uncut hair of graves."[18] Both hunches seem right to me, and they are reminiscent of our earlier attempt to grasp the hydra-head of naturing.

Others come upon us as we walk in the world. Most often the greeting is apparently benign, a routine "how are you?" Actually and strictly speaking, we cannot answer this, for it would involve our telling how it is that we came to be the being who we are, or at least think we are. Watch out for that question, the one which we turn on ourselves by asking, "who am I?" Have you ever thought about how we walk in and through the world and that it seems less that we are doing the walk and more that we are carrying someone along who is doing it. Please notice that I am talking about walking and not about talking. For the most part, we own up to our talking but less so to our walking.

At times the initiating response of another person to our presence is accosting or dazzling in its recognition. Of the thousands of such greetings, I offer you but two, each symbolically rich, as we ferret out the meaning of our journey. The first goes like this: "My God, you look awful." Unless we are clinically and masochistically hypochondriacal, our response is immediate, armoring, walling, and denying. We say, "who, me?" A second and far more cheering greeting of our presence has someone say to us, "Hey there, you with the stars in your eyes . . ." To which we respond coyly, "me?" I trust that both of these encounters are in your existential memory. If the first has not happened to you, the odds are that in time, it will. As for the second, I certainly hope that it happens, and happens again and again. I see these little vignettes as instances of experiential neighbors, transacting with us as poles of possibility, ever-present, circling around us, penetrating us as if they were a dance of a Texas turkey vulture and a plumed peacock.

I take it that this eternal yet not infinite dance was meant by Whitman in his double answer to the child. Once again, we have the oscillation between naturing exquisite and naturing carcinogenic. No dead, no grass. So say I to the child: listen, little one, if you wish to come unto your own, pay attention, look at, think about, both how and where you are taking this walk. Like breadcrumbs in the forest, signs abound to help. Do not forget, however, the warning of Heraclitus, who as an ancient, reflective dew-line wondered why if the Logos speaks, we are unable to understand.[19] Of the many signs extant in this walk of ours, after some painful misreading, I now find three of these signs to be of singular help, to be fortuitous, and to be the least capable of miring us in self-deception, the most vaunted and dangerous of our opponents. These signs function integrally for us because they are not clear; in fact, they are experiential paradoxes. On this walk, watch, then, for the sign that announces nature as ethereal and beneficent, yet also maleficent. Watch also for the one that says spiritual loneliness is the only way to grasp the meaning and the nectar of a journeying community. Third, pay special attention to the surprising admonition that surprises come to those who create situations in which they are welcome. Of course, what I have in mind here are patterns of amelioration, healing *en passant*. This has nothing to do with ultimate salvation, for such a belief wrecks the possibility of authentic nectaring during our journey. Nor can these signs—or any others, of which there are many—totally obviate our being ill-at-ease, for our disconnectedness is ontological and incurable.

III. Nature as Ethereal, Beneficent, and Maleficent

Controverting centuries of received opinion and dogmatic judgment, I offer that the most powerfully prescient work in the history of Christian theology is the *Periphyseon* of Johannes Scotus Eriugena. Unhappily translated into Latin as *De divisione naturae*, and subsequently into English as *The Division of Nature*, the title indicates a sort of wooden scaffold, a logical schema imposed on the mysterious utterances of the Neoplatonists, especially Pseudo-Dionysius. Eriugena, however, was not Porphyry, and the *Periphyseon* is not a logical manifold. To the contrary, it is a masterpiece of relational metaphysics, and it long ago tipped me off to the abiding confluence of the Augustinian tradition and the American philosophers of experience and nature, especially Emerson, James, and Dewey.[20] In Book 4 of the *Periphyseon*, Eriugena speaks of his treatise as "our physiology," and I understand his title to mean "on the phasing of nature"—that is, a discussion of the contention that everything is in some way everything else, a sort of, shall we say it, *perceptual entailment.*[21]

William James would have no difficulty with this physiological metaphysics of Eriugena, for himself a physiologist, James wrote: "There can *be* no difference anywhere that doesn't *make* a difference elsewhere—no difference in abstract truth that doesn't express itself in a difference in concrete fact and in conduct consequent upon that fact imposed on somebody, somehow, somewhere and somewhen."[22] The theological ramifications of this position of Eriugena are quite profound and for many, unsettling, for it leads to what I take should be the orthodox view of Christianity, namely, pantheism. Continuing the parallel, this is also intriguingly close to what William James means by "The Compounding of Consciousness" in his last major work, *A Pluralistic Universe.*[23]

For Eriugena, the relationship between the created, the uncreated, the creating and the uncreating is bound together by the abiding presence of the Divine Ideas, read by me as reflective energies. Each of these phasings of Nature is entwined with the other such that if one stops speaking, all go silent. Notably, the metaphysical lattice-work invoked by Eriugena is not ontological—that is, in utter, ultimate place—but rather, in his own word, "physiological," irreducibly organic. What we have here in the *Periphyseon* of Eriugena is eternal transactional making, chattering, doing and losing. As human naturals we appear, Neoplatonically participate, and then disappear. Hegel was not the first to diagnose our situation in these accurate, albeit for him more morose and baleful, terms.

In the present context, a more obviously secular vein, I offer that the rhythmic transactions of nature can never be isolated into hierarchies, sheerly negative and positive poles, or be had by us in a moral anthropomorphism, as if somehow Nature, writ large, had us in mind. It, he, she does not award us any privileged place. Certainly it is pro forma, especially in an elocutory situation as is the present occasion, to wax eloquent about the plumaging of nature. I, too, have had my fair share of rhapsodic moments when in the presence of natural grandeur, the awesome and the splendidly fey. Coming upon the Rocky Mountains for the first time as they jagged their way high, high above the soft, flat plains of eastern Colorado; winding my way around the Grand Tetons; coursing through the allegedly sparse but actually flora-rich Mojave Desert; and training through the stubborn sluices of the upper Missouri. I have crossed and recrossed the vertebrate of America, our Mississippi, countless times and never fail liturgically to place hands and feet in its unpredictable flow, mostly benign but capable, as we now know, of a savage roiling. Yes, I, too, as you, have been present, caught up, done in, amazed, frightened by naturing in its snowing, deserting, oceaning, mountaining, lakeing, fogging, rivering, raining, sunning and mooning. It is doubtless that these comings and goings of naturing frequently have an ethereal quality, one which enables us, in an embodied way, to transcend our obviousness, our being sucked into the humdrum. Such natural events provide adventure to the adventureless.

How does it go? A bird on the wing, a furtive cat on the window box, a snake in the sun, and the omnipresent urinary lovemaking by a dog to a fencepost. At times our transaction rivets us in a way that is supremely convincing that although we are natural, equivalently of nature as are the creatures, still we are, shall we say, at a distinctive disadvantage. I recall having a conversation with a black leopard in the San Diego Zoo. My opening gambit was affectionate, genial, and admiring of both her prance and her silky coat. She did not act out, roar, or otherwise be unpleasant. This leopard simply looked me in the eye and raised her upper lip: not a snarl and not a waft, just a statement revealing two incisors that meant business. I froze and decided that I shall not invite my leopard to our next dinner party. Still more memorable is the encounter with a black bear in Yellowstone National Park. At that instant, I learned both the phylastic and experiential difference between a domestic animal and a wild animal. The difference is incalculable and serious, that is, having to do with the genesis of terror.

As we are fond of saying, nature has its way, which is something of a quietist natural theology, an attitude of resignation. Of recent vintage, there is much talk of "androcentrism" and its pernicious role in the destruction of our ecosystem. No doubt the deep-ecology, "green" critique of our long history, now frighteningly revved to dangerous heights, of our trashing the planetary, and even astral, environment is on the mark. I caution, however, that this diagnosis is but one side of the debacle. Surely, one has to grant that nature is beneficent and provisionary of our sustenance as human naturals. The frequent experience of nature as ethereal awards to this beneficence a still further quality deserving of admiration, affection, and, historically, even adoration. Once again, however, there is more here than meets the eye, or, as my ninety-year-old mother has been saying for all of my sixty-two years, he, she (nature) says more than its prayers.

If we take at dead-reckoning, as I do, the inevitability of our own death to mean that our future-time prospect is zero, non-existent, then I believe that we must come to grips with nature as also maleficent. How else can we describe a journey in which succulent berries alternately feed us and poison us? The ocean is truly an ethereal phenomenon, yet some of us swim, some of us bob, and some of us drown.

Many years ago, traveling through the Sunflower State of Kansas, I was taken by the distant appearance of an authentic Dorothy-in-Oz–sized tornado. Deeply charred in color, this outburst of naturing was funneling, sporting a seductive tail as it hovered over the land and cityscape, a conical, cyclonic marauder. This image I have before me today as vividly as thirty years ago. I then went on my way, having a storied memory, a romance with nature, safely ensconced elsewhere in its beneficence. Some decades later, the unfortunate souls of the persons of Wichita Falls, in the Longhorn State of Texas, also saw a tornado. No romance this time, for the tornado visited with a vengeance, flattening the city and bequeathing carnage of every stripe. We could continue indefinitely with these rotations of meaning when faced with the erupting instances of naturing. How, for example, does the soft rain of an Irish mist become the violent, raging water of the Irish West Coast bringing about the endless parade of grieving "Riders to the Sea"? Further, is that mist of Ireland behind the monsoon burial of the people on the coastal edges of Bangladesh? Why is it that at the very same time the Mississippi River rises from its haunching banks, smashing our poor levees, flooding millions of acres of arable, human-sustaining land, Texas croaks in the parched and cracked soil of a drought? Do the Mississippi River and the Texas sun ever have a conversation with each other? Maybe they do; that would be even more worrisome, for then naturing could turn out to be a Cartesian *mal genie*.

Mutatis mutandis, we might cast a similar net of paradox over other imposing dramatis personae of naturing. I have in mind those natural events that, when undergone on behalf of a human setting, can only be said to have run wild. Under such consideration could be the less-than-benign arrival of blizzards, hurricanes, volcanoes, visiting meteors, and, above all, the sneaky one, the earthquake, certainly the most "unsettling" natural disaster of all. (Why, by the way, do we call these eruptings of nature "disasters"? Etymologically, at least, the issue is clear; "disaster" means the activity of a bad, irascible, misbehaving, even nasty, star. Does this call for a reworking of our earlier lyric line, "you with the stars in your eyes," so that on occasion we hear, "you with the 'disaster' in your eyes"? Is not that what the Italians mean by the *mal occhio*, or by those who, when steeped in guilt, say, "don't look at me that way!")

Let us return to the quixotic threat from under our feet, the stealth bomber that cruises very slowly within the crust of what appears as the solidity of the planet Earth, an earthquake. We say that some of us live on top of a "fault," called the San Andreas, the Santa Susana, or the New Madras, among other appellations. Why do we call this situation that results from the restless play of naturing inside our earth a "fault"? Whose fault is it? Did I do that? Did you do that? Who did that? Own up, whose fault is this fault? Not mine!

In the above litany of natural disasters, the one which most sustains my claim of our ontological disconnectedness is precisely that of the earthquake. My son David, who was on scene at San Francisco's last major earthquake and is presently an environmental officer with the Peace Corps amid the jungles and volcanoes of the Kingdom of Tonga in the South Pacific, a master ecologist and naturalist, a very tough guy who has lived domestically with tarantulas, water moccasins, and a giant boa constrictor, said to me: "Dad, it was weird! I was scared! I never felt so disconnected." Other interviewees of my acquaintance, even if their experience was only due to tremors, say exactly the same. The opening of the ground under our feet deeply counters our abiding religious and spiritual expectation that our final journey will be up and out, that is, to the above. We feel comfortable with the seemingly seamless garment of the astral, the heavens.[24] Contrariwise, to be plunged below, as the very grounding of our person drops into the crevice of a renting and rending earth, causes in us the distinctively abject terror of being permanently lost, out of sight, buried alive. I recall as a child that the most vivid and frightening expectation had by me and my childhood friends was to find ourselves in quicksand, which in retrospect has all of the characteristics, softly had, of an earthquake.

Suddenly, I hear you say, hold it John J. These reports from the fielding of nature are too ominous. Rather, take us for a stroll through the sylphing glen that loafs beneath the high piney woods. Look up and see the early twilight dancing in shafting ribbons deflecting and reflecting a cone, a thistle, a branch, and, finally, an elongated proud trunk. That move is more than fine with me, for I, too, have my share of "biophilia,"[25] the term used by Edward O. Wilson, the leading proponent, ironically, of sociobiology. Unfortunately, however, I am not finished with this philosophical probe into the Janus face of naturing.

My earlier admonition about berries succulent and berries poisoning, the pleasing and the nefarious, was not a throw-away line. Pressing it further, the performance of a single berry could be either, both, or neither, dependent on which creatures partake, and, for that matter, dependent as well on a partaking by the same creature in a different state of physiological activity, readiness, or lack thereof. William James knows of this possibility when he tells us of "the self-same piece of experience taken twice over in different contexts,"[26] and when he asserts, "There is no property ABSOLUTELY essential to any one thing."[27] From this perspective, can we offer another play on the aforementioned idiom, which now turns out to say, "what we get is who we are, at that time." Your time may not be my time, and the berry time may not be the time for either of us. Some berry time may not at any time be for us. It may be curtain time. Should we blame the berries?

I do not mean to pick on the berries, nor do I hold that so far as naturing is concerned, we are in the hands of a potential *mal genie*. Nor do I say here that I believe in the existence of a conscious nature writ large which means or intends to do us harm. Prior to what John Dewey refers to as the appearing of "warranted assertions" of human "funded experiences," I think it would be accurate to describe and diagnose our natural transaction with nature as initially a form of Russian roulette. The pangs, pains, and tragedy of our historically hardscrabble experience with the things and affairings of nature, as subjected to "creative intelligence," again evoking Dewey, led us to a very careful and cautious inventory of the revolving roulette chambers, looking for those that we can pull with impunity. Slowly, we advanced to those diagnoses of nature's presence that enabled us to pull the chambers on behalf of healing, balming rather than embalming. One thinks here of the roots, plants, bark, and, yes, (even at least some) of the berries.

The strategy of caution and the search for ameliorative naturals lasted until the nineteenth century—in the advanced world, that is. At that time we began a program of curing by the method now known as *scorching* the earth. We started this policy for reasons still difficult to discern. Was it willy-nilly, conspiratorial, ecologically masochistic, or merely a lay-over from Original Sin? Whichever, whatever possessed us to refill the roulette chambers with live, nasty bullets? A DDT cartridge here, an asbestos blanket there, and on through herbicides, pesticides, PCBs, toxins and a canopy of strontium 90. I take the covering word, pesticide, as a metaphor describing the recent "helping" past. Does it not seem strange to use a "-cide" word, for its congeners are extraordinarily dangerous; matricide, patricide, egocide, suicide, and ecocide. Quite simply, "-cide" means "to kill," too often indiscriminately and transiently by "fall-out," or by the subsequent permutations of naturing.

I was only thirty when, in 1962, a woman wrote something which said to me, John J., you and yours are in for trouble. How so, Miss Carson? It is so because you are facing a *Silent Spring*.[28] The discovery of North American DDT in fish residing in the seas which shore the distant Pacific Ocean of the Far East should have taught us that when set into motion, we cannot control the randomness of even well-intentioned ecological violence. What comes to mind here is the execrable but revealing line of the Papal Legate during the Inquisitional crushing of the Albigenses in the early thirteenth century. When asked whether the Catholics should be spared, and, if so, how would we know their identity, his response was chillingly and instructively clear. "Kill them all, for God knows his own."[29] Releasing toxins, of whatever chemical bonding and for whatever reason, is a no-search but yet a destroy mission, with the flora and fauna of the planet identical to the hapless believers trapped inside the onslaught directed to the Cathari of Albi in medieval southern France.

Lest these baleful ruminations about the planet Earth, inclusive of oceans, ozone layers, and other vast natural phenomena, cause the listener to fog over, drift away, and self-counsel that this is too much, too big, and anyway not my existential affair, I turn to closer, more intimate quarters. More than a decade ago, when confronted with the sudden erupting of naturing in a frightening way—namely, the presence of gynecological cancer in the body of a deeply loved one—I took to finding out how this went, what was up, so to speak. Learning the then-used nomenclature of malignancy—or is it the malignant nomenclature of our fate?[30]—I came to know the stages on cancer's way; dysplasia, severe dysplasia, carcinoma in situ, and metastasis, the last one signaling fatality. I innocently asked the oncologist, himself brilliant, caring, and a superb gynecological surgeon, why did not our bodies, specifically our fighting and protecting cells, come to the rescue as these stages progressed, from the dysplasing—that is, misbehaving—cells to the roaming killer cells of metastasis? Were our good cells overmatched? No, he answered. It appears rather that they lay out, that is, they do not seem to give a damn. I found this contention to be quite remarkable, and I pondered its implications for many years. At first, I had great difficulty in squaring my romantic view of naturing and my abiding trust in the good will of our bodies with the now-obvious presence of human cells variously described as "wise guys," lazy, indifferent, cowardly, hapless, or adolescently petulant.

This disquiet within me lasted for several years until I came upon the far-more-disquieting yet clarifying phenomenon of HIV, the Human Immunodeficiency Virus, known globally as AIDS: Acquired Immune Deficiency Syndrome.[31] Simply put, a virus, originating in Latin as a slimy liquid or poison, is an organism composed mainly of nucleic acid within a protein coat and it acts differently at each of two stages in its life-cycle. In the one stage, the virus is free and infectious and does not carry out the functions of other living cells. In the other stage, the virus enters a living organism, whether it be a plant, animal, or bacterial cell, and then makes use of the host to replicate itself. That appears quite straightforward and helps us to understand the studied, repetitive vagueness of that frequent and frustrating medical diagnosism, "you probably have caught a virus." To which diagnosis is usually added the attempted healing phrase, "wait it out," and the efforted, conflicting re-mark, "it is going around." This latter piece of information tries to cre-ate a passive community brought together by the presence of the communicable. It was never clear to me when given these personal, fam-ily, and especially pediatric diagnoses that such uninvited visitations of our viral neighbors constituted the presence of a disease. But, then, has that not been the lineage of long-standing diagnostic punting, found over and over in answer to our plaintive complaint, "I feel lousy"? The "diagnosis" comes in as "you have a cold" (the single most mysterious word in the English language) or subsequently, it is probably the flu, and recently, it's a virus; "they" say it is going "around."[32]

The arrival of the AIDS virus has put an end to any innocence that we might still have with regard to the embattled character of our entwin-ing with the affairings of nature. The AIDS virus has two distinctively distressing and, as it turns out, deadly characteristics. First, its coat is a masquerade, blinding us to both its early presence and its intentions. Strictly speaking, as of the present (1994), I should not use the singular for this virus and its misleading coat, for we now know of at least six variations of the viral presence, of which, at this time, we test only for one. The second characteristic of the AIDS virus is that its docking place is in those very blood cells, the T cells, which have been called out to repel and destroy the intruder. Too late! The AIDS virus penetrates the membrane of the T cell, then takes off its coat and goes to work subverting our T cells in many nefarious ways, only one of which is the final destruction of the T cell itself. Replicating itself, the AIDS virus seditiously produces aberrant host-cell behavior, soon to generate dangerous pathologies. In time, our T cells drop from many hundreds (as measured in absolute numbers of cells per volume of blood) to below 200 and, finally, into "double digits" as the pronouncement is made on behalf of the presence in the patient of "full-blown AIDS." I have visited with a dying AIDS patient who had but six T cells, as measured above, still functioning. He died within that week.

Now if we hold up here for a brief, reflective time and think of this disease anthropomorphically, which is the only way that I know how to think, it turns out something like this. Somehow, somewhere, somewhen, someway this virus shows up, and it turns out to be a con man. Further, this conning, cunning virus figures out just how to accomplish its mission of destruction by choosing the entry to our bloodstreaming bodies that is the second most frequented, the second most needed, and, most tellingly, the one which is fraught with the energy of headless passion—namely, the orificial openings of human sexuality. Only the mouth, the opening for nutrition, takes precedence in frequency, but it has the major advantage of controlling that which enters, and even has alternatives for entering: for example, intravenously. To the contrary, the sexual entrances are circumscribed, proscribed, and without alternatives. Is it possible that our AIDS virus remembers its Latin and works off the phrase *occasio furem facit* (opportunity makes the thief)? Further, upon entry, this con man has the venal foresight to cut the phone line, dismantle the burglar alarm, and force its hosts into a process by which they victimize themselves, a claim sustained by recent scientific investigation, which contends it is precisely the response of our immune system that drives the AIDS virus from its hosting cover and sets it free for maleficent activity. As Hegel once said of history, and as is now said of alcoholism, the major diagnostic word here is *cunning*.

Does it occur to you that what we have described here is not a fair fight? Does it not seem apparent that this conflict is not taking place on a level playing field? In fact, is not this playing field in reality a killing field, hosted by none less than ourselves? I think that the answer to each of these questions is a lachrymose yes! I think also that whatever comes of the battle against AIDS, it is clear that the meaning of nature is not, on a priori terms, beneficent. Rather, as we say, it all depends.

A time ago, when adoring one of my six grandchildren, this one Damon, then five, I queried rhetorically and publicly, I wonder what his future will bring? His father, my son-in-law, a physician of note, answered dourly and resignedly that Damon's only problem will be to reach age forty without falling victim to AIDS. When I was little, I did not think that way. When my five children were little, none of us thought that way. What is it to think that way?

IV. Loneliness

The upshot of what I have offered here thus far is that when all is said and done, when the bread is baked, the car is fixed, the plane arrives, and whoever says yes to one deep, pleading question or another, I am still ontologically alone. For me, to be alone, to experience systemically my self-consciousness as implacably one of "loneliness," is not to evoke the geometric method, nor is it to be trapped in a "spatial metaphysics" so incisively deprecated by Maurice Blondel. I am not referring to loneliness or describing loneliness as "being alone," as one, as only one, with no one else near and hereby. Rather than holding loneliness to be the result of absenting, of something gone or as not having come, I see loneliness as a palpable, thick, even aggressive, presence in each of our personal worlds: in short, the personal space of our embodied, yet ontologically disconnected, selves. Actually, if we were to be self-diagnostically honest (no small feat, that), I believe that we would own up to the presence of the Augustinian *irrequitur cor* as omnipresent and incurable.[33]

Obviously, we are not without our resources, strategies of coping, cleaning, placing, making, fixing, changing, rendering aesthetically, observing, cataloguing, and moves desperate, searching for a hook, hoping for a reef, a landfall, a preserver, or, best of all, a friend, a trustworthy friend. Do you have a friend? The etiology and morphology of the AIDS virus taken as symbolic of the wider fabric of naturing has sustained my hunch that our being-in-the-world is a masterpiece of attempting to overcome our melancholy fate, one stated baldly as follows: having evolved to being human naturals, we now find that we do not belong—we are ontologically homeless. There may be a naturing reason for this situation, but I rather think that Camus has it right: "Man is the only creature who refuses to be what he is."[34] If that is so, and I believe it to be so, then my suggestion is that we relocate our point of departure. Instead of coming to consciousness under the assumption that we "belong" and have to deal with things and events that go awry, we proceed, rather, under the assumption that we do not belong and therefore must work to make the best of our situation, such that things and events will here, there, sometime, and somewhere be celebratory, occasions for joy. In this vein, the diagnosis would run something like this.

We do not fit into the world as a Lego piece or a Lincoln Log. In fact, I believe that we have no *special* place in the organic constituency of nature. Our consciousness, so different, so extraordinary, so bizarre, especially in its dream state, is a marvelous and pockmarked perturbation of the conic history of DNA. Following Dewey, we are in, of, and about nature.[35] We are nature's creature, its consciousness, its conscience, however miscreant and quixotic; its organizer, namer, definer, and defiler; a transient in search of a needful, probably unrealizable, final consummation. The human organism is surrounded, permeated, and contexted by both the natural and social environment. In speaking of William James's doctrine of the self as a relational manifold, John E. Smith writes, "Radical empiricism is a radically new account of how the self penetrates and is penetrated by the world."[36] This penetration is not without its rhythmic threats, as John Dewey warns:

> Man finds himself living in an aleatory world; his existence involves, to put it baldly, a gamble. The world is a scene of risk; it is uncertain, unstable, uncannily unstable. Its dangers are irregular, inconstant, not to be counted upon as to their times and seasons. Although persistent, they are sporadic, episodic. It is darkest just before dawn; pride goes before a fall; the moment of greatest prosperity is the moment most charged with ill-omen, most opportune for the evil eye. Plague, famine, failure of crops, disease, death, defeat in battle are

always just around the corner, and so are abundance, strength, victory, festival and song. Luck is proverbially both good and bad in its
distributions. The sacred and the accursed are potentialities of the
same situation; and there is no category of things which has not embodied the sacred and the accursed: persons, words, places, times,
directions in space, stones, winds, animals, stars.[37]

The way in which the human self abides in the world is an extraordinarily complex affair. The self projects itself into the world. The self constructs a personal world, a habitation.[38] The self, when threatened,
retreats, even attempts to eject from the world, a form of dropping out.
The rhythm of these transactions is often lost in the macroscopic setting
of getting through the day. The algorithmic subtleties of our movements, shifts in attitude, and construction, deconstruction, setting, shifting, and bypassing of barriers are often buried in the frequently graceless
syntax of duties, obligations, and habituations. So typical are our routines that the virtually infinite number of plans, plots, and variations in
the rhythm of our bodily movements are lost to our attention. Recent
investigations in biochemistry, especially in the human liver and in cell
surfaces and molecular biology, reveal an utterly amazing transacting
network. The electron microscope has revealed a dazzling array of complexity in an endless chain of relationships. The human skin is a battleground of bacteria colonies—symbiotic, voracious, and with long
memories—as found in the unerring recurrence of dermatitis, repeatedly appearing on an isolated finger or toe, over and again.[39]

The embodied happenings of the everyday, our affectings, skinnings,
dreamings—some comforting, some discomforting—allow us to feel
connected, or at least so we tell ourselves. Yet should we come at our
loneliness from the back side, that is, our missings, the truth may out.
To miss is to be lonely, to be alone, even, perhaps more so, in a crowd.
It is to be without, to be adrift while yet stationary. For us, when lonely,
it is as if "I can't get started," I cannot get it together, and I have a
pervasive sense of separateness, of disconnectedness. I am out of place,
I am no place, I am nowhere, I am nobody, no one, although as seen by
others I am here, there. That they see me whereas I do not see myself
gives me an eerie pain of discomfort. Not only is something, someone
missing, but I am missing from myself as others have me.

To miss is to be in a state of spiritual hunger. It is not so much that we do not have personal food as that the food, for us, is not nutritional. Or again, still more baleful, the spiritual food we have is potentially nutritious, but we do not have the capacity to make the *conversion*. We may eat the world and yet are not sated. We become more of a viaduct than an organism. That is why we seek "company"—etymologically, to be "with bread," the stuff, the staff of life, of nutrition. We may receive nutrition from flora and fauna, from the bugs, the birds, the animals, the ferns, the weeds, the water—always the water—in which we frolic, into which we dive, for fun, for alleged mastery, for suicide. The water which feeds us, calms us, frightens us, drowns us—the water as deep, as grave and as a grave, as a home for creatures, strange, mysterious, and now, in a temporary halt, recession, but someday to wash over us, to wash us away, to take us back to our first home, the uterine fluids of our mother.

Further, although we do not seem to be aware in the same way, systemic loneliness is due also to the separation from our things. Such a separation is obviously severe when it is spatial, as in our things are somewhere else or, tragically, when we are ripped from them as we are forced to flee. Yet more subtly, it can also be severe when we are still in the presence of our things if we do not let them speak to us, or if when they speak, we shut them off and refuse to hear their comforting words.[40]

As with all human experiences, our loneliness finds itself wrapped around a time-space matrix. For most, time and space are taken as naturals, the fabric, the very meaning of nature. Following Immanuel Kant, and may I add, modern physics, I demur. Rather, time and space are imposed human constructs by which we live our mortal, emboxed, natural lives. Nonetheless, whatever may be the potentially resolute physics and metaphysics of this matter, I believe that the following phenomenological diagnosis holds.

Is the space I am "in" my space (as in being someplace), my place, or is the space alien space? The same space can be comforting and alien dependent on its peopling (as in a hotel after a convention—the loss of faces, community, common endeavor, bonds assumed without having to be publicly articulated); or when the space is transformed by light, or lack thereof, or sound, or smell; or when the space is mobile, as in an automobile or a train, constantly visited by shifts—some dramatic, some prosaic—all telling, such that my experience of my present space is a flighting, a process, forcing me to claim and reclaim my place in this ever-changing space, despite its apparent stasis. The domestication of space—as in a hotel room, a picnic ground, a shelter, a long train ride or bus ride—tells of our ability to build any thing and every thing into our bodies such that it, they, become aspects of our inner, personal space. The inability to domesticate our space, to turn it into an embodied, personal place, is a sign of severe, unwanted disconnectedness, and it foretells our experience of loneliness no matter where we are or what is happening around us, by us, or to us. I would extrapolate even further and claim that to be simply in and of the world is to be able to participate in a panoply of shifting spatial contours, facades, depths, alleys, heights, and reaches. Loneliness appears when this panoply fades into a sameness resulting in the irony that the absence of difference thereby structures not recognition (habituation in any positive sense) but rather bequeaths an aloneness, a desiccated, second-hand person, alone with himself or herself.

The second matrix in and through which we live, move, and have our being is time, the inevitable source of our erosion and the harbinger of our death, our dismissal from the journey. To escape from this insistent, persistent presence which appears in microseconds, we adopt strategies, all of which cut us off from nutrition and are contrary to the salvation we seek. All too often, we find ourselves in one bunker or another, and once again, despite our best effort, lonely. For example, some of us retreat into a vicious nostalgia, whereby the past takes on a glow that it never had in its present and seduces us into living our lives backward. Increasingly the present loses its reality, and we become tied to a chimera, with our experiences being lived both vicariously and by hindsight. When we are reminded of the unreality of our nostalgia, we become defensive and further enlarge our dependence on a past which never happened and which prevents us from experiencing our own present. In effect, we have dropped out and back, isolating us from continuous nutrition and trapping us in a world that cannot be understood or shared by anyone else. We become our own glass menagerie.

Some others of us deny the call of the present by entering into the seduction of a projected future, laced with the deep, although most often unrequited, nostrum that "things will get better." In the meantime, we either hunker down, waiting for forces other than our own to propel us or even to rescue us, or we tint every experience with its alleged future-time prospect, in the hope, most often vain, that things will (must?) get better. In both strategies, the present has no feet, no past, for that disappears into a redeeming, albeit vague, future. And, further, the power of the present, the existential moment, has no bite, for we are always waiting for something else, something different, something better—a wait which is futile, for only the experience of the present can lead to a viable future. And now we understand why the great originating antique cultures believed in the cycle, historical and natural. If everything which goes around comes around, then all of the existential worries that I lamentably describe herein become vapid, a no-go, of no existential import. Is not this the proffered personal peace of the *Te-Tao Ching*, as given to us by Lao-tzu?[41]

In all of our previous remarks, especially those which diagnose our spatial and temporal context, the danger is involuntary disconnectedness. To disconnect *voluntarily* is not to be lonely, for in such a decision, we affirm the process most congenial, and the forced absence is on behalf of our building, kneading, constructing, and creating. Conversely, to be disconnected without our personal approbation is to risk self-deception as to the worth of that with which we are left. The message here is that loneliness is a given; it is our ontological state of being human. We must fight it by forging contexts, situations, and attitudes, each of which opens us to possibilities not given to simply being here or there. I do not accept the Scholastic philosophical maxim that *actus sequitur esse. Sed contra*, I offer that in and through our relating, our experiencing is no less than who we are. As human naturals, we must listen carefully and warily to both the consonant and dissonant voices of naturing. We are both fed and destroyed by nature. The natural rhythm for being in the world is more akin to a rollercoaster than to a hammock. At the very least, we should watch for what is behind our back, whether it be bacterial, viral, or cyclonic.

V. Surprise

Do not fret. This is but the voice of one turtle. All is not lost. There may be gold in them thar' hills. Surprises abound, if we make ready for them by trimming our system of denial.[42] It is, after all, the philosophical logician and scientist par excellence, C. S. Peirce, who tells us that "experience is our only teacher," and then adds, "how does this action of experience take place? It takes place by a series of surprises."[43]

And so, the dolorous phrase "what's next?" could also be a harbinger of juvenescence, of song, of fragrance, and of healing experiences. When the little ones say to me, "what's next, Grandpa?" I intone the lyrics of Ray Bolger, sung on behalf of being "once in love with Amy": "someday, there will be horseless carriages and stereopticons that fly." That someday is today and, as for tomorrow, on the morrow, I hope to see you around the block.

THIRTEEN

"TURNING" BACKWARD

The Erosion of Moral Sensibility

I have to say that I am aware that my presentation of a stand-up, belt-it-out-in-public lecture at this time has the odor of a troglodyte. We seem to be caught between two depressing "stools" (the pun is intended); the first features the glitz of pop culture, showboat sports, and preening politicians. The second features the dreary databases of academic analyses and in-house jargonic puff. In the first, eros has degenerated into ahistorical sleaze, and, in the second, eros has disappeared. For those among us who believe in intellectual passion rather than settling for intellectual inquiry, I say that we are a remnant and, as such, so be it, for we believe that the integrity of the journey is all that we share so as to live, move, and have our being.

The remarks which follow have as their ambience my having to re-think, and thereby relive, my tried (and assumedly true) assumptions as a result of being savagely derailed from the neat clicking wheels of a life onward and upward. Some ten years ago, having, as they say, bottomed out, I was faced with the other side of the Janus mask directly, asking not just second questions but even third questions. Life, as philosophy, echoing William James, is the habit of always seeing an alternative. A life and person threatening experience (they are not identical—each of us needs both at some time) effects a profound transformation of what one already "knew" to be so but did not "know" to be so. The American poet Wallace Stevens has it best:

> You have a blue guitar
> You do not play things as they are
> . . . Things as they are
> Are changed upon the blue guitar

And so, I offer here, some comments on the obvious, the quotidian, put sufficiently different, I trust, so as to prompt you to ask at least a second question.

Preamble

Remember that in life you ought to behave as at a Banquet.
—Epictetus, *The Enchiridion*, 15

In a relievedly brief vein, I offer here my personal stance as a context for the diagnosis to follow. I am not a Cassandra, who in the *Agamemnon* of Aeschylus, stands in the chariot facing the great doors of the palace which homes the House of Atreus, and issues her prophecy of doom. Although I can be Cassandra-like, especially on the vexing problem of world population, I keep going on in the hope of better times. Conversely, I am not the eighth dwarf who awakes every morning singing, "Hi-Ho, Hi-Ho, it's off to work we go," proceeding to tell us that if you sing all day long, your troubles will go! Work may save, but it can also punish. Consequently, please hear my remarks tonight as neither pessimistic nor optimistic. Rather, take them as melioristic, a sort of moral Dew line, an early (late?) warning system for me and for thee!

In the parlance of medical practice, it is now virtually a truism that compassionate care in the face of serious medical illness requires the presence of a wounded healer. The analogy to the moral question has not been forthcoming but it is pertinent and overdue. I put it this way. Moral pedagogy requires the presence of a "judge-penitent," in the telling phrase of Albert Camus. Different from the self-destructive protagonist of Camus' last novel, *The Fall*, my emphasis is on "penitent," and who among us is not one of those, or one who should admit to being one of those, thereby obviating the besetting sin of casting the stone. Moral outrage frequently masks systemic hypocrisy. See, for example, the official rhetoric during the war in Vietnam, in which the moral posturing on behalf of democracy was in fact a cover-up for jingoistic scapegoating. Try one closer to our time, that is, now, alas. Many ill veterans of the Gulf War have been accosted with the moralistic attitude that they are actually hypochondriacal and medical malingerers. Despite these bravado pronouncements from paragons of official *dissemblement*, with each passing day it becomes both startling and obvious that once again the public moral take is but a smokescreen, blocking us from the malodorous underbelly. Put directly, the word in question is not "dissembling." It is "lying." There is a difference and, once more, if you have lied, you know what I mean. (For every gloss here, I am just as aware as you that there exist exceptions. They are just that, exceptions. Further they are used in the manipulative form of co-optation, namely, to throw us off track, off the scent. It is the bad faith of an appeal to bootstrapping by those who have no such experience.)

It goes something like this, or, with Kurt Vonnegut, "and so it goes." Hey there, John J., have you ever done anything wrong? Have you ever flouted, flaunted, trashed, ignored, or violated the moral law? First response: Who me? Not me? Second response, well, perhaps, a time or two. Third response, yes, big time. Now, and only now, can I suggest that there may be a better way. To sustain this proposal of the wounded moralist, you reach for St. Augustine who offers to the infinite God that "if we had not sinned, you would not have loved us." Or you can appeal to the antique and deeply Christian moral tradition of the *felix culpa*, the happy fault which sees sin as the way to grace. A more recent invocation would be that of John Dewey, for whom we lived by the funded experiences of our personal and collective historical past, learning equally from the negative and damaging. Whatever, however, the paradox is that unless I say I am sorry, unless I apologize, I am not in any position to offer advice, let alone wallow in moral outrage. (Parenthetically, I trust that you have noticed this form of authorial confessional critique is noticeably absent in the long history of ethical theory.)

So, having said that I am sorry on more than one occasion, I set forth on the text in hand.

The American Setting: A Tale

I was a young child in the bleak decade of the American 1930s. Three of my grandparents were dead. My paternal grandfather was buried on the nasty January day that I was born in 1932. My remaining grandparent was my maternal grandmother, known in our family as Nana. Widowed at an early age, with three young children, she made a living for them by scrubbing fire-house floors and sewing men's ties. She was a follower of the New York Giants of John McGraw and a whiz at pinochle. My entire extended family was shanty Irish. We had nothing, except the American dream, Irish style.

I correct myself, for I should not say "nothing." For the shanty Irish did manage to obtain, grab, or perhaps even purloin one precious possession, lace curtains, to be had no doubt in defiance of our often offensive and patronizing peers, the lace-curtain Irish. My Nana had such a set of curtains. Each spring they would be ceremoniously washed, starched, and tacked to a long, nail-pronged stretcher. For decades, I helped to do that. And then, as she failed in strength, I did them for her. Some thirty years ago, when she was in her eighties, I said to her, "time for the curtains." Nana replied, not this year. What! Why not? They were *threadbare*. A stretch was beyond their reach. They would fray and the threads would unravel, spinning dizzily out of control, dangling footless, homeless, gnomic, and pathetically lonely, each and all of them, lonely together. Nana Kelly was dead within the year.

I think here of America, our "strand" of hope and I ask, do we still have that long-standing, self-announcing confidence in our ability to meet and match our foes, of any and every stripe—political, economic, natural, and, above all, spiritual—arising from without and within our commonwealth? I do not ask this as a rhetorical question but rather one of direct, existential contemporaneity, the intention of which is to elicit an equally direct response. For most of my life, even through the turbulent and bewildering decade of the 1960s, I would answer, yes. Subsequently, my reply became halting and had the cloak of "maybe" about it. Of late, I carry with me, resonant of many others among us, a lamentable dubiety about whether, in fact, we are still able to tap that eros of community, which has served us so well for the past three centuries.

This dubiety does not trace to events so much as to mood. To be sure, events such as the Oklahoma City bombing and the precipitous rise in acts of violence as traceable to the increasing presence of estrangement, and ontological rather than functional frustration, is of central moment. The issue in question, however, cuts deeper and may presage our having lost the capacity to rework and reconstitute the viability of a pluralistic and mosaic communal fabric which, in truth, is simply quintessential if we are to survive as a nation.

Taking heed of botanical and physiological metaphors, far more helpful in telling us what is happening than is the language of logic and conceptual schemas, I hear the following conversations. After an ice storm, a flood, a fire, or just the constant, searing sun of the Texas summer, one asks of the tree, the plant, the bush, or perhaps a tendril or two, can it come back, will it come back? I do not know. There exists a line of viability, for the most part invisible and even, and, despite modern science, mysterious. Cross that line and the leaves wither, announcing the death of the botanical life-form.

So, also, with physiological metaphors. We speak of atrophy, as when a muscle loses its febrility. The common watch in our mediated society is for the rampant, destructive cell, as in cancer. Far more present, however, is the malodorous activity of inanition, wasting away, loss of tone—in short, he, she seems to be failing. In what, of what, we ask? I do not know, just failing, in general. You can tell! The many diseases of the central nervous system carry on by *via negativa*. Neurons do not fire. Cellular messages are not sent, or, if sent, are not received, or, if received, are not heeded, as in the biblical admonition, they who have eyes, but do not see, they who have ears, but do not hear. The terror of addiction and Alzheimer's disease is that we do not know how far to go with it until it is too late and we cannot turn back for a fresh start.

"Turning Backward": The Erosion of Moral Sensibility

It is best to begin by glossing the title. The meaning of "turning" descends from the Jewish notion of *teshuvah*, from the Hebrew, "to recover," as being "in recovery." It is a turn of the heart, not simply of the mind, even if there be such a phenomenon as mind, on its own. A *teshuvah* is not primarily an enlightenment, as when John Dewey first read *The Principles of Psychology* by William James. Nor is it akin to the "dream" of Descartes, or to the separate, but equivalent, intellectually shattering discovery of Kant's *Prolegomena* by Nicholas Berdyaev and Martin Buber. We come closer if we think of the *tolle lege* episode in Augustine's life, or Kierkegaard's decision to "make trouble" as his *Point of View*. Further, we find proximity to a *teshuvah* in William James's reading of Charles Renouvier and patently in Josiah Royce's retrospective version of his defining moment in the mining camp of his California childhood.

Versions of this experience of turning abound in our lives, in yours I hope and trust. I could extemporaneously offer one or more of these "turnings" in the life of each of my children. These events, these explosive stories are transforming of our deepest sensibility and in Spinoza's version, they are constitutive of an *emendatione*, a healing of the preternatural wounds that for some reason come with our coming to consciousness. Lamentably, the *teshuvah* is not necessarily permanent. In the language of addiction-recovery therapy, one can, and often does, relapse. Further, a second turning is difficult to come by, for disappointment, self-abnegation, and skepticism dog the second effort. Still, even given these obstacles, a deep personal struggle can generate a return to the original turning.

At issue here, however, is an event, personal or culturally systemic, which is more foreboding by far and largely unsung, namely, a "turn" backward. This baleful undoing of the moral fabric is unsung because it rarely, if ever, is accompanied by an announcement, a pronouncement, or even an acknowledgment that it has taken place. Actually, the turn backward is a form of spiritual arteriosclerosis, accompanied by a hardening of the heart. The remonstrances of the "everyday" echo here in these "deadening" walls of the chambers of the heart, as in, he has no heart, she is heartless, can't you find it in your heart to, don't you have a heart, please have a heart, they are hard of heart, and, as famously wailed by Jack Haley in his Tin Man persona, "if [they] only had a heart."

The downshot of this hardening of our hearts is the existential instantiation of amorality. This is the Pontius Pilate syndrome, made infamous by Adolph Eichmann and now found planet-wide in response to one or the other frequenting atrocities that pollute the human landscape of our epoch. It is of sour note that even creative moral pedagogy is helpless when faced with amorality. The "turn" backward is most often quite subtle, and instead of being characterized by a decisive and personal-public event, its etiology reflects rather the postcolonic phrase in our title, namely, the erosion of moral sensibility. The word at issue here is "erosion," not "implosion" or "explosion." Erosion is subtle and masks its foreboding of catastrophe. By contemporary example, you can replace millions of coconut trees but you cannot replace any of the Pacific black coral now being foraged for commercial trinkets. In time the island-dwelling merchants of this egregious theft will be under water.

When the eroded is gone, it is gone. Forever? Hard to say for sure, but probably. We ask of others (rarely, of ourselves), will he ever "turn" around? She seems to have "turned" around, but I have my doubts. He, she is hopeless. The recidivist rate in turns of *attitude* is constant, high, and seemingly defiant of moral pedagogy, assuming that such a distinctively human effort still exists other than in isolated precincts of the culture. The present discussion is of moral sensibility and not of ethics. The latter, ethics, in our time has become bowdlerized of the patterns of human affectivity. The teaching of contemporary ethics features the use of wooden case studies often introduced by the hapless phrase, "let us suppose. . . ." Let us suppose she is pregnant; let us suppose you have end-stage renal failure—or pancreatic cancer, or you are HIV-positive—positively. Or let us suppose that you are a clinical alcoholic—who, me? For those of us who have received one or more of these "announcements," among others extant, the use of "suppose" takes on the dull face of abstraction.

The absence of existential, experiential affections in these discussions wilts the eros of imagination and turns the moral question into a game of checkers—or, for self-announced, really smart philosophers, a game of chess. Antique ethics, of whatever culture, the *Analects*, the *Te-Tao Ching*, the *Enchiridion*, and Native American moral pedagogy have ethical prescriptions and proscriptions but they are entailed within a living and affective cultural setting. In the words of Jonathan Edwards, they have to do with "holy practice." One thinks here of the Stoic ethics as found in Book 2 of the *Meditations* by Marcus Aurelius. He tells us that no matter how long we live, even for thousands of years, we live only the life we live. And of that human life, he offers, "the time is a point, and the substance is in a flux, and the perception dull, and the composition of the whole body subject to putrefaction, and the soul a whirl, and fortune hard to divine, and fame a thing devoid of judgment. And, to say all in a word, everything which belongs to the body is a stream, and what belongs to the soul is a dream and vapour, and life is a warfare and a stranger's sojourn, and after fame is oblivion."[1]

Well, what of the Aurelian "take" on being in, of, and about the world? Is this an ethical position? I think not. Rather, it is a matter of attitude, of sensibility. The American apothegm tells us that you cannot legislate morality. Fair enough, but that phrasing is an emptying derivation from the far richer original line of the Roman, Horace: *quid leges sine moribus vanae proficiunt*—that is, no use of idle laws in the absence of moral civics. What could be more enervating to a human life than to have few or no moral affections and at the same time to have parental, familial, societal, and legislated moral dicta hanging around one's neck?

If we were to come clean on the issue, we could ask ourselves who among us makes ethical decisions? Who among us, when faced with the travails of living, seek out ethical principles, weigh the options, and then act? I never did, I don't, and I hope I never do. If we live shallow lives, then we shall act shallowly. If we live deep lives in which the moral question is one of sensibility rather than one of rule, we shall act accordingly. You say, no way. Cannot happen. We have to rein in the instincts. We have to get this straight once and for all. It is said that moral attitudes are too murky. The affective life lacks objectivity. Feelings are not to be trusted. It is said, as well, that there is a clear right and clear wrong and that distinction must prevail in everyone's life (except in my own life). The classic question is, can virtue be taught? My question is, can compassion be taught? The above approach is not an issue of moral pedagogy. To the contrary it is an issue of law and authority, a moral *regula*. Yet, if you peel away this self-righteous rhetoric on behalf of getting things straight on the moral business, once and for all, you look directly into the underlying "attitude," one of cynicism about the possibility of moral sensibility, moral growth, and, above all, moral transformation— that is, the possibility of a "turning." The erosion of this belief in the "turn" is of paramount importance in any diagnosis of contemporary American culture. How has this happened? Why has this happened? How could it be that collectively we seem to have lived the life of the fabled Mr. Jones of the Bob Dylan lyric, around whom the wind was blowing, but he did not know it. So, a word or two here, about the wind.

Losing Our Way

Over against the modus vivendi of affection and compassion, we seem to be slipping into a *modus moriendi*, willing victims of the virus of cynicism in what I think to be an obviating of our once deeply held commitment to the possibility of possibility. If I were to ask the following question, as I frequently do, "How is it with you, America?" or better, "How is it with me, America?", diagnostically I come up with a dolorous intake. It is very important to ask such questions, constantly, for one powerful characteristic of a culture awash in cynicism is the abandonment of self-reflection, let alone self-critique. The need for our doing this intake was nailed to my forehead by a down-home, homely, brief story. While scouring America this last spring and summer, I found myself on Northern Boulevard in Nassau County on Long Island in the state of New York. Not surprisingly, I had left my gas cap at the last filling station. So, in transit, I was delighted to find an old-fashioned auto parts and hardware store. In our transaction, I mentioned—with some rhetorical wonder to the effect, "just what is happening here?"—to "Mr. Hardware" that the night before, some wise guy had keyed the side of my rental car. He said, happens all the time, and last week "they" (who, by the way, are they?) blew up the telephone booths on Northern Boulevard. I was leaving with the ironically cheering news that I was not alone, so to speak, when he opined, "Something has gone wrong along the way." Indeed! And just what has gone wrong such that the way is no longer a Tao, or even a journey, so much as it is the pursuit by a basset hound of the mechanical rabbit. In short, no cigar!

If we were to scan the recent decades of this cluttered trip we are taking—a sort of spiritual MRI of how we have lost our way—I suggest that the following culturally palpable signs, in fact, are mis-directions, deceiving directions, or no directions at all. Every wayfarer should take some time at a wayside so as to reflect upon whence they have come, whither they are heading, and, as they say, how it is going. Well then, how is it going?

First, I believe that we are witnessing the collapse of inherited expectations, especially those which were appropriate only as a shell game or three-card monte. And this holds, whether the expectation emerged from the religious motif, that all will go well for those who love God; the political motif, that democracy will bring both equity and peace; or the economic motif, that in time everyone will have their needs fulfilled. (The tenor of this last motif now has escalated to having our wants fulfilled.) So penetrating in the American psyche were these expectations, they soon began to function as assumptions, or, remarkably, as eschatological, redemptive clots to happen in our very own generation. Surely, however, even the casual observer, let alone those more reflective, cannot fail to see that these promises are bogus. For us, they are broken promises. The ensuing malady comes about in our inversion of the usual phrasing; that is, we see, yet we do not believe. In consequence, we become disconnected from our experiences—from our empirical, affective sensibilities—and continue to chase a chimera. Sorry about this, but we are not going to live forever. More, it is not simply that we shall die. We are going to be zapped out of existence. Non-being awaits us. No, we are not going to be remembered beyond a generation or so, if that. No, America is not eternal. No, the planet Earth is not eternal. Worse, far worse, baseball is no longer a game. It is a business. Of equal pathos, or should we say bathos, the university is no longer a cathedral of learning, a birthing of sensibility. See it rather as a placement center with athletic teams.

And so it goes. How quaint now is the earlier refrain, "Where have all the flowers gone?" or, more forebodingly, "Where do the children play?" Think about that one. As we prep in "expectation" of the global economy for the twenty-first century, hard census data figures reveal that millions of American children do not have sufficient food to eat and are trapped in what can be appropriately called an "ontological" cycle of poverty.

Too strong? I think not. Take some substantial time and monitor all that advertising that comes your way—by print, by radio, by video, by billboard, by the Web and the Internet, by whatever. Does it not promise more than most of us can have, ever? And does not this unctuous farrago of promises have as the thematic hook that we deserve to have, to be, to experience the object of the pitch? Does not this mode of communication move from announcement to expectation and, self-deceivingly, to birthright?

The spiritual message here is crystal clear. As the biblical admonition warns us, in time our foot will slide. Either we become totally consumed by the chase, thereby losing our bearings, our way, or we fail to be requited and turn bitter. Worse still, we become envious and jealous, the most destructive of the human vices.

Second, it is this *ressentiment*, in the language of Nietzsche, which feeds the media frenzy to expose cynically those who are successful in whatever way. If I can't have it, then you can't have it. Bring them down. The time-honored assumption that all of us have feet of clay, are penitents for one reason or another, is now escalated to the judgment (in journalism, I trust you note, there are few penitents) that anyone who steps forward has feet of rotting clay. These naked public figures are then judged retroactively and punished presently. Although a penitent in some areas of my life, I am basically a decent fellow and could conceivably be of some public help. Yet if I were to announce my candidacy for public office, it would not take longer than fifteen minutes and a few phone calls to obtain enough allegedly damaging information sufficient to destroy me, my family, and those close to me. The cynicism here pertains to the erosion of belief in *penitence*, recovery, and growth. The affectionate childhood phrase, "give them another chance," has disappeared under the intentional onslaught on behalf of bringing everyone down.

A third source for this cynicism can be found in the fraying of even the bronze parachutes. We no longer trust the viability of those social programs constructed precisely to prevent our being subject to the catastrophic in our lives. I refer here to the post hoc disappearing pension, the savage inequities in our health-care delivery system, the threat to both Medicare and Social Security, and the terrifying future for an exponentially ever-increasing geriatric population. A word about the latter collective and widespread fear. Retirement homes, well-appointed, are available to the very few who have substantial resources after retirement. We are speaking of at least $30,000 per year. Although there are exceptions, "nursing homes" are often a euphemism for "warehouses." A battle taking place at present between operators of nursing homes and state regulatory officials is revealing. The state of Texas, for example, has banned the use of the antiparanoia drug Haldol from use in nursing homes. The reason is simple and instructive. Haldol was being used, indiscriminately, to render the residents of the nursing homes zombies. This is convenient, but cruel and clearly dehumanizing. Yet without such a drug the trapped, often abandoned, aged population acts out and creates a situation of institutional dysfunction. One might ask, not rhetorically I trust, how did we get ourselves into this situation? Quite directly, it descends from the diagnosis sketched above. If a society is trapped in the chase, those who worked with us and for us are exiled as soon as they are no longer in harness. Most of us live lives as flotsam, carried by forces not of our own making, a sort of second-hand living. When aged, we find ourselves hooked, impaled, or simply wrapped around one jutting stream branch or another, now only jetsam.

Listen to Mary Tyrone in Eugene O'Neill's *Long Day's Journey Into Night*: "But I suppose life has made him like that, and he can't help it. None of us can help things life has done to us. They're done before you realize it, and once they're done they make you do other things until at last everything comes between you and what you'd like to be, and you've lost your true self forever."[2] We should not be surprised at any of this if we focus on the following, startling irony, one mentioned to me by dozens of persons from most walks of life. As we "downsize" personnel, tossing them out on the street, we are asked contemporaneously to celebrate the entailing fact that the stock market is consequently healthier, richer, and, dare I say it, more secure. If that does not generate cynicism, nothing will. For many among us, it does! What we indulge here is a Dow—not a Tao.

These signs have nefarious companions, which I have discussed elsewhere. One could consider the afflictions of public school education: the inequities, the frequent shabbiness, the embattled teachers, the de facto segregation, and the drop-out rate. Or, one could discuss the epidemic facts of mindless violence, and, if I may, the bizarre, and ever more popular, move to legalize concealed weapons. And riding well beneath the surface, yet perilous, nonetheless, is the decades-long failure to maintain our physical and environmental infrastructures: bridges, tunnels, and roads, air and water quality. We seem to be heading, inexorably as it were, toward a bottom, in which we no longer care about the things we care about. One can never claim to care *about* something or someone if they do not care *for* that someone or something. We note a systemic state of personal depression hidden by a pasty smile. In his *Treatise Concerning Religious Affections*, Jonathan Edwards offers twelve signs of conversion. Forebodingly to the contrary, we are moving toward twelve signs of *reversion* to a form of moral acedia, an inner decay.

I tell you a story. When my son, David, was with the Peace Corps in the kingdom of Tonga, a group of islands on the International Date Line in the Pacific Ocean, he had occasion to educate the children in matters environmental. At one point, with the children in the last remaining rain forest on Tongatapu, he told them that their trees had a disease. They were astonished and said, how could that be, Tevita, for there is no industrial pollution of any kind in Tonga. Taking his vaunted knife, David slit open the bark of a tree to show them the fetid presence of disease. He then taught them about acid rain and global wind currents. The decay was hidden but, believe me, palpable and lethal.

At the "Turning"

What to do! Is it too late? Is this DEW-line already hanging shards over a moral landscape which has undergone the tipping phenomenon, the algae of cynicism everywhere? Recall your reading of the opening pages of *The Plague* by Albert Camus. One rat appears and then three rats. The concierge, M. Michel, is adamant, "there weren't no rat here." So begins the plague of Oran. Do you remember that line from your childhood? I *smell a rat*. Think about that line, once again. Think about it. In the face of our denial, the rats revealed that something had gone wrong along the way! Well, now let us make a "turn" ourselves. The above jeremiad is in place. What to do! First, I tell you a story from the life of Martin Buber. After speaking to a group of students in an adult-education program in Jerusalem in 1947, Buber is accosted by one listener, a tough guy, a warrior in those fractious, dangerous early days of modern Israel. The man chided Buber for his seemingly ethereal thoughts and asked, aggressively, how could he possibly be expected to achieve that sensibility, that form of affectionate relations with nature, with persons, and especially with profound ideas. Buber heard this outcry of frustrated rage but did not respond in kind. To the accoster, Buber said simply and directly, "You are really able." You can do it, for you have the strength.

Note that Buber did not chastise this man for his feelings of contempt. He had these feelings. They do not lie. They can, however, be turned around and of that turn, Buber believed him to be "able." Clearly, the task here was to undergo a *teshuva* and the pedagogy was not one of admonition or instruction. The pedagogy was that of the midwife, a mediator, of one who appeals to the dormant, but not dead, energies and strength of the other. Martin Buber assumed to be so what Josiah Royce had written earlier, that "the popular mind is deep and means a thousand times more than it explicitly knows." Buber asks us to live pedagogically in the creative zone of the *zwischenmenschen*, that between each of us, free of manipulation, nominal authority, and patronizing. In effect, can I help you? How can I help? Let me try to help you. And, by the way, can you help me?

The "turn" I question here has to do with the awareness of human fragility, ontologically. Your fragility and my fragility. This gives rise to virtues not of the legalistic type, those falling under the rubric of justice, important though that be, but flowing from *caritas*, which I render as "caring," for and about, with affection. The moral pedagogy would then direct itself to the nurturing of compassion, gratitude, and loyalty. In so doing, we would drop, or at least mute, the acquisitive chase, and so turn toward healing. The assumption here, as I have written elsewhere, is that by the very nature of being human, we are disconnected, personally and systemically lonely, *ontologically*. The pursuit of inherited, societally driven expectations which now characterizes most of our lives, mine included, is a journey without nectar and without an awareness, let alone a celebration of the sacrament of the moment. Proximate goals are necessary and can even be salutary as we forge our own version of being in the world, on this trip. Ultimate goals and goals beyond our reach, beyond our means, beyond our abilities, turn out to be manacles dragging us forward in a manner that causes us to be oblivious to the very experiences we are now having. Following Kafka, as we should, the "castle" of our dreams turns out to be a burrow in which we are self-entombed.

In *The Myth of Sisyphus* (no myth, that), Camus writes "I want to know whether I can live with what I know and with that alone."[3] Subsequently, in *The Rebel*, he tells us that we are the only creatures who refuse to be what we are.[4] What, then, are we? We are creatures in need, ever, always. Josiah Royce has it right. The most dangerous among us is the "detached individual," that person who comes to realize, to say to himself, to herself, "I have nowhere to turn." A person comes to have nowhere to turn if they have "lost the way to turn." Ironically, sadly, threateningly, these detached individuals, lacking a way to turn, then "turn" on others. Why has she "turned" on me? He is "turning" on everyone around him. Why are they "turning" so? It is because they have lost the *way* to "turn."

And given our cultural penchant for obsolescence, it is surprising that, as with most of these depressing cultural trends, there is more here than meets our complaining eye. Although always somewhat characteristic of American society, the nefarious instantiation of obsolescence as a modus vivendi is now both rife and systemic. If I come to consciousness with the belief that if something is out of sync, toss it; or, if I subscribe to the now common attitude that, on the face of it, new is better; or, if my puerile philosophy of history is of the linear vein by which the march forward is cannibalistic, eating its past and hopelessly naive about its future, then I stand bereft of roots, aesthetic comparisons, and, in short, become an "isolated individual" among hordes of "isolated individuals."

Now it is precisely the task of moral pedagogy to assist in having us "turn" toward compassion, affection, gratitude, and loyalty, and away from "turning" backward, scapegoating in response to our journey going sour, as if it must be derivative of false and second-hand expectations. Centuries ago, Jean-Jacques Rousseau told us that if you are not free, then I cannot be free. Recasting this admonition, if I am not compassionate, if I am not loyal, then I cannot expect others to so be. As ye sow, so shall "we" reap. Speaking in November of 1951, to a group of young persons in New York City, Martin Buber said that we were "at the turning." Buber asked:

> Where does the world stand? Is the ax laid to the roots of the trees—as the Jew on the Jordan once said, rightly and yet wrongly, that it was in his day, today, at another turn of the ages? And if it is, what is the condition of the roots themselves? Are they still healthy enough to send fresh sap into the remaining stump and to produce a fresh shoot from it? Can the roots be saved? How can they be saved? Who can save them? In whose charge are they? Let us recognize ourselves: we, in whom, and in whom alone, that mysterious affirmation and negation of civilization—affirmation and negation in one—was implanted at the origin of our existence, we are the keepers of the roots. *We are? How can we become it? How can we become what we are?* [5]

My version of this "turning" was written some thirty years ago as a passage in which I still believe, only more so, with the scars to sustain that belief. Do not await salvation while the parade passes by. Surprise and mystery lurk in our experiencing the obvious, the ordinary. Salvation may be illusory, but salving experiences can occur day by day.

FOURTEEN

THE INEVITABILITY OF OUR OWN DEATH

The Celebration of Time as a Prelude to Disaster

> Their foot shall slide in due time.
>
> —Deuteronomy 32:35

I. Untimely Meditations

How strange, how singular, how unusual is our understanding of death! Each of us claims to know of death, yet our experience is necessarily indirect, vicarious, and at a distance. It is always someone else's death that we experience. Yet the power of that experience of the death of an other is such as to suffuse our very being with an intimacy of awareness, virtually equivalent to our own death. No reader of this chapter has died. Nonetheless, we speak of death as though we knew of which we speak. I do not contravene or even doubt such an assumption. Rather, I ask, how it is possible that a vicarious experience can have such a direct hold on our deepest feelings and our most intense of personal anticipations? My response to this question is unpleasant and unsettling, but it is true. In the test of time, we are all terminal. And that fact, of which history, thus far, has allowed no exceptions, is the most repressed and denied of all facts in the human condition. In turn, it is this repression which makes the formal announcement that a person is terminally ill so devastating. Such an announcement is unnecessarily vulgar, for it acts to separate some of us from others of us in a drastic and absolute way. Yet it is only time which is in question here, for to be terminal is the foreordained future of each of us.

Why have we allowed this situation to develop? The major reason is not cheering to those of us who seek to attribute the best motivations to the activities of human life. It is as though we lived our lives in the context of a global roulette wheel, so that the announcement of someone else's impending death somehow lessened the possibility of ours. David Cole Gordon writes:

> The thought of our finitude and ephemerality is so frightening that we run away from this basic fact of existence, consciously and unconsciously, and proceed through life as though we shall endure forever. When we recognize the inevitability of death by the making out of our wills and buying life insurance, it is as though the wills and the insurance related to someone other than ourselves, and we live our actual life as though death is not likely to touch us. Insofar as we consider the possibility of our own death at all, it is as an event that is as remote as the end of time, and so we tend unconsciously to repress the fear and the fact of our ultimate doom, or consciously to forget it.[1]

This foolhardy version of our own demise is verified by the habituation of our obituary reading. What, for example, are we to make of a recent Associated Press story?

> TROY, N.Y. (AP): The switchboard at the [Troy, N.Y.] *Times Record* was flooded with calls this weekend, many of them from "really irate" citizens wondering what had become of the newspaper's obituaries. Not a single paid death notice or local obituary appeared in the paper Saturday. "Some people accused us of dropping the obituary page altogether," said Frank Dobisky the managing editor. "We haven't. Frankly, it never occurred to me that we should tell our readers that no one had died."

It should have occurred to the obituary editor to state publicly that no one had died. At a minimum, this would have brought reality to bear on the readers for whom only others die.

Irony aside, we have to face this peculiar masking of the inevitability of our own death. It is simply a matter of time passing before this inevitability emerges as personal, existential reality. In the opening lines of her brilliant essay "Illness as Metaphor," Susan Sontag presents the irre-ducibility of our fundamental situation: "Illness is the night-side of life, a more onerous citizenship. Everyone who is born holds dual citizen-ship, in the kingdom of the well and in the kingdom of the sick. Al-though we all prefer to use only the good passport, sooner or later each of us is obliged, at least for a spell, to identify ourselves as citizens of that other place."[2]

Sontag proceeds to discuss the metaphoric versions of two diseases, tuberculosis and cancer, as ones which have acquired the status of sepa-rating them from us, or us from them. Both diseases have been associ-ated with death and a sense of fatalism in those who have been afflicted. Yet tuberculosis is now curable and cancer is under medical siege, with the cure rate, depending on the bodily location, ranging from 1 to 90 percent. Sontag's point, however, and mine as well, is that century by century we seem to need a scapegoat—that is, a disease which, ostensi-bly at least, bears terminality for the rest of us. The invidious compari-son between the terminally ill and the rest of the population, which is a temporary distinction at best, serves no legitimate purpose except to fos-ter alienation, on the one hand, and self-indulgence, on the other.

Let us pursue this question of terminality somewhat further. In addi-tion to the contemporary classic case of terminal cancer, we have a series of euphemistic versions of terminality. No matter what the illness, the physician may say to family and friends that the patient "has no chance." In itself, this is an interesting phrase from the point of view of scientific, allopathic medicine. Or the statement may be that all potential remedies have been exhausted, which in turn leads to the comment that it is now in the hands of whomever or whatever. These last categories embrace religious overbelief, the salvific arm of divine providence, a brace of homeopathic nostrums, or the utilization of banned "miracle" drugs. Each of these in turn are desperate efforts to reverse or forestall the inevitable. With the exception of the occasional instance in which such efforts release hidden energies in the body, they are, for the most part, futile, although pursuing them is profoundly understandable. Even the slightest time gained in these approaches constitutes an important personal victory, for it is not death which is the opponent in these situa-tions. Rather, it is the intrusive finality of the announcement of termi-nality that constitutes the offense against the person. Time gained is a profoundly human advantage set over against the obstreperously public announcement, which summarily and objectively curtails our right to live.

Similarly, I offer that it is precisely this presumptuous seizure of the natural flow of events that is the offensive strand in capital punishment, rather than the asking for death as compensation. Terminality is no more dramatically announced than when a person is sentenced to death at an appointed time and place. The nomenclature of the waiting space is even more vivid: death row. Literature, journalism, and film are especially interested in the event of capital punishment, for they act as our stand-in, enabling us to vicariously grab the power of awarding death from its more traditional sources—nature or, for some, God. Nowhere were the macabre dimensions of the death announcement more pronounced than in the city of Ossining, New York. Formerly, at that city's Sing Sing prison, the activating of the electric chair caused many of the lights in the city to dim, as if much of the citizenry had a hand in bringing about the final moment of a human life.[3]

Still other instances of terminality abound, some of them potential, as in entering a combat zone or participation in daredevil sports. In such activities, the risk of death is an enlarged, and even necessary, specter which hovers over the event itself. The last days of the battles of Bataan and Stalingrad are grim reminders of the imminence of death. A German soldier, awaiting his fate at Stalingrad, writes as follows: "Tomorrow I shall set foot on the last bridge. That is the literary way of saying 'death,' but as you know, I always liked to express things figuratively, because I took pleasure in words and sounds. Give me your hand, so that crossing it won't be so hard."[4]

In all of these instances of terminality, our death is due to forces outside of our control, even if we place ourselves in situations of jeopardy. One type of terminality, however, is of a decidedly different cast. I refer to that most prepossessing and intriguing of human acts: namely, the decision to commit suicide.[5] In so doing, it is we who announce to ourselves our own death. It is we who seize the time, the place, and the means. Modern Western civilization, especially in its Judeo-Christian version, has been largely unsympathetic toward suicide and has placed negative religious and legal sanctions on it. We often work off the naive notion that the act of suicide entails some form of insanity, despite the fact that the certifiably insane rarely kill themselves.

One form of suicide that we tend to indulge somewhat is that of the person who responds to the announcement that he or she has a terminal disease. It is assumed that the reason for suicide in this case is due to the desire to avoid pain. To the contrary, I believe that this decision traces more to the refusal to have one's death announced by others, as though we were innocent bystanders to our own demise. More to the point of our present discussion are those suicides which are neither a response to impending death nor a result of temporary mental aberration. Consider those suicides which are self-conscious and self-possessed human acts designed to articulate a distinctive personal statement. Albert Camus once wrote, "There is but one truly serious philosophical problem, and that is suicide."[6] One can gainsay Camus's claim of singularity, but not his claim of its import. Having played no role in our own coming into being, with all of its attendant cultural, familial, psychosocial, and genetic trappings, it should not strike us as perverse that we seek to preside over our own cessation from being. The most pessimistic version of the interval between our birth and our death is found in the writings of Søren Kierkegaard. "What is reflection? Simply to reflect on these two questions: How did I get into this and how do I get out of it again, how does it end? What is thoughtlessness? To muster everything in order to drown all this about entrance and exit in forgetfulness, to muster everything to re-explain and explain away entrance and exit, simply lost in the interval between the birth-cry and the repetition of this cry when the one who is born expires in the death struggle."[7] This description of the bare bones of our situation is accurate, but it need not be indulged. After all, we can go against the grain. Camus writes, "I want to know whether I can live with what I know and with that alone."[8] And, I argue, it is precisely the integrity of living within the boundaries of such knowledge that can occasion our decision to withdraw from the fray, in our own time and on our own terms. By this reasoning, and I emphasize reasoning, suicide becomes a rejection of a dehumanizing determinism, while simultaneously signaling an existential choice, a true act of human freedom.

William James, for one, saw such a decision in precisely those terms. In the midst of a personal crisis at the age of twenty-eight, he wrote in his diary: "Hitherto, when I have felt like taking a free initiative, like daring to act originally, without carefully waiting for contemplation of the external world to determine all for me, suicide seemed the most manly form to put my daring into."[9] Although many deeply reflective persons have committed suicide and are doing so at this moment, it is important to realize that neither Camus nor James did so. In fact, they developed imaginative and ameliorative strategies for coping with the stark reality of their own defense of the plausibility of suicide. I, too, have some suggestions for a human response to the avoidance of suicide and for dealing with the inevitability of our own death. Before turning to that discussion, however, we must consider a major way in which many persons shun the trauma of death—by belief in some form of salvation or immortality.

I do not refer here to a hope that somehow, somewhere, somewhen all will go well for all of us who are, have been, or will be. Certainly, such a hope is a legitimate and understandable human aspiration. But to convert this hope into a commitment, a knowledge, a settled conviction is to participate in an illegitimate move from possibility to actuality. It's understandable that we wish to escape from peril, but it is unacceptable to translate that desire into an assured belief that we have so escaped. The history of culture has presented many varieties of immortality. Perhaps the most ingenious, although the least plausible, is that of traditional Roman Catholicism, wherein each of us, bodily, is resurrected glorious and immortal or damned and immortal. The attraction here is that our eternal life will be affectively continuous with our mortal life. Other versions of the doctrine of immortality involve claims of reincarnation, metempsychosis, immersion, or absorption, each attempting to perpetuate the me which is me, in one form or another. Obviously, I have no final knowledge of these claims nor do I know of anyone who has. Evidence on their behalf is scanty, scattered, tentative, highly personal, and empirically dubious. Yet many of us cling to one or more of these solutions, as a redoubt, a trump card, or a last-minute reprieve from the overwhelming evidence that we are terminal.

Philosophical, political, and even religious thought of the last century and a half has been characterized by increasing dubiety about the possibility of immortality. Attention also has been given to the complex cultural reasons for the persistence in the belief in immortality, and the explanations are as varied as the doctrine in question. Marx, Freud, the existentialists, Dewey, and Norman O. Brown, among others, have all attempted to account for the persistence of this belief. Brown's version is especially fascinating, for, in his judgment, the quest for immortality is the locus classicus of the human disease. Following the Freud of *Civilization and its Discontents*,[10] Brown contends that our refusal to face our own death (Thanatos) has led us to repress the life force (Eros) in favor of comparatively permanent civilizational monuments. In short, our greatest neurosis is history, through which we attempt to transcend the burdens of time and project ourselves as having meaning beyond our own lives. In this regard, the monument par excellence to our flight from temporality and from finitude is the "having" of children. By that means, we assert our transcendence from the sheerly local and death-bound character of our lives. In so doing, however, we abandon access to the nectar that comes to those who live the life of Eros, hear the call of immediacy, and, as such, for Brown, cease to be human organisms in any profound sense of that meaning. In his chapter "Death, Time and Eternity," he writes:

> If death gives life individuality and if man is the organism which re-presses death, then man is the organism which represses his own individuality. Then our proud views of humanity as a species endowed with an individuality denied to lower animals turns out to be wrong. The lilies of the field have it because they take no thought of the morrow, and we do not. Lower organisms live the life proper to their species; their individuality consists in their being concrete embodiments of the essence of their species in a particular life which ends in death.[11]

Here, we have the height of irony, for in our effort to transcend the life of the lower organisms, we fail to realize even the level of Eros, wallowing rather in a self-deceptive flight from the burden of time passing.[12]

Brown's prescription for overcoming this false transcendence, this escape into self-deception, is complex and personally radical. At this point, I bypass the details of his resolution in order to say, quite directly, that, in my judgment, he asks us to marry our own death. He cautions against a preening narcissism, in which we take ourselves too literally, as well as against the fruitless flight from the temporal, the immediate, and transient Eros. At some point in our life, the sooner the better, we should confront the inevitability of our own death and absorb this awareness into the most active forefront of our consciousness. The message is clear and twofold: avoid the temptation to invest in meaning which transcends our own experience of the life-cycle; and affirm the imminence of death as the gateway to an unrepressed life in which the moment sings its own song, in its own way, once and once only.

Although I regard Brown's critique of immortality as devastating, his resolution in *Life Against Death*, and again in *Love's Body*,[13] is beyond the pale of possibility for all but the heroic figure, the person who lives perpetually on the horizon, on the furthest edge of each and every experience. The fundamental question is whether there is a median way between the self-deception of personal immortality, on the one hand, and the radical commitment to the moment, on the other. If we live within the bowels of the temporal process, can we not have also a sense of the future, a sense which does not delude us into thinking that we have transcended time? Put directly, can we experience ourselves as terminal and yet live creative, probing, building lives which, nonetheless, ask for no guarantees and for no ultimate significance to be attributed to our endeavor? I, for one, believe that we can live this way; nay, I believe that it is *only* in this way that we live a distinctively human life. In fact, I offer that a life lived consciously in the shadow of our own death is one which can prehend the scents of the most subtle of messages—namely, those intended only for creatures who risk living within the rhythm of time. With such an attitude, categories basic to human life and understanding undergo a change in our experience of them. As our fundamental expectation for human life changes, so, too, does our perception of time, growth, history, and experience undergo comparative changes. Let us now map these developments in some detail.

II. The Life of the Live Creature

I believe that we should experience our own lives in the context of being permanently afflicted, that is, of being terminal. This is not to propose a morbid personal style, but rather to ask that this attitude ride as an abiding presence in the active recesses of our conscious life. Surely, the shift from ancient to contemporary cosmology has doomed the doctrine of the equivalence of cosmic space with human life. The unintelligible distances, activities, gestations, and denouements of contemporary cosmology have dwarfed us and rendered illusory any human effort at ultimate accountability by our appeal to our proper place. The place we claim in the infinite universe is precisely that, a claim, an assertion, a seizing, an activity unknown to and unfelt by infinite space. The cosmology of human life is scarcely more extensive than our sociology. We have domesticated one planet and one lunar satellite and have probed several other planets. Electronically and mathematically, we have extended ourselves somewhat further. Nonetheless, relative to galactic plurality, let alone infinite space, these extraordinary human efforts are scarcely more than explorations of one city block or of a fifty-acre farm. Further, we are told as one active possibility that cosmic reality itself is entropic, winding down on its inexorable way to nothing.[14] In short, whatever may be the long-range future of cosmology, I do not see any auspicious signs that it will provide a resolution of present personal plight.

Historically, a paradox emerges which is intriguing and instructive. When, in antique times, we held the universe to be finite, we also held that it was eternal. Human life had a fixed and natural place in this version of the world, and only sub specie aeternitatis could it play a permanently meaningful role in the cyclically repetitive flow of time. Modern cosmology, for the most part, holds reality to be infinite and, on behalf of the doctrine of relativity, denies that we have a natural and fixed place.[15] The paradox is that in the modern view time has no ultimate meaning, yet it does take on profound human meaning, for it is both unrepeatable and the distinctive way in which human life asserts its presence and significance in the context of infinite reality. Infinite space becomes increasingly domesticated by being subjected to human time.

Given this cosmological context, our fundamental situation is transiency. We are of the species *Homo viator*, persons on a journey, human travelers in a cosmic abyss. Actually, in my judgment, "transients" is a better word than "travelers," for the latter often connotes a definite goal, an end in view, or at least a return home. A transient, however, is one who is passing through. The meaning of a transient's journey is precisely that: the journey itself. In transiency, paraphrasing John Dewey,[16] it is the quality of the journeying which counts, not the end in view and certainly not the claim that we have journeyed. The quality of transiency is achieved by passing through rather than by passing by. We should make our journey ever alert to our surroundings and to every perceivable sensorial nuance. Our journey is a kaleidoscope of alternating experiences, mishaps, setbacks, celebrations, and eye-openers, all undergone on the *qui vive.*

I repeat that space becomes meaningful for us to the extent that, through time, we build ourselves into it and convert space to place, to our place. It is necessary for us to make a place, for I do not believe that we have any inherited or natural place, as awarded. Just as the bottom line of death is that we are not around and about anymore, so, then, does life mean to be in a place, from someplace, on the way to someplace. We cannot do this by ourselves, for to be in place is to be relative to some other place, someone else's place. Friendship, family, media all serve to context our place, as they set over against us another place. Our memories are thereby crucial to a human life, for they carry past places to a present place, enabling a single place to be laced with all of the places we have been. Memories save the loss of places and the loss of persons from total disappearance. Actually, our losses often become more intense aspects of our present experience than our present itself. In the flow of the journey we hook ourselves to persons, places, things, and events, allowing us to reconnoitre, while passing through. A classic and profound hook is that of our junk drawer. Scraps and pieces of memorabilia tumble over one another, unworthy aside from their endowed meanings, given in a prior experience. An opera ticket, a ring, a watch, a baseball, a rejection slip, a cancelled check defy their ejection from our junk drawer, for they are laden with meaning and they act as personal clots in the onrushing flow of our lives.

Nonetheless, despite the richness of our memoried past, we cannot allow ourselves to be trapped in nostalgia. Following William James, life is as much in the transitions as it is in the events we experience directly.[17] No doubt our past experiences should remain alive in our consciousness and should be stirred and restirred so that they envelop and enrich our present experiences. But it is to the future that we wend. We cannot stand still. If we do, atrophy awaits us. Our deepest personal need, then, is to grow, for personal growth is the only sure sign that we are not yet dead. And by growth we mean here the capacity to convert our environment into sources of personal nutrition—to eat experience, as it were. The deeper meaning of growth is not an increase of size, length, height, or any other quantitative measure. Rather, it has to do with fructification, enriching, enhancing, and the pregnant provision for still further growth. Dewey's much maligned comment—"since in reality there is nothing to which growth is relative save more growth"—yields more than meets the eye.[18] In Dewey's understanding, growth is not characterized by a teleological movement to a final end. Rather, it is the quality of being humanly enriched by our experience, even if it be failure or loss. Further, growth is not simply an outcome or a result. It is the very nature of the live creature when participating in the flow of experience. In the following text, Dewey is referring to children, but he refers equally to all of us. "Where there is life, there are already eager and impassioned activities. Growth is not something done to them; it is something they do."[19] It is doing to the world and being done by the world which constitute the fundamental human transactions and allow for the possibility of growth. Hanging back while waiting to be rescued ultimately from the flow will not generate growth. Indulging and preening our ego, impervious to the messaging of the world, will not generate growth. In order to grow—that is, to live the life of a live creature rather than a life of second-handedness—we must forge a self-conscious relationship between our acceptance of our irreversible fragility and our creative energies. The most revealing focus of developing this relationship is our own version of the meaning of time and its attendant significance for the meaning of things, events, and history.

And now I come straight out and say where I stand on this issue. I believe that time is sacred. It is not sacred, however, because it has been so endowed by God, the gods, nature, or any other force. I believe that time is sacred because human history has endowed it with our meaning, our suffering, our commitments, and our anticipations. Can we sustain this position if we place it over against our previous discussion of the inevitability of death? What can we say, for example, when faced with the following text from the ancient Roman philosopher Marcus Aurelius? "And, to say all in a word, everything which belongs to the body is a stream, and what belongs to the soul is a dream and vapour, and life is a warfare and a stranger's sojourn, and after fame is oblivion."[20]

The Aurelian text is candid and accurate. He resolves it by an appeal to the cycle of nature, which gives human explanation for the existence of the human organism. This resolution, however, does not remove the bite from the fact that we are born to live and destined to die. I contend that the utter frustration of this contradiction in our personal situation cannot be resolved. Rather, speaking for the living, I take my point of departure from a text by John Dewey: "We always live at the time we live and not at some other time, and only by extracting at each present time the full meaning of each present experience are we prepared for doing the same thing in the future. This is the only preparation which in the long run amounts to anything."[21] Here, Dewey joins hands with the thought of Norman O. Brown and with the medieval tradition of the sacrament of the moment. Contrary to those positions, however, Dewey acknowledges no forces at work, neither Dionysian nor divine, other than the constitutive transactions of human life with the affairs of nature and the world. For better and for worse, we make the world and we endow nature with our presence, our values, our arrogance, and our fealty. You and I inherit thousands of years of human formulation, human judgment, human management, human violence, and human affection. Still, we come upon the world fresh, as if for the first time. The historically encrusted implications rush out at us as we seek to see, hear, touch anew. The novelty is not the world, for the world is tired, even jaded, with millennia of human hands and minds kneading it into a human image. No, the novelty, if it is to be at all, is found in us, in you, in me. It is not the monumental or the charismatic which provides the clue to the magnificence of being human. Rather, it is the celebration of the ordinary that enables us to make our way as truly human, avoiding the twin pitfalls of the humdrum, ennui and boredom, and the equally dehumanizing attempt to escape from the rhythm of time on behalf of a sterile, and probably self-deceptive, eternal resolution. Most likely, we have no ultimate future. This should not keep us from participating in the explosive possibilities of our present, no matter what the situation. Setback enriches as well as breakthrough.

Our impending death is not the major obstacle to our becoming truly human. The obstacle is found in our running for cover on behalf of our escape from death. We sell ourselves short. We should listen to the poet Rainer Maria Rilke, who praises our very ephemerality.

> But because being here amounts to so much, because all
> this Here and Now, so fleeting, seems to require us and strangely
> concerns us. Us the most fleeting of all. Just once,
> everything, only for once. Once and no more. And we, too,
> once. And never again. But this
> having been once, though only once,
> having been once on earth—can it ever be cancelled?[22]

Indeed, can it, can we, ever be cancelled? I think not. Celebrate!

FIFTEEN

ISOLATION AS STARVATION

John Dewey and a Philosophy of the Handicapped

It is not enough to insist upon the necessity of experience, nor even of activity in experience. Everything depends upon the *quality* of the experience which is had.

—John Dewey, *Experience and Education*

I

As to the word "handicapped," never has a historical definition, as found in our great dictionaries,[1] been so out of touch with the contemporary meaning. Originally defined as a "capping of the hands" that would provide equity between the superior and inferior in sport and games, the word only later became associated with disabilities, physical and emotional. In our time, however, the word has undergone a profound transformation. It now refers to a situation different but not necessarily inferior. Indeed, there is now a political aura to the term "handicapped," one which connotes growing power and respect. This development is a far cry from the condescension and ignorance characteristic of the public's reaction to the handicapped only two decades ago. Witness the following statement in the litigation between Ms. Lori Case and the State of California, which occurred as recently as 1973:

> With minor exceptions, mankind's attitudes toward its handicapped population can be characterized by overwhelming prejudice. [The

handicapped are systematically isolated from] the mainstream of society. From ancient to modern times, the physically, mentally or emotionally disabled have been alternatively viewed by the majority as dangers to be destroyed, as nuisances to be driven out, or as burdens to be confined. . . . [T]reatment resulting from a tradition of isolation has been invariably unequal and has operated to prejudice the interests of the handicapped as a minority group.[2]

After an extended series of court cases, this prejudice was finally overcome, at least in the legal sense. In the following comment, the importance of the Public Act of 1975 is detailed.

> The Education for All Handicapped Children Act of 1975, Public Law (P. L.) 94-142, is not revolutionary in terms of a role for the federal government. P. L. 94-142 represents the standards that have over the past eight years been laid down by the courts, legislatures, and other policy bodies of our country. Further, it represents a continued evolution of the federal role in the education of children who had handicaps. For example, much of what is required in P. L. 94–142 was set forth in P. L. 93–380, the Education Amendments of 1974.
>
> Most importantly, P. L. 94-142 reflects the dream of special educators and others concerned about the education of children with handicaps, for it has been the hope of our field that we as special educators would one day be able to assure every child who has a handicap an opportunity for an education, that we would be free to advocate for appropriate educational services for these children, that we would be unfettered by inappropriate administrative constraints, and that we would not always have to temper critical decisions about children's lives by the inadequacy of public resources. In this sense, P. L. 94-142 becomes the national vehicle whereby the promise of state and local policy that we have heard for so long, and the dreams that we in the profession have hoped for, for so long, may become a reality.[3]

Although this public act is directed at children, it sets a tone for all handicapped people in the United States, now a considerable portion of the population. In fact, to refer to the handicapped as a minority may well be a euphemism, for the figures are quite staggering. Ranging from a low of 13 million handicapped, as provided by the Urban Mass Transportation Administration, to a high of 41 million, as provided by the

Department of Health, Education, and Welfare, the cautious mean indicates that American society is characterized by a substantial number of citizens with operative disabilities.[4] As a nation we face a social, political, psychological, and moral problem of sizable proportion and of existential exigency.

It may be of assistance to our understanding of the meaning of "handicapped" if we were to make a distinction between the temporarily and the permanently handicapped. Many of us, at one time or another, have suffered a severe disability. Nonetheless, despite the pain, the inconvenience, and loss of personal power in our activities, we were buoyed by its transiency. The assumption that we would get better, be healed, and get back to normal carried us through our temporary plight. Lurking in the background, although functionally repressed, was the specter of permanence, and a foreboding that we would not get better and that our condition was here to stay. The difference between a transient disability, no matter its length of time, and a permanent disability is akin to the immeasurable and qualitative difference between the finite and the eternal. The difference between the *healing* of a smashed and severely damaged human limb, on one side, and an amputation, on the other, is incomparable.

As human beings we fear closure not only in its ultimate sense, as in our own death, but in any number of proximate senses, as in the permanent inability to perform in a way considered natural to human life. Looked at objectively, to be permanently blind, deaf, or crippled to some considerable extent is to be denied an avenue of access to the world. Some activities, some experiences, are thereby simply not possible. Despite our previous sufferings and disabilities, those of us who are not permanently handicapped actually have no experience of the dramatic force of closure which permeates permanent disability. Nonetheless, as found in those memorably heroic figures of the past and present, and in startling numbers, those so handicapped have been able to overcome in such a way as to magnify the alternative avenues of experience. Indeed, so extraordinary has been this development in the activities of the handicapped that it is legitimate to see them as performing in a way superior to those of us for whom our sense-life is desultory, haphazard, and taken for granted. Paradoxically, it is the nonhandicapped who often face closure, albeit of another, more subtle kind. It is they who have eyes but do not see, ears but do not hear, for they have taken their bodies for granted. The handicapped, to the contrary, although ostensibly they do not see, or hear, or walk, do each of those things, in their own way, for their bodies are supremely sensitized to the slightest sensorial nuance. In Dewey's sense, it is they who are "live creatures."

Significantly, the new education of the handicapped mirrors Dewey's philosophy in an accurate and creative way. Indeed, it realizes Dewey's vision more than most other contemporary forms of education. Two primary reasons for this relationship between Dewey's philosophy and the education of the handicapped can be cited. First, Dewey's diagnosis of the human condition is to see us all as continuous with nature and therefore, in general, "handicapped" in the attempted resolution of our problems, because nature gives no quarter and often demands of us a response that is not humanly possible. Second, he sees education as a form of deep "coping," problem solving, and assisting, rather than as any final solution to the irreducibly problematic situation of being in the world. I shall consider these two aspects of Dewey's thought in turn.

II

This is neither the time nor the place to undo the many gratuitous misinterpretations of the philosophy of John Dewey. One such mistaken view of Dewey, however, has to be opposed straight out. I refer to the view of Dewey's thought as a Pollyanna vision, innocent of mishap and evil and too trusting in human ingenuity. Not only is this view unfair to Dewey's thought, it actually reverses his fundamental position. For Dewey, existence involves risk and chance and is indeed an ontological gamble. He writes that "luck is proverbially both good and bad in its distributions," for "the sacred and the accursed are potentialities of the same situation."[5]

Dewey then proceeds to detail the deleterious effects of a long-standing philosophical tradition which divides the experience of reality into higher and lower orders of experience, thus emptying out the complex content of our actual situation. By defining reality as that which we wish existence to be, we render defect as unnatural and "render search and struggle unnecessary."[6] The higher order, which remains only in philosophical imagination, yields perfection. Of this unreal turn of events, Dewey writes: "What is left over, (and since trouble, struggle, conflict, and error still empirically exist, something is left over) being excluded by definition from full reality is assigned to a grade or order of being which is asserted to be metaphysically inferior; an order variously called 'appearance,' 'illusion,' 'mortal mind,' or the merely 'empirical,' against what really and truly is."[7] In so proposing, philosophy has abandoned its task, namely, a description of the generic traits of existence as undergone, empirically, by human life. For Dewey, when so undergone, the most primitive of these generic traits show themselves to be a "mixture of the precarious and the problematic with the assured and the complete."[8] The point is clear; all human experience is riven with the presence of a dialectic between the stable and the precarious; no existence, event, or quality escapes this dialectic. In effect, at every moment of our lives we alternate between being free to do and being handicapped, each in our own way. Called in to map our way through this thicket, Dewey laments the frequent effort of philosophy to bypass it.

> Under such circumstances there is danger that the philosophy which tries to escape the form of generation by taking refuge under the form of eternity will only come under the form of a bygone generation. To try to escape from the snares and pitfalls of time by recourse to traditional problems and interests:—rather than that let the dead bury their own dead. Better it is for philosophy to err in active participation in the living struggles and issues of its own age and times than to maintain an immune monastic impeccability, without relevancy and bearing in the generating ideas of its contemporary present.[9]

For Dewey, to the contrary, the method of philosophy must confront the "teachings of sad experience."[10] The most dramatic upshot of such teachings is the irrational and inequitable distribution of suffering among human lives. The following text from Dewey can be read as a direct response to the existence of the handicapped. "There is no need to expatiate upon the risk which attends overt action. . . . Fortune rather than our own intent and act determines eventual success and failure. The pathos of unfulfilled expectation, the tragedy of defeated purpose and ideals, the catastrophes of accident, are the commonplaces of all comment on the human scene."[11] Further, we should avoid any "doctrine of escape from the vicissitudes of existence by means of measures which do not demand an active coping with conditions."[12] The stark realism of Dewey, which owns up to our human plight, does not presage a drift to pessimism. In fact, it is precisely the nature of the difficulties that we face which leads him to develop a doctrine of coping and healing. Like Emerson before him, Dewey stresses the doctrine of possibility. Setback and mishap are unavoidable, yet they set the stage for growth and human activity. The crucial factor in the assessment of the quality of human life is the affective quality of the transaction. It is how we undergo the necessary alternations between the stable and the precarious which reveals the quality of our lives. Perfection or consummation is rarely attained, but the rhythm of the human struggle carries with it deep moral and aesthetic significance. The "live creature" even makes friends with its stupidities, "using them as warnings that increase present wariness."[13] Indeed, at one point, Dewey even states that periodic alienation is necessary if genuine growth is to occur.

> Life itself consists of phases in which the organism falls out of step with the march of surrounding things and then recovers unison with it—either through effort or by some happy chance. And, in a growing life, the recovery is never mere return to a prior state, for it is enriched by the state of disparity and resistance through which it has successfully passed. If the gap between organism and environment is too wide, the creature dies. If its activity is not enhanced by the temporary alienation, it merely subsists. Life grows when a temporary falling out is a transition to a more extensive balance of the energies of the organism with those of the conditions under which it lives.[14]

It is important to notice that the most severe difficulty encountered by a human being is that of isolation from the flow of events. This isolation prevents the making of relations and prevents recoveries and consequently growth. Periodic alienation enhances the rhythm of our transactions with nature and the world of experience, but isolation drops us out and away from the very leads and implications which the flow of experience harbors for our needs. The historical isolation of the handicapped from the flow of events resulted in precisely this devolutionary situation, wherein the actual handicap became a minor and subsidiary problem in comparison to being cut off from the avenues and possibilities of future experience. Following Dewey's basic metaphysical scenario, the pedagogy of the handicapped, above all, must be a pedagogy of involvement and not one of isolation.

The variant ways, then, of managing these phases of alienation and growth in human life give rise to the multiple approaches of Dewey relative to the classic methods and fields of inquiry. The fundamental setting is the transaction of the human organism with nature or with the environment. Nature has a life of its own, undergoing its own relatings, which in turn become what we experience. Our own transaction with the affairs of nature cuts across the givenness of nature and our ways of relating. This is *how* we experience *what* we experience. Dewey was a realist in the sense that the world exists independent of our thought of it, but the meaning *of* the world is inseparable from our *meaning* the world.

Experience, therefore, is not headless, for it teems with relational leads, inferences, implications, comparisons, retrospections, directions, warnings, and so on. The rhythm of how we experience is an aesthetic process, having as its major characteristic the relationship between anticipation and consummation, yet having other perturbations, such as mishap, loss, boredom, and listlessness. Pedagogy becomes, then, the twin effort to integrate the directions of experience with the total needs of the person and to cultivate the ability of an individual to generate new potentialities in his experiencing and to make new relationships so as to foster patterns of growth. And politics is the struggle to construct an optimum environment for the realizing and sanctioning of the aesthetic processes of living. Finally, the entire human endeavor should be an effort to apply the method of creative intelligence in order to achieve optimum possibilities in the never-ending moral struggle to harmonize the means-end relationship for the purpose of enhancing human life and achieving growth.

I turn now to the ways in which Dewey developed the method of creative intelligence with regard to the problem of education. In my judgment, both his theoretical underpinnings and his concrete suggestions for practice are germane and viable for our time. In addition, although he did not develop his philosophy of education with the handicapped specifically in mind, Dewey's position, as we have just hinted, is remarkably apropos for any formulation of a pedagogy for the handicapped.

III

In Dewey's thought, all experiencing, except the inchoate, is a knowing of some kind. To be in the world is to be in a learning situation or, to coin a phrase for Dewey, experience is pedagogical. Of this contention, Dewey writes:

> Now, old experience is used to suggest aims and methods for developing a new and improved experience. Consequently experience becomes . . . constructively self-regulative. What Shakespeare so pregnantly said of nature, it is "made better by no mean, but nature makes that mean," becomes true of experience. We do not merely have to repeat the past, or wait for accidents to force change upon us. We use our past experiences to construct new and better ones in the future. The very fact of experience thus includes the process by which it directs itself in its own betterment.[15]

The fact that for Dewey experience is pedagogical does not account for the specificity or distinctive importance of pedagogy, although it does provide the setting for the task of pedagogy. The human organism transacts with nature, with the environment, and thereby finds itself in a situation which is problematic. Relative to the interests and goals of the organism, the task is to make one's way through the flow of experience while attempting resolutions of the obstacles to human growth. If philosophy is called upon to map the terrain of this transaction, pedagogy seeks to forge a mutuality between the possibilities active in experience and the strengths and predispositions of the person in question. When teaching takes place, it takes place. It does not have as its justification some future time: "Education, therefore, is a process of living and not a preparation for future living."[16] Dewey unites the process and the goal of learning. The nectar of awareness and accomplishment does not await an ultimate future, for it is gathered on the way, as a testament to the richness and finitude of experience. Learning for Dewey is not an epiphenomenon, tacked onto a regimen of mental flagellation. Rather, it is a process, yielding its rewards en route and from time to time, consummating in an insight, a skill, a breakthrough to the mastery of a handicap or even, occasionally, a mastery of a discipline, an activity, or an area of vital concern. Attention to detail and rigor of method are not separated in Dewey's purview from the joy and celebration that accompany the process of learning. The worse things are, the more dramatic is the need for a creative pedagogy: "The intellectual function of trouble is to lead [us] to think."[17]

Long before the work of Maria Montessori and Martin Buber, John Dewey, with the imaginative assistance of his wife, Alice Chipman, rejected the view of children as but small adults. He had an uncanny sense of the spatial and emotional aesthetics necessary to creative learning. The classrooms of the Deweys' laboratory school at the University of Chicago were furnished for the physical needs and abilities of children. The Deweys provided classrooms for children which responded to both their emotional and physical needs, thereby formulating an optimum environment for learning and for interpersonal transaction of the most fruitful kind. Dewey would have strongly approved of the recent movement to arrange for access to buildings and for appropriate materials for study on behalf of the handicapped.

And he would have realized both the advantages and the disadvantages to "mainstreaming" handicapped children in traditional settings. I believe that Dewey, facing today's problems, would opt for functional "mainstreaming," in which handicapped children would be integrated into the emotional and social life of the school and yet would have access to the distinctive pedagogical and physical strategies necessary to their educational well-being. Dewey had a life-long commitment to opposing artificial and economic obstacles to the learning process, especially on behalf of those to whom unhappy chance had dealt a debilitating injury.

In Dewey's philosophy, growth is relative to the situation in which one finds oneself. Growth is not a linear notion but rather signifies the transaction with nature as problematic. Also, it connotes the ability to resolve, if only contextually, to overcome, and, above all, to recover from loss. Growth is an "on-the-way" fruit of experiencing as subject to intelligence and purpose. It is not solely dependent on habitual responses, accepted customs, or on reaching preconceived goals, especially those determined by persons who do not have the experiences, difficulties, or strengths of those undergoing the transaction.

Although subject to critical and often unreflective abuse, Dewey's position on the importance and nature of growth is quite clear.

> Since in reality there is nothing to which growth is relative save more growth, there is nothing to which education is subordinate save more education. It is commonplace to say that education should not cease when one leaves school. The point of this commonplace is that the purpose of school education is to insure the continuance of education by organizing the powers that insure growth. The inclination to learn from life itself and to make the conditions of life such that all will learn in the process of living is the finest product of schooling.[18]

Learning from life connotes a fidelity to the situation, capacities, and limitations of the learner. Each of us brings anticipations, possibilities, and relative abilities to the learning process. Such a context is always complicated and that of the handicapped is more so. But the basic process holds, nonetheless. Relative to our possibilities, we seek achievements. Dewey's warning in the epigraph to this chapter is a telling one. "Everything depends upon the *quality* of the experience which is had."[19] The achievement of quality is inseparable from the making of relations and from seizing the implications of what we are doing. The learner, in Dewey's understanding of education, is neither a mere spectator nor a listener. Learning is by doing, mastering, managing, as well as by losing and failing. Setback, mishap, and even failure are not disasters. Rather, they can serve as creative wedges back into the tissue of experience, prophesying a renewed effort to attend, assist, or perhaps even resolve the problem in question. Surely, the handicapped understand and welcome this approach to the practice of education.

Dewey's stress on activity and the making of relations as central to the process of education has been known as the "project method"—that is, one in which we propel ourselves into the environment and make a distinctively personal version out of its givenness. It has been alleged that this approach of Dewey is overly experiential and lacks the intellectual character necessary to a proper educational experience. This judgment is wrong on two accounts. First, consistent with Dewey's total philosophical outlook, the undergoing of experience is itself a learning experience. He writes that "there is, apparently, no conscious experience without inference; reflection is native and constant."[20] Second, Dewey is aware of the strategic character of reflection when brought to bear on an organized set of experiences as found in the educational process. It is in the reflective relating of doing to undergoing that the person has a genuinely educational experience.

> Mere activity does not constitute experience. It is dispersive, centrifugal, dissipating. Experience as trying involves change, but change is meaningless transition unless it is consciously connected with the return wave of consequences which flow from it. When an activity is continued into the undergoing of consequences, when the change made by action is reflected back into a change made in us, the mere flux is loaded with significance. We learn something.[21]

Dewey, however, does warn us against the reverse error; namely, one in which theory floats loose, innocent of the experience from which it is to proceed and to which it is to point. Such self-aggrandizing theoretical activity is the bane of genuine education, for it renders tawdry the activities which actually make up our life-situation and casts dubiety on the importance of our ordinary activities. On this matter, Dewey counsels wisely:

> An experience, a very humble experience, is capable of generating and carrying any amount of theory (or intellectual content), but a theory apart from an experience cannot be definitely grasped even as theory. It tends to become a mere verbal formula, a set of catchwords used to render thinking, or genuine theorizing, unnecessary and impossible. Because of our education we use words, thinking they are ideas, to dispose of questions, the disposal being in reality simply such an obscuring of perception as prevents us from seeing any longer the difficulty.[22]

If Dewey's philosophy of education makes as much obvious sense as I think it does, why is it not more influential in our own time? Dewey would not be surprised at this neglect, for he believed always that the political and sociological structures were more determinant of institutional life than were philosophical ideas, no matter how perceptive. The key resolution of that disproportion, of course, was to develop a doctrine of political and social life which would find its way into influence and perhaps even power. Dewey made efforts in this direction, especially in the second, third, and fourth decades of the twentieth century. In that some of these efforts have significance for his philosophy of education, I shall consider them at this time.

IV

Although public consciousness of the needs and rights of the handicapped has been raised considerably, the level is not yet sufficient to ensure the social, economic, and political breakthroughs necessary to a national program amelioration and personal adjudication. The final report of the now moribund Carnegie Council on Children makes this clear; the report is entitled "The Unexpected Minority: Handicapped Children in America." A *New York Times* commentary on this document reads as follows:

> [The report] cites the disabled child as the most oppressed member of contemporary American society and advocates a new civil rights movement to create major social changes in public institutions and in attitudes about handicapped children.
>
> Among its recommendations: that parents—not teachers, doctors, or counselors—exercise final authority over disabled offspring; that the handicapped organize into political groups; that the Federal Government help integrate these children into the educational and social mainstream by redistributing existing public funds and creating new ones.[23]

The classic paradox in American life—the tension between the rights of the individual and the often necessary intervention of the federal government to insure those rights—clearly surfaces here. It is laudable to insist that parents have ultimate authority over the education of their disabled children, but local bureaucracies often act as an insuperable obstacle in this regard. The major difficulty is that these parents are too often regarded by the rest of the community as adversaries, as competitors for tax revenues. This view of the community is atomistic and its only future is strife. The handicapped children are the inevitable losers. Dewey, no stranger to this development, urged a far more expansive communal attitude toward the education of children. "What the best and wisest parent wants for his [her] own child, that must the community want for all of its children. Any other ideal for our schools is narrow and unlovely; acted upon, it destroys our democracy."[24]

The educational rights of children, handicapped or not, do not constitute, in Dewey's view, a special interest group. Rather, the education of all of our children to their fullest capacity is an irreducible necessity if we are to survive as a nation and as a people. Long ago, our great Puritan forebear John Winthrop warned us that unless we be knit together, we shall be shipwrecked. The obstacles to such community sensibility are considerable, and Dewey was deeply cognizant of them. He was especially concerned with the deleterious and self-deceiving effects of a nostalgia for a form of "bootstrap" individualism. Although he had great confidence in the capacity of the individual to overcome obstacles, he deplored the naiveté that ignored the vast social, political, and economic forces which contrived to hinder and even prevent personal growth. Dewey held that "the educational task cannot be accomplished merely by working upon men's minds, without action that effects actual changes in institutions."[25] Yet attempts to bring about institutional change run afoul of the deepest special interest in American life, that of those who control the economic sector: "The notion that men are equally free to act if only the same legal arrangements apply equally to all—irrespective of differences in education, in command of capital, and the control of the social environment which is furnished by the institution of property—is a pure absurdity, as facts have demonstrated."[26] Not surprisingly, then, we are faced with two major problems in our effort to forge a new, equitable, and viable philosophy of education for the handicapped: namely, the need for a public consciousness raising, and a transformation of institutional priorities. These two needs are of a piece, neither taking political precedence, for they are mutually necessary. Dewey's strategy is based on neither charity nor revolutionary fervor. Rather, he sees the need for social action on behalf of those who need ameliorative efforts as precisely a reflection of the democratic ethos. He writes that "to cooperate by giving differences a chance to show themselves because of the belief that the expression of difference is not only a right of the other persons but is a means of enriching one's own life-experience, is inherent in the democratic personal way of life."[27]

Only when we as a people take on seriously the obligations attendant upon the democratic ethos shall we have the will to effect the necessary transformations of our educational, social, political, and economic structures sufficient to a provision for the needs of the handicapped. No worse fate can befall a self-conscious human being than to be regarded as a pariah in his or her own culture. Isolation from the flow of experience is a fate worse than death, for it mocks the potentialities, expectations, and yearnings of the live creature. In Dewey's philosophy, "A true wisdom . . . discovers in thoughtful observation and experiment the method of administering the unfinished processes of existence so that frail goods shall be substantiated, secure goods be extended, and the precarious promises of good that haunt experienced things be more liberally fulfilled."[28]

Unless we move expeditiously and imaginatively in the direction of a systematic response to the needs and rights of the handicapped, it is we—as a nation, as a people, and as individuals—who shall in the eyes of subsequent history be judged as morally handicapped. To be physically and emotionally handicapped is to be a luckless victim of the roulette wheel of natural history. To be morally handicapped is a result of self-indulgence, arrogance, and a blindness to the plight of others. Those of us who have been fortunate to be spared severe physical and emotional disability have an obligation to assure that we avoid the collective moral turpitude that follows from building a world fit only for ourselves. On behalf of John Dewey, and in my judgment as well, we have no other moral choice than to build a world in which the apertures of accessibility are as wide and as many as the variant styles and abilities of each and every one of us. To do less is to abandon the human quest.

PART FOUR

BEQUEATHING

DEADLINES

A festering presence
takes
on the inappropriate
Label
of
Dead
As in no life
no play, no more
How does a line
Die
only to live
forever
as a sign of
failure
if one goes over
the line
But if we meet
the dead
line
Then the line
dies
Living only when
not
met.

SIXTEEN

HAST ANY PHILOSOPHY IN THEE, SHEPHERD?

Preamble

I am deeply grateful to Professor Pat Alexander for her invitation to address this distinguished gathering. Gratitude is offered, also, to my two former doctoral students at Texas A&M, who will offer a panel discussion on the significance of philosophical perspectives for educational psychology. Preambling still, I appear here to offer some potential help for those whose life-mission is to help others. For my take, such is the irreducible and ever-present calling of all inquiry and pedagogy. The question before me, if I am to be of service, is, in what way can I be of help? First, the diagnosis. I am told that the discipline of educational psychology has lost its philosophical roots and, of late, has been mesmerized by the demanding quest for right answers, echoing the Cartesian point of departure enhanced by cybermethodology.

Briefly, I respond that the absence of historical, let alone historical-philosophical, insight and sensibility is not unique to educational psychology. I am embarrassed to say that ahistoricism of all stripes is a paramount characteristic of contemporary mainstream philosophy and has found its way into literary studies as well, mutatis mutandis. To the contrary, I offer that every discipline pedagogically should open with its history, inclusive of engineering. The usual response to the noxious and exponentially increasing obsolescence of the past is that our lives now move so fast, and we now know so much, that there is no time for acknowledging, let alone probing, the past. I have another response to the systematic penchant for obsoleting our past. When I look back to the ancients, to the medievals, to Dante, to Goethe, to Jonathan Edwards, to Emily Dickinson, and especially to *The Confidence Man* of Melville, it becomes apparent that my vaunted knowledge and occasional personal wisdom is often second-hand. For the most part, on the deep and central issues, it has been said before and usually better.

As to the second affliction, the intellectual drive for answers, surely that mode of inquiry has been obviated since Darwin, Hegel, Wittgenstein, the existentialists, quantum physics, Picasso, Martha Graham, John Coltrane, and now chaos theory. More simply, the philosophy of William James, in a variety of ways, yielded a way, that is, a Tao, that reinstated the vague and the inarticulate to the center of our reflective life. James has a name for this methodological anality. He calls it "vicious intellectualism," by which we define A as that which not only is what it is but cannot be other. Proceeding this way, answers abound and clarity holds sway. Missing is surprise, novelty, the wider relational fabric, often riven with rich meanings found on the edge, behind, around, under, over the designated, prearranged conceptual placeholders. Percepts are what count, and the attendant ambiguity in all matters important presage more and deeper meaning, not less. Following John Dewey, method is subsequent and consequent to experience, to inquiry. Method can help fund and warrant experience, but it does not grasp our doings and undergoings in their natural habitat. For that, we must begin with and experimentally trust our affections—dare I say it, trust our feelings. They may cause trouble, but they never lie.

Hast Any Philosophy in Thee, Shepherd?

Some may reply to the question posed in the heading above, fortunately no philosophy that I admit. Further, you say, what does philosophy have to do with this dolorous diagnosis? In what way, in what sense, in whatever, can philosophy be of help to disciplinary practice? After all, we know of what we do, what we are about. Please do not meddle.

I say, philosophy is one of one. It is the reflective activity that grounds all other reflections. John Dewey tells us that "reflection is native and constant." I believe that to be true. And as a careful Yiddish watcher of things, events, and persons allegedly ordinary, I offer the reverse text of Shakespeare's *Hamlet*, to wit: "There are more things in heaven and earth, Horatio, than are dreamt of in your philosophy." Now these two versions feed off each other. The philosophy needed by the shepherd, that is, by me, the teacher, is that which holds these to be more than any philosophy can offer. It is a cardinal insight of William James that there is always a "more," to all that we claim to be so. Concepts, judgments, definitions, names, labels are always beggars before the vast implications of reconnoitered experience. The bequest of philosophy in this atavistic human situation is to provide both a landscape and an inscape or to provide both a lodestone and a lodestar. For William James, philosophy is "the habit of always seeing an alternative."[1] For J. J. McDermott, it is pushing our native reflection until it faces an *Urfrage*, a question to which there is no answer, such as, why is there something rather than nothing? Closer to your work would be the version of this question as given by Billie Holiday, "Why was I born?" Put more evocatively, listen to the plea of that famous taxi dancer, the late, lamented Gwen Verdon, who offers that "there has got to be something better than this." Does there? And again, the American chanteuse Peggy Lee asks, "Is that all there is?" Probably!

These existentialist, albeit rhetorical, questions dog all of us, no matter the cultural and personal rendering by which they are shaped. I talk of this as our social cosmology—namely, our effort to build a place that is distinctively personal yet ineluctably tied to a relational mosaic as wide as it is defining. Just what is it to be a person and just where am I? For Plato and Freud, there is a secret, a veil that renders the rational a self-deceiving strategy, ne'er to break the lock, the cave, the trap of embodiment. For Aristotle and Dewey, what you see is what you get. We are ontologically continuous with nature, its rhythms, and our rhythms with that of nature. For William James, seeing is the least of it.

The affective life is multisensorial and diaphanous. Messages are riotously present, and to survive we must carve out a stand, a place, a mooring, wary always of the consequences. For Camus, following the overwhelming evidence for nihilism as both obviously and dramatically present in human history, the initiating and primary philosophical question is suicide.

One could continue this gloss on the history of philosophy, seen as a series of points of departure, so as to enable us to get at the question of our own social cosmology. Try Lucretius, Marcus Aurelius, Maimonides, Averroes, Bruno, Descartes, Spinoza, Leibniz, Kant, Hegel, Shopenhauer, Nietzsche, Sartre, and Foucault. Of paramount importance here is the radical plurality of these versions and the stark absence of agreement on the most fundamental assumptions. If one seeks a seamless thread of accruing wisdom or certitude on contentions, then the history of philosophy is barren terrain. Contrariwise, if one seeks to widen, deepen, and thicken the way in which one has experiences reflectively undergone, then philosophy is delta soil: rich, fecund, and, on being turned over, yielding growth. The exploration of any of these philosophers, as well as of others, is as arduous as it is rewarding. Philosophical wisdom cannot be attained by way of sound bites or word bites (and certainly not by gigabytes). The study of philosophy requires a bath, not a shower. The mode of philosophical inquiry is not one of "poking around" but rather one of suffusing until philosophical sensibility becomes au naturel.

I turn here from an ambient approach to the importance of philosophical inquiry to one closer at hand relative to what I take to be mutual concerns: namely, the well-being of a person in an educational setting. More specifically, our question is how that person has his or her experiences relative to the psychological dimensions—that is, genetic inheritance, environmental intrusions, failure, potential, self-esteem, and the gnawing ontological underbelly, "why bother?" (I postpone in this setting any discussion of whether educational psychology is, in fact, a different animal than philosophical pedagogy.)

I believe that every human being is called to forge an originating presence in what, for lack of a better word, we call the "world." Etymologically, "world" (*woruld*) comes from the Old English and means quite simply "human existence," circular though that be. Long, long ago, I was taken with the plea of Emerson as to why I could not have an "original relationship to the universe." Subsequently, I was warned by Whitman not to live a second-hand life. And Josiah Royce cautioned me to never forget that "the popular mind is deep and means a thousand times more than it explicitly 'knows.'"[2] In common parlance, thick and abiding philosophical questions are put as follows, subject to cultural evocative variants. Who am I, who are you? Where am I, where are you? What's up, what's happening, and the most telling of questions, how do you feel?

I soon realized that these questions were afloat—nay, disconnected—unless and until I announced to myself, by whatever version of articulation (for example, poetry, dance, and craft), my own singular, personal bedding, that on which I stood, that in and through which I have my being. Any psychotherapeutic inquiry, any counseling psychological inquiry that focuses on symptoms but has no access to this bedding finds itself in an "intake" that at bottom is chimerical. Jargonically, we are putting the cart before the horse. (Not here and now, but a salutary way to get at this bedding is to ask for stories, what they say, and why those stories.)

The construction of that on which I stand and that by which I project myself into the world can be innocent of explicit philosophical positions. Indeed, for most persons, such is the case. For us, however, who have taken it upon ourselves to read the experiences of others for the purpose of amelioration, we have the obligation and the responsibility to know how we have come to this bedding and to know why we have rejected alternatives. Further, for us, at some point, we have to own up to our decisions and face the inevitable price that comes with saying yes to this contention and no to that contention.

The following is a telescoped presentation of that on which I stand. If time were capacious, it would be helpful if I gave you my history and told you my stories. Today, however, time is stingy. Suffice to say that events in my youth propelled me to ask some questions. As I move through this, I urge you to reflect, analogously, as it were, such that you evoke your own bedding. The first question is whether there is any ultimate intelligibility. The living response for me is no. Intelligibility, yes;

ultimate, no. Please note that I say "living response," for I have no answer, no certitude on this question. Second question, does human history have a meaning other than the meaning we impose? The response is also no. The third question asks whether essences, objects, Platonic forms are *ab initio*, from the beginning, or whether they are human constructs. As with William James, I came to believe that essences are teleological weapons of the mind. Read here that all of our precious labels, definitions, and categories—for example depression, or, more dangerously, bipolarity—are but constructs, pragmatic loci, for better or worse. Further, are relations between the just-noted essentials, objects, and nominations simply logical connectors or do they have a life of their own? Indeed they do, and so, with James, I hold that "life is in the transitions" and that "experience grows by its edges." Lastly, in this short diagnosis, is life worth living? To which I say, barely but not necessarily. Can it be, then, that suicide, despite its being the final insulating cut, can be an act of nobility, of amelioration for self and others, a moment of existential freedom? Yes.

So with the attitudes that these responses generate, I have put together the following bedding by which I try to live my life. Whatever we do, whatever we think, whatever we believe, we are natural organisms, live creatures (no redundancy here), ineluctably so. Consequently, mortality is our calling card—only the when and where are yet to be decided. Thus our deep, pervasive, mostly inchoate landscape shrouds all of our living. Inevitably, for each of us, that inchoateness explodes: an impacted bowel; a failing kidney; the announcement of a terminal disease; the death, especially the tragic death, of one dearly loved; a recognition that I am an abject failure; a radical destruction; a burning, flooding home, photographs and letters gone forever; or simply a growing awareness that in the long run, nothing makes sense and inner loneliness becomes the hidden, not to be shared, modus vivendi.

I want to assume that, given your profession as educational psychologists, you, too, have forged a bedding, one that is as thick and as free as is possible from self-deception. Yet, think now, how all of us, inclusive of myself, are prey to conducting our pedagogical relationships as if this bedding were not present. Think of the puerile concern with GPA, extracurriculars, speed and retention of atomistic bits of flotsam—all of it masquerading as knowledge, much less understanding. Think of the attention paid to that twiddle—SAT, GRE, LSAT, MCAT, and other autocratic acronyms that measure what my great teacher Robert Pollock called "dreadful externality." Surely, for each person who comes before us seeking help, it is a given that there is more here than meets the eye or the measure, for they, too, have bedding, or, alas, do not!

Quite simply and directly, all I am saying here is that when constructing your bedding, taking your point of departure for your personal social cosmology, if you are fed by the wisdom of the philosophers and by an ability to probe philosophically all that you hold to be so, then the result will be distinctively personal and open to transformation at the behest of experience—yours and that of those who come to you for help.

Invoking hard currency, cash not credit, I offer now an *explicatio de texte* of some lines from *Art as Experience* by John Dewey. He wrote: "The time of consummation is also one of beginning anew. Any attempt to perpetuate beyond its term the enjoyment attending the time of fulfillment and harmony constitutes withdrawal from the world [read here death]. Hence it marks the lowering and loss of vitality. But through the phases of perturbation and conflict, there abides the deep-seated memory of an underlying harmony, the sense of which haunts life like the sense of being founded on a rock."[3] I try to live by that text. It is not easy, for anality is a pervasive discourse. Note how Dewey tells us that the ontological haunting is like a rock, although he is stern in his warning that we do not indulge any permanence for our halcyon times. Conceptually, those two affirmations do not hang together. Yet, perceptually, affectively, could anything be more so? Can there be anything more grounding than the interstitial presence of mortality in my every act, every thought, every dream? Is there anything more treacherous than the hankering for immortality, as if we could bypass our finitude, our transiency? I cannot tell you how ameliorative this text has been for me and for those countless souls I have counseled. Of course, this text is lifted from the vast canopy of Dewey's philosophical naturalism. I have to know, *in extenso*, that canopy, if this text is to have life. So, too, do I have to know Spinoza's canopy if I am to embrace his meaning of epistemology as a *de emendatione intellectus*, a healing of the understanding. Again, Sartre in the round, so as to understand his meaning of "bad faith." And, by analogy, Augustine and Peirce on the necessity of doubt for knowledge and belief; Hegel, that all judgments take place on a historical matrix; Kant, that space and time are mock-ups, human constructs; Gabriel Marcel, on the differences between being and having; and Marx, what you get is not what you see.

Probing the insights of a philosopher or the underlying strands in a long-standing philosophical tradition presses me to reconstruct the often-haphazard, rickety, derivative shell in which and from which I purport to live. It is not, I repeat not, to become smart about ideas, to drop names, and to use intellectual slogans. Nor is it to adopt an ideology and to pin myself into a procrustean bed, such that enhancing and warning experiences are jettisoned for reasons of a bad fit. Literal-mindedness and the quest for objectivity in matters human constitutes the death of the soul. The distinctively personal ingredient should color all of our activities, otherwise we live in the gray of correctness, external and dead to the world and to ourselves. We should widen the frame of relations and avoid being hung out to dry, like jetsam, or carried by the mob or by the occult or by the socially acceptable, like flotsam. Reach and touch. When you are touched, touch back. The key is not in objects, names, and definitions. The key is in the relations and symbols. Not by the obvious, alone, doth man live.

In that regard, I close with a story. I call it the story of the cigar man. Long dead, long ago on a dreary Sunday morning, he taught me about the difference between the literal and the symbolical. In 1948, I was a volunteer at the *Catholic Worker* in New York City, headed by the indefatigable and famous Dorothy Day. One of my tasks was to visit hospitals and to attend to the indigent sick. On early Sunday mornings, I would go to Bellevue Hospital and do what I could to assuage the suffering in the cancer ward, known as the death ward, because this was before contemporary therapies were available. Among my assignments was the pathetic effort to fit the patients with appropriate reading glasses, collected randomly at the *Catholic Worker*. I also made phone calls, ran errands, and assisted the crippled patients to chapel services.

One rainy Sunday morning, I came on a quadruple amputee, sitting totem-like on the bed, as if he were a runaway torso. He was Puerto

Rican, and his black eyes had the defiance known only to a beaten person, for he was terminal. I passed by his bed, at a quickened pace, afraid to look or stare. He called to me in Spanish. Not knowing the language, I asked a nurse for help. Our patient wanted two cigars. It was a rainy Sunday morning and not propitious for finding a store open. I groused but said I would try to get them for him.

As I was about to leave, he barked again to the nurse. He wanted a special cigar, a Puerto Rican cigar. At that point, I became stressed, for the task was becoming onerous. I told the nurse to tell him I would try for his cigars, but failing, I would bring him some American cigars. On being told that, he became furious and all of his anger, as befits a quadruple amputee, rushed to his face. He blurted: no Puerto Rican cigars, no cigars at all. As embarrassing as it now seems to me, I became irritated at his obduracy. After all, I was doing a "good thing," being helpful and solicitous. But enough is enough. Yet, as an Irish Catholic, I had been steeped in guilt and the moral obligation of service, so I set out to get two Puerto Rican cigars—no easy task. After much hassle, I did obtain the cigars and brought them back. I placed one in his mouth and lit it. His face shone like an evening star.

It was not until fifteen years later that I realized what had happened, what I had missed, and what I had to learn. I was teaching the philosophy of Albert Camus, and the theme was personal authenticity. In a flashback, my Puerto Rican patient taught me of authenticity, of the aesthetic moment, and of the quality of life in a pretechnological medical setting. His message came to me as a revelation, an epiphany. Surely, only those special cigars would do, for only they, their smell and taste, would bring back the rich memories of Puerto Rico, the cocoa-brown skin of the women, the mist hanging over the coast between the Condado of San Juan and the city of Mayaguez. Only those cigars were authentic, existential, freighted with experienced relations. Only they sang his song, his personal song.

I missed the meaning in 1948. Now I have it. No pedagogy is worth its salt if it does not know the difference between one cigar and another, between the literal and the symbolical. As help to being sensitive to this difference, I carry with me always the admonition of William James, who asks us to be alert to "an 'ever not quite' to all our formulas, and novelty and possibility forever leaking in."[4]

SEVENTEEN

THE CULTURAL IMMORTALITY OF
PHILOSOPHY AS HUMAN DRAMA

For it is owing to their wonder that men both now begin and at first began to philosophize; they wondered originally at the obvious difficulties, then advanced little by little and stated difficulties about the great matters, e.g., about the phenomena of the moon and those of the sun and of the stars, and about the genesis of the universe. And a man who is puzzled and wonders thinks himself ignorant (whence even the lover of myth is in a sense a lover of Wisdom, for the myth is composed of wonders); therefore since they philosophized in order to escape from ignorance, evidently they were pursuing science in order to know, and not for any utilitarian end. And this is confirmed by the facts; for it was when almost all the necessities of life and the things that make for comfort and recreation had been secured, that such knowledge began to be sought. Evidently then we do not seek it for the sake of any other advantage; but as the man is free, we say, who exists for his own sake and not for another's, so we pursue this as the only free science, for it alone exists for its own sake.

—Aristotle, *Metaphysics*

I. Introduction

The history of philosophy in Western civilization is a vast intellectual map characterized by periods of speculative explosions followed by larger periods of absorption and redress. If we accept the common wisdom that Western civilization began with the Greeks, then the paramount role of philosophy is obvious, for philosophical speculation was the formative dimension of Greek civilization. Philosophy is the mother of most of the intellectual and academic disciplines as we now know them. Rhetoric, logic, the sciences, the social sciences, economics, and politics all trace their lineage to philosophy. And Western theology would be bare-bones if it were not for philosophical ideas. Indeed, as late as the eighteenth century, scientists were actually philosophers. Mathematics and physics were brought into being by philosophers—as witness the invention of calculus, an attempted philosophical resolution of the problem of infinity. If, in the twentieth century, the sciences contend that they are independent of philosophical ideas, we can still point to the work of Niels Bohr and Werner Heisenberg, who were profoundly influenced by philosophy and wrote philosophical treatises. Quantum mechanics is as much a philosophical hypothesis as a scientific one, as is the biology which points to the molecular structure of beings.

The influence of philosophers throughout the centuries is dazzling and way out of proportion to the number of philosophers recognized in the canon of important thinkers. We note Aristotle's organization of the intellectual disciplines and his pioneering work in biology and astronomy. Of significance also is Francis Bacon's stress on the inductive method and Descartes's invention of analytic geometry. The doctrine of toleration, so central to our democratic form of government, traces to Locke, whereas Western civilization owes much to the defense of liberty by John Stuart Mill. Virtually the only interesting theories of education trace to philosophers: Plato, Rousseau, Herbart, Montessori, and, above all, John Dewey. The major reason contemporary educational theory is so utterly boring is precisely that it has been shorn of philosophical imagination. Finally, we should not forget that Karl Marx, perhaps the single most influential thinker in human history, was a philosopher.

I could continue this pantheon of influential philosophers indefinitely, but suffice it to say that to be ignorant of the history of philosophy while pursuing a study of the meaning of human life is akin to studying the human body while remaining ignorant of the brain and the liver. Socrates once said that the unexamined life is not worth living, and for William James philosophy was the habit of always seeing an alternative. For me, the importance of philosophy proceeds from the fact that it is not afraid of anything. No idea is too daring to be pursued to its realization. Please notice that I did not say "afraid of nothing," for "nothing" is a serious problem in philosophy. In fact, the most important philosophical question, still with us, reads, "why is there something rather than nothing?" To this question there is neither a perceivable nor a conceivable answer; yet having asked it over 2,000 years ago, we are burdened with re-asking it and probing its significance. In effect, philosophy does not become tired and does not jettison its old questions; rather, it adds new ones. It is in this way that we can speak of philosophy as culturally immortal, for so long as life exists, questions as to its origin, meaning, and future are of paramount concern. On occasion, the responses to these perennial questions take on a dramatic and novel formulation, so much so that they become permanent deposits in our cultural history and in our collective consciousness, even if not so acknowledged by those who have had the deep misfortune not to have studied philosophy. I turn now to a presentation of several of these paradigmatic moments in the history of Western thought.

II. Plato's Cave and the Search for Light

In Book 7 of the *Republic*,[1] Plato (427–347 BC) introduces an allegory to describe what he takes to be our fundamental situation. We are imprisoned in a cave, fettered by the neck and the legs so that we can only look forward to a wall in front of us. On the wall are cast shadows of human figures with baskets of food on their heads and of animals carried by bearers. The shadows are projected by the light of a fire in back of a parapet (behind us) on which pass the figures. A slight diffusion of daylight breaks in from the entrance to the cave, high above and to the side of the parapet. Because, as prisoners, we see only shadows, we take these images to be real. For reasons not given in the allegory, one of the prisoners is compelled to leave his chains and make his way to the upper world. After a period of adjustment to the emergence of light, the former prisoner stands in the glare of the sun. Returning to the cave, he attempts to instruct his fellow prisoners that they see only shadows and that he brings to them the knowledge of the real, sensible world. The prisoners threaten to kill him if he persists in this attempt to unmask their view of the world—a clear reference to the trial and death of Socrates for comparable activities in classical Athens.

In order to explicate this deceptively simple allegory by Plato, I have to introduce at least one more theme, this one from Plato's dialogue "Meno."[2] Socrates asks Meno to tell him the nature of virtue. Meno responds with a series of definitions which Socrates rejects as instances of virtue but not equivalent to its nature, that is, its *eidos*, or form. Meno becomes irritated at Socrates for constantly confusing him and strikes back with two devastating questions. First, if you do not know what you seek, how do you know that it exists? Second, should you find it, how would you know that it is what you have been seeking?[3] To these questions, Socrates, representing Plato, introduces a myth, the upshot of which is that before our present embodiment, our souls had access to another world wherein we knew the true forms of reality. Our task now is to recall these forms and to shed ourselves of the material world which blocks our vision. True pedagogy moves us from the world of shadows, through the world of material things, and then through the mathematical forms until we have access to the forms themselves, especially of truth, beauty, and the good.

The paradox of Plato's position can be stated as follows: we know more than we should but less than we can. As human beings, we sense the world one thing at a time: a chair, a book, a person. Yet we can speak of chair, book, and person to include endless individual instances. Our percepts are singular but our concepts are general. How is this possible? The history of philosophy is faced with a variety of responses to this basic and puzzling question. It is not Plato's response so much as the question itself which is intriguing. More than 2,000 years before Freud, Plato informs us that the world is not what it seems to be. Further, he tells us that we can be in touch with powers beyond our immediate ken. Physics is only a local discipline, for our minds can penetrate the physical world and reach to the forms of things, independent of their singular, sensate characteristics.

Now, if we return to the cave, we find our situation deepened considerably. The cave is a description of our life, our neighborhood, our region, our university, our state, our career, our family, our religion, and our politics. Where we are at any given time is in one cave or another. The task is to know that, a task more subtle and more arduous than at first glance. The height of self-deception is to think that where we are, what we do, and what we believe is where others are, what they do, and what they believe. Worse, we think that this is where others ought to be, what they should do, and should believe. The crucial question pertaining to Plato's cave has to do with the person leaving. How did that happen? Was there a fight in the cave, such that some helped one to escape?[4] If so, who informed him of the self-deception in which he was mired? And why did they not respond positively when he returned? Or is it that the escaped prisoner was in touch with powers which transcended the cave, powers given only to the few? Or still further, perhaps the fetters are self-inflicted and can be dropped by an act of the will, if we but had the will.[5]

As I see our situation, there are three possible positions of people regarding the cave. First, there are those who have broken out and are proceeding toward the light. I have not met any such persons and am dubious about reports that they exist, although my reading tells me of occasional instances. Second, there are those of us who are in the cave but are aware of its self-deception. We are restless and of good will, yet we lack either the energy, the courage, or the originality to escape. Finally, there are opponents: those who are in the cave and refuse to admit to their situation. They become hostile to any effort which is directed toward enlightening them as to their actual plight. The more we insist on the existence of the cave, the more stubborn they become as to the righteousness of their way, of their cause, and, above all, in their blindness. The Greeks had a word for this attitude. They called it *hubris*, roughly translated as stubborn pride in an unworthy, unworkable, inelegant, and self-deceiving cause. For Plato, the dissolving, unmasking, or disarming of this attitude was the key issue in pedagogy. And that is why, for Plato, philosophy is *therapeia*, an attempted healing of our wounded and encapsulated psyche. Thus, Shakespeare was a Platonist when he wrote, "There are more things in heaven and earth, Horatio, than are dreamt of in your philosophy."[6] Plato's dreams may not be yours or mine, but his philosophy makes it clear that we should dream of things unseen and unknown.

III. The Augustinian Self as Divine Image

I turn now to a second paradigmatic event in the history of Western consciousness, that of the doctrine of the Trinity as promulgated by Augustine (354–430 AD). Those unfamiliar with philosophy may be unaware that Christianity would have been an empty shell were it not for its marriage to Greek philosophy, especially of the Neoplatonic variety.

Augustine, of course, is not the founder of the doctrine of the Trinity. Indeed, the currents and crosscurrents of Greek philosophy, pagan ritual, Jewish ethics, and Christian belief constitute a dazzling intellectual enterprise of the first four hundred years after the death of Christ. Nonetheless, Augustine was the most original spokesman for the doctrine of the Trinity as well as being the most explicitly philosophical of the fathers of the early church. It is precisely the philosophical fallout from Augustine's doctrine of the Trinity which interests philosophers, for it continues Plato's view of the world and casts a spell over the intellectual life of Europe for 1,000 years, until it is replaced by the secular Platonism of Descartes. The doctrine of the Trinity is a brilliant intellectual construction of one of the most implausible contentions in the history of religion: namely, that one God is three persons, each exactly and equivalently God. Augustine puts the quandary clearly.

> Some persons, however, find a difficulty in this faith; when they hear that the Father is God, and the Son God, and the Holy Spirit God, and yet that this Trinity is not three Gods, but one God; and they ask how they are to understand this: especially when it is said that the Trinity works indivisibly in everything that God works, and yet that a certain voice of the Father spoke, which is not the voice of the Son; and that none except the Son was born in the flesh, and suffered, and rose again, and ascended into heaven; and that none except the Holy Spirit came in the form of a dove. They wish to understand how the Trinity uttered that voice which was only of the Father; and how the same Trinity created that flesh in which the Son only was born of the Virgin; and how the very same Trinity itself wrought that form of a dove, in which the Holy Spirit only appeared. Yet, otherwise, the Trinity does not work indivisibly, but the Father does some things, the Son other things, and the Holy Spirit yet others: or else if they do some things together, some severally, then the Trinity is not indivisible. It is a difficulty, too, to them, in what manner the Holy Spirit is in the Trinity, whom neither the Father nor the Son, nor both, have begotten, although He is the Spirit both of the Father and of the Son. Since, then, men weary us with asking such questions, let us unfold to them, as we are able, whatever wisdom God's gift has bestowed upon our weakness on this subject.[7]

The rudiments of the doctrine itself are quite simple. God is infinite and therefore has infinite knowledge. Further, in that God knows all, he knows himself. Infinite knowledge of himself is equivalent to an infinite person, the Son. Where there are two there is a relationship, in this case an infinite relationship, equivalent to the Spirit, the third part of the Trinity. The entire argument hinges on the philosophical proposition that what is infinite must exist, for if it were only conceptual, then any existing thing would be superior, thereby denying the infinite. There is no question that philosophical difficulties abound in this formulation. Aside from the obvious one that we have no rational verification that the infinite God exists in the first place, we have to ask also, why do these infinite relationships stop at three? Should it not follow that the Son and the Spirit have such a relationship and, likewise, the Spirit and the Father? Fortunately, these problems are not at the center of the present discussion. Rather, we focus on the nature of the Son and the remarkable contention that in the person of Christ, God became human. Our concern here is not with the religious claim but rather with its import for epistemology, that is, for what and how we know.

Et verbum caro factum est is the message of the Christian Scriptures, namely, and the Word was made flesh.[8] In the original Greek of St. John, the word for the Word, for the Christ, was *logos*. For 500 years of Greek philosophy, beginning with Heraclitus, *logos* was the term used to describe the deepest manifestation of *phusus*, of nature, of all that was or could be. John writes: In the beginning was the *logos*.[9] This was not new to the Greeks. That God the Son was an idea, an *eidos*, would not have been new to Plato. But what was new, staggeringly new, was that the *logos* chose flesh, matter, to appear to the world. The appearance of God, the theophany, in early Christian thought uses the Platonic tradition, yet makes a radical break with its most cherished assumption. The Platonists believed that the material world was an obfuscation which had to be transcended if one were to reach for the *eidai*, the ultimate forms.

Augustine, however, was influenced not only by the Platonists but also by the Greek and Roman Stoics. They taught him that the human world was penetrated by the *eidai*, known as, significantly, *logoi spermatikoi*, or, in the Latin of Augustine, *rationes seminales*. These seeded reasons or ideas were open to us if we practiced the doctrine of *apatheia*, that is, allowed nature to take an unhindered course within the very fabric of our being. The task, then, is for each of us, as a microcosm, to become continuous with nature as a macrocosm and, in so doing, we shall be consumed in the fire of an ultimate harmony. Despite the power of this position, we face a serious difficulty in accepting it. If Plato's world of forms is unreachable, the Stoic doctrine of consummation in nature obliviates our personal lives. Nowhere is this more graphically stated than by Marcus Aurelius, Roman emperor and Stoic philosopher:

> Of human life the time is a point, and the substance is in a flux, and the perception dull, and the composition of the whole body subject to putrefaction, and the soul a whirl, and fortune hard to divine, and fame a thing devoid of judgement. And, to say all in a word, everything which belongs to the body is a stream, and what belongs to the soul is a dream and vapour, and life is a warfare and a stranger's sojourn, and after fame is oblivion.[10]

Despite the philosophical problems with Plato's world of ideas and the Stoics' doctrine of *apatheia*, if we merge them, as Augustine does, they provide an excellent explanatory framework for the person of Christ in relation to the problems of knowledge. Christ is the supreme *eidos*, the idea that God has of himself. He is also the *logos*, the way in which God appears to the world. And it is extremely noteworthy that the "way" of the Christ is to be the true light that enlightens every man who comes into the world.[11] Following Plato and the Jewish-Christian teaching of original sin, we are born prisoners in the cave of our own making. Following the doctrine of the Trinity, Christ, the *logos*, is the light which appears to us in the cave and summons us to liberation. Augustinean epistemology holds that to be a Christian is to be in a world which is bathed with light, and to be able to behold the seeded reasons of the Stoics as alive and obvious. For Augustine, the world is laced with *vestigia dei*, the traces and shadows of God.

Yet this scenario is definitely that of Plato, for both the world of ideas and the cave are central themes in early Christian teaching. The radical difference is that by virtue of the Incarnation, Christian thinkers, especially Augustine, find a way for the supreme idea, the *logos*, to be both supreme and to penetrate the cave. Plato is vague about how and why the one prisoner escapes. Augustine is not vague. We have it within our power, if called, to convert toward the light. In the Jewish sense of a *teshuvah*, we must turn our whole body, not just our mind, if we are to truly seek and find the light. In the words of Baruch Spinoza, the great Jewish philosopher of the seventeenth century, we must be prepared for a *de emendatione intellectus*, a moral healing of the understanding, if we are to know at all.[12] And still later, in the nineteenth century, William James can say that belief helps to create its own verification.[13] It was Augustine who gave decisive impetus to a moral epistemology. His person and his thought dominated medieval culture. He is a key figure in the powerful doctrines of conversion as found in Luther and Calvin. And long after Christianity ceased to be at the center of European intellectual life, Augustine's stress on a change of heart, if we are to see and to know, remains with us, an abiding remembrance of the omnipresence of Plato's cave and of mine and of yours.

IV. The Cartesian Self as Infinite

Despite the bold, speculative character of the Western revealed religions—Judaism, Christianity, and Islam—each of them accepted the finite cosmology of the Greeks, especially as promulgated by Aristotle. Although this commitment can be understood historically and aesthetically, it was unfortunate from a theological vantage point. How, for example, can one believe that God is infinite and still accept a version of nature as closed, fixed, and intelligible? The commitment to Aristotle's cosmology is especially strange for Christianity, for as we have seen in the Trinitarianism of Augustine, Christians believe in a material continuity between the earth, human life, and the infinite God. Aristotle, brilliant philosopher and scientist, was no match for the extraordinary vision of nature which was implicit in Christian theology. Indeed, only post-Copernican quantum cosmology can fulfill the intentions of Augustine. (The naiveté of Christianity with regard to the physical world has reappeared in our time under the nostrum of creationism. This is not only nonsense from the side of science, it is also heterodox Christianity, for it traps the infinite God into an unimaginative, one-shot creation and, more seriously, denies the Christian claim that human history is a cocreator in the evolution of nature such that we culminate in the richness of a freely wrought realization of the intentions of a nondeterministic God.)

Returning to the center of our discussion, the medieval Christian cosmological, theological, and cartographical assumptions come apart at the seams in the tumultuous sixteenth century. In 1507, the Waldseemuller map, for the first time, presented the world in two distinct hemispheres. To Europe, Asia, and Africa, there was added the fourth part of America. The medieval assumption of a single continent, as protected by God from the violence of the oceans, was shattered. In 1517, Luther posted his theses on the castle door at Wittenberg and the Reformation began. The unity of medieval Christendom was soon to be in disarray. In 1543, the Polish astronomer Nicolaus Copernicus published his *De revolutionibus orbium coelestium libri IV*, a work which was to spell the end of the Aristotelian-Ptolemaic geocentric cosmology. The controversy surrounding the heliocentric theory of Copernicus was to become one of the most fascinating and complex in European intellectual history, and in time would involve the Roman Catholic Church, the Inquisition, and the persons of Galileo, Cusanus, Melancthon, Bruno, and, finally, Newton. In the midst of the ferment, the most intriguing thinker is Rene Descartes (1596–1650), for it is he who most directly responds to the implications of the Copernican revolution.

One of the casualties of Copernicanism was the Aristotelian doctrine of natural place, whereby everything that exists, celestial or terrestrial, has its proper place in the rational scheme. The most important implication of this doctrine was that the earth was the center of the universe and, concomitantly, that human life, as the center of the earth, was thereby central to cosmic life. Copernicanism rendered the earth as but a satellite, moving both around the sun and on its own axis. The crisis was clear. If stability and physical centrality were essential for metaphysical importance, the post-Copernican version of human life rendered us dwarfed and inconsequential. The English poet John Donne says it best in his "Anatomy of the World."

> And new Philosophy calls all in doubt,
> The Element of fire is quite put out;
> The Sun is lost, and the earth, and no man's wit
> Can well direct him where to look for it.
> And freely men confess that this world's spent,
> When in the Planets, and the Firmament

They seek so many new; then see that this
Is crumbled out again to his Atomies.
'Til all in pieces, all coherence gone;
All just supply, and all Relation:
Prince, Subject, Father, Son, are things forgot,
For every man alone thinks he hath got
To be a Phœnix, and that then can be
None of that kind, of which he is, but he.[14]

Or perhaps you prefer the plaintive remark of Pascal: "The eternal silence of these infinite spaces frightens me."[15] Whether it be Donne or Pascal, among others, a crisis in the meaning of the human self had erupted in the late sixteenth century. With Copernicanism came a new doctrine of place. In Aristotelianism everything had a natural place, and the human organism was not an exception. Copernicanism dealt a devastating blow to this living-room version of the cosmos by casting deep doubt on the fixed character of the planets. In Aristotelian perspective, the importance of human life was inextricably tied to the importance of the planet earth as nothing less than the physical center of the cosmos. Copernicanism eradicated that centrality and engendered a deep disquiet about the ontological status of human life. The intervening centuries between Copernicanism and the twentieth century witnessed an effort at temporary repair by Newtonian physics. But the remedy could not hold and the full implications of Copernicanism finally arrived in our century, sustained by quantum mechanics, a new cosmology, and the social collapse of religious, political, and ideological eschatologies. The deepest contemporary ontological problem is that of homelessness. The vast, limitless, perhaps infinite universe does not award us a place. The planet earth is a node in the midst of cosmic unintelligibility. According to Aristotle, who we are is where we are. And where anything is, is a function of where everything is, in relation to a center and a periphery. If that is so, we are now no one, for we are nowhere, in that we do not know the extension of the cosmos or, for that matter, whether it has any periphery at all.

It is in the context of this dramatic situation that we consider one aspect of the philosophy of Descartes. He was clearly sympathetic with Copernicanism, as we see in his early work *Le Monde* (1634), which he had to suppress after the condemnation of Galileo. The implications of Copernicanism acted as a specter behind all of the works of Descartes. If heliocentrism is true, then the Aristotelian doctrine of natural place is wrecked. Further, if the earth is not the center of the universe, then human life cannot count on physical centrality for the source of its epistemic certitude. In a series of bold and ingenious methodological and philosophical moves, Descartes sets out to reanchor the possibility of human certitude. He proceeds in the following way. It is conceivable that God does not exist. In that God is the guarantor of our sense experience, it is also conceivable that I am deluded as to the existence of the physical world, including my body. What is not conceivable, however, is that I, as a thinking being, do not exist, for, in one of the most famous of all philosophical phrases, *Cogito ergo sum*: in that I think, I exist. In the *Discourse Concerning Method*, Descartes writes: "But immediately afterward I noticed that, while I thus wished to think that everything was false, it was necessary that I who was thinking be something. And noting that this truth—I think, therefore I am—was so firm and so assured that all the most extravagant suppositions of the skeptics were not capable of disturbing it, I judged that I could receive it, without scruple, as the first principle of the philosophy I was seeking."[16] The philosophy he sought was one in which the foundation was not subject to doubt, especially not subject to the foibles and snares of sense experience. To that end, he opposes Aristotle and Scholastics such as Thomas Aquinas by holding that the *res cogitans*, the thinking thing, the human mind, has no need of the physical world, the *res extensa*, for its existence. The *res cogitans* is a complete substance and, as such, is self-guaranteeing of its existence and its knowledge. The thinking self comes equipped with innate ideas of such power that they are able to reconstruct the existence of God and of the material world with indubitability. In order to achieve this power, however, Descartes began a tradition known as "psycho-physical dualism," which shattered the experiential unity of the human self and caused serious disarray in the behavioral sciences until the middle of the nineteenth century and the birth of experimental psychology.

Nonetheless, Descartes bequeathed also an intriguing possibility—namely, that the human mind has innate powers which are independent of sense experience and which are independent of the physical place that the mind occupies at any given time. Further, as with Plato, he holds that we can know infinitely more than we do, even to knowing the ultimate principles of reality equivalent to the knowledge of perfect being. This is a heady claim, but we should not forget that Descartes was the father of modern mathematics. As we of the twentieth century know, modern mathematics creates physics, and physics makes worlds of which nature knows not nor even dreamt. Looked at from a traditional view, Pascal was right; infinite space does terrify us. In the philosophy of Descartes, however, even infinite space is but a local box, potentially transcended by the power of the human mind.

V. Immanuel Kant: The Self as Constructing the World

Not all philosophers accepted the claims of Descartes or of the two major thinkers who continued his work, Spinoza and Leibniz. I refer especially to the British tradition in philosophy, which had always stressed the irreducible importance of sense experience in the activity of human knowing. Beginning with Francis Bacon, and on through Hobbes and Locke, the empirical method of observation was regarded as necessary if reason were to function in a trustworthy way. It was the eighteenth-century philosopher David Hume, however, who issued the most trenchant critique of the European continental philosophers. Focusing on the principle of causality, Hume made it clear that judgments proceeding from the intuitive power of reason were faulty. Hume's opponents were the Newtonians, who, following the philosophical speculation rather than the empirical physics of Newton, had promulgated increasingly unlikely hypotheses. The chastising and skeptical voice of Hume was heard across the English Channel by the German philosopher Immanuel Kant (1724–1804). Awoken from his "dogmatic slumber" by the attack of Hume, Kant set out to address his criticism and save Newtonian physics.

However much they disagreed on fundamental issues, Descartes, Spinoza, and Leibniz did agree that the human mind had access to the principle of causality. For David Hume, the principle of causality was a mock-up due to habit and custom rather than to any intuitive grasp of the mind. Hume admitted that we can say that A caused B again and again, but he denied that we experienced the principle of A causing B. What we experience is a series of repetitive acts, no one of which provides reason with the right to claim that such a causal nexus will always be so. If Hume were right, scientific propositions would be limited to single elements. Correspondingly, Newtonian physics would be shipwrecked. Despite the extensive and intense outcry against Hume, Kant, for one, was wise enough to admit that he was fundamentally correct. A way had to be found to accept Hume's criticism and yet save science.

Kant's move in this direction is not only a mark of genius but also of speculative ingenuity. He rightly refers to his work in this regard as a "second Copernican revolution." There is considerable complexity in Kant's response to Hume, but I shall trim the sails and set it out in bald terms. Hume insisted that propositions which were analytic, a priori, had no merit. By this he meant that any proposition which claimed more than a single event or sense datum could reveal was an illegitimate claim. To the contrary, the only propositions of merit were synthetic, a posteriori, by which Hume meant a description of our sense of experience, that could be accounted for only by single sense impressions. Kant accepted Hume's dictum that legitimate propositions had to be based on experience. But Kant sought also to have these propositions function as a priori, that is, as universal laws, which did not have to be evaluated on each appearing occasion. The latter was necessary if Newtonian science were to prevail. Kant's strategy was to develop an entirely new type of proposition, one which was synthetic but also a priori. This proposition would be based on experience and yet would function as a universal law. How in the name of all that was sacred in the 2000-year history of epistemology would such a hybrid be possible? In fact, nothing less than a philosophical Copernican revolution would suffice if Kant were to succeed.

As early as his "Inaugural Dissertation" in 1770, Kant anticipates this revolution in consciousness. In a series of extraordinary claims, Kant turns the history of philosophy and science upside down: "The idea of time does not originate in the senses, but is presupposed by them. Time is not something objective and real. The concept of space is not abstracted from outer sensations. Space is not something objective and real."[17] In technical terms, Kant holds that space and time are presensuous intuitions had by us prior to our experience of the physical world. In a more simple format, Kant tells us that space and time are homemade blankets which condition all of our experience. We time the world and we space the world. If we, as human life, did not exist, then neither would time nor space. His answer to Hume is now clear. All of our a priori judgments on the physical world, as found in physics and mathematics, are based on experience, for they always assume the existence of space and time, which we experience as presensuous intuitions, had by each human being. The world is experienced as it appears, that is, as phenomenal. It comes to us already contexted by our formulation of space and time. In this way, synthetic a priori propositions are possible in physics and mathematics, for they are laws which are nonetheless based on common experience. Science is saved. The concession made by Kant is both beguiling and serious. The world which does not appear in space and time cannot be known with apodictic or scientific certainty. So we have only indirect knowledge of the existence of God, the immortality of the soul, and the eternality of the world. In fact, because these concerns are not limited to space and time, they are antinomic and can be both supported and opposed equally by reason. Metaphysics, then, is not a science.

Kant has taken the first step in the second Copernican revolution. The world we experience is a construct of the human imagination. Its laws are home-grown and have no ultimate or even astral significance. He does not take the subsequent step, although it will be taken in subsequent centuries. The universe will become a construct of human imagination and so, too, in the twentieth century, will God become one of our imaginative formulations, and nothing will have any meaning unless we endow it with meaning.

VI. Karl Marx: Human Life as Self-Deceived and Alienated

In spite of the inordinate brilliance of philosophy from the early Greeks to the nineteenth century, one naive strand awaited challenge. Philosophy, and other disciplines as well, assumed that events took place one after the other, in serial fashion, playing out the transcendent rubric of

Judaism, Christianity, or Islam. Until the eighteenth-century thought of Vico and Herder, the inner, complex fabric of historical forces was largely unsung. This naiveté about the complexity of history was given a rude awakening by the publication of the philosophy of Hegel, who introduced us to the dialectic of historical events and who put into perspective the power of historical forces which transcend the intentions and interpretations of human chronicle. For Hegel, history is a matrix in and through which all persons and all events are given their meaning. Hegel was the first to see history, correctly, as a "slaughter-bench," in which the private affairs of human life are carried on in the context of forces over which they have no control. He writes: "But in contemplating history as the slaughter-bench at which the happiness of peoples, the wisdom of states, and the virtue of individuals have been sacrificed, a question necessarily arises: To what principle, to what final purpose, have these monstrous sacrifices been offered?"[18]

To this question, there are any number of responses, and they range from the Pollyanna attitude of the religious zealot to the laissez-faire cynicism of the determinist. A more realistic and creative response emerges from the thought of Karl Marx (1818–83), who studied Hegel's writings with care. The central philosophical position of Marx was brilliantly paradoxical. On the one hand, he accepted the Hegelian view that human life is in the inextricable throes of history. On the other hand, he, like the Jews and the Christians, believed in *kairos*, a moment in historical time which can be seized such that the flow of history is irreversibly changed. Marx was the first genuine and intentional revolutionary of consciousness in the history of philosophy.

Schopenhauer once said that anyone who studied philosophy and was unaware of Kant was in a state of innocence. I agree, but I add that in the twentieth century, anyone who studies anything and is unaware of Marx is in a state of innocence, or, as the Roman Catholicism of my childhood would say, in a state of vincible ignorance—that is, guilty of not knowing what one should know in order to make an intelligent moral decision. I concentrate here on only two of Marx's salient contentions: first, that institutions condition consciousness rather than the reverse; second, that our fundamental situation is to be in a state of alienation. For the first, I cite the famous passage from Marx's 1859 work, "A Contribution to the Critique of Political Economy": "The mode of production of material life conditions the social, political and intellectual life process in general. It is not the consciousness of men that determines their being, but, on the contrary, their social being that determines their consciousness."[19] Marx is telling us that we come to consciousness in a maelstrom of competing institutional conditions. For him, it was church and state, bourgeois and proletariat, capitalist and worker that formulated our consciousness. For us in twentieth-century America, additionally it is male and female; urban and rural; black, brown, and white; East and West; North and South; having access to money and education and being denied such access—all of which conditions our coming to consciousness. Marx's point is clear. Who we are is a function of our anticipations, expectations, and the burdens promulgated by those around us, who accept or reject our efforts at becoming either like them or different from them. The self-generating, self-motivating individual is largely a myth, as we find ourselves slotted into one groove or another, for the good of the family, the economy, the nation, or some religious or political ideology, none of which function on behalf of individuals.

It is no wonder that originality, imagination, and boldness on behalf of social and political change are hard to come by, for, as Marx points out, the social structure so conditions us that we regard such changes as anathema. Given this lamentable state of affairs, we find that Marx, perhaps surprisingly, is in the tradition of Plato, Augustine, and Spinoza, for he, like they, holds that only a moral conversion will free us from the fetters of social conditioning and illegitimate expectation. Remarkably, Marx calls upon us to seize the process of history, enter into its bowels, and redirect society toward human liberation. To this end, in continuity with the entire tradition of moral epistemology, it is necessary for us to become aware of how we have been had. And this leads to a second important insight of Marx, the deleterious character of our alienation from our own humanness.

Although the experience of human alienation has been made notorious by the existentialists Sartre and Camus, its original explication traces to Marx's early "Economic and Philosophic Manuscripts of 1844." The manuscripts are a brilliant analysis of a broken promise. Contexted by the Industrial Revolution, they detail how "workers" become estranged from their work, and, in time, from nature, from other workers, and, finally, from themselves.[20] Marx's complex and detailed argument centers around the failure of society to structure social and economic life such that we fulfill our *Gattungswesen*. Awkwardly translated as "species-consciousness" or "species-being," *Gattungswesen* is best explored through its referent, "worker." Because of the rise of laissez-faire capitalism, the free-market economy, and the economic exploitation of surplus value, the interpretation of workers as equivalent to overhead became accepted policy. In time, workers became estranged or alienated from their work, for the products were not distinctively theirs and they became estranged from each other by virtue of piecework competition. Due to land enclosure and the development of the urban factory system, the workers became alienated from nature. Finally, stung with the burden of what the classical economist David Ricardo approvingly conceived as the capitalist necessity of sustaining a subsistent, lumpen proletariat, the worker became alienated from himself/herself. Although considerable controversy has been generated relative to Marx's appraisal of industrial capitalism, we should not allow this to distract us from the universality of Marx's notion of alienation. The greatest offense is for those in power to promise that which they have neither the power nor the intention to redeem. This is as true of socialism as it is of capitalism, as true of religion as it is of egalitarian democracy. Marx is right. The major offense is to structure a society in which promises are made but knowingly aborted. Political, social, and religious power exists as dependent on the rampant, imposed self-deception of the common person. This is an egregious offense against humanity which can be changed only by an extensive revolution in human consciousness. Marx had the courage to call for that change. His commentary on his philosophical predecessor, Ludwig Feuerbach, is apropos: "The philosophers have only *interpreted* the world, in various ways; the point, however, is to *change* it."[21] Ironically, Marx was too modest about philosophy, for philosophy has always changed the world, and he as a philosopher has changed the world more than any other single person.

VII. Nietzsche: Live Dangerously

As surprising as it might be to casual students of modern intellectual history, Marx was not the radical thinker of the nineteenth century. That designation is more appropriately applied to either Søren Kierkegaard (1813–1855) or Friedrich Nietzsche (1844–1900). Marx believed that the lumpen proletariat would be redeemed if we were to have a systemic extirpation of social mores. Kierkegaard and Nietzsche, to the contrary, had no such confidence in the possibilities of the common person. Although all three thinkers showed a contempt for organized religion, bureaucracy, and the faceless ideologies of their time—a contempt shared, incidentally, by their peer, the great Russian novelist Fyodor Dostoevsky—nonetheless, Kierkegaard and Nietzsche saw hope only for those few among us who were able to break through the systematic hypocrisy of modern religion, society, and politics. I focus here on Nietzsche. From the time of Jean-Jacques Rousseau, in the middle of the eighteenth century, until the middle of the twentieth century, we have witnessed an extraordinary rash of creative thinkers and artists whose personal lives, predilections, and attitudes, to say the least, have been neurotic. In this tradition, which I refer to as that of the "tangled genius," Nietzsche is clearly the dominant figure.

As a young man in his twenties, Nietzsche was hailed as the greatest philologist in the history of the European languages. Yet from the time of the publication of his first work, *The Birth of Tragedy*, in 1872, Nietzsche was progressing toward the insanity which was to claim him in 1888, some twelve years before his death. There are scholarly arguments over the cause of his insanity, with the three favored explanations being a syphilitic infection contracted in his youth, a brain lesion resulting from an early fall, and genetically induced paranoid schizophrenia. Whatever may be the correct cause, it is unsettling to read that Freud speaks of Nietzsche as knowing more about himself than anyone in the history of literature. Still more unsettling is that to read Nietzsche is to read someone who knows more about me than I know about myself, indeed, knows more about us than we know about ourselves.

In one of his last writings, Nietzsche tells us that "since Copernicus, man has been rolling from the center toward X."[22] In effect, we have lost our hold on the life-force necessary to a fully human and liberated culture. For Nietzsche, civilization makes a tragic mistake when it advances the cause of Apollo, the God of order and form, over that of Dionysus, the God of eros and energy. Nietzsche cites the paradox that when Apollo is supreme, we have neither creative energy nor form, but when Dionysus is supreme, the Apollonian call to order is present and enhancing. Nietzsche is the most strident figure in the history of philosophy because of his doubt about the significance of clear reason. He contends that Socrates, by virtue of his introduction of the rational method of philosophical questioning to Greek culture, single-handedly brought about the demise of Greek tragedy—namely, the move from the supreme madness and magic of Aeschylus and Sophocles to the deus ex machina of Euripides.[23]

It is not germane to the present discussion that we adjudicate the scholarly controversies over Nietzsche's inflammatory interpretation of the evolution of Greek tragedy. To the point, however, is that Nietzsche, in siding with the Sophoclean chorus, which foretells the doom of Oedipus, also encourages acceptance of the underground energies available to us as a gift from Dionysus, if we had but the will to shuck off the tired truisms of our politics, our religion, and our ethics. Nietzsche's call, to each of us, is for a *Versuch einer Umwertung aller Werte*, an attempt at a transvaluation of all values. In order to bring off the instituting of new values, we must overcome our primary opponent, bourgeois Christian ethics, especially as found in the glorification of humility and self-abnegation. Nietzsche charges Christianity with the historical guile of convincing its followers to be humble, whereas its leaders were the acme of pride and arrogance. For Nietzsche, the traditional hierarchy of values is to be inverted. The supreme values are the aesthetic, especially the dance, whereby the entire body resonates through our consciousness. He anticipates the momentous closing scene in Ingmar Bergman's film *The Seventh Seal*, in which the flagellants do the dance of death as their response to the plague. In Nietzsche, as in Bergman, better to dance to the death than to humbly accept the will of God. No surprise here, for it is Nietzsche who is the first modern thinker to announce the death of God. In a brilliant parody of the Gospel of St. John, Nietzsche writes in *The Gay Science*:

Have you not heard of that madman who lit a lantern in the bright morning hours, ran to the market place, and cried incessantly, "I seek God! I seek God!" As many of those who do not believe in God were standing around just then, he provoked much laughter. "Why, did he get lost?" said one. "Did he lose his way like a child?" said another. "Or is he hiding? "Is he afraid of us?" "Has he gone on a voyage? Or emigrated?" Thus they yelled and laughed. The madman jumped into their midst and pierced them with his glances.

"Whither is God," he cried. "I shall tell you. We have killed him—you and I. All of us are his murderers. But how have we done this? How were we able to drink up the sea? Who gave us the sponge to wipe away the horizon? What did we do when we unchained this earth from its sun? Whither is it moving now? Whither are we moving now? Away from all suns? Are we not plunging continually? Backward, sideward, forward, in all directions? Is there any up or down left? Are we not straying as through an infinite nothing? Do we not feel the breath of empty space? Has it not become colder? Is not night and more night coming on all the while? Must not lanterns be lit in the morning? Do we not hear anything yet of the noise of the gravediggers who are burying God? Do we not smell anything yet of God's decomposition? Gods, too, decompose. God is dead. God remains dead. And we have killed him. How shall we, the murderers of all murderers, comfort ourselves? What was holiest and most powerful of all that the world has yet owned has bled to death under our knives. Who will wipe this blood off us? What water is there for us to clean ourselves? What festivals of atonement, what sacred games shall we have to invent? Is not the greatness of this deed too great for us? Must not we ourselves become gods simply to seem worthy of it? There has never been a greater deed; and whoever will be born after us—for the sake of this deed he will be part of a higher history than all history hitherto."

Here the madman fell silent and looked again at his listeners; and they, too, were silent and stared at him in astonishment. At last he threw his lantern on the ground, and it broke and went out. "I come too early," he said then, "my time has not come yet. This tremendous event is still on its way, still wandering—it has not yet reached the ears of man. Lightning and thunder require time, the light of the stars requires time, deeds require time even after they are done, before they can be seen and heard. This deed is still more distant from them than the most distant stars—*and yet they have done it themselves.*" It has been related further that on that same day the madman entered divers churches and there sang his *requiem aeternam deo*. Led out and called to account, he is said to have replied each time, "What are these churches now if they are not the tombs and sepulchers of God?"[24]

What an extraordinary text. Tombs and sepulchers, indeed! What are we to do? Nietzsche tells us, straight out, that we are to become *Ubermenschen*, that is, we are to transcend the banalities of our lives and drink deeply of the saving energies of Dionysus, the god of eros. Above all, we are to avoid being seduced by the fraud, the hokum, the hypocrisy, and the false promises which surround us. We are called, as the Gospel of Jesus teaches us, to come unto ourselves, to be ourselves, and to transcend the petty bureaucracies which dominate our lives, be they Christian, democratic, or socialist. Above all, we should avoid living second-hand lives handed down to us by parents, teachers, ministers, and assorted functionaries. Nietzsche reminds us of the parable of the snake and the need to shed our skin, regularly. "The snake that cannot shed its skin perishes. So do the spirits who are prevented from changing their opinions; they cease to be spirit."[25] More, we must risk our lives and our values, if we are to prevail as human. "For believe me, the secret of the greatest fulfillment and the greatest enjoyment of existence is: to *live dangerously*! Build your cities under Vesuvius! Send your ship into uncharted seas."[26] And, if I read Nietzsche right, do not turn back.

VIII. *William James: To be Human is to Risk*

Despite the vast disparities of style and deep disagreements on fundamental issues, a common thread binds the thinkers just considered. And that thread would wend through most other philosophers of the period in question. Each of them in his own distinctive way was convinced of the certitude of his respective position. We come upon an entirely new phenomenon in philosophy with William James (1842–1910), for whom pluralism was not a fall from grace but rather a permanent and positive condition of human inquiry. In 1876, James published an essay in the *Nation* entitled "The Teaching of Philosophy in Our Colleges." Midway through that piece, he wrote:

If the best use of our colleges is to give young men a wider openness of mind and a more flexible way of thinking than special technical training can generate, then we hold that philosophy . . . is the most important of all college studies. However sceptical one may be of the attainment of universal truths . . . one can never deny that philosophic study means the habit of always seeing an alternative, of not taking the usual for granted, of making conventialities fluid again, of imagining foreign states of mind. In a word, it means the possession of mental perspective. Touchstone's question, "Hast any philosophy in thee, shepherd?" will never cease to be one of the tests of a well-born nature. It says, Is there space and air in your mind, or must your companions gasp for breath whenever they talk with you? And if our colleges are to make men, and not machines, they should look, above all things, to this aspect of their influence.[27]

The search for alternatives characterized both the life and thought of William James. As a young man, under the baleful influence of his father, who insisted that he choose a career, James underwent a series of profound personal disturbances, which forced him to consider suicide as an alternative to the bland Protestant ethic that suffused his early conscious life. After undergoing an intense vastation experience, dramatized by the appearance to his consciousness of a loathsome creature, James realized *"that shape am I*, I felt, potentially."[28] Convinced of the utter fragility of his personal self, he subsequently writes in his diary that he is trapped between living out the bequest of a stale, inherited ethic, on the one hand, and suicide, on the other. Faced with Scylla and Charybdis, James makes a bold personal move to extricate himself. In his diary entry of April 30, 1870, he rejects suicide and writes: "Now, I will go a step further with my will, not only act with it, but believe as well; believe in my individual reality and creative power. My belief, to be sure, *can't* be optimistic—but I will posit life (the real, the good) in the self-governing *resistance* of the ego to the world. Life shall be built in doing and suffering and creating."[29]

James remained loyal to this provocative announcement. His subsequent life and thought was based on two active assumptions. First, he was convinced that human beings have extraordinary reservoirs of untapped energy which can be brought into play by an act of the will. In this regard, he had confidence also in the wisdom of common people, and he shared the belief of his philosophical colleague, Josiah Royce, that "the popular mind is deep, and means a thousand times more than it explicitly knows."[30] James was especially fond of drawing from the insights and experiences of underground, bizarre, or highly idiosyncratic people. In his introduction to his father's *Literary Remains*, James wrote that "the sanest and best of us are of one clay with lunatics and prison-inmates."[31] In this vein, James's popular essays, among them "The Will to Believe," "Is Life Worth Living?," "The Sentiment of Rationality," and "The Energies of Men," constitute an effort on behalf of a nineteenth-century American philosophical evangelism. Unfortunately, they have been often misunderstood because they have been read apart from James's second, and more important, assumption: namely, that the nature of reality and the human process of knowing have been dramatically misconstrued by the history of philosophy.

Proceeding from his brilliant study of the psychology of human behavior, which culminated in his classic work *The Principles of Psychology*, James contended that reality was not made of things, substances, or blocks of any kind. Rather, the key to understanding the nature of reality was relations. Before we absorbed the philosophical import of modern art, quantum mechanics, depth psychology, and modern mathematics, James had told us of the narrowness and misplaced emphases of classical metaphysics and epistemology. The cardinal insight of James occurs in 1884, in an essay entitled "Some Omissions of Introspective Psychology." Therein, he affirms that our prehension of reality does not occur through the denotation of separate objects but rather is best described by a "stream of consciousness," by which our experience of the relational transitions between objects is as affectively real as our experience of the objects themselves. James's phenomenological description of how we actually experience the world as a processive, relational field is not given full justice until James Joyce's magnificent version of the stream of consciousness appears in *Ulysses*.

James cuts between the ideational pretensions of the classical idealist philosophy, in which our common, ordinary experience is distrusted, and the narrow, unimaginative claims of the British empiricists, for whom the world comes as a simple, contiguous string of single sense perceptions. To the contrary, for James, the world is thicker and is teeming with inferences, anticipations, and leads, each of which awaits our active, constituting presence. James writes: "In our cognitive as well as in our active life we are creative. We *add*, both to the subject and to the predicate part of reality. The world stands really malleable, waiting to receive its final touches at our hands. Like the kingdom of heaven, it suffers human violence willingly. Man *engenders* truths upon it."[32] James's commitment to the active and constituting presence of the human mind in any version of reality leads to several radical conclusions. First, the world as we know it is inseparable from how we know it. Second, shifts in the human version of the world result in nothing less than shifts in the world itself. Third, and most extraordinary, a diagnosis of the history of philosophy, speculative science, and the arts is equivalent to a diagnosis of the evolution of reality. In short, the history of human life is a history of reality, for without human life, the source of intelligence so far as we now know, the blunt existential reality of the physical world would have no meaning whatsoever.

James's philosophy is unashamedly anthropocentric. He calls it "radical empiricism," for it is based on experience undergone and it takes at full cognizance the equivalent experiential character of relations to that of things and objects. James is unabashedly post-Copernican. He regards the world as ultimately unintelligible, fraught with chance and novelty, and subject to the constitutive role of human life. In 1903, James made the following entry in a notebook:

> All neat schematisms with permanent and absolute distinctions, classifications with absolute pretensions, systems with pigeon-holes, etc., have this character. All "classic," clean, cut and dried, "noble," fixed, "eternal," *Weltanschauungen* seem to me to violate the character with which life concretely comes and the expression which it bears of being, or at least of involving a muddle and a struggle, with an "ever not quite" to all our formulas, and novelty and possibility forever leaking in.[33]

The fundamental contribution of William James to any morphological analysis of the human condition is that he thickens the discussion. Radical empiricism involves an acceptance of a far wider range of continuous and experienced relationships than that usually associated with the normal confines of the human self. It gives to novelty and chance a much greater role in our understanding of the fabric of the world. The philosophy of James calls for a never-ending series of descriptions and diagnoses, each from a specific vantage point with no one of them burdened with having to account for everything. For James, the world is much like "the pattern of our daily experience,"[34] loosely connected, processive, and pluralistic. The crucial factor in our understanding of the world in which we live is the affective experiencing of relations. So multiply involved are we that the attainment of deep insight to our "inner life" leads us to participate in no less than the very rhythm of the world at large. If we live at the edge, what we most find in this rhythm are surprises, relational novelty everywhere. Nothing is clear until the last of us has our say and the last relation is hooked. Rare among philosophers, William James believed this.

In principle, then, as I said, intellectualism's edge is broken; it can only approximate reality, and its logic is inapplicable to our inner life, which spurns its vetoes and mocks its impossibilities. Every bit of us at every moment is part and parcel of a wider self; it quivers along various radii like the wind-rose on a compass, and the actual in it is continuously one with possibles not yet in our present sight.[35]

IX. *Conclusion*

The message of William James is that there are possibilities "not yet in our present sight." That is also the message of philosophy. We could have chosen seven other thinkers to represent the dramatic importance of philosophy. Philosophy abounds with troublemakers, thinkers who are restless about the status quo and who bring the human mind to bear upon our situation with an attitude of skepticism, belligerence, and openness to new ideas, resolutions, and possibilities unheard, even undreamt. Finally, a personal note. How can anyone who speaks a Western tongue, especially those among us who purport to be educated, afford not to study philosophy? I ask you! I implore you! Quo vadis? Whither goest thou without any understanding whence we have come and who we are? And this is to say nothing of where we hope to go. In the works of Voltaire, we find a reference to a letter from Henry IV, the King of France, to an ill-knighted person by the name of Crillon, who, most unfortunately, arrived after a great battle had been fought. To the tardy Crillon, Henry IV wrote: "Hang yourself, brave Crillon! We fought at Arques, and you were not there."[36]

We stand today on the edge of another great battle, that between humanistic learning in our nation and in our universities, on the one hand, and the shallow, opportunistic, and personally aggrandizing appeal to the bottom-line principle of sheerly economic accountability, on the other hand. Unlike Crillon, I plan to be at this battle and I trust that you will do likewise, for to do less is to abandon all that is distinctively human. I tell this to our children and to my students. I ask them to pass the message to their children and to their students. Philistines and purveyors of the shallow are everywhere. They pervade the university as well as the marketplace. It is our task to sustain and celebrate the wisdom of the past on behalf of our obligation to make possible the wisdom of the present.

More than seventy years ago, William James said that philosophy bakes no bread. True enough; nor does it build bridges, or clone cells. Yet a society that only bakes bread, builds bridges, and clones cells is a society that has failed to realize its deepest mission. The ancients knew well that time will seize us—in time. Our task is to think deeply about the most quixotic of all cosmic events—namely, the utterly transient yet powerful existence of a human life. Three millennia of philosophical speculation have addressed that paradox. And it is to that same ambivalence between power and fragility that we address ourselves once again. Ultimate conclusions are beyond our reach, but the quality of our endeavor is a gauge of the worthiness of our cause. Those of us who have bartered the present for a paradisaical future, much less a career, have missed the drama of the obvious. Philosophy teaches us that every day, everyone has access to the depth of being human. We should not await salvation while the parade passes by. The nectar of a guaranteed human future is illusory and the height of self-deception. Our death is imminent. Philosophy sanctifies our reflective effort to ask why and, above all, philosophy makes an effort to tell the truth. In our time, what could be a more outlandish and coveted activity?

EIGHTEEN

TO BE HUMAN IS TO HUMANIZE

A Radically Empirical Aesthetic

It is . . . the reinstatement of the vague and inarticulate to its proper place in our mental life which I am so anxious to press on the attention.

—William James, *Psychology: Briefer Course*

Two themes occupy us in the present essay. First, we contend that modern art works a revolution in man's view of himself; it broadens the ways in which he relates to the world and the ways by which he is informed.[1] Second, we hold that the most fruitful philosophical statement of the meaning of modern art is to be found in the thought of William James and John Dewey, interpreted as a radically empirical philosophy of experience. From the time of the nineteenth-century impressionists to the Second World War, these two themes were historically and imaginatively interwoven. We want to make up for the recent neglect of these two themes, in order to show the unusual significance of radical empiricism for contemporary art. We make no effort to develop a complete aesthetic.

The problems we face focus on the relationship of impressionism to the nature of inquiry,[2] the role of philosophy relative to modern art, and the pre-eminence of a doctrine of relations in a contemporary aesthetic. We shall see that the thought of James and Dewey, so long trapped in the narrow epistemological problems of a pragmatic theory of truth, has extraordinary resiliency when looked at from the viewpoint of a generalized aesthetic. Further, the possibility of an aesthetic in our technological world poses a challenge of considerable importance for the future.

I. Modern Art as an Attitude

Technique is the very being of all creation.
— Roland Barthes, "The Structuralist Activity"

It is now a truism to affirm the decisive importance of modern science for the development of philosophical method and philosophical language. The methodology of contemporary science has been especially effective in forcing philosophy to abandon many of its presuppositions and working categories. Less well known is the fact that no corresponding transformation of philosophical language has taken place in response to the drastic changes effected by the artistic activity of the last seventy-five years. The revolution in art is as embracing as that in science, and, relative to the life of the person, a more immediate one. We should not underestimate the extension of modern art as a general cultural attitude. Permeating our advertising, decorating our living space, reconstructing our sense of sound, making hybrids of all the classical art forms, modern art is so pervasive an influence that even the most radical departure from the commonplace fails to cause any consternation.[3] Has any culture heretofore found itself nostalgic for objects and experiences a decade or so removed in time but totally obliterated in experienced form? The revolution in primal shapes, colors, and textures wrought by the influence of modern art on industrial design is now so complete an aspect of our living that it would be difficult to single out a set of visual experiences which has not undergone considerable transformation within a single generation. In his essay on "The Man-Made Object," Gillo Dorfles refers to this characteristic as "formal instability."[4] Coupled with the acknowledgment of such restless formal identity is the effort of man to create forms. Surrounded by what he has "made" and aware of his ability to change its character at rapid intervals, modern man takes seriously his role as constitutor of reality. The shift from a denotative to a constitutive response to the world is rooted not only in modern technology but in modern aesthetics as well.

Moreover, the ingrained dependence on the visual and auditory senses is now experienced as inseparable from the sense of touch. The new art forms struggle against the conceptual domination of our traditional patterns of response. The arts of assemblage, kinetic sculpture, and mixed media make the tactile experience central. Modern in theme, these art activities reinvoke the primitive affection for the hands and symbolically restate the case for *Homo faber*.

No longer separated from his world like a spectator from a picture, modern man has slowly acknowledged the presence of an irreducible factor; how he formulates the environment becomes the environment itself.[5] Recently this insight has been stated in cryptic form by Marshall McLuhan as "the medium is the message."[6] We should not, however, be so surprised at this claim, for early in our century the traditional stranglehold on the meaning of nature, exercised through rigid conceptual models, was dramatically broken by the artistic revolution in the use of "media." Subsequently spurred on by the influence of the generic attitude known as "Dada," modern art assaulted the established aesthetic values. In art as in science, the obviousness of common sense was rejected as a resource for creative work. "Nouns," "things," and the consensus of meaning rooted in an "objective" framework were now taken to be but abstractions from a distinctively personalized aesthetic. While the acceptance of this iconoclastic attitude varied widely, the critical and nonconforming edge of Dada as an attitude is still residual in the activity of modern art to this day. Further, in response to these experiences of negation, modern art sets out to formulate new contexts for the articulation of aesthetic values. The most important factor in this development is the new understanding of technique. For the most part located in the very choice of media to be used, technique often becomes the primary locus for the generating of artistic insight. As the medium is shifted, the nature of aesthetic experience and the attendant questions of meaning, participation, and enhancement undergo a like transformation.[7] In these preliminary remarks we insist only that the notion of reality which emerges from this activity is one which affirms a reality whose very being is its process.

With these factors in mind let us return to our initial question. Those sympathetic to the metaphors of process philosophy usually trace the roots of their awareness to the revolution in speculative science and to certain perspectives in recent philosophy, particularly the thought of Bergson and Whitehead. Modern art, on the other hand, despite its being a more directly experienceable phenomenon, and despite its having extensive implications for the meaning of inquiry, has not been brought to bear on the basic philosophical issues of our time. The philosophical discipline known as "aesthetics" continues to deal largely with antique problems, seemingly innocent of the fact that the art-experience of the last half-century has rendered the questions of beauty, truth in the arts, and the search for objective criteria as simply not to the point.[8] If we survey contemporary American philosophical works on aesthetics, it is astonishing to see how little they have to do with our experience of contemporary art—a situation made clear if we were to think of the philosophy of science as still dominated by the problems of classical mechanics. Likewise, in any number of broadly based attempts to deal with the aesthetic dimensions of modern culture, the participation of the contemporary philosopher is at a minimum.[9] Can we offer an analysis of this situation or must we admit to the contention that philosophical discourse and modern art are separated by a linguistic, and even experiential, gulf too immense to allow for mutual inquiry?

From one side, certain critics and the more articulate artists have become increasingly concerned with a reflective statement of their activities; in a word, have become increasingly philosophical about art.[10] For the most part, however, critics and artists rarely turn to philosophy itself when conducting such inquiries, and seem to boycott even those philosophers who have made an attempt to address themselves to aesthetic concerns. Should we agree with Herbert Read, in his commentary on Naum Gabo? "He is virtually creating a new language, a symbolic language of concrete visual images. This language is necessary because our philosophical inquiries have brought us to a point where the old symbols no longer suffice. Philosophy itself has reached an impasse—an impasse of verbal expression—at which it hands over its task to the poets and painters, the sculptors and other creators of concrete images."[11] We would argue that Read takes philosophy too literally and condemns us to an unreflective participation in the experience of art and to discourse which signifies sterility of experience. To the contrary, if one is located in a wider philosophical tradition, discourse can have philosophical intention and yet be continuous with the basic attitude and creative direction of contemporary art. Although at times a noble goal, clarity is not the only objective of philosophical discourse. In some instances, particularly those referring to the plastic arts, philosophical discussion of the experiences in question may be illuminating in its inability to provide adequate linguistic corollaries as well as in its effort to create new metaphors of articulation. These latter would refer not to ingrained philosophical language, but to the aesthetic qualities of the artistic experiences. The crucial question has to do with one's expectations of inquiry. To the extent that we seek a final statement, or a methodology able to put the vagaries of experience in fixed categories, the tendency is to push the philosophical enterprise beyond the limits of experience. For some, this is precisely the task of philosophy, namely, to transcend experience. But to those for whom the qualities of our experience are inseparable from their peculiarities in the concrete, such a method is fruitless.

A glance at the ambiguity in the basic attitude toward modern art in philosophical circles will give us some perspective. It will also serve as an introduction to the American philosophy of experience begun by William James and crystallized in the essays on the "live creature" by John Dewey. It can be said that modern art needs no justification beyond its very presence. Yet when philosophers reflect upon the phenomenon of artistic creation, two distinct viewpoints emerge. The first and more generally accepted perspective sees modern art as a distortion of the "real world." This evaluation arises from a base extrinsic to the creative process itself; it has at its core the claim that the new forms which characterize contemporary art are a function of the widespread dehumanization afflicting the twentieth century generally. For support of this position, not only are we directed to the obvious "distortion" in canvases of Rouault, the surrealists, and expressionist protest art, but we are also asked to respond to the overall presence of Dadaistic elements as if they were statements of content rather than an attempt to relocate the aesthetic experience. Recent examples of collage, combine-paintings, pop art, and, especially, the mysterious versions of assemblage found in the "boxes" of Joseph Cornell seem to sustain the charge that modern art violates our conceptual order and has only a topical significance, of a negative cast.

The major obstacle in the way of this interpretation is its notion of form. Dehumanization in art is taken to be the aberration or distortion of finalized forms, recognized as such by a centuries-old tradition of philosophical and aesthetic sanction. We must acknowledge the depressing truth that twentieth-century man has turned on his brother as never before. And there is no doubt that these circumstances have directly influenced the art of our time, which is said to represent the dark shadow hovering over the human face and the human place. Dehumanization, however, proceeds from still another source. Modern man is also a victim of clarity. Much of our difficulty proceeds from the demand for certitude and an inability to recognize and live with the irreducibility of shadows. Who among us knows the human face, or the nature of man? Have the myriad forms through which man humanizes his environment been approached, let alone exhausted? The departure from the moorings once so clearly recognized and accepted by Western man does not seem to be a fall from grace; it may be a liberation of creative human activity. Dehumanization, then, is often due to the blind defense of traditional versions of human life, now vestigial and no longer able to sustain human needs. Modern art accuses Western culture of sterility and narrow defensiveness. The accusation, often couched as a "manifesto," is at once a rejection of tired forms and a call for a new statement about human creative possibility. The extremes expressed in modern art occur in proportion to the lack of flexibility and imagination characteristic of the cultural attitudes under attack.

If it is folly to think that the old aesthetic values shall return as they were, it is equally true that the new artistic movements are so radical that they preclude any stable, final order. What is at stake seems to be nothing less than reconstruction of the modes and expectations of inquiry, in which we are constantly obligated to fuse the critique of previous forms with an attempt to create new forms.[12] Thomas Hess, writing on the painter Willem de Kooning, supports this interpretation: "The crisis of modern art presupposes that each shape, even a plain oval, be reinvented—or rather, given an autochthonous existence in paint. Nothing could be accepted or received on faith as a welcome heritage."[13]

Here then is the second way to view modern art, as an articulation of modern man's most distinctive activity, the creation of forms. Whether it be due to simple shifting of context, as in the "creation" of the haunted forms of *objet trouvé* or in the more aggressive structuring of totally new environments as brought off by the ever-changing styles of assemblage, modern art has made innovation a central theme.[14] It is not difficult to find an acknowledgment of this dimension in the assessment of modern art; indeed, it has become almost a commonplace. The full implications, however, of such an attitude have not been developed thus far. For the most part, the understanding of innovation has been along the lines of "replacement," an echo of the old metaphysics of objects. The key to the meaning of originality in modern art is not found in a doctrine of the "wholly new" but, rather, in a metaphysics of relations.

Fundamental to this new perspective are two contentions, both of direct philosophical importance. First is the recognition of the inability of nature to act any longer as the objective referent for the creative affairs of men. Rooted in the impressionistic attitude, this development owes much to the modern meaning of symbolism and the acceptance of ambiguity as a persistent dimension in human inquiry. Second is the affirmation that no entity can be experienced in isolation but has to be encountered as a field of relations.[15] Better, the term "entity" should be replaced by "event"—that is, a network of relations, historically understood, with a past, present, and future. Furthermore, no matter how these "events" come into being and however diverse their lineage,[16] whenever they become subject to our awareness and touch us in a human way, they become realities of the most direct and intense kind. Citing Thomas Hess once more: "Life as we live it, obviously, is a matter of endless ambiguities and proliferating meanings; transparencies upon transparencies make an image that, while it blurs in superimpositions, takes on the actuality of rocks."[17] Concretion need not be associated with the meaning of "thing," for if we are willing to live with ambiguity, the flow of relations is also concrete and real.

In order to grasp the import of these contentions about nature and relations, we should examine two traditions. One is obvious: the plastic arts from Monet to the present. The other is not so obvious: the metaphysics of relations as rooted in the philosophy of William James. The remainder of this chapter will have as its task to show that these traditions, however different in expression and parallel in historical development, proceed from a single vision and can be allied to each other as philosophical metaphor to artistic creation.

II. Impressionism as Breakthrough: William James and Claude Monet

L'exactitude n'est pas la verité.

—Henri Matisse, in Herbert Read, "The Modern Epoch of Art"

The presence of nuance and shading as a function of the gigantic manifests itself in the impressionistic attitude. Unity is achieved not by a decisive appeal to an objective referent but, rather, by a gentle fading into continuous but ever-more-obscure edges. It is an attitude whereby all insight is fringed, as if we were reaching for a horizon with what William James calls an " 'ever not quite' to all our formulas, and novelty and possibility for ever leaking in."[18] Writing in the *American Journal of Psychology* in 1891, G. Stanley Hall evaluates James's *Principles of Psychology*: "Passing now to the work as a whole, the author might be described as an impressionist in psychology. His portfolio contains sketches old and new, ethical, literary, scientific and metaphysical, some exquisite and charming in detail and even color, others rough charcoal outlines, but all together stimulating and suggestive, and showing great industry and versatility."[19] James's *Principles* is, like an impressionist canvas, a virtuoso performance, technically proficient and characterized by extraordinary detail. Yet it has an elusive center and its major theme is the fluidity of consciousness. Further, its concluding chapter, "Necessary Effects and the Truths of Experience," renders the entire effort subject to doubt or at best, in James's judgment at least, renders it a bare hint of the desired statement. James shares, then, in the nineteenth-century breakthrough in sensibility. In an essay on James's aesthetics, Jacques Barzun writes:

> One can begin abstractly by saying that through this book [*The Principles*] James struck a deathblow at Realism. The then prevailing views of the mind were that it copied reality like a photographic plate, that it received and assembled the elements of experience like

a machine, that it combined ideas like a chemist. For this "scientist" mind, James substituted one that was a born artist—a wayward, creative mind, impelled by inner wants, fringed with mystery, and capable of infinitely subtle, unrecordable nuances. Dethroning the sophistical Realist, in short, James revealed Impressionism native and dominant.[20]

In but a line—indeed, the epigraph to this essay—too infrequently noted by commentators, James responds to the call of experience: "It is, in short, the reinstatement of the vague to its proper place in our mental life which I am so anxious to press on the attention."[21] Apparently not satisfied with this phrasing, James is bolder in his *Psychology: Briefer Course*: "It is, the reader will see, the reinstatement of the vague and inarticulate to its proper place in our mental life which I am so anxious to press on the attention."[22] This affection for the "penumbra" of experience is no isolated insight in James. It everywhere sustains his contention that conceptual statements are but truncations of the flow of concrete life. Such insulating cuts in the flow are merely functional and should not prevent us from maintaining a reflective confrontation with those areas of our conscious experience not given to systematic definition.

In a more advanced statement of his views, James tells us: "Our fields of experience have no more definite boundaries than have our fields of view. Both are fringed forever by a more that continuously develops and that continuously supersedes them as life proceeds."[23] The experiencing of this fringe yields awareness while defying any conceptual formulation. For James, the crucial area of human activity is found precisely where the conceptual order breaks down, for it is in those conscious but inarticulable environs, wherein we experience religiously, aesthetically, psychedelically, that we are open to demons.[24] Although most often not subject to explanation, the meanings of these situations are intensely personal and, in a way proper to their own modalities, crystal clear.

In 1890, the year of the publication of James's *Principles*, Monet tells us of the struggle he has in painting the "haystack" series: "I am working terribly hard, struggling with a series of different effects (haystacks), but . . . the sun sets so fast that I cannot follow it. . . . I am beginning to work so slowly that I am desperate, but the more I continue the more I see that a great deal of work is necessary in order to succeed in rendering that which I seek: 'Instantaneity,' especially the 'envelope,' the same light spreading everywhere, and more than ever I am dissatisfied with the easy things that come in one stroke."[25] Ambiguity bathes our experience and the one-to-one correspondence between the perceptual act and the objective order is challenged. For Monet, the shift in light was decisive, but there can be a multiplicity of other activities (in James's phrase, "the halo of felt relations") which challenge the finality of our conceptual view of the universe.[26] The important thrust of the impressionist attitude is to see the object as a locus from which to allow the full range of shades and meanings to show. The vagueness is relative; it depends on how prematurely one cuts off inquiry and attempts to answer the question, what is that? The painter Wassily Kandinsky understood this revolution better than most, for it was a decisive factor in transforming his own artistic activity. In 1895, Kandinsky stood before a Monet "haystack" exhibited in Moscow. Of this experience, he writes:

> Previously I knew only realistic art. . . . Suddenly, for the first time, I saw a "picture." That it was a haystack a catalogue informed me. I could not recognize it. This lack of recognition was distressing to me. I also felt that the painter had no right to paint so indistinctly. I had a muffled sense that the object was lacking in this picture, and was overcome with astonishment and perplexity that not only seized but engraved itself indelibly on the memory and quite unexpectedly, again and again, hovered before the eyes down to the smallest detail. All of this was unclear to me, and I could not draw the simple consequences from this experience.
>
> But what was absolutely clear to me was the unsuspected power previously hidden from me, of the palette which surpassed all my dreams. Painting took on a fabulous strength and splendor. And at the same time, unconsciously, the object was discredited as an indispensable element of the picture.[27]

The discrediting of the object is no small event in the history of human consciousness. All too often this development is analyzed as the other side of the growth of subjectivism. Such an interpretation is narrow and misguided, for the dispersal of objects does not necessarily throw us back on an introverted self-consciousness, although it does enhance the role of the self in the creative process. By far, the more significant implication has to do with the emergence of relational activity as the focus for meaning. The subject-object duality is no longer to the point, for at both ends these terms are but abstract statements of actually dynamic processes. Pushing further, inquiry moves steadily to an analysis of the interaction between the relational qualities of self-consciousness and the relational qualities of constructed environments. In effect, analysis focuses on "fields" of relationships, rather than on subjects and objects in isolation.[28] From such a viewpoint, the role of "names" undergoes a serious shift. They stand for loci or gathering places of ongoing relational activities, and thereby merely focus attention. In modern art, names of art objects are not to be taken as descriptions of the work. Rather, they merely announce the presence of activity and are bypassed as soon as we tie into the peculiar qualities of such activity. More often than not, such nominal delineations of works of modern art become increasingly less relevant as we broaden our participation. Thus, to speak consistently, there is no single canvas in modern painting; for, experienced as an event, the physical environment of such a canvas, the psychic thrust of one's own personal activity at that time, and the myriad historical and cultural factors involved in such aesthetic participation are all irreducible dimensions of the painting. If we can apply such criteria, retrospectively, to traditional works of art, this does not gainsay the fact that such a possibility emerges primarily from the method of modern painting. Among artists, Kandinsky, for one, was aware of the nature of this shift away from the object to the relational event as the real source of meaning. He offers a metaphorical statement of this new philosophical insight: "This isolated line and the isolated fish alike are living beings with forces peculiar to them, though latent. . . . But the voice of these latent forces is faint and limited. It is the environment of the line and the fish that brings about a miracle: the latent forces awaken, the expression becomes radiant, the impression profound. Instead of a low voice, one hears a choir. The latent forces have become dynamic. The environment is the composition."[29] Kandinsky's statement is inseparable from the fact that the plastic arts since Monet have set a dizzying pace in the creation of new environments. At first limited to radical shifts within the context of the "painting" or the "sculpture," their activities soon spilled out into "assembled" environments, often creating the need for entirely new evaluative criteria. The task of a modern aesthetic is to achieve discursive continuity with such constructs. Just as single "things" gave way to "environments," so, too, the single arts of painting and sculpture have become antique, giving way first to hybridizations with other aesthetic forms and now to new aesthetic creations, sui generis, often with no recognizable tie to what was only recently known as "art." What is most needed, therefore, is a philosophical outlook which does not ask dead questions, that is, questions which focus simply on content. Whether we say, with Kandinsky, "the environment is the composition," or, with McLuhan, "the medium is the message," the problem is clear from the philosophical side—the need for a doctrine of relational activity phrased in aesthetic metaphors.

At this juncture, William James again offers a point of departure. James has an original approach to relations: they are rooted in a psychology of experience. His view of self-consciousness is characterized by process and function rather than by entity and faculty. And finally, his anthropology, which is Promethean in outlook, is fully aware of chance, novelty, and the centrality of human creativity. Rather than a structured aesthetic theory, it is his life and his philosophical approach to the problem of inquiry which gives us the basis for a modern aesthetic.[30] Using the assumptions of James, let us make an effort to consider the problems of modern art in a way which shows philosophical concern but maintains fidelity to the quality of modern experience.

III. A Relational Aesthetic

Monumentality is an affair of relativity.

—Hans Hofmann, cited in William Seitz, *Hans Hofmann*

William James took his stand over against the associationist psychology of the nineteenth century. Although he shared the empirical temper of that tradition, he could not accept its view that experience is composed of atomistic elements. The reigning opposition was idealism, which, in James's understanding, provided an overarching principle of unity, without any experiential sustenance. Rejecting both views, he countered with his doctrine of radical empiricism.[31] The clearest statement of this position was made by James in the preface to *The Meaning of Truth* (1909):

> Radical empiricism consists first of a postulate, next of a statement of fact, and finally of a generalized conclusion.
>
> The postulate is that the only things that shall be debatable among philosophers shall be things definable in terms drawn from experience. (Things of an unexperienceable nature may exist ad libitum, but they form no part of the material for philosophic debate.)
>
> The statement of fact is that the relations between things, conjunctive as well as disjunctive, are just as much matters of direct particular experience, neither more so nor less so, than the things themselves.
>
> The generalized conclusion is that therefore the parts of experience hold together from next to next by relations that are themselves parts of experience. The directly apprehended universe needs, in short, no extraneous transempirical connective support, but possesses in its own right a concatenated or continuous structure.[32]

The crucial aspect of this position is unquestionably found in his claim for the "statement of fact." Central to James's radical empiricism, this affirmation has its roots in a phenomenology of the processes of consciousness. He tells us in his essay on "The Stream of Thought" that "if there be such things as feelings at all, then so surely as relations between objects exist *in rerum natura*, so surely and more surely, do feelings exist to which these relations are known."[33] Quite concretely, we should say a "feeling of and, a feeling of if, a feeling of but, and a feeling of by, quite as readily as we say a feeling of blue or a feeling of cold."[34] And to the extent that we do not, we accept the empiricist prejudice "of supposing that where there is no name no entity can exist."[35] In this way, "all dumb or anonymous psychic states have, owing to this error, been coolly suppressed."[36]

The search for "what" inevitably ends with a "noun" as a response. The epistemology of common sense seeks names, definitions, and categories. From its critical side, modern art, particularly in its Dadaistic overtone, has led an assault on such an approach. In refusing to name its artifacts, or in naming them abstractly, as "#1," or again, in naming them specifically but with no visual correspondence to the work, this art denies to itself and to the participant any substantive identity. Such a denial does not, however, imply an absence of meaning or of intelligibility. Rather, meaning is located in the ongoing fabric of relations, by which we mean it is found neither in an isolated self nor in an isolated thing but, rather, in the environment constituted by shared participation. Any attempts to extrapolate a fixed meaning for other than functional purposes are denials of this process. James had warned of the dangers involved when connections were thought to be but logical bridges instead of experienced continuities: "Continuous transition is one sort of a conjunctive relation; and to be a radical empiricist means to hold fast to this conjunctive relation of all others, for this is the strategic point, the position through which, if a hole be made, all the corruptions of dialectics and all the metaphysical fictions pour into our philosophy."[37]

If we wish to understand the meaning of modern art, we have to place ourselves in continuity with the interiorized structuring of each creation. At all costs, we must avoid the temptation to evaluate this art by virtue of criteria derived from a source extrinsic to the qualities of the creative process. Support for such a contention is offered to us in the following text of James: "Knowledge of sensible realities thus comes to life inside the tissue of experience. It is made; and made by relations which unroll themselves in time."[38] In order to sustain this claim, James takes a position which is bold relative to philosophy but obvious from the side of modern painting and sculpture. "Life is in the transitions as much as in the terms connected; often, indeed, it seems to be there more emphatically. . . . These relations of continuous transition experienced are what makes our experiences cognitive. In the simplest and completest cases the experiences are cognitive of one another."[39] The crucial problem, therefore, in the search for the "form" of a modern painting is the inability to relate it to a reality already given.

In the concrete, to seek a morphology of a modern painting, say, of the abstract expressionist school, turns up the following. We do not confront an object but an event;[40] or, in a name used recently for one kind of modern art but more widely applicable, a "happening." The origins of such an event are obscure, unless we accept a psychoanalytic or sociological reductionism. Should we do so, the experiencing of such an event would likewise be conditioned and we would still be faced with the problem of ever-varying qualities in such influence.[41] Despite the absence of an inherited identity, we are able to enter into meaningful relationship to modern art. We enjoy, undergo, and are carried along by it. Its form seems to be its process, although with no fixed goal. This does not imply looseness of endeavor or of craft. In the paintings of Mark Rothko, for example, one is fascinated by the intense effort to deal with relationship as such, under the specifics of shading, dripping, and ever-so-subtle internal shifts of color and canvas size. This concern becomes almost obsessive in the work of the late Ad Reinhardt, known as "minimal" art. The point at issue here is that this galaxy of interiorized relations cannot be rendered meaningful by any appeal to a known object. This does not mean that such paintings are locked up within themselves, but any opening out of their meaning must follow the same nonliteral processes which were central to their creation originally.[42] That the human self can enter into such a process we shall discuss further on.

Expressions such as "ongoing," "process," "reconstruction," "event," "interaction"—so central to a metaphysics of experience, and so often criticized by philosophers as vague—show up again and again in writings by painters and critics.[43] Perhaps the most explicit statement of the position that an ongoing fabric of relations is the source of meaning and intelligibility in a work of modern art was offered by Hans Hofmann. A painter of the first rank, Hofmann was also a teacher and made a serious effort to render in discursive terms his view of modern painting. Holding that a color interval is "analogous to a thought-fragment in the creative process," Hofmann sees such intervals or fragments taking their meaning from their "aesthetic extension," for "any isolated thing can never surpass its own meaning."[44] Actually, he goes beyond James, for according to William Seitz, Hofmann will hold that "the relation between elements, whatever they may be, is always more significant than the elements themselves."[45] Should we not take seriously Hofmann's belief that "relations," rather than isolated "actualities," account for the quality of our response? Seitz clarifies our attitude toward these matters thusly: "Traditionally, a painting used to begin as a rough sketch of the main lines or areas of a preconceived image, and this is still often the case; but with Hofmann, painting is from the first stroke a continuing establishment and re-establishment of life relationships. As it progresses, the work moves toward a more perfect integration of all its parts—toward a relational unity."[46]

We need not remain within the rhetoric of painting in order to establish the significance of relations for the modern theme. Perhaps if we were to look at a more aggressive art form, like modern jazz, our meaning would become clearer. Outside of a relational setting, jazz is meaningless, for it proceeds by a series of interwoven tensions. A jazz group is especially revealing, as single members create their music in line with their respective insight but over against other members of the group. We have tension between personal mastery of the instrument and the demand for improvisation, between the developing structure of each contribution and, overall, an open system. The entire performance is carried on with a sense for group responsibility.[47] The viability of these tensions is manifested only as experienced; it cannot be predicted or planned, as there are no formal or abstract correlations. The qualities of a jazz performance cannot be extrapolated and taught as such. The jazz master is one whose distinctive originality enables the fledgling to create in his own vein: thus, each to his own vision but as a shared experience. Such indirect communication is necessary, for we do not have duplication of experiences or the performance of others' versions. Yet, in a jazz group, the participant senses when the group is not sharing the same experience, articulated by each in his own manner. And, in turn, the experiencing public senses when it "comes off." As in the plastic arts, intelligibility is manifest when one is carried along by the possibilities and relations of the medium in question. This is a cardinal instance of Dewey's contention that "connections exist in the most immediate noncognitive experience, and when the experienced situation becomes problematic, the connections are developed into distinctive objects of common sense or of science."[48]

In jazz, the experienced situation becomes meaningful because of the technique. More than any other single factor—as, for example, the instruments used or the melody as point of departure—it is technique which is decisive in bringing about a creative advance. In the plastic arts, correspondingly, every shift in material used creates a new locus of relations, new problems, and, lately, entirely new art forms. In his essay on

"The Structuralist Activity," Roland Barthes states: "It is not the nature of the copied object which defines art (though this is a tenacious prejudice in all realism), it is the fact that man adds to it in reconstructing it: technique is the very being of all creation."[49]

At this point, it should be obvious that modern art sustains an important shift in the meaning of person. No mere copier of forms or even a discoverer of forms hidden, man becomes the creator of forms.[50] The rhetoric of the artist and the critic, on this issue, has often been extreme. Apollinaire, for example, in *The Cubist Painters*, traces the existence of the "world" to the creative work of the artist:

> It is the social function of great poets and artists to renew continually the appearance nature has for the eyes of men.
>
> Without poets, without artists, men would soon weary of nature's monotony. The sublime idea men have of the universe would collapse with dizzying speed. The order which we find in nature, and which is only an effect of art, would vanish. Everything would break up in chaos. There would be no seasons, no civilization, no thought, no humanity; even life would give way, and the impotent void would reign everywhere.[51]

In an exchange of views between the critic Herbert Read and the founder of constructivism, Naum Gabo, a similar position is taken, although more modestly stated. Gabo puts it this way: "I maintain that knowledge is nothing else but a construction of ours and that what we discover with our knowledge is not something outside us or a part of a constant and higher reality, in the absolute sense of the word; but that we discover exactly that which we put into the place where we make the discoveries."[52] In his essay on "Human Art and Inhuman Nature," Read simply maintains that some modern artists set out "to invent an entirely new reality."[53] But these contentions, and they are representative of the many manifestoes-declarations of novelty that abound in modern art, are too pat; they protest too much. They have meaning in that they clearly delineate the opponent, a mimetic or spectator view of the world. The problem, however, is more complex and surely the creative capacity attributed to the modern artist is more subtle than the replacing of one total view by another. A "new reality" is only one kind of novelty and it is rarely achieved. Further, in time, it too shall be replaced and rendered obsolete. The revolution of modern art is better found in the attitude it takes to all reality, whether obvious to common sense, surreal, or invented.[54] What is novel is not simply new creations, but a way of approaching all art.

The genuine sense of novelty is achieved by virtue of our focusing on processes rather than on products, and by our energizing of relationships, both given and created. If we wish, this approach can be applied retrospectively to classical art, for although it may violate the original intention, the implications of such art would then be considerably widened. No doubt this is why so many modern artists claim profoundly personal relationships with individual classical artists, while creating, in their own vein, a radically different style. From the outside, the well-known fact of the influence of classical drawing on abstract expressionism is difficult to absorb and seems to demand a massive reconstruction of the notion of continuity. Yet, in morphological terms, the internal struggles to achieve the dynamics of line are quite continuous. The key is to dwell within and capture the rhythm, the ongoing dialectic. The identity or nonidentity of extrapolated forms is peripheral to real aesthetic insight, and is not necessary for purposes of understanding or comparison. Gardner Murphy describes a wider sense of creative activity that parallels our description of artistic creation: "creative activity is the very nature of the primitive life-process itself. The concept of the open system really means that living things are not only intent on their own growth and development, but that they are directing evolutionary processes in accordance with a dynamic which is organismic, rather than mechanical."[55] That such an inner dynamic, with its own logic, is characteristic of the processes of experience and amenable to human interaction is a distinctive position of William James. In a series of texts, written at different times, he lays the problem bare.

James, in a morbid state and on the edge of suicide, entered this liberating text in his "Diary": "Life shall [be built in] doing and suffering and creating."[56] The full meaning of his commitment at that point is made clear in his subsequent essay on "The Sentiment of Rationality": "If we survey the field of history and ask what feature all great periods of revival, of expansion of the human mind, display in common, we shall find, I think, simply this: that each and all of them have said to the human being, 'The inmost nature of the reality is congenial to powers which you possess.'"[57] The confidence in the capacity of man to transform his environment proceeds from James's view that the human self and the flow of experience share the same basic relational patterns. The human self, in James's view, has no inherited identity. Gordon Allport writes of James: "There is, he thinks, no such thing as a substantive self distinguishable from the sum, total, or stream of experiences. Each moment of consciousness, he says, appropriates each previous moment, and the knower is thus somehow embedded in what is known."[58]

The interaction between the human self and the environment is the decisive factor in engendering the experience of identity. The fabric of man's life is a relational schema; it not only deals with the exigencies for human identity but, within conditioned structure, yields the imaginative construction of the meaning of the world. In his *Principles*, James had held to the natively formulating character of conscious activity.[59] The selective work of the mind follows interest, practical or aesthetic: "Out of what is in itself an undistinguishable, swarming continuum devoid of distinction or emphasis, our senses make for us by attending to this motion, and ignoring that, a world full of contrasts, of sharp accents, of abrupt changes, of picturesque light and shade."[60]

By the time of *Pragmatism* (1907), James sees the activity of man as even more aggressively constructive. "In our cognitive as well as in our active life, we are creative. We add, both to the subject and to the predicate part of reality. The world stands really malleable, waiting to receive its final touches at our hand. Like the kingdom of heaven, it suffers violence willingly. Man engenders truth upon it."[61] As with the modern artist, James's world does not give itself to any conceptually extrapolated or finalized version. "Whatever separateness is actually experienced is not overcome, it stays and counts as separateness to the end."[62] The world cannot be had whole—from any single perspective. Indeed, two minds cannot know one thing, except by a pragmatic verification of a shared experience.[63] Unity is a process achieved only *durcheinander* and not all *einheit*. He rails against the "block universe," holding rather to a "multiverse": unfinished, tychastic, and shot through with novelty.[64] In the search for meaning in a processive world, James gives to man the decisive role—man is the creator of forms.

Notwithstanding all these positions of James and the strength of their supporting texts, rendered almost stereotypical by the commentaries on his thought, we should focus on another perspective too often overlooked. First, we should not forget the full text of James's remark in "The Sentiment of Rationality."[65] While it is true that he emphasizes the "powers which you possess," he describes man's relationship to his environment as one of "congeniality" and not one of dominance.[66] Further, he stresses the presence of the "inmost nature of the reality," to which such "congeniality" is directed.[67] It can be said that James did not stress adequately his insight into the relational fabric of the affairs of nature, concentrating, rather, on the "energies of men" and the fluid quality of the human self.[68] Yet he was aware of such dynamics and came to hold that only by acknowledging this texture in the activities of nature as experienced can we do justice to the creative thrust of human activity. Rather than the oversimplified emphasis on novelty, as proceeding wholly from the self (a caricature of the modern artist), James presents a taut relationship between a constructing and manipulating consciousness, and the activity of a continually related flow of experience.

A second balancing factor in James's view was found in our earlier discussion, when we indicated James's contention that "life is in the transitions." A text in *Pragmatism* spells out this belief and gives meaning to his affirmation of that "inmost nature of the reality" which challenges the creative activity of man. "Our experience meanwhile is all shot through with regularities. One bit of it can warn us to get ready for another bit, can 'intend' or be 'significant' of that remoter object."[69] Relative to man's needs, including his desire to enhance, experience is malleable. But it is no dummy, for "experience itself, taken at large . . . grows by its edges. That one moment of it proliferates into the next by transitions which, whether conjunctive or disjunctive, continue the experiential tissue, can not, I contend, be denied."[70]

Man, therefore, is called upon to create meaning, to engender truth. This activity places man at the center of the flow of experience. The modern artist has shown that the resources of human imagination are virtually limitless and that man has only begun to articulate the possible dimensions of the human self. Nevertheless, we must maintain that it is a "world" which we wish to create. We seek more than a dazzling array of self-preening evocations of the human psyche. Relations must be forged between the processes of the human self and the affairs of our living space, our topography, our cities, and our artifacts. Modern art, in the last decade, has become aware of this need and, as we shall attempt to indicate, has begun to offer a viable aesthetic for contemporary man. So that modern art on behalf of modern man, in carrying on this endeavor, may avoid the temptation to become overly impressed with the novelty of the effort, at the expense of the task, let us close this section with a stern and incisive warning by William James: "Woe to him whose beliefs play fast and loose with the order which realities follow in his experience; they will lead him nowhere or else make false connexions."[71]

IV. Experience of the Ordinary as Aesthetic

Works of art are . . . celebrations, recognized as such, of the things of ordinary experience.

—John Dewey, *Art as Experience*

The philosophy of radical empiricism, with which John Dewey was fundamentally in accord, is thematically rearticulated in his *Art as Experience*.[72] Published in 1934, the book was a development of Dewey's remarks as the first William James Lecturer at Harvard University. Dewey's range of concerns and the incisiveness of his judgments make this one of his outstanding contributions and deserving of ever more analysis.[73] Quite aside from these significant general considerations, recent artistic events press us to evaluate the book, especially the first three chapters, from a perspective quite unknown to Dewey. In a word, his sections on the "live creature," "ethereal things," and "having an experience" are profound philosophical delineations of the art of the last decade. Dewey's views provide a point of departure for a contemporary aesthetic, rooted in the very fabric of the human condition and capable of transforming our cultural attitudes. Taking James's sense for relations and his processive anthropology, Dewey deals with the interaction of man with his environment. He goes beyond James, by virtue of his insight into the sociological dimension of all inquiry, his ever-present sensitivity to the struggle for values and his acute awareness of man's effort and need to control his social environment. It is not excessive to say that Dewey has initiated an inquiry into experiences of which the contemporary art of the ordinary—collage, assemblage, found-objects, mixed media, environmental sculptures, ready-mades, junk art, pop art, kinetic art, and happenings—are intensifications and symbolizations. His view of the aesthetic situation as a phenomenology of the live creature, rhythmically tied to his environment, was anticipatory of today's artistic structurings of such interactions. And, in line with the contention of the present essay, Dewey's book offers sustenance for our belief in the viability of the American philosophy of experience for purposes of enlightened analysis of the contemporary cultural situation.

At the very outset of his book, Dewey tells us that our "task" is to "restore continuity between the refined and intensified forms of experience that are works of art and everyday events, doings and sufferings that are universally recognized to constitute experience."[74] Given the full implication of Dewey's subsequent analysis, the term "restore" is to be read as "build"—that is, to achieve relational continuity between the intrinsic rhythms of the human self as a live creature and the attempts to structure enhanced versions of his environment. Two obstacles prevent successful rendering of this continuity. First, our approach to art has been dominated by theoretical statements of its meaning and, more seriously, has failed to maintain the relationship between aesthetic refinement and experiential bedding from which such art proceeds: "Theories which isolate art and its appreciation by placing them in a realm of their own, disconnected from other modes of experiencing, are not inherent in the subject-matter but arise because of specifiable extraneous conditions. [This approach] deeply affects the practice of living, driving away esthetic perceptions that are necessary ingredients of happiness, or reducing them to the level of compensating transient pleasurable excitations."[75] Aesthetic enhancements are too often things apart, and when sought out, are approached for reasons extraneous to the very mode of experiencing which generated them in the first place. The second obstacle then becomes clear, for having systematically separated aesthetic delight from reflective awareness, we become correspondingly anaesthetized to the aesthetic qualities inherent in the live creature. The establishing of continuities between the life of the person and artistic creation cannot take place by the acknowledgment of this art as "great," but only by the intensification and qualitative reconstruction of patterns of feeling already deeply felt: "Theory can start with and from acknowledged works of art only when the esthetic is already compartmentalized, or only when works of art are set in a niche apart instead of being celebrations, recognized as such, of the things of ordinary experience. Even a crude experience, if authentically an experience, is more fit to give a clue to the intrinsic nature of esthetic experience than is an object already set apart from any other mode of experience."[76]

Dewey then devotes an entire chapter to an examination of the rhythms of ordinary experience.[77] He speaks of the "humdrum," "slackness," "dissipation," and "rigidity" as factors in preventing the integration of personal anticipations and affections with the larger patterns of the human situation.[78] In this aesthetic ecology, Dewey stresses the need to be continuous with animal life and to have one's senses on the *qui vive*.[79] All should be turned to living tissue; suffering and celebration become related aspects of maturation. "The live creature adopts its past; it can make friends with even its stupidities, using them as warnings that increase present wariness."[80] He repeats, in a number of different ways, the significance of having sensitivity to relations. Order is a becoming, a transactional relationship between "doing" and "undergoing." Consistent with our viewpoint on modern art, Dewey insists that "order is not imposed from without but is made out of the relations of harmonious interactions that energies bear to one another."[81] Said another way, form in modern art is the theme of continuity which wends its way through the creation of the work of art, acting not as a constant element but as a living function, holding in tension that narrow otherness of vision and technique. Entering into this process, the live creature must do more than witness. "For to perceive, a beholder must create his own experience."[82] And, finally, the person must create the continuities between the rhythm of his own life lived and the experienced participation with those refinements and enhancements present in the world of art.

The recent explosion of that art generally referred to as "art of the ordinary" is created out of the very texture of the continuities sought by Dewey. It takes seriously his claim that "art is thus prefigured in the very processes of living."[83] As early as the *Futurist Manifesto* (1912), Umberto Boccioni tells us that we can use "furry spherical forms for hair, semicircles of glass for a vase, wire and screen for an atmospheric plane" and in our artistic work overall, we can incorporate "glass, wood, cardboard, iron, cement, horsehair, leather, cloth, mirrors, electric light, and so on."[84] Taking assemblage as a cardinal instance of art of the ordinary,[85] we isolate two attitudes, each of which have importance for a contemporary aesthetic. First, any material, found or constructed, can be aesthetically meaningful. What is most important—and here the plastic arts have broken far more ground than other art forms—is the willingness to abandon a hierarchy of material, of composition, and to deny the delineation of acceptable aesthetic forms. The most dramatic instance of this is to be found in the "Watts Towers" of Simon Rodia.[86] Built singlehandedly and under construction for thirty-two years, Rodia abandoned the "Towers" as forever unfinished. They are found in his yard, hard by a railroad siding, in the now well-known and depressed area of Watts, Los Angeles. Soaring some one hundred feet high, they are built of steel webbing, concrete, broken dishes, cups, 7-Up bottles, tiles, and scrap of every kind. Enclosed by a high wall, they are multicolored and shaped as rising spirals or simulations of crowns and grottoes. Crossing and recrossing the lines of sculpture, architecture, and industrial design, they threaten always to be sentimental or grotesque. But they are not. As assemblage, they press upon us a renewed experience of the regenerative powers of the human hands,[87] and bring to the surface how deeply affectionate we are toward our entire setting and all that touches us as human. It would be good to admit to this natively aesthetic quality in our ordinary experience.

A second attitude emerging from the art of the ordinary is the narrowing of the gap between nostalgia and immediacy. Following the criteria of Marshall McLuhan, we render environments aesthetic when they are no longer experienced. Thus, romantic poetry is written in the machine age.[88] Our age is one in which the gap between differently experienced environments has shrunk almost to an imperceptible level. The metaphor of our times is "instantaneity"; the transistor replaces the wire. One experience is "had" differently, at different times and for different purposes. Aspects of our present environment have many aesthetic qualities, heretofore unacknowledged. If we widen the scope of the meaning of aesthetic quality, immediate experience yields new riches. Junk art, found objects, and ready-mades, all aspects of our immediate experience, are offered to us for purposes of aesthetic participation. Lawrence Alloway draws the following implications from these activities:

> Junk culture is city art. Its source is obsolescence, the throw-away material of cities, as it collects in drawers, cupboards, attics, dustbins, gutters, waste lots and city dumps. Objects have a history: first they are brand new goods; then they are possessions accessible to few, subjected often to intimate and repeated use; then as waste they are scarred by use but available again. . . . Assemblages of such material come at the spectator as bits of life, bits of environment. The urban environment is present then, as the source of objects, whether transfigured or left alone.[89]

This art tends to draw us in from the side of creation rather than observation. The artist, himself or herself, makes of us a more intimate aspect of his art. "By actively participating in the aesthetic transaction the spectator becomes himself a part of the artist's total material."[90] Correspondingly, the extraordinary range of what is offered as aesthetic and the variant number of ways in which this can take place encourages all of us to render aesthetically our immediate environment. Collage alone has revolutionized the experience of art for young children. Liberated from dealing with formal design perspective and encouraged to utilize all materials, especially those at hand, the child can now forge experienced continuity between what he feels deeply and what he creates as artifact. The end of the Euclidean values of proportion, symmetry, and total accountability has opened the way for each of us to work at a new kind of structuring; one that is continuous with our experience rather than irrelevant to it or even a violation of our actual sensibilities.

The decisive insight of contemporary art is that it does not claim hold of an eccentric, albeit exciting, aspect of human life but, rather, creates out of a sense of the most properly human dimensions. Its credo is, in effect, that to be human is to humanize. The art process is the human process brought to a specific angle of vision, with a claim about man's activity which throws light on the entire range of human affairs. We stand then with Dewey who, in a paraphase of Keats, held that the truly ethereal things are made by man.[91]

V. A Psychedelic/Cybernetic Aesthetic

We have stressed the lag between philosophical articulation and the activities of the contemporary art scene. Even if we were able to generate some energy devoted to closing this gap, we might still find ourselves badly dated. For as we write, two movements of great vitality appear upon the cultural scene. Each has an unusual potentiality for reworking the human situation: the effort to expand human awareness psychedelically and the attempt to extend the human perimeter by means of electronic technology.[92] Both of these revolutions are continuous with the concerns stated above and both share, with modern art, the critique of man's confinement within the geometric or linear view of human experience. Positively these efforts are directed to the massive and crucial problem of how to structure affectivity in a technological society.

The relationship of personal life to the need and experience of community is characterized in our time by a major tension. On the one hand, the scope of our experience has been broadened in a shattering way. Paradoxically, this has also increased the intensity of our experiences. "As electrically contracted, the globe is no more than a village. Electric speed, in bringing all social and political functions together in a sudden implosion, has heightened human awareness of responsibility to an intense degree."[93] Politics enjoins astral physics. We domesticate the heavens and cut distances in a savage onslaught on the limitations of time and space. From another side, and at the same time, we have an equally profound effort to probe the inner man, from both a behavioral and speculative point of view. Perhaps we can say that the poles of contemporary experience are nothing less than the astral and the nuclear.[94]

For some, in order to develop a sense of community in our present environment, it is necessary to shift the focus of concern from the biological, and even the sociological, to the activities of cybernetic technology as a resource for metaphors used to articulate the human endeavor.

In a quite different direction, we find those thinkers who hold that we should reconstitute human experience, and thereby human feelings and language, by virtue of psychedelic activity. Both of these commitments, whether to have us "tuned in" or "turned on," stress total involvement. Institutions such as the school, the church, and our political bureaucracy have shown themselves largely bankrupt in providing nutrition for the human person. Sensibility, affectivity, and a relevant liturgy of celebration are hard to come by. Still we must admit that the psychedelically inspired "trip" has major difficulties, since the landscape for such a trip often (though not always) remains painfully introverted. The total resource for the lived experience becomes heightened but correspondingly narrowed. The psychedelic community has exclusivity at its core. On the other hand, the revolution in electronic technology extends the hegemony of man and even, some contend, renders our planet but a probe. Yet here, too, we face divisiveness. Few of us can participate directly in planetary experience and many of us find ourselves hopelessly cut off from a world so distant from common experience, from the use of our hands, and even from the use of our machines.

Modern art has moved steadily in the direction of liberating the human person to enjoy his immediate experience. As Martin Buber says, "all is hallowed" and the ordinary sings a distinctive song of its own. Is the psychedelic-cybernetic revolution continuous with this attitude or is it to be another catastrophic break in our experience? Perhaps we are once again faced with the paradoxical situation wherein the dazzling quality of our insights moves us forward at one level only, but generates a feeling of anomie and loneliness for the larger community. The question confronting us can be asked in simple terms. Given the increased extension of man and his growing hegemony over nature, can he achieve a response, in concert, equal to those startling intensifications of personal experience brought on by psychedelics? In a cybernetic technology, can we achieve affectivity and personal sensibility in all aspects of the human situation and on a communitywide basis? If philosophy has a contribution to make, it could urge that the last half of the twentieth century would do well to view the economic and political questions as, at bottom, aesthetic.

NINETEEN

EXPERIENCE GROWS BY ITS EDGES

A Phenomenology of Relations in an American Philosophical Vein

All my knowledge of the world, even my scientific knowledge, is gained from my own particular point of view, or from some experience of the world without which the symbols of science would be meaningless.

—Maurice Merleau-Ponty, *Phenomenology of Perception*

I t is to take a precarious and even treacherous path to begin an essay on philosophy with an acknowledgment of one's "own particular view." Foundationalism, in either its Cartesian or contemporary analytic formulation, forbids such an allegedly subjective point of departure. Yet it is precisely here that phenomenology and classical American philosophy share both assumptions and endeavor. And both traditions can resonate to the description of phenomenology by Merleau-Ponty: "The opinion of the responsible philosopher must be that *phenomenology can be practiced and identified as a manner or style of thinking, that it existed as a movement before arriving at complete awareness of itself as a philosophy.*"[1] Both American pragmatism and phenomenology have been called "methods" rather than "philosophies." So be it. Practitioners of both know the differences which exist between pragmatism and phenomenology. Despite these acknowledged differences, some have made efforts to close the gap or at least to stress similarities.[2] My own predilection on this issue, if I can be forgiven a violation of the ostensible objectivity now required in philosophical discussion, comes to this: phenomenology has taught me to take things, attitudes, ambience, and relations straight up, with no excuses. I pay little attention to the famous Husserlian bracket, which seeks for the pure essence of things, for I regard such efforts in his work and those of his followers as a form of epistemological self-deception, a result of the rigid science it deplores in a fruitless search for true objectivity. To the contrary, nothing, nothing, is ever totally bracketed, for leaks are everywhere.[3]

Yet the effort of phenomenology is salutary. Pay attention, says the phenomenologist. I listen to that warning. Intentionally, pay attention, says the phenomenologist. I listen more intently. This attending to the flow of experience is multisensorial, for it involves not only hearing but feeling, touching, seeking, smelling, and tasting as well. What, then, is it for a human being to be in the world?

I

Taken straight out, and day by night, to be in the world is not to be inert, a thing among things, a bump on a log. However surprising for the tradition of Aristotelian natural place and Newtonian mechanics, quantum physics merely confirms the multiple processing which is endemic to the activity of the human organism. Merleau-Ponty writes: "Our own body is in the world as the heart is in the organism: it keeps the visible spectacle constantly alive, it breathes life into it and sustains it inwardly, and with it forms a system."[4] We do not fit into the world as a Lego piece or a Lincoln Log. In fact, I believe that we have no *special* place in the organic constituency of nature. Our consciousness—so different, so extraordinary, so bizarre, especially in its dream state—is a marvelous and pockmarked perturbation of the eonic history of DNA. Following Dewey, we are in, of, and about nature. We are nature's creature, its consciousness, its conscience, however aberrant and quixotic; its organizer, namer, definer, and defiler; a transient in search of an implacable, probably unrealizable, final consummation. The human organism is surrounded, permeated, and contexted by both the natural and social environments. In speaking of William James's doctrine of the self as a relational manifold, John E. Smith writes, "Radical empiricism is a radically new account of how the self penetrates and is penetrated by the world."[5]

The way in which the human self abides in the world is an extraordinarily complex affair. The self projects itself into the world. The self constructs a personal world, a habitation. The self, when threatened, retreats, even attempts to eject from the world, a form of dropping-out. The rhythm of these transactions is often lost in the macroscopic setting of "getting through the day." The algorithmic subtleties of our movements, shifts in attitude, and construction, deconstruction, setting, shifting, and bypassing of barriers are often buried in the frequently graceless syntax of duties, obligations, and habituations. So typical are our routines that the virtually infinite number of plans, plots, and variations in the rhythm of our bodily movements are lost to our attention. Recent investigations in biochemistry, especially with respect to the human liver, as well as cell surfaces and molecular biology, reveal an utterly extraordinary network. The electron microscope has revealed a dazzling array of complexity in an endless chain of relationships. The human skin is a battleground of bacteria colonies—symbiotic, voracious, and with long memories, as found in the unerring recurrence of dermatitis, repeatedly appearing on an isolated finger or toe, over and again.[6]

The phenomenological approach to the "lived body" has been an auspicious point of departure for philosophical speculation. The arrival of phenomenological and existentialist literature after the Second World War was a bracing antidote to the positivism and logical empiricism of the émigrés from the Vienna circle. As early as 1958, Rollo May and others introduced us to the empiricism of phenomenological psychiatry and existential analysis.[7] Following the path set by Ludwig Binswanger, Kurt Goldstein, and, indirectly, by Aron Gurwitsch, Richard Zaner correctly sees the medical model as the most propitious for understanding the activity of the human body, since it exaggerates medical case histories, which cast light on the hidden drama of simply being in the world as a body, as an organism, and as a conscious person.[8]

For most of us, most of the time, being in the world has an obviousness to it. We move about, little aware of our gait, presence, and interruptive activities. From time to time, an event, a startle, a happening will jog us to immediate consciousness. A snake in the yard, a tarantula in the bathtub, or the rolling red neon lights of a police cruiser in our driveway is required if we are to shake off our studied state of mesmerism, of ontological lethargy.

From 1916 until 1927, a pandemic swept the European continent. Technically called "Encephalitis lethargica," it is known to us as "sleeping sickness." Its victims numbered in the millions and very few avoided death. Those who did slumbered on, kinaesthetically anonymous, until the advent of the drug L-dopa, prescribed in the late 1960s. The subsequent "awakenings" have been described in a brilliant book by the neurologist Oliver Sacks.[9] In contrast to the way most of us are in the world, moving about in our unreflective, programmed way, I offer you, courtesy of Sacks, the movements of Lillian T., who, when she awoke, found her bodily movements, in an understatement, to be a chore. Burdened by violent "head movements" as a result of the pharmacological therapy, she was never in control of her body by instinct, only by detailed plotting. Sacks details her attempt to simply move from one place to another.

> One such patient had managed to maintain an independent life outside institutions for years, in the face of almost incredible difficulties—difficulties which would instantly have broken a less determined or resourceful person. This patient—Lillian T.—had long since found that she could scarcely start, or stop, or change her direction of motion; that once she had been set in motion, she had no control. It was therefore necessary for her to plan all her motions in advance, with great precision. Thus, moving from her armchair to her divan-bed (a few feet to one side) could never be done directly— Miss T. would immediately be "frozen" in transit, and perhaps stay frozen for half an hour or more. She therefore had to embark on one of two courses of action: in either case, she would rise to her feet, arrange her angle of direction exactly, and shout "Now!", whereupon she would break into an incontinent run, which could be neither stopped nor changed in direction. If the double doors between her living-room and the kitchen were open, she would rush through them, across the kitchen, round the back of the stove, across the other side of the kitchen, through the double doors—in a great figure-of-eight—until she hit her destination, her bed. If, however, the double doors were closed and secured, she would calculate her angle like a billiard-player, and then launch herself with great force against the doors, rebounding at the right angle to hit her bed. Miss T.'s

apartment (and, to some extent, her mind) resembled the control room for the Apollo launchings, at Houston, Texas: all paths and trajectories pre-computed and compared, contingency plans and "fail-safes" prepared in advance. A good deal of Miss T.'s life, in short, was dependent on conscious taking-care and elaborate calculation—but this was the only way she could maintain her existence.[10]

Sacks also details the baleful motile effects of Parkinson's disease. The person afflicted with festination is subject to "forced hurrying of walking, talking, speech or thought" and takes steps which "tend to become smaller and smaller, until finally the patient is 'frozen'—stepping internally, but with no space to step in."[11]

A case history of a different kind is also illuminating. Reported by A. R. Luria, the distinguished Russian psychologist, it details the recovery efforts of a young soldier who was wounded with a bullet to the brain. He suffered "impairment of vision, loss of memory and the ability to speak, read and write."[12] This man, Zasetsky, made a heroic effort to retrieve his faculties. Over a twenty-five-year period, he wrote of his journey to possible recovery. The result is a 3,000-word document, or no more than 120 words per year, for twenty-five years. By contrast, the present chapter is 6,000 words and was written in four weeks, without either the human or clinical significance of that by Mr. Zasetsky. The space-time-place-object relationships that you and I take for granted were, for our brain-wounded colleague, a nightmare. Zasetsky reports on some disasters in doing the obvious:

> When the doctor learned what my first name was, he'd always address me that way and try to shake hands when he came over. But I couldn't manage to clasp his hand. He'd try it a second time, but as luck would have it, I'd forget I had a right hand since I couldn't see it. Suddenly I'd remember and try to shake hands again but would only manage to touch his fingers. He'd let go of my hand and try once more. But I still wasn't able to do it, so he'd take my hand and show me how.
>
> Ever since I was wounded I've had trouble sometimes sitting down in a chair or on a couch. I first look to see where the chair is, but when I try to sit down I suddenly make a grab for the chair since I'm afraid I'll land on the floor. Sometimes that happens because the chair turns out to be further to one side than I thought.

Luria comments: "These 'spatial peculiarities' were particularly distressing when he was sitting at a table. He'd try to write and be unable to control a pencil, not knowing how to hold it. He encountered similar problems in the hospital workshops where he went for occupational therapy, hoping he'd be given some work to do and thus convince himself he could be useful, fit for some kind of job. There, too, he was up against precisely the same difficulties."

Zasetsky continues:

> The instructor gave me a needle, spool of thread, some material with a pattern on it, and asked me to try to stitch the pattern. Then he went off to attend to other patients—people who'd had their arms or legs amputated after being wounded, or half their bodies paralyzed. Meanwhile, I just sat there with the needle, thread, and material in my hands wondering why I'd been given these; I sat for a long time and did nothing. Suddenly the instructor came over and asked: "Why are you just sitting there? Go ahead and thread the needle!" I took the thread in one hand, the needle in the other, but couldn't understand what to do with them. How was I to thread the needle? I twisted it back and forth but hadn't the slightest idea what to do with any of these things.
>
> When I first looked at those objects, but hadn't yet picked them up, they seemed perfectly familiar—there was no reason to think about them. But as soon as I had them in my hands, I was at a loss to figure out what they were for. I'd lapse into a kind of stupor and wouldn't be able to associate these two objects in my mind—it was as though I'd forgotten why they existed. I twisted the needle and thread in my hands but couldn't understand how to connect the two—how to fit the thread in the needle.
>
> And then another annoying thing happened. By then I'd already learned what a needle, thread, thimble, and material were for and had some vague notion of how to use them. But I couldn't for the life of me think of the names for these or other objects people had pointed out to me. I'd sit there stitching the material with the needle, completely unable to remember what the very things I was using were called.
>
> The first time I entered the shop and saw people working there, I noticed various things—a workbench, a slab of wood, a plane—and I thought I recognized these objects and knew what they were called. But when I was actually given a plane and a slab of wood, I fiddled

with them for quite a while before some of the other patients showed me how to use these and other tools. I started to sand some wood but never learned to do it right, never did get it sanded. Each time I'd try, the surface would come out lopsided and crooked or had pits and bumps in it. And what's more, I got tired very quickly. While I was sanding the wood or looking at some of the other tools in the carpentry shop (a block of wood or a workbench) it was the same old story—I couldn't remember what any of these was used for.

When I went to a workshop to learn shoemaking, the instructor explained everything to me in great detail, since he was convinced I was very muddled and thick-headed and didn't know the first thing about making shoes. He showed me how to hold a hammer, drive nails in and pull them out, but all I learned to do was drive wooden nails into a board and pull them out again. And even then that was hard, because I couldn't see where the nails were supposed to go but kept missing the spot and banging my fingers until they bled. And I was very, very slow at it. So the only thing they let me do was bang nails into a board.[13]

Cases such as those of Lillian T. and Mr. Zasetsky abound in the literature and, tragically, in the everyday—our neighbors, friends, and family. They are a witness to the indolent response we have to our everyday movements, perfunctory and blind to the gift that a healthy DNA double helix awards to us, idiosyncratically. These extreme versions of what it takes to be in the world, versions which are extremely intensified by anyone who has had experience with the handicapped, are intensive role models for our untapped capacities and sensibilities. The richness of the everyday, had we the will to savor our possibilities, would far exceed our fantasies. Indeed, our penchant for the fantastic is but an indictment of how casual and unreflective has become our daily posture in a world which screeches at us, though we hear not.

Classical American philosophy, represented by James and Dewey, offers us some insight into the way in which we are in the world. James stresses human energy, human proclivity, and human daring. His self is Promethean: making, constructing, reconstructing, and bold in its effort to transcend the accepted conceptual frames of human experience, which often tie us down, and are often chary of suspension of disbelief. James invokes the "will to believe" as an antidote to our premature resignation to limits in the variety, reach, or implication of our experiences.

Acceptance of the routine, the humdrum, and the obvious results in a flaccid, inert, and dull personal presence. James writes: "Some men and women, indeed, there are who can live on smiles and the word 'yes' forever. But for others (indeed for most), this is too tepid and relaxed a moral climate. Passive happiness is slack and insipid, and soon grows mawkish and intolerable. Some austerity and wintry negativity, some roughness, danger, stringency, and effort, some 'no! no!' must be mixed in, to produce the sense of an existence with character and texture and power."[14] As described by James, especially in his *Principles of Psychology*, the human self is Promethean and picaresque: a venturesome, risk-oriented, and experimental prober into the widest and furthest reaches of the flow of experience.

John Dewey accepts this profile as an ideal. Dewey, for example, believes, "If it is better to travel than arrive, it is because traveling is a constant arriving, while arrival that precludes further traveling is most easily attained by going to sleep or dying."[15] Yet Dewey, a proletarian, in contrast to James, a New England Brahmin, realizes that the traveling is not done by an isolated self. To the contrary, Dewey's sense of a person being in the world is conflicted by the vagaries of natural forces and, above all, by the bottom-line admission that we are social selves: contexted, conditioned, herded, institutionalized, and tradition-laden. Despite the attraction of James's Promethean self, the cautions of Dewey with regard to the trappings that work on us as we confront the human condition must be taken with seriousness. One may lament the absence of an aboriginal approach to being in the world, but lamentation does not obviate the hard, irrepressible facticity of natural and social conditioning, a context provided throughout the work of John Dewey and George Herbert Mead.

One can posit still a third version of our being in the world, although the American intellectual scene pays little attention to it: that of the cosmological. In truth, James is right. We must seek to be prepossessive and creative in our dealings with the world in which we find ourselves. Yet Dewey is also correct in his stressing of the natural and social ambience which restricts our doings, limits our travelings, and short-circuits our desires. Still, not by the planet Earth alone do we live. In our time, increasingly, the stellar—indeed, the vaunted mystery of the moon—has become accessible to us, an extended neighborhood. Contemporary astral physics has enhanced our reach a millionfold. Although our new and approximate knowledge of the age and extent of the universe has been dwarfing in the ultimate sense, nonetheless, paradoxically, the human odyssey takes on the hue of a remarkably novel and originally self-conscious presence in an otherwise vast, unfeeling, unknowing, and uncaring panoply of sheerly natural events. Extraterrestrial consciousness is a possibility, but we have no evidence. Until such appears, the universe is not aware of itself except for the activity of human life. Merleau-Ponty tells us that "because we are in the world, we are *condemned to meaning,* and we cannot do or say anything without its acquiring a name in history."[16]

The task of building a liberating human future, as I foresee it, assumes the Promethean self of James and the social sophistication of Dewey, Mead, the Marxists, and cultural anthropology, all rendered within a burgeoning social cosmology. That task, of course, remains to be done. For now, let us start at the beginning and discuss the lineaments of the potentially Promethean self and the dangers therein. The key to such a consideration is the understanding of relations, as first proposed by William James in his doctrine of radical empiricism.[17]

II

For James, and subsequently for Dewey, the human self is urged to build a personal world, although not as *ab ovo.* Rather, this personal world is to be built in response to the "push and press of the cosmos," as James would have it, or, as Dewey suggested, as a response to the irreducible and ineluctable problematic which resides at the very point of transaction of the human organism with nature. Rather than there being one world, which we acknowledge from an alleged separately distant place, we have a series of worlds as constructs, as mock-ups. In the words of the neopragmatist Nelson Goodman, there are "ways of worldmaking" which he calls "versions and visions."[18] Anticipating modern quantum physics, James sees the world as a relational webbing with objects as results of our conceptual intrusion, rather than as fixed givens in an already structured setting. Referring to essences as *"teleological weapons of the mind,*"[19] and affirming that *"there is no property absolutely essential to any one thing,"*[20] James inverts the classical assumption that the world comes as given and need but be defined, denoted, and arranged. To the contrary, what in common parlance we take to be objects are bundles of relations, gathered first conceptually, and then, by habit, perceptually. Speaking of the names of things—in this case, a painting—Michel Foucault criticizes the supposed one-to-one correspondence between our language and the object: "And the proper name, in this context, is merely an artifice: it gives us a finger to point with, in other words, to pass surreptitiously from the space where one speaks to the space where one looks; in other words, to fold one over the other as if they were equivalents."[21]

In modern art, the names of the paintings are often but placeholders, vestibules for entry into a world of relations that prevent any denomination or definition. If we could break the lock placed upon us by our inherited syntactical conceptual scheme, we could come to see, hear, feel, smell, and taste bundles of relations rather than objects, hardly more alive than the nouns used to name them. I believe that James is right. Aboriginally, the world is not made up of objects but rather is a continuum of concatenated relations. Scandalous though it may be to those for whom logic tells the only truth, if we were to focus on a single object and detail its relations, we would have access to a perceptual entailment which would involve us in everything that exists. Unfortunately, we do not even attempt this, for as James notes, "We actually ignore most of the things before us."[22] Far less do we follow the relational leads which spring from these linguistically ordained things. When alert, we do better. James describes our active sense life in the following way: "Out of what is in itself an undistinguishable, swarming *continuum,* devoid of distinction or emphasis, our senses make for us, by attending to this motion and ignoring that, a world full of contrasts, of sharp accents, of abrupt changes, of picturesque light and shade."[23] The way in which an object is denoted on the macroscopic scale is due to one or more functional characteristics: for example, shape, size, texture, color, odor, place in space, or mobility. Once having been designated, except for occasional aesthetic considerations, the object falls into a class of conceptually identical companions: chair, glass, book. Thus we repress or ignore the relational run in every object, as in *this* book, with *that* kind of paper, smell, size, and as found on *this* table in *that* room in *this* house on *that* street in *this* neighborhood, county, state, region, country, hemisphere, planet, solar system, galaxy, and pluriverse. There is no doubt that we cut off the relations. The important question has to do with both *what* relations are cut and *how* we cut them. Who was the first human being to eat a lobster? Surely a more foreboding and less appetizing creature has not appeared to the culinary search. Yet, as with sheep brains, pigs' feet, and squid, the human being, here and there, follows a different relational trail. In those cases, relational plurality leads to delight and leaves the definition of pleasing as simply not sufficient for the longer reach.

If we were to follow each thing and event to its full perceptual implication, we would explode from experiential overload. James gives us a taste of this:

> Only in some pitiful dreamer, some philosopher, poet, or romancer, or when the common practical man becomes a lover, does the hard externality give way, and a gleam of insight into the ejective world, as Clifford called it, the vast world of inner life beyond us, so different from that of outer seeming, illuminate our mind. Then the whole scheme of our customary values gets confounded, then our self is riven and its narrow interests fly to pieces, then a new centre and a new perspective must be found.[24]

Cutting off relations is therefore necessary for personal survival. But how do we cut? Do we snip, and so leave a small wound which heals in time? Do we hack, and so leave a gaping wound which festers and, when closed, leaves an unsightly scar? Do we fold over the rejected relation, biding time until we can recover and savor it? Do we let the relational lead or inference dangle, awaiting a propitious moment to reconnoitre and relive its possibility? Do we send the relation on a journey, hoping for a return? Or do we give it a one-way ticket? Finally, do we bury the relation, hoping for its continued interment, although worried about periodic reappearance through the cracks in our vulnerable psyche?

The world we build is exactly akin to the way we cut relations, indulge relations, and celebrate relations. More, our world takes off as novel and as distinctively ours precisely in response to how we make new relations of the relations already at work in the environ in which we find ourselves. It is clear, although not for the present setting, that the way we best understand this activity of making relations is to pursue the life of the young child. Genetic epistemology has much to teach us, for children naturally make their own relations until we teach them that the world has already been named and properly codified. Against their aboriginal bent, they are told to march in step, name by name, definition by definition, until they, too, see the world as an extension of local grammar and hidebound conceptual designations. The social and moral result of this aberrant pedagogy is deleterious, as stressed, for example, by Merleau-Ponty in his discussion of the presence of "psychological rigidity" as a lamentable but typical characteristic of young children.[25] Yet, for both young children and adults who are, or who wish to become, alive to possibilities heretofore undreamt, the making of relations is the way to build a distinctively personal world. I turn now to some of the obstacles to a salutary making of relations.

III

Being in the world is not a cakewalk. Our surroundings, personal, natural, and social are fraught with potential deception, actual invasion, and an omnipresent indifference. To make a world as distinctively ours by the making of relations is too often a rarity. The other-directedness made famous by David Riesman and his colleagues in *The Lonely Crowd* can be raised to the status of an ontological category.[26] In ideal terms, a person comes to consciousness and begins to work out one's place, one's version, and one's taste for this or that. Yet we now know that the burgeoning self is fraught with personal freight: genetic, familial, linguistic, bodily, climatic, ethnic, gendered, racial, and even the subtleties of gait, weight, and smile. As I see it, the fundamental challenge is to convert the personal weaknesses into strengths and to drive our strengths into the teeth of a personally neutral, but relatively pregnant, world. The ancient philosophers, especially the Stoics and the Epicureans, offered sage advice on how to be in the world without getting maced. Taken overall, their warnings focused on the dangers of excess, indolence, and self-aggrandizement.[27] This was and is wise counsel. The intervening 2,000 years, however, have bequeathed a far more sophisticated environment as a setting for the constructing of a personal world. The dangers, the traps, and the obstacles are more subtle, more extensive, and more seductive than they were in antiquity.

The scriptural rhetorical question, Lord, what must I do to be saved? can be reinvoked by our children as follows: What shall I do to make a world which is personally mine, although it inheres, coheres, borrows, and lends to others who are making a world personally their own? Couched more indirectly, this is the question that our children and our students ask us. The initial response is obvious. Make relations! Build, relate, and then reflect. Reflect, relate, and then build. Seek novelty, leave no stone unturned. Fasten on colors, shapes, textures, sounds, odors, sights. Above all, never close down until the fat person sings. The only acceptable denouement is death. Until then, all signs are go—that is, make relations until the maker is unmade. Still, in the making of relations, dangers lurk. We detail them as follows:

Relation Starvation

Stinginess is omnipresent in the human condition, as anyone who has lived on tips will attest. The novel experience carries for some of us a warning signal. We are often suspicious of the new, an unfamiliar face, a turn in the road, a break from the routine. We tend to huddle with the familiar. Even the more flamboyant of us have our schedule, our pigeonhole for person and event. Novelty is unsettling. We prefer the recognizable, the repetitive, for that awards personal control. In time, everything is forced to resemble something else, something prior, something already experienced. Have not I seen you before? Have not I heard you before? Repetition becomes so comforting that genuine novelty is reduced to prior experience. The width of our vision shrinks. We become more defensive about what we already know, less open to what we do not know. Relation starvation is the incarnation of the a priori. All that happens has happened, for us, before. At least we think so. And that is because we focus only on famliarity, sameness. The novel is repressed, transformed into the familiar. We tend to chatter, over and over, about our experiences, warding off the novelty brought to us by others. We become monologic rather than open to dialogue and to those potentially liberating, yet frightening and unfamiliar, experiences out of our ken. We become shrill, repetitive, and overindulgent of the significance of our own past. Others' histories hold no interest for us, for they become indices of our deprivation rather than communal undergoings to share, however vicariously. The more committed we become to the significance of our own experiences, the less capacity we have to participate in the experiences of others. In time, the ultimate bane of human health emerges: jealousy. We soon become trapped in our own world, one which is shrinking, increasingly lonely and overesteemed. Relation-starved, we are less and less able to make relations, to break out, to build a world in which our personal style takes on meaning not by insularity but by contrast.

Relation Amputation

In making relations, we run the risk of being strung out. Granted that shutting out relational possibilities leads to relation starvation and an encapsulated self, yet in our countereffort to reach out, we often fail to read the map of possibilities. Knowing when to desist, to withdraw, and to close down is very difficult. How much testing is enough testing? How much experimentation is enough experimentation? The explosive world of pharmacological nostrums is constantly blindsided by late-appearing side-effects. Pesticides, thalidomide, birth control pills, L-dopa, and countless other substances bequeath later "hits," events which are severely damaging to human life and which on retrospect call for earlier amputation.

On the one hand, risk is often avoided at the expense of possibility and breakthrough. The human odyssey is replete with stories of those courageous persons who defied the present data in favor of that which might emerge if one were to take the next step. One must never be cavalier. Nonetheless, surprise often awaits us as we forge a relationship heretofore banned or simply unthought. The burden is that we must learn to read the signs of implicitness. An early amputation of a lead will throw us back into the obvious. Persistence in following a relational possibility beyond its capacity to ameliorate and sustain the worth of the risk of the endeavor is foolhardy. We should not hang back and endorse the accepted slavishly. Premature amputation denies the long-standing historical message that taking a chance is usually fortuitous. Cut when necessary, but not out of fright or habit.

Relation Saturation

There are those of us who get the message that the making of relations is liberating. For some, this awareness turns into a frenetic activity of multiple involvement, as though the quantity of experience were sure to ensure a significant life. We face here an overindulgence in the having of experiences, as though one need not bring to bear a reflective self in these transactions. Most often, for those persons whose lives have been constricted by mores, repressions, and systemic habituation, any opportunity to break them open is responded to with alacrity. New experiences are collected like hash-marks. We become impervious to their significance, their dangers, their relationship to our past, our person, and our future. Unreflective in anticipation, undergoing and retrospection, these experiences follow one after the other into an unknowing bin, marked only "accomplishment." The relations, the potential implications, tumble about shy of significance and of no import to either our person or our prospects.

Relation saturation describes the fate of the person who eats without tasting. It is a relation-saturated person whose sexual activity is more characterized by a desire to do it again than to experience the doing of it in the first place. The depth of a single relation, the mastery of a technique—or an instrument, as in the cello of Pablo Casals—is lost to the saturator. Endless variation replaces the nectar of a rich, single experience. The relation-saturator writes his or her autobiography at a tender age, failing to realize that it is subsequent personal history which casts genuine light on the relative importance of events once undergone without reflection. Sheer quantity of experience is misleading in its import. Following John Dewey, "Everything depends on the *quality* of the experience which is had."[28]

Relation Seduction

William James was fond of urging us to live on the fringe, beyond the ken of normal, everyday experience. To that end, he experimented with hallucinogens and spent considerable time in pursuing investigation of the claims made on behalf of extrasensory perception. James was also fascinated by persons who claimed to attain extraordinary insight by virtue of religious, aesthetic, or even dietary experiences. He found saints, yogis, and clairvoyants of equal fascination. For James, the present reach of the normal consciousness was puerile when compared with what he regarded as possibilities as yet unseen except by a few unusually bold and gifted persons.

Actually, James points to a double fringe. The first we have discussed, for it refers to the implicitness hidden in every object, event, and situation. That fringe holds the ongoing relational leads which we too often prematurely cut in the name of obviousness and definition. The second fringe is more fascinating and more dangerous. Some persons are driven by the temptation to transcend the boundaries of common experience and belief. Through intense, single-minded commitment, they fasten on a vision of reality not given to the rest of us. Rooted in political or religious belief, this commitment can be liberating for others, but it can also be a snare of major self-deception. For every Abraham, Jesus, Mohammed, Marx, or Nietzsche, there are hundreds of self-benighted souls who become so enamored of their personal goal that they find themselves cut off from the stark claim of reality.

Still more dangerous is the fringe which is accessible by means of pharmacology. Mind-altering drugs are now a fact of public and familial life.[29] Yet the leap over the relational chain to experiences which are literally *de novo* and beyond normal capacity tends to freeze in a world of experience that has no connection with our body, our things, and our space-time relations as normally experienced. I do not deny that the trip to the fringe is exhilarating. The question is whether one can ever return without experiencing severe depression in response to the comparative tawdriness of the everyday. The trouble with relation seduction, be it local fanaticism on behalf of a visionary goal or pharmacologically induced, is that it is addictive, and therefore more a manacle than liberation.

Relation Repression

Often we have experiences which are potentially threatening to our well-being, at least as we conceive it to be so. Instead of allowing these experiences to play out their hand, we repress them. The relational implications of the experience cannot be severed once and for all. Rather they are shoved down into the labyrinth of our unconscious, but nonetheless active, self. We act as if we were in a World War I pillbox complete with flamethrowers, burning out the ground around us. Bunkered down, we seem to feel on top of things. And that is precisely the problem. The repressed experiences take on a life of their own, sifting their way up and into the nooks and crannies of our conscious life, designated here as our stomach, nervous system, dreams, tics, and temperament.

In the terminology of classical psychoanalysis, relation repression is often discussed under the rubric of trauma. Franz Kafka traces his comparative creative and interpersonal impotence to such an event. In a letter to his father—typically, and fittingly, unsent—Kafka tells of an event which set the stage for his life-long sense of alienation. As a very young child, Franz annoyed his father by constantly demanding attention while a guest was in the apartment. After repeated warnings, his father seized him and placed him outside on the *pavlatche*, the outside ledge, closing the doors on Franz in his pajamas. Locked out, cut off, and bewildered, Kafka concluded, "I was a mere nothing for him." This event, repressed and never worked out, did him "inner harm."[30] Even the final revealing of the event was posthumous and to an audience who knew neither Kafka nor his father. Such relation repression, repeated over and over in our own lives, is baleful and insidious.

IV

Being in the world is not a position of stasis. It is active, energizing, and potentially creative. Of course, it can also be enervating, treacherous, and self-deceiving. For those of us who wish to become persons, the world does not come ready-made. The doctrine of natural place was a provincial fallout from the enclosed geography and cosmology of the Greek world of Aristotle, a point made in detail by Heidegger.[31] Our world is infinitely more expansive, more complex, more furtive, more demanding, and, if we have the will, more rewarding. The lattice-work of nature is intriguing. Still more intriguing is the set of relations which we ourselves fashion, knead, and impose.

Most of us have barely scratched the surface in our efforts to build a truly personal world. And few of us bequeath the ability to make relations to our children, choosing rather to pass on a shopworn box of maxims, shorn of relational excitement. On behalf of our possibilities, I tell you the story of the Polish mathematician. Our colleague, something of a dissident within the last decade, was arrested and placed in solitary confinement. He was left to himself with only a slop-pail for company, having been refused his request for a pencil and paper. Seeking to keep personally alive, he did mathematical formulae in his head. Shorn of physical replication, he soon began to repeat the same mathematical relations, over and over, until they became frayed from repetition and lack of novelty. When released several years later, he said that he was about to eat his brain, for he had run out of relations and had no new formulae to revivify the inherited and so stalk out new ground. Surely, surrounded by the richest of novel possibilities, we can do as well. Or can we, oh we of little faith in the prevalence of surprise.

TWENTY

THE AESTHETIC DRAMA OF THE ORDINARY

> I wish I could see what my eyes see.
>
> —Vanilla Fudge

T raditionally, we think of ourselves as "in the world," as a button is in a box, a marble in a hole, a coin in a pocket, a spoon in a drawer; in, always *in* something or other. And yet, to the contrary, I seem to carry myself, to lead myself, to have myself hang around, furtive of nose, eye, and hand, all the while spending and wasting, eating and fouling, minding and drifting, engaging in activities more descriptive of a permeable membrane than of a box. To feel is to be felt. To be in the world is to "world" and to be "worlded." No doubt, the accepted language of expository prose severely limits us in this effort to describe our situation experientially. Were I to say, for example, "my presence in the world" or "my being in the world," I would still fall prey to the container theory and once again be "in" as over against "out." Is this not why it is necessary to describe an unusual person, situation, or state of being as being "out of this world," or "spaced out," or simply "out of it"? Why is it that ordinary language, or our language as used ordinarily, so often militates against the ways in which we actually have—that is, undergo—our experiencing? Why is it that we turn to the more specialized forms of discourse, such as jokes, fiction, poetry, music, painting, sculpture, and dance, in order to say what we "really" mean? Does this situation entail the baleful judgment that the comparative bankruptcy of our ordinary language justly points to the comparable bankruptcy of our ordinary experience?

In gross and obvious empirical terms, it is difficult to say no to the necessity of this entailment. Surely, it is true that we are surrounded by the banal, monumentalized in a miniature and trivial fashion by the American shopping center. And it is equally—yea, painfully—true that the "things" of our everyday experience are increasingly deaestheticized, not only by misuse and failure to maintain, but, forebodingly, in their very conception of design and choice of material, as witnessed by the recent national scandal in our urban bus fleet, when millions of dollars were spent on buses that were not built for city traffic, city streets, or for frequent use. How striking, as well, is the contrast between those Americans at the turn of the century, who built the IRT subway in New York City—complete with mosaics, balustrades, and canopied entrances—over against their descendants, our peers, who seem unable to find a way to eradicate the stink and stain of human urine from those once-proud and promising platforms and stairwells. So as not to contribute any further to the offensive and misleading assumption that our main aesthetic disasters are now found in the great urban centers of the Northeast, let us point to one closer to my home.

The city of Houston, in paying homage to a long-outdated frontier myth of every "building" for itself, proceeds to construct an environment which buries an urban aesthetic in the wake of free enterprise. Houston gives rise to tall and imposing buildings whose eyes of window and light point to the surrounding plains, but whose feet are turned inward. These buildings do not open in a merry maypole of neighborhood frolic and function. Houston buildings are truly sky-buildings, for they look up and out, leaving only the sneer of a curved lip to waft over the enervated neighborhoods below, most of them increasingly grimy and seedy. As an apparent favor to most of us, Houston provides a way for us to avoid these neighborhoods, allowing us to careen around the city, looking only at the bellies of the titans of glass and steel, astride the circular ribbon of concrete known, appropriately, as the beltway, marred only by the dead trees, broken car jacks, and the intrusively omnipresent Texas-sized billboards.

Perhaps it is just as well that we, too, rise above the madding crowd, for in that way we miss the awkwardness of wandering into one of those walled-off, sometimes covenanted and patrolled, fancy enclaves which make the city tolerable for the rich. And as we make our "beltway," we miss as well that strikingly sad experience of downtown Houston at 6 P.M. of a weekend evening, when the loneliness and shabbiness of the streets are cast into stark relief by the perimeter of empty skyscrapers and the hollow sounds of the feet of the occasional snow-belt émigré traveler, emerging from the Hyatt Regency in a futile search for action. What is startling and depressing about all of this is that the city of Houston is the nation's newest, and allegedly most promising, major city.

Actually, whether it is North, South, East, or West matters little, for in general the archons of aesthetic illiteracy have seen to it that on behalf of whatever other ideology they follow, the presence of aesthetic sensibility has been either ruled out, or, where traditionally present, allowed to erode. Further, to the extent that we prehend ourselves as a thing among things or a functioning item in a box, then we get what we deserve. Supposing, however, we were to consider the major metaphorical versions of how we carry on our human experiencing and, in so doing, avoid using the imagery of the box. Instead, let us consider ourselves as being in a uterine situation, which binds us to nutrition in a distinctively organic way. James Marston Fitch, a premier architectural historian, writes about us as follows: "Life is coexistent with the external natural environment in which the body is submerged. The body's dependence upon this external environment is absolute—in the fullest sense of the word—uterine."[1] No box here. Rather we are floating, gestating organisms, transacting with our environment, eating all the while.

The crucial ingredient in all uterine situations is the nutritional quality of the environment. If our immediate surroundings are foul, soiled, polluted harbors of disease and grime, ridden with alien organisms, then we falter and perish. The growth of the spirit is exactly analogous to the growth of the organism. It, too, must be fed and it must have the capacity to convert its experiences into a nutritious transaction. In short, the human organism has need of two livers. The one, traditional and omnipresent, transforms our blood among its five hundred major functions and oversees the elimination from our body of ammonia, bacteria, and an assortment of debris, all of which would poison us. The second is more vague, having no physical analogue. But its function is similar and crucial. This second liver eats the sky and the earth, sorts out tones and colors, and provides a filter through which the experienced environment enters our consciousness. It is this spiritual liver which generates our feelings of queasiness, loneliness, surprise, and celebration. And it is this liver which monitors the tenuous relationship between expectations and anticipations, on the one hand, and realizations, disappointments, and failures, on the other. We are not simply in the world so much as we are of and about the world. On behalf of this second type of livering, let us evoke the major metaphors of the fabric, of the uterus, through which we have our natal being. Our context for inquiry shall be the affairs of time and space, as well as the import of things, events, and relations. We shall avoid the heightened and intensified versions of these experiential filters and concentrate on the explosive and implosive drama of their ordinariness.

Time

Time passing is a death-knell. With the license of a paraphrase, I ask, for whom does the bell toll? It tolls for thee and me and for ours. We complain about the studied repetition, which striates our lives, and yet, in honesty, we indulge this repetition as a way of hiding from the inexorability of time passing, as a sign equivalent to the imminence of our self-eulogy. Time is a shroud, often opaque, infrequently diaphanous. Yet, from time to time, we are able to bring time into our own self-awareness and to bring time to its knees. On those rare occasions when time is ours rather than we being creatures of time, we feel a burst of singularity, of independence, even perhaps of the eternal import of our being present to ourselves. How has it happened that we have become slaves to time? Surely as children of Kant and Einstein, we should know better. For them and for modern physics, time is a mock-up, an earth phenomenon, no more relevant cosmically than the watches which watch time, supposedly passing. Still, Kant notwithstanding, "time" is the name given to the process of our inevitable dissolution. On the morrow, our kidney is less quick, our liver less conscientious, our lung less pulsatile, and our brain less alert. Is it possible, without indulging ourselves in a Walter Mittyesque self-deception, to turn this erosive quality of time passing to our own advantage?

I suggest that we can beat time at its own game. Having created time, let us obviate it. Time, after all, rushes headlong into the future, oblivious to its damages, its obsoleting, and its imperviousness to the pain it often leaves in its wake. A contrary view is that in its passing, time heals. But it is not time which heals us, it is we who heal ourselves by our retroactive reconstruction of history. It is here that time is vulnerable, for it has no history, no past. Time is ever lurching into the future. We, however, can scavenge its remains and make them part of ourselves. For us, the past is existentially present if we have the will and the attentiveness to so arrange. I offer here that we recover the detritus of time passing and clot its flow with our freighted self-consciousness. We can become like the giant balloons in the Macy's Thanksgiving Day parade, thick with history and nostalgia, forcing time passing to snake around us, assuring that it be incapable of enervating our deepest feelings of continuity. What, for example, could time do to us if every time we met a person, or thought a thought, or dreamt a dream, we involved every person ever met, every thought ever thought, and every dream ever dreamt? What would happen if every event, every place, every thing experienced, resonated all the events, places, and things of our lives? What would happen if we generated a personal environment in which the nostalgic fed into the leads of the present, a self-created and sustained environment with implications fore and aft? In so doing, we would reduce time passing to scratching on the externals of our Promethean presence. Time would revolve around us rather than passing through us. Time would provide the playground for our activities rather than the graveyard of our hopes. We would time the world rather than having the world time us. And we would reverse the old adage, to wit: if you have the place, I have the time, for time is mine to keep and to give. And, in addition to telling our children, "now is your time," we would tell ourselves, no matter how old, "now is our time."

Space

It is equally as difficult to extricate ourselves from the box of space as it is to escape from the penalties of time. Here, too, we have failed to listen to Kant and Einstein, for space, just as time, has no existential reality other than our conception of it. Yet we allow the prepossessing character of space to dwarf us. Nowhere is this more apparent than in Texas, where the big sky of Montana is outdone by the scorching presence of a sun that seems never to set, frying our brains in the oven of its arrogance. In the spring of the year, the bluebonnets and Indian paintbrush state our position: fey, lovely, quiet, reserved, and delicate of manner. The Texas sun indulges this temporary human-scaled assertion while hovering in the background with vengeance on its mind. As the flowers fade, the horizon widens and the sun takes its place at the center of our lives, burning us with the downdraft of its rays. Listen to Larry King on the sun and sky in West Texas:

> The land is stark and flat and treeless, altogether as bleak and spare as mood scenes in Russian literature, a great dry-docked ocean with small swells of hummocky tan sand dunes or humpbacked rocky knolls that change colors with the hour and the shadows: reddish brown, slate gray, bruise colored. But it is the sky—God-high and pale, like a blue chenille bedspread bleached by seasons in the sun— that dominates. There is simply too much sky. Men grow small in its presence and—perhaps feeling diminished—they sometimes are compelled to proclaim themselves in wild or berserk ways. Alone in those remote voids, one may suddenly half believe he is the last man on earth and go in frantic search of the tribe. Desert fever, the natives call it. . . . The summer sun is as merciless as a loan shark: a blinding, angry orange explosion baking the land's sparse grasses and quickly aging the skin.[2]

Texans pride themselves upon being larger than life. But this is just a form of railing against the sun. The centuries-long exodus from the Northeast and the coastal cities was in part an escape from urban claustrophobia. In that regard, the escape was short-lived and self-deceptive, for it soon became apparent that the West presented a claustrophobia of another kind—paradoxically, that of open space. The box was larger, the horizon deeper, but the human self became even more trivialized

than it was among the skyscrapers and the crowded alleyways and alcoves of the teeming urban centers. No, to the extent that we are over-
shadowed by an external overhang, be it artifact or natural, we cower in
the presence of an *other* which is larger, more diffuse, still threatening,
and depersonalizing. In response, just as we must seize the time, so, too,
must we seize the space, and turn it into a place, our place.

The placing of space is the creating of interior space, of personal
space, of your space and my space, of our space. I am convinced, painful
though it be, that we as human beings have no natural place. We are
recombinant organisms in a cosmic DNA chain. Wrapped in the mystery of our origins, we moved from natural places to artifactual ones,
from caves to ziggurats to the Eiffel Tower. We moved from dunes to
pyramids and then to the World Trade Center. The history of our architecture, big and small, functional and grandiloquent, lovely and grotesque, is the history of the extension of the human body into the abyss.
We dig and we perch. We level and we raise. We make our places round
and square and angular. We make them hard and soft and brittle. We
take centuries to make them and we throw them up overnight. In modern America, the new Bedouins repeat the nomadic taste of old and
carry their places with them as they plod the highway vascular system of
the nation, hooking up here and there.

Some of our idiomatic questions and phrases tell us of our concern
for being in place. Do you have a place? Set a place for me. This is my
place. Why do we always go to your place? Would you care to place a
bet? I have been to that place. Wow, this is *some* place. Win, place, show.
The trouble with him is that he never went any place and the trouble
with her is that she never got any place. How are you doing? How is it
going? Fine, I am getting someplace. Not so well, I seem to be no place.
Recall that poignant scene in *Death of a Salesman* when Willy Loman
asks Howard for a place in the showroom rather than on the road. In
two lines, Howard tells Willy three times that he has no "spot" for him.
I knew your father, Howard, and I knew you when you were an infant.
Sorry, Willy! No spot, no place, for you. Pack it in. You are out of time
and have no place.

Listen lady, clear out. But this is my place. No lady, this place is to be
replaced. The harrowing drama of eviction haunts all of us as we envi-
sion our future out of place and on the street.[3] Dorothy Day founded

halfway houses, places somewhere between no place and my place, that is, at least, someplace. And, finally, they tell us that we are on the way to our resting place, a place from which there is no return.

These are only anecdotal bare bones, each of them selected from a myriad of other instances which point to our effort to overcome the ontological *angoisse* which accompanies our experience of *Unheimlich-keit*, a deep and pervasive sense of ultimate homelessness. We scratch out a place and we raise a wall. The windows look out but the doors open in. We hang a picture and stick a flower in a vase. We go from cradle and crib to a coffin, small boxes at the beginning and end of journeys through slightly larger boxes. Some of us find ourselves in boxes underneath and on top of other boxes in a form of apartmentalization. Some of our boxes are official boxes and we call them "offices," slightly less prestigious than the advantage of a box seat. Everywhere in the nation, the majority of our houses are huddled together, sitting on stingy little pieces of ground, while we ogle the vast stretch of land held by absentees. One recalls here "Little Boxes," a folksong of the 1960s that excoriates the ticky-tacky boxes on the hillsides, as a preface to the yuppiedom of our own time. For the most part, our relation to external space is timid, even craven. From time to time, we send forth a camel, a schooner, a Conestoga wagon, or a space shuttle as probes into the outer reaches of our environ, on behalf of our collective body. Yet these geographical efforts to break out are more symbolic than real, for after our explorations we seem destined to repeat our limited variety of habitat.

The locus classicus for an explication of the mortal danger in a sheerly geographical response to space is found in a story by Franz Kafka, "The Burrow." In an effort to protect his food from an assumed intruder, the burrower walls off a series of mazes sure to confuse an opponent. This attempt is executed with such cunning and brilliance that his nonreflective anality is missed as a potential threat. The food is indeed walled off from the intruder—from the burrower as well. He dies of starvation, for he cannot find his own food. The way out of the box is quite different, for it has to do not with the geography and physicality of space, but rather with our symbolic utilization of space for purposes of the human quest. We manage our ontological dwarfing and trivialization at the hands of infinite space, and the rush of time passing and obsoleting, by our construction, management, placing, and relating of *our* things. It is to our things, to creating our salvation in a world without guarantee of salvation, that we now turn.

Things

"Thing," orthographically and pronouncedly, is one of the ugly words in contemporary American usage. Yet it is also, inferentially and historically, one of the most subtle and beautiful of our words. It is lamentable that we do not speak the way Chaucer spoke. From the year 1400 and a work of Lydgate, *Troy-Book*, the text reads: "That thei with Paris to Greece schulde wende, To Brynge this thynge to an ende." The Trojan war was a thing? Of course it was a thing, for "thing" means concern, assembly, and, above all, an affair. Thing is a woman's menses and a dispute in the town. Thing is a male sex organ and a form of prayer. (The continuity is not intended, although desirable.) Thing is what is to be done or its doing. I can't give you any thing but love, baby. That is the only thing I have plenty of, baby. When you come, bring your things. I forgot to bring my things. My things are packed away. Everything will be all right. And by the way, I hope that things will be better.

What and who are these things to which we cling? An old parimutuel ticket; a stub for game seven of the World Series; a class ring; a mug; a dead Havana cigar, loved but unsmoked; my snuff box; my jewelry drawer; an album; a diary; a yearbook—all tumbled into the box of memories, but transcendent and assertive of me and mine. Do not throw out his things—they will be missed. Put her things in the attic, for someday she will want them as a form of reconnoitering her experienced past. Do you remember those things? I know that we had them. Where are they? They are in my consciousness. Can we find them? We didn't throw them out, did we? How could we? The making, placing, and fondling of our things is equivalent to the making, placing, and fondling of our world. We are our things. They are personal intrusions into the vast, impersonal reach of space. They are functional clots in the flow of time. They are living memories of experiences had but still viable. They are memorials to experiences undergone and symbolically still present. The renewed handling of a doll, a ticket, a toy soldier, a child-hood book, a tea cup, a bubble-gum wrapper evokes the flood of experiences past but not forgotten.[4] How we strive to say "hello," to say "here I am," in a cosmos impervious, unfeeling, and dead to our plaintive cry of self-assertion. To make is to be made and to have is to be had. My thing is not anything or something. Your thing is not my thing, but it could be our thing. The ancients had it right—bury the things with the person. We should do that again. Bury me with a copy of the *New York Times*, a Willie Mays baseball card, a bottle of Jameson, my William James book, a pipe, some matches, and a package of Seven Seas tobacco.

The twentieth-century artist Alexander Calder once said that no one is truly human who has not made his or her own fork and knife. Home-made or not, do you have your own fork, your own knife, your own cup, your own bed, desk, chair? You must have your own things! They are you. You are they. As the poet Rilke tells us, "Being here amounts to so much."[5]

Our things are our things. They do not belong to the cosmos or to the gods. They can be had by others only in vicarious terms. Commendable though it may be for those of us who are collectors of other people's things, nonetheless, those who burn their papers or destroy their things just before they die are a testament to both the radical self-presence and transiency of human life. Those of us, myself included, who collect other people's things, are Texas turkey vultures, seizing upon the sacred moments hammered out by transients and eating them in an effort to taste the elixir of memory for our own vapid personal life. Ironically, for the most part their experience of their things were similar efforts, sadly redeemed more by us than by them. Now to the crux of the matter before us. It is not, I contend, humanly significant to have the primary meaning of one's life as posthumous. We and our things, I and my things, constitute our world. The nectar of living, losing, loving, maintaining, and caring for our things is for us, and for us alone. It is of time but not in time. It is of space but not in space. We and our things make, constitute, arrange, and determine space and time. The elixir garnered by the posthumous is for the survivors. It cannot be of any biological significance to us, although many of us have bartered our present for the ever-absent lilt of being remembered. St. Francis of Assisi and John Dewey both taught us the same *things*: time is sacred, live by the sacrament of the moment, and listen to the animals. We may have a future. It is barely conceivable, although I doubt its existence. We do have, however, a present. It is the present, canopied by our hopefully storied past, that spells the only meaning of our lives. Still, the present would be empty without our things.

You, you out there, you have your things. Take note. Say "hello," say, "hello, things." They are your things. Nay, they are you. No things, no you, or, in correct grammar, you become *nothing*. So be it. Space and time are simply vehicles for things, our things, your things, my things. These things do not sit, however, in rows upon rows, like ducks in a shooting gallery. These things make love, hate, and tire. Like us, they are involved. We consider now this involvement of persons, things, things and persons, all struggling to time space and space time—namely, the emergence of events as relations.

Things as Events As Aesthetic Relations

We have been in a struggle to achieve nonderivative presence for ourselves and our things over against the dominating worlds of space and time. Fortunately for us, space and time do not necessarily speak to each other. Our canniness can play them off, one against the other. The triumph is local, never ultimate, although it does give us staying power in our attempt to say "I," "me," "you," "we," "us" and other asserted pronominal outrages against the abyss. A happy phenomenon for human life is that things not only are; they also happen. I like to call these happenings "events." The literal meaning of "event" is intended: a coming out, a party, a debutante dance, a bar mitzvah, a hooray for the time, given the circumstance. In my metaphysics, at least, things are bundles of relations—snipped at the edges, to be sure. Usually, we give our things a name and this name takes the place of our experience of the thing. It does not take long to teach a child a list of nouns, each bent on obviating and blocking the rich way in which the child first comes upon and undergoes things. It is difficult to overcome this prejudice of language, especially since row upon row of nouns, standing for things, makes perfectly good sense, if you believe that space is a container and time is the measure of external motion. If, however, you believe as I do, that space and time are human instincts, subject to the drama of our inner lives, then things lose their inert form. Emerson says this best when he claims that every fact and event in our private history shall astonish us by "soaring from our body into the empyrean."[6]

The clue here is the presence of a person. Quite aside from the geographical and physical relationships characteristic of things and creatures, we further endow a whole other set of relations: the aesthetic. I refer to the rhythm of how we experience *what* we experience. The most distinctive human activity is the potentially affective dimension of our experiencing ourself, experiencing the world. I say potentially, for some of us all of the time and most of us most of the time are dead to the possible rhythms of our experiences. We are ghouls. We look alive but we are dead, dead to our things and dead even to ourselves. As John Cage warned us, we experience the names of sounds and not the sounds themselves. It is not the things as names, nouns, which are rich. It is how the things do and how they are done to. It is how they marry and divorce, sidle and reject. The aesthetic drama of the ordinary plays itself out as a result of allowing all things to become events—namely, by allowing all things the full run of their implications. This run may fulfill our anticipations and our expectations. This run may disappoint us. This run may surprise us, or blow us out. Implicitness is everywhere and everywhen. Were we to experience an apparently single thing in its full implicitness, as an event reaching out to all its potential relations, then, in fact, we would experience everything, for the leads and the hints would carry us into the nook and cranny of the implicitness of every experience.[7]

We are caught between a Scylla and Charybdis with regard to the drama of the ordinary. The scions of the bland and the anaesthetic convince us that nothing is happening, whereas the arbiters and self-announcers of high culture tell us that only a few can make it happen, so we are reduced to watching. My version is different. The world is already astir with happenings, had we the wit to let them enter our lives in their own way, so that we may press them backward and forward, gathering relations, novelties all the while. Our affective presence converts the ordinary to the extraordinary. The world is made sacred by our handling of our things. We are the makers of our world. It is we who praise, lament, and celebrate. Out of the doom of obviousness and repetition shall come the light, a light lit by the fire of our eyes.

PART FIVE

TEACHING

lurking

A writing fellow
Freud
By name
Taught me
That the
world
Is not the
way
It seems to
Be ———
When I am
Ailing
From whatever
A response is
Immediate
And confident
Take
A
Pill
Say they
But
Pills are not the
way
They seem to
Be ———
Lurking
Are the many
Blindside-effects
Neuro-transmittering
with forked
tongues
The din of serotonin

crashes
Shaking, itching
In the midst
of unrequited
sleep
what is wrong
With me?
My ailing has
Been replaced
By
Flailing
Courtesy of a
Neuro-Pharmo
Pill
So
Skip the cure
Slide-effect the
lurking
Switch to
Chicken soup
And Ginger Ale

John J. McDermott
June 2006

TWENTY-ONE

THE GAMBLE FOR EXCELLENCE

John Dewey's Pedagogy of Experience

What the best and wisest parent wants for his [her] child, that must the community want for all of its children.

—John Dewey, *School and Society*

I n 1977, Elizabeth Flower and Murray G. Murphey published a stunning work of historical exposition and commentary on the development of American philosophy. The task of writing the long, detailed chapter on the thought of John Dewey fell to Elizabeth Flower, who for decades has been celebrated in philosophical circles for her analytic acumen, capacity for trenchant critique, and wise, informed grasp of the swirling currents in American thought. (Parenthetically, I recall, vividly, some years ago, her brilliant defense of the St. Louis Hegelians against some wags who knew nothing of their importance or the seriousness of their endeavor.)

The chapter on the philosophy of John Dewey by Elizabeth Flower is a masterpiece of intellectual scrutiny. She weaves the tapestry of Dewey's early thought, isolating for clarity, and then reintegrating, the many themes, strands, and influences that fed the complexity and subtlety that he carried into his mature work. On the thorny issues of the relationship between means and ends, the difference between truth and warranted assertions, and the theory of inquiry and the ethical context of Dewey's thought, she is unfailingly accurate and perceptive. Frequently Flower offers us a line or a cameo version of Dewey's philosophy, which provides us with a quick, startling insight to his work. For example, of Dewey she writes that "the environment is changing progressively as the activity progresses." And, "after all, we live in a network of affections; the qualities of virtue are the qualities which help us feel and assign worth in such a network."[1]

Although Flower concentrates on the epistemological and methodological facets of Dewey's work, she is ever alert to the enduring social and educational matrix that is riven throughout all of his thought. She states that "growth or development of selves, not attainments, is the primary educational goal, although of course education is not confined to formal schooling."[2] Indeed not, especially in a democratic society where all of the apertures of insight are called upon to teach us how to be human. At the end of her chapter on Dewey, Flower points us in the direction of the next step, Dewey's philosophy of education. She cites Dewey as follows: "If we are willing to conceive education as the process of forming fundamental dispositions, intellectual and emotional, toward nature and fellow-men, philosophy may even be defined *as the general theory of education*."[3]

With considerable modesty and some trepidation, I offer the following pages as a personal perspective on Dewey's philosophy of education, set in our contemporary situation and in honor of the bequest of our colleague, the philosopher Elizabeth Flower. Entropy, the loss of energy in a closed physical system, is now regarded as an eschatological cosmic threat. For those of us who think closer to home—say, in decades—the entropic character of American society with regard to the education of its children is no less a threat, given our values in a democratic society. I do not think it hyperbolic to state that a dismal cloud of systemic lethargy has settled over the American educational process, one that seems to have weaned both imagination and energy from the process of inquiry. The reasons for this development are no doubt both complex and many. One reason is certainly the self-aggrandizing and soulless mills known as colleges of education and their political ties to the nefarious and self-perpetuating sources of mediocrity, state accrediting agencies.

Another reason is the drab school curriculum with its multiple daily interruptions and the omnipresence of the weary but oracular pronouncements of the social sciences, ever out-of-date and always cast in a prose that no one ever has occasion to use again.[4] A third reason is the extraordinary dilution of intellectual sophistication and accrued wisdom in our teachers. Having been taught nothing, except how to "manage," they know nothing. Although this is dramatically true of most teaching in the elementary and secondary schools, it has permeated colleges and universities as well. No doubt that there are exceptions to the above jeremiad. Ms. X, Mr. Y, and Professor Z dot the landscape of our schools, colleges, and universities. They are heroic, brilliant, embattled, and often excoriated exceptions to my judgment. But they are precisely that: exceptions.

Lest you think that I speak from some intellectual ivory tower, allow me to assure you that my remarks are based on experience and not from a jaundice generated by distance. I have taught students for more than thirty-five years, inclusive of preschools and kindergartens, secondary schools, community colleges, private colleges, city and state universities, labor colleges; I have taught the handicapped, prison students, and adult-education extension students. As a member of the National Humanities Faculty, I have visited many classrooms throughout the United States. My students number more than twenty thousand, from all walks of life and with a range of values, needs, and ambitions that mirrors our nation in the last four decades. Their message to me—in an increasing crescendo, especially in the last decade—was in a variant of verbal and prose forms of articulation, but it always came to a muted, embarrassed, yet forthright, complaint that the vast majority of their educational experiences were repetitive, dull, insouciant, and paradigmatically *boring*. Should we wonder why an inner-city school district in a major city in California can have more than 60 percent daily absenteeism, or why, just recently, the New York City public school system can announce concern about the fact that more than 40 percent of their students are not finishing secondary school, drop-outs to personal and economic oblivion? Must it be so? I think not.

I recently returned from an assignment in Budapest, Hungary. While there, I volunteered to teach two seminars in contemporary American civilization to the students in Eötvös Lorand University, the major academic institution in Budapest. The building was ancient and decrepit. The halls and the stairwells were jammed. The classrooms were funky, tiny, dirty, and victims of socialist craftmanship, complete with splattered paint, dead windows, a blackboard from 1890, and a dirty cloth for an eraser. The students, selected from the eight hundred students in the English-language program, jammed into the room, elbow by knee, crowded, alert, burning with the fire of inquiry, and hungry for new stuff, new ideas, new names, and another way to build themselves into a wider world. I felt the pressure on me to be enormous. I could not let them down; I could not disappoint them. I had to deliver. What to say? How to say it? I did my best, finally hitting on pluralism as a key to contemporary America, its history, its present, and its best future. I left time for questions. Shyness pervaded at first until a young woman student looked right at me and said in beautiful English: so far, so good for American pluralism, but how, then, do you make a decision if everyone has a right to their point of view? She wanted to understand the meaning of consensus. Off we went, into constitutional issues, abortion, school busing, food stamps, nuclear deterrence. It was exhilarating. After the second seminar, a young male student asked me, why did they kill Malcolm X? In the conversation, he also cited an article from *Der Spiegel* on James Baldwin and the exilic propensity of American writers. Could I explain that phenomenon to him, he gently asked: that is, why were Henry James, Ernest Hemingway, Gertrude Stein, James Baldwin, the countless painters and poets, all seeking America away from America?

During this heady experience, I kept thinking of my own students past and present. I thought of the brilliant students, mostly Jewish, at Queens College in the 1950s. The best of them devotees of psychoanalysis, they were headed for law at Harvard, medicine at Johns Hopkins, and philosophy at Yale. Their social conscience was trapped in the narcissistic mirror of Dostoevsky's "Underground Man." I thought of the Roman Catholic intellectual high-rollers and the Jesuits I taught at Fordham University Graduate School in the 1960s: brilliant, accomplished, multilingual, and experientially repressed. I thought of my Queens College students in the late 1960s—hopheads, acidheads, movement cretins—all sensitive, and woefully uninformed. I thought of my Queens

College students in the middle 1970s: well-meaning, dull, plodding, spiritless. I thought of my labor college students of the late 1970s, mostly black and Hispanic, and found a flame in their eyes kindred to my Budapest guests. Finally, I thought of my Texas A&M students of the past decade. They are smart, National Merit Scholarship smart, the cream of this wounded crop coming from our best secondary schools. Unfortunately, they have no symbolic bank. They cannot convert the literal to the symbolical. Let me tell a story.

A few years ago at Texas A&M University, I taught a seminar course entitled The Philosophy of Literature. The gathering theme was that of the family, and the readings were appropriate to that theme. Among them were: Aeschylus's *Agamemnon*; Sophocles' *Oedipus Rex*; O'Neill's *Long Day's Journey into Night*; Baldwin's *Go Tell It on the Mountain*; Plath's *The Bell Jar*; McCullers's *The Heart Is a Lonely Hunter*; Roth's *Call It Sleep*; Dostoevsky's *Brothers Karamazov*; and other readings from Ellison, Camus, and Kafka. On the way to class one morning I met one of my students. He was a white male, intelligent, and a graduating senior in mining engineering. He had only one three-credit elective and, by virtue of a happenstance student grapevine conversation, he enrolled in my course. He had lined up a position after graduation that paid $30,000 per year to start. I asked him how he was doing. He became very agitated and blurted out, "terrible." He said it was my fault or someone's fault but this course had knocked his socks off, blitzed him. He was up every night, all night, reading the books, avoiding his engineering obligations. He was appalled at how little he knew about other cultures, about the way in which the world gets itself on through the endless varieties of attitudes, values, fears, and foibles. He asked me why no one had ever introduced him to this literature, and he realized that it happened for him serendipitously. Finally, he commented that the family name, Tyrone, in *Long Day's Journey* was misnamed, for it should have had his own family name. The play was for this young man a rendition of family autobiography.

Poignant though the story may be, our young man is not an exception. In the thousands of student semester-long journals that I have read, the most constant theme is the "shock of recognition" upon first facing great philosophy and literature. Due to the extreme emphasis on preprofessional education within the last decade, the woeful character of our students' grasp of the historicity and complexity of life has heightened considerably. I am aware that this conflict between getting things done and speculation is not new to our generation. It is found in the first book of Aristotle's *Metaphysics*, and the dispute has periodic refrains in the history of Western education. John Henry Newman phrased this conflict as the unawareness that not everything useful is good but that everything good is useful. In "Discourse VII" of his classic *The Idea of a University*, Newman considers "Knowledge Viewed in Relation to Professional Skill."

> This process of training, by which the intellect, instead of being formed or sacrificed to some particular or accidental purpose, some specific trade or profession, or study or science, is disciplined for its own sake, for the perception of its own proper object, and for its own highest culture, is called Liberal Education; . . . And to set forth the right standard, and to train according to it, and to help forward all students towards it according to their various capacities, this I conceive to be the business of a University. Now this is what some great men are very slow to allow; they insist that Education should be confined to some particular and narrow end, and should issue in some definite work, which can be weighed and measured. They argue as if every thing, as well as every person, had its price; and that where there has been a great outlay, they have a right to expect a return in kind. This they call making Education and Instruction "useful," and "Utility" becomes their watchword. . . . "Good" indeed means one thing, and "useful" means another; but I lay it down as a principle, which will save us a great deal of anxiety, that, though the useful is not always good, the good is always useful.[5]

Newman represents a different century and a different cultural context, but his vision is telling and it still faces the same kind of opposition, one that has no awareness of the ambience of all human activity and of the necessity to integrate our hands with our affections. Closer to our own necessity to integrate our hands with our affections, closer to our own time and clime, the version of John Dewey, an understanding of which is our task in this essay, is different but comes to the same result. For Dewey, the cardinal sin is the separation of concepts from percepts—that is, the separation of pedagogy from lived experience. Being a quintessential American, in a way that was not characteristic of William James, who was a Europhile and did not understand America as a society, Dewey turned Newman's ideal back on itself. With Dewey, the everyday carried with it pregnant possibilities that would emerge and occasionally explode, if attention—that is, "creative intelligence"—were brought to bear. The traditions of the arts, the humanities, and the sciences become horizons rather than fixed ends and sources of elitism or academic patronizing, such that all experience vibrates with potential insight. This is not only the goal of a university, as in Newman, but it is the ideal for all pedagogy: for children, for adults, for young and old, and for outcasts. To bring this off, nothing less than a systemic revamping of present national policy is necessary, a salutary and worthy goal, a gamble for excellence. In order for us to grasp this position of Dewey, it would be necessary to retrack all of his writing and his life. No such opportunity is available in the present setting, so we provide only benchmarks and highlights before turning to the upshot of Dewey's thought for our contemporary situation.[6]

In both his undergraduate education at the University of Vermont and his graduate education at Johns Hopkins, Dewey came under the sway of disciples of continental idealism, especially the Hegelian variety. In this, he was like most of his peers in late-nineteenth-century American philosophy, with the notable exceptions of William James and C. S. Peirce. Dewey took a logic course with the beleaguered and fractious Peirce at Hopkins, although he did not realize its significance until many decades later. While teaching at the University of Michigan, Dewey began to undergo deep changes in personal, religious, and philosophical outlook, much of which change was initiated by his alert, modern, and socially conscious young wife, Alice Chipman Dewey. Suffice to say that Dewey began to break from the abstractions of neo-Hegelian idealism, a development that was consummated by his reading of William James's *Principles of Psychology* (1890).[7] Yet, in an important way, Dewey retained the thought of Hegel as "a permanent deposit" in his thinking.[8] The character of that deposit was to separate him from his pragmatist companions, James and Peirce, for Dewey maintained an abiding awareness of the social and institutional context in all of his thinking, a characteristic that was to be central to the development of his subsequent philosophy of education. Dewey soon began to follow the route laid out by James, one that was to lead to his naturalistic metaphysics as a bedrock for his pedagogy and his aesthetics. In 1905, Dewey joins the fray in an effort to make experience the major metaphor in an understanding of how we find ourselves in the world:

> The criticisms made upon that vital but still unformed movement variously termed radical empiricism, pragmatism, humanism, functionalism, according as one or another aspect of it is uppermost, have left me with a conviction that the *fundamental* difference is not so much in matters overtly discussed as in a presupposition that remains tacit: a presupposition as to what experience is and means. . . . Immediate empiricism postulates that things—anything, everything, in the ordinary or non-technical use of the term "thing"—are what they are experienced as.[9]

To be "experienced as" is to realize, following James, that "life is in the transitions," that "experience itself, taken at large, can grow by its edges," and "in the simplest and completest cases the experiences are cognitive of [one] another."[10] *Experience, itself, is pedagogical.* Dewey states this in the following passage:

> Generalizing from the instance, we get the following definition: An experience is a knowledge, if in its quale there is an experienced distinction and connection of two elements of the following sort: *one means or intends the presence of the other in the same fashion in which itself is already present, while the other is that which, while not present in the same fashion, must become so present if the meaning or intention of its companion or yoke-fellow is to be fulfilled through the operation it sets up.*[11]

Now what does this sortie into the denizens of epistemology and metaphysics come to so far as our effort to present Dewey's philosophy of education? The answer is that such an awareness of Dewey's position is the linchpin necessary to understanding his aesthetics and, consequently, his pedagogy. The reason for this judgment is simple and straightforward. Unless one knows how Dewey diagnoses experience, then his approach to education takes on an obviousness, so castigated by the legions of casual commentators and critics who have never read his work in the round.

Allow me to be explicit and direct. There are many thinkers who believe that to be in the world is to be a spectator to a picture or an actor upon a stage. Neither James nor Dewey believe this to be so. There are many thinkers who believe that knowledge is an affair of concepts, definitions, and proper nouns. Neither James nor Dewey believe this to be so. There are many thinkers for whom experience is mute, rendered only articulate by the language of mental activity. Neither James nor Dewey believe this to be so.[12] What, then, does Dewey hold to be so insofar as we have experiences? I put this in my own words with an attempted textually informed editorial license on behalf of the position of John Dewey. The human organism, strikingly akin to other advanced organisms, transacts with the affairs of nature. The human organism, however, is paradoxical in that it knows whereof, whereat, and whereby this transaction takes place; in short, the human organism is aggressively self-conscious.[13] This transaction between the human organism and nature is experience. The transaction is ever striated not only with problems, knots, but with the problematic as an ontological condition of being in and of and about the world. To be human is to be constantly, ineluctably, irreducibly faced with the problematic.

For Dewey, one can make one's way through this network of difficulties, although attempted resolutions inevitably generate new difficulties. Life has *no final perch*. Many years ago Dewey described this viewpoint to a lay audience. An elderly woman approached Dewey after the lecture and said to him as follows: "Mr. Dewey, you describe life as though one climbed a mountain to the top and then descended, only to climb another mountain to the top. Mr. Dewey, what happens when there are no more mountains to climb?" Dewey answered in properly laconic Yankee form and true to his metaphysics, "You die, Madam!" Make no mistake, we have a major difficulty spelled out in Dewey's version of the human quest—namely, the absence of closure, of ultimate certitude, and of transcendent meaning. In short, there is no immortality. Yet, equivalently, make no mistake, we do *not* have nihilism.

Dewey accepts the claim of James that experiences are indeed cognitive of one another, so that the transaction is not without a guide, a source, a leaning, a hint, a hunch, an Indian-head watch. Keep your eye on the ball; it speaks. Listen to the wind; it speaks. Hear the murmurs, read the gestures, mark the gait, catch the tone, eye the color, reach and keep one foot on the ground. Formal education teaches us that experience can be denoted. The brilliant phyla of Aristotle is a masterpiece of local organization. Modern molecular science has shown that the makeup of nature can be put differently, although still in a conceptual structure. It is Dewey's wisdom to insist that experience is also connotative. More, as Dewey stresses, all inquiry—that is, all reflective experience of nature—has an experimental potential. Inquiry is not limited to naming and placing, for it can forge, shift, and reconstruct the way in which our experiences come at first hand. At an intitial glance this seems to make considerable sense as a description of our basic transaction with the world. Alas, the description turns out to be far more ideal than characteristic.

Two major obstacles loom in the way of our capacity to enter into an experimental, resolving, healing, and future-oriented transaction with the world as it comes to us. First, as Dewey stresses over and over, we tend not to trust our own experience to be significant, leading, warning, and revealing. In fact, we have been taught to either deride the importance of our own experience, and therefore enter an incommunicative shell, or, from insecurity and a hesitant sense of the true worth of our experiences, we rattle on in a monologue as self-aggrandizing as it is empty. Second, in our confrontation with our own experience, we are all too often severely hobbled by the trappings of our own education, informal and formal—especially the latter. Although the world-as-experienced speaks in dulcet, loud, peremptory, cajoling, and symbolic ways, it is rare that we hear anything. Although the world-as-experienced struts its colors—carried by blossom, bird, and sky—it is rare that we see anything. Although the world-as-experienced preens its scents—floated from sea, cave, animal, and cuisine—it is rare that we smell anything. Although the world-as-experienced flaunts its texture by bristle, horsehair, cactus, and spider web, it is rare that, in touching, we feel anything. It is not as Yeats warned, that the center does not hold; rather, it is that the senses do not grasp, do not reach, for they have become captives of the denotative mind rather than extensions of our bodies.

Given the riot of possibilities in the ancient world, who can fault Aristotle for putting "things" and "species" in order, according to his own light? Before Aristotle, in the writings of Plato, and from Aristotle to this day, the poets have been struggling to free our experience from the clutches of definition and the roster of self-defining names, which have rendered our experience more from the inert than the symbolical. No one says this more perceptively than Dewey's mentor, Ralph Waldo Emerson. "We learn nothing rightly until we learn the symbolical character of life. Day creeps after day, each full of facts, dull, strange, despised things, that we cannot enough despise,—call heavy, prosaic and desert. The time we seek to kill: the attention it is elegant to divert from things around us. And presently the aroused intellect finds gold and gems in one of these scorned facts,—then finds that the day of facts is a rock of diamonds; that a fact is an Epiphany of God."[14] Granted that Dewey does not use the theological imagery of Emerson, he is nonetheless in complete accord with Emerson's belief in the epiphanic character of reality. Such a belief is rooted in the ancient Stoics and finds subsequent articulation in the thought of Augustine, Scotus Eriugena, the Franciscans of the High Middle Ages, and Jonathan Edwards. The tradition is quickly caught in the lines of the poet Gerard Manley Hopkins: "And for all this, nature is never spent; / There lives the dearest freshness deep down things."[15] With the exception of the Stoics, these are alien bedfellows for the thought of John Dewey. Yet the tradition comes to him through Emerson and is reinforced by the richness of the American landscape and by the puritan Yankee tradition, in which nature is refractory and speaks directly to us, for better or for worse.

> Man finds himself living in an aleatory world; his existence involves, to put it baldly, a gamble. The world is a scene of risk; it is uncertain, unstable, uncannily unstable. Its dangers are irregular, inconstant, not to be counted upon as to their times and seasons. Although persistent, they are sporadic, episodic. It is darkest just before dawn; pride goes before a fall; the moment of greatest prosperity is the moment most charged with ill-omen, most opportune for the evil eye. Plague, famine, failure of crops, disease, death, defeat in battle, are always just around the corner, and so are abundance, strength, victory, festival and song. Luck is proverbially both good and bad in its distributions. The sacred and the accursed are potentialities of the same situation; and there is no category of things which has not embodied the sacred and accursed: persons, words, places, times, directions in space, stones, winds, animals, stars.[16]

Dewey writes this text in a chapter called "Existence as Precarious and as Stable." He had an uncanny sense of the rhythms at work in the transaction between ourselves and nature. Like James, Dewey never lost his fidelity to the organic, to the physiological as the source of major metaphors to describe our comings and goings, our ups and downs, our systolic and diastolic binding to the flow of our experiences as they articulate the personal way in which each one of us has the world. Yes, our experiences are articulate, for just as nature speaks to us, so, too, by our experiencing of nature do we speak to ourselves. How we experience the world—that is, how we speak to ourselves—is the script of our personal consciousness. I am not a person who experiences the world as sheerly other. My experiencing the world is who I am. The task is to grow, to mature by virtue of insight, affection, and, notably for Dewey, setback. In *Art as Experience*, Dewey describes this rhythm of our transaction with nature as constitutive of our "career and destiny."

> No creatures lives merely under its skin; its subcutaneous organs are means of connection with what lies beyond its bodily frame, and to which, in order to live, it must adjust itself, by accommodation and defense but also by conquest. At every moment, the living creature is exposed to dangers from its surroundings, and at every moment, it must draw upon something in its surroundings to satisfy its needs. The career and destiny of a living being are bound up with its interchanges with its environment, not externally but in the most intimate way.[17]

Dewey then proceeds to claim that setback, and even "temporary alienation," are *necessary* if the human organism is to grow. Failure, disappointment, missing when reaching are as constitutive of our person as is fructification.

> Life itself consists of phases in which the organism falls out of step with the march of surrounding things and then recovers unison with it—either through effort or by some happy chance. And, in a growing life, the recovery is never mere return to a prior state, for it is enriched by the state of disparity and resistance through which it has successfully passed. If the gap between organism and environment is too wide, the creature dies. If its activity is not enhanced by the temporary alienation, it merely subsists. Life grows when a temporary

falling out is a transition to a more extensive balance of the energies of the organism with those of the conditions under which it lives.[18]

Given this setting, in which our transactions are fundamentally aesthetic, Dewey deplores the tendency of education to divide our activities between high and low culture or between the fine and the useful arts. He is not attempting to level the world of art to some form of proletarian socialist realism; rather, he is pointing to the extraordinary potentialities of the ordinary, if we would only learn how to diagnose the rhythm of our own experiences. For Dewey, so-called high art and culture act more like a beacon light, a luminous cloud, a dawn, a sylvan path through the great pines, a symbolic jolt to our constant tendency toward habituation than as an arbiter of acceptable experiences as bathed in condescension. The best of art and culture casts light, not stones, at our everyday experience, although the light often focuses on the murky, the dangerous, the evil that seem to inevitably accompany our human journey. He insists on the continuity between our artistic activities, our crafts, and the texture of our ordinary experience.

> When artistic objects are separated from both conditions of origin and operation in experience, a wall is built around them that renders almost opaque their general significance, with which esthetic theory deals. Art is remitted to a separate realm, where it is cut off from the association with the materials and aims of every other form of human effort, undergoing, and achievement. A primary task is thus imposed upon one who undertakes to write upon the philosophy of the fine arts. This task is to restore continuity between the refined and intensified forms of experience that are works of art and the everyday events, doings, and sufferings that are universally recognized to constitute experience.[19]

The separation of art from the everyday "deeply affects the practice of living, driving away esthetic perceptions that are necessary ingredients of happiness, or reducing them to the level of compensating transient pleasurable excitations."[20] We find here Dewey's profound concern for the quality of the life lived by the average person, those millions who flocked to America in the immigrant decades from the late nineteenth century until well into the twentieth century. Consequently, just as his pedagogy is informed by the central importance of the aesthetic, so, too, does it have a political bite.

The political side to Dewey's lamentation about the separation of art from the everyday is his concern for what he calls "the lost individual," that person who has been cut adrift by the erosion of the classical loyalties that permeated previous societies in Europe and previous generations in America. Writing in 1930, Dewey provides a text that has the eerie ring of contemporaneity.

> It would be difficult to find in history an epoch as lacking in solid and assured objects of belief and approved ends of action as is the present. Stability of individuality is dependent upon stable objects to which allegiance firmly attaches itself. There are, of course, those who are still militantly fundamentalist in religious and social creed. But their very clamor is evidence that the tide is set against them. For the others, traditional objects of loyalty have become hollow or are openly repudiated, and they drift without sure anchorage. Individuals vibrate between a past that is intellectually too empty to give stability and a present that is too diversely crowded and chaotic to afford balance or direction to ideas and emotion.[21]

The attempted resolution of this anomie by a revival of evangelical self-righteousness or by the separation of American society into stratified classes, as identified by aesthetic taste and by educational opportunity, appalls Dewey, for whom neither "dogmatic fundamentalism," nor "esoteric occultism," nor "private estheticism" can cultivate the social binding necessary to ensure a creative human life for all.[22]

Despite Dewey's lifelong commitment to egalitarian education, we find nothing of the Pollyanna attitude in his views. He has a firm grasp on the obstacles that face any attempt to achieve educational equity, and he wants that equity to be not only of opportunity but of remediation as well. Dewey has no patience with a simply external qualification for opportunity, as found in the standardized tests of our time. On the contrary, he sees it as the responsibility of society to prepare our children sufficiently so that equal opportunity will not become a hollow promise or a door opening to a corridor that leads to the back door and the junk heap of failed expectation. Dewey believes, as I do, in the educability of all persons, each to the full realization of the limits of their capacities.

He regards the realization of these potentialities as a primary obligation of the community, spelled out as you and me. Equality does not signify that kind of mathematical or physical equivalence in virtue of which any one element may be substituted for another. It denotes effective regard for whatever is distinctive and unique in each, irrespective of physical and psychological inequalities. It is not a natural possession, but rather is a fruit of the community when its action is directed by its character as a community.[23]

One of the obstacles confronting us is naiveté about the corporate world and its ties to the political process. Dewey has no illusions that a gathering of scholars and educators can do any more than scratch with a fingernail a sheet of aluminum. We make a grievous mistake, he warns us, if we think that stentorian rhetoric and plea-bargaining for equity will effect a sufficient change in what is an essentially arrogant and unconcerned echelon of self-centered entrepreneurs, sustained and funded by bureaucratic hacks. In 1935, Dewey's *Liberalism and Social Action* was an attack on American society worthy of Marx, although without the self-defeating specter of revolutionary intent. His diagnosis is revealing. "The conditions that generate insecurity for the many no longer spring from nature. They are found in institutions and arrangements that are within deliberate human control. Surely this change marks one of the greatest revolutions that has taken place in all human history. Because of it, insecurity is not now the motive to work and sacrifice but to despair."[24] In his own way, Dewey had developed an analysis of American society which paralleled that of Marx's critique of European society in the *Economic and Philosophic Manuscripts of 1844*.[25] Dewey, however, was not prone to emulate the inflammatory prose of the American Marxists of the 1930s, for he believed that the transformation of institutions, especially the schools, was possible without resorting to a violent overthrow of an elected government. Still, Dewey realized that good intentions and affectionate rhetoric on behalf of the American "lumpen proletariat" was insufficient and, in fact, may have simply been used by the "power elite"—to quote the phrase of C. Wright Mills, an epigone of Dewey—to co-opt those who thought that they were making headway in the transformation of American society, when actually all was business as usual.[26] Dewey knew that the rhetoric on behalf of the schools had to be accompanied by political power such as to effect institutional values, goals, and priorities.

> The educational task cannot be accomplished merely by working upon men's minds, without action that effects actual change in institutions. The idea that dispositions and attitudes can be altered by merely "moral" means conceived of as something that goes on wholly inside of persons is itself one of the old patterns that has to be changed. Thought, desire and purpose exist in a constant give and take of interaction with environing conditions. But resolute thought is the first step in that change of action that will itself carry further the needed change in patterns of mind and character.[27]

More, much, much more needs to be said about Dewey's metaphysics, epistemology, aesthetics, and politics if we seek to obtain a true grasp of his pedagogy, for all his endeavors are of a piece, quiltlike, none of them fully intelligible without each of the others as a backup, a refrain, or a continuation. Nonetheless, in this cramped setting we are forced to push on and thus we take a look at Dewey's pedagogy itself. In the midst of Dewey's voluminous writings, four works stand out as directly significant for his pedagogy and as having extensive influence. The first two were published at the turn of the century, *School and Society* and *The Child and the Curriculum*.[28] As is obvious, these works represent an integrated quadrant of concerns, no one of which can function successfully without a satisfactory relationship with the remaining three areas of consideration. Dewey wrote these works while in the midst of his ten-year tenure as administrator of the Laboratory School at the University of Chicago, the first such program in experimental education in the United States. With his wife, Alice Chipman Dewey, who was the bellwether of the program, Dewey developed a pedagogy that was child-centered and that did not treat children as small adults. Before the powerful and incisive work of Maria Montessori in Italy, the Deweys had discovered the extraordinary capacity of children to learn when there was continuity between the educational program and their own experiences.[29] From their work in the Laboratory School, the Deweys developed the famous "project method," by which children both design and respond to scenarios in which the context for learning is that of actual situations. This approach is in keeping with the process metaphysics and the pragmatic epistemology that Dewey was constructing at that time. Dewey writes that "development does not mean just getting something out of the mind. It is a development of experience and into experience that is really wanted."[30] The burden is clearly on the teacher to provide a pedagogical situation that is both geared to the needs of the child and that will open horizons for growth and a richer experience of the future.

In 1916, Dewey published *Democracy and Education*, his most famous book in the precincts of professional educators, although most of them read it independently of his wider philosophical enterprise and therefore approach the book unintelligently. The pervading theme of this book is Dewey's emphasis on the importance of human growth. "Taken absolutely, instead of comparatively, immaturity designates a positive force or ability—the power to grow. We do not have to draw out or educe positive activities from a child, as some educational doctrines would have it. Where there is life, there are already eager and impassioned activities. Growth is not something done to them; it is something they do."[31] The "doing" is central to Dewey's view of how children become educated. He is opposed to all forms of rote learning unless they can be integrated with an ongoing project, as in the learning of mathematics or a language. Growth is not a casual word for Dewey, for its absence denotes dying, as when children, by virtue of the pedagogical ennui which so often envelops them, become dead unto themselves. In our time, they escape into varieties of electronic media, a hyped-up version of the comic books and Saturday movie serials of Dewey's time. He sees serious social and political results in the estrangement of children from formal learning. In our contemporary language, Dewey foresees a creeping narcissism, sure to beget either anomic drifters or Yuppies who have no compassion for the underclass: "Only gradually and with a widening of the area of vision through a growth of social sympathies does thinking develop to include what lies beyond our direct interests: a fact of great significance for education."[32]

How do we widen "social sympathies," such that our children assume the mantle of the egalitarian and democratic ethos? Dewey is very explicit on this matter, invoking the possibilities and risks attendant on the radically empirical process metaphysics sketched above. Like James, Dewey is not naive that all will go well. I have made it clear that he has a heightened sense of the pervasive disasters that await us in our journey. Nonetheless, Dewey has a trust that experience, whatever may be its constant travail, provides its own potential source of healing. "To 'learn from experience' is to make a backward and forward connection between what we do to things and what we enjoy or suffer from things in consequence. Under such conditions, doing becomes a trying; an experiment with the world to find out what it is like; the undergoing becomes instruction—discovery of the connection of things."[33] Unfortunately, the followers of the thought of John Dewey lacked his depth of understanding relative to the complex question of how one has experience, does experience, and receives experience. His opponents, still afflicted with the diseases of metaphysical foundationalism, a penchant for the a priori or assorted self-verifying conceptual schemes, mocked his emphasis on anything so homely, so prosaic as experience. The first camp, under the banner of progressive education, turned his thought into an endorsement of education as a circus, free of restraint, unstructured, and socially irresponsible. The second camp plodded on, teaching fewer things to fewer people until the decade of the 1960s, when the watchword was to "tune in and drop out," often fueled by cerebral acid in response to the wailing cry of Grace Slick of the Jefferson Airplane—"feed your head."

In 1938, approaching the age of eighty, Dewey struck back in a small but trenchant book entitled *Experience and Education*. He attacked the either/or options just sketched and then proceeded to revivify his own meaning of what is meant by experience as central to a liberating and *effective* pedagogy. He immediately makes clear that "it is not enough to insist upon the necessity of experience, nor even of activity in experience. Everything depends upon the *quality* of the experience which is had."[34] Such quality does not emerge casually. The child must be assisted to diagnose his or her own experiences, as they take place, in time and in space. The traditional approach to education that stresses preparation for a future that may or may not happen strikes Dewey as deadly and counterproductive to the needs of the child. What, then, is the true meaning of "preparation" in the educational scheme? In the first place, it means that a person, young or old, gets out of his present experience all that there is in it for him at the time in which he has it. When preparation is made the controlling end, then the potentialities of the present are sacrificed to a supposititious future. When this happens, the actual preparation for the future is missed or distorted. The ideal of using the present simply to get ready for the future contradicts itself. It omits, and even shuts out, the very conditions by which a person can be prepared for his future. We always live at the time we live and not at some other time, and only by extracting at each present time the full meaning of each present experience are we prepared for doing the same thing in the future. This is the only preparation which in the long run amounts to anything.[35]

If Dewey is right, as I believe he is, that we live only at the time we live and at no other time, then our present approach to education is caught between an insufficient sense of the necessary past we must carry and an emphasis on a future which most likely will not happen. To the contrary, we must find a way to assist and convince our children, and those adults who seek to renew themselves, that it is necessary to constantly diagnose the messages of their own experiences while at the same time submitting these messages to the supporting and countervailing responses of their peers. Further, they must build into their diagnosis the experiences and insights of those who have gone before them, making allowance for the shift in historical context while still remaining open to wisdom from another setting.

I do not suggest that Dewey's approach to pedagogy is a panacea, any more than I would endorse a competing viewpoint. In our pluralistic society, it is impossible to have any single version of the educational process become able to account for all needs, all situations, and all desires. Still, Dewey's emphasis on the centrality of experience carries with it enormous good sense, empirical sustenance, and a capacity to involve our attention to the past, the present, and a future that is experientially linked to our present. I am not unaware that to cast one's education into the vagaries of experience has a treacherous aspect to it, for experience, despite its obviousness, as the philosopher Charles Sanders Peirce holds, is that which "takes place by a series of surprises."[36] The enemy, however, is the humdrum, the habitual, the routine. Better to love and be crushed than not to love at all.

My awareness of the dangers that lurk in opening ourselves to experience as the source of pedagogy prompted the title of this essay, for in fact we must gamble for excellence. We must take a chance that if we cast off the chains of the obvious and ride with the flow, we may very well drown. Then again, we may not drown. We may cavort, play, suck air, and rise again. Better to drown in the water of life than to be suffocated in the rote of obviousness.

TWENTY-TWO

LIBERTY AND ORDER IN THE EDUCATIONAL ANTHROPOLOGY OF MARIA MONTESSORI

U nfortunately, except when it is centered on a notable and preco-cious performance here or there, the media's attention to children is generally focused on the heinous crime of child abuse. For those of us for whom children are a sacred trust, the increase of such abuse is bewildering. Part of the cause of such social violence is that as a society, we have not sufficiently articulated both the fragility and the potentiali-ties of the child. The moguls of national education seem to be of little help in this matter, for they concentrate on quantitative scores in their evaluation of children, as though preparing little creatures for a fatten-ing, for entrance into the churning and anomic gears of postindustrial society.

Though many of our children suffer from the deep maladies of inner loneliness, alienation, cultural sadness, and the confusion that often re-sults from troubled families, many educators now think that the num-ber-one priority for a child in our society is the attainment of computer literacy. Surely by now, in the first decade of the twenty-first century, we should realize that mere technological gimmicks do not address the needs of the inner life of the child. Maria Montessori (1870–1952), for one, knew better. It was she, more than any other person in the twentieth century, who realized that the life of the child demanded an education that was ordered, creative, and distinctively personal.

Maria Montessori had great hope that the twentieth would be the century of the child. For that hope to be realized, one thing above all was necessary—that Western civilization cease viewing the human situation as hierarchical, as a ladder on which our first steps take meaning only from the last. Within such a conceptual framework, the child was required to become an adult as quickly as possible, and the education was characterized by the imposition on the child of the needs and the frame of reference of the adult world.

Freud, by proving that the phenomena of childhood pervade the human situation, demonstrated the inadequacy of such a viewpoint. He held that adult life could be understood only as a continuance of phases and tensions at work not only in the child but in the infant as well. Unfortunately, the original power of this insight has not been sustained; contemporary psychiatry, occupied with casing the plight of the beleaguered modern adult, has failed to make a breakthrough on the problems posed when Freud's view of the child is placed within the total fabric of society, particularly as related to elementary education. Instead, what were originally placeholders in a fascinating descriptive analysis of infantile and child psychic life have tended to become doctrine closed to experimental reworking; open terms have become locked categories which cut us off from the freeing experiences that should spring from insights as seminal as those of Freud.

Now the biology that informs Maria Montessori's view of the child is of a different cast. She shares with William James, Henri Bergson, and John Dewey the late-nineteenth-century awareness of the developmental nature of humankind in an evolutionary context. The theory of evolution caused most people to look behind them toward the origins of humankind; but the more explosive insight—to use Montessori's metaphor—was achieved by those who took seriously the fact that matter had a history and then boldly affirmed that it must also have a future. An understanding of human life, they held, depends on a new formulation of the unique way in which we live through matter while not equivalent to it. This tradition, central to contemporary thought, offers a series of insights and methods that assume a developmental framework and simultaneously point the way to sustenance of those values central to the genuine growth of personal life. It seeks in addition to create new values capable of moving the human situation to the "unheard-of-heights" dreamed of by Thoreau.

Though Americans have begun to realize it only within the last five decades, the work of Maria Montessori is in the forefront of such efforts. It is a unique contribution to a distinctly modern movement. She began her work with mentally retarded children and thus, in a sense, shares a point of departure with Freud, who started with people suffering aberrant personality problems. Yet Montessori soon became far more concerned with the wider possibilities offered by the application of these new scientific methods of inquiry to the normal personality, particularly that of the child. She shares with Dewey an evolutionary and experimental pedagogy, but she is far more willing than he to submit religious and spiritual qualities to the rigorous demands of concrete educational processes. Deeply committed to Catholicism, Montessori nevertheless opposes that type of religiously oriented school which is characterized by an educational theory outmoded in language and insight and negligent of empirical data about the human personality. Montessori demands that the data of anthropology and the natural sciences take their place at the base of educational practices, including those of a religious nature. By comparison, then, with other modern efforts, Montessori's view of the child is perhaps the most comprehensive available. And for this reason, she does not see children as an element in a series of overarching concerns, but rather sees them as an experimental touchstone of both educational methods and the human experience as a whole.

In his biography of Maria Montessori, E. M. Standing brings together the main lines of her thought and places them in the context of their concrete application in the Montessori schools. After a discussion of her early career as a pioneer woman physician in Italy, he turns to an analysis of her remarkably successful work with slum children in 1907. Standing rightly holds that the search for the "normalized child" is at the heart of the Montessori approach and is the catalyst that allowed her so many fruitful insights into the genuine situation of childhood. Reversing the usual approach that considers the child a fertile field in which the

adult plants the seeds of sound development, or a formless being awaiting the molding of the educator, for Standing Montessori "discovered
that children possess different and higher qualities than those we usually
attribute to them. It was as if a higher form of personality had been
liberated and a new child had come into being."[1]

Just as the liberation of the inner life of the child is the point of origin
for Montessori's work, so, too, is liberty the atmosphere in which the
life of the child is to develop. She then offers us a truly amazing set of
interdisciplinary elements as necessary to pedagogy. Her basic atmosphere for the educational process is freedom; her basic methodology is
experimental. Montessori seeks as the goal of freedom the ordering of
the inner life of the child as well as the ordering of the relationship existing between the highest activities of the mind and those fundamental
sense activities so brilliantly described and analyzed by her under the
name of "sensorial foundations." Montessori is also profoundly aware
of the necessary communal setting for all individual life; she has bequeathed to us some remarkable instances of successful miniature life-
communities carried on in her schools, better known as "prepared environments." So intriguing is her notion of freedom that she claims as a
result of its proper nourishment, children prefer "work" to "play," or
at least the distinction is rendered as not to the point.

If we are given a new set of perspectives for viewing human life, a
new set of values and relationships emerges. What has been said of William James by Bergson is certainly true of Montessori; with her "the
whole man [woman] counts." And she shares with James the belief that
religious experience is a legitimate, and indeed profound, aspect of the
philosophy of the person. In the same decade that Montessori makes
her discovery of the "normalized child" and attempts in her Casa dei
Bambini to realize experimentally each heretofore hidden dimension of
the child's life, James tells us in the conclusion to his *Varieties of Religious Experience* that "so long as we deal with the cosmic and the general, we deal only with the symbols of reality, but as soon as we deal
with private and personal phenomena as such, we deal with realities in
the completest sense of the term." Maria Montessori was fascinated by
such private and personal phenomena, particularly as found in the child,
and she utilized all of the available empirical data and experimental

techniques. But her insights into the child soon outstripped the techniques she inherited. She was now forced to couple her vision with technical innovations in materials and methods. Only these would enable her to solve the educational problems she clearly diagnosed.

Readers who find themselves enthusiastic about Montessori and her achievements as a result of Standing's exposition should not allow their enthusiasm to flower in a cultural vacuum. Rather, they should acquaint themselves with the intentions, accomplishments, and weaknesses of the American educational establishment. It makes no sense to adhere to Montessori's program at the expense of that of John Dewey and other pioneers in early-childhood education, most of whose vision has been distorted in the competitive atmosphere so characteristic of early-learning centers. To do so would be the height of irony, since one reason the Montessori method did not take root earlier in America, despite its effort to do so, was the fact that it was too often seen as an antidote to American educational practice and values when, in fact, Montessori schools can be structured to sustain those values that are worthy. The gap between the philosophical, psychological, and social perception of the child as held by Montessori and that held by John and Alice Chipman Dewey and their followers is small and not significant. Montessori had a richer grasp of the life of the child, whereas the Deweys knew more of the social and environmental context in which children come to consciousness and learn.

A second problem is the temptation to accept the Montessori system whole and entire rather than as one set of seminal insights among several, all of which can be used to formulate an expandable educational theory. (The adherents of Freud face this difficulty, as do the adherents of Montessori.) Certainly, the varied exercises of Montessori's pedagogy form a remarkably coherent and unified lattice-work of theory and practice. Yet she herself regarded that splendid creation as *un tentativo*: the person who ceases to be experimental ceases to follow Montessori's example. The cultish atmosphere that at times surrounds her followers does violence to her basic concerns. For example, the famous Montessori materials used for teaching reading and mathematics lack contemporary aesthetic qualities; there is no reason they cannot and should not be radically improved through experiment. Some followers, however, consider them sacrosanct, an indication perhaps that they have lost Montessori's commitment to scientific inquiry. Rigid devotion to the details of her method might permit Montessori schools to spread, but they would do so as a parallel system—something foreign, something that did not penetrate to the heart of the contemporary scene. It would be far wiser to be an advocate of those elements essential to Montessori's view of the child, for they can stand not only the test of time but the fluid nature of the society in which we live.

The most striking feature of Montessori's work is that her method, her teachers, and the learning children in her programs are to be found throughout the world. No other educator has such global influence, for although Pestalozzi, Rousseau, Herbart, and Piaget have each made their contributions, they are restricted for the most part to Western culture. John Dewey, it is true, has had enormous influence in East Asia but not in Western Europe, Latin America, or Africa. Montessori, to the contrary, has struck a more universal chord. I trace this important fact to three sources. First, she wisely believed that children of very early age had an ability to learn—independent of their peer-group cultures—that was rarely tapped in any formal way. Second, it was not necessary to import teachers who had a secret message to deliver. Indeed, teachers in the usual sense were not part of the Montessori picture. What was important was the presence of Montessori directresses, and later directors, who could be either imported or homegrown so long as they honored the autodidactic activities of the children. It was the children, after all, who taught themselves, so long as the environment was prepared, the materials utilized, and the goals or directions made clear. In very young children this could take place, and has taken place, in a wide variety of cultures throughout the world. Third, the Montessori children were not class-structured. From the first days of the Casa dei Bambini, Montessori was convinced that children of all backgrounds and all cultural limitations were capable of self-learning. Indeed, it is often characteristic of a Montessori program that the children are representative of a far wider range of cultural and economic advantages than is true in the more traditional programs.

The global influence of Montessori was not an accident of history. Long before our own awareness of the inextricability of our lives on this planet, she saw the need for the recognition and development of the abilities of children throughout the world. As early as 1910, she resigned her lectureship at the University of Rome, struck her name from the list of practicing physicians, and committed herself to "all the children in the world, born and as yet unborn." She then began a lifelong journey on behalf of children's rights and of their liberation from the darkness of unknowing. Her work was to take her beyond Italy to the United States, Latin America, India, Ceylon, France, Germany, Holland, Ireland, Spain, Austria, and Pakistan. UNESCO had its spiritual if unsung founder, and the global consciousness of our time can he traced back to its remarkable anticipation by this extraordinary educator.

When Maria Montessori died in 1952, she was all but unknown in the United States. But her view of education can contribute to the solution of problems facing contemporary America. In 1984, there were close to one thousand Montessori schools in the United States. Further, there is increasing evidence of the influence of the Montessori method on early-learning programs of every persuasion. To those concerned with religious education, she speaks of the role that experiment and awareness of the child's developmental nature must play if true religious education is to be achieved. For those concerned with public and secular education, she cuts through the peculiar dilemma that arises from the affirmation of the continuity of school and society and the simultaneous denial of the teaching of values central to that very same continuity. To all, the work of Maria Montessori proclaims that the role of the spirit in the development of the child—a role that experimental methods help us define—can be wedded to a methodology harmonious with the nature of the child and pointing toward the direction modern pedagogy must take. In this way, the work of Maria Montessori presents a vigorous challenge to American thought and culture, particularly as ramified in education. After all, if we are to have a future, every century should be the century of the child.

The Present Setting

The current interest in Montessori results in part from a willingness to read her afresh in the light of new contributions to learning theory, and in part from the urgent need for guidance, new or old, in facing the crushing problems of school systems that are not fulfilling their function of educating all of the children. Almost a century ago, the rejection of Montessori after an initial burst of interest was largely the result of an unnecessary and false tension that developed between "Progressivism in American Education" and Montessori.[2] The basic criticism of Montessori, as offered by William Heard Kilpatrick, seemed to center on her failure to provide for "self-directing adaptation to a novel environment."[3] And the Deweys, although more sympathetic to Montessori than Kilpatrick was, could say that "Montessori, in common with the older psychologists, believes that people have ready-made faculties which can be trained and developed for general purposes, regardless of whether the acts by which they are exercised have any meaning other than the training they afford."[4] I would suggest that both of these attitudes result from a misreading of the Montessori method and fail to consider her already published *Pedagogical Anthropology*. The notion of structure, so central to Montessori's thought, does not of itself preclude the variety of experiences that is indispensable for learning. The entire criticism is rendered ineffectual by Montessori's explicit remarks relative to novelty, as found in *Spontaneous Activity in Education*: "As a fact, every object may have infinite attributes; and if, as often happens in object-lessons, the origins and ultimate ends of the object itself are included among these attributes, the mind has literally to range throughout the universe."[5] It is not simply a question of quantity that is at stake here, but rather the relationship between the potentialities of the child and the kind of experiences offered. It is not the number of options that constitutes novelty, for "it is the qualities of the objects, not the objects themselves which are important."[6] In his own language, Dewey comes to the same conclusion when he laments the lack of order in progressive education. He cautions that "it is not enough to insist upon the necessity of experience, nor even of activity in experience. Everything depends upon the quality of the experience which is had."[7]

There were, of course, other reasons for the rejection of Montessori in her first American phase. As J. McV. Hunt points out in his introduction to *The Montessori Method*, she ran into several of the more firmly held psychological clichés relative to "fixed intelligence" and the "unimportance of early experience."[8] By the 1960s, the commitment to early learning of a prekindergarten kind had finally found its way into actual school operations. This applies particularly to "culturally disadvantaged" children, for whom there was then under way, partially by government sanction, a program of learning beginning at age four. Montessori, by name, is rarely mentioned in the framing of the new programs, although they were an obvious concession to the broadest dimensions of her revolution in educational practice—namely, the view that six years of age is late in life to begin the formal learning process.[9]

  This development, devoted as it was to early learning, would seem to have bypassed Montessori and rendered her work an historical footnote. But there is a major difficulty in such a judgment: it is one thing to begin schooling at age three and quite another to know what to do for such children. In the American tradition, there exists a great gap between sophisticated learning theory and actual classroom practice. This is particularly true for programs centering on ages three to five, where, aside from the nursery school tradition, we have had very little practical experience of a public kind. With regard to those programs which look to early learning as a crucial step in alleviating some of the difficulties engendered by children coming to self-consciousness in an enervating environment, we are starting from scratch. In this situation it seems reasonable to study anew the liberal and seminal side of Montessori's thought for its relevance not only to the "culturally disadvantaged" child but also to the broader needs of early education.

Process and Structure

Montessori is most fruitfully read within the framework of the late-nineteenth-century upheaval in experimental and philosophical psychology.[10] She shares the metaphors and concerns of Bergson, James, and the early Dewey.[11] The methodological breakthrough that characterized the nineteenth century had two sources of energy. First, an insight into the historical as a matrix for all inquiry. Found as early as the eighteenth century in the thought of Vico and Herder, it is primarily identified with the work of Hegel. Second, the emphasis on the developmental character of nature and, thereby, of behavior. This emphasis is essentially the result of the Darwinian version of evolution. Parenthetically, it is also the basic theme of Montessori's *Pedagogical Anthropology*, where she states that "man changes as he grows; the body itself not only undergoes an increase in volume, but a profound evolution in the harmony of its parts and the composition of its tissues; in the same way, the psychic personality of man does not grow, but evolves, like the predisposition to disease which varies at different ages in each individual considered pathologically."[12] From the contemporary vantage point, we see the historical and developmental strands as actually a single contention, to wit: that the object of inquiry can no longer be seen as fixed or as "standing out" in such a way as to yield intelligibility from a single perspective. The implications for a methodology of inquiry were clear. If the object under scrutiny is found to be developmental, whether it be from the side of its history or from the side of its behavior, then the method of analysis must recognize and manifest development. Put another way, the insight into structure or order would have to be a function of activity or of process. To isolate the object of inquiry from this process and claim for it the reality in question would be a denial of the transformation implicit in all activity, and, in effect, would close off novelty from the act of inquiry.

The nineteenth century, then, reversed the classical priority, in which order was assumed and the difficulty centered on how to account for change. Transformation, development, and process became primary, whereas order and structure seemed subsequently imposed.[13] Perhaps the most revealing testimony to this state of affairs in the nineteenth century was found in impressionism, directed as it was to an evocation of the world consonant with the ways in which we experience, rather than to a statement of the nature of its underlying constituents. This attitude is crystallized in the work of Claude Monet, whose painting in terms of the flow of light suggested the view that there were no fixed objects but only a series of momentary versions which we catch on the run. William James puts it best when he urges that "we reinstate the vague and inarticulate to its proper place in our mental life."[14] There were, however, severe problems in this reversal of the relationship between structure and process.

If structure were but a function of an ongoing development, did this not raise a question about the fundamental intelligibility of the world? After all, how could science and philosophy maintain their role in dispensing cognitive certitude in a world in which the very points of mooring, so trustworthy in the past, were to be seen merely as functional ways of managing the ever-changing flow of experience?[15] In our day, the struggle between process and structure must be carried on within the context of process. This new beginning, with its roots in Hegel and Darwin, created an extraordinary ferment at the end of the nineteenth century, a ferment which remains active today. Three thinkers of that time made this question basic in their work: William James, John Dewey, and Maria Montessori. Their thought had tremendous repercussions for a theory of education.

Notwithstanding the difference in her style and subject matter, Montessori breaks through to offer specific contributions to the nagging problems that accompany the need to formulate this ongoing, developmental view of humanity. Further, it is Montessori, above all others, who holds to the entwining of empirical method, scientific data, and human aspirations—specifically as they are found in the world of the child—as the irreducible elements in any theory of education.[16] What of the oft-heard charge that the Montessori version of early learning is committed to structure at the expense of potential growth? This charge holds that Montessori contravenes the most consistent insight of the behavioral sciences—namely, the primacy of the developmental and the processive. A more profound awareness of the generalized context in which she developed her thought would render this charge false. In fact, the situation is reversed. Not only does Montessori share this developmental point of view, but she makes a notable contribution by formulating it in pedagogical terms. In a sense, she can be said to have reoriented the philosophical question of the relationship between structure and process from the side of personal life, phrased as the relationship between liberty and order.

We are long past the time when it is possible to take a stand for one side of a disjunction between liberty and order.[17] The present way of stating this problem clearly posits a delicate web of relationships that enable liberty and order to feed each other, although Montessori makes it clear that of the two categories, it is liberty that is seminal and the way of experience. In *The Montessori Method*, she tells us that "the pedagogical method of observation has for its base the liberty of the child; and liberty is activity."[18] Furthermore, in *Pedagogical Anthropology*, Montessori has indicated that liberty, as the sponsor, is the source from which one proceeds to delineate order. "It is this liberty that makes it possible for us to pursue experimental investigations, without fear that our brains may become sterile. And by liberty we mean readiness to accept new concepts whenever experience proves to us that they are better and closer to the truth that we are seeking."[19] But coming full circle, with her characteristic sense of balance she tells us in *Spontaneous Activity* that "creation finds its expansion in order." Again, "the consciousness may possess a rich and varied content; but where there is mental confusion, the intelligence does not appear." It is precisely within this framework of liberty and order that Montessori generates a series of new insights into the life of the child and the most effective way to educate him or her.

Sensitive Periods, Materials, and Environment

There are three major dimensions to Montessori's view of the child. First, she holds to the existence of sensitive periods in which the child is most amenable to personal development along specific lines. She delineates sensitive periods for language, order, and manners, among other areas of development, and contends that they occur most sharply in the very young child and cannot be artificially induced at a later time. In what is an obvious commitment to a behavioristic point of departure, she declares these sensitive periods to be the foundations for fruitful interaction between emergent personal life and the environment. In explaining how the child assimilates his environment, Montessori declares that "he does it solely in virtue of one of those characteristics that we now know him to have. This is an intense and specialized sensitiveness in consequence of which the things about him awaken so much interest and so much enthusiasm that they become incorporated in his very existence. The child absorbs these impressions not with his mind but with his life itself."[20] It is important to realize that Montessori, in contrast to many Montessorians, does not construe these sensitive periods as fixed levels of development, but rather as phases of response on the part of the organism to the environment. Montessori is certainly closer to Dewey's refinement of the "Reflex Arc Concept" than she is to the fixed developmental schema of Spencer.[21] Indeed, in *Spontaneous Activity*, she clearly breaks with Spencer. Further, her chapters on "Attention," "Will," and "Intelligence" are explicitly indebted to William James's *Principles of Psychology*. And, above all, her notion of the "sensitive periods" is not to be seen as a hangover from the older, discredited faculty psychology. Dewey's above-cited opinion notwithstanding, Montessori tells us in *The Absorbent Mind* that she in no way intends an atomistic conception of the mind but rather holds to the view that "the mental organism is a dynamic whole, which transforms its structure by active experience obtained from its surroundings."[22] From one point of view, Montessori would heartily agree with William James, who believed that "revival" in the human endeavor was consonant with the belief that "the inmost nature of the reality is congenial to powers which you possess."[23] But she would hold equally to the need for specifying the ways in which this congeniality can be structured. As a result of this concern, she develops the notion of didactic materials and its sociological correlate, that of a "prepared environment."

Even those who are out of sympathy with Montessori acknowledge the fundamental genius of her materials. Introduced in *The Montessori Method*, they are carefully described in Dr. Montessori's own *Handbook* and in *The Montessori Elementary Material*, which is volume 2 of the *Advanced Montessori Method*. Devoted to education of the senses and to preparation for work in the arts, and conceived as a basic method for stimulating reading, writing, and mathematical ability, these materials are still of considerable value, although not completely adequate for our present situation.[24] But what should occupy us here are the implications of the very notion of didactic materials. It has long been an attitude of the "humanist" view that apparatus of whatever kind can never adequately perform the personalizing function of the teacher-pupil relationship. In our time, this prejudice is confronted by the tremendous pressure of those who wish to effect a technological revolution in the schools. From the latter point of view, those who hold to the supremacy of the interpersonal situation for educational growth stand in the way of an absolutely necessary transformation of the schools. So critical a problem is this transformation that even those who side with the traditional use of materials are about to be bypassed. In a 1964 essay on "Technology and the Instructional Process," James D. Finn could write that "the concept of programming and systems analysis it implies completely absorbs the idea of materials. Instructional materials becomes an outmoded atomistic, pretechnological concept useful mainly to the historians of education."[25] And again in 2001, the same claim can be made, and, sadly, must be made again.

Montessori materials may be pretechnological, perhaps even preindustrial, but they symbolize a breakthrough of major importance to both the defenders of the status quo and the new technologists. Montessori's use of materials reminds us, first, that the teacher is not necessarily the dispenser of learning, for the child may very well find himself in a more liberating and instructive situation when utilizing carefully structured physical correlates to his instinctual learning powers. Second, and of great significance from the other side, Montessori sees the didactic materials as of a piece with the entire classroom setting. They share with the furniture, the activity of the teacher, and the exercises of practical life an orientation to the experience of the child, and are thereby inseparable from what she calls the "prepared environment." It would be of great peril for contemporary education, particularly in its coming technological phase, to ignore this insight into the organic continuity between materials, environment, and the inner life of the child. The technological revolution in education—be it in the direction of the earlier Skinner boxes, or the teaching machines of O. K. Moore, or the now-emerging automated classroom—must be chastened by a sober awareness of the role played by the school environment.

Montessori has shown that it is not the teacher by himself or herself that is crucial, but rather the humanizing effect of the setting, including the teacher, in which children are to learn. There is no reason for us to limit ourselves to Montessori's specific suggestions on the nature of the "prepared environment," although they seem to be based on more solid observational evidence than many other options offered to us. Furthermore, in their broader considerations of mobility and classroom furniture, her insights have already been absorbed. What we must take seriously, however, is her fundamental vision of the living context in which learning takes place. Seeing this context rather as a "preparing environment," we must demand that innovations, no matter how capable of solving individual learning problems, must prove themselves within the total fabric of learning. This is an awareness that should characterize the schools and, for that matter, the whole of the human situation.

Montessori and the "Culturally Disadvantaged" Child

In addition to the generalized insights that would result from a careful analysis of Montessori, there is a more pressing reason to examine her approach: its peculiar relevance to the problem of "cultural deprivation." The early 1960s saw imaginative educators and social critics urging the larger community to address itself to the educational crisis spawned by racial ghettoes (now the "inner city") and poverty, and to view it within the context of an increasingly complex and mobile society.

It is well known that the restriction of childhood experiences to a narrow and drab environment results in serious personal damage. We are no longer distracted from this problem by "Horatio Alger" stories, however gratifying in themselves, about the singular few who have transcended their environment. It makes little difference whether we draw the implications for education from the broad perspective given to us by Michael Harrington's *Other America* or from the more specific statement by John Silberman,[26] which charged that "neither the large cities nor the nation as a whole can afford a public-school system which fails to educate between 50 and 80 percent of its Negro and white slum students."[27] The problem was conceived of as needing an imaginative program addressed directly to this situation, described by Kimball and McClellan as "where there is a basic difference between the mobility culture of America as a whole and the aspirations of a locality, as in the racial ghettoes of our large cities, the standard fare is a failure. We have yet to design anything for areas like these."[28] So staggering an influence is the local environment, especially when coupled with the absence of positive family life, that it was understood that many a child of six years of age was already beyond substantial transformation, despite the best intentions and efforts of the school. This being so, the significance of early learning—not only from ages three to five, but into the period of kindergarten and the first grade—was not primarily a matter of learning theory or procedures. The question was rather one of basic human nutrition, for poor children were understood for the most part as being cut off from growth experiences which would be of a more significant quality than the intellectual emphasis fostered in today's schools. The necessity for a freshly structured and incisive approach to these problems took precedence over any more speculative theory of learning. Such theories were of questionable relevance in the face of a widespread application. It is not enough to describe the children as "broken" or the schools as "delinquent." At his best, Martin Deutsch stated the position well: "it is unfair to imply that the school has all the appropriate methods at its disposal and has somehow chosen not to apply them. On the contrary, what is called for is flexible experimentation in the development of new methods, the clear delineation of the problem, and the training and retraining of administrative and teaching personnel in the educational philosophy and the learning procedures that this problem requires."[29]

Of course, added to this specific social structural problem of the "culturally disadvantaged" child is the more generalized one of the increased automation and bureaucracy that characterizes our American society, with its ensuing demand for a comprehensive retooling of the entire school process. It is true that the resolution of these difficulties, particularly those involving estrangement from the community, demands a reworking of the environment. It is also significant to note, however, that a major contributing factor would be the ability of the schools to offer a realistic program to meet the actual situation in which these or any children find themselves. Clearly we can no longer assume the standard school operation, with or without increased expenditures, to be adequate. What seems to be needed here is an educational program that will recognize, accumulate, and encompass hostile environmental structures, and thereby encourage a development in the child that is personally expansive and socially conscious.[30] The "prepared environment" of Montessori, so successful with the Italian slum children among whom her work began, deserves renewed study with the effort to alleviate the alienation of an ever-growing number of children in our communities.

More specifically, then, what can the Montessori perspective contribute to the contemporary renewal of the schools? John Silberman puts it this way:

> The Montessori approach may be particularly relevant to our time for a number of reasons. It emphasizes what psychologists call "intrinsic motivation"—harnessing the child's innate curiosity and delight in discovery. Each child is free, therefore, to examine and work with whatever interests him, for as long as it interests him, from the materials that are available. What is available is determined by the Montessori concept of "prepared environment," which places great stress on training the sensory processes: cognition is enhanced by providing stimuli to all the senses.[31]

Of particular importance is Montessori's contention that the young child is characterized by self-creating energies, which can be sustained and enhanced by the imaginative and controlled use of environmental materials. It is not that this "prepared environment" denies the power or centrality of the neighborhood or family, but rather that it stresses experience options heretofore largely neglected. A fascinating parallel to this effort of Montessori can be seen in the work of Sylvia Ashton-Warner,[32] whose experience also shows how extraneous to the life of the child are the great majority of educational materials. In emphasizing the active interrelationship of the personal and the instinctive, the Montessori approach encourages human growth, which is ever characterized by a genuine physical and psychical development proportionate to the demands placed on intelligence.

The constant, and often unnecessary, appeal to conceptualization that generally prevails in school experience is for many youngsters an overwhelming and illegitimate demand. This results not so much from lack of intelligence as from the arrangement of institutionalized education that renders intellectual activity largely irrelevant. When we are asked to develop an assessment of "experience" age rather than of "chronological" age at the same time we are asking teachers to develop rich environments for enhancing the activities of their children, then we are in the tradition of Montessori's primal insight into the relationship between awareness and achievement, an insight that enabled her to pioneer the notion of "ungraded primaries." After all, isn't Jung basically correct when he states that "one consequence of repressing the instincts is that the importance of conscious thinking for action is boundlessly over-estimated"?[33] Such excessive concern for conceptual learning causes endless invidious comparisons to the substance of education, even for the very young. This is so powerful a tradition that, in one of the classic ironies of our time, Montessori schools are often sought out by parents so that their children will distinguish themselves intellectually at an early age. Such an objective reflects, of course, a serious misinterpretation of Montessori. It is offensive to her vital concern for an integral, personal development of the child, in which the activity of intelligence would be liberating for self and community, and not developed for the purpose of giving an edge to the youngster as he enters the competitive arena. And what a disaster that intellectual competition has become the hallmark of new interest in early learning, a development that advances the "drop-out" syndrome of the "culturally disadvantaged" child by some three years!

It is not the purpose of early learning, especially for the "culturally disadvantaged," simply to simulate the school experience at an earlier period. Rather, it is to effect a liberation of the personality, and to establish a living and fecund relationship with the environment that can make subsequent learning possible. In effect, Montessori attempted to recast the very mode of inquiry in a way that would bypass the reigning dualism between the task of intelligence and the development of instinctual life. In so doing she moves directly to the problems afflicting those children who are cut off from taking advantage of the school as the major vestibule through which they might have access to the society. By the very fact that it concentrates on early learning, beginning at age three, the Montessori approach frees itself of the burden of making its first achievements primarily intellectual. The emphasis on muscle control, or the "exercises of practical life," introduces the child to the dialectic of activity with respect to the body. In such an approach, the child is seldom put to an irremediable disadvantage as he or she begins to create an explicit tie to the world through mastery of the physical environment. Socially conditioned within the "prepared environment," the child thereby begins the process of self-realization, so indispensable because of the burdens subsequently placed upon all children in the name of intelligence and achievement.

Montessori's position is clear: the school environment should be organized to reflect the actual potentialities and needs of the child rather than the superimposed compensations and burdens of the adult world. At this state of the discussion, Montessori's specific ideas as to the "prepared environment" are not crucial but her insight into the need for such an environment and her assertion that it takes its lead from the life of the child are absolutely critical. Jung has told us that "we do not usually listen to children at any stage of their careers, in all the essentials we treat them as non compos mentis and in all the unessentials, they are drilled to the perfection of automatons."[34] It is in this spirit that Montessori insists that the revamping of the "prepared environment" should take place always in terms of hard or observational data gathered from the children themselves. This applies to all teachers, in all teaching situations. Each teaching situation develops its own insights. The insight developed in the "laboratory" school, whose insights are not easily applied elsewhere, often loses relevance when shifted to a less favorable environment.[35]

Montessori saw the "school itself in action" as a "kind of scientific laboratory for the psychogenetic study of man."[36] Sharing with Dewey a keen pragmatic concern, she insists on the inseparability of intellectual modes of inquiry, that we have neglected studying the countless other ways in which the child humanizes his environment—and this in spite of the major currents of contemporary thought, especially in art and social psychology, which continually reveal new ways of conducting inquiry.

American education, hurried on by the demands of information technologies, on the one hand, and large numbers of "culturally disadvantaged" children, on the other, may very well have to make a radical breakthrough in the area of inquiry. It would seem that we have come to the end of the classical mode of inquiry characterized by its dualism of subject/object, cognitive/noncognitive, and mind/matter. Philosophy and psychology have been struggling to abandon them, but in the realm of public language these polarities are more persistent, particularly as formulated in educational terms. We tend to speak of "tracks" and "drop-outs," both mechanical metaphors, and in our personal evaluations we systemically bypass experience in favor of externalized categories, such as diplomas and degrees. In a word, we are committed to a single version of the educational process and have failed to incorporate into our basic school structure what many disciplines have shown in a smaller setting to be the untapped ways in which the human personality opens itself to learning experiences. Montessori certainly has no specific answer to this gnarl of problems, but she stands with Freud, James, and Dewey in pointing to the misleading, and even self-deceptive, character of an education derived primarily from the activities of the intellect.

Spontaneous Activity in Education

After reading and analyzing *The Montessori Method*, one is moved to inquire about the nature of the ideas that support such insights. Further, one wonders whether Montessori's views are limited in application to ages three to seven. Her *Spontaneous Activity in Education* attempts to sketch out a reply to the first question, and, in conjunction with *The Montessori Elementary Material*, extends her concerns to children aged seven to eleven.

Like most of Montessori's writing, *Spontaneous Activity* has an impressionistic quality. There are long stretches, particularly in the chapter "Imagination," which are almost conversational in tone and seem to refer to experiences and concerns of a local kind, never clarified in the text. But the way to read Montessori is to allow her to introduce large problems in such a way that we may subsequently break through the encrusted prejudices surrounding them and encourage a reworking of the most fundamental kind. The very notion of "spontaneous activity" as the source for curriculum development is a typical Montessori insight. This was not only a major revolution in her time but is still useful, for, in our own age, "spontaneity" is honored as a watchword but rarely reflects actual practice. In any event, the basic simplicity of Montessori's thought, and its expression in a type of rambling, colloquial prose, should not keep us from dwelling on the extremely important problems she brings to light.

Her primary concern is the problem of liberty. She early anticipates one type of subsequent criticism,[37] as expressed in her statement that "the principle of liberty is not therefore a principle of abandonment."[38] Indeed, true order in the life of the child is a hopeless endeavor outside the atmosphere of liberty. "Hitherto the liberty of the child has been vaguely discussed; no clearly defined limit has been established between liberty and abandonment."[39] Montessori felt that even the newly won admission of the child's hygienic rights was but a prelude to what she called "the civil rights of the child in the twentieth century." And "civil rights" they are, as the term is used today: the right to make optimum use of the environment, to achieve the fullest realization of one's personal life. This theme preoccupied Montessori throughout her life; elsewhere she writes of the need "to educate the human potential."[40]

In *Spontaneous Activity*, she sets down the basic structure as consisting of an inseparability between the growth patterns of physical and psychical life, as understood within a specific environmental setting. Put another way, it is the dialectic between liberty and the demands of the environment that brings the child to self-realization. This theme is expressed effectively in the chapters treating "Experimental Science," "Attention," and "Intelligence," the strongest in the book. In line with this concern she tells us that "it is necessary that the spontaneous activity of the child should be accorded perfect liberty."[41] Liberty does not mean for Montessori that the children be sated with what we think they want. Indeed, "overabundance debilitates and retards progress; this has been proved again and again by my collaborators."[42] And of course, deprivation of stimulus material will all but eliminate spontaneity.[43] The thing to be exactly determined is: what is "necessary and sufficient as a response to the internal needs of a life in process of development, that is, of upward progression, of ascent?"[44] Is there a more important question in the education of young children?

For many, this concern for the interweaving of physical, psychical, and intellectual growth is a truism. But they have often given up hope of utilizing current institutions to achieve social amelioration, whence the favor shown the creation of imaginative parallel structures, such as Walden II, Summerhill, and the suggestions of Paul Goodman. These ideas have an important critical effect, but to function as a transforming element in our society, they must demand that our basic institutions— for example, the schools—start virtually anew. Now the exciting aspect of Montessori's revolution in education is that, taken as a point of departure, it does not involve the creation of a parallel and totally different social structure. In accordance with the American commitment to public education, the approach of Montessori should urge us to redirect our energies to bring about a more integral development of all children by means that are liberating in educational content and gentle in extraneous effects.[45] The question at stake is fundamental. Do we believe that the school introduces the child to the rote assimilation of an already-structured version of human life, or do we believe that the school is the arch through which the process of insight, liberation, and human growth proceeds? It is clear where Montessori stands.

TWENTY-THREE

THE EROSION OF FACE-TO-FACE PEDAGOGY
A Jeremiad

Their foot shall slide in due time.

—Deuteronomy 32:35

The jeremiad is rooted in wisdom literature and has many variations. Nominally, in this chapter I use that which has come to us
courtesy of the prophet Jeremiah—neither a full lamentation nor a
Cassandra-like prophecy of doom, but rather a DEW line, an early-
warning system, or the ever present and ever dangerous "tipping
phenomenon."

In modern times, the jeremiad is an American cultural staple, first
appearing in the election sermon of Samuel Danforth in 1670. Two
recent major jeremiads have to do with the subject at hand: high technology—that is, electronic technology, or more directly, with the potential loss of our sense of person as primarily felt, as embodied. The first
is the 1995 "Unabomber Manifesto" of T. J. Kaczynski, which linked
technological prowess with the systemic destruction of the environment
necessary to sustain and foster human life. Surprisingly, a guardedly
sympathetic response to the concerns of this manifesto was presented
by Bill Joy, a major technology wizard and founder and chief scientist of
Sun Microsystems. Although clearly opposed to the person and violent

activities of the Unabomber, Joy nonetheless sees merit in that section of the manifesto, "The New Luddite Challenge," where Kaczynski writes: "If the machines are permitted to make all their own decisions, we can't make any conjectures as to the results, because it is impossible to guess how such machines might behave." Bill Joy adumbrates this worry by stating: "Perhaps it is always hard to see the bigger impact while you are in the vortex of a change. Failing to understand the consequences of our inventions while we are in the rapture of discovery and innovation seems to be a common fault of scientists and technologists; we have long been driven by the overarching desire to know—that is the nature of science's quest, not stopping to notice that the progress to newer and more powerful technologies can take on a life of its own."[1] The language in both documents is simple and straightforward. The message is identical. The issue is consequences and the worrisome context is that consequences can yield both amelioration and disaster. How do we know which of these upshots is forthcoming? Can we know which will emerge? Most often we think we do know. Yet, frequently, we do not. Think here of the baleful consequences of so-called side-effects in the use of pharmacological regimens to treat assorted afflictions and diseases.

Consequences

In the "Meno" of Plato, Socrates is pressed to answer the following questions: How do you know what you are looking for? And if you find that, how do you know that it is what you sought? At this point, Socrates backpedals and appeals to a priestess, who has a claim staked on knowledge beyond our experience. That will not do. One is reminded here of that telling and poignant piece of dialogue in Eugene O'Neill's *Long Day's Journey into Night*. After chastising her son, Jamie, Mary Tyrone opines: "But I suppose life has made him like that, and he can't help it. None of us can help the things life has done to us. They're done before you realize it, and once they're done they make you do other things until at last everything comes between you and what you'd like to be, and you've lost your true self forever."[2]

This is how I view contemporary technology: dazzlingly creative, exponentially explosive in its speed, spatial shortcuts, and shrinking of equipment necessary to the endeavor. Nonetheless, the working strategy is single-minded and often oblivious to consequences beyond the ken of immediacy. For an increasing number of us, the dominance of this approach to technological "breakthrough" is foreboding. The difficulty here is a paramount problem for all pedagogy: namely, how to build an awareness of consequences into the fabric of all decisions.

Infrequently considered in discussions of these matters are the underlying philosophical assumptions. For many, the point of departure is that we, human beings, "belong," inherit a purpose, and have a fixed end that is both explanatory and exculpatory. In this view, progress, however one-dimensional, is good and the nefarious instances of fallout are the price we pay. Or, contrariwise, we could work off a different philosophical bedding, one that holds that we do not so "belong," and therefore have to create, to build, to protect, and to endow as sacred a human place, a human abode. If this is so, as I hold it to be, then we as the human community are responsible for all that has taken place and for all that we choose to take place from here forward. Given that, the consequences of all thoughts and actions are inseparable from the quality, the merit, the worth of what we think and do. Scoping and scaping, evaluatively, is a major task of pedagogy. Echoing Dewey here, "it is the quality of the experience which counts."

In order to understand how one assesses consequences we must have an awareness of processes as they press into future experience. Put simply and directly, we have to grasp the ongoing web of relations that adhere, inhere, cohere, surround, penetrate, obviate, float, shrink, squash, deceive, render inert, cause perversion, erupt idiopathically, iatrogenically, and just lurk as a buried landmine. These are some of the sensibilities and concerns that should be at the forefront of the present attempt to impose electronic technology as the prime medium for pedagogy. Lamentably, for the most part none of these beacons for spotting consequences are under consideration.

Who among us has the temerity to sound an alarm with regard to the overwhelming explosion of computer technology as addressed to matters educational? The term "distance learning," in a remarkably short time span, has become a talisman for the resolution of educational problems, globally. The claims of accessibility to online education are astounding. We have been told that in one area of India more than 700,000 persons are online. In that conversation, we have not been told that in the very same geographical area, several hundred thousand women rise very early to squat on the railroad tracks before the arrival of the commuter trains, for they have no toilet facilities. This conjunction of glaring opposites can be played out over and again when technological prowess is set against the dolorous circumstances that plague the lives of most people on the planet.

Such is the larger setting. Here, I address a more immediate question—namely, should we be distressed by the escalating influence of computer technology in the affairs of pedagogy? How seriously are we to take the erosion of face-to-face encounters in the pedagogical environment? And how seriously are we to take the obsoleting of our language, our embodiment, and our intentional communities, the latter understood here as the teaching classroom, the seminar room, and the counseling session, respectively?

Surely, even a neo-Luddite, of whom I am not one, cannot gainsay the extraordinary achievements of computer technology. In many areas of concern, accessibility has been increased dramatically, or in some cases made available for the first time. One thinks here of families separated throughout the nation and from other nations, for whom the opportunity to exchange information, relay messages of affection and announcements of disaster, act as a binding hitherto never seen. Analogously, we recall the difference between the sending and arrival of letters before the advent of the telephone. We cite as well the contributions of medical informatics such that health-care professionals in areas egregiously distant from the most advanced diagnostic equipment can have virtually immediate access to information protocols and advice that would otherwise be unavailable to them. True, also, is it that the arrival of the computer-generated database has enabled us to store vast sources of information that are easily retrievable, and yet to do so without needing the existence of comparatively vast physical space. (I mention here a small example of the space question. By domestic standards I have a large personal library. Recently a student acknowledged the size of the library and waggishly stated that in a short time I would be able to put all of it in a shoebox.) So, I repeat, who among us would display the

audacity to stand up, chafing in the face of this scientific and technological power? Yet, apace, there emerge demurrers. We isolate here the dilution of embodiment and the worship of speed.

Embodiment

Thinkers as different as Aristotle, Freud, and Dewey warned against patterns of disembodiment as a vestibule for conducting and understanding human life. Even the mystics, in spite of their constant and intense
concentration on the ever present sensuality of the spiritual, were persons in bodies. Unless one is an orthodox Cartesian or embraces some
other type of psycho-physical dualism, all knowing is irreducibly and
patently embodied. A colleague once remarked to John Dewey, "The
trouble with you, Dewey, is that you think philosophy is done with
the hands rather than with the eyes." Dewey responded, "Thank you
for the compliment."³ Following Alfred North Whitehead, we are prehensile animals. And as such to touch is to be touched. To obviate the
tactile, whether it be of the face or of the hand, is to run the risk of
severe disconnection from the way in which we experience ourselves as
organisms. To fly in an airplane from Honolulu to New Zealand is not
to be a Polynesian voyager, nor is it even to be outrigging. To fly from
St. Louis to San Francisco is not to be a mountaineer. In fact, in both
instances one has traveled through space but has neither traversed nor
overcome space. In these travels, neither the ocean nor the mountain
has been experienced as embodied, only seen from afar. Put simply, no
feet, no hands are at work.

Certainly it is impressive and, upon reflection, startling to "travel"
distance online. And, as we have noted, much is salutary about this rev-
ving up of accessibility. Yet, citing the insight of Whitehead, we must be
wary here of committing the fallacy of "misplaced concreteness." An
e-mail message to Bangkok has its "place," but we are not in Bangkok,
not in Thailand, nor, for that matter, anywhere but where we are. The
fallacy of misplaced concreteness tells us that contemporary physics
holds there to be no solids, so this table on which I write is a rush of
electrons. Coming up from this table hurriedly and awkwardly, I hit my
knee. The resultant hematoma tells me that though some things may be

true, they are not so. Consequently, I hold that the "traveling" of distance by online technology is true, but there is a crucial way in which it is not so. By analogy, and with regard to the anecdote above, my "library" may very well be reprised in a shoebox. In what sense is it still my library if I say, goodbye colors, goodbye scents, goodbye shape and size, goodbye touch, and goodbye the personal history of this book?

Since the time when the first human beings evolved or emerged, speaking generically, all humans have experienced the same bodily functions, physiologically and emotively. Defecating and urinating, laughing and crying, sweating and breathing are constants, among other responses appropriate for a "natural" in the world. In this consistent mix are the presence and the activity of the human face, which is not the sole way but the most revealing way by which we communicate with each other. To wit: I can see it in her face; his face is tight, grim, lined, furrowed, distressed; her face is laced with mirth; he uses his face to hide his depression, or to reveal his depression; she has the look of confidence; I see rage in his face; ad infinitum. The human face is not flat. The human face is not one-dimensional. It is textured, contoured, and expressive beyond words. The human face has reach and finds its way into the voice, the smile, the hands, and even the gait. Our face sends messages by a myriad of gestures, some continuous, some discontinuous, some mysterious, answering and resonating to affects deep within our person. The human face is rarely bland and if so, that, too, is a messaging. Human facing connotes joy, sorrow, guilt, shame, fright, repression, anxiety, alienation, anomie, perplexity, curiosity, and intellectual hunger, an attitude incomparably more profound than the seeking of information.

I am aware that faces are beginning to show up online. Such a development, no matter how sophisticated it becomes, cannot gainsay the implacable power of face-to-face experience, physiognomically undergone. The wider the physical gap, the more indirect the experience. Following William James, we have knowledge only "about" rather than "by acquaintance." As an example of the diluting character of distance, I point to the distance between voice-to-voice and "voice" mail, another technological marvel that has a negative hook. Quite aside from the mounting complexity of the "convenience," of the "step-(fast)-forward," and the ensuing corporate strategy for its use to deter messages rather than accept them, I find that the protected person on the other end of the voice mail carousel frequently welcomes a live, personal voice with whom to speak. By now, all of us know how it goes with voice mail. After pushing anywhere from five to twenty buttons in response to Byzantine directions, the caller is chastised for hitting the wrong button, providing information that does not compute, or simply for falling off the carousel. Obviously irritated with our incompetence, voice mail tells us, tough luck, call back. Still, once in a while the system will give up on us and track us into the voice of a live person. Usually, they are friendly, sympathetic with our voice-mail travails, unabashedly confessing that they also are unable to navigate the system. Sometimes it is my lead, sometimes theirs, whatever—the conversation slowly transcends the business at hand, yielding conversations about geographical location, the weather, medical ailments, and sports: embodied concerns, all. Although these conversations are not face-to-face, they are not voice-to-machine or communication-by-password. We do not hold that voice mail, especially for personal reasons, does not have a salutary place in our lives. The problem is that having such a place, it has quickly ratcheted itself up to an overarching place, thereby replacing my place and replacing your place with a place that is no place. In the interest of efficiency and on behalf of speed, we have further enervated embodiment herein found as the human voice.

The just-noted marriage of efficiency and speed is a reigning characteristic of the revolution in electronic technology. On closer look, this marriage sits on very rocky soil. In the history of American attitudes, efficiency has been a frequent target of critics who hold that when used single-mindedly, "the cult of efficiency" blocks imagination, innovation, and, ironically, when locked up in its stubbornness, fails to see the inefficiency of efficiency. I cite but one illustration. Now rarely heard, less than ten years ago we were told that e-mail would lighten our workload and introduce us to efficiency undreamt of. That rhetorical nostrum has vanished, taking its place as one of the truly authentic canards.

What, then, of the second partner in this efficiency-speed conjugation? One of the more misleading, actually treacherous, American mantras is "safe at any speed." Not so. Speed is deceptive on two accounts.

First, it is not simply an arithmetic progression. Speed picks up force, exponentially, as we know from our attempts to stop an automobile when adding five-mile-per-hour increments; we quickly proceed from difficult to perilous to impossible. In a different vein, writing long-hand, typing, and computer word processing is not only a question of speed. These three viaducts for sentences, paragraphs, and pages are working under a very different timing gear, sufficient to result in a very different outcome. Yes, speed is energizing, but we must beware of its impatience, its reluctance to stop, to reconnoitre, and to maintain those boundaries that cannot be violated with impunity. For instance, I note the execrable prose of e-mail communication. This is now a genre overrun with abbreviations, many intelligible only to self-styled initiators, and well on the way to a private language, ostensibly on behalf of widening and extending connections.

A second deception is that increased speed has an endless future, and, in time, ironically, all speed barriers will evaporate. Think of poor Mr. Bernard Lagat, who won the fabled Millrose Mile run in the year 2003. He was criticized for running that mile in a "slow" 4:00.36. Now, it is just several decades since the centuries' long-standing barrier to the 4-minute mile was broken. Today, that speed is slow. So determined are we to go faster, we have added hundredths of seconds to our measurements and then thousandths of seconds. Soon we will measure our human speed in millionths—billionths? trillionths?—of seconds, using a measurement that has no connection to how fast we are going, as experienced by us. We then have a measurement that relates only to itself—namely, the heightened speed, the heightened capacity that is the hallmark of computer worth.

Community

To cut to the quick, here is my response to the aggressive takeover of pedagogy by variant, ever-more powerful, and intrusive versions of electronic technology. The fundamental claim is that contemporary technological innovation forges, widens, and intensifies connections between human beings, especially in a pedagogical setting. That this can happen and, at times, does happen has some evidential support. That it always happens is false. That it most often happens is also false. To the contrary, paradoxical though it be, this vaunted claim on behalf of generating connections has fostered, in reverse, an abiding pattern of disconnections. In my understanding of pedagogy, a systemic move away from interpersonal embodiment is a move away from who we are and how we experience ourselves as human beings, ineluctably.

In his work *The Hope of the Great Community*, Josiah Royce, a philosopher committed to globalization long before that term was coined, writes of the danger of becoming a "detached individual."[4] He has in mind a person who, despite access to communication and information, remains isolated from the burdens and nectar of social union—in short, the community. I do not see us obviating this warning if we shed embodiment and face-to-face intentional community life. To bypass, to transcend, to move beyond the pace, the gait, the deliberate, the considered, the slow is to ignore the taproots of genuine communal growth. Fructification has no future without roots. Globalization is hollow if it does not embrace the centrality of an affective, liturgical, and aesthetic binding, none of which seems to be the province of the mavens of speed, heightened capacity, and communication absent reflection. A plethora of information and electronic contact will not suffice for comprehending the issues in globalization that demand simmering rather than boiling, watching and waiting rather than seizing and managing by intrusion. Is that why, traditionally at least, we always shake hands, even in times of tension? I repeat, to be touched is to touch.

Pedagogy is at its best when one person touches another by virtue of imaginative and intelligent reconstruction of experiences had and experiences novel. For me, teaching is a response to the most fundamental of all human questions, "Can you help me?" I believe that you can see the existential urgency of this question in the faces before us, given, of course, that we remain face-to-face.

TWENTY-FOUR

CULTURAL LITERACY
A Time for a New Curriculum

I n our time and in our nation, public precollegiate education is in serious disarray. It is now a nationally observed phenomenon that despite good intentions on the part of teachers and despite generally intelligent students, even those students who proceed to colleges and universities seem culturally deprived. They exhibit a staggering ignorance of history and letters, and their symbolic resources for imaginative reconstruction seem bankrupt. It is as if the soul has disappeared, leaving only a more or less satisfactory standardized test as the approach to learning.

The reasons for this state of affairs are complex and obviously not amenable to easy solutions. This is not the place to probe the educational politics of the situation, although they are decidedly relevant, as the Conant report attested decades ago.[1] We are faced with something of an institutional fait accompli, in that colleges of education prepare most of our teachers in a decidedly nonhumanistic and nonspeculative framework.[2] It should not come as surprising that these teachers then teach our children in a similar vein. Nothing less than a radical transformation of the curriculum in teacher-education programs, a transformation long overdue, can resolve this dilemma.[3]

It is now obvious that many students with high test scores and class rank are nonetheless unaware of even the pre-eminent events in the history of Western civilization, and totally innocent of the very existence of major cultural traditions other than their own. In a recent effort to assess the knowledge of highly qualified and academically successful juniors and seniors in a major American university, I was startled to learn that thirty of forty students could not identify Socrates, the Roman Empire, the Protestant Reformation, Newton, or Beethoven. In fact, of the thirty simple identifications requested, the average score for the forty students was six correct. Despite the fact that we now live in a truly global culture, requests for information or insight about Oriental, Indian, African, or Islamic cultures are met with utter bewilderment.

Still more serious than this appalling absence of awareness of our historical and cultural past is the spiritual context of contemporary public education. Although exceptions exist, it is a safe generalization to describe the ambience of "being in school" as an alternation between boredom and violence. The major escapees from these nefarious poles are those children who, due to family, or occasionally ethnic, pressure, concentrate on "making it" and see one or more careers as the delineation of their human future. These judgments as to the plight of our schools are not novel. In fact, ample literature, both popular and scholarly, details this situation on a regular basis.

Admittedly, the critique of the studied emptiness of middle-class education and the warnings about the baleful future of those children who know only a career as the meaning of education are comparatively subtle in a nation that is increasingly characterized by the quick, the shallow, and the ersatz. Not so subtle, however, is the diagnosis of the school systems of our great urban centers. In such settings, involving millions of children, historical and cultural illiteracy is not, alas, the primary concern. Rather, we face dramatically high rates of absenteeism and adolescent drop-outs. We face strife, social disorder, and plummeting scores in basic verbal and mathematical skills. Administrators, teachers, and community leaders are often called upon to undertake heroic efforts in their attempt to structure a meaningful educational environment. Despite their efforts, increasingly, even liberal and pluralistically oriented parents are choosing to squirrel their children away in one of the urban private schools which now multiply like mushrooms after a constant rain. When added to the postwar flight of the self-announced gentry to the suburbs, the rise of urban private schools leaves the urban public school something of an embattled redoubt, an abandoned but peopled bunker, left behind.

In America, historically and morally committed to a democratic polity, it is essential that we continue, generation by generation, to educate all of our children in the best of our warranted wisdom so that they may take their rightful and necessary place in the ongoing presentation and continuance of our attempt to build a truly human future. The erosion of humanistic sensibility, awareness of the past, and basic competency in literacy and science, as often found in contemporary public education, constitutes a major threat to this essential national endeavor. Granted the occasional worthiness and even curricular imagination of private education, we must acknowledge that it is the quality of public school education which holds the key to the spiritual future of this republic. Therefore, we cannot be sanguine, for it is precisely public school education that mirrors the deepest crisis in contemporary America: the economic and social bifurcation between a struggling and cynical lumpen proletariat confined to poor rural and inner urban schools, and an affluent, morally laissez-faire middle class, making their way through private or suburban educational institutions. The separation of blacks and Hispanics from whites is, of course, a looming factor in this division, but it is not the decisive source of the division. Looming larger is the gap between the poor and the affluent, for that gap, regrettably and undemocratically, constitutes the major reason for the double standard as to what constitutes acceptable education for an American child. Despite the penchant for crisis management in American society, the crisis in American public school education remains obdurate, discussed only sotto voce. Highways, potholes, prisons, illegal aliens, and interest rates rank far ahead of the debilitation of millions of our children. The politics of this situation seem impervious to resolution, short of revolution, which, in this century, seems to bring only repression under a different rubric.

Given the skepticism about the salutary effect of recent federal programs for the solution of problems besetting the public schools, and given the economic climate of America in this decade, it is very unlikely that we will witness the appearance of an educational Marshall Plan in the near future. Consequently, the finances, the neighborhoods, and the clientele of the public schools will remain basically the same in this decade. The curriculum, however, need not remain the same. And we can move in the direction of a significant shift in the focus of the teaching process. I now offer some suggestions as to the ingredients necessary for a transformation of public education. (Parenthetically, I do not have in mind the simplistic resolution, often put forth by university faculty, of adding materials and subject matter in the earlier years. As one who has taught Latin and English in secondary school, I can attest that this would only introduce increased confusion to the current curricular bedlam. Adolescent students who now take six, seven, and even eight different subjects a day in short time snatches are in no position to have more subject matter added. Although it is generally lamentable that such areas of important intellectual endeavor as philosophy, sociology, psychology, anthropology, the history of religion, and the history of science are not staples in a typical secondary school curriculum, I see no possible way in which they could become so except by ousting equally important concerns or by making the curriculum more of a patchwork quilt than at present. No, the needed change is in a different direction entirely. We must demythologize the discipline structure of our approach to education.)

I believe that humanistic learning is present in every endeavor and that it is dramatically present in the traditional endeavors of precollegiate education. How did it happen that the discipline known as "history" became responsible for the history of everything, such that other disciplines became ahistorical? If I am teaching physics to secondary school students, is it not germane to the discussion that for more than 2,000 years physics and philosophy were identical? Is it not significant that the ancient philosopher Democritus anticipated modern atomic theory? Should not these students be told that the history of science is pockmarked with errors, many of them propagated far beyond the time of exposure because of political or ideological reasons? Would not the teaching of science be served well if we were to introduce the students to the contrasting conflicts found in the life and work of Galileo and Lysenko? In this way, the teaching of science might involve not only history, but ethics and biography as well. A further example from the sciences pertains to biology. In Western civilization, biology was founded by Aristotle, and the phyla are his creation. Could there be a better model for students to emulate for developing the power of observation? And would it not be a contribution to these students for them to know that while learning Aristotle's approach to biology, they were also learning his method of philosophy, a method which infused Western culture until the late nineteenth century? Similar examples from the sciences can be multiplied indefinitely, and the historical dimension of every discipline should be an integral aspect of its presentation.

We do not quarrel with the fact that it is necessary and salutary that precollegiate education spend time on mathematics, and on reading, writing, and speaking English and at least one other language, all taught very early in the schooling process. And, whenever possible, computer-assisted instruction should be utilized. But for the rest of the curriculum, at the outset for some years and then periodically thereafter, we should concentrate on autobiography/biography, the science of living things (that is, botany and physiology), sculpture, and theater. These suggestions are neither final nor definitive, although their interdisciplinary width makes them especially attractive. Properly structured and taught, they would be the filter through which all of the "subjects" now in the curriculum would be introduced. Before I attempt to justify the significance of these approaches to a new curriculum, I offer the following commentary on the importance of a cultural pedagogy, by which I mean the common source of our personal expectations, sensibilities, and evaluations.

Pedagogy is hapless and empty if it does not face directly the deep and pervasive dialectic between the historical and genetic conditioning of the person, on the one hand, and, on the other, the impress of the novelties of the physical and social world. This confrontation between our human heritage and the world in which we find ourselves is the stuff out of which we weave that fragile creature we call our very own "self."

The key to a successful mapping of this conflictual terrain is the making of relations: that is, the forging of a distinctively personal presence in the doings and undergoings which constitute our experience. The making of relations is a lifelong endeavor, but it is especially crucial in the lives of children, as they struggle to achieve self-consciousness in a vast, complex, and initially undefined environment. Helping our children to learn how to make relations is the central and most important task of pedagogy. To the extent that they do not learn to make their own relations, children are doomed to living second-hand lives. They become creatures of habituation who merely follow out the already programmed versions of their experience as inherited from parents, older siblings, and self-appointed definers of reality, such as teachers. Ironically, a child who knows how to make relations can convert even authoritarian and repressive treatment into paths of personal liberation, whereas a child who does not make relations converts invitations to free inquiry into derivative and bland repetition. This irony is made vivid for us when we realize that most often the lives of those whom we regard as "great" are characterized by affliction, suffering, and frequent rejection. In the hands of those who can make and remake relations, even negative events become the nutrition for a creative life.

Just what is it for a child to make relations and why do I regard it as crucial to a humanistic pedagogy? First, we must dispel any naiveté about the allegedly virginal character of the emerging self. The profound and complex preconscious conditioning of the self is a fact of our time. Modern sociology, with its roots in the thought of George Herbert Mead, stresses the social origins of the self, holding that without the me, the socially derived "generalized other," there would be no I. Modern psychology, with its roots in Freud and Jung, stresses the irreducible presence and power of our unconscious. Or conversely, modern psychology, here following B. F. Skinner, holds that we are totally conditioned by the operative impress of external stimuli. The sociology of knowledge founded by Karl Marx contends that our consciousness, far from being original, is derivative of institutions. For Marx, "institutions" referred to church, state, family, and money, whereas recent thought adds gender, race, ethnicity, language, climate, and region as initiating boxes from which we never really escape.

It is now culturally obvious that as we come to self-consciousness in our early years, we are playing out our inherited genetic and social trappings. None of us can ignore the conditioning power of this inheritance. The existence of a pristine self, free of the entangling alliances of one's genetic and social past, is a myth. To be born white or black, male or female, Irish or Jewish, is an inherited context as thick as the earth itself. To experience one's postnatal years in the city or on a farm, in the snow or in the desert, is an informing crucible that our consciousness can repress but never totally dismiss. One could multiply these inheritances indefinitely, and a diagnosis of their significance in the lives of children could become a rich source of self-awareness as well as of awareness of others by contrast. In fact, these diagnoses would be the beginning of the child's self-understanding and the beginning of the child's attempt to build a new, distinctively personal world.

My point here is that the only way to obviate the deleterious second-handedness of our inherited trappings is to bring them to the fore and diagnose them as to their richness, their narrowness, and the role they play in our assumptions. Under careful and probing guidance, even very young children are capable of fleshing out their distinctive sense of time, space, place, size, color, tone, and ever more subtle ambiences of the world in which they "find" themselves. In this way, the inheritances are transformed from conceptual boxes, in which the child is unknowingly encased, to perceptual fields fit for romping and reconstructing in the light of present experiences. This is precisely what I mean by the making of relations—namely, taking these inherited conditionings and turning them from conceptual rocks into something more diaphanous, crossed and recrossed with variant images, attitudes, and styles. There is nothing arcane in this, for children, despite their inheritances, seek novelty naturally, unless they are prevented by a pedagogy which attempts to reduce all of their experiences to a common denominator. For example, just recently, a teacher was queried in a newspaper article as to how she would begin her teaching after the children returned from their Hanukkah/Christmas holiday. She replied that if they insisted, they could take a "few minutes" to say what they did during that time, but then it would be "back to the routine." One can hardly dignify this approach as educational, for the classroom is a morgue and the children are cadavers, passive witnesses to an anatomical dissection on behalf of a fixed curriculum.

Is not this the time to assist in the conversion of the children's ordinary reportage of these remarkable events, celebrated for two millennia, into something extraordinary and within their reach? Is not this the time to read them O. Henry's "Gift of the Magi" and appropriate selections from the *Diary of Anne Frank*? Is not this the time to introduce them to Ramadan, the holy period of Islam, and then to contrast Judaism, Christianity, and Islam with Buddhism and Hinduism? Is not this the time to assist the children in leaping upon an experience about to be had and/or undergone so that they may open it up and reach out to neighboring experiences, both similar and starkly different? It is necessary for one to have experience if one is to make relations and create a personal world, tied to others, but yet distinctive. To have experience without making relations, especially of dissimilarity, is to be left with the inert, repetitious, and routine.

Like William James, I, too, believe that experience grows by its edges.[4] By nature, the child comes into the world on edge, on the *qui vive*, with a penchant for making relations. Traditional education, however, seems perversely determined to block this run of the imagination, opting rather for a world made up of boxes, separate one from the other, each defined and named, impervious to the rash of potential relations that yield themselves only to the reflection born of experienced perception. Is it not long overdue that contemporary educational practices integrate the accrued wisdom of this century and come to realize that names, categories, schema, and definitions are but functional placeholders in our experiencing the flow of events, linked to each other in a myriad of ways? With the exception of speculative mathematics and formal logic, percepts should reign over concepts. Definitions should never be taken to exhaust the meaning, texture, tone, or implication of that defined. Ambiguity should be restored to its proper place as the proper response in direct proportion to the importance of the experience undergone. Love and loyalty, for example, are exquisitely ambiguous; no amount of quantitative social science methodology can clarify them sufficiently, such that they become fully understood or manipulable.

I have no objection to the proper utilization of quantitative methodology, and I am aware of the necessity of scientific rigor. Similarly, I endorse the importance of high technology and the utilization of the computer in the attainment of ever more sophisticated and accurate access to data. No, my concern is quite different. I lament the suffusion of the elementary and secondary school curricula with disciplines and approaches whose major task is to prepare students for successful functioning in an ostensibly high-tech future, as though such activity were to be the primary activity of a human life. If we are to survive as an originating human culture, we cannot view the reflective awareness of our past, the extensive knowledge of other cultures and other languages, literature, the arts, and speculative science as activities merely desirable but actually peripheral to the more important task of "getting along" in the future. This approach may enable us to survive as a nation—that is, as the saying goes, "to hold our own." On the other hand, we shall become spiritually bankrupt.

As an antidote to the drift away from having the humanities as the centerpiece of public elementary and secondary school education, I offer that we should make use of four curricular modules: autobiography/biography, the science of living things (botany and physiology), sculpture, and theater. My justification is as follows.

Autobiography/Biography

How are young persons to find a wedge into the tissue of experience in a way which transcends the narrowness of their own ego-development? One way, of course, is to be driven by an event, either magnificent or disastrous. Such events are rare in our lives and even they become meaningful only in proportion to our reflective awareness of their significance. A second possibility exists, less intense but more available. I refer here to the way in which we can be carried beyond our immediate ken by participating in the recorded lives of the many startling and creative persons in our collective lineage. Think, for example, how extraordinarily rich is the prose and the historical content of the life and death of Socrates, as written by Plato. Here we introduce the student to a raft of central concerns: classical Greek culture, philosophy, religion, ethics, politics, and, finally, the important and profound question of our death, as raised in the discussion as to whether Socrates committed suicide. Equal wisdom is to be gained from the life of Thomas Jefferson, who also introduces us to architecture and to his deep feeling for the land, on behalf of an agrarian ethic. The meaning of courage and indomitability in the face of adversity is brought to our consciousness by the study of the lives of Queen Elizabeth or Joan of Arc. Virtually every human characteristic and every cultural and intellectual movement is represented by one or more biographies and autobiographies. Through this medium, we have access to the achievements and the plight of every race, region, ethnic group, religion, and cultural persuasion. And we need not confine our materials to happy endings, for we have much more to learn from the slave narratives and from the stories of survivors of the Holocaust, the Gulag, and Hiroshima. I do not see the study of biography and autobiography as a replacement for systematic study. Rather, I view it as propaedeutic and an accompaniment. The plaintive cry, "Why do I have to study physics?" is not well met by the stock reply, "Someday you will use it." Far better to study the lives of Newton and Heisenberg and develop a hunger for the activities of physics.

The biographies of the famous, the great, and the notorious are an obvious way to have students begin to understand the multiplicity of cultures and life-experiences, which then cast light on their own lives. Equally important are the reported lives of those persons who are comparatively unsung or known only for their prowess in a limited area or for a single accomplishment. Their stories do not have a fabled backdrop, but the human quotient may be even closer to the experiences of the students. Of special value may be the lives of the totally unknown, as pieced together from diaries and letters found posthumously. In 1963 and 1967, I traveled with our five children across America, some 40,000 miles in and out of every continental state. One of the most moving sets of experiences resulted from our indefatigable effort to stop at hundreds of local museums throughout the country. In those modest buildings, on those modest streets, we found the letters and diaries of the founders: men, women, and children. Beautifully written both in prose and in penmanship, belying the fact that their formal education, mostly in the nineteenth century, was limited in scope and time, these documents evoked a sense of the past, of human misery and triumph equal to the legendary figures we celebrate. It is of importance to note that the beauty of the style and the depth of feeling in these documents is accompanied by a simplicity of access. They can be read by children without difficulty. I think of the letters of the people of the former whaling communities of Sag Harbor and Cold Spring Harbor on Long Island, New York. I think of the letters of the settlers in Texas and Minnesota and Colorado. For every Lewis and Clark, for every Daniel Boone, there are hundreds of people like you and me who wrote of their experience in a moving and telling way.

In addition to the students bathing in the reflective waters of the experience of others, ordinary as well as extraordinary, the pedagogical task is to urge them to keep their own diaries and to save their letters. The suggestion of keeping a diary at a young age is often met with an embarrassed incredulity. The responsive refrain is often in the plaintive vein of "Who, me?" or "Who would care?" Perhaps no one would care. Perhaps someone would care. Perhaps many would care. The significance of the diary does not depend on these future possibilities. Rather, the writing of a diary, influenced by the reading of others' lives, provides the student with a private landscape for self-diagnosis and for the integration of the past with the present. The diary will provide the glare of self-examination. The prose will improve and the life of the student will be privately exposed to the twin canons of evaluation: the niggardliness of the everyday and the occasional breakthrough or conquest. The personal importance of the student's diary will not achieve the significance of the spotlight cast upon the *Meditations* of Marcus Aurelius, but the rhythm of a life will be notably similar.

The Science of Living Things (Botany and Physiology)

Despite our many differences, one from the other, creature from creature, we share a rich and incontrovertible common bequest: that of being a live creature. The plants, the animals, and human beings are living things. (Some say the stars are as well, but we shall leave that discussion for another time.) With the exception of those few who believe in panpsychism, an intriguing although as-yet-unverified hypothesis, most people accept the distinction between the organic and the inorganic as fundamental to any understanding of reality. The science of living things would introduce the student to the life and death cycles of plants, vegetation, insects, animals, and human beings. Ideally, this should involve both laboratory and field work. The task here is not only to introduce the student to the names and functions of organisms, but also to stress the dramatic sharing and conflict that is a permanent characteristic of living. It is easy to replicate the life and death cycles of vegetation, plants, insects, and small animals in a classroom setting. Objections to the existence of these living things in the classroom are often bureaucratically self-serving, because of alleged inconvenience. The death of a geranium or a hamster, especially one giving birth, provides an unending and, ironically, fertile source for the exploration of the most important event in our life, our own death.

Moving to the human organism, considerable time should be given to the liver and the brain, organs which are masterpieces of perturbation, consummation, and messaging. The rhythms of setback and recovery are salient characteristics of these organs. The liver, for example, nicely and appropriately named in English, has as its obligation the managing of more than five hundred activities, each essential not only to human well-being, but to life itself.[5] I am reminded of the ancient text from the Book of Ezekiel (21:21): "For the King of Babylon stood at the parting of the way, at the head of the two ways, to use divination: he made his arrows bright, he consulted with images, he looked in the liver." And from the Greek doctrine of the four humors, through the medieval period and into Shakespeare's time, the amount of liver bile was thought to have a direct bearing on a person's temperament. Modern medical science has abandoned these anthropomorphic versions of the liver, yet the urgency and centrality of its function still hold. A biochemical marvel, the human liver is a sorter, a dispatcher, a condemner, a welcomer, and the arbiter of what stays in our body and what leaves. In short, the human liver is a supreme maker of relations, our biological brain. Its malfunction is our serious illness. Its death is our death. For the children, the obvious fallout of this study of the liver, as well as of the brain and of the kidneys, each a maker of relations, is an awareness of the simultaneous power and fragility of the human body, a dialectic which is repeated in our religious, ethical, social, psychological, and imaginative transaction with the world.

Sculpture

What the liver is to the inner world of our bodies, the hands are to the outer world in which we live out our lives. Different from fish and from snakes, we are prehensile creatures. With our hands we touch, we grab, we hold, we push, and we pull. More subtly we caress, we knead, we feel, and with our hands, we make sounds and things and signs. Our hands are the major way in which we penetrate the world, seeking to learn its texture and occasionally seeking to remake the world in our image, be it a representation, fantasy, or an original construct. It is with our hands that we touch and care for the most intimate and private parts of our bodies and, as adults, care for the bodies of those we love. Our hands enable the violin and the piano to yield their enchanting sounds. Our hands enable us to write and type the messagings of our person. Our hands go still only in our sleep or at our death. It is well known that the most human and "living" aspect of a human cadaver is the hand; the fingers are crooked over the palms, seemingly clinging to life when all else has failed.

In this vast variety of activities of the hand, the most distinctive and powerful version is to be found when we sculpt. In so doing, we render the external world in our own image. No matter what the material, we can fashion it into shapes and contours which bespeak the press of our desire to build a world that is singular and original. Pedagogically, the intention is to have the student create his or her own imaginative image of the world, experiencing deeply the extension of human intimacy, the hands, into the obduracy of materials. Accompanying this creative and managing activity would be research into the textual makeup and history of the materials utilized. Each student would provide analysis of the materials to be used, and share this information with the others; the result would be a common appraisal of the history and texture of cloth, paper, clay, plastics, woods, and metals. Shared too would be the range of skills necessary to an effective managing of these materials, such as carpentry, welding, the use of a kiln, and an array of decorative abilities. Salutary as well would be the collapsing of the pernicious distinctions between the fine arts, the practical arts, and the industrial arts. Sculpture is remarkable precisely for its capacity to integrate every conceivable human way that we have to effect a change in the nature of the material before us—in effect, to make something undreamt of in nature.

In addition to the mastery of technique and the understanding of the potentialities and limitations in the nature of materials, the making of sculpture offers students an excellent opportunity to forge relationships between themselves and the world in a personal and imaginative medium. On the basis of my experience with this approach to learning, I have no doubt that the results will range from the obvious to the surreal and from the beautiful to the grotesque, thus bequeathing a mirror image of the dazzling, albeit too often hidden, plurality as potential to human creative activity. In time, these sculptures would be in every classroom, in homes, and perhaps even in public places. In this way, the community would relive its own fantasies, histories, and personal perspectives through the hands of its children.

Theater

The last of our suggested curricular modules is that of theater. Of all the ways to educate, theater is the most demanding and complex, both in preparation and execution. The rewards in learning and experience, however, more than justify the effort. Basically, we can either select our source of theater as pedagogy from plays that have already been written and performed, or we can have the writing of the play as part of the activity.[6] Each option has its advantages. The former provides the students with a play that has been evaluated and represents approved wisdom, style, and dramatic effect. All of the details necessary to staging are provided, so that the students can concentrate on effecting a successful production. I would suggest several attempts at utilizing plays already written and produced before trying to write an original script, since starting from scratch would probably not produce the quality of plays already extant. Still, the advantages here are considerable. Learning to write dialogue, developing a plot, generating believable characters, and setting out the specifications for stage directions are all extraordinarily valuable in teaching students how to write and how to set up a human world. It would be especially valuable if the development of the script

could be done in concert, thereby introducing the students to an ongoing and shared community of inquiry by which they as generational
peers would evolve their view of the world, its values, and its pitfalls.

Whichever of the two methods described above is followed, the pedagogical rewards are considerable. First, theater is contextual; it is set
somewhere. The setting may be ancient Greece, as in the *Agamemnon* of
Aeschylus, or in England during the late medieval age of the history
plays of Shakespeare. Or, the setting could be more modest, say Willy
Loman's unbecoming home in New York and a small hotel room in
Boston, as found in Arthur Miller's *Death of a Salesman*. Additional sites
abound: airplanes, farms, ghettoes, ships, war sites, mountains, and even
totally imaginative sites such as alien planets. Whatever the site, the pedagogical bequest is that the students must enter a world other than their
own. Costume, jargon, climate, and an endless set of cultural assumptions will differ from theirs. By virtue of participating in a theatrical presentation of this other world, they would be forced, by contrast, to
sharpen their experience of their own world while thus avoiding the
subtle danger of habituation and repetition.

A second positive result of the pedagogy of theater results from the
preparation of the play. Ideally, all of the ingredients necessary to the
production should be made by the students. Lighting, costumes, scen-
ery, and other appurtenances also should be the responsibility of the
students. As with sculpture, this responsibility will bring together the
fine arts and the applied arts. As an example of this merging of disciplines and technical skill, take the problem of costumes. They should
not be obtained ready-made but rather should be made by the students.
What, then, is a toga? Of what material was it made? How did it fit?
Were they all identical? What of those worn by a male, female, slave, free
person, citizen, or child? And did the dress differ by the time of the day,
the year, the season, or ceremonial occasion? Equally tantalizing is the
nature and history of footwear, undergarments, and personal weaponry.
This historical research is only the first step, for when the knowledge of
"what" was worn "when" and "why" is attained, the students must then
attend to "how" it was made and make it themselves.

One could go further and have the students make the technology,
however primitive, which made the clothing and utensils of other, earlier cultures. Not only will this provide a deep and lasting insight into

the ingenuity and steadfastness of the children's forebears, it also will cast a light of appreciation and even marvel on the achievements of contemporary technology. Two anecdotes will illustrate this point. At the end of the nineteenth century, John and Alice Chipman Dewey founded a laboratory school for children. One of the exercises was to bring in a bushel of raw cotton plants and have the children pick the cotton and prepare it for processing. After a day of this, they barely had enough cotton for a pair of socks, and their untutored hands were sore and abrased. The children were then introduced to Eli Whitney and the invention of the cotton gin. The second anecdote comes firsthand. When our son Brian was in the fourth grade, his public school teacher devoted a major part of the year to having the class build a replica of the Mercury capsule, launched just a year earlier. The children read articles on aerodynamics, the mysteries of space, and were taught the elementary physics of this astonishing phenomenon. They did all the carpentry and other material preparation. The capsule grew, imposing, dazzling, and mysterious, although accessible to its creators. It stood in the center of the classroom and each day took on portentous stature as it neared completion. For our son, now a secondary school teacher of the industrial arts and a master carpenter, the experience in the fourth grade was incomparably the richest of his eighteen years of schooling. Depressingly, although not surprisingly, this story has a bitter ending. Despite the protests of irate parents, our fourth-grade teacher was fired at the end of that memorable year. It seems that he did not complete the fourth-grade syllabus.

A third reason for introducing the pedagogy of theater as a central module in our curriculum is the re-enforcement of effort and experience by doing the play for an audience, either one composed of student peers or perhaps parents and relatives. The best of these dramatic productions could even be shared with the community at large. As a medium, theater surpasses the symphonic concert and even cinema in its ability to draw the audience out of its consciousness and into a different and often novel setting. The legendary excitement of the "opening" is deserved, for the footlights are just that, lights which illuminate the walking of an audience into the lives of others. Theater is rhetorically and scenically embracing. Song and dance are infinitely more alive and captivating when they are aspects of theater; hence the power of opera and ballet. The most ordinary of plots and banal of prose turn into excitement in the context of music and song, as when the libretto of *La Bohème* is rendered operatically by Puccini. The simplest of tales rise from their obviousness when Tchaikovsky offers us the ballets *Swan Lake* and *The Sleeping Beauty*. Even the dramatic starkness of Thornton Wilder's *Our Town* draws the audience into its environment and then back again to their own consciousness for a nostalgic rumination on their childhood. To create theater is not only to create a human world. It is to create so that others—the audience—can participate, can share, and can enter into the process. No other medium, no other art form, no other human activity, can make relations in so many ways, so expansively, so extensively, so multiple in style and theory and artifact, so subtle, so explosive, so clear, so ambiguous, so deft, so explicit, and so rich in implication. If I am correct in this assessment, then our children must have the opportunity to develop these theatrical skills, attitudes, abilities, experience these failures and successes, from their preschool years through their adult life.

I do not have an idée fixe on these four modules for a revised precollegiate curriculum. Other possibilities come to mind: archaeology, pathology, dance, and comparative anthropology, to cite some of many. Frankly, they and others seem absorbable and able to be taught within the imaginative pedagogical approach to autobiography/biography, the science of living things, sculpture, and theater. Actually, adjustments to these curricular suggestions and even replacements are not destructive to the above discussion, so long as we remember that the irreducible task of pedagogy is to help others to make relations, such that the deepest recesses of personal privacy transact with human others, with an external world, and with the images gleaned from a storied and even repressed past. In this way we build our world. It is a world borrowed, stolen, hidden from others, shared, lamented, celebrated, and, occasionally, the result of personal triumph.

Surely, in a nation ostensibly committed to excellence and to equality, we cannot afford to deprive our children of access to the wisdom of the past and to the stirring and value-laden modalities and media of the arts and the humanities. They have every right to be taught how to write, listen, read, and speak with a deep understanding of our full cultural heritage. The computer, in the end, will be only as meaningful as the quality of our input. If we render generation after generation culturally deaf and dumb, the rising spires of high technology will be but a contemporary parallel to the Tower of Babel.

TWENTY-FIVE

TRUMPING CYNICISM WITH IMAGINATION

J ohn J. McDermott is Distinguished Professor of Philosophy at Texas A&M University. Professor McDermott is one of the leading scholars of American philosophy and a renowned educator. A riveting, animated speaker, John McDermott demonstrates a vast knowledge of the history of philosophy from Plato to Dewey and the remarkable ability to apply these great thinkers to a modern context. He is interviewed below by host Michael Malone.

Michael Malone (MM): Okay, John, I've been wanting to ask you a question. I've been waiting for you to come on to ask you this, because you're the great pragmatist. Here we are at the end of the twentieth century, 100 million people dead, probably the bloodiest century in human history. The Holocaust, the great famine, all of these events—what exactly has philosophy done to help get us through all this? It seems to me philosophy has been off in a corner devising new language and symbolic logic.

John J. McDermott (JM): Yes, but no. The difficulty is that current philosophy has lost its purchase and, consequently, even things which are helpful have not received attribution.

MM: What do you mean by that?

JM: Well, philosophy is the lodestone for the wisdom tradition and it has been much less ideologically burdened than religion and politics. And so philosophy has been able to have a living, accruing, creating tradition which has much to say of great significance to the overall questions, but certainly less so since the thirties.

MM: Because of the Vienna circle.

JM: The Vienna circle, but also since Oxbridge analysis and since they adopted the manners of sciences—not the best of the sciences, not the intuitive character of the sciences, not the experimental sensibility of the sciences. But of the quest for certainty, as Dewey would say—that part of the sciences.

MM: But why did philosophy suddenly fall so in love with the sciences?

JM: Because in philosophy, there's a deepened insecurity in the twentieth-century intellectual which generates arrogance.

MM: Okay.

JM: And so this insecurity, wanting to get this right and so on, when, as a matter of fact, if you really return to tradition, you discover that ambiguity is everywhere. It is true that the Cartesian move was a move in the direction of certitude, but it was a very modest move because it didn't involve the body, it didn't involve sensorial foundation. See, he was smart enough to know that. So I want to get back to the business about the Holocaust and so on; it has to do with authority and absolutism. This does not have to do with inquiry. It has to do with taking positions before there was any evidence. And so it is the reverse of everything we believe in philosophy. There is no inquiry characteristic of the fascist movement, whether it's on the left or on the right. The fascist movement is a move which is a function of absolutism. And it is a function of nonreflection.

MM: So did philosophy fall victim to absolutism at the beginning of the century, too, in a sense that they [philosophers] looked around, they said, look what Rutherford's doing, look what Einstein's doing.

They're coming up with answers. Maybe if we turn scientific we'll come up with answers, too.

JM: That has been said and you can say that. But let me say something else to you. I think that there was a reluctance to confront the fact that the really powerful questions are never going to be answered. And so what they did is they backed out, you see, into language. One of the lines was that the task of philosophy is not to diagnose experience, but analyze language. Now that line is, I think, a line that takes us nowhere. If I keep the first part of the line, to diagnose experience, I'm constantly confronted with setback, with mishap, with ambiguity, right? I'm confronted with, ah . . .

MM: Failure.

JM: Yes, yes, with failure, you see. And if you think that failure is not part of the meaning of growth and the meaning of the human spirit and so on, well, then, of course, you are looking for smaller and smaller versions, of which you are more and more sure.

MM: But philosophers, of all people, should have been the people *not* afraid of failure, by definition. Is that because of the Academy? Once you go inside the walls you've got to publish, you've got to . . .

JM: Well, that's another question and it's a question which is in all realms. It's a small question compared to the one you opened up with.

MM: Yes, well I'm asking because now we're at the brink of the twenty-first century. Is anything changing?

JM: No, things are getting worse and universities are infinitely more pompous, more bloated, more insensitive, more unaware of what they were supposed to be about, and less involved in what we would call "pedagogy." So the American experiment, which is the greatest of all the experiments in the history of the world, was to strive for equality across the board. That is to take seriously that everyone is educable. You know Royce once said, the popular mind is deep, knows a thousand times more than it knows, and the task of pedagogy is to enable people to see. Or in Buber's phrase to the man who challenged him in Jerusalem in '47, listen buster, you are able. You can do it, you see. I believe that; I mean, it's hard to believe that in a world in which you see less and less that's that significant. Huh? So, the university is no help.

MM: Yes.

JM: All right. I mean, the university is no help. More and more, it looks like corporate life. Less and less does it look like the agora, does it look like the monastery walk, less and less does it look like, you know, Emerson's stuff or whatever. So, more and more, I see myself and others like me, my friends, too, and all these people and so on as a remnant. It's really quite extraordinary, Mike. But then in the last . . .

MM: Do you see yourself just as a remnant?

JM: Don't say "just" because that's a very deep term.

MM: No, but I mean, you're talking to an Irishman.

JM: Ah, as if I didn't know.

MM: Yes, but there came a point when there was just a handful of Irishmen keeping the tradition going. Hanging on the coast.

JM: That's right.

MM: So is that what you are? Do you see yourself as that—is your duty to carry it?

JM: But, you see, the difference is that they [Irish] were keeping something right for our future.

MM: Yes.

JM: You see, we aren't keeping something that has been bypassed and remanded and absolute. It's very different.

MM: But it always comes back; it's waiting out there to come back.

JM: Well.

MM: People need it. If, because official philosophy hasn't done the job, people have looked to philosophy in other ways. They've gone to other sources. But still there is a need. You've always said, philosophy comes down to a handful of simple questions.

JM: Right.

MM: People ask those questions every single damn day. They're asking them in the offices out here in Boston right now.

JM: That's right, that's right. Well, you see, you say they look for it in other ways. Now here's my sadness, okay? I think that there's been this movement toward pop stuff, quick fixes, right? And yet it's sort of a cheap, and even spiritually salacious, road. When, certainly you know this, but the deep things are irresolute, okay? There's a lot of trouble even in this room here, a lot of suffering, broken stuff, and so on. Now I think, you see, that I can do much better than that stuff by teaching the meditations of Marcus Aurelius. Or, for example, open with the line from Epictetus, "You should live life as if it were a banquet." Marcus Aurelius says at one point to the centurion, look, he said, see the mouse? Ah, you, me, it's all the same. How long would you live, Mike? Six years, sixty years, six hundred? What difference does it make? My friend, life is a warfare and a stranger's sojourn and after fame is oblivion. That's all there is. So warriors are frightened by this; the centurion is horrified. So he tries to do something with them. That's that whole doctrine of a Stoic bond and my position is that each of the powerful philosophers has a diagnosis of this wound, you call it what you want, the fall, or, I call it a walk-on, DNA, everybody has their way of doing it. Now the task is, what can I do? So then you reach for healing metaphors and these healing metaphors don't have to be chintzy, I mean, they can be built into deep stuff, like a metaphysics.

MM: Yes.

JM: Spinoza says that I have an adequate idea of the mind of God. William James says the whole thing runs in a current, it's all in a flow. Dewey says, basically, we're tied to nature. We have to just see this stuff as a kind of problematic and do the best we can, and each of these, you see, they've got forty people out there. Ten said Dewey's might work, right? Okay. And then they have something to move onto. Once I teach in such a way as it's arcane, then no longer is it something that they can in any way tie to the quality and nature of their own experiences, they drop out.

MM: Right.

JM: Okay, but that's what's going on. Somehow the philosophy crowd thinks that I'm less if I'm understood. How'd we get into that—will you explain that to me?

MM: Well, it must be doubly troubling to you as a pragmatist because you know you can look out there and say, well, the whole principle of pragmatism is, pick what works, and this obviously isn't working, but nobody's dropping it.

JM: Okay, that's very good.

MM: Nobody's putting the thing down and picking up something else and saying, well, let's try this, maybe this is going to work better.

JM: Well, just for clarification, I don't use the term "pragmatist" for myself. I mean, I'm basically a guy who's interested in the diagnosis of experiences, so I'm just as much into Camus as I am into Dewey. But you're right, you use the term "works." And that was a term that James used, that's a beautiful American word, right? You know, in the thirties, my old man was out of work, I lived in the Depression, so in the line they would say, hey, Mac, did you get work? And when, even in the forties and I was going to school and this and that, they'd say, do you have a job? Did you get work? I'm going to school. I didn't ask you that—did you get work? What does "work" mean? "Work" means, you see, this way, in which possibilities, consequences, I mean hopes, aspirations, expectations that there's some kind of organic way in which the thing works, that's what it means—it's a beautiful word. Yeah, you're right, it's not working.

MM: We have another phrase, too. Which is, you manage to accomplish something together. Whether it's a car motor or it's your life. And it's barely going, but people point that out and you say, what the hell, it works.

JM: Exactly, exactly. And you cobble, see, that's nice, life's a cobblestone.

MM: Yeah.

JM: You say "cobbles," right. You get through it—not smooth, not smooth. It's like the streets in the Bronx, right, they're not smooth. See, but you can get on them. So you're right, now. I mean there's this thing about "enrollment is dropping." People aren't interested in philosophy, you know, nobody is, they just keep going. But I think another thing you see is that we, you know, John Smith, my friend, used to say that ideas die in England and come here to be reborn. And we seem to be having this thing about the intellectual. I mean, we don't seem to see it in this Emersonian, Deweyian way. Do you see? I mean, for example, Whitman opens his *Leaves of Grass* and he says, hey, he says, Mike, would you like to be taking a walk with me, and he said, remember, I don't want you to be seeing what I see. I want you to see what you see.

MM: Yeah.

JM: And that's the famous *Leaves of Grass*, we take this walk. And so, the task of pedagogy is to have you come with me, right? And then, you know, after a while you begin to see what you see. And then you tell me what you see and I say, wow. Well, we've lost a lot of that, you know that?

MM: Sure.

JM: Right. What's the word, what is the word that persons use when they say how do you feel about going to school? Boring. That's the word. You see, there is no eros.

MM: Yes, boring.

JM: Well, the possibilities are extraordinary. For example, take the canon. My position is you keep the canon and you fire it. You just throw it wide open, right? So I mean all the blacks and the women and everybody goes in the canon, you know what I mean, wide open, and so. And I would say . . .

MM: See what works.

JM: Yes, exactly, exactly. And I'm teaching Eugene O'Neill's *Long Day's Journey into Night*. And I'm going around and so on, and this young female student, she puts up her hand and she says, I'll tell you where it is, page whatever it is, you know, sixty-one, I think. When Mary Tyrone says, well she says, it's not his fault. These things happen to you. There's nothing you can do about them, and then you've lost your own true self. She says, that's what happened to me. Okay? Now, for someone else, it's a paragraph in *Go Tell It on the Mountain*, for someone else, it is a paragraph from Carson McCullers. For someone else, you see, it is what Aeschylus says: wisdom comes only through suffering. I mean, I don't know, but you create this theater of possibility. Well, then, why philosophy at all? Well, because, you see, the philosophers have this girth, you know what I mean, you understand? They're not just . . . there's girth here. You see. So you do the *Meditations* and they say this is serious business—you can't do this overnight. There's girth and there's a seriousness. And that takes away, then, you see, the whole "pop" aspect of it. They say, what are you going to do this weekend, Mike? Say, I'm going to read the *Meditations* of Descartes. I say, I'll see you in a month.

MM: Going in the steambath with Descartes.

JM: Okay. All right, see, and that seriousness is important because when mama dies, right? When the little one gets run over, you know what I mean. When they foreclose the house and so on, that's serious.

MM: And serious is important because life's important.

JM: Exactly. Life is serious.

MM: Yeah, it's damn serious, it's deadly serious.

JM: Deadly serious.

MM: So behind the pop side seems to me is a manifestation of the craving for somebody to help give people answers to these things, help me deal with this thing, help me take these terrible problems in my life and deal with it. Cause they're . . . I'm not getting it at school.

JM: Right.

MM: I'm not getting it from the academics. I'm not getting it from the people who are supposed to be giving it to me.

JM: Right.

MM: So, let me ask you then. Take all the craving that's out there—250 million people. Is there still a uniquely American philosophy hidden behind all this that's not being taught? That we're living?

JM: Well, you know, yes, that's a controversial issue. Rorty, I think, is a brilliant guy and he worries about the jingoism of this thing, you see. I don't worry about that because I think all the great cultures have their version of the world, I mean, cultural anthropology is a discipline of the twentieth century. And so everybody does this differently. And then it gets into other questions, as you well know, being Irish. I mean, guilt, they say. You know, relationships and so on. Yeah, I think there's—I wrote this forty years ago—what I call an "American angle of vision."[1] I mean, it's like what we would call on the street a "take"—you got a take on this, John? I got a take on this. What's the take on this? Okay, you ready? The take on this, have you ever thought about why there's no Hegel in American thought? Have you ever thought about why Marx never took? Have you ever thought about why we don't like, you know, hierarchy and Roman Catholics and so on? Right. Because, basically, you see, we're a three-generation people. Margaret Mead said we live in three generations. We are a group of people, you see, for whom the fabric of history is episodic, and it's built in. The genealogy is tight. And that's a very bold, spiritual move. There's no canopy of explanation. We ain't going anyplace else, you see? Now, what's the negative upshot of this? The negative upshot of this is that when we trash somebody, it's all that they have. They're not going to get, you know, worked out some other place, some other time. You see.

MM: Right.

JM: Now Dewey has a marvelous sense of this. This is a very serious calling. This work is very serious. Really? Because these students, my children, you know, my relationship, spousal, whatever they are, and so on, this is it. Okay. So, that's, you see, why you have this extraordinary, intense kind of literature and certain kind of philosophical tradition.

MM: And that's the American take?

JM: That's the American take, the American take. See, no eschatology, no ultimate goals, and so on. And, of course, it's very dangerous because it also means you don't look to the future. I quoted this thing from the Iroquois Confederation this morning, that every time we make a decision, we should think in seven generations. We never think in seven generations, right? We think in how to clean up from the last generation, you see.

MM: Right, right.

JM: But those of us who . . . maybe, we think in two or three generations. I have grandchildren, six grandchildren now.

MM: Yeah, that'll do it to you.

JM: Well, obviously it means I'm going to die soon. It does. It means, I'm coming to the end and so I'm beginning to see this thing now in terms of expectations and losses, and you know, suffering, sadness, joys, and so on and I get this American thing. There's nothing else working, man, this is it, you see? This is it. And I think that at our best, the tradition of literature and philosophy in America—for example, Royce—that nobody reads at all, that's powerful stuff about this business of the community and so on. So the take then is the utter, irreducible, illogical seriousness of these events in our time and of this conversation with you, my friend, right? This is what's going on right now in my life.

MM: That's why we have to get it right, because you ain't going back.

JM: You're not going back, I got to go ahead. And the thing is that there's no wager, no Pascalian wager here. This is really up front, and . . .

MM: That's the wager. Well, you might as well lead a good life just in case there is God.

JM: There's none of that, no. There's none of that in the best of American thought. See, the best of American thought is the secular religious tradition, what I call "secular spirituality." And it's chary of all institutions and hierarchies and bishops and all that stuff. What it has to do with, you see, is the community. It's the old New England bequest of the face-to-face community and it's what we used to do in the schools, it's what we used to do in the university. It's what we used to do in the grocery store, it's what we used to do in a ballpark. It's what we used to do at a local bar. It's what we used to do in a funeral home. You see, it's what we used to do.

MM: You're teaching down at Texas A&M; they do it in Texas a little bit.

JM: They do it in Texas a little bit.

MM: You walk in to a 7-Eleven and get to know somebody behind the counter in thirty seconds.

JM: Well, yes, and I'll tell you this, that those people are totally disenfranchised from the university, completely. I was talking about this this morning. This is a great university, land-grant tradition and so on, so I mean Mr. and Mrs. Texas should not be disenfranchised from the, I mean, there's a lot of yahoo stuff, but I'm talking about deep— see what I mean? We are not open, right? See, I believe every university, every school, should be open twenty-four hours a day, seven days a week, and that people should be able to come and go. All the time. So, if the Wal-Mart's open, the school should be open. To be able to go in there and take Philosophy I at two in the morning, if you're a fireman, whatever you are and so on, two to three in the morning, you go in . . .

MM: 24–7 school.

JM: That's right, twenty-four hours a day, the whole thing you see, and that credentialing should all be functional in terms of all these needs, and they just cut everybody off. The whole thing is quite scandalous; it's sort of like a European high-culture model dropped on a democratic ethos—it doesn't make any sense.

MM: And underneath, underneath it though, like at Texas A&M, it's still that old land-grant model, which it was that, wasn't it?

JM: It was beautiful. Oh yes, it was. Of course, but it's not only that, you see, Morrill, in the Morrill Act, this guy was great, he says, look we're going to have this act. We're going to have this act for the young people in the Plains states, man. And he said we're not going to be narrow like the big shots: Harvard, Yale, and so on. He said, they teach Latin and Greek, but they don't teach the mechanical-agricola arts. He said we are going to teach the mechanical-agricola arts and Latin and Greek as well. And when Texas A&M University opened up in 1876, Latin and Greek were required. You see? He got it. You see what I mean? Now, that's all gone, that's just everybody's nostalgia, man. So the degree has been, has become a $50,000 bill. Do you understand what I mean? You don't carry it or you cannot get it, right? And I see no way to deal with the spiritual crisis in America. Except that every community, as we used to say, every "hitching post," right, is a source, you see, of this thing.

MM: Is it happening? Is it not going on anywhere in America?

JM: No, no, because, I mean, corporate capitalism is not going to let this happen. I mean, you know, Marx was right about this. He was right about this, you know.

MM: What about entrepreneurial capitalism?

JM: Well, they're not going to let it happen either.

MM: Look at those little start-ups and those are like little families.

JM: Yes, but, you see, I see the only way this can happen is, that's why Rorty used that phrase, "Achieving Our Country," which comes at the end of James Baldwin's essay. I mean, it's not my phrase. My phrase, you see, would be the Jewish *teshuvah*, which means "recovery." I mean a recovery of the real meaning of the democratic ethos. And the real meaning of the democratic ethos, to do a paraphrase of Rousseau's famous line: If you are not free, I'm not free, and so on, you see? My understanding of this is, if everyone doesn't have access—I don't mean to the Internet—I mean access your right through the community with sanctions, you understand? With sanctions, but if everyone doesn't have access, then the kind of conversation we're having and the words that we're having and so on, then we're not going to make it.

MM: Let's talk about the Internet, then. Is that a hope?

JM: I don't know, I'm not . . .

MM: It's another way. Another linkage. And it's access. It's access to all of that out there.

JM: Right, but as Dewey says, all, everything, depends on the quality of the experience which has happened. You see, I am not at all impressed. As a matter of fact, I'm distressed by information pile-up.

MM: Yes.

JM: Look, in philosophy, there's just a few questions. One question which is a tough one and nobody knew what to say: Why is there something rather than nothing? One question is, are we in on something which has meaning beyond our ken or are we responsible for the meaning, right? The third one is, you know, what should I do? I mean, Kant had this right. What should I do, what should I know, what can I hope? And so these are the only questions. They're variations on a theme. They're really aesthetic variations. I mean, in a deep sense of that. So the question—I have my version, you have your version. So if we turn toward them, we would have two different versions of really the same thing. Well, basically, you know, the question is, what the hell's going on here, man? You see, it's like when my little ones were growing up and so on, and you know the youngster, she gets acute leukemia, thirteen years old, she goes, hey, dad, what does this mean? Now, what *does* that mean? I mean, what does *all* this mean? I don't *know* what all this means. But then we enter a community, right? You go with the parents and the siblings and talk and that's community. The meaning then, you see, emerges from the situation.

MM: You walk together in the woods.

JM: Yeah, exactly.

MM: Right, and grandpa can show them things, but hopes that they'll see it their own way.

JM: That's right, that's right. But, no one, no one in a democratic politic should be cut off from the best that can be for their lives. In other words, I mean, no one should be walking around not knowing that Hobbes said, it may be, right, that we can't do it without authority. Nobody should be walking around without knowing that Locke says, maybe if we sit down and work out a contract, we could do it, right? Nobody should be walking around not knowing that Dewey said, if you hook your strap on your horse to the ridge there, and what is known in New England as "horse shedding," you see you're face-to-face with someone, you can work some of these things through, and on and on and on. I mean, all of that, to me, should be available to everyone. It should—all, all the way from the beginning.

MM: The questions are simple.

JM: They're very simple. . . .

MM: Then you can teach the questions in first grade.

JM: I could teach Royce's famous third term, which he took from Peirce, and so on—the triad, all that stuff. Here it goes, like this, you're seven or eight years old. Say, what do you think the best way would be to resolve a dispute? Well, you know, bop! Well, you sit down and talk it out. I know what; I got an idea. What's your idea? My idea is that if there were a third person here, so this third person is a person who is an interpreter. Why do we need an interpreter? We all speak the same language. I said, spiritually we don't. Some speak the language of hate, some speak the language of jealousy, some speak the language of insecurity, some speak the language begotten by trauma. This person, this third one, you see, is going to help interpret this, okay. So we're all going to meet here. Well, I could show the passage in Royce, it's very difficult, but that's what it is. And I think you can teach it to a seven year old. And you want to know something else, as you well know, they'll understand it. Of course they will.

MM: Sure they will.

JM: Sure they will. I gave this thing at Bainbridge Island—that's outside of Seattle—a guy teaching philosophy at the high school. So anyway, I get up early at six in the morning and take the ferry over there. I get over there, there are 150 high school students sitting on the floor and I talked to them about the difference between Plato and Aristotle.

Half of them walked me back to the ferry. You know, they wanted to come on the ferry and go back and keep talking. Why? Because I told them, I said, look, there are two big ways to do this. One is maybe there's a secret—Plato. The other way, there ain't no secret—you know, you just look at that stuff and say I want to talk about that, man. They wanted to talk about it. Or another way is, do you move through the world with your hands or with your eyes? Do you move with your feet? Woodbridge said to Dewey, you know, the trouble with you, he said, you're always talking about the hands and not the eyes. And Dewey said, I take that as a compliment, the thing with the hands, right?

MM: Right.

JM: Descartes is the eyes. See the seventeenth-century guys were optic guys. In the nineteenth century, they are hands guys. All that stuff is teachable to everybody, Mike.

MM: What are twentieth-century guys, word guys?

JM: Very deeply constipated, man. Yes, we're chronically constipated, you know. I think it's more and more complicated.

MM: All right, if you can teach this stuff to seven-year-olds, how come when you look at a philosophy library on campus, there are 250 books of symbols and logical languages and all that? Why aren't they out teaching that to the seven-year-olds? Teaching the good stuff to seven-year-olds?

JM: Well, I mean, you know, the philosophy-of-children crowd teach logic and so on, but you know, Buber says how we're educated by children and by animals.

MM: Or grandchildren, in your case.

JM: But, here's something, let's talk about this for a minute. See, I don't believe that directness and simplicity of articulation necessarily betray depth or complexity. I don't believe that. Now, that doesn't mean I'm a wise guy, in other words, I don't think you could take Kant's *Critique of Pure Reason*, you know, and just pass it around. I have as much trouble with that as the next person. But I happen to be the kind of guy who likes to read that, you understand?

MM: Yeah, yeah.

JM: And that's okay. I'm not talking about that, you understand. But, what's behind that, you see, is quite extraordinary. It's in the dissertation of 1770. The only dissertation that's ever been written—the rest of them were all . . . just forget it. There's only one ever been written. It's the dissertation of 1770. And in there, he says, I got to tell you something, Mike. What do you have to tell me, Kant? I have to tell you that space and time are made up. And you say, what? Right. Now some of us can do the deduction of the categories and all that sort of stuff. I'm not asking everybody to do that. But I do want to say this. I do have to say to him, now look, why did Kant say that this had to do with Copernicus? What does Copernicus have to say to us? Well, I say what Copernicus has to say is, things will never be the same. They'll never be the same. We used to think we could get it together. Now we can't get it together—just try that, you see? So I think that, just as there are only three or four or five questions, there are three or four or five very deep things to worry about. You see, deep things to worry about. And my own death is one. The death of those people I love is one, and sadness and brokenness and inequity and, you know, all this stuff.

MM: Yes. How about doing the right thing?

JM: Well, doing the right thing, you know, that's Spike Lee. It's also a line in the AA program, and, by the way, you know where I first found it? It's in Emerson. Yes, it's in Emerson. I'm sure it's in some Chinese philosopher, too, but anyway, it's doing the right thing. What does it mean to "do the right thing"? Well, who knows what the right thing is, you see? And that's where the American stuff is interesting because you'll know pretty soon, because there are consequences.

MM: Well, we've seen the consequences of twentieth-century philosophy. What's the right thing for philosophy to do in the twenty-first?

JM: Well, the right thing for us to do is to not tie being real, real smart with pedagogy. In other words, the right thing, you see, is to begin to develop a pedagogy of pedagogy.

MM: Yes.

JM: It's really remarkable that there is no effort made in the graduate schools to teach people how to teach, not to be smart, you see. I did a seminar at [the State University of New York at] Stony Brook for many years and they would teach and we would just—it's really quite extraordinary—say "wow." But it's not just how to teach in a classroom. I mean, it's how to, I taught in a medical school, you know, I've been teaching in medical school fifteen or sixteen years and a guy once said to me, what do you know?, he said, you don't cut anyone. He was going to be a surgeon or something. I said, I don't? I said, let me tell you something. I can cut. Mike comes to me and he says, McDermott, I'd like to go on to study philosophy and I say to Mike, you don't have it, Mike. I mean, there ain't no surgery equivalent to that.

MM: Yes, the deepest cut of all.

JM: Deepest cut of all. I don't do that, by the way, I'd never do that; God forbid I would do that. But, Michael, that's done all the time. Do you understand? You see, so that being smart is dangerous, you know what I mean? So when you say, what's it to do the right thing? Well, to do the right thing, see, is to re-enter the community.

MM: Well, let me ask one last question. In the time you have left, what's the right thing for you to do for philosophy?

JM: Well, I have to avoid one thing. I must avoid cynicism because all the evidence is there, Mike, right? So I guess what I have to do, you see, is, like old Dewey, just keep going. And you hope that the cry for help, that the passion for inquiry is taken up by others. But I'm not burned out, I'm not giving up. But we're up against tough odds here because the intellectual life has become conflicted, insular, self-centered, arrogant, and suspicious.

MM: We've got to start working with our hands, again.

JM: You bet, you bet.

MM: Thank you.

Finis

In April 1988, I spoke to the Conference of National Health Care Professionals on the topic of "Vulnerability, Dignity or Despair." At the end of my presentation, I told the "Cigar Man Story." More than a year later, I received a letter from a psychiatrist in Baltimore. She wrote of being moved by the story, although she felt that the deeper meaning eluded her at the time. She then recounted a recent experience which brought back the "Cigar Man Story" with both personal force and equivalent clarity. I call this event, on her behalf, the "Napkin Story."

The Napkin Story

Quite regularly our psychiatrist would participate in celebratory occasions for the less fortunate, the egregiously lonesome and the geriatrically disabled. The occasion in question was a birthday party, featuring a luscious and well-appointed chocolate cake, festooned with candles representing many, many decades of life. A good time was had by all. As the psychiatrist was leaving, the women chimed in unison, "Thank you for the cake."

As the door was about to close, still another voice was heard, one that was jagged and struggling. It came from a very aged woman, off to the side, with gnarled limbs and severely crumpled posture, cronish-like. She raised her arthritic finger and said, "Forget the cake, thank you for the napkins."

I offer my hope that these essays have provided my readers with a napkin along the "way."

Notes

CHAPTER ONE
THREADBARE CRAPE
Reflections on the American Strand

This essay was the keynote address at the Interdisciplinary Group for Historical Literary Study Conference, "Fascism's Return: Scandal, Revision, and Ideology Since 1980," Texas A&M University, College Station, Texas, November 10–11, 1995.

1. Thomas Hobbes, *Leviathan* (Indianapolis, Ind.: Library of Liberal Arts, 1958 [1658]), 287–88.

2. G. W. F. Hegel, *The Phenomenology of Mind* (New York: Macmillan, 1931), 564–65.

3. Cf. John J. McDermott, "Ill-at-Ease: The Natural Travail of Ontological Disconnectedness," in *The Proceedings and Addresses of the American Philosophical Association* 67, no. 6 (June 1994): 18–19. See also chapter 12 in the present volume.

4. John J. McDermott, "Transiency and Amelioration: An American Bequest for the New Millennium," in *Streams of Experience: Reflections on the History and Philosophy of American Culture* (Amherst: University of Massachusetts Press, 1986 [1980]), 63.

5. John Dewey, *Art as Experience* (1987), vol. 10 of *The Later Works* (Carbondale: Southern Illinois University Press, 1981–), 19–20.

6. John Dewey, *Human Nature and Conduct* (1983), vol. 14 of *The Middle Works* (Carbondale: Southern Illinois University Press, 1976–83) 227.

7. Cf. John J. McDermott, "America: The Loneliness of the Quest," in *Streams of Experience*, 76–91.

8. Cf. Roger Eatwell, *Fascism: A History* (New York: Viking-Penguin, 1995), and Stanley G. Payne, *A History of Fascism, 1914–1945* (Madison: University of Wisconsin Press, 1995).

CHAPTER TWO
AN AMERICAN ANGLE OF VISION, PART 1

1. This is not to say that the Roman Church has no future. Perhaps it does. But as the burden of this essay will attempt to show, an institution that hopes to participate in future growth, of a qualitative rather than simply quantitative kind, will not only have to come to terms with the irreversible character of modernity but also learn how to live within the demands of contemporary experiences, as soon as they come to the fore.

2. Cf. Sidney E. Mead, "The Rise of the Evangelical Conception of the Ministry in America (1607–1850)," in *The Ministry in Historical Perspectives*, ed. H. Richard Niebuhr and Daniel D. Williams (New York, 1956), 209–10: "Thus, foreshadowing what we have come to regard as something typical of the American mentality when 'all of Europe's logic found itself, arrayed against all of New England's experience' it was the experience that won and became decisive." Mead's reference here is to Perry Miller, *The New England Mind, From Colony to Province* (Boston, 1961), 97. Miller's entire section on the Half-Way Covenant, 93–104, can be read as a statement in miniature on the problem of tradition and experience in American life.

3. This "American style" is an anticipation of much contemporary effort in the behavioral sciences. Cf. Robert K. Merton: "The Mosaic of the Behavioral Sciences," ed. Bernard Berenson (New York, 1964), 250: "As European ideas were transplanted in the American scientific culture, they were often transformed. Characteristically, these ideas were converted into an array of hypotheses requiring systematic investigation rather than remaining intact as final truths. One question has been typically put in each of these instructive ideas: Is it really so? And to answer this question, it was judged necessary to look and see. All this, presumably, is caught up in what is often described as the strongly 'empirical temper' of behavioral science in the United States." Also, for further support of the type of language used in the present essay and for a tighter and more explicit development of the overall methodological approach, cf. Kurt Lewin, *Field Theory in Social Science*, ed. Dorwin Cartwright (New York, 1961), and John Herman Randall Jr., "Substance as a Cooperation of Processes," in *Nature and Historical Experience* (New York, 1958), 143–94.

4. The literature relating to the peculiarities of the American way is voluminous and never-ending. Some of the more recent generalized approaches to this question are: Roger Shinn, ed., *The Search For Identity: Essays on the American Character* (New York, 1964); Roland van Zandt, The *Metaphysical Foundations of American History* (Gravenhage, 1959); Sigmund Skard, *The American Myth and The European Mind* (Philadelphia, 1961); Seymour Martin Lipset, *The First New Nation* (New York, 1963), and an excellent anthology with annotated bibliography, Michael McGiffert, ed., *The Character of Americans* (Homewood, 1964).

5. John Higham, "The Construction of American History," in *The Reconstruction of American History* (London, 1962), 9.

6. Strong support for the affirmation of indigenous institutional formulation, filtered through a pluralistic cast of expression, is found in the history of American religion; see H. Shelton Smith, Robert T. Handy, and Lefferts A. Loetscher, eds., *American Christianity*, 2 vols. (New York, 1960, 1963).

7. The difficulties in such a parallel interpretation are raised but not adequately met in Adrienne Koch, *Power, Morals and the Founding Fathers: Essays in the Interpretation of the American Enlightenment* (Ithaca, 1961), esp. the introduction and concluding chapter, "Toward an American Philosophy." An explicit rejection of such a parallel interpretation is found in Daniel J. Boorstin, "The Myth of an American Enlightenment," in *America and the Image of Europe* (New York, 1960), 65–78. A different and more imposing objection to the use of this parallel interpretation is that the European Enlightenment itself has undergone a radical reinterpretation in our time. In this regard, see the work of Ernest Cassirer, Alfred Cobban, Peter Gay, Lester Crocker, and Henry Vyverberg, which, taken together, points to the conclusion, among others, that the apellation "Age of Reason" was a serious misnomer.

8. In the most specific sense, the European Enlightenment was a philosophical revolution, thereby further differentiating it from the American eighteenth century. Notable here is the remark of D'Alembert, "Our century is called, accordingly, the century of philosophy *par excellence*" ("Essai sur les Elements de Philosophies," in *Œuvres* [Paris, 1805], 2:9). This position is fully supported by Ernst Cassirer, *The Philosophy of the Enlightenment* (Boston, 1951), 3–36.

9. Ralph Waldo Emerson, *Complete Works*, 12 vols. (Boston, 1903), 1:417. This is a note to his remark in "The American Scholar," 1:81, that "our day of dependence, our long apprenticeship to the learning of other lands draws to a close."

10. Even so astute a cultural historian as Perry Miller will use the term "uniqueness"; see his preface to *Errand Into Wilderness* (New York, 1964), ix. Looking back at America from his adventure in the Congo, he tells us that "what I believe caught my imagination, among the fuel drums, was a realization of the uniqueness of the American experience."

11. Herbert W. Schneider, *History of American Philosophy* (New York, 1946; 2nd ed., 1963), vii–viii.

12. Ibid., xiv. This is not a warm endorsement to be sure, but it is a sign of a shift in concern, at least by Schneider's critics.

13. Although his general context is somewhat different, this would seem to be the position of R. W. B. Lewis, *The American Adam—Innocence, Tragedy and Tradition in the Nineteenth Century* (Chicago, 1955), 8–9: "There may be no such thing as 'American experience'; it is probably better not to insist that there

is. But there has been experience in America, and the account of it has had its own specific form. That form has been clearest and most rewarding when it has been dialectical."

14. Emerson, *Works*, 1:3. Lewis, in *American Adam*, contends that "only recently has the old conviction of a new beginning seemed to vanish altogether, and with it the enlivening sense of possibility, of intellectual and artistic elbow-room, of new creations and fresh initiatives" (9).

15. See, for instance, Neil Leonard, *Jazz and the White Americans* (Chicago, 1962).

16. See, for instance, Maurice R. Stein, *The Eclipse of Community—An Interpretation of American Studies* (New York, 1964), esp. "Toward a Theory of American Communities," 94–113.

17. Daniel J. Boorstin, *The Americans, The Colonial Experience* (New York, 1958), 150. Boorstin calls part V of this work "An American Frame of Mind," 147–68. See also Ralph Barton Perry, "An American Cast of Mind," *Characteristically American* (New York, 1949), 3–33.

18. Ibid.

19. Cf. Boorstin, "The Place of Thought in American Life," *America and the Image of Europe*, 44, for a more explicit misunderstanding of the role of philosophy, especially in its European setting. But despite his difficulties with the role of philosophy, Boorstin is a most incisive interpreter of what is meant by "knowing" in the American tradition. Further, his work on the place of thought in American culture has ultimately more philosophical significance than the corresponding effort of the philosopher Ralph Barton Perry.

20. An important effort in this direction, stated in the light of American theology, is that of Daniel D. Williams, "Tradition and Experience in American Theology," in *The Shaping of American Religion*, 4 vols. (Princeton, 1961), 1:443–95.

21. See the preface to John E. Smith, *The Spirit of American Philosophy* (New York. 1963). The richest statement of the American notion of experience is found in Robert C. Pollock, "Process and Experience: Dewey and American Philosophy," *Cross Currents* 9 (Fall 1959): 341–66.

22. The second problem, that of the American philosophical tradition as a locus for examining the American cultural tradition, will be treated in a subsequent essay.

23. See H. Stuart Hughes, "The Historian and the Social Scientist," *American Historical Review* 66 (October 1960): 20–46, for an analysis of the problem of historical generalizations.

24. John Dewey, *Logic, The Theory of Inquiry* (New York, 1938), 236. Strong exception to this position is taken by Burleigh Taylor Wilkins, "Pragmatism

as a Theory of Historical Knowledge: John Dewey on the Nature of Historical Inquiry," *American Historical Review* 64 (July 1959): 884.

25. See Randall, *Nature and Historical Experience*, 63: "A knowledge of the history of things is essential to an understanding of them and, ultimately, of ourselves and our world; yet when we ask *Why* and *How*, we are at once plunged into a thicket of thorny questions."

26. In a popular Columbus Day oration in 1792, Elhanan Winchester focuses on this triple breakthrough but chooses the discovery of printing rather than heliocentrism as the third decisive factor. Printing, although overwhelming in importance, was rather an expansive and continuing type of event and did not sever off the past; see idem, *An Oration on the Discovery of the New World* (London, 1792), 4.

27. For a provocative analysis of the American response to this novelty, see Charles L. Sanford, "The American Cult of Newness: A Rebirth Out of Hell," in *The Quest For Paradise: Europe and the American Moral Imagination* (Urbana, Ill., 1961), 94–113.

28. Edmund O'Gorman, *The Invention of America* (Bloomington, Ind., 1961), 123. We follow O'Gorman in the meaning given to "world" as over against universe: "First and foremost, the World was at that time and is still the cosmic dwelling place of man, his home within the universe, a notion best expressed by the ancient Greek term *oikoumene*" (61). Again an instance of the term lingering on, after the meaning has shifted violently.

29. Samuel Eliot Morison, in a review of O'Gorman's writings on this problem, *History and Theory, II* (New York, 1963), 295.

30. O'Gorman, *Invention of America*, 128–29.

31. These motives are subtly analyzed in the opening chapters of Ola Winslow, *Meetinghouse Hill* (New York, 1952).

32. De Tocqueville, *Democracy in America*, ed. Phillips Bradley, 2 vols. (New York, 1964), 1:301–3. See also Loren Baritz, "The Idea of the West," *American Historical Review* 66 (April 1963): 618–40, for a detailed history of the notion of "going West," with its culmination in the American situation, and also Henry Nash Smith, *Virgin Land* (New York, 1957). The question, of course, is not one simply of geography. See, too, David Donald in his preface to Clarence L. Ver Steeg, *The Formative Years: 1607–1763* (New York, 1964), vi, where he speaks of Ver Steeg having "carefully avoided the crude environmentalism that has characterized too much writing on the colonial era." Recognizing the "invaluable legacy" the colonists brought from Europe, he shows how cultural conditioning, not mere geography, caused the pattern of New England settlement to differ from that in Virginia. At the same time, in analyzing how abundant land, expanding trade, and immigration modified the European heritage, he persuasively argues that Frederick Jackson Turner's frontier hypothesis, now so often

controverted by historians, is valid when applied to the settlement of the Old West.

33. In his farewell sermon to John Winthrop's company, then leaving for the New World, John Cotton took as his text 2 Samuel 7:10: "Moreover I will appoint a place for my people Israel, and I will plant them, that they may dwell in a place of their owne, and move no more" (John Cotton, "God's Promise to His Plantation" [London, 1630], *Old South Leaflets*, no. 3).

34. Cf. the remark of Thoreau, "Eastward I go only by force; but westward I go free" ("Walking," in *Excursions* [New York, 1962 (1863)], 176).

35. So that John Cotton, once in the New World, can say in "A Reply" to Roger Williams that "the jurisdiction (whence a man is banished) is but small, and the Countrey round about it, large and fruitful: where a man may make his choice of variety of more pleasant, and profitable seats, than he leaveth behinde him. In which respect, Banishment in this countrye, is not counted so much a confinement, as an enlargement" (cited in Sidney E. Mead, "The American People: Their Space, Time and Religion," in *The Lively Experiment* [New York, 1963], 13).

36. So Boorstin will say of colonial Americans that "they lacked the leisure; they were far from ancient libraries and centers of learning, and their New World beckoned with many varieties of unthought-of phaenomena. In Europe, discovering something new in the natural world required the concentration of a philosopher, the researches of a scholar, or the industry of an encyclopedist. In America it took effort to avoid novelty" (Boorstin, *The Americans*, 168).

37. Karl Jaspers, *Man in the Modern Age* (New York, 1957), 4–15.

38. J. H. Parry, *The Age of Reconnaissance* (London, 1963).

39. Relative to the English experience of this period, see the careful countervailing effort of Allan French, *Charles the First and the Puritan Upheaval* (London, 1955), and also Wallace Notestein, *The English People on the Eve of Colonization 1603–1630* (New York, 1954).

40. Winslow, *Meetinghouse Hill*, 315. Mark Twain draws out the full legend imbedded in the American view toward novelty when he tells us that "the world and books are so accustomed to use, and over-use, the word 'new' in connection with our country, that we early get and permanently retain the impression that there is nothing old about it" (Twain, *The Family Mark Twain* [New York, 1935], 7).

41. Cf. Miller, *Errand*, ix. Seeking the beginning of American thought, he tells us that it was "inevitably—being located in the seventeenth century—theological." And again, "the first articulate body of expression upon which I could get a leverage happened to be a body of Protestant doctrine" (ibid.).

42. Protestantism as the "marrow" of early American culture is given convincing and incisive support by the work of Smith, Handy, and Loetscher, *American Christianity*.

43. Miller, *Errand*, ix.

44. On this matter, see Winthrop Hudson, *American Protestantism* (Chicago, 1961), 1–48, and Shelton Smith, Handy, and Loetscher, *American Christianity*, vol. 1.

45. Although he tends to handle the religious question in an inadequate way, Sumner Chilton Powell gives us an excellent portrayal of the social and economic dialectic that exists between the European deposit and the Puritan experience in the New World; cf. Powell, *Puritan Village—The Formation of a New England Town* (Middletown, 1963). Cf. also French, *Charles the First and the Puritan Upheaval*, 323–418.

46. Cf. Wilkins, "Pragmatism as a Theory of Historical Knowledge," 888–89, for judicious support of this view: "While William James may have been correct in saying that the relationships among the items of experience are as real as the items in themselves, the relationships remain infinitely harder to recover; and it is this task that should tantalize the historian, even to such an extent that his imagination and sympathy might cautiously take up where the documents leave off. We hasten to add, however, that imagination and sympathy do not give us license to build prefabricated houses upon any historical lot we may choose."

47. Paul Tillich, *The Religious Situation* (New York, 1956), 192. And even with its existentialist language, Tillich's *Courage To Be* (New Haven, 1952) can be read as a tract in the tradition of classic American Protestantism, with its emphasis on "awakening" and reconstitution of the self.

48. The historical framework for this tension is sketched, although inadequately analyzed, by Merle Curti, *American Paradox: The Conflict of Thought and Action* (New Brunswick, N.J., 1956).

49. Even those sympathetic to American religious thought have difficulty with this affirmation of novelty within the very tradition of revelation. Daniel Williams, for example, in his excellent article on "Tradition and Experience," 492 (see n. 20) cites the prophetic text of Edgar Quinet from the "Revue des Deux Mondes" of 1831: "A new idea of God will surge from the Lakes of Florida and the peaks of the Andes; in America will begin a new religious era, and will be born a new idea of God." Williams holds, however, that this may be "dubious prophecy from a Christian point of view, which holds that God, the Logos of all things, has already decisively disclosed Himself." But this, in turn, is dubious orthodoxy, for at least one strand of classical Christianity holds to the historicity of the Logos. Isn't the problem one of having a doctrine of experience and novelty without being willing to face up to the dimension of process and growth in the Revelation itself? To hold that the Logos has appeared once and for all is to confuse Christian thought with the Unmoved Mover of Aristotle. A theology which reflects the American tradition should have no such problem.

50. Cf. Hudson, *American Protestantism*, and H. Richard Niebuhr, *The Social Sources of Denominationalism* (New York, 1957). See also the horrified response to this denominational shifting by the Jesuit Giovanni Grassi in his nineteenth-century travels through America in "The Jesuit Scholar," in *This Was America*, ed. Oscar Handlin (New York, 1964), 147–50.

51. See the writings of Martin Marty, particularly *The Infidel—Freethought and American Religion* (Cleveland, 1961).

52. See John Herman Randall Jr., *Aristotle* (New York, 1960).

53. Mircea Eliade, *Cosmos and History—The Myth of the Eternal Return* (New York, 1959).

54. Sanford, "The Renaissance Standard of Nature," in *Quest for Paradise*, for an analysis of this new view of nature.

55. O'Gorman, *Invention of America*, 129–30.

56. We use the term "Copernicanism" advisedly. The specific place of Copernicus in this matter shall not occupy us at this point. Actually, a great cluster of figures—Kepler, Bruno, Galileo, Nicholas Cusanus, and Thomas Digges, among others—all play important roles. The publication of the *De Revolutionibus Orbium Caelestium* by Copernicus in 1643 remains, however, the seminal work in this revolution, although it is soon rendered technically obsolete; see Alexandre Koyré, *From the Closed World to the Infinite Universe* (New York, 1958), and Edward Rosen, ed., "Annotated Copernicus Bibliography, 1939–1958," in *Three Copernican Treatises* (New York, 1959), 199–269.

57. See Thomas S. Kuhn, *The Copernican Revolution* (New York, 1959), 186: "From the start the *Revolutionibus* was widely read, but it was read in spite of, rather than because of, its strange cosmological hypothesis."

58. See John Herman Randall Jr., *The Career of Philosophy* (New York, 1963), wherein he cites a text from Galileo: "As to the earth, we seek to make it more noble and perfect, since we succeed in making it like the heavenly bodies, and in a certain fashion place it almost in heaven, whence your Philosophers have banished it." Randall then adds that "this was the real religious issue involved in the Copernican revolution, so soon as Galileo made it clear that it was no mere shift in mathematical hypotheses. The earth, and man, and the practical science of his environment and daily living, are as important as the contemplation of heavenly things, as theology" (ibid.).

59. John Donne, "An Anatomie of the World," in *The Complete Poetry and Selected Prose of John Donne* (New York, 1952), 191.

60. Randall, *Career of Philosophy*, 309–10.

61. See Kuhn, *Copernican Revolution*, 195–96; Randall, *Career of Philosophy*, 309; and George Sarton, *Six Wings—Men of Science in the Renaissance* (Bloomington, Ind., 1957), 61–62.

62. See David Hume, *Dialogues Concerning Natural Religion* (New York, 1948).

63. G. W. F. Hegel, *The Phenomenology of Mind* (New York, 1955), 560. The section "Spirit in self-estrangement; the discipline of culture and civilization" is a brilliant analysis of the human difficulties to be faced when a culture challenges what had been, up to that time, its fundamental way of formulating itself. Such, I would contend, is the import of our increasing realization of the Copernican revolution.

64. No doubt many of these "meanings made" were pegs below the value-level of European civilization, but it is a shift in the nature of inquiry and in the locus for determining meaning that concerns us here; see Arthur K. Moore, *The Frontier Mind* (New York, 1957).

65. Smith, *The Spirit of American Philosophy*, viii.

66. Boorstin, "Place of Thought in American Life," 43–61.

67. See Jagjit Singh, *Great Ideas and Theories of Modern Cosmology* (New York, 1962), 3, wherein, speaking of cosmology, he states that it "is the one branch of knowledge where our deepest plumbing will fail to reach bottom for a long time to come, perhaps forever."

68. Immanuel Kant, *Critique of Pure Reason* (New York, 1953), 22. Of course, for some, this revolution is simply a shift in philosophical method and does not involve a reconstituting of the physical universe; cf. Jules Vuillemin, *L'Heritage Kantien et la Revolution Copernicienne* (Paris, 1954).

69. This ascendant version of modern science is articulated in basic terms by Werner Heisenberg, *Physics and Philosophy* (New York, 1958). The introduction, 1–26, is an acute statement of the philosophical revolution engendered by modern science, giving empirical structure to the historical beginnings sketched above. Opposition to this, and to the entire import of Copernicanism as herein discussed, is found in David Bohm, *Causality and Chance in Modern Physics* (New York, 1957).

70. William James, "Notebook," cited in Ralph Barton Perry, *The Thought and Character of William James*, 2 vols. (Boston, 1935), 2:700.

71. The sociological dimensions to this philosophical attitude are cogently summarized by the English historian Frank Thistlethwaite, *The Great Experiment* (Cambridge, 1961), 319–20: "In the mid-twentieth century the American people still pursue their Revolutionary ideal: A Republic established in the belief that men of good will could voluntarily come together in the sanctuary of an American wilderness to order their common affairs according to rational principles; a dedicated association in which men participate not by virtue of being born into it as heirs of immemorial custom, but by virtue of free choice, of the will to affirm certain sacred principles; a gathered community of Protestants, 'separatists,' nonconformists, from whom the individual conscience alone is

sovereign; a community of the uprooted, of migrants who have turned their backs on the past in which they were born, who have thrown off the disciplines of traditional authority, for whom continuing institutions command only tentative allegiance and have only an attenuated personality; a caravan on the move; squatters sojourning in a mansion where all the cluttering furniture of the past has been banished to the attic; a commonwealth where authority, reduced to a minimum, is hedged about with safeguards and government serves the limited purpose of a framework within which individuals find their levels in voluntary and ever-shifting groups and minorities preserve their identity in a plural order; a society fluid and experimental, uncommitted to rigid values, cherishing freedom of will and choice and bestowing all the promise of the future on those with the manhood to reject the past."

72. Cited on the frontispiece of Thistlethwaite, *The Great Experiment*.

73. See Gilbert Chinard, *L'Amerique et le Rève Exotique* (Paris, 1934). The French disappointment in eighteenth-century America is graphically stated by W. Stark, *America: Ideal and Reality, The United States of 1776 in Contemporary European Philosophy* (London, 1947).

74. Of course, not all commentators are as sanguine about America. One thinks immediately about the brilliant and bitter critique of the American approach to experience, as found in Melville's *The Confidence Man*. In a recent commentary on Melville, Lorenz Baritz concludes with the statement: "With civilization in America came the ultimate tragedy: the eternal passing of the Typee valley from mankind's sober hope. America now took her place among the nations as a land like any other. Americans now were merely men. The land had come of age, and age was time and tragedy and the end" (Baritz, *City on a Hill—A History of Ideas and Myths in America* [New York, 1964], 831).

75. George Santayana, "The Genteel Tradition in American Philosophy," in *Winds of Doctrine* (New York, 1957), 186–87. We would not, of course, support the imagery of "old wine in new bottles."

76. Speaking of the American, Henry Bamford Parkes states that "his character was molded not by the complex moral and social obligations of an ordered hierarchical system, but by the struggle to achieve victory over nature" (Parkes, *The American Experience* [New York, 1961], 9).

77. These problems will be given further analysis in a sequel to this essay; see chapter 3 of the present volume.

CHAPTER THREE

AN AMERICAN ANGLE OF VISION, PART 2

1. America will not have forever to articulate her specific "angle of vision"; cf. James Bryce, *The American Commonwealth*, ed. Louis Hacker (New York,

1959 [1888]), 1:1. In 1888, Bryce wrote about American institutions as follows: "They represent an experiment in the rule of the multitude, tried on a scale unprecedently vast, and the results of which everyone is concerned to watch. And yet they are something more than an experiment, for they are believed to disclose and display the type of institutions towards which, as by a law of fate, the rest of civilized mankind are forced to move, some with swifter, others with slower, but all with unresting feet." The scene has shifted drastically, and this is no longer so, for there are again several options extant as to structuring basic political and social institutions, and in many areas the American version is out of favor. No small reason for this is the often inept and unfeeling way in which America has expressed the qualities of her own tradition.

2. "The American Angle of Vision—I: Historical Dimensions," *Cross Currents* 15 (Winter 1965): 69–93; see also chapter 2 in the present volume.

3. Ralph Waldo Emerson, "Introduction," *Works* (Boston, 1903), 1:3.

4. Sidney E. Mead, "The American People: Their Space, Time and Religion," in *The Lively Experiment* (New York, 1963).

5. Ibid., 7–8; emphasis added.

6. The statement of Rathenau is taken from Andre Gide, *Imaginary Interviews*, as cited by Harry Levin, "Some European Views of Contemporary American Literature," in *The American Writer and the European Tradition*, ed. Margaret Denny and William H. Gilman (New York, 1964 [1950]), 180.

7. Daniel J. Boorstin, *The Genius of American Politics* (Chicago, 1953), 183–84.

8. John A. Kouwenhoven, *Made in America: The Arts in Modern Civilization* (New York, 1962 [1948]).

9. John W. Ward, "The Meaning of Lindbergh's Flight," *Studies in American Culture—Dominant Ideas and Images*, ed. Joseph J. Kwiat and Mary C. Turpie (Minneapolis, 1960), 39.

10. Daniel Boorstin, *The Image—A Guide to Pseudo-Events in America* (New York, 1964), 245–46.

11. The absence of an ancient tradition is itself often seen as a mixed blessing. On the one hand, Rilke can speak of the "ever swifter vanishing of so much that is visible, whose place will not be supplied. Even for our grandparents a 'House', a 'Well', a familiar tower, their very dress, their cloak, was infinitely more, infinitely more intimate: almost everything a vessel in which they found and stored humanity. Now there come crowding over from America empty, indifferent things, pseudo-things, DUMMY-LIFE. . . . A house, in the American understanding, an American apple or vine, has NOTHING in common with the house, the fruit, the grape into which the hope and meditation of our forefathers had entered. . . . The animated, experienced things that SHARE OUR LIVES are coming to an end and cannot be replaced. WE ARE PERHAPS THE LAST

TO HAVE STILL KNOWN SUCH THINGS" ("Appendix 4," *Duino Elegies*, trans. J. B. Leishman and Stephen Spender [New York, 1939], 129). But D. W. Brogan, *American Aspects* (New York, 1964) states that "it was because the American wasn't so burdened with the past, had no such *damnosa hereditas* to live down or live with that Goethe declared: *"Amerika du has es besser"* (155).

12. Herman Melville, *The Confidence Man* (New York, 1949 [1847]). Among countless instances, cf. 64–65: "Now tell me, sir," said he with the book, "how comes it that a young gentleman like you, a sedate student at the first appearance, should dabble in stocks and that sort of thing?"

"There are certain sophomorean errors in the world," drawled the sophomore, deliberately adjusting his shirt-collar, "not the least of which is the popular notion touching the nature of the modern scholar, and the nature of the modern scholastic sedateness."

"So it seems, so it seems. Really, this is quite a new leaf in my experience."

"Experience, sir," originally observed the sophomore, "is the only teacher."

"Hence am I your pupil: for it's only when experience speaks that I can endure to listen to speculation."

"My speculations, sir," dryly drawing himself up, "have been chiefly governed by the maxim of Lord Bacon; I speculate in those philosophies which come home to my business and bosom—pray, do you know of any other good stocks?"

13. George Santayana, "The Genteel Tradition in American Philosophy," in *Winds of Doctrine* (New York, 1957 [1913]), 186.

14. John Dewey, *The School and Society* (Chicago, 1943), 154–55.

15. William Bradford, *Of Plymouth Plantation*, ed. Harvey Wish (New York, 1962), 60.

16. Boorstin, *Genius of American Politics*, 161.

17. Charles L. Sanford, *The Quest for Paradise—Europe and the American Moral Imagination* (Urbana, Ill., 1961), 107.

18. Cited in Richard C. Brown, ed., *The Human Side of American History* (New York, 1962), 76.

19. Sanford, "The American Cult of Newness," in *Quest for Paradise*, 97.

20. Perry Miller, *Errand Into the Wilderness* (New York, 1964), 15.

21. Cited in Frederick Jackson Turner, "The Significance of the Frontier in American History," *Frontier and Section* (New York, 1961), 57.

22. Henry Nash Smith, *Virgin Land* (New York, 1957), 54–63.

23. Arthur K. Moore, *The Frontier Mind* (New York, 1963), 3.

24. An excellent example of such a clustering of self-awareness is found in Charles Sanford, ed., *Quest for America 1810–1824* (New York, 1964), part I, "The Character of American Experience," and esp. 25–114, "The Structure of Experience."

25. A similar transformation was effected in American economic theory of the nineteenth century. The basic theme at that time was the American environmental experience over against the *homo œconomicus* of the reigning Classical school. Cf., for example, Ernest Teilhac, *Pioneers of American Economic Thought in the Nineteenth Century* (New York, 1936).

26. Lewis Mumford, *The Brown Decades—A Study of the Arts in America, 1865–1895* (New York, 1955 [1939]), 59.

27. For a working bibliography, cf. Daniel J. Boorstin, *The Americans* (New York, 1958), 394–96.

28. Sanford, *The Quest for Paradise*, vi. An important and different way of stating the Edenic myth is found in George H. Williams, *Wilderness and Paradise in Christian Thought* (New York, 1962), esp. part IV, "The Enclosed Garden in the Wilderness of the New World," 98–131, and part V, "Conclusion: Wasteland and Wilderness," 132–37.

29. Sanford's work is a partial exception to this, for he tries to "make clear the view that the paradisiac impulse and metaphor does not depend solely upon nature as its setting, but has been broadly associated with a rich abundance of inward and outward life in contrast to the fancied poverty of existing conditions" (Sanford, *The Quest for Paradise*, vii). But the framework of the Edenic myth is so eschatological in emphasis, that the full import of the American approach to time consequently is underplayed.

30. Mead, *American People*, 5.

31. William James, "The Relation Between Knower and Known," in *The Meaning of Truth* (New York, 1932 [1909]), 111.

32. Paul Tillich, "The Struggle Between Time and Space," in *Theology of Culture* (New York, 1964), 30.

33. Ibid., 31.

34. Paul Tillich, "Autobiographical Reflections," in *The Theology of Paul Tillich*, ed. Charles W. Kegley and Robert W. Bretall (New York, 1961), 60.

35. Cited in Arthur A. Ekirch Jr., *Man and Nature in America* (New York, 1963), 85. There is an intriguing parallel to this attitude as found in a later approach of the Soviet Union; cf. Albert E. Burke, "Influence of Man Upon Nature—The Russian View: A Case Study," in *Man's Role in Changing the Face of the Earth*, ed. William L. Thomas Jr. (Chicago, 1956), 1048. Burke cites a 1929 textbook written for children of the Soviet Union. "We must discover and conquer the country in which we live. It is a tremendous country, but not yet entirely ours. Our steppe will truly become ours only when we come with columns of tractors and plows to break the thousand-year-old virgin soil. On a far-flung front we must wage war. We must burrow into the earth, break rocks, dig mines, construct houses. . . ." And again, the remark of a Russian plant scientist that "we can expect no favors from Nature: our job is to take them."

Ideology aside, there is still an inadequately analyzed parallel between the relationship of frontier and technology as operative in both societies. The difference seems to be located in the articulated symbolism of the meaning of frontier for American life in all its endeavors.

36. John M. Anderson, *The Individual and the New World* (State College, Pa., 1955), 10.

37. Ibid., 181 n. 41.

38. Sanford, *The Quest for Paradise*, 112–13.

39. Anderson, *Individual and the New World*, 89.

40. Winthrop Hudson, *American Protestantism* (Chicago, 1961), 126.

41. The primitive strain in the American view of time and nature is particularly fascinating because it is structured outside of the "primitive" and prehistorical doctrine of nature as cyclic; cf. Mircea Eliade, *Cosmos and History—The Myth of the Eternal Return* (New York, 1959), esp. 1–92.

42. Cf. Tillich, "Struggle," 34, where, speaking of Greek culture, he claims that "they have no dynamic trend to go beyond it. They are in space, fulfilling it with divine force, bound to their space, expressing the tragic limitation of it. Greek reason never was able to overcome this limitation. Even the logic of Aristotle is a spatial logic, unable to express the dynamic trend of time. There is no philosophy of history in Greek thought, and where history is dealt with it is considered as only a section of the long circular motion of the whole cosmos from birth to death, of one world replacing the other. Time is swallowed by space in this cosmological tragedy."

43. The necessarily anthropomorphic character of all views about man's place in the world is argued by Martin Versfeld, "Reflections on Evolutionary Knowledge," *International Philosophical Quarterly* 5 (May 1965): 221–47.

44. Paul Tillich, "The Conquest of Intellectual Provincialism: Europe and America," in *Theology of Culture*, 176.

45. Nature and time have been much less adequately treated from the philosophical side in American thought. An exception is the classic work of John Dewey, *Experience and Nature* (New York, 1952 [1929]). Actually, all three themes are analyzed in a series of essays by John Herman Randall Jr., *Nature and Historical Experience* (New York, 1958).

46. Robert O. Johann, "The Return to Experience," *Review of Metaphysics* 17 (March 1964).

47. Ibid., 329.

48. Each commentator attempts this from a different angle, that of Johann being the potentially fruitful one of a metaphysical personalism. Another recent attempt, from the side of the behavioral sciences, is that of B. A. Farrell, "Experience," in *The Philosophy of Mind*, ed. V. C. Chappell (New York, 1962), 23–48.

49. William James, *Essays in Radical Empiricism* (New York, 1947 [1912]), 10. Johann, "Return," 324, arrives at a similar position.

50. John Dewey, *Experience and Nature*, 2nd ed. (New York, 1958 [1929]), 8.

51. Johann, "Return," 329.

52. Cf. Seymour Martin Lipset, "American Intellectuals: Their Politics and Status," in *Political Man* (New York, 1963), 332–71. Lipset, correctly I believe, argues that the anti-intellectualism found in American life does not result in low status for intellectuals.

53. Richard Hofstadter, *Anti-Intellectualism in American Life* (New York, 1968), 49–50.

54 Gulian C. Verplanck, "The Advantages and Dangers of the American Scholar," in *American Philosophic Addresses, 1700–1900*, ed. Joseph L. Blau (New York, 1946), 126–27.

55. John Dewey, "The Need For a Recovery of Philosophy," in *On Experience, Nature, and Freedom*, ed. Richard J. Bernstein (New York, 1960), 66–67.

56. William James, *The Varieties of Religious Experience* (New York, 1902), 489.

57. James, *Letters*, 2:270.

58. Ibid., 260.

59. Dewey, *Experience and Nature*, 38.

60. Cf. John Dewey, *Philosophy and Civilization* (New York, 1963 [1931]) and idem, *Logic: The Theory of Inquiry* (New York, 1938).

61. In an earlier series of essays, Dewey had argued in great detail that "knowledge" is a narrow category and falls short of revealing the manifold ways in which experience teaches; cf. *The Influence of Darwin and Other Essays in Contemporary Thought* (New York, 1951 [1910]), esp. "The Experimental Theory of Knowledge," 77–111; "Experience and Objective Idealism," 198–225; and "The Postulate of Immediate Empiricism," 226–41, which are particularly relevant.

62. These texts are found in Dewey, "The Need For a Recovery of Philosophy," 23. Dewey takes an historical point of view on this issue in "An Empirical Survey of Empiricisms," in *On Experience, Nature and Freedom*, 70–87.

63. An unassimilated but fascinating account of the sociological dimensions in American classical philosophy is to be found in C. Wright Mills, *Sociology and Pragmatism*, ed. Irving Louis Horowitz (New York, 1964).

64. Alan Pasch, *Experience and the Analytic—A Reconsideration of Empiricism* (Chicago, 1958), 5.

65. One of the few treatments of this setting is found in George H. Mead, "The Philosophies of Royce, James and Dewey in Their American Setting," in *Selected Writings*, ed. Andrew J. Reck (New York, 1964), 371–91.

66. John Herman Randall Jr., *How Philosophy Uses Its Past* (New York, 1963), 88. For an earlier and more general assessment, see idem, "Spirit of American Philosophy," in *Wellsprings of the American Spirit* (New York, 1948), 133. In speaking of the contribution of American thought, he comments that "it adds a new level to the long tradition of Western philosophical thought because it brings the lessons learned from American experience to all the lessons men had learned before and left for us in the embodied philosophical wisdom of the past."

67. Tillich, "Conquest of Intellectual Provincialism," 164; emphasis added.

68. Ralph Waldo Emerson, "Compensation," in *Works* (Boston, 1903), 2:95.

69. Cited in Edmund Fuller, *Tinkers and Genius—The Story of the Yankee Inventors* (New York, 1955), 34.

70. The persistent biblicism of American life has been insufficiently treated or else viewed in narrow doctrinal terms. A good introductory statement is found in Joseph Gaer and Ben Siegel, *The Puritan Heritage—America's Roots in the Bible* (New York, 1964); cf. also Williams, *Wilderness and Paradise*.

71. The complex symbolism that accompanies America's attempt to retain the biblical metaphor but yet avoid the literalism and religious orthodoxy that accompany such a tradition is of central importance to the development of American thought, at all levels. It is unfortunate that the important work of Robert Pollock in this critical area remains largely unpublished; see his "Ralph Waldo Emerson—The Single Vision," in *American Classics Reconsidered*, ed. Harold Gardiner (New York, 1958), 15–58.

72. Henry Thoreau, "Our Country," in *Collected Poems*, ed. Carl Bode (Baltimore, 1964), 135, lines 43–45.

73. Robert Frost, "The Gift Outright," in *Major American Poets*, ed. Oscar Williams and Edwin Honig (New York, 1962), 241.

74. Daniel Boorstin, "The Place of Thought in American Life," in *America and the Image of Europe* (New York, 1960), 58–59. See also Tillich, "Conquest of Intellectual Provincialism," 164, for a similar judgment about the distinctive American approach to theory and practice.

75. Robert C. Pollock, "James: Pragmatism," in *The Great Books*, ed. Harold Gardiner (New York, 1953), 191.

76. Dewey, "Need For a Recovery of Philosophy," 68.

77. Education as a discipline offers an instructive illustration. To the extent that it remains tied to its own categories, aridity and pretense dominate. To the extent that it opens itself up to the language and concerns of the wider culture, as, for example, technology or the sociology of the school, the discipline is revivified; cf. Ronald Gross and Judith Murphy, eds., *The Revolution in the Schools* (New York, 1964).

78. William James, *Pragmatism* (New York, 1947 [1907]), 222, and idem, *A Pluralistic Universe* (New York, 1947 [1909]), 212: "Reality, life, experience, concreteness, immediacy, use what word you will, exceeds our logic, overflows and surrounds it."

79. Cf. James Feibleman, *An Introduction to Peirce's Philosophy* (New York, 1946), 200, where, in a paraphrase of Peirce, he states that "experience contains an element which is forceful and unavoidable, and yet requires an act of attention to appreciate fully."

80. Charles Sanders Peirce, *Collected Papers*, ed. Charles Hartshorne and Paul Weiss (Cambridge, 1934), 5:37, §§ 50–51.

CHAPTER FOUR

SPIRES OF INFLUENCE

The Importance of Emerson for Classical American Philosophy

1. *American Philosophic Addresses, 1700–1900*, ed. Joseph L. Blau (New York: Columbia University Press, 1946); *Men and Movements in American Philosophy* (Englewood Cliffs, N.J.: Prentice-Hall, 1952); "Emerson's Transcendentalist Individualism as a Social Philosophy," *Review of Metaphysics* 31, no. 1 (September 1977): 80–92.

2. Robert C. Pollock, "Ralph Waldo Emerson—The Single Vision," in *American Classics Reconsidered*, ed. Harold Gardiner (New York: Scribner's, 1958), 15–58.

3. George Herbert Mead tends to speak of Emerson only in the context of Concord transcendentalism. Ironically, in lamenting the failure of the transcendentalists to develop a distinctive doctrine of American self-consciousness, Mead overlooks the powerful voice of Emerson in precisely that regard; Mead, "The Philosophies of Royce, James and Dewey in Their American Setting," in *Selected Writings*, ed. Andrew J. Reek (Indianapolis, Ind.: Bobbs-Merrill, 1964), 377–78.

4. Charles Sanders Peirce, *Collected Papers of Charles Sanders Peirce*, ed. Charles Hartshorne and Paul Weiss (Cambridge, Mass.: Harvard University Press, 1934), 6:86–87 (§102). Peirce also was fond of quoting and mocking Emerson's poem on the Sphinx, especially the line, "Of thine eye, I am eyebeam" (ibid., 1:153–54 [§310], and 3:252 [§404]). Some unpublished material on Peirce's "boyhood impressions" of Emerson can be found in "Manuscript—296," as recorded in the *Annotated Catalogue of the Papers of Charles S. Peirce*, ed. Richard Robin (Amherst: University of Massachusetts Press, 1967), 31.

5. Ralph Waldo Emerson, "The American Scholar," in *The Complete Works of Ralph Waldo Emerson* (Boston: Houghton Mifflin, 1903–4), 1:86.

6. Emerson, "Nature," in ibid., 1:3.

7. Emerson, "The Divinity School Address," in ibid., 1:135.

8. Ibid., 1:151.

9. Emerson, "American Scholar," 1:95. The use of "he" and "man" in this text and in subsequent texts is to be read in the present essay as referring also to "she" and "woman."

10. Ibid., 1:99.

11. Emerson, "Fate," in ibid., 6:3. For a similar attitude, see William James, *The Varieties of Religious Experience* (New York: Longmans, Green, and Co., 1902), 489: "Knowledge about life is one thing; effective occupation of a place in life, with its dynamic currents passing through your being, is another."

12. Texts in support of this position abound in the writings of John Dewey. Among others are Dewey, *Reconstruction in Philosophy* (1982), vol. 12 of *The Middle Works* (Carbondale: Southern Illinois University Press, 1976–83), 132: "Experience carries principles of connection and organization within itself." And: "What Shakespeare so pregnantly said of nature, it is 'made better by no mean, but nature makes that mean,' becomes true of experience" (ibid., 134).

13. For an historical and philosophical treatment of the genesis of James's doctrine of radical empiricism, see John J. McDermott, introduction to William James, *Essays in Radical Empiricism* (Cambridge, Mass.: Harvard University Press, 1976), xi–xlviii. Dewey's doctrine of radical empiricism is best found in Dewey, *The Influence of Darwinism on Philosophy and Other Essays in Contemporary Philosophy* (New York: Henry Holt, 1910).

14. Emerson, "American Scholar," 1:111. For a richer description of the extreme variety of audience responses to Emerson's oration of 1837, see Bliss Perry, "Emerson's Most Famous Speech," in *Ralph Waldo Emerson—A Profile*, ed. Carl Bode (New York: Hill and Wang, 1969), 52–65. Oliver Wendell Holmes heard the oration as an "intellectual Declaration of Independence" and James Russell Lowell viewed it as "our Yankee version of a lecture by Abelard, our Harvard parallel to the last public appearances of Schelling" (ibid.)

15. Emerson, "American Scholar," 1:111.

16. Emerson, "Experience," in *Works*, 6:308n1: "Everything in the Universe goes by indirection. There are no straight lines."

17. Ibid., 6:68. William James holds a similar position; see his "Notebook" entry of 1903, in Ralph Barton Perry, *The Thought and Character of William James* (Boston: Little, Brown and Co., 1935), 2:700.

18. Ralph Waldo Emerson, *The Journals of Ralph Waldo Emerson* (Boston: Houghton Mifflin, 1909–14) 9:277–78.

19. Emerson, "Nature," 1:34.

20. Emerson, "Education," in *Works*, 10:132.

21. Emerson, "The Poet," in *Works*, 3:118.

22. Emerson, "Nature," 1:32.

23. Peirce, *Collected Papers*, 5:37.

24. John Dewey, *Experience and Nature* (1981), vol. 1 of *The Later Works* (Carbondale: Southern Illinois University Press, 1981–), 43.

25. Emerson, "Nature," 1:31.

26. Josiah Royce, *The Letters of Josiah Royce*, ed. John Clendenning (Chicago: University of Chicago Press, 1970), 586.

27. Josiah Royce, *The Problem of Christianity* (Chicago: University of Chicago Press, 1968 [1913]), 294.

28. William James, *Pragmatism* (Cambridge, Mass.: Harvard University Press, 1975), 9.

29. Ibid., 99.

30. Ibid., 123.

31. William James Papers, Houghton Library, Harvard University (bMs AM 1092, box L, notebook N²).

32. James, *Essays in Radical Empiricism*, 42.

33. Cited in Gay Wilson Allen, *William James—A Biography* (New York: Viking, 1967), 186–87.

34. Emerson, "American Scholar," 1:89–90.

35. William James, "Address at the Emerson Centenary in Concord" (1903), in *Essays in Religion and Morality* (Cambridge, Mass.: Harvard University Press, 1982), 109–15. For a contrast of James's hagiographic approach to others more critical and substantive, the reader should consult two collections of essays: *Emerson*, ed. Milton Konvitz and Stephen Whicher (Englewood Cliffs, N.J.: Prentice-Hall, 1962), and *The Recognition of Ralph Waldo Emerson—Selected Criticism since 1837*, ed. Milton Konvitz (Ann Arbor: University of Michigan Press, 1972). It is striking that in the vast secondary literature on Emerson, distinctively philosophical considerations are virtually absent.

36. James was not always complimentary to Emerson. In *The Varieties of Religious Experience*, for example, he criticized Emerson for tending toward "abstraction" on the religious question (32, 56). For a discussion of James's ambivalence toward Emerson, see F. O. Mathiessen, *The American Renaissance* (New York: Oxford University Press, 1941), 53–54n.

37. James, *Essays in Religion and Morality*, 114.

38. Emerson, "American Scholar," 1:96–97.

39. James, *Essays in Religion and Morality*, 114. The potential capacity for "transfiguration" of fact as subject to human will is not a strange contention for William James, as can be seen in his own doctrine of "The Will to Believe." Could it have some expressive origin in Emerson's "Nature"? "Build therefore your own world. As fast as you conform your life to the pure idea in your mind, that will unfold its great proportions. A correspondent revolution in things will attend the influx of the spirit" (*Works*, 1:76).

40. What could be more Emersonian than James's remark in his "Sentiment of Rationality" that "the inmost nature of the reality is congenial to powers which you possess" (James, *The Will to Believe* [Cambridge, Mass.: Harvard University Press, 1979], 73)? See also *The Writings of William James*, ed. John J. McDermott (Chicago: University of Chicago Press, 1977), 331. In preparation for his "Address," James did read Emerson, "volume after volume," but came away with "a moral lesson" rather than distinctive philosophical insight; see *The Letters of William James*, ed. Henry James III, 2 vols. (Boston: Atlantic Monthly Press, 1920), 190.

41. James, *Letters of William James*, 234–35. For another contrast of Emerson and Santayana, see John Crowe Ransom, "Art and Mr. Santayana," in *Santayana: Animal Faith and Spiritual Life*, ed. John Lachs (New York: Appleton-Century–Crofts, 1967), 403–4.

42. George Santayana, *The Letters of George Santayana*, ed. Daniel Cory (New York: Scribner's, 1955), 81–82.

43. George Santayana, "The Optimism of Ralph Waldo Emerson," in *George Santayana's America*, ed. James Ballowe (Urbana: University of Illinois Press, 1967), 84. Another little-known piece of Santayana on Emerson is "Emerson the Poet," a centennial contribution of 1903. Although in this essay Santayana speaks of Emerson as often bland, he praises him for self-direction and a deep and unyielding sense of personal liberty; see *Santayana on America*, ed. Richard C. Lyon (New York: Harcourt, 1968), 268–83.

44. George Santayana, "The Genteel Tradition in American Philosophy," in *Winds of Doctrine* (London: J. M. Dent, 1913), 192–93.

45. George Santayana, "Emerson," in *Interpretations of Poetry and Religion* (New York: Scribner's, 1900), 218.

46. Ibid., 233.

47. Santayana, *Letters*, 225–26.

48. Ignas K. Skrupskelis, "Annotated Bibliography of the Publications of Josiah Royce," in *The Basic Writings of Josiah Royce*, ed. John J. McDermott (Chicago: University of Chicago Press, 1969), 2:1167–226.

49. Josiah Royce, *William James and Other Essays* (New York: Macmillan, 1911), 3–4, 5–6.

50. John Dewey, "Ralph Waldo Emerson," in *Characters and Events* (New York: Henry Holt, 1929), 1:71.

51. Ibid., 74.

52. Ibid., 70.

53. Ibid., 75.

54. Dewey takes a similar position in *Art as Experience* (New York: Capricorn, 1958 [1934]), 11: "Theory can start with and from acknowledged works of art only when the esthetic is already compartmentalized, or only when works

of art are set in a niche apart instead of being celebrations, recognized as such, of the things of ordinary experience. Even a crude experience, if authentically an experience, is more fit to give a clue to the intrinsic nature of esthetic experience than is an object already set apart from any other mode of experience."

55. Dewey, "Ralph Waldo Emerson," 75.

56. Ibid., 77.

CHAPTER FIVE

JOSIAH ROYCE'S PHILOSOPHY OF THE COMMUNITY

Danger of the Detached Individual

1. Josiah Royce, *The World and the Individual,* 2 vols. (New York: Macmillan, 1899, 1901); cited hereafter as *WI*.

2. Gay Wilson Allen, *William James* (New York: Viking Press, 1967), 387.

3. Bruce Kuklick, *The Rise of American Philosophy: Cambridge, Massachusetts, 1860–1930* (New Haven: Yale University Press, 1977).

4. See John J. McDermott, "Spires of Influence: The Importance of Emerson for Classical American Philosophy," in *History, Religion and Spiritual Democracy,* ed. Maurice Wohlgelerntner (New York: Columbia University Press, 1980), 181–202; see also chapter 4 in the present volume.

5. Charles Sanford, *The Quest for Paradise: Europe and the American Moral Imagination* (Urbana: University of Illinois Press, 1961), 82.

6. Sarah Royce, *A Frontier Lady,* ed. Ralph Henry Gabriel (New Haven: Yale University Press, 1932). Gabriel tells us that Josiah Royce had asked his mother to recount her journey overland to California so as to assist him in his writing of the history of California, which he published in 1886. It is an informal document, but then all the more does it convey the authenticity of those exciting, courageous, and treacherous days as lived by the westward settlers of 1849.

7. Josiah Royce, "Words of Professor Royce at the Walton Hotel at Philadelphia, December 29, 1915," in *The Hope of the Great Community* (New York: Macmillan, 1916), 122–23; cited hereafter as *HGC*. This work is reprinted in John J. McDermott, *The Basic Writings of Josiah Royce,* 2 vols (Chicago: University of Chicago Press, 1969), 1:31–32.

8. Josiah Royce, *California from the Conquest in 1846 to the Second Vigilance Committee in San Francisco: A Study of American Character* (Boston: Houghton Mifflin, 1886), 240–46 (excerpted); cited hereafter as *CAL*. For literature on the final destination of the Forty-niners, the mining camps, see Remi Nadeau, *Ghost Towns and Mining Camps of California* (Los Angeles: Ward Ritchie, 1965), and Charles Howard Shinn, *Mining Camps: A Study in American Frontier Government* (New York: Scribner's, 1884).

9. See, for example, Royce's address of 1898, "The Pacific Coast: A Psychological Study of the Relations of Climate and Civilization," in *Race Questions,*

Provincialism and other American Problems (New York: Macmillan, 1980), 169–225; cited hereafter as *RQP*. See also Mcdermott, *Basic Writings*, 1:181–204.

10. Josiah Royce, "Meditation before the Gate," in *Fugitive Essays*, ed. Jacob Loewenberg (Cambridge, Mass.: Harvard University Press, 1920), 6–7; cited hereafter as *FE*.

11. See Ralph Barton Perry, *The Thought and Character of William James* (Boston: Little, Brown and Company, 1935), 1:781. The complete letter, longer by far, is found in *The Letters of Josiah Royce*, ed. John Clendenning (Chicago: University of Chicago Press, 1974), 66–68.

12. George Herbert Palmer, "Josiah Royce," in *Contemporary Idealism in America* (New York: Macmillan, 1932), 9.

13. Josiah Royce, *The Religious Aspect of Philosophy* (Boston: Houghton Mifflin, 1885); cited hereafter as *RAP*.

14. Royce, *CAL*.

15. Josiah Royce, *The Feud of Oakfield Creek: A Novel of California* (Boston: Houghton Mifflin, 1887); cited hereafter as *FOC*.

16. See Frank M. Oppenheim, *Royce's Voyage Down Under: A Journey of the Mind* (Lexington: University Press of Kentucky, 1980).

17. Citations for works by Royce not cited above are as follows: *Studies of Good and Evil: A Series of Essays upon Life and Philosophy* (New York: Appleton, 1898); cited hereafter as *SGE*. *The Philosophy of Loyalty* (New York: Macmillan, 1908); cited hereafter as *PL*. *The Sources of Religious Insight* (New York: Scribner's, 1912); cited hereafter as *SRI*. *The Spirit of Modern Philosophy* (Boston: Houghton Mifflin, 1892); cited hereafter as *SMP*. *The Conception of God*, with commentary by S. E. Mezes, J. Leconte, and George Holmes Howison (Berkeley: Philosophical Union, 1895; 2nd ed., with Supplementary Essay by Royce, 1897); cited hereafter as *CG*. *The Conception of Immortality* (Boston: Houghton Mifflin, 1900); cited hereafter as *CI*. *Lectures on Modern Idealism*, ed. J. Loewenberg (New Haven: Yale University Press, 1919); cited hereafter as *LMI*. *The Principles of Logic*, ed. Arnold Ruge (London: Macmillan, 1914); cited hereafter as *PrL*. *The Problem of Christianity*, 2 vols. (New York: Macmillan, 1913; reprinted, with a new introduction by John E. Smith, in a one-volume edition, at Chicago: University of Chicago Press, 1968); cited hereafter as *PC*.

18. Royce, *FE*, 152.

19. Royce, *SGE*, 16; McDermott, *Basic Writings*, 2:845.

20. Royce, *RAP*, 431; McDermott, *Basic Writings*, 350–51.

21. McDermott, *Basic Writings*, 452–53; emphasis in original.

22. Royce, *CG*, 108–9. It may be of significance here to reflect on the idiosyncratic events which brought Royce to Harvard University instead of, at the time, the more deserving Howison. The biographers of Howison point to the irony of this reversal of roles for Howison and Royce. They cite James in a letter to

Thomas Davidson of August of 1883, to the effect that "Royce has unquestionably the inside track for any vacancy in the future. I think him a man of genius, sure to distinguish himself by original work." They add, however, that James goes on to remark: "But when I see the disconsolate condition of poor Howison, looking for employment now, and when I recognize the extraordinary development of his intellect in the past four years, I feel almost guilty of having urged Royce's call hither. I did it before Howison had returned, or at least before I had seen him, and with my data, I was certainly right. But H. seems now to me to be quite a different man, intellectually, from his former self; and being so much older, ought to have had a chance, which (notwithstanding the pittance of a salary), he would probably have taken, to get a foothold in the University" (John Wright Buckham and George Malcolm Stratton, *George Holmes Howison* [Berkeley: University of California Press, 1934], 70).

23. See Royce, "Professor Royce on His Critics," in *CG*, 333, where he objects to Howison's "failure to comprehend that self-consciousness and the unity of consciousness are categories which inevitably transcend, while they certainly do not destroy, individuality."

24. In my view, Royce's 1895 essay "Self-Consciousness, Social Consciousness and Nature," in *SGE* is a forerunner to the work of the American philosopher George Herbert Mead. In fact, Mead's *Mind, Self and Society* reflects the original table of contents in Royce's papers as a task to be done.

25. Royce, *WI*, 1:ix–x.

26. Ibid., 1:338–39.

27. Morton White, "Harvard's Philosophical Heritage," in *Religion, Politics and the Higher Learning* (Cambridge, Mass.: Harvard University Press, 1959), 53.

28. See McDermott, *Basic Writings*, 2:787; originally in Royce, *PrL*.

29. See McDermott, *Basic Writings*, 2:813; originally in Royce, *PrL*.

30. Royce, *PL*, 16–17; McDermott, *Basic Writings*, 2:861.

31. Royce, *PL*, 357; McDermott, *Basic Writings*, 996.

32. See Royce, *RAP*, 289: "We go to seek the Eternal, not in experience, but in the thought that thinks experience."

33. Royce, *SRI*, 279–80.

34. See Kuklick, *Rise of American Philosophy*, 376.

35. Royce, *PC*, 337, 339.

36. Ibid., 253, 255–56.

37. Ibid., 294.

38. Ibid., 294.

39. In 1914 Royce attempted to structure a program of indemnification for victims of the burgeoning war. This effort of Royce, although it received little support, is a remarkable anticipation of the type of international activity found

in the present United Nations; see Josiah Royce, *War and Insurance* (New York: Macmillan, 1914).

40. Royce, *HGC*, 51–52.

1. William James to Carl Stumpf, January 1, 1886, in *The Correspondence of William James*, ed. Ignas K. Skrupskelis and Elizabeth M. Berkeley (Charlottesville: University of Virginia Press, 1998), 6:106.

2. William James, "The Teaching of Philosophy in Our Colleges," in *The Works of William James*, ed. Frederick Burkhardt (Cambridge, Mass.: Harvard University Press, 1978), 4. The full text of the passage reads: "one can never deny that philosophic study means the habit of always seeking an alternative, of not taking the usual for granted, of making conventionalities fluid again, of imagining foreign states of mind."

3. William James, *Pragmatism and the Works of William James* (Cambridge, Mass.: Harvard University Press, 1975), 106.

4. From "Notes for Philosophy 20C: Metaphysics Seminar" (1903–4), in William James, *Manuscript Lectures—The Works of William James* (Cambridge, Mass.: Harvard University Press, 1988), 326.

5. James, "The Sentiment of Rationality," in *Works* (Cambridge, Mass.: Harvard University Press, 1979), 73.

6. James, *Pragmatism*, 123.

7. Ibid., 99.

8. Gerard Manley Hopkins, "God's Grandeur," in *Poems* (New York: Oxford University Press, 1948), 70.

9. Charles Sanders Peirce, *The Collected Papers of Charles Sanders Peirce*, ed. Charles Hartshorne and Paul Weiss (Cambridge, Mass.: Harvard University Press, 1934), 5:37 (§§50–51).

The Significance of the Thought of William James and John Dewey for Global Culture

1. William James, *The Will to Believe* (Cambridge, Mass.: Harvard University Press, 1979), 144. See also idem, *The Writings of William James*, ed. John J. McDermott (Chicago: University of Chicago Press, 1977), 2:613. James was not unaware of the danger involved in revolutionary ideas, for in 1878 he writes that "we have never had an example in history of a highly intellectual race, in which prudence was the ruling passion" (James, cited in Ralph Barton Perry, *The Thought and Character of William James* [Boston: Little, Brown, 1935], 35).

2. William James, *The Meaning of Truth* (Cambridge, Mass.: Harvard University Press, 1975), 6–7. See also idem, *Writings of William James*, 136.

3. William James, *The Principles of Psychology* (Cambridge, Mass.: Harvard University Press, 1981), 2:961; emphasis in original.

4. For a more detailed analysis of radical empiricism, see John J. McDermott, introduction to William James, *Essays in Radical Empiricism* (Cambridge, Mass.: Harvard University Press, 1976), xi–xlviii; and idem, "Life Is in the Transitions," in *The Culture of Experience: Philosophical Essays in the American Grain* (New York: New York University Press, 1976), 99–117.

5. William James, *Pragmatism* (Cambridge, Mass.: Harvard University Press, 1975), 30; emphasis in the original. See also James, *Writings of William James*, 379.

6. John J. McDermott, "To Be Human Is to Humanize: A Radically Empirical Aesthetic," in *Culture of Experience*, 21–62.

7. William James, *A Pluralistic Universe* (Cambridge, Mass.: Harvard University Press, 1977), 145; emphasis in the original. See also James, *Writings of William James*, 806–7.

8. Perry, *Thought and Character of William James*, 2:700.

9. James, *Will to Believe*, 6–7; see also James, *Writings of William James*, 135.

10. William James, *Essays in Religion and Morality* (Cambridge, Mass.: Harvard University Press, 1982), 162–73; see also James, *Writings of William James*, 660–71.

11. John Dewey, "The Development of American Pragmatism," in *The Philosophy of John Dewey*, ed. John J. McDermott (Chicago: University of Chicago Press, 1981), 1:50–51.

12. See John Dewey, *Lectures in China, 1919–1920*, ed. Robert W. Clopton and Tsuin-Chen Ou (Honolulu: University Press of Hawaii, 1973).

13. A balanced view of Dewey's contributions and limitations during his China sojourn is found in Thomas Berry, "Dewey's Influence in China," in *John Dewey: His Thought and Influence*, ed. John Blewett (New York: Fordham University Press, 1960), 199–232.

14. John Dewey, *Democracy and Education* (1980), vol. 9 of *The Middle Works* (Carbondale: Southern Illinois University Press, 1976–83), 153; emphasis in the original.

15. John Dewey, *Experience and Nature* (1981), vol. 1 of *The Later Works* (Carbondale: Southern Illinois University Press, 1981–), 172.

16. John Dewey, *The Quest for Certainty* (1984), vol. 4 of *The Later Works*, 224; see also Dewey, "The Construction of Good," in *Philosophy of John Dewey*, 2:595.

17. Dewey, *Experience and Nature*, 12–13.

18. Clifford Geertz, *The Interpretation of Cultures* (New York: Basic, 1973), 24–25. See also idem, *Local Knowledge* (New York: Basic, 1983).

19. Dewey, *Experience and Nature*, 392.

20. Dewey, *Philosophy of John Dewey*, 2:539.

21. Dewey, *Experience and Nature*, 40–41.

22. Dewey, *Democracy and Education*, 200.

23. John Dewey, *Education Today* (New York: G. P. Putnam's Sons, 1940), 298.

24. Cited in Jacques le Goff, *The Birth of Purgatory* (Chicago: University of Chicago Press, 1984), 49–50.

CHAPTER EIGHT

NATURE NOSTALGIA AND THE CITY

An American Dilemma

1. A cardinal example of generalizations creating their own evidence is to be found in David Riesman, Nathan Glazer, and Reuel Denney, *The Lonely Crowd* (New Haven: Yale University Press, 1950). Our deep contemporary self-consciousness about directedness and manipulation dates from that book.

2. Daniel Boorstin, *The Image: A Guide to the PseudoEvents in America* (New York: Harper Colophon, 1964).

3. Leo Marx, "Pastoral Ideals and City Troubles," in *The Fitness of Man's Environment* (Washington, D.C.: Smithsonian Institution, 1968), 142–43. Marx claims that the contention of an antiurban bias as existent in American literature is a misreading of the metaphoric intention of that tradition. He may be correct about the "intention," but the fact is that the popular interpretation of American literature has sustained a nature romanticism and a distrust of the city.

4. George H. Williams, "The Enclosed Garden in the Wilderness of the New World," in *Wilderness and Paradise* (New York: Harper and Bros., 1962), 98–131. See also Roderick Nash, *Wilderness and the American Mind* (New Haven: Yale Universty Press, 1967).

5. Edward L. Morgan, *Visible Saints* (Ithaca: Cornell University Press, 1962), 67–73, and Daniel B. Shea Jr., *Spiritual Autobiography in Early America* (Princeton: Princeton University Press, 1968).

6. For a brilliant analysis of the edenic theme in America, see Charles L. Sanford, *The Quest for Paradise: Europe and the American Moral Imagination* (Urbana: University of Illinois Press, 1961).

7. Morton and Lucia White, *The Intellectual versus the City* (New York: New American Library, 1962), 19.

8. Samuel Sewall, "Phaenomena," in Perry Miller and Thomas H. Johnson, *The Puritans* (New York: Harper Torchbooks, 1963), 1:377.

9. Jonathan Edwards, "Personal Narrative," in Clarence H. Faust and Thomas H. Johnson, eds., *Jonathan Edwards* (New York: Hill and Wang, 1962), 67.

10. Cited in Perry Miller, "Nature and the National Ego," in *Errand into the Wilderness* (New York: Harper Torchbooks, 1956), 210.

11. Ibid., 211.

12. Cited in Williams, *Wilderness and Paradise*, 130.

13. Cited in Freeman Tilden, *The National Parks* (New York: Alfred A. Knopf, 1970), 22.

14. Thomas Jefferson, *Notes on the State of Virginia* (New York: Harper Torchbooks, 1964), 157–58 (query 414).

15. Ibid., 158.

16. See White and White, *Intellectual versus the City*, for an excellent survey of the deep-seated animus against the city that pervades American thought. The Whites, however, seriously underplay the spiritual significance of the land in American life.

17. John M. Anderson, *The Individual and the New World* (State College, Pa.: Bald Eagle Press, 1955), 12.

18. Lucy Lockwood Hazard, *The Frontier in American Literature* (New York: Frederick Ungar, 1927), 152.

19. Ralph Waldo Emerson, "The American Scholar," in *The Complete Works of Ralph Waldo Emerson* (Boston: Houghton and Mifflin, 1904), 1:95.

20. Leo Marx, *The Machine in the Garden: Technology and the Pastoral Idea in America* (New York: Oxford University Press, 1967), 232.

21. Emerson, "Culture," in *Works*, 6:13.

22. Ibid.

23. Carl Bode, ed., *Collected Poems of Henry David Thoreau* (Baltimore: The John Hopkins University Press, 1964), 135.

24. Perry Miller, *Nature's Nation* (Cambridge, Mass.: Harvard University Press, 1967).

25. Anderson, *Individual and the New World*, 41.

26. Sidney E. Mead, *The Lively Experiment* (New York: Harper and Row, 1963), 5.

27. See Leslie Fiedler, *The Return of the Vanishing American* (New York: Stein and Day, 1969), 187, for a similar remark.

28. See the excellent chapter on "The Mountain Man" in Henry Nash Smith, *Virgin Land: The American West as Symbol and Myth* (New York: Vintage, 1957), 88–89.

29. Emerson, introduction to "Nature," *Works*, 1:3.

30. Cited in Smith, *Virgin Land*, 296n4.

31. William James, *The Meaning of Truth* (New York: Longmans, Green and Co., 1909), 111.

32. This passage, with slight changes, is taken from an earlier effort to ground an American metaphysics of history; see John J. Mcdermott, *The American Angle of Vision* (West Nyack, N.Y.: Cross Currents, 1966), and chapters 1 and 2 in the present volume.

33. Josiah Royce, *Basic Writings of Josiah Royce*, ed. John J. McDermott (Chicago: University of Chicago Press, 1969), 1:117. See also the chapter on "The Temper of the West" by James Bryce in *The American Commonwealth* (London: Macmillan, 1891), 1:696–706, for a vivid description of open land from a European point of view.

34. Cited in Frederick Jackson Turner, "The Significance of the Frontier in American History," ed. Ray Allen Billington, *Frontier and Section* (New York: Prentice-Hall, 1961), 57.

35. Out of an extensive literature, I will mention only William Hinds, *American Communities* (New York: Corinth, 1961 [1875]).

36. Compare contemporary social diagnosis with the reports of the depression as found in *The Great Depression*, ed. David A. Shannon (New York: Prentice-Hall, 1960), and Studs Terkel, *Hard Times* (New York: Pantheon, 1970).

37. Cited in Peter J. Schmitt, *Back to Nature: The Arcadian Myth in Urban America* (New York: Oxford University Press, 1969), 20. For many further instances of such nostalgia, see Samuel R. Ogden, ed., *America the Vanishing: Rural Life and the Promise of Progress* (Brattleboro, Vt.: Stephen Greene Press, 1969).

38. Lewis Mumford, *The Golden Day* (Boston: Beacon, 1957), 38.

39. Van Wyck Brooks, "Emerson at Sea," in Carl Bode, ed., *Ralph Waldo Emerson* (New York: Hill and Wang, 1968), 68.

40. By contrast, see the stark reality in instances of urban photography, for example the remarkable set of photographs in Susan Cahill and Michele F. Cooper, eds., *The Urban Reader* (New York: Prentice-Hall, 1971).

41. Peter L. Marks, "A Vision of Environment," *American Scholar* 40, no. 3 (Summer 1971): 426. This essay is a utilization, albeit imaginative, of nature nostalgia, revealing contempt for city life, which he describes by reference to the cliché, "urban anonymity."

42. What, for example, are we to make of this broadside from the landscape architect Ian McHarg? "I contend that . . . the modern city inhibits life, that it inhibits man as an organism, man as a social being, man as a spiritual being, and that it does not even offer adequate minimum conditions for physiological man; that indeed the modern city offers the least humane physical environment

known to history" (McHarg, "Man and Environment," in Leonard J. Duhl, *The Urban Condition* [New York: Simon and Schuster, 1969], 49).

43. For a discussion of urban aesthetic metaphors, see John J. McDermott, "Deprivation and Celebration: Suggestions for an Aesthetic Ecology," in James Edie, ed., *New Essays in Phenomenology* (Chicago: Quadrangle, 1969), 116–30.

44. John Dewey, *Art as Experience* (New York: Capricorn, 1950), 11.

45. Even in a terribly afflicted neighborhood, the "block" maintained a deep spiritual hold on its residents; see the extraordinary photographic essay by Herb Goro, *The Block* (New York: Random House, 1970).

46. Cited by Ray Ginger, *Modern American Cities* (Chicago: Modern American Cities, 1969), 3.

47. Kevin Lynch, *The Image of the City* (Cambridge, Mass.: MIT Press, 1959), 47. See also the refreshing experimental perspectives in Stanley Milgram, "The Experience of Living in Cities," *Science* 167 (March 13, 1970): 1461–68. Some of these perspectives are taken into consideration in the exciting new work of Paolo Soleri, about which see Donald Wall, *Visionary-Cities: The Archology of Paolo Soleri* (New York: Praeger, 1971).

48. Richie Orange, "Harlem," in Cahill and Cooper, *Urban Reader*, 143.

49. For a poignant description by young Juan Gonzales of his "being renewed" into a project, see Charlotte Leon Mayerson, "Two Blocks Apart," in Cahill and Cooper, *Urban Reader*, 76–81. See also the review article by Roger Sale, "Cities and the City," *New York Review of Books* (January 28, 1971): 40, where he tells of the ramifications in the taking down of a basketball hoop on a city block.

50. See Marc Fried, "Grieving for a Lost Home," in Duhl, *Urban Condition*, 151–71.

51. Francis X. Clines, *New York Times*, December 2, 1970.

52. See Josiah Royce, "The Hope of the Great Community," in *Basic Writings*, 1156.

CHAPTER NINE

SPACE, TIME, AND TOUCH

Philosophical Dimensions of Urban Consciousness

1. One recent effort on this behalf has been made by A. K. Bierman, *The Philosophy of Urban Existence* (Athens: Ohio University Press, 1973). It is highly idiosyncratic and is more a sociology of persons than an analysis of cities.

2. See Herbert Marcuse, "Love Mystified: A Critique of Norman O. Brown," and Norman O. Brown, "A Reply to Herbert Marcuse," in *Negations* (Boston: Beacon, 1969), 227–47.

3. For two examples of urban jeremiads, see Mitchell Gordon, *Sick Cities* (Baltimore: Penguin, 1965), and Nathan Glazer, ed., *Cities in Trouble* (Chicago: Quadrangle, 1970).

4. Glazer, *Cities in Trouble*, xi.

5. A recent verbal contention from some who are responsible for the care of urban parks is of interest here. Vandalism unanswered begets further vandalism, whereas vandalism to which there is an immediate response of repair and renewal tends to cure, the so-called Broken Windows theory.

6. For the significance of "modern art" in this "turning," see John J. McDermott, "Deprivation and Celebration: Suggestions for an Aesthetic Ecology," in *New Essays in Phenomenology*, ed. James Edie (Chicago: Quadrangle, 1969), 116–30.

7. We add "feel" to that list of words begun by William James and supplemented by John Dewey—namely, "experience," "life," and "history"—as words which are double-barreled, connoting that which we do as well as that which we undergo. To "feel about" is not only "to have feelings" but also "to touch," as when one goes on hands and knees or follows sounds and smells—that is, to be up and around; see John Dewey, *Experience and Nature* (La Salle, Ill.: Open Court, 1929), 10.

8. For a discussion of the gap between how we actually feel about our environment and how we are assumed to feel, see John J. McDermott, "Feeling as Insight: The Affective Dimension in Social Diagnosis," in *Hippocrates Revisited*, ed. R. J. Bulger (New York: Medcom, 1973), 166–80.

9. Grady Clay, *Close-up: How to Read the American City* (New York: Praeger, 1973), 18.

10. See, for example, Morton and Lucia White, *The Intellectual versus the City* (Cambridge, Mass.: Harvard University Press, 1962).

11. John J. McDermott, "Nature Nostalgia and the City: An American Dilemma," in *The Family, Communes, and Utopian Societies*, ed. S. Te Selle (New York: Harper Torchbooks, 1972), 2. An interesting dimension of American nature nostalgia was mentioned in conversation by Judah Stampfer, who pointed out that, contrary to the case in Europe and most of the rest of the world, American military history took place on the land, rarely, and less importantly, in and around cities.

12. Theodore Roszak, *The Making of a Counter-Culture* (New York: Anchor, 1969), and idem, *Where the Wasteland Ends* (New York: Anchor, 1973).

13. Charles Reich, *The Greening of America* (New York: Random House, 1970).

14. Cited in White and White, *Intellectual versus the City*, 35.

15. Norman O. Brown, *Life Against Death* (New York: Random House, 1959), 283. In response to a question about contemporary American cities, Brown

stated that in his judgment an urban Armageddon had already taken place and that he wrote for the fleeing remnant.

16. We ask of metaphor something more than its technical, dictionary meaning. Rather, we have in mind the version of George Steiner, for whom "metaphor ignites a new arc of perceptive energy. It relates hitherto unrelated areas of experience." (Steiner, "The Language Animal," *Encounter* [August 1969]: 11, as cited in Clay, *Close-up*, 21).

17. John J. McDermott, "Nature Nostalgia," 2–11.

18. Cited in Perry Miller, "The Romantic Dilemma in American Nationalism and the Concept of Nature," in *Nature's Nation* (Cambridge, Mass.: Harvard University Press, 1967), 201.

19. Eliot Porter, *In Wildness Is the Preservation of the World* (San Francisco: Sierra Club, 1962).

20. Germane to our discussion is the remark of Peter Farb: "If it were possible to X-ray a patch of soil to a depth of a few feet, it would look very much like a busy intersection in a city, for the soil is a great concourse of throngs which jostle through the particles" (Farb, *The Living Earth* [New York: Harper Colophon, 1968], 51).

21. Los Angeles is often cited as an exception to this generalization. Strictly speaking it is not, for Los Angeles has more tall buildings than most other American cities. It is true, however, that Los Angeles conceived itself in radically different terms than other American cities by adopting a horizontal rather than a vertical approach overall, and therefore endowed roads, automobiles, spatial proximity, and distance with entirely different meanings than traditional urban environments. If it is true that nature and open land are the sources of a distinctive American ethos, then Los Angeles is the most distinctive urban rendition of America.

22. Kevin Lynch, *What Time Is This Place?* (Cambridge, Mass.: MIT Press, 1972).

23. Perhaps urban buildings share the double meaning of an urban "pad," namely, a place to repose and a place from which one can launch.

24. A city "block" is a miniature world. The best of the recent efforts to capture its peculiar life-rhythms is the photographic essay of Herb Goro, *The Block* (New York: Vintage, 1970).

25. Kevin Lynch writes that "a landmark is not necessarily a large object. Its location is crucial: if large or tall, the spatial setting must allow it to be seen; if small, there are certain zones that receive more perpetual attention than others: floor surfaces, or nearby facades at or slightly below eye-level" (Lynch, *The Image of the City* [Cambridge, Mass.: MIT Press, 1960], 101).

26. An earlier generation of New Yorkers was more self-conscious about this need, choosing to meet, quite literally, under the clock at the Biltmore Hotel.

27. Plotinus *redivivus*, stated simply and with regard to our problem, comes to this: as superior is to inferior, so is one to many—nous to body and "body to artifact." It is relevant to think here of the computer as the disembodying of artifact, in much the way mathematics purifies the visible world in a Platonic pedagogy.

28. Herbert Schneider reports John Dewey as having said: "I think this whole problem of understanding should be approached not from the point of view of the eyes, but from the point of view of the hands. It's what we grasp that matters" (Corliss Lamont, ed., *Dialogue on John Dewey* [New York: Horizon, 1959], 95).

29. Among others, we have in mind here the work of Herbert Marcuse, Norman O. Brown, Ronald Laing, and the late, lamented Ernest Becker.

30. John Dewey, *Art as Experience* (New York: Capricorn, 1958 [1934]), 3.

31. Ibid., 11.

32. Material in this section is taken from two public lectures: "A Methaphysics of Relations: William James's Anticipation of Contemporary Experience," delivered at the William James Seminar at Winterthur, Switzerland (1973); and "Human Existence and Human Violence," delivered at the Fifteenth World Congress of Philosophy at Varna, Bulgaria (1973).

33. *John Dewey and Arthur F. Bentley, A Philosophical Correspondence*, ed. Sidney Ratner and Jules Altman (New Brunswick, N.J.: Rutgers University Press, 1964), 646.

34. William James, *The Principles of Psychology* (New York: Henry Holt, 1890), 1:285.

35. Ibid., 2:333.

36. William James, "Reflex Action and Theism," in *The Will to Believe* (New York: Longmans, Green and Co., 1897), 114.

37. For James's statements as to the meaning of "radical empiricism" and his "radically empirical" version of classic philosophical problems, see John J. McDermott, ed., *The Writings of William James* (New York: Random House, 1967), 134–310.

38. James, "The Stream of Thought," in *Writings*, 38.

39. See A. J. Ayer, *The Origins of Pragmatism* (San Francisco: Freeman, Cooper and Co., 1968), 288–93.

40. Of an escalating number of efforts to show the aesthetic import of artifacts, see, for example, Sterling McIlhany, *Art as Design: Design as Art* (New York: Van Nostrand-Reinhold, 1970), and the "Vision and Value" series, edited by Gyorgy Kepes, especially the *The Man-Made Object* and *Arts of the Environment*. A psychological litmus test of artifact sensibility would take this form: When you hear the word "crane," do you think of a pond or of a building?

41. Nature time is not always kind and regenerative, as the Dakota sod-farmers of the nineteenth century and the Okies of the twentieth century discovered. A recent, extraordinarily powerful, and original version of the systematic madness often found in nature time is the photographic essay by Michael Lesy, *Wisconsin Death Trip* (New York: Pantheon, 1973). The setting is rural Wisconsin from 1895 to 1900 and the common experience is laced with misery and affliction.

42. See Robert Sommer, *Design Awareness* (San Francisco: Rinehart, 1972), 66. In his chapter on "SpaceTime," Sommer tells us that "a San Francisco radio station announces the exact time 932 times a week."

43. Surveying big-city newspapers, one finds that the screeching headlines of the first edition frequently do not merit even a paragraph in the last editions. Are these instances references to pseudo-events, or is it the pace?

44. We refer here not only to the erosion of aesthetic quality in the urban environment, symbolized by the faceless projects of the days of urban renewal, but to the more subtle and equally important fact that we fail to articulate, let alone sanction, the still-existing, aesthetically rich experiences of city life. The development of such an articulation is equivalent to an urban pedagogy. For an important step in this direction, see Jonathan Freedman, *Crowding and Behavior* (New York: Viking, 1975).

45. James, *Writings*, 205.

CHAPTER TEN

GLASS WITHOUT FEET
Dimensions of Urban Aesthetics

1. From countless sources, to experience the child experiencing the world, I suggest Henry Roth, *Call It Sleep* (New York: Avon, 1962 [1934]).

2. Earlier versions of this relationship can be found in John J. McDermott, "Nature Nostalgia and the City: An American Dilemma," and "Space, Time and Touch: Philosophical Dimensions of Urban Consciousness," both in *The Culture of Experience: Philosophical Essays in the American Grain* (New York: New York University Press, 1976), 179–231.

3. Samuel Sewall, "Phaenomena," in *The Puritans*, ed. Perry Miller and Thomas H. Johnson (New York: Harper Torchbooks, 1963), 1:377.

4. Granting statehood to Hawaii, therefore, ranks as one of our most saving decisions, for Hawaii ties us back to the beginning, to the Orient, and enables us to rejoin the new hegira of East to West, just at the time when the original journey, begun more than one thousand years ago, has come to an end.

5. Ralph Waldo Emerson, "Education," in *Works* (Boston: Houghton Mifflin, 1903–4), 10:132.

6. See *The Journals of Ralph Waldo Emerson* (Boston: Houghton Mifflin, 1909–14), 9:277–78. For fuller treatment of this theme, see chap. 2 of the present volume.

7. I am aware that beginning with the Astrodome in Houston, and continuing on with the Silverdome in Pontiac, Michigan, and the Kingdome in Seattle, baseball is now frequently played indoors. Despite customer convenience, this is blasphemous and should be stopped. It is as if an Indian rain dance were held inside a wigwam. After all, is not being "rained out" the stuff of life?

8. The absence of personscape in the new urban architecture is depressingly obvious, as noted in a recent article by Bob Schwaller, "Pillars, Pedestals and Porticoes," *Texas Business* (November 1983): 57–66. Apparently, money and the size of buildings are the dominant theme. A second article in the same edition of that publication, this by Michael McCullar, "Scanning the Skylines, Citing the Singular," 68–73, discusses monumentality and the turf of architects. Speaking of the new Southwest Center building in Houston, McCullar writes that it "will reaffirm the apparent fact that because of land values, human egos and an almost primal need for man to be awestruck by his architecture, big buildings are getting more monumental all the time." This is macho, male-chauvinist America at its worst. Cities are for people and not for the aggrandizement of architectural egos. We do not live in the sky. We live on the ground, where we walk seeking to be at home.

CHAPTER ELEVEN

WHY BOTHER

Is Life Worth Living? Experience as Pedagogical

This paper enlarges and revises my "Why Bother: Is Life Worth Living?" *Journal of Philosophy* 88, no. 11 (November 1991): 677–83. It appears here by permission of *Journal of Philosophy* and its managing editor, Michael Kelly.

1. John Dewey, *Art as Experience* (1987), vol. 10 of *The Later Works* (Carbondale: Southern Illinois University Press, 1981–), 23.

2. William James alerts us to the importance of the vague. He writes, "It is, in short, the reinstatement of the vague to its proper place in our mental life which I am so anxious to press on the attention" (James, *Principles of Psychology*, in *The Works of William James* (Cambridge, Mass.: Harvard University Press, 1981), 1:246.

CHAPTER TWELVE

ILL-AT-EASE

The Natural Travail of Ontological Disconnectedness

1. T. Lucreti Cari, *De Rerum Natura, Libri Sex*, ed. William Ellery Leonard and Stanley Barney Smith (Madison: University of Wisconsin Press, 1968), 91, 319–20.

2. Marcus Aurelius, "The Meditations," in *The Stoic and Epicurean Philosophers*, ed. Whitney J. Oates (New York: Random House, 1940), 501.

3. St. Augustine, *The Confessions* (New York: Modern Library, 1949), 3.

4. Martin Buber, *I and Thou*, trans. Ronald Gregor Smith (Edinburgh: T. and T. Clark, 1937), 16.

5. Friedrich Nietzsche, *The Will to Power*, ed. Walter Kaufmann (New York: Vintage, 1967), 8.

6. Friedrich Nietzsche, "On the Genealogy of Morals," in *Basic Writings of Nietzsche*, ed. Walter Kaufmann (New York: Modern Library, 1968), 591, §25 (third essay).

7. Ibid.

8. Surely the lament of Francis is more ennobling for us than the systemic regret of Leo Tolstoy's Ivan Ilych, who asks himself, "what if my whole life has really been wrong?" (Tolstoy, *The Death of Ivan Ilych and Other Stories* [New York: New American Library, 1960], 152).

9. John Dewey, *Experience and Nature* (1981), volume 1 of *The Later Works* (Carbondale: Southern Illinois University Press, 1981–), 43.

10. William James: "A World of Pure Experience," in *Essays in Radical Empiricism*, in *The Works of William James*, ed. Frederick Burkhardt (Cambridge, Mass.: Harvard University Press, 1976), 42.

11. As with most everything that is important for understanding ourselves, "periwinkle" is one name for two very different organisms. The first preens and cheers, the second fights off desiccation, to wit:

PERIWINKLE: any of several trailing or woody evergreen herbs (genus Vinca) of the dogbane family; esp: a European creeper (V. minor) widely cultivated as a ground cover and for its *blue or white flowers*; emphasis added; and PERIWINKLE: any of a group of marine Gastropod mollusks having conical, spiral shells and considered to be a variety of snails. Periwinkles feed on algae and seaweed. *They are found at the water's edge; out of water, they resist drying by closing themselves into the shell with a horny plate*; emphasis added.

12. *The Diary of Alice James*, ed. Leon Edel (New York: Dodd, Mead and Co., 1964), 206, 207. Another penetrating, and increasingly widespread, experience of the potential relief which comes with the announcement of a disease as replacement for an ongoing malady occurs over and over at meetings of Alcoholics Anonymous and related "twelve-step" groups. Here, the awareness must be self-announcing, consequently enhancing the nightmare by an extensive quotient. If one were to go to their first meeting and say, "My name is John, and I am an alcoholic," the immediate inner sense would be one of disbelief, guilt, shame, and terror. Yet riven inside those feelings exists also a profound sense of relief, for one now has a real disease at last, and the trap of the malady has a door, albeit still stuck by denial and covered by the physiology of DNA. No

matter, this side of a natural death, that trap-door can now be wedged as the dis-ease slowly replaces the penetrating presence of our being ill-at-ease.

13. Albert Camus, *The Myth of Sisyphus* (New York: Alfred A. Knopf, 1955), 40, 3.

14. John J. McDermott, "Teaching Philosophy-Historically," in *Newsletter on Teaching Philosophy*, ed. Tziporah Kasachkoff (Newark, Del.: American Philosophical Association, 1988), 88, no. 1: 55–60.

15. William James, *The Principles of Psychology*, in *Works*, 2:961.

16. John J. McDermott, "Experience Grows by Its Edges," in *Streams of Experience* (Amherst: University of Massachusetts Press, 1986), 151.

17. Walt Whitman, "Song of Myself," in *Whitman*, ed. Leslie A. Fiedler (New York: Dell, 1959), p. 29 (#2).

18. Ibid., 32, 33 (#6).

19. Heraclitus, *An Introduction to Early Greek Philosophy*, trans. and comm. by John Mansley Robinson (Boston: Houghton Mifflin, 1968), 94 (#5.30, 5.31; #1.2 in most other editions).

20. Johannis Scotti Eriugenae, *Periphyseon* (*De divisione naturae*), ed. L. P. Sheldon-Williams (Dublin: Dublin Institute for Advanced Studies, 1968). The initial tip to read Eruigena was neither *ab ovo* nor *sui generis*. It came from Robert C. Pollock of Fordham University, who for many decades taught the deep similarities existent between the Augustinian tradition and that of Jonathan Edwards and R. W. Emerson.

21. Scotus Eriugena, "On the Division of Nature," in *Medieval Philosophy*, ed. John F. Wippel and Allan B. Wolter (New York: Free Press, 1969), 132, and cf. J. P. Migne, *Patrilogia latina*, 122, no. 4, 1, 741c.

22. William James, *Pragmatism* (1975), in *Works*, 30.

23. William James, *A Pluralistic Universe* (1977), in *Works*, 83–100.

24. The long-standing comfort of an astral future, a salvific beyond, may be eroding. What are we to think of the latest fright now frequently shown in contemporary films, wherein a person, tethered to a space vehicle, has the life-line cut? The stern message sent to us is that the victim will float eternally into an endless void. If this is not disconnectedness, then what is?!? (Subsequent to the presentation of this address, we were visited by the Los Angeles earthquake. There, too, the diagnosis focused on the eerie disappearance of terrestrial stability. My stepdaughter, Lynne Elizabeth, caught in that earthquake, echoed David's feelings, cited above, and harbored a deep sense of impending doom for more than a month. She was not alone in that ontological queasiness.)

25. *The Biophilia Hypothesis*, ed. Stephen R. Kellert and Edward O. Wilson (Washington, D.C.: Island, 1993).

26. William James, *Essays in Radical Empiricism*, in *Works*, 27.

27. William James, *Principles of Psychology*, 2:959; emphasis in original.

28. Rachel Carson, *Silent Spring* (Boston: Houghton Mifflin, 1962). It should be remembered that Carson dedicated that clarion warning of a book to Albert Schweitzer and took as her epigraph Schweitzer's equivalent warning, "Man has lost the capacity to foresee and to forestall. He will end by destroying the earth." Ironically my children, too, faced a seasonal disaster, referred to as a nuclear winter. And my grandchildren?

29. Kenneth Scott Latourette, *A History of Christianity* (New York: Harper and Brothers, 1953), 456.

30. No one seems to be as curious as I about the medical-scientific claim that all males, by the age of 100, have prostate cancer. DNA? Environment? Life-style? How could that be?

31. For an excellent and brief primer on the medical-scientific and epidemiological significance of AIDS, see *AIDS: A Guide for Survival* (Houston: Harris County Medical Society–Houston Academy of Medicine, 1988).

32. I trust that I am only guilty here of "eclectic" rather than "agnostic" skepticism in my presentation of the routining of diagnosis. This helpful distinction is found in Patrick Romanell, *John Locke and Medicine* (Buffalo: Prometheus, 1984), 67.

33. It is of note that for several decades we have attempted to transform the presence of "ill-at-ease" by means of a "pill-at-ease." Known in the medical trade as antidepressants, these psychotropic drugs come to us on behalf of a distinct interpretation of human naturals, such that the key to well-being resides in the biochemistry of the neural transmitters. My language of relations, connections, and disconnections is also the language of neural pharmacology, now the dominant tactic of psychiatry. Some psychiatrists even talk of "remaking the self"; see Peter D. Kramer, *Listening to Prozac* (New York: Viking, 1993). The philosophical significance of pharmacological psychiatry begs to be addressed.

34. Albert Camus, *The Rebel* (New York: Alfred A. Knopf, 1954), 17.

35. John Dewey, *Experience and Nature*, 12–13: "These commonplaces prove that experience is of as well as *in* nature. It is not experience which is experienced, but nature—stones, plants, animals, diseases, health, temperature, electricity and so on."

36. John E. Smith, "The Course of American Philosophy," in *Themes in American Philosophy: Purpose, Experience and Community* (New York: Harper Torchbooks, 1970), 135.

37. John Dewey, *Experience and Nature*, 43.

38. Martin Buber sees this quest for habitation as having alternate success, epochally. I see it as both personal and epochal; see Martin Buber, *Between Man and Man* (London: Routledge and Kegan Paul, 1947), 126: "In the history of the

human spirit I distinguish between epochs of habitation and epochs of homelessness. In the former, man lives in the world as in a house, as in a home. In
the latter, man lives in the world as in an open field and at times does not even
have four pegs with which to set up a tent." What would Buber say of that
scabrous contemporary American phenomenon, the homeless among the
urban (urbane?) crowd?

39. This diagnosis of our "place" rests on an earlier essay, "Experience
Grows by Its Edges," 142–48.

40. We should not underestimate the profound symbolic significance of the
social fact that the "bag ladies," forerunners of the now-pandemic urban homeless, carried their "things" everywhere and had as a mooring no place, but only
and rather their "things."

41. Lao-Tzu, *Te-Tao Ching*, trans., with an intro. and comm. by Robert G.
Henricks (New York: Ballantine, 1989).

42. Often our battle, the personal fight, is waged deep within our heart,
where resides a *Binnenleben*, that region described by William James as the one
in "which we dwell alone with our willingness and unwillingness, our faiths
and our fears" (William James, "Is Life Worth Living," in *The Will to Believe*,
in *Works*, 55). My version of this central question can be found in John J. Mc-
Dermott, "Why Bother: Is Life Worth Living? Experience as Pedagogical," in
Philosophy and the Reconstruction of Culture, ed. John J. Stuhr (New York: State
University of New York Press, 1993); originally published without the "Deweyan Pedagogical Appendix" in the *Journal of Philosophy* 11 (November 1991):
677–83, and see chapter 11 in the present volume.

43. Charles Sanders Peirce, *Collected Papers* (Cambridge, Mass.: Harvard
University Press, 1934), 5:37 (paragraphs 50, 51).

CHAPTER THIRTEEN
"TURNING" BACKWARD
The Erosion of Moral Sensibility

1. Marcus Aurelius, *Meditations* (Chicago: Regnery, 1956), 18–19.

2. Eugene O'Neill, *Long Day's Journey into Night* (New Haven: Yale University Press, 1956), 61.

3. Albert Camus, *The Myth of Sisyphus* (New York: Alfred A. Knopf,
1955), 40.

4. Albert Camus, *The Rebel* (New York: Alfred A. Knopf, 1955), 17.

5. Martin Buber, *At the Turning* (New York: Farrar, Straus, and Young,
1952), 25–26.

CHAPTER FOURTEEN

THE INEVITABILITY OF OUR OWN DEATH

The Celebration of Time as a Prelude to Disaster

1. David Cole Gordon, *Overcoming the Fear of Death* (Baltimore: Penguin, 1972), 13.

2. Susan Sontag, *Illness as Metaphor* (New York: Vintage, 1979), 3.

3. For a profound analysis of capital punishment, see Albert Camus, "Reflections on the Guillotine," in *Resistance, Rebellion and Death* (New York: Alfred A. Knopf, 1961), 175–234.

4. Anonymous, *Last Letters From Stalingrad* (New York: New American Library, 1961), 125. See also Edith Wyschogrod, "Sport, Death and the Elemental," in *The Phenomenon of Death* (New York: Harper and Row, 1973), 166–97: "To engage in sport as a mode of being in the elemental is not merely to want to die, but to be willing to do so" (197).

5. A. Alvarez, *The Savage God: A Study of Suicide* (New York: Random House, 1972).

6. Albert Camus, *The Myth of Sisyphus* (New York: Alfred A. Knopf, 1955), 3.

7. Søren Kierkegaard, cited in Alvarez, *Savage God*, 114.

8. Camus, *Myth of Sisyphus*, 40.

9. William James, "Diary," in *The Writings of William James*, ed. John J. McDermott (Chicago: University of Chicago Press, 1977), 8.

10. Sigmund Freud, *Civilization and Its Discontents* (London: Hogarth, 1953): "If the evolution of civilization has such a far-reaching similarity with the development of an individual, and if the same methods are employed in both, would not the diagnosis be justified that many systems of civilization—or epochs of it—possibly even the whole of humanity—have become 'neurotic' under the pressure of the civilizing trends?" (141).

11. Norman O. Brown, *Life Against Death* (Middletown: Wesleyan University Press, 1970), 105.

12. Brown himself, subsequently, is to disappoint us in this regard, opting for a doctrine of the cycle, which effectively removes the novelty from time passing. See Norman O. Brown, *Closing Time* (New York: Random House, 1973).

13. Norman O. Brown, *Love's Body* (New York: Vintage, 1968): "The world annihilated, the destruction of illusion. The world is the veil we spin to hide the void. The destruction of what never existed. The day breaks, and the shadows flee away" (261).

14. Jacques Merleau-Ponty and Bruno Morando, *The Rebirth of Cosmology* (New York: Alfred A. Knopf, 1976), 275–76.

15. Strictly speaking, we should no longer speak of "world," "cosmos," or "universe," all of which connote an order, a singularity, which is not verified by contemporary cosmology. Perhaps we should adopt the position of William James and speak of a "pluralistic universe"; see William James, *A Pluralistic Universe* (Cambridge, Mass.: Harvard University Press, 1977).

16. John Dewey, "The Need of a Theory of Experience," in *The Philosophy of John Dewey*, ed. John J. McDermott (Chicago: University of Chicago Press, 1981): "Everything depends upon the quality of the experience which is had" (2:508).

17. William James, *Essays in Radical Empiricism* (Cambridge, Mass.: Harvard University Press, 1976), 42. See also John J. McDermott, "Life is in the Transitions," in *The Culture of Experience: Philosophical Essays in the American Grain* (New York: New York University Press, 1976), 99–117.

18. John Dewey, *Democracy and Education* (1980), vol. 9 of *The Middle Works* (Carbondale: Southern Illinois University Press, 1976–83), 56. See also John Dewey, "Education as Growth," in *Philosophy of John Dewey*, 2:492.

19. Dewey, *Democracy and Education*, 47.

20. Marcus Aurelius, *Meditations* (Chicago: Henry Regnery, 1956), 18–19.

21. John Dewey, "Criteria of Experience," in *Philosophy of John Dewey*, 2:523.

22. Rainer Maria Rilke, "The Ninth Elegy," in *Duino Elegies* (New York: Norton, 1939), 73.

CHAPTER FIFTEEN

ISOLATION AS STARVATION

John Dewey and a Philosophy of the Handicapped

As of 2006, The Education for All Handicapped Children Act of 1975 (P. L. 94-142) has been serially modified—in 1990 and 2004. It is now known as the Individuals with Disabilities Education Improvement Act. Of note here is that the term "disabilities" has replaced "handicapped," "individuals" has replaced "children," and, of much importance, the act now uses "people-first" language. I am grateful to Linda Parrish for assistance on this sensitive issue.

1. The term "handicapped" is no longer current precisely because of its traditional meanings, as suggested below. We have chosen to leave it in the text, however, because it reflects the time in which this essay was written and matches the usage of other literature of the day. The Random House Dictionary (unabridged), Webster's International (unabridged), and the multivolume Oxford English Dictionary all stress the meaning of "handicapped" as a penalty to the superior for the purpose of equalization. A secondary meaning of an emotional or physical defect is also given.

2. *Lori Case v. State of California*, 1973, page 2a, as cited in Alan Abeson and Jeffrey Zettel, "The End of the Quiet Revolution: The Education for All Handicapped Children Act of 1975," *Exceptional Children* (October 1977): 115–28.

3. Frederick Weintraub, editorial comment, in ibid., 114.

4. Raymond S. Nickerson, "Human Factors and the Handicapped," *Human Factors* 20, no. 3 (June 1978): 259–72.

5. John Dewey, *Experience and Nature* (1981), vol. 1 of *The Later Works* (Carbondale: Southern Illinois University Press, 1981–), 43.

6. Ibid., 51.

7. Ibid., 51–52.

8. Ibid., 52.

9. John Dewey, "The Practical Character of Reality," in *The Philosophy of John Dewey*, ed. John J. McDermott (Chicago: University of Chicago Press, 1981), 1:222.

10. Ibid., 221.

11. John Dewey, *The Quest for Certainty* (1984), vol. 4 of *The Later Works*, 6. The chapter in question is entitled, appropriately, "Escape from Peril."

12. Ibid., 14. Still, Dewey's aspiration is for "shared experience," which "is the greatest of human goods" (*Experience and Nature*, 157).

13. John Dewey, *Art as Experience* (New York: G. P. Putnam's Sons, 1934), 18.

14. Ibid., 14.

15. John Dewey, *Reconstruction in Philosophy* (1982), vol. 12 of *The Middle Works* (Carbondale: Southern Illinois University Press, 1976–83), 134.

16. John Dewey, *My Pedagogic Creed* (1972), vol. 5 of *The Early Works* (Carbondale: Southern Illinois University Press, 1969–72), 87.

17. John Dewey, "Science and Society," in McDermott, *Philosophy of John Dewey*, 2:397.

18. John Dewey, *Democracy and Education* (1980), vol. 9 of *The Middle Works*, 56.

19. John Dewey, *Experience and Education* (New York: Macmillan, 1938), 16.

20. John Dewey, *The Need for a Recovery of Philosophy* (1980), vol. 10 of *The Middle Works*, 6.

21. Dewey, *Democracy and Education*, 146.

22. Ibid., 151.

23. Nancy Rubin, "Carnegie Council Raised Storms—and Some Dust," *New York Times*, March 2, 1980.

24. John Dewey, *The School and Society* (1976), vol. 1 of *The Middle Works*, 5.

25. John Dewey, *Liberalism and Social Action* (New York: G. P. Putnam's Sons, 1935), 61.

26. John Dewey, "Philosophies of Freedom," in *Philosophy and Civilization* (New York: Minton, Balch and Co., 1931), 281.

27. John Dewey, "Creative Democracy—The Task Before Us," in *Classic American Philosophers*, ed. Max Fisch (New York: Appleton-Century–Crofts, 1951), 393. See also Dewey's perceptive remark in a similar vein, as found in *Democracy and Education*: "Only gradually and with a widening of the area of vision through a growth of social sympathies does thinking develop to include what lies beyond our *direct* interests: a fact of great significance for education" (155).

28. Dewey, *Experience and Nature*, 67–68; see also Dewey, "Existence as Precarious and Stable," in McDermott, *Philosophy of John Dewey*, 300.

CHAPTER SIXTEEN

HAST ANY PHILOSOPHY IN THEE, SHEPHERD?

This is a direct transcript of John J. McDermott's address given at the annual meeting of the American Psychological Association, Division 15, San Francisco, California, in 2001.

1. William James, "The Teaching of Philosophy in Our Colleges," in *Essays in Philosophy—The Works of William James* (Cambridge, Mass.: Harvard University Press, 1978), 4.

2. Josiah Royce, *The Letters of Josiah Royce* (Chicago: The University of Chicago Press, 1970), 586.

3. John Dewey, *Art as Experience* (1987), vol. 10 in *The Later Works* (Carbondale: Southern Illinois University Press, 1981–), 23.

4. James, *Manuscript Lectures*, in *The Works of William James* (Cambridge, Mass.: Harvard University Press, 1988), 326.

CHAPTER SEVENTEEN

THE CULTURAL IMMORTALITY OF PHILOSOPHY AS HUMAN DRAMA

1. Plato, *Republic*, in *Plato: The Collected Dialogues* (New York: Pantheon, 1961), 747–53.

2. Plato, *Meno*, in *Plato: The Collected Dialogues*, 354–84.

3. Ibid., 363.

4. See Herbert Marcuse, "Love Mystified: A Critique," in *Negations* (Boston: Beacon, 1969), 243: "Waking up from sleep, finding the way out of the cave is work within the cave, slow painful work with and *against* the prisoners in the cave. Everywhere, even in your own land which is not yet found, not yet free, there are those who do this work, who risk their lives for it—they fight the real

fight, the political fight. You have revealed the latent, the true content of politics; you know that the political fight is the fight for the whole—not the mystical whole, but the very unmystical, antagonistic whole of our life and that of our children—the only life that is."

5. See Norman O. Brown, "Love Mystified: A Reply," in *Negations*, 246: "The next generation needs to be told that the real fight is not the political fight, but to put an end to politics. From politics to metapolitics." For a commentary on this dispute between Brown and Marcuse about the meaning of the "cave," see John J. McDermott, *The Culture of Experience: Philosophical Essays in the American Grain* (New York: New York University Press, 1976), 126–32.

6. William Shakespeare, *Hamlet*, in *The Complete Works of William Shakespeare* (London: Oxford University Press, 1905), 878.

7. Augustine, "On the Trinity," in *Basic Writings of Saint Augustine* (New York: Random House, 1948), 2:673.

8. John 1:14.

9. John 1:1.

10. Marcus Aurelius, *Meditations* (Chicago: Henry Regnery, 1956), 18–19.

11. John 1:9.

12. Baruch Spinoza, "On the Improvement of the Understanding," in *The Chief Works of Benedict De Spinoza* (New York: Dover, 1951), 1–41.

13. William James, *"Quelques considerations sur la methode subjective,"* in *Essays in Philosophy* (Cambridge, Mass.: Harvard University Press, 1978), 24: *"Il y a donc des cas ou une croyance cree sa propre verification."*

14. John Donne, *The Complete Poetry and Selected Prose of John Donne* (New York: Modern Library, 1952), 191.

15. Blaise Pascal, *Pensees* (New York: Modern Library, 1941), 75.

16. Rene Descartes, "Discourse on Method," in *The Essential Writings* (New York: Harper and Row, 1977), 134.

17. Immanuel Kant, *Kant's Inaugural Dissertation and Early Writings on Space* (Chicago: Open Court, 1929), 53, 56, 59, 61.

18. G. W. F. Hegel, *Reason in History* (New York: Liberal Arts, 1953), 27.

19. *The Marx-Engels Reader*, ed. Robert C. Tucker (New York: Norton, 1978), 4.

20. Ibid., 70–79.

21. *Marx and Engels: Basic Writings on Politics and Philosophy*, ed. Lewis S. Feuer (New York: Anchor, 1959), 245.

22. Friedrich Nietzsche, *The Will to Power* (New York: Vintage, 1968), 8.

23. Friedrich Nietzsche, "The Birth of Tragedy," in *Basic Writings of Nietzsche*, ed. Walter Kaufman (New York: Modem Library, 1968), 56–121.

24. Friedrich Nietzsche, "The Gay Science," in *The Portable Nietzsche*, ed. Walter Kaufman (New York: Viking, 1943), 95–96.

25. Nietzsche, "The Dawn," in ibid., 92.

26. Nietzsche, "The Gay Science," 297.

27. William James, "The Teaching of Philosophy in Our Colleges," in *Essays in Philosophy*, 4.

28. William James, *The Varieties of Religious Experience* (New York: Longmans, Green and Co., 1902), 160. Masked as coming from a "French correspondent," this text is actually autobiographical. The term "vastation" is taken from the eighteenth-century mystic-philosopher Emmanuel Swedenborg and refers to the projecting of our inner self outward, such that we behold ourself anew, usually in a grotesque form. The attempt is to purify inner evil, although the frightening character of the experience holds the center of the attention.

29. William James, "Diary," in *The Writings of William James*, ed. John J. McDermott (Chicago: University of Chicago Press 1977), 8.

30. *The Letters of Josiah Royce*, ed. John Clendenning (Chicago: University of Chicago Press, 1970), 586.

31. William James, "Introduction to the Literary Remains of the Late Henry James," in *Essays in Religion and Morality* (Cambridge, Mass: Harvard University Press, 1982), 62.

32. William James, *Pragmatism* (Cambridge, Mass.: Harvard University Press, 1975), 123.

33. Ralph Barton Perry, *The Thought and Character of William James* (Boston: Little, Brown and Co., 1935), 2:700.

34. William James, *A Pluralistic Universe* (Cambridge, Mass.: Harvard University Press, 1977), 39.

35. Ibid., 130–31.

36. Voltaire, "La Henriade," in *Les Oeuvres Completes de Voltaire* (Geneva: Institut et Musée du Voltaire, 1970), 2:575.

CHAPTER EIGHTEEN
TO BE HUMAN IS TO HUMANIZE
A Radically Empirical Aesthetic

1. Although we use the term "modern art" as a functional canopy for all of the major art activities of the twentieth century, in this essay the plastic arts are mainly in focus. The references to contemporary art stand for recent events in the modern art tradition.

2. "Inquiry" as used throughout this discussion refers to man's transactional quest. He is informed by the world at every turn, literally through his skin and in his dreams, as well as by virtue of more conventional means. Man also informs the world—again, literally by creating the contexts in which his awareness takes place. Rooted in Kant, this tension between man getting and begetting the world is of irreducible importance in modern art.

3. Has any major cultural prognostication turned out to be so wide of the mark as the judgment of José Ortega y Gasset on the viability of the new art? See Ortega y Gasset, *The Dehumanization of Art* (Garden City, N.Y.: Doubleday-Anchor, 1956), 5: "Modern art, on the other hand, will always have the masses against it. It is essentially unpopular; moreover, it is antipopular."

4. Gillo Dorfles, "The Man-Made Object," in *The Man-Made Object*, ed. Gyorgy Kepes (New York: George Braziller, 1966), 2.

5. The driftwood sculpture of Louise Nevelson is a notable contemporary effort to create "environments" or, better, "worlds," out of apparently relation-less materials. In an interview in the *New York Times*, April 28, 1967, she said: "I am asking for an environment to suit me. Look darling, there is no world. We objectify the world in form. That is the world." The combine-paintings of Robert Rauschenberg and the mixed media of Edward Kienholz are other imaginative examples of the limitless array of new human constructs.

6. Marshall McLuhan, *Understanding Media: The Extensions of Man* (New York: McGraw-Hill, 1964), 7–21. The same point is made from the side of a theory of criticism as found in Roland Barthes, "The Structuralist Activity," *Partisan Review* (Winter 1967): 82–88.

7. An interesting comment on the machine—that is, a typewriter—as a shift in poetic media is found in an analysis of the poetry of Charles Olson by M. L. Rosenthal, *The New Poets* (New York: Oxford University Press, 1967), 146.

8. There are exceptions to this charge, although they are rarely found within the context of philosophy itself. One effort to construct a modern aesthetic is reaching its zenith with the publication of the first volume in Susanne Langer's *Mind: An Essay on Human Feeling* (Baltimore: The Johns Hopkins University Press, 1967).

9. An outstanding example of this problem is found in the six-volume study edited by Gyorgy Kepes under the general title of *Vision and Value* (New York: George Braziller, 1965–66). With multiple contributors to each volume ranging over the cultural and aesthetic problems which challenge us, philosophical perspective can be garnered only indirectly. The issues in question, however, have philosophical significance at almost every turn.

10. See Allen S. Weller, "Art: U.S.A.: Now," in *Art: U.S.A.: Now*, ed. Lee Nordness (New York: Viking, 1962), 249–52, for a commentary on the increased importance of the reflective statement by the contemporary artist.

11. Herbert Read, "Realism and Abstraction in Modern Art," in *The Philosophy of Modern Art* (New York: Meridian, 1957), 99. See also idem, "The Limitations of a Scientific Philosophy," in *The Forms of Things Unknown* (New York: Meridian, 1963), 15–32.

12. Dore Ashton, "From Achilles' Shield to Junk," in Kepes, *Man-Made Object*, 194. In speaking of the Dadaists, she comments that "when they incorporated shreds of daily life in their work they did so with a dual and often equivocal purpose—both to deride and explore."

13. Thomas B. Hess, *Willem de Kooning* (New York: George Braziller, 1959), 15–16.

14. For a significant comparison, see "Innovation in Science," *Scientific American* 199, no. 3 (September 1958).

15. An illustration of our meaning of "field" is found in an analysis of "field composition" by Charles Olson, "Projective Verse," in *The New American Poetry, 1945–1960*, ed. Donald M. Allen (New York: Grove, 1960), 386–97.

16. An important but separate endeavor would take on the interrelated origins of the artistic event. Sociological, historical, and psychoanalytical matrices of interpretation, no one of them wholly reductionistic, are themselves irreducible conditioners of the aesthetic quality in each of our experiences. For a preliminary statement, see Arnold Hauser, *The Philosophy of Art History* (New York: Alfred A. Knopf, 1958), 21–116.

17. Hess, *Willem de Kooning*, 15.

18. William James, "Notebook," cited in Ralph Barton Perry, *The Thought and Character of William James* (Boston: Little, Brown and Co., 1935), 2:700.

19. Perry, *Thought and Character of William James*, 2:108–9.

20. Jacques Barzun, "William James and the Clue to Art," in *The Energies of Art* (New York: Harper and Row, 1956), 325.

21. William James, "The Stream of Thought," in *The Writings of William James: A Comprehensive Edition*, ed. John J. McDermott (New York: Random House, 1967), 45.

22. James, *Psychology: Briefer Course* (New York: Henry Holt, 1892), 165.

23. William James, "A World of Pure Experience," in *Writings*, 207. See also idem, "Pragmatism and Common Sense," in *Writings*, 442: "Everything that happens to us brings its own duration and extension, and both are vaguely surrounded by a marginal 'more' that runs into the duration and extension of the next thing that comes."

24. Only by an acknowledgment of man's dwelling on the fringe can we understand the risk-oriented, strenuous ethic of James, as well as his much-maligned doctrine of "the will to believe."

25. William C. Seitz, *Claude Monet: Seasons and Moments* (New York: Museum of Modern Art, 1960), 24.

26. William James, "The Stream of Thought," in *Writings*, 46.

27. Wassily Kandinsky, "Reminiscences" (1913), in Robert L. Herbert, *Modern Artists on Art* (Englewood Cliffs, N.J.: Prentice-Hall, 1964), 26.

28. We draw here from the tradition of American social psychology, especially the work of Charles Horton Cooley, George Herbert Mead, and Gardner Murphy; see, for example, Murphy, "The Human Natures of the Future," in *Human Potentialities* (New York: Basic, 1958), 302–29.

29. Robert Goldwater and Marco Treves, eds., *Artists on Art* (New York: Pantheon, 1947), 451. See also Weller, "Art: U.S.A.: Now," in Nordness, *Art: U.S.A.: Now*, 12: "In a sense, the physical facts of nature become less and less important to us in themselves; we have gone beyond a stage in which recognition and identification of material forms is of primary significance. It is the tension between forms, the effects of movements on shapes and qualities, the active spaces which surround solid masses, which seem to be the most tangible things with which many artists need to work. There are of course striking parallels to the social and economic situation of our times. The great problems of our period are not material ones; they are problems of basic relationships."

30. The contemporaneity of James's questions and attitudes becomes obvious to the reader of the biography by Gay Wilson Allen, *William James* (New York: Viking, 1967).

31. The historical and philosophical factors in the development of James's radical empiricism are extensively presented by Perry, *The Thought and Character of William James*, vol. 2. The relevant texts are found in James, *Writings*, esp. 134–317.

32. James, *Writings*, 314. This mature view is consistent with James's essay "On Some Omissions of Introspective Psychology" (1884), which became the basis for his chapter in the *Principles of Psychology* entitled "The Stream of Thought." Further, this position maintains the fundamental viewpoint of "The Function of Cognition" ([1885]; James, *Writings*, 136–52) and is rephrased throughout James's writings, particularly in the group of essays published in 1904 and 1905 under the generic theme of "radical empiricism." Of significance for our subsequent remarks in section IV, above, these essays of James play a decisive role in the maturation of John Dewey's metaphysics; see John Dewey, "Experience, Knowledge and Value-A Rejoinder," in *The Philosophy of John Dewey*, ed. Paul Arthur Schilpp (New York: Tudor, 1951), 533n16: "Long ago I learned from William James that there are immediate experiences of the connections linguistically expressed by conjunctions and prepositions. My doctrinal position is but a generalization of what is involved in this fact."

33. James, "The Stream of Thought," in *Writings*, 38.

34. Ibid.

35. Ibid.

36. Ibid.

37. James, "A World of Pure Experience," in *Writings*, 198.

38. Ibid., 201.

39. Ibid., 212–13. See also John Dewey, "The Experimental Theory of Knowledge," in idem, *The Influence of Darwin on Philosophy* (New York: Henry Holt, 1910), 90: "An experience is a knowledge, if in its quale there is an experienced distinction and connection of two elements of the following sort: one means or intends the presence of the other in the same fashion in which itself is already present, while the other is that which, while not present in the same fashion, must become so present if the meaning or intention of its companion or yoke fellow is to be fulfilled through the operation it sets up." A later statement on relational continuities, notably in the realm of aesthetics, is found in Christopher Alexander, "From a Set of Forces to a Form," in Kepes, *Man-Made Object*, 96–107.

40. See Daniel Abramson, in Nordness, *Art: U.S.A.: Now*, 134. "De Kooning's painting is never a situation but, rather, an entire event."

41. The problem of reductionism in aesthetic interpretation deserves far more analysis than it has received. For strong statements, see Norman O. Brown, "Art and Neurosis," in *Life Against Death* (New York: Random House, 1959), 55–67; Erich Neumann, *Art and the Creative Unconscious* (New York: Harper and Row, 1966); and Arnold Hauser, *Philosophy of Art History*, 43–116.

42. See Robert Goldwater, *Primitivism in Modern Art*, rev. ed. (New York: Vintage, 1967), 98. Without objects, we have "implications far beyond the canvas itself." He cites a remark of Georges Duthuit that "the painter remains in intimate contact not alone with a motif, but also with the infinite nebulousness." Goldwater then states that "emotionally as well as in its formal structure, the picture becomes a symbol whose very generality increases its possible meaning." We can crystallize this in Jamesian terms by holding that the lines of meaning stretch out beyond the finished work and are picked up by any number of responses, be they primitive rejoinders to sheer color and shape, aesthetic in the formal sense, or historical and sociological evaluations. Each work of art has a future as well as a past, in that it extends and proliferates its connections out beyond the field in which it was brought to fruition.

43. See, for example, Herbert, *Modern Artists*; and *Hans Hofmann, The Search for the Real and Other Essays*, ed. Sara T. Weeks and Bartlett H. Hayes Jr. (Cambridge, Mass.: MIT Press, 1967); and Hans Hofmann, "The Color Problem in Pure Painting—Its Creative Origin," in Frederick Wight, *Hans Hofmann* (Berkeley: University of California Press, 1957).

44. William Seitz, *Hans Hofmann* (New York: Museum of Modern Art, 1963), 50.

45. Ibid.

46. Ibid.

47. See André Hodeir, "On Group Relations," in *Toward Jazz* (New York: Grove, 1962), 73–93.

48. John Dewey, in Schilpp, *Philosophy of John Dewey*, 532–33.

49. Barthes, "The Structuralist Activity."

50. The reigning confusion involved in our notions of creativity, innovation, and discovery is given incisive analysis from the side of a philosophy of science by Norwood Russell Hanson, "The Anatomy of Discovery," *Journal of Philosophy* 64, no. 11 (June 1967): 321–52. An interdisciplinary approach to discovery and innovation, especially with regard to the problem of form, is found in Lancelot Law Whyte, ed., *Aspects of Form* (Bloomington: Indiana University Press, 1961).

51. Guillaume Apollinaire, *The Cubist Painters* (New York: George Wittenborn, 1962), 14–15.

52. Naum Gabo, cited in Herbert Read, "Realism and Abstraction in Modern Art," in *Philosophy of Modern Art*, 97.

53. Herbert Read, "Human Art and Inhuman Nature," in *Philosophy of Modern Art*, 76.

54. Andre Malraux, cited in *The Modern Tradition*, ed. Richard Ellmann and Charles Feidelson Jr. (New York: Oxford University Press, 1965), 517: "I name that man an artist who creates forms, be he an ambassador like Rubens, an image-maker like Gislebert of Autun, an *ignotus* like the Master of Chartres, an illuminator like Limbourg, a king's friend and court official like Velázquez, a *rentier* like Cézanne, a man possessed like Van Gogh or a vagabond like Gauguin; and I call that man an artisan who reproduces forms, however great may be the charm or sophistication of his craftsmanship."

55. Gardner Murphy, "The Enigma of Human Nature," *Main Currents* (September 1956): no pagination.

56. James, "Personal Depression and Recovery," in *Writings*, 8.

57. James, "The Sentiment of Rationality," in *Writings*, 331.

58. Gordon Allport, *Becoming* (New Haven: Yale University Press, 1955), 51.

59. James, "The Stream of Thought," in *Writings*, 71.

60. Ibid., 70. Texts like this abound in the *Principles*; see McDermott, introduction to *Writings*, xxxi–xxxv. James makes a specific reference to the artistic activity as "notoriously" selective and, therefore, having "superiority over works of nature" (*Writings*, 72). Compare these texts to that of the American painter Robert Motherwell, in William C. Seitz, *The Art of Assemblage* (New York: Museum of Modern Art, 1961), 97: "One cuts and chooses and shifts and pastes, and sometimes tears off and begins again. In any case, shaping and arranging such a relational structure obliterates the need, and often the awareness of representation. Without reference to likeness, it possesses feeling because all the decisions in regard to it are ultimately made on the grounds of feeling."

61. James, "Pragmatism and Humanism," in *Writings*, 456; and, with Lawrence Durrell, "Does not everything depend on our interpretation of the silence around us?" (Durrell, *Justine* [New York: Pocket Books, 1961], 250).

62. James, "A World of Pure Experience," in *Writings*, 212.

63. James, "How Two Minds Can Know One Thing," in *Writings*, 227–32.

64. See William James, *A Pluralistic Universe* (New York: Longmans, Green and Co., 1909); or *Writings*, 277–304, 482–581.

65. See note 57, above.

66. Ibid.

67. Ibid.

68. Ibid.

69. James, "Pragmatism's Conception of Truth," in *Writings*, 432.

70. James, "A World of Pure Experience," in *Writings*, 212.

71. James, "Pragmatism's Conception of Truth," in *Writings*, 432.

72. In addition to material in Schilpp, *Philosophy of John Dewey*, a recent statement of Dewey's aesthetics is found in Monroe Beardsley, *Aesthetics: From Classical Greece to the Present* (New York: Macmillan, 1966), 332–42. For a relevant collection of Dewey texts, see Richard J. Bernstein, *Experience, Nature and Freedom* (New York: Liberal Arts, 1960). Creative reinterpretations of Dewey's thought are found in Robert C. Pollock, "Process and Experience," in *John Dewey, His Thought and Influence*, ed. John Blewett (New York: Fordham University Press, 1960), and John Herman Randall, *Nature and Historical Experience* (New York: Columbia University Press, 1958).

73. For the scattered work on Dewey's aesthetics, see references in Beardsley, *Aesthetics*, 391–92.

74. John Dewey, *Art as Experience* (New York: Capricorn, 1958), 1.

75. Ibid., 10.

76. Ibid., 11.

77. Speaking of anticipation of what is to come, Dewey gives depth of meaning to James's contention that "life is in the transitions": "This anticipation is the connecting link between the next doing and its outcome for sense. What is done and what is undergone are thus reciprocally, cumulatively, and continuously instrumental to each other" (ibid., 50).

78. Ibid., 40.

79. Ibid., 19.

80. Ibid., 18.

81. Ibid., 14.

82. Ibid., 54.

83. Ibid., 24.

84. Seitz, *Art of Assemblage*, 25.

85. We acknowledge the complexity of the contemporary art scene. From the side of the artist, for example, differences between assemblage and pop art are considerable. In addition to Seitz, *Art of Assemblage*, one can find these distinctions in Lucy R. Lippard et al., *Pop Art* (New York: Praeger, 1966), and Gregory Battcock, *The New Art* (New York: Dutton, 1966).

86. It is extraordinary and depressing that the pathos of the "Watts Towers," relative to our time, has not, to my knowledge, been discussed. The "Towers" were constructed by Simon Rodia, an Italian immigrant and tile-setter, as a monument to opportunity for the disfranchised. Just recently, they looked down upon a new group of deprived, who at the time were destroying Watts as a monument to the hopelessness of their plight. The setting was the same, but some continuities are not as fruitful as others.

87. Henri Focillon, "In Praise of Hands," in *The Life of Forms in Art* (New York: George Wittenborn, 1948), 65–78.

88. Marshall McLuhan, "Address at Vision 65," *American Scholar* 35 (Spring 1966): 196–205.

89. Seitz, *Art of Assemblage*, 73.

90. Weller, "Art: U.S.A.: Now," in Nordness, *Art: U.S.A.: Now*, 462.

91. Dewey, "The Live Creature and 'Ethereal Things,'" in *Art as Experience*, 20–34.

92. R. E. L. Masters and Jean Houston, *The Varieties of Psychedelic Experience* (New York: Holt, Rinehart and Winston, 1966).

93. McLuhan, *Understanding Media*, 5.

94. R. Buckminster Fuller, "Conceptuality of Fundamental Structures," in *Structure in Art and Science*, ed. Gyorgy Kepes (New York: George Braziller, 1965), 66–88.

CHAPTER NINETEEN
EXPERIENCE GROWS BY ITS EDGES
A Phenomenology of Relations in an American Philosophical Vein

1. Maurice Merleau-Ponty, *Phenomenology of Perception*, trans. Colin Smith (New York: Humanities Press, 1962), viii; emphasis in original.

2. See Sandra B. Rosenthal and Patrick L. Burgeois, *Pragmatism and Phenomenology: A Philosophic Encounter* (Amsterdam: B. R. Gruner, 1980). Pioneer efforts in this direction were provided by the work of James M. Edie; see his introduction to Pierre Thévenaz, *What is Phenomenology? and Other Essays* (Chicago: Quadrangle, 1961), 113–36, and idem, "Notes on the Philosophical Anthropology of William James," in *An Invitation to Phenomenology*, ed. James M. Edie (Chicago: Quadrangle, 1965), 110–32; and Bruce Wilshire, *William James and Phenomenology* (Bloomington: Indiana University Press, 1968).

3. See John Dewey, "Having an Experience," in *The Philosophy of John Dewey*, ed. John J. McDermott (Chicago: University of Chicago Press, 1981), 2:555. Dewey writes here of the inchoate, of the "distractions," "dispersions," "extraneous interruption," and "inner lethargy" which dog all of our attendings.

4. Merleau-Ponty, *Phenomenology of Perception*, 203.

5. John E. Smith, "The Course of American Philosophy," in *Themes in American Philosophy: Purpose, Experience and Community* (New York: Harper Torchbooks, 1970), 135.

6. Arthur Bentley, "The Human Skin: Philosophy's Last Line of Defense," in *Inquiry into Inquiries* (Boston: Beacon, 1954), 195–211.

7. Rollo May et al., *Existence* (New York: Basic, 1958), esp. "The Case of Ellen West," 237–364.

8. Subsequent steps in a phenomenology of the body have been taken in *The Philosophy of the Body*, ed. Stuart Spicker (Chicago: Quadrangle, 1970), and in Richard M. Zaner, *The Context of Self: A Phenomenological Inquiry Using Medicine as a Clue* (Athens: Ohio University Press, 1981).

9. Oliver Sacks, *Awakenings* (New York: Dutton, 1983).

10. Ibid., 316.

11. Ibid., 328

12. A. R. Luria, *The Man with a Shattered World* (New York: Basic, 1972).

13. Ibid., 46–49.

14. William James, *The Varieties of Religious Experience* (New York: Longmans, Green and Co., 1902), 298–99.

15. John Dewey, *Human Nature and Conduct* (1983), vol. 14 of *The Middle Works* (Carbondale: Southern Illinois University Press, 1976–83), 195.

16. Merleau-Ponty, *Phenomenology of Perception*, xix; emphasis in original.

17. For a discussion of James's radical empiricism, see Smith, *Themes*, 26–41, and John J. McDermott, introduction to James, *Essays in Radical Empiricism: The Works of William James*, ed. Frederick Burkhardt (Cambridge, Mass.: Harvard University Press, 1976), xi–xlviii.

18. Nelson Goodman, *Ways of Worldmaking* (Indianapolis, Ind.: Hackett, 1978). Acknowledging the influence of James, Goodman writes, "Our universe, so to speak, consists of these ways rather than of a world or of worlds" (3); "universes of worlds as well as worlds themselves may be built in many ways" (5).

19. William James, *The Principles of Psychology* (Cambridge, Mass.: Harvard University Press, 1981), 2:961; emphasis in original.

20. Ibid., 959; emphasis in original.

21. Michel Foucault, *The Order of Things* (New York: Pantheon, 1970), 9. See, too, the ironically perceptive critique of the deception of words in idem, *This Is Not a Pipe* (Berkeley: University of California Press, 1982).

22. James, *Principles*, 1:273; see also William James, "The Stream of Thought," in *The Writings of William James*, ed. John J. McDermott (Chicago: University of Chicago Press, 1977), 70.

23. James, *Principles*, 1:274; see also James, *Writings of William James*, 70.

24. William James, *Talks to Teachers on Psychology* (Cambridge, Mass.: Harvard University Press, 1983), 138; see also idem, "On a Certain Blindness in Human Beings," in James, *Writings*, 634.

25. Maurice Merleau-Ponty, *The Primacy of Perception*, ed. James M. Edie (Evanston, Ill.: Northwestern University Press, 1964), 100–108.

26. David Riesman et al., *The Lonely Crowd* (New Haven: Yale University Press, 1950).

27. For an exquisite instance of a symbiotic relationship, witness that of the jellyfish and the nudibranch in the Bay of Naples, as described by Lewis Thomas, *The Medusa and the Snail* (New York: Bantam, 1980): "Sometimes there is such a mix-up about selfness that two creatures, each attracted by the molecular configuration of the other, incorporate the two selves to make a single organism. The best story I've ever heard about this is the tale told of the nudibranch and medusa living in the Bay of Naples. When first observed the nudibranch, a common sea slug, was found to have a tiny vestigial parasite, in the form of a jellyfish, permanently affixed to the ventral surface near the mouth. In curiosity to learn how the medusa got there, some marine biologists began searching the local waters for earlier developmental forms, and discovered something amazing. The attached parasite, although apparently so specialized as to have given up living for itself, can still produce offspring, for they are found in abundance at certain seasons of the year. They drift through the upper waters, grow up nicely and astonishingly, and finally become full-grown, handsome, normal jellyfish. Meanwhile, the snail produces snail larvae, and these too begin to grow normally, but not for long. While still extremely small, they become entrapped in the tentacles of the medusa and then engulfed within the umbrella-shaped body. At first glance, you'd believe the medusae are now the predators, paying back for earlier humiliations, and the snails the prey. But no. Soon the snails, undigested and insatiable, begin to eat, browsing away first at the radial canals, then the borders of the rim, finally the tentacles, until the jellyfish becomes reduced in substance by being eaten while the snail grows correspondingly in size. At the end, the arrangement is back to the first scene, with a full-grown nudibranch basking, and nothing left of the jellyfish except the round, successfully edited parasite, safely affixed to the skin near the mouth" (3–4).

28. John Dewey, "The Need of a Theory of Experience," in *Philosophy of John Dewey*, 2:508; emphasis in original.

29. R. E. L. Masters and Jean Houston, *The Varieties of Psychedelic Experience* (New York: Dell, 1966).

30. Franz Kafka, *Letter to His Father* (New York: Schocken, 1953), 17.

31. See Martin Heidegger, *What Is a Thing?* (South Bend, Ind.: Gateway Editions, 1967), 82–85.

CHAPTER TWENTY

THE AESTHETIC DRAMA OF THE ORDINARY

1. Cited in Serge Chermayeff and Christopher Alexander, *Community and Privacy* (New York: Anchor, 1965), 29.

2. Larry L. King, "The Last Frontier," in *The Old Man and Lesser Mortals* (New York: Viking, 1975), 207.

3. See the moving and poignant scene of "eviction" in Ralph Ellison, *Invisible Man* (New York: Vintage, 1972 [1952]), 261–77.

4. The master of "things" and "boxes" is, of course, Joseph Cornell. Indeed, he is the master of things *in* boxes, known forever as "Cornell boxes." Only those who have experienced these "boxes" can appreciate Cornell's extraordinary ability to merge the surrealism of the imagination and the obviousness of things as a "memorial to experience"; see Diane Waldman, *Joseph Cornell* (New York: George Braziller, 1977), and Kynaston McShine, *Joseph Cornell* (New York: Museum of Modern Art, 1981). As with Cornell, by "things" we mean, as does William James, bundles of relations. Things are not construed here as Aristotelian essences, much less as conceptually rendered boxes.

5. Rainer Maria Rilke, "The Ninth Elegy," in *Duino Elegies* (New York: Norton, 1939), 73.

6. Ralph Waldo Emerson, "The American Scholar," in *Works* (Boston: Houghton Mifflin, 1903–4), 1:96–97.

7. See William Blake, "Auguries of Innocence," in *The Poetry and Prose of William Blake*, ed. David V. Erdman (New York: Anchor, 1965), 481:

> To see a world in a grain of sand
> And a heaven in a wild flower,
> Hold Infinity in the palm of your hand
> And Eternity in an hour.

CHAPTER TWENTY-ONE

THE GAMBLE FOR EXCELLENCE

John Dewey's Pedagogy of Experience

For critical consideration of the above material, I am grateful to the participants in the conference on Education at Risk: Directions for the Future from the Wisdom of the Past as sponsored by Rockford College, Rockford, Illinois.

1. Elizabeth Flower and Murray G. Murphey, *A History of Philosophy in America* (New York: G. P. Putnam's Sons, 1977), 2:848, 865.

2. Ibid., 2:866.

3. John Dewey, *Democracy and Education* (1980), vol. 9 of *The Middle Works* (Carbondale: Southern Illinois University Press, 1976–83), 338.

4. See John J. McDermott, "Cultural Literacy: A Time for a New Curriculum," in idem, *Streams of Experience: Reflections on the History and Philosophy of American Culture* (Amherst: University of Massachusetts Press, 1986), 180–95.

5. John Henry Newman, *The Idea of a University* (New York: Longmans, Green, and Co., 1896), 152–53, 164.

6. For a systematically and chronologically representative selection of Dewey's writings, see John J. McDermott, ed., *The Philosophy of John Dewey*, 2 vols. (Chicago: University of Chicago Press, 1981). The entire corpus of Dewey's writings is being edited in a critical edition by Jo Ann Boydston. *The Early Works*, 5 vols., covering publications from the period 1882–98, and *The Middle Works*, 15 vols., covering publications from the period 1899–1924, have been published by Southern Illinois University Press. Eight of sixteen projected volumes of *The Later Works*, covering publications from the period 1925–53, have thus far been published. See also Jo Ann Boydston, ed., *Guide to the Works of John Dewey* (Carbondale: Southern Illinois University Press, 1970), which is a detailed analysis of Dewey's writings and a bibliographical checklist by subject. Thus far, the only thorough biography extant is George Dykhuizen, *The Life and Mind of John Dewey* (Carbondale: Southern Illinois University Press, 1973). An excellent starting point for the study of Dewey's thought is the above-mentioned chapter by Elizabeth Flower in *History of Philosophy*.

7. See John Dewey, "From Absolutism to Experimentalism," in McDermott, *Philosophy of John Dewey*, 1:1–13.

8. Ibid., 8.

9. John Dewey, "The Postulate of Immediate Empiricism" (1977), in *The Middle Works*, 3:158.

10. William James, *Essays in Radical Empiricism: The Works of William James*, ed. Frederick Burkhardt (Cambridge, Mass.: Harvard University Press, 1976), 42.

11. John Dewey, "The Experimental Theory of Knowledge" (1977), in *The Middle Works*, 3:114–15.

12. In fact, for James, the reverse position is on specific record. See William James, "The Stream of Consciousness," in *Psychology: Briefer Course* (Cambridge, Mass.: Harvard University Press, 1984): "It is, the reader will see, the reinstatement of the vague and inarticulate to its proper place in our mental life which I am so anxious to press on the attention" (150). (Parenthetically, I spend many comparatively fruitless hours trying to teach this to my students in the College of Medicine.)

13. I do not preclude other creatures from this power. I simply do not know. Evidence seems to suggest that some organisms, such as chimpanzees and dolphins, have a nascent capacity for such awareness. So be it. The fact is that

human organisms are obviously, treacherously, and delightfully self-conscious. Such is a fact of our situation.

14. Ralph Waldo Emerson, *The Complete Works of Ralph Waldo Emerson* (Cambridge, Mass.: Houghton Mifflin, 1903–4), 4:132; see also Emerson, "Works and Days," in ibid., 7:155–85. For the influence of Emerson on the classical American philosophers, inclusive of John Dewey, see John J. McDermott, "Spires of Influence: The Importance of Emerson for Classical American Philosophy," in McDermott, *Streams of Experience*, 29–43; see also chapter 4 of the present volume.

15. Gerard Manley Hopkins, "God's Grandeur," in *Poems* (New York: Oxford University Press, 1948), 70.

16. John Dewey, *Experience and Nature* (1981), vol. 1 of *The Later Works* (Carbondale: Southern Illinois University Press, 1980–), 43.

17. John Dewey, "The Live Creature," in McDermott, *Philosophy of John Dewey*, 2:535.

18. Ibid., 2:535.

19. Ibid., 2:526.

20. Ibid., 2:532.

21. John Dewey, "The Lost Individual," in ibid., 2:599.

22. Ibid., 604.

23. John Dewey, *The Public and Its Problems* (1984), vol. 2 of *The Later Works*, 329–30.

24. John Dewey, "Renascent Liberalism," in McDermott, *Philosophy o f John Dewey*, 2:646.

25. Karl Marx, *The Economic and Philosophic Manuscripts of 1844* (Moscow: Foreign Languages Publishing House, n.d.). See also T. B. Bottomore, ed., *Karl Marx: Early Writings* (New York: McGraw-Hill, 1963).

26. See C. Wright Mills, *Sociology and Pragmatism* (New York: Paine Whitman, 1964), 277–463.

27. John Dewey, "Renascent Liberalism," in McDermott, *Philosophy of John Dewey*, 2:647.

28. John Dewey, *School and Society* (1976), vol. 1 of *The Middle Works*, 3–109; John Dewey, *The Child and the Curriculum* (1976), vol. 2 of *The Middle Works*, 273–91.

29. See Maria Montessori, *The Montessori Method* (New York: Schocken, 1921).

30. Dewey, *The Child and the Curriculum*, 282.

31. Dewey, *Democracy and Education*, 47.

32. Ibid., 155.

33. Ibid., 147.

34. John Dewey, "The Need for a Theory of Experience," in McDermott, *Philosophy of John Dewey*, 2:508.

35. John Dewey, "Criteria of Experience," in ibid., 2:523.

36. Charles Sanders Peirce, *Collected Papers*, ed. Charles Hartshorne and Paul Weiss (Cambridge, Mass.: Harvard University Press, 1934), 5:37 (§51). Peirce also says, "But without beating longer round the bush, let us come to close quarters. Experience is our only teacher" (5:37, §50).

CHAPTER TWENTY-TWO

LIBERTY AND ORDER IN THE EDUCATIONAL ANTHROPOLOGY OF

MARIA MONTESSORI

1. E. M. Standing, *Maria Montessori—Her Life and Work*, with an introduction by John J. McDermott (New York: New American Library, 1984 [1957]), 33.

2. The complexity of this early-twentieth-century period in American education is carefully analyzed by Lawrence A. Cremin, *The Transformation of the School* (New York: Alfred A. Knopf, 1962).

3. William Heard Kilpatrick, *The Montessori System Examined* (Boston: 1914), 10; see also Robert H. Beck, "Kilpatrick's Critique of Montessori's Method and Theory," *Studies in Philosophy and Education* 1 (November 1961): 153–62. This essay, like that of Kilpatrick, rests solely on an interpretation of *The Montessori Method*, and no attempt is made to redress Montessori's reputation in the light of her other writings, as, for example, *Spontaneous Activity in Education*, with an intro. by John J. McDermott (New York: Schocken, 1965 [1917]).

4. Evelyn Dewey and John Dewey, *Schools of Tomorrow* (New York: E. P. Dutton, 1962 [1915]), 118.

5. Montessori, *Spontaneous Activity*, 207.

6. Ibid., 203.

7. John Dewey, *Experience and Education* (New York: Macmillan, 1956 [1938]), 16. A further anticipation by Montessori of pragmatic concerns is found in her *Spontaneous Activity*, 154–57 and 159–65.

8. Maria Montessori, *The Montessori Method* (New York: Schocken, 1964 [1912]), xx–xxiv. This essay is by far the best statement of Montessori's significance from a psychological point of view.

9. An historical note: however halting may have been the work of the American Montessori Society, founded nearly a decade ago by Nancy McCormick Rambusch, there is little doubt that it has been one of the decisive catalysts in forcing educators to look again, not necessarily at Montessori, but certainly at early learning. Of itself, this will prove to be a major contribution.

10. We do not, of course, deny the often acknowledged influence of Jean Itard (1775–1838) and Edouard Seguin (1812–1880) on Montessori. The work of Seguin, devoted to "mental defectives," was especially influential in her early thought.

11. With regard to James and Bergson, this tie to Montessori was recognized as early as 1912; see Harriet Hunt, *The Psychology of Auto-Education* (Syracuse, N.Y.: 1912).

12. Maria Montessori, *Pedagogical Anthropology* (New York: 1913), 17–18.

13. Edwin Boring states that "it seems fair to say that the process-nature of consciousness, the fact of change and flux, has been pretty clearly recognized since about 1890" (Boring, *The Physical Dimensions of Consciousness* [New York: 1933], 216n).

14. William James, *Psychology: Briefer Course* (New York: Collier, 1962 [1892]), 179.

15. See G. W. F. Hegel, *The Phenomenology of Mind* (New York: Macmillan, 1955), 589, for the dangers of self-deception that accompany such cultural changes.

16. J. McV. Hunt, intro. to *The Montessori Method*, xxxiv, is no doubt right when he states that Montessori "confused experimentation with clinical observation." I simply mean to stress, at this point, her demand that pedagogy be open to the specific conclusions of science. Even today, this is no mean request and, given her time, it was a position of great boldness and imagination.

17. See the chapter "Liberty within Limits" in Nancy McCormick Rambusch, *Learning How to Learn* (Baltimore: Helicon, 1962), 24–28.

18. Montessori, *The Montessori Method*, 86.

19. Montessori, *Pedagogical Anthropology*, 22–23.

20. Maria Montessori, *The Absorbent Mind* (New York: Adyar, 1959), 23.

21. See John Dewey, "The Reflex Arc Concept in Psychology," *Psychological Review* 3 (July 1896): 357–70.

22. Montessori, *Absorbent Mind*, 82.

23. William James, "The Sentiment of Rationality," in idem, *The Will to Believe* (New York: Dover, 1956 [1882]), 86.

24. An acute appreciation of the didactic materials and their limitation is given by Martin Mayer in his introduction to another edition of Montessori, *The Montessori Method* (Cambridge: Robert Bentley, 1964), xxx–xxxviii.

25. James D. Finn, "Technology and the Instructional Process," in *The Revolution in the Schools*, ed. Ronald Gross and Judith Murphy (New York: Harcourt, Brace and World, 1964), 29–30.

26. See Michael Harrington, *The Other America* (New York: Macmillan, 1962), 56, 65–66.

27. John Silberman, "Give Slum Children a Chance," *Harper's* (May 1964): 42.

28. Solon T. Kimball and James E. McClellan, *Education and the New America* (New York: Random House, 1962), 8.

29. Martin Deutsch, "The Disadvantaged Child and the Learning Process," in *Education in Depressed Areas*, ed. A. Harry Passow (New York: Teachers College, 1963), 178.

30. See the pertinent remark of Deutsch, "Disadvantaged Child": "Part of an hypothesis now being tested in a new pre-school program is based on the assumption that early intervention by well-structured programs will significantly reduce the attenuating influence of the socially marginal environment" (178).

31. Silberman, "Slum Children," 41–42.

32. See Sylvia Ashton-Warner, *Teacher* (New York: Simon and Schuster, 1963).

33. C. G. Jung, *The Development of Personality* (New York: Pantheon, 1954), 15n5.

34. Ibid., 14.

35. See Hunt, intro. to Montessori, *The Montessori Method*, xxxiv, for a careful statement of the continuing significance of Montessori's position on the relationship between observation and pedagogy.

36. Montessori, *Spontaneous Activity*, 125.

37. Montessori is often criticized for (a) a rigidity of setting and (b) giving too much freedom to the young child. I find this ambiguity in Montessori's critics to be indicative of the actual balance in her doctrine of liberty.

38. Montessori, *Spontaneous Activity*, 9–10.

39. Ibid., 71.

40. Maria Montessori, *To Educate the Human Potential* (New York: Adyar, 1961).

41. Montessori, *Spontaneous Activity*, 71.

42. Ibid., 79.

43. Montessori's insight into stimulus deprivation is powerfully set forth in *Spontaneous Activity*, 25–26, in a brief analysis of prison life. For her, significantly, starvation of the spirit occurs when one is cut off from a richness of colors, sounds, and forms.

44. Ibid., 78.

45. The significance, possibilities, and limitations of Montessori within the American cultural context are examined by John J. McDermott, "Montessori and the New America," in *Building the Foundations for Creative Learning*, ed. U. H. Fleege (New York: American Montessori Society, 1964), 10–28.

CHAPTER TWENTY-THREE

THE EROSION OF FACE-TO-FACE PEDAGOGY

1. Bill Joy, "Why the Future Doesn't Need Us," in *Ethics and Values in the Information Age*, ed. Joel Rudinow and Anthony Graybosch (London: Thomson Learning, 2002).

2. Eugene O'Neill, *Long Day's Journey into Night* (New Haven: Yale University Press, 1956), 61.

3. John Dewey, *Experience and Nature* (1982), vol. 2 of *The Later Works* (Carbondale: Southern Illinois University Press, 1980–).

4. Josiah Royce, *The Hope of the Great Community* (Freeport, N.Y.: Books for Libraries Press, 1967).

TWENTY-FOUR

CULTURAL LITERACY

A Time for a New Curriculum

1. James B. Conant, *The Education of American Teachers* (New York: McGraw-Hill, 1963). Although published over twenty years ago, this report retains its significance. The situation is now worse and the reforms suggested have not been implemented. Of the twenty-six recommendations, the most telling is that fledgling teachers be certified after having successfully majored and graduated in a field or discipline in the arts, sciences, and social sciences and after having completed successful student-teaching. This procedure enables some prospective teachers to bypass the usual "college of education" curriculum and offers a new source of competent teachers in our schools. Learning how to teach, after all, is significant in direct proportion to whether one knows something worth teaching others. For a recent statement on this issue, see David Stewart, "Schools of Teacher Education Should be Eliminated," *English Journal* 71, no. 8 (December 1982): 10, 12.

2. Unfortunately, it is necessary to clarify the term "humanistic." In my use, it has no relation to the contemporary conflict between the Moral Majority and its alleged opponent, secular humanism. To the contrary, humanistic education appeals to the entire history of human activity, including religion and religious experience, as reflectively undergone and aesthetically articulated. Equally germane to this effort are the thoughts of Cicero and those of St. Teresa, the Revelation Scriptures, and Goethe's *Faust*.

3. The re-education of teachers so that the humanities become the matrix on and through which education takes place is precisely the ongoing legacy of the work of the National Humanities Faculty, which arranges for outstanding university scholar-teachers to visit secondary schools and assist in developing new approaches to the teaching of the humanities. It is extraordinary to witness

the impact of a visiting NHF member, when he or she provides insight into how to galvanize and enliven an existing curriculum.

4. William James, *Essays in Radical Empiricism: The Works of William James*, ed. Frederick Burkhardt (Cambridge, Mass.: Harvard University Press, 1976), 42; see also idem, "A World of Pure Experience," in *The Writings of William James*, ed. John J. McDermott (Chicago: University of Chicago Press, 1977): "Experience itself, taken at large, can grow by its edges. That one moment of it proliferates into the next by transitions which, whether conjunctive or disjunctive, continue the experiential tissue, cannot, I contend, be denied" (212).

5. See *Evaluation of Liver Function in Clinical Practice* (Indianapolis: Lilly Research Foundation, 1965).

6. Another alternative is to have the students rewrite an extant play in their own words, or, again, to put an extant biography or short story into dramatic form. The latter was done some years ago at Huntington High School in Huntington, Long Island, New York. The students rewrote and dramatized Kurt Vonnegut's "Harrison Bergeron," with electrifying success.

CHAPTER TWENTY-FIVE

TRUMPING CYNICISM WITH IMAGINATION

This text is a transcript from a discussion with Michael Malone for *A Parliament of Minds: Philosophy for a New Millenium*. The segment was produced by KTEH-TV of San Jose, California, and JMT Productions of Los Angeles, California.

1. See chapters 2 and 3 in the present volume.

Index

John J. McDermott, *The Drama of Possibility: Collected Essays*, ed. Douglas R. Anderson.

Kenneth Laine Ketner, ed., *Peirce and Contemporary Thought: Philosophical Inquiries.*

Max H. Fisch, ed., *Classic American Philosophers: Peirce, James, Royce, Santayana, Dewey, Whitehead*, second edition. Introduction by Nathan Houser.

John E. Smith, *Experience and God*, second edition.

Vincent G. Potter, *Peirce's Philosophical Perspectives.* Edited by Vincent Colapietro.

Richard E. Hart and Douglas R. Anderson, eds., *Philosophy in Experience: American Philosophy in Transition.*

Vincent G. Potter, Charles S. Pierce: *On Norms and Ideals*, second edition. Introduction by Stanley M. Harrison.

Vincent M. Colapietro, ed., *Reason, Experience, and God: John E. Smith in Dialogue.* Introduction by Merold Westphal.

Robert J. O'Connell, S.J., *William James on the Courage to Believe*, second edition.

Elizabeth M. Kraus, *The Metaphysics of Experience: A Companion to Whitehead's "Process and Reality,"* second edition. Introduction by Robert C. Neville.

Kenneth Westphal, ed. *Pragmatism, Reason, and Norms: A Realistic Assessment—Essays in Critical Appreciation of Frederick L. Will.*

Beth J. Singer, *Pragmatism, Rights, and Democracy.*

Eugene Fontinell, *Self, God, and Immorality: A Jamesian Investigation.*

Roger Ward, *Conversion in American Philosophy: Exploring the Practice of Transformation.*

Michael Epperson, *Quantum Mechanics and the Philosophy of Alfred North Whitehead.*

Kory Sorrell, *Representative Practices: Peirce, Pragmatism, and Feminist Epistemology.*

Naoko Saito, *The Gleam of Light: Moral Perfectionism and Education in Dewey and Emerson.*

Josiah Royce, *The Basic Writings of Josiah Royce.*

Douglas R. Anderson, *Philosophy Americana: Making Philosophy at Home in American Culture.*

James Campbell and Richard E. Hart, eds., *Experience as Philosophy: On the Work of John J. McDermott.*